Laboring Classes
and Dangerous Classes

Louis Chevalier

Laboring Classes
and Dangerous Classes

In Paris During the First Half of
the Nineteenth Century

Translated from the French by Frank Jellinek

PRINCETON UNIVERSITY PRESS

Princeton, New Jersey

Published by Princeton University Press, Princeton, New Jersey

Originally published as *Classes Laborieuses et Classes Dangereuses à Paris pendant la première moitié du XIXe Siècle* by Librairie Plon
Copyright © 1958 by Librairie Plon

Library of Congress Cataloging in Publication Data
Chevalier, Louis, 1911–
    Laboring classes and dangerous classes in Paris
    during the first half of the nineteenth century.
    Includes bibliographical references.
    1. Crime and criminals—Paris—History. 2. Paris—
    Social conditions. I. Title.
    HV6970.P3C513   364'.944'36   80-8678

ISBN 0-691-00783-7 pbk.

Typography by Albert Burkhardt

First PRINCETON PAPERBACK printing, 1981
Published by arrangement with Howard Fertig, Inc.

Contents

BOOK III
CRIME, THE EXPRESSION OF A PATHOLOGICAL STATE: ITS EFFECTS

Laboring Classes
and Dangerous Classes

General Introduction

NOTE

It has not proved feasible to standardize or complete the bibliographic citations beyond the form originally given in the French edition. Where possible, however, additional information has been included.

I
The Problem of Crime: Its Importance

The writers who have dealt with the economic, social and political history of Paris in the first half of the nineteenth century have gone astray by ignoring the problem of the socially dangerous classes and the vast mass of documentation on it, as if crime were merely a secondary, virtually negligible aspect of urban development and the description of crime merely a passing literary fashion of dubious historical value.

Yet crime was one of the major themes in all writing in Paris and on Paris during the period running from the last years of the Bourbon Restoration to the early years of the Second Empire, when there arose amid the debris of the older city a new Paris, monumental and spacious, with its government and business quarters, a Paris fit for human habitation, a city far more like the one in which we live today than the Paris of the past, racked and branded as it was by the Ancien Régime. About no other city, even London, except for a few in our own time—Chicago between the two world wars, for example—has so much been written. From the most famous novels and the most important philosophical and sociological treatise to the most insignificant pamphlet, from works of imagination to pedestrian surveys, this writing has dwelled insistently on every aspect of crime, as if the proliferation of the criminal classes really was, over the years, one of the major facts of daily life in Paris, one of the main problems of city management, one of the principal matters of general concern, one of the essential forms of the social malaise. No matter what groups we take, whether the bourgeois, apparently secure behind their triple bars and bolts, or the lower classes, menacing and menaced; no matter what trend we study in the events, whether social or political, however artificially divorced from such sordid considerations, this documentation and this weight of testimony loom on the threshold as we enter the Paris of the period and present us inescapably with a sanguinary preview of it. However repugnant it may be, we simply cannot burke the sight of a city in which crime assumed an importance and an implication which we can hardly appreciate today, living as we do in a capital where crime is of interest only as a minor news item, except when it happens to bring to mind certain ancient terrors and some recollection of an earlier age not unlike the period we shall be dealing with in this study.

"Criminal" is the key word for the Paris of the first half of the nineteenth century; first of all, because of the increase in the number of crimes committed, as recorded in the crime statistics, but brought out even more strikingly in other documents such as the economic and demographic statistics. For even though these are not directly concerned with crime, yet when they are correlated with the crime statistics proper, they enable us to pierce through the criminality reflected simply in the number of arrests and convictions to criminality in its broadest sense, the only form of criminality that really counts.

"Criminal," secondly, because of the imprint of crime upon the whole urban landscape. No part of the contemporary Paris was unshadowed by crime. At the old gates and on the outer boulevards, the barrières, where, until the railroads were built, highwaymen carried on the traditions of the Ancien Régime and, as the lower classes drank and danced nearby, forgathered in the shadows with criminals of a new type spawned by the recent outward sprawl of the city. And in the central quarters themselves, where the capital's complex and disordered growth had engendered a tangle of lanes, passageways, courts and blind alleys and had ranged cheek by jowl sunny street and cesspool, the affluent mansion and the slum, areas of light and shade in a landscape we can now barely make out, and had almost everywhere left nooks and corners ideally suited to robbery with violence by day or night— and, indeed, in some places day hardly differed from night. For risk to life, or at best, to purse, our Parisian had no need to linger in the purlieus of the place Maubert or the Cité, or to push on as far as the sinister boulevards bordering on the faubourg Saint-Jacques or the faubourg Saint-Marcel; for every route running from the Temple to the Seine, from the Palais-Royal to the place des Vosges, through the huddle of houses barely threaded by the rue Saint-Denis and the rue Saint-Martin, must at some point pass through a district far from secure, brush by some thieves' kitchen, or worse.

"Criminal," above all, because of the citizens' overwhelming pre-occupation with crime as one of their normal daily worries. Crime was an abiding cause of fear, a fear which reached heights of terror in certain winters of cold and destitution. Deadly fear and terror were the main theme of police reports and newspaper reports alike in the winter of 1826–27, when the crime rate and the death rate rose in parallel;[1] and, too, in the last years of the July Monarchy, when every form of urban poverty was aggravated, accumulated and intermingled. "We are back in the palmy days of the Middle Ages, when the streets were dark and deserted," the vicomte de Launay wrote in his *Lettres parisien-nes* on December 21, 1843:

For the past month the sole topic of conversation has been the nightly as-saults, hold-ups, daring robberies. . . . What is so terrifying about these nocturnal assaults is the assailants' noble impartiality. They attack rich and poor alike. . . . They kill at sight, though they may get the wrong man; but little do they care. At one time the advantage of being poor was that at least you were safe; it is so no longer. Paris is much perturbed by these sinister occurrences. A concern for self-defense greatly troubles family gatherings especially. Evening parties all end like the beginning of the fourth act of *Les Huguenots,* with the blessing of the daggers. Friends and relatives are not allowed to go home without a regular arms inspection. . . .

More important than the fear of crime, however, was the interest in crime and everything connected with it. Besides the persistent daily murmur nourished by the ordinary crimes and the small change of minor brawls which the Parisians could tot up each morning, there was the mighty reverberation of the great crimes, inspissated with horrid gloom and haloed, as it were, with a somber glory, occurrences in the social history of the Paris of this period at least as important as the major events in foreign and domestic policy. For instance, the crime of Dautun in 1817, described by Hugo as one of the principal events of that year: "The most recent Paris sensation was the crime of Dautun, who threw his brother's head into the fountain in the Flower Market." The murder of the goatwoman of Ivry, too, which for some ten years was the burden of street ballads and is mentioned several times in *Les Misérables.* Again in 1833, Regey's murder of Ramus, the cashier's messenger, whose body was found beside the Seine at the outlet of the sewer in the rue de la Huchette, the first instance of the conjunction of sewer and crime, the two by-products of urban life, whose inter-relationship we shall discuss later. And, above all, the crimes of Lace-naire, whose trial in 1835 and execution in 1836 were to shake Paris to the core and to give rise to peculiar manifestations of collective terror, which have often been described but generally misconstrued.

For the interest in crime was not restricted to these phenomena of terror and alarm. It was one of the forms of contemporary popular culture, of the ideas, images and words, the beliefs, the lore and language, and the forms of behavior which the people rather evolved spontaneously and discovered for itself than took from others, precisely when it seemed to be imitating and adopting these forms. Crime assumed a truly astonishing bulk in conversations in the workshop and café and on the street, as our documentation shows over and over again, as well as in the serials and novels—which were discussed or retold orally or in mime far more often than read, and thus themselves became a topic of conversation with a speed that can be measured by the success of *Les Mystères de Paris*;[2] in street ballads and popular songs; in dances and entertainments; in performances at the theater or out of doors; and finally in the vast drama of the city itself, in which every inhabitant was a performer.

Crime, indeed, was itself the theme of a dramatic performance in the shape of exposures in the pillory on the place du Palais de Justice, regularly recorded in the newspapers and in contemporary memoirs as important events in the city's life, as well as the crowds they attracted, the tumults, and even riots they sometimes caused, the popular customs they revealed, and the echoes of them that persisted long afterwards. For this there is ample material to be drawn from the contemporary press, from novels and memoirs, and from the crude illustrations pinned up on the walls of the rooms in lodging houses. One extraordinary case was the pillorying of the priest Joseph Contrafatto, exposed and branded in January 1828. The *Journal des Débats* described this as follows:

The preparations made as usual on the place du Palais de Justice began at nine in the morning. The sensation in the crowd, thronging more thickly from minute to minute, when Contrafatto was tied to the post, and especially when the board was nailed up with his name, occupation and address in large capitals, was indescribable. The square itself and all the streets running into it were soon congested with throngs of spectators pressing around the pillory throughout the performance. The attendants laid the red-hot iron to Contrafatto's shoulder. We can hardly bring ourselves to record the ferocious glee with which part of the crowd greeted it. The jeers, shouts and cheers lasted for several minutes. For a long way, a crowd giving vent to foul language wholly improper in any circumstances followed the carriage in which the wretch was taken back to Bicêtre.[3]

But the truly great performances were the capital executions, announced by town criers at every street crossing in Paris, which, before they were transferred to the barrière Saint-Jacques in the early years of the July Monarchy and were there carried out at dawn, provided a sanguinary and sumptuous spectacle in the very heart of Paris, on the place de Grève, amidst one of the most splendid architectural settings in the world and in the full blaze of noontide, to the accompaniment of outbursts of atrocious collective frenzy.

II
The Problem of Crime: Its Implications

While the conventional histories of Paris are unduly impoverished by ignoring or misinterpreting crime, the many recent studies of criminal literature and criminality in the nineteenth century also labor under a similar misconception. They concentrate on crime alone and are, so to speak, fascinated by it, while wholly ignoring general history. Hence they treat criminality in the Paris of this period in exactly the same way as they would treat it in any other city or at any other period.

But crime in the Paris of the Restoration and the July Monarchy was something quite different from crime in the sense in which the term is used today. The malaise of the Parisians of that period would be almost inexplicable if it related only to such trivial and inevitable byproducts of city life as fraud, picking pockets, theft or even murder, matters for the police and the courts alone to study and cope with. Crime in the sense we are using here involved a menace of a wholly different kind, with wholly different implications. It was not an incidental and exceptional consequence of social existence, but one of the largest consequences of the growth of the city; not something abnormal, but one of the most normal aspects of the city's daily life in this phase of its development. This is amply borne out by the position and significance given to crime in both the qualitative and the quantitative documentation.

The qualitative documentation

Both major contemporary literary works and social treatises stressed the importance of crime—the former far more strongly than the latter. But since they lacked the tools to measure it with and were concerned solely with sources and influences, they failed to realize the true implications of what they were describing.

The description of the criminal classes and the places in which they were born, lived and died undoubtedly forms part of a traditional description of Paris on lines originally laid down by Mercier and Restif de la Bretonne.[4] Mercier was the first to draw up the rules of the genre, codify its subjects and establish its topography so definitively that no subsequent account could dispense with them: the prisons, especially Bicêtre, the most horrible of the lot, crouching like an ancient monster on the city skyline and embodying in itself all the city's destitution and criminality; and the place de Grève, "the populace leaving workshops and stores to flock around the scaffold, eager to watch how the victim performs the great act of public dying in torment." The setting for the execution was fixed once and for all. No subsequent writer made any substantial change. "The people watch the clock face on the Hôtel-de-Ville," Mercier said, "and mark the hour as it strikes; they shudder, horror-stricken, gaze and are silent." "The Hôtel-de-Ville," Hugo wrote much later, "is a sinister edifice. . . . As night falls, its clock, which had struck the fatal hour, remains luminous on the grim façade." As for the executioner, his name and lair were perfectly well known to Gavroche. "The lowest class of the people," Mercier had written, "is familiar with his looks; in the eyes of the ugly mob which throngs to these hideous performances he is the great tragic actor."[5]

The influence of social romanticism, which has often been analyzed, is also incontrovertible. And equally incontrovertible are the other, more clearly defined and more easily identified and dated influences, thus summed up by *L'Univers* in a review of *Les Mystères de Paris* in February 1843:

So this is what you call the Mysteries of Paris! All you have done is to unearth the *Gazette des tribunaux*—which has had 12,000 subscribers these twenty years past. Could you find nothing more mysterious in Paris? You must have forgotten that we read the Memoirs of Vidocq at high school, that the *Dernier jour d'un condamné* interrupted our classical education. . . . There is nothing special about vice and crime nowadays, nothing less shrouded in mystery.

Novelists and journalists lifted much of their material from the *Gazette des tribunaux*, the first issue of which appeared on November 1, 1825. This is easily demonstrated, and indeed, often has been. More important, perhaps, is the way in which this paper contributed so greatly to the development of the psychosis of crime. Day after day the Parisians, finding assembled in its columns a mass of facts which they had previously heard about piecemeal, gained a growing impression—growing, indeed, to a certainty—that the capital was even less safe than they had thought and that their security was in truth threatened by large and well-organized gangs of robbers. Particularly impressive was the way in which the great crimes were dramatized to the utmost and the immense publicity given to the lethal ceremonies on the place de Grève.

As for Vidocq, it would be idle to overlook the influence of his Memoirs, the first two volumes of which appeared early in October 1828—a few weeks before Hugo began *Le dernier jour d'un condamné* —upon Balzac, Hugo, Eugène Sue and other less known writers. The influence of the book, and of the man himself, upon popular thinking was equally strong, though this has been noted less often. Viennet wrote in the *Nouveau journal de Paris* as early as October 28, 1828, that "the book must have already moved down from the drawing room to the servants' hall, from the reading rooms to every shop counter in town." The legend of Vidocq, combining in one person as he did order and disorder, police and crime, dirty work and high politics, was an important element in popular thinking. The massive silhouette, now reassuring and now terrifying, not only loomed in the background of the major contemporary works, but also dominated the people's fears and beliefs. Nor can we overlook the influence of the descriptions of crime and criminals by Balzac, Sue and Hugo upon the contemporary literature of crime and upon contemporary popular thinking.

But the study of sources and influences, which discusses the attention paid to crime in the contemporary writing merely in terms of a literary fashion, does not give sufficient weight to the theme of crime and its development.

The role of crime in the quantitative documentation least concerned with crime as such, as well as in the qualitative documentation, immediately impresses us—without further verification—with the idea that something more than a merely literary element was embodied in this literature itself: a far more general and spontaneous element, which was a fact of popular thinking, a terror not related to the problem of crime in the narrow sense of the word but rather to that of crime as a threat to society. This implication of the problem of crime is not to be measured solely by the relative quantitative dimensions of the theme of crime, that is, by checking it by statistics of the number of works, chapters or pages published. It is demonstrated rather by the transformation of the theme, nothing less than a complete metamorphosis, the phases of which we shall chart in our study.

The quantitative documentation

The amount of space given to criminal statistics in the contemporary quantitative documentation (very different from that given it both in earlier periods and today) provides further evidence of the social implications of crime.

Criminal statistics imply official registration. The remarkable progress in this registration during the period is accounted for in part by the general progress in this respect and by what may be called an enthusiasm for figures, but in part too by the aggravation of criminality in Paris, which called for commensurate registration. It was now that that admirable series the *Comptes rendus de la justice criminelle et civile* began publication. Cournot later said of it in his *Mémoire sur les applications du calcul des chances à la statistique judiciaire* that "it will one day become the source of a mass of documents of inestimable value for improving legislation and for the study of the moral and civic structure of society."

Of greater importance, however, was the place accorded to criminal statistics in the general population statistics. We are concerned not so much with the recording of crime by criminologists as an abnormal fact, or for preventive or punitive purposes, as with its recording by demographers as a normal fact of urban life in order to acquire a more intimate knowledge of its forms.

A normal fact it was, inasmuch as the measurement of crime was one of the first procedures in a statistical survey of the city, and one of the most ordinary procedures, as if crime were simply one among the many facts of urban life. The series was not separated from the general statistics concerning Paris, nor was it introduced in a final section incidentally and as an afterthought; the tables were included in the first instance and as a matter of course.

The municipal statistician painted precisely the same picture as the skilled Parisian potboiler novelist or the country cousin—or even good old Agricol Perdiguier[6] himself—whose visit to the big city included as a matter of course the place de Grève, the hell's kitchens of the Cité, the place Maubert and les Halles, the hospitals, the cemeteries and the Morgue.

It was a normal fact, too, inasmuch as the figures for crime were accorded precisely the same space in the general population census and in the measurement of the changes in it as those for illegitimacy, child desertion, infanticide and suicide (themselves forms of criminality), and practically the same space as births and deaths, distinct from them in some tables, combined with them in others.

It was a normal fact, above all, inasmuch as it reflected the general conditions of urban living, providing an accurate and convenient method of measuring them in the same way as, but perhaps more accurately and fully than, the major demographic events. While the implications of the rates embodied in the population statistics can be accepted as a valid tool of social measurement, these implications and their validity were not the same at all periods. For centuries the inequalities in the incidence of the death rate have provided a valid measurement of social inequalities, so much so that we are able irrefutably to deduce social distribution from the distribution of deaths at certain periods of high mortality and extreme destitution.

Nowadays, however, we in the cities of the Western world would be more inclined to look at the fertility rate; for advances in health and education have mitigated the former biological inequality, with its fundamental injustice, and the death rate has consequently lost much of its previous significance. To a yet greater degree, child desertion, infanticide and even suicide are no longer so important for social research, and crime even less so, since the criminologist is apt to be the only specialist concerned today with measuring, describing and accounting for it. These demographic events have now become abnormal and their importance and implications insignificant. And this trend is rapidly reducing the privileged position in social description enjoyed by demographic measurement not so long ago. Social research must henceforth use its own techniques in exploring its own field.

But this is not true of our period. Here, all the methods and applications of demographic measurement are given full scope and, indeed, priority—to the exclusion, in the last resort, of any other type of measurement. We do use the fertility rate, with its high illegitimacy content and wide variations, depending on year and locality; and the death rate, both the normal daily rate and the rate in major disasters. But the figures for crime are at least as useful as the figures for the general death rate, for the crime rate forms part of the normal death rate and is separated from it only by many imperceptible transitional stages. Thus, we are speaking not only of crime in the broad sense—including infanticide and what we may consider a habitual and, so to speak, insti-

tutional form of infanticide, the method by which the Parisians and the
authorities of the period rid themselves of superfluous children and the
aged by exporting the children to the lethal provinces and packing the
old people into asylums where they would never make old bones—but
crime, too, in the ordinary legal sense. This gives us at least as good a
means of measurement for the social description of the city as the
general mortality tables, so close and consistent are the correlations of
time and place for both of them. The method is incontrovertible and
also convenient, because it combines the basic data condensed in relatively few figures more simply and usefully than the unwieldy fertility
and mortality tables. Thus, Quételet in his *Recherches sur le penchant
au crime aux différents âges* (1831), inaugurating a quantitative description which took the criminal statistics as the starting point for a
description of the conditions of urban living as a whole, maintained
that living conditions could be deduced from the statistics on crime
and that they provided a more accurate means of measurement for this
than any of the other population and social statistics. Most of the
authors using the municipal statistics of population composition and
movement in those years took a similar view; they at once focused
their main interest and made their fullest comments upon the crime
statistics. This does not mean that they were satisfying some sort of
morbid curiosity; rather, it was here that they found in one place the
quantitative data for one of the city's major problems, the evidence
for, and measurement of, an unhealthy state of affairs, not reflected in
crime alone but expressed more clearly in it than anywhere else.
Investigating the causes of the Revolution of 1848, Daniel Stern wrote:
"The abundant publication of irrefutable statistics gave overwhelmingly
convincing figures for the state of the jails, convict prisons, brothels
and asylums and fully justified condemning a government which was
impotent to heal such running sores."[7]

We are no longer dealing simply with the criminal classes; behind the
final degradation of selected individuals and through the specific experience provided by such individual cases, we perceive the socially
dangerous condition of the vast majority, a common plight, a formidable
brotherhood. What we have here is not crime itself so much as the
pathological nature of urban living, revealed with greater certainty
by the quantitative investigation of crime than by investigating any
other problem of Paris.

III

*Crime and the Biological Aspects of the
Social History of the Period*

The pathological state of the city is, indeed, suggested by the amount of space given to the series on crime and by the prevalence of the theme of crime in the quantitative and qualitative documentation respectively, from the closing years of the Restoration to the advent of the Second Empire and the new order instituted by it. "Paris must change. Its constitution is diseased," Doin and Charton wrote in January 1830. "Paris must change. Paris is incompatible with the Republic," Lecouturier echoed in 1848.[8] A sick city, a city perpetually racked by all kinds of crises and conflicts, a city perpetually agitated—and more intolerably than at any other period—by disturbances ranging from random street brawls and fights in the workshop to the great revolts, riots and revolutions of the workers; from continual brutalities in workshop and street and the daily settlement of scores to the most formal affray; from personal hatreds to the great hatreds of the people. A sick city indeed; even the textbook account of the period shows beyond the shadow of a doubt that social and political antagonisms were never so ferocious, breaches of the peace never so frequent and—despite economic expansion and even periods of undoubted prosperity—the misery of the vast majority never so implacable. The characteristics and causes of this lingering disease attributed to it by the conventional historian, however, make for a wholly inadequate description.

Although even the conventional history of Paris can show clearly enough, simply by means of political, economic and social analysis, that these years were among the most somber in the capital's history from the beginning of the nineteenth century to the present day, it habitually omits some of the characters in the drama. Perhaps not the most important characters nor those which, if studied thoroughly, would remove the need for any other kind of study, but characters which are indispensable if we are to paint the whole picture of destitution, violence, hatred and fear. It fails, too, to observe these characters in those intermediate phases which were unmarked by any economic, social or political crisis, and so furnishes an imperfect interpretation of the periods when the private and public distress was reflected in a different way, disclosed by a different set of documents. Since it sees nothing but prosperity, tranquility and public concord in years which we know from other sources to have been years of private discord, secret poverty, deep degradation and fury, it is not only self-condemned to misinterpret the history of these periods of apparent public tranquility, but is also inevitably bound to ignore the real causes of the major conflicts to which it rightly devotes most space and which are described in most detail.

The Crises and Their Biological Characteristics

Whether we consider the long crises that persisted throughout the last years of the Restoration and the early years of the July Monarchy—"that cloud of tragedy into which the story of *Les Misérables* feels its way," as Hugo wrote—or the final storm that swept away the régime, we find a parallel development between the aggravation of political and economic disturbances and the forms of the same unnoticed dramatic development. Thus we see crimes multiplying around the place de Grève and the shuttered workshops; an increase in incidents of working-class violence both by day and night, at places ranging from the unquiet districts in the heart of the city to the sinister and solitary stretches of the outer boulevards; a steep rise in the figures for suicides among the lower classes, noted by the municipal statisticians; cases of infanticide, from the anonymous and individual acts penalized by law recorded in the reports from the Sewers Department to such forms of officially recognized and long-term infanticide as abandoning infants in the street, or on church steps, or on the threshold of some bourgeois or charitable mansion—the numbers rising to such heights at certain periods that the foundling institutions were crowded out and whole cartloads would have had to be dispatched to the provinces had not a providential mortality intervened to relieve the burden on public and private charity; and finally a general mortality rate casting up the balance of the whole and swelling till it reached, around 1830 and 1848, its highest totals for the first half of the century.

Death itself rather than the general mortality rate is what must engage us here. Death in all its forms is the measure of a misery which at certain periods exceeded individual powers of endurance, with a lower depth that cannot be sounded by any economic description. It provides, too, a means of measuring the acts of violence, for the ideological and political descriptions do not bring out clearly enough the fact that they settled in terms of life and death a problem which itself was a matter of life or death.

An instance of great significance is the appearance of cholera on two occasions, each coinciding with the severest crises—in 1832 and 1849. In both years, and even more certainly in the dark days as the Restoration moved on to the July Monarchy, the biological drama cannot be isolated from the economic and political drama; for the former reinvested the latter with its true causes and characteristics, which, in this instance too, were reduced to matters of life or death.

It may be said, no doubt, that the cholera epidemic of 1832, coming as it did after a long period during which there was every reason to believe that such plagues had vanished forever, was an exceptional disaster. "Very severe mortality has become rare," the municipal statistician wrote, somewhat prematurely, in introducing the second volume of the *Recherches statistiques concernant Paris* in 1823. Yet should we not rather regard this abnormal mortality simply as an aggravated form of the normal one, a solemn and monstrous experience of the ordinary mortality in a more visible and incontrovertible shape? The real cause of both was the same. It was not the infection gradually creeping up from the Ganges delta, but the age-old accumulation of poverty, the ancient foundation of malnutrition, fatigue and exhaustion, breeding ground at all times for the heaviest mortality among the poorest of the poor. It fostered the epidemic, it is true, but only as an accessory and subsidiary factor; and it is noteworthy that the epidemic took no hold on the areas of France, even urban areas, where poverty and, concurrently, the normal mortality were least severe.

There was an even closer parallel in the similarity of the figures for both normal and abnormal mortality in relation to the losses by social groups. The only difference is that, the figures for deaths from cholera being higher, the distribution by class is clearer in 1832 and can be broken down into very small categories which do not appear in the statistics of the normal death rate—that is to say, not merely into the bourgeois and the common people but, within those categories, into occupational groups with their levels of living and ways of life, their material and moral conditions, their work, earnings, pleasures and passions; not merely by arrondissement and district, described as bourgeois or working-class according to the predominating type of inhabitants, but by street and dwelling, with comments on such features as exposure to sun and air and humidity and cleanliness. An entire social classification is embodied in this breakdown of the death rate: rentiers, small employers, workers in shops or at home, outdoor workers, workers on

the river and even such lower categories—or categories so regarded—
as day laborers, water carriers, and the very ragpickers who dealt with
the city's garbage and were universally regarded as repulsive; an entire
urban landscape, too, with full details of its streets and alleys in a
thorough, detailed classification that can be derived simply from the
nomenclature of the deaths.

To the municipal statistician the epidemic was a primary, incontrovertible experience of social inequality; it revealed the inequality before
death, the phases of which we shall describe later. But to the city's
inhabitants, too, and most of all to the lowest of the low, those worst
savaged by the plague, it was a revelation, and a revelation brought
home immediately to them. Jules Janin in the midst of the epidemic
rightly referred to this "plague attacking a populace which is dying
solitary and sooner than the rest, providing in its very death a re-
doubtable and savage denial of the doctrines of equality with which it
has been beguiled for half a century."[9] A denial inasmuch as the plague
first appeared in the poorest districts. The first to be stricken, on February 13, 1832, was a porter in the rue des Lombards; then a small
girl in the rue du Haut-Moulin in the Cité district; then a woman
pedlar in the rue des Jardins-Saint-Paul; then an eggseller in the rue
de la Mortellerie. A denial embodied in the cynical comments in the
bourgeois press: "The cholera morbus is within our walls," wrote the
Journal des Débats on March 28.

Yesterday a man died of it in the rue Mazarine. Today nine persons were
carried to the Hôtel-Dieu and four of them are already dead. All the persons
stricken by this epidemic disease are members of the lower classes, though
it is not thought to be contagious. They are cobblers and people working at
the woolen blanket manufacture. They live in the narrow dirty streets of the
Cité and the Notre-Dame district.

While the description of the cholera epidemic emphasized the biological aspects of the general crisis in the early days of the July Monarchy, as well as in the last years of the Restoration, by the close
correlation between the cholera mortality and the normal mortality, it
threw light equally upon the biological bases of antagonisms where the
conventional documentation merely delineated their political, religious
and social contours. These struggles were of course undoubtedly political,
religious and social; but the experience of the cholera epidemic enables
us to look through and beyond them and to discern between the lines
the sanguinary settlement of scores. "No voice was raised amid this

silence," to quote Jules Janin again, "except, eventually, the voice of the people—and how did that formidable voice speak? It expressed itself as the people does, in arson, savage blows, curses, in blood, fury and turmoil of every kind." A remark that went to the heart of the matter, reducing the whole thing to its essentials.

Were these antagonisms political, expressed as they were in the progress from one riot to the next toward revolution, as has often been described? Certainly they were. It should be noted, however, that at any given moment this political agitation was simply the sum of other forms of agitation, in which it is hard to determine what was the public element and what the private, and equally hard to say what derived from republican conviction and what was merely a form of criminality, what was to be ascribed to the laboring classes and what to the dangerous classes, as closely correlated in fact as they were in the flickering shadows of Victor Hugo's barricades. It was these lower forms of the proletarian revolt which the cholera epidemic developed, raised and revealed, elevating the worst to the level of the best, justifying crime by the belief that the cholera itself was simply a form of criminality. "An invention by the bourgeoisie and the government to starve the people," a workman cried in Roch's book, written immediately after the events.[10]

For nearly two years now the people has been racked by the most appalling poverty. They lack work, bread, clothes, they are hunted down, jailed, murdered. Now, on the pretext of preventing an epidemic, they are being shot down in the prisons. On Sunday a swarm of police sneaks burst into the Sainte-Pélagie Prison and the scoundrels opened fire on the patriots imprisoned there.

The cholera once again dressed out political revolt in varied guises practically imperceptible at other periods; some brought others into relief, some strengthened others; some were transformed into others and some substituted for others, depending on the season, the day of the week or the time of day or night. But the cholera also conferred upon this protest a deeper chronological unity and kept constantly in being the menacing undercurrent of restless agitation, whose persistence can be understood only when we realize that, despite political and social appearances, it was in fact a long-standing disease. The people was murdered, but the people was also sick. Hugo undoubtedly sensed this in speaking of "political disease and social disease," and in describing the epic of the barricades only after he had depicted that strange spring when "the door of winter, still ajar, let out gusts of cold and death."

The epidemic defined, or rather summed up, the unity of the period. In relation to the previous period, the heavy cholera mortality totaled up and multiplied the destitution of the last years of the Restoration and the earliest days of the July Monarchy. And in relation to the following years, the rising in June 1832, coming as it did immediately on the heels of the epidemic, was in every respect merely the political continuation of a single biological crisis so far as the principal actors, the main places and the fear propagated throughout the city were concerned, the physical hatreds it bred in rioters and bourgeois alike, in vanquished and victor, the violence of both, and the determination to exterminate the adversary, where both sides seemed to be blaming not so much their adversaries as those responsible for the epidemic. At the end of his book Roch posed the question correctly. "After the firing on June 5," he wrote, "there was no need to traverse the barricades on the sixth. What lay in the immediate future was the state of siege and, consequently, the revival of the political malaise, indistinguishable from a renewed outbreak of the cholera; the subject was complete in itself." And he concluded, well summing up the biological unity of the story: "Ah, Paris! You are cured of the cholera, but you are close to civil war; you are still sick indeed."

Nor should we fail to recognize the biological characteristics of those acts of religious and social violence brought together in the political history of the period. It would be more correct to say that the cholera epidemic revealed the biological bases of the religious and social antagonisms, whose ideological aspects alone are described in conventional history. During these days—but in the previous period, too—the problems were posed and settled in terms of life and death. This was what the people did in the many demonstrations of irreligion, the most startling being that which led to the Archbishop of Paris's visit to the Hôtel-Dieu. "In other times," Roch wrote, "he would have had to push his way into the forecourt of the Hôtel-Dieu through crowds prostrating themselves as he passed, imploring his blessing; but not so now. Their demeanor simply expressed indifference, defiance or fury. Neither priest nor sister was spared the most mendacious and atrocious accusations." This was equally true of the interpretation of the cholera epidemic by the devout, as summed up by Roch, and was also expressed in the vengeful and apocalyptic sermons of the time: "All these wretches are dying impenitent. But the wrath of the God of Justice is waxing, and soon each day will see a count of thousands stricken; the crime of the destruction of the Archbishop's Palace is far from expiated."

Expressed in terms of life and death, too, were the class hatreds, seen in the murderous fury which seemed suddenly to grip the city. Among the lower classes first. Murders redoubled; but the crowd also indulged in collective massacres. Unfortunate passers-by, convicted by their ill looks of propagating the disease by poisoning fountains or food, were murdered on the streets and squares or thrown into the Seine. Louis Blanc vividly depicted the workers' fury when abandoned by the bourgeoisie, who hastened to shut up shop and flee.[11] "Between the cholera and hunger, what was to become of them?" History, even the history closest to the events, was strangely silent on this point. "It has been said," Guizot wrote in his Memoirs,

that when the plague first broke out, M. Casimir Périer's imagination was so struck that he instantly fell sick, especially as the rumors of poisonings and the murders among the lower classes caused by these rumors troubled his spirits almost as if they were a personal insult. He was outraged by these deplorable scenes of ferocious cruelty. "This is not the thinking of a civilized people," he said. "It is that of a race of savages."

There was a murderous fury among the bourgeois, too, expressed in the many merciless administrative orders for the purpose of clearing the ground by sacrificing the working class and the working-class districts, if need be, to the ferocious deity of the disease.

Hardly any trace of all this remains either in the later political and social documentation or in the contemporary accounts. But are we to believe that these events were effaced so rapidly from the minds of those who experienced them? The vast convulsion of the cholera epidemic of 1832 long remained graven on the memory of the people of Paris—for as long as it left its mark in the deep clefts of the statistical age pyramids. For many years, the street ballads and popular novels handed on and amplified its memory. "And your parents?", Rodolphe asked La Goualeuse in *Les Mystères de Paris*. "The cholera got them." It stayed alive in every family in the memory of the departed until the epidemic of 1849 revived the experience in similar form and with similar violence—the experience of a fundamental injustice and a great popular fraternity, both of them unforgettably demonstrated in the ordeal of death. How has it been possible for conventional social history, which pays so much attention to identifying the earliest traces of class consciousness in this period, to overlook the inevitable effects of the cholera mortality?

The Periods Between Crises

While these biological facts were evident, though generally misinterpreted, in times of crisis, they were equally evident, though even more generally misinterpreted, in the periods between crises, when the absence of political or industrial disturbances and the existence of economic expansion apparently betokened prosperity, social concord and tranquility.

It is here that the demographic documentation most plainly belies the appearance of tranquility. The figures measuring the phenomena that disclose the city's unhealthy biological and social condition remained consistently high and in some cases increased, despite prosperity. This applies to the statistics of the general death rate and even more clearly to the figures for the poorest districts, for children and for the aged. If there were no other evidence, the mere fact that the marriage rate rose far less than might have been expected from the growth of the city and the influx of migrants, mainly young workers, reveals a fluidity of sex relations or, at best, a working-class cohabitation leading to illegitimacy, child desertion and a high rate of infanticide. This emerges, too, from the study of infanticide supplemented by the quantitative documentation generated by the activities of the Board of Health and the daily reports of the Sewers and Street-Cleaning Departments, as well as the sinister accountancy of the Seine. Then there is suicide, too, the high figures and police identification reports proving that this was not due simply to a bourgeois fashion or to romantic behavior. There are the statistics of madness, the madness of the destitute and the newcomer to the city; and of misery, the misery of the vast majority, quite unmistakable in the many administrative enumerations of the indigent population, but equally so in the vital statistics of deaths, marriages and fertility themselves. These, as we shall see, are so far from being incompatible with the undoubted prosperity of numerically large social groups that they may indeed be its consequence and, in some sort, the price to be paid for it. And, lastly, the increase in crime, which had so little connection with economic prosperity that contemporary statisticians assumed a constant relation to a given figure for population and a given distribution by sex and age rather than a relation to a general state of poverty or prosperity.

It is true that these quantitative data for the periods between crises were overwhelmed by the striking contrasts with the periods of actual crisis between which they were recorded and by which they were over-shadowed. They barely show up between the peaks for death, crime and inhuman destitution. Since they cannot be totally denied, conventional historians prefer to ignore them or to minimize their importance and implications. This position is untenable, and it becomes even more so if we simply ask ourselves what these figures would mean in relation to the population of our cities of the Western world and, more particularly, of modern Paris. It may perhaps be said that notions of life and death have changed. This is unconvincing. There is no reason to believe that the measure of popular suffering, of both bodily affliction and moral anguish, has not always been the same.

The impressive statistics mentioned briefly above give us this incontrovertible measurement of suffering even when the people itself was silent and even though similar conditions in later periods seem to indicate the opposite. The many documents overlooked by historians concerned only with describing the major economic and political events, simply because they are commonplace and fugitive publications, also bring this fact home to us in connection with the periods of profoundest tranquility—"the time of profound royalist peace" mentioned by Hugo in *Les Misérables*—and the ensuing period of bourgeois felicity and "dreamless slumber." Can it be said that in such periods the city was prosperous and quiet, preoccupied with work and thrift, eagerly pursuing self-enrichment (and succeeding tolerably well), eager, too, for moral as well as material cónquests, tranquilly cultivating the public and private weal within its families, parishes and its own bourgeois districts, enamored of order in all things, in its affairs, its ideas, its habits, its laws and regulations? Certainly it can; but only if we look no further than the level of political and economic history or a relatively superficial social history. The city which emerges at a far deeper level—the level of the street, the workshop, the scatter of petty day-to-day happenings derived from the administrative files, the daily police and gendarmerie reports, and even more clearly from small items in the newspapers—is a very different place. This city emerges, too, from the muted roar that rises from the great bulk of qualitative documents, and especially from the popular novels of every kind and at every level, whose testimony acquires its full value when checked by quantitative research. This was a criminal and violent city, and even more, a city sick to such a degree that its social structures and relationships were perpetually confronted by issues of life or death.

Social history, drawing on this primary experience in the highly simplified form provided by the study of Paris in the first half of the nineteenth century, reaches down to biological bases whose existence it had never suspected.

IV
The Biological Bases of the History of Paris
in the Period

Throughout this study we shall be discovering the nature and implications of these biological bases—that is to say, everything in the past or contemporary social facts that closely relates to the physical characteristics of individuals—and we shall conclude with an attempt to define a biological theory and to show how this points to a method of recasting social history and social description. By way of introduction to this piece of research and of throwing some light, however dim it still may be, on a method of analysis which will compel us to go a long way round in approaching our ultimate subject, we need merely stress at this point that, first, we simply cannot ignore biological facts in the social history of Paris in the first half of the nineteenth century; and, secondly, that such facts have been neglected or given little place in research on later periods, rather as if urban societies and Parisian society itself had become progressively disincarnate and as if economic or moral inquiry could adequately account for the social facts, which would thereby be reduced to data purely economic and/or moral.

It is easy to see that the reason for such a radical simplification lies in the general evolution of societies, and, perhaps even more strikingly, of urban societies. From the second half of the nineteenth century onward, living conditions improved so greatly that the very term "living conditions" lost the pregnant significance it had in a period when it meant a margin between life and death that might be wiped out by the slightest increase in the price of bread. It is easy to see that research evolved in a similar way and that it came to seem unnecessary to dig down to the biological facts beneath the vast layer of economic, political and moral facts deposited over them.

The old wisdom vanished even from demographic research, though it is true that some trace of the human vocation of population studies was still to be found in a few scattered observations. Thus, [Louis-Adolphe] Bertillon wrote in his introduction to a census of Paris:

It is obvious that if the Paris community has a smaller proportion of children and the aged and if, on the other hand, there is an abundance of adolescents and adults, this fact alone will endow the community with special qualities; its marriage and birth rates and its productive force should be greater; while, unless it is subjected to any abnormally damaging factors, it should register fewer sick persons and fewer deaths for the same number of inhabitants. Production and consumption should notably increase, since the population is of an age at which vigor, mental and physical activity and productive force, and consequently all the appetites and sexual needs, are at their height. Unless environmental factors restrict these capacities, the sharper these differences in composition, the stronger should be all the motions of society.[12]

This sums up well, and in terms which still hold good, the implications of the age distribution of an urban population, and especially the importance of sexual needs, which moreover (as we know from other sources) were more precocious than usual in this instance. Urban civilization is erotic; on the one hand, it develops sexual needs; on the other, it receives a stimulus from sexuality that is reflected in every sphere, the economic, the social and the cultural. This factor called for a real effort to discover the biological content of the demographic phenomena, of everything that lives, suffers, struggles and breathes beneath the figures—without which, indeed, figures are meaningless. It called for determining the contribution of demographic investigation to the general investigation of societies. In vain, however; for Bertillon, the statistician of the city, who had neither the time nor the inclination to exploit what he had discovered, or rather rediscovered; who could exploit it, moreover, only by applying this statistical tool to disciplines other than his own; and who was a most eminent expert in his own specialty but fatally impoverished by his very specialization, Bertillon left the material in a forgotten corner of a statistical annual which no one would ever read except another statistician, that is, the very person least equipped to understand it; and even he would read it rapidly, furtively, almost as if ashamed of it and, as it were, without the author's knowledge.

Social history and social description henceforward operated at a level well above the biological depths disclosed by the first half of the nineteenth century. Upon those depths history closed its books, never to revisit them save in exceptional cases when major cataclysms stirred them up once again, like earthquakes which rip open settled structures, subvert the order of natural strata and men's constructions and bring the subterranean forces to the surface. This was to happen in the Commune, which released to the surface of history something akin to a lava stream of buried and forgotten biological facts. Contemporary social description has behaved in the same way, and has discerned the biological bases of the developments it was observing only in the investigation of such purely pathological circumstances as criminality.

But we must surely consider that these biological conditions exist and that it is important to have some knowledge of them; that we should not merely regard them as something exceptional and abnormal. And so far as history is concerned, we must surely find that they are at least as active in the periods in which they are not apparent as during the crises; but active in a different way. So far as the description of modern societies is concerned, we must surely assume that normal people are tied to these physical characteristics at least as strongly as criminals are, that to obtain a knowledge of everything in people's behavior which is intimately connected with the structure, needs, imperatives and functions of their body is one of the most important procedures in social observation, and that this should be exactly the same element in the social study as in the literary description of the urban environment. The pictures of Paris painted by the sociologists and the novelists differ so widely that they seem to be about two different cities and two different societies, each of them equally exaggerated, incomplete and over-simplified: a city and a society in which all problems—even that of leisure—are reduced to a single problem, that of labor; a city and a society in which all problems—even the problems of labor—are reduced to problems of passion. Surely it is clear enough that in the period we are dealing with, just as in previous periods, the biological facts, though overlaid with a dense layer of economics and morals, played their normal and ordinary part in the development of society?

This is true of the earlier periods but applies even more obviously to the first half of the nineteenth century, which provides us with an experience of the relationships between biological and other historical factors so complete that we can determine the biological bases of a social history and with a social description applicable not only to that period, but to all others.

But before we come to the theoretical exposition and attempt to discuss it, we shall have to obtain figures for, define and appraise, the basic data of the problem. It might perhaps have been more logical to identify these data at the outset, to isolate them in successive stages and then to regroup them in a general description of Parisian society in the first half of the nineteenth century. However, we have thought it better to give a conspectus of them at the start: both the facts as a whole and their interrelations, confused and complex, it may be, but living and incontrovertible, as they appeared to their contemporaries and to the actors in the drama and as we find them in the documents which transmit and reconstruct them for us.

It is, then, the general problem of daily life in Paris during the period—in its entirety and in detail—as presented in the qualitative documentation which dictates our initial approach, because it is there that we find, set out in a form which we could find nowhere else, all the developments that we shall later have to identify, break down and analyze. For it is the literary documentation, above all, haunted as it is by crime, which enables us to perceive that the causes and effects of crime are simply the expression of the pathological state of the city—which is, in short, the whole problem we are dealing with; although this documentation simply sets it out rather than breaks it down, experiences it rather than expounds it.

BOOK I

The Theme of Crime:
Its Importance
and Implications

Introduction

This study might well have been arranged in a different order: the actual order of the research which brought home to us the conviction that the theme of crime was in fact the principal theme in the history of Paris in the nineteenth century, a notion calculated to set social history on a new course. We might first have discussed the quantitative documents, the series of figures, since what they disclose at a first glance is the wholly exceptional character of the growth of Paris during our period, seen in the statistics for mortality and fertility and in all those pathological facts which reveal and measure the diseased state of the city, physical and moral, which was the consequence of that growth. The study of the qualitative documents, especially the literature, might have been expected to come second, once we had mastered our quantitative tools.

We shall not proceed in this way, however, but shall begin with the qualitative documentation. We shall leave the observation of the quantitative facts themselves till later, since we consider we already know enough about them from an earlier study[1] to interpret the qualitative documentation, and particularly because we consider that this qualitative documentation potentially contains all the facts we shall be discussing, especially the testimony about their own time and their own plight supplied by contemporaries. It is the qualitative, and above all the literary, documentation that most immediately and most readily records—most visibly in the transformation of the theme of crime—a collective disquiet, relating not so much to crime itself as to the development of society as a whole, and that imparts to a great number of works of literature an invariable cast which is not adequately accounted for by the influence of romanticism. "No one should be surprised," one of

Eugène Sue's correspondents wrote, "if we deal in the terrible; it is because everything around us is terrible."[2]

It is one and the same dangerous and diseased city that looms large on the horizon in these books, no matter how indifferent they may themselves be to the convulsions of society. One and the same society is described throughout, stamping the most personal, the most subjective and the most exceptional dramas with the powerful imprint of this basic imbalance, the demographic, economic and social aspects of which we shall describe later. The correlations between the qualitative documentation and the most elementary contemporary statistical documentation which suddenly come to light are so frequent, so incontrovertible and so overwhelming that there is no reason to begin with one rather than the other; on the contrary, there are many reasons for starting with this testimony and for giving the images precedence over the figures. The literature invades our research from the very outset.

What is the value of its testimony? Before assessing this we must define the new correlations we believe we can establish between the qualitative and the quantitative documentation.

CHAPTER ONE

The Demographic Approach

I

From Rejection to Approach

In his initial approach, the social historian must inevitably reject the evidence of the literature.

One of the principal reasons for the almost complete absence in France of a social history—defined as a continuous, homogeneous and numerical description of the material and moral aspects of the population—is the existence of great works of literature, which certainly look like irrefutable documents and which, moreover, by their verbal magic solidly reconstruct things past and generate, so to speak, a recurrent experience of them. This is true of the social history of the period from the beginning of the nineteenth century down to our own times, but especially of the first three quarters of that century, when testimony of this sort is notably abundant, brilliant and convincing. It is true of France as a whole, both the countryside and the towns, but especially so of Paris. Balzac, Hugo, Sue, Daudet and Zola, to name only the greatest, have left such a complete and concrete description of the capital that historians tend to neglect the apparently unnecessary archival research and jejune statistics and for the most part simply take their raw material from the large range of famous novels. Alongside the political and the economic history, laboriously built up on well-checked documents, there exists a social history, compounded, curiously enough, almost wholly of fiction.

How this renunciation of professional standards operates is beside the point. We shall merely remark here that of all writers it is Balzac whose novels provide an obvious clue to an attitude so much at variance with the rigorous methods of conventional history. Balzac's works alone suffice to dispel the distrust engendered by the disorderly descriptions of a Hugo or a Zola. They alone can do this because of their impersonal registration of facts, persons and places undistorted by the interposition of any subjective viewpoint; not nearly so much because of the leading characters and principal locations in the *Comédie humaine* as because of the manifold and apparently incidental links between these characters and society as a whole and between the districts and the city as a whole, the detailed information on relatives, neighbors and friends, on business transactions and customers and clients, for example, and addresses which look as if they had been taken from registration offices or trade directories. From such dry and succinct notes history draws the most vivid and convincing consequences; in brief, not nearly so much from what may be called their upper levels, whose appreciation involves considerations and techniques outside our competence, as from their lower levels, which, by their very imperfection and lack of polish, are barely distinguishable from the ordinary material of social history and really do look like files of archival materials similar to the actual archives which have survived to this day. Thanks to Balzac's works and, so to speak, under Balzac's auspices, historians have come to look upon most of the major social novels of the first three-quarters of the nineteenth century, even those with the largest purely literary content, if not as actual historical documents, at any rate as credible evidence. The descriptions by Balzac, Hugo, Sue and Zola of Paris during the Restoration, the July Monarchy and the Second Empire account for the lack of research in social history on the period, despite the ample documentation both published and unpublished. Such research should have begun by resolutely rejecting this literature and its whole world of obsessive images.

Nevertheless, at a second stage a different attitude towards the literature has become feasible, owing to the progress in quantitative social history. The conclusions derived from a quantitative research which has by now gained a better grasp of its documentation and methodology, and better access to adequate statistical material, can be collated with the literary evidence. The historian can now undertake a demographic appraisal of the literary documentation and make proper use of the literature.

Indeed, this has become inevitable. The advances in quantitative research stress the potentialities of the statistical survey, but they also soon define its limitations both as to the facts and to the extent and speed with which contemporaries became aware of them.

Statistics are the necessary framework of social research. They identify and measure incontrovertible facts. In some cases, they even reveal facts which would certainly not show up otherwise. They cannot, however, replace social description. Two towns may record the same number of inhabitants, the same distribution by sex and age, the same rates of mortality, fertility and marriage, the same social mobility and the same levels of living, and yet may differ profoundly.

An exclusive bias toward measurement would condemn sociologists to a view far more abstract and a description far more inaccurate than the most disparate of literary descriptions. This is frequently the deplorable outcome of tremendous spadework, as is to be seen even in the splendid sociological research of the Chicago school; the huge accumulation of urban facts laboriously compiled in the capital of contemporary urban sociology may well itself one day become a dead letter unless literary testimony, worked up in some instances by novelists who began as sociologists, continuously and consistently imbues it with a higher and more immediate form of life.

Let us go further. The qualitative procedure is not so irreplaceable in the case of modern surveys as it is for the description of earlier periods. In the last resort the statistical annuals would nowadays suffice, if a strictly quantitative description, that is to say, a measurement of all the social facts, is feasible—nay, desirable—today; the most complete description of a country would be that condensed in a compilation of figures. This, indeed, is now the ultimate aim of social research in certain countries, the United States in particular, where a method for measuring almost all the facts has been worked out. These multiple and detailed, but scattered and dispersed, statistics are synthesized automatically. Living as they do at the time when and in the environment where these documents have been prepared, their authors and users compare, correct and complete the figures, convert them into real situations and reinvest them with color, passion and real life.

Similarly, to a Quételet, a Villermé, a Parent-Duchatelet, to the authors and users of the city's *Recherches statistiques*, the figures for contemporary Paris, of all orders of magnitude and however scattered and heterogeneous, were as concrete as a chapter of *Les Misérables*; they made it unnecessary to read the book. They were resurrected for use precisely because they reflected realities so well and because their contemporaries found in them a means of measuring appearances.

This measurement has survived; it is readily available to us in the statistical documents we are going on to survey. The appearances have vanished, together with beliefs which we no longer find intelligible, old fevers and revolutions which no longer alarm us, the colors of the sky, the sounds, the forms of a Paris which we can barely imagine. For we may well get its images and epochs confused when we come to reconstruct them at random. A few shreds, perhaps, still hang here and there in the disembodied architecture of the statistics, traces of color, fragments of material, outlines of forms. But it may be, too, that these appearances have not totally vanished, since the literary evidence helps us to rediscover what they may have been, to reconstruct them, to breathe into the most antique and defunct statistics something of a life comparable to that with which our modern experience invests the statistics of our own time.

This entails working through the problem of the facts to the problem of the awareness and opinion of them. Death, fertility and crime statistics are historically meaningful only by virtue of the relative importance people accord them. The highest death rates do not necessarily identify the groups of people who are most moved by death. Indeed, the reverse is true, for dismay at death and the sense of the value of life are usually strongest in the areas and at the periods when the death rate is tending to fall or even where and when it is lowest. An awareness of the facts is at least as important to historical description as their measurement. Of this awareness the statistical documentation preserves scarcely a trace, whereas it can be discerned in the literary documentation; and this is yet another reason for correlating statistical research with literature.

II

The Demographic Approach to the Facts

While these are the reasons for the historian's taking a different view of the literary documentation, what are the main features of this historical evaluation? It can be defined, firstly, as the confrontation of the literary evidence with the numerical data; and, secondly, as the comparison of the literary evidence with the basic trends revealed by statistical research. The first form of this evaluation is wholly external and fragmentary, in that it does not embrace the works as a whole but only certain relatively incidental observations, certain details which can be verified by the statistics, details which are of no great importance in relation to the works themselves, but whose relative authenticity may enable the historian to form some judgment of the authenticity of the works themselves. The second stage in this approach is far more essential to our research, in that it relates not to the details but to the works in the aggregate, confronting the social developments described by the novelist with those shown up by the figures.

An Approach by Detail

Granting that the social history of Paris in the first half of the nineteenth century can be divested of its obsessive images only by subjecting to measurement the facts it tries to describe, it is evident that the historian's first, and almost instinctive, procedure is to confront the literary evidence with the numerical data he has already collected. Regardless of a work's literary value, and without going so far as to embark upon a historical study of it, the historian cannot accept a literary description as evidence unless it tallies with the statistical measurements, not merely as a whole but in its details, and precisely in those details which are of only incidental importance relative to the work as a whole and which—quite rightly—are wholly irrelevant to any purely literary reading of it.

Economic Authenticity: We shall be dealing hardly at all here with the economic appraisal, the most obvious, the best known and the one most usually made. A comparison of wages, rents, land prices, the price of bread or wine at different periods, or a mason's or dressmaker's budget, with the figures given in novels is often, and perhaps wrongly, taken to be sufficient guide for the historian's assessment of the authenticity of a work.

Balzac's prestige among historians is due in large measure to the quality of the figures he gives for certain economic facts, such as his delight in demonstrating the way certain things work or the details of speculations in which he involves our attention. He goes so far as to provide us with a precise observation of the time span, the character and the consequences of economic situations as a whole. Noteworthy is the accurate registration of the deadly effects of the years 1816, 1817, 1818 and 1819, which are confirmed by the statistics for the death rate and are the theme of a great deal of discussion in the medical topographies. "It will be recalled," Lachaise wrote, "that the other years in question were remarkable for brief periods of dearth and severe winters; it is well known that such temporary crises exert their most lethal effects on women and children."[1] It was the crisis of 1816 that was responsible for the drama in Balzac's *Une double famille*, which begins in the rue du Tourniquet-Saint-Jean, where M. de Granville one day caught sight of an embroideress and her mother at a window:

In these circumstances and towards the end of December, when bread was dearest and the beginning of the rise in the price of corn which made the year 1816 such a cruel one for the poor was already making itself felt, the stroller observed on the face of the young girl, whose name he did not know, the terrible marks of some secret preoccupation which his benevolent smiles failed to dissipate. He soon recognized in Catherine's eyes the dark signs of night work. . . .[2]

The crisis of 1819, aggravated by a merciless winter, is the denouement of *La Vendetta*, a story of revenge, love and poverty narrated with incomparable precision in the observation of the relationships between the progressive ravages of poverty, hunger and death.

Sue's works do not seem to stand up so well to appraisal by economic historians. His earliest readers, themselves contemporaries of the events narrated in the book, subjected *Les Mystères de Paris* to detailed criticism in a number of letters which have been preserved. Thus one correspondent, referring to the character of the Slasher, the driftwood docker on the quai Saint-Paul and murderer in his off moments, wrote on November 21, 1843:

Dear M. Sue, I find that your Slasher (for a fellow as good at his job as you make him out to be) does not earn enough. If you were better informed, you ought to know that a good hauler earns 7 to 8 francs and that 35 sous a day is what a good paddler gets. I'm not surprised he has to visit Mère Ponisse's dive.

In many respects the historian is even more exacting than the contemporary reader because less swayed by appearances, better informed and more familiar with the statistics and their implications. No matter how fine a work may be, the historian finds it hard to take it seriously as a whole and to concede it the slightest evidential value if the figures in it do not tally with those which his knowledge of the general economic situation tells him must be correct.

Demographic Authenticity: There is, however, an even more exacting type of statistic, the demographic. In the description of Paris society presented in Balzac, Hugo and Sue, the historian will accept in the first place only those observations which square with what he has learned from the statistics of the composition of the population and the changes in its growth. Here we shall give only a few examples of this procedure, taken at random from various authors—it will be the theme of most of what we shall be discussing hereafter—yet we cannot but point once more to Balzac's superiority and the quite exceptional quality of his demographic observations. In Balzac, population structures are not fused with the biologically determined elements described by Zola, or rather the elements which Zola asserts to be hereditary even in a work which he nevertheless describes as "the natural and social history of a family under the Second Empire"; in Balzac, they are assimilated rather with less obscure facts, such as family relationships, the generations, age structures, the process of ageing itself—Rastignac becoming a statesman when Marshal Hulot has grown old—individual facts backed by contemporary historical facts, which date and leave their mark upon them.

The historian has to discover how far the description of the population of Paris, or at least the random and rapid clues scattered more or less haphazardly throughout the works, corresponds with what he knows of the composition of that population in the period, that is to say (to take only the demographic characteristics) what he knows of the inhabitants' provincial origins and their distribution by age and sex.

As to the first, certainly the careers of Remonencq, Monistrol, the Brezacs, Sauviat and Bourgeat, the foundling from Saint-Flour, give a picture of the Auvergnat immigration in Paris in the first decades of the century and of its rate, habits and success which wholly agrees with the case histories and graphs that can be constructed from contemporary statistics and the bankruptcy dossiers and with the many reports by the Prefecture of Police. But it is equally certain that the space given in the works of Balzac and of most of the nineteenth-century novelists to people from the Massif Central does not at all correspond with their real proportion relative to the Paris population as a whole.

It is quite clear that Balzac was far more interested in the immigrants from the south of France than from the north, yet we know that the latter accounted for the higher proportion. It is true that a more detailed statistical survey—which has yet to be made—would perhaps show that immigration from the south was the larger, at least within the restricted society Balzac was depicting. Be that as it may, the Parisian population was swollen in the first decades of the nineteenth century by an immigration from the northern provinces. On this point statistical analysis concurs with medical topography. Describing the Parisian, Lachaise wrote in his *Topographie médicale* in 1822: "His soft, white complexion contrasts markedly with that of the inhabitant of the small town and especially the countryside, who is more exposed to bad weather and sun and light. The Parisian has fair or chestnut hair and blue eyes." The predominance of fair hair in *Les Mystères de Paris* is striking. There are so many descriptions of physical characteristics in that book that we could practically compile statistics of them. La Goualeuse is fair: "A braid of magnificent ash-blond hair curled halfway down her cheek . . . "; the Slasher has "pale fair hair, verging on white, shaggy eyebrows and huge, very fair sideburns"; the members of the horrible Martial family are fair-haired or redheads; and as for Tortillard, the son of Bras Rouge, "the child's forehead was half-hidden by a thicket of coarse yellowish hair as stiff as a horse's mane." In brief, fair hair predominates in the Paris underworld. A character must be a really sinister criminal for Eugène Sue to give him brown hair and red cheeks, to Sue—but also to the contemporary criminologists—signs of genuinely deep-seated viciousness.

No less important is the precision of observations concerning the distribution of the population by age and sex, with due weight to period, district and occupation.

The relative youth of a population and its normal or abnormal distribution by sex and age determine what the statistician Bertillon called "a relative social exaltation,"[3] the effects of which may be found in the contrasts recorded in the literary descriptions collected by the historian, such as the contrast between districts peopled by the young, like Les Halles, and districts of retired and aged persons, like the Ile Saint-Louis or the Marais, where Cousin Pons lived "in a quiet house in the quiet rue de Normandie." Such, too, is the contrast, of which Proudhon often complained, between the trades eagerly sought by the young and those despised by them, as well as the essential, and usually forgotten, aspect of social struggles referred to in the confession by Champmathieu, the former wheelwright in Paris, in *Les Misérables*: "One gets old when one's still quite young in that job—A man's done for at forty.—I was fifty-three, that was hard—And the young workmen are so nasty! When you're not as young as you were, they jeer at you as a stupid old gaffer!" The breakdown of the proportion of the female population in Paris, the uneven distribution of the sexes by class and district—the luxury districts, where the proportion of the female population was highest, and the Hôtel-de-Ville district, where masons and laborers crowded the sordid lodging houses in the little streets off the place de Grève where hands were taken on—have left traces in the literature. The 1851 census giving the distribution of the female population and the number of households by district and street enables us to assess the value of certain literary evidence, to mention only the authenticity of the description of the rue aux Fèves in the heart of the Cité, where Sue places the first scene in *Les Mystères de Paris*.

In brief, a historian reading the major novels which have some claim to describe Paris society in the first half of the nineteenth century cannot fail to observe, almost by instinct, how the clues in them, usually in matters of detail, coincide fairly closely with the incontrovertible statistics of population composition. A work will be of appreciable value to him only if it contains a great many instances of exact correspondences of this kind, unintended by the writer.

Observations concerning changes in the population and especially in the death rate are, however, more frequent in these works and more authentic. Since we know the high death rates in Paris in the first half of the nineteenth century, this is not surprising. Sickness and death are very definitely the most important facts in the social, and even the general, history of Paris in the period. This is well symbolized in the Paris landscape by the high-lying cemetery to which the novelists so often take their characters and by the somber mass of the hospitals which inspired the Parisians with a terror stressed by Sue and Balzac: "The popular classes' obstinacy in this respect is such," Balzac wrote in *Le Cousin Pons*, "that sick people's repugnance to going to the hospital comes from the fact that they believe that they kill people there by giving them nothing to eat." There are many references to illnesses and epidemics such as cholera, but also to smallpox, which killed one-half of the newborn infants, supplying Victor Hugo with the story of the Thénardier children and Gavroche, and disfiguring or engendering some of the monsters in *Les Mystères de Paris*. Even more frequent is the confirmation of inequality before sickness and death. In the first half of the nineteenth century, as under the Ancien Régime, the workman, the artisan and the bourgeois showed the kind of sickness and death and life expectancy corresponding to their occupation in the same way as they bore the speech, dress and even body marks peculiar to their occupation. The diseases of tailors and concierges were described in almost exactly the same terms by Lachaise in his *Topographie médicale de Paris* and by Balzac in his depiction of the death of Cibot in *Le Cousin Pons*:

Dr. Poulain acquitted his own and the scientific conscience by assuming that because of his sedentary life in a damp porter's lodge, the blood of this tailor, squatting on a table behind a lattice window, might have decomposed for lack of exercise and especially by his continually inhaling vapors from a foul gutter. . . .—"What disease has my poor Cibot got?", the concierge asked Dr. Poulain.—"My dear Madame Cibot," the doctor replied, "he is dying of the concierge's disease."

There is striking agreement between Villermé's and Quételet's[4] studies of the stature of city dwellers and inequality of stature by social class and Victor Hugo's observations in *Les Misérables*:

It was the period when Anglès, the Prefect of Police, ended a special confidential report to the King on the Paris faubourgs: "All things well considered, Sire, there is nothing to be feared from these people. They are as carefree and indolent as cats. The lower classes are active in the provinces; in Paris they are not. They are all small men. Two of them, Sire, would be needed end to end to make one of your grenadiers. There is nothing to be feared from the capital mob. It is noteworthy that their stature has shrunk in the past fifty years; the people of the Paris faubourgs are smaller than before the Revolution. They are not dangerous. In a word, they are scum."

This is an observation drawn from a reliable source, the report by Anglès,[5] who had personal knowledge of the statistics, later to be used in demographic research.

These few examples sum up the main aspects of an initial demographic reading paying more attention to the details of the works than to those works as a whole, the findings being of more interest to the historian than to the specialist in literary research. But not much more. If the latter finds these random observations only of slight interest as a matter of curiosity, the historian, starting from his statistical description, does not even find that they confirm what he considers he knows already. A mere matter of curiosity, that is, for both of them alike. We should add that such historical evaluation does not enable us to classify the works very precisely in relation to their value as history. Certainly, Balzac's authenticity shines out in scores of details, almost always subsequently confirmed; but we should observe that far less notable works, even imaginary descriptions, abound in equally accurate and verified details. This is not surprising, for this authenticity is, to some degree, involuntary; Sue's Parisians are fair-haired for the same reasons and in the same way as they would inevitably be brown-haired in a twentieth-century description.

An Aggregate Approach

The second form of demographic evaluation is very different and far more important for our subsequent research. It does not deal with the

incidental and fragmentary aspects of these works, dwelling on correspondences that are perhaps no more than chance pieces of luck, and
collecting, as we have just been doing, harmless curios. Instead it
embraces and, so to speak, quizzes the entire work: its aggregate, its
unity, the cohesion of the developments it traces, the whole scope of
the dramatic events it unleashes, its irreplaceable theme and, in some
cases, even its title. The tool of measurement it uses is not an isolated
rate taken from the statistics, not some partial breakdown, but the
totality of those breakdowns, the aggregate of the statistics of population composition and changes, a mass of figures bringing out the major
trends in population and social development, that is, the rapid growth of
the population in the first half of the nineteenth century and the inadequate adaptation of the urban environment to that growth, which
accounts in part for many of the material and moral characteristics of
the Parisians of the time.

In the light of this evaluation, what certainly emerges as the dominant
characteristic of the vast literary documentation on Paris in this period
and, even more plainly, of the major works, is the astonishing correspondence between the social facts confirmed by demographic research
and those most frequently described. The essential demographic fact
governing the evolution of Paris during these years (one which earlier,
nonstatistical research could not get at) is the major theme of the
description which most of these works embody or assume, state or imply.
This accounts for the importance given to social problems in them and
for the way in which they are treated; and above all for the attention to
the biological characteristics of inequality and the physical content of
the class antagonisms which inflame most of these narratives, from the
great dramas of the people to the fate of individuals.

Strange indeed is the authenticity of most of these works, but perhaps
even stranger the authenticity of those which the historian is bound to
view with the most suspicion. While conventional social history, rightly
distrustful of grand romantic outbursts, is readier to accept Balzac's
evidence than Hugo's or Sue's, quantitative research by the social
historian paradoxically discovers a truth no less important, though of a
different kind, in works which seem overcharged with noise, color and
passion. Is not the main theme of the history of Paris in our period that
identified by and summed up in the very title of Hugo's novel, *Les
Misérables*? Is it not the actual subject of Sue's novel, from whose
opening pages we may take the definition which best expresses it in the

actual choice of terms: "We are about to try to place before the reader some episodes in the life of barbarians as far outside civilization as the savage tribes so well depicted by [James Fenimore] Cooper. Only, the barbarians we are speaking of are in our midst. . . ."

"Barbarians," "savages," "vagrants," the terms generally used by Sue and Hugo—all of them evoking a picture of a primitive race living apart from civilized people—designated a large proportion of the Paris population, all those who lived in what Sue called "the sinister regions of poverty and ignorance," as well as the dwellers in the lower depths and "the great cavern of Evil." Even in the very terms he used, Sue here identified the processes of the demographic evolution governing the general evolution of Paris, its tremendous expansion and transformation, to be discussed later; indeed, they are to be the major theme of this survey because they were the major facts in the history of Paris.

The conclusions to be drawn from a demographic reading of this sort of literature are of historical importance. We find that these documents confirm the conclusions derived from statistical research and supply, too, a mass of facts previously uncompiled, suggesting applications of them previously unsuspected and posing problems which had hitherto remained outside its scope. Above all, we discover a concrete and total experience hitherto inaccessible to statistical research. Moving out of the world of figures, statistical research emerges into the light of reality in the heart of a Paris whose communal and private dramas had seemed to lie outside its field, and thus surpasses its limitations.

But the conclusions from a demographic reading are equally important to literary criticism, since they add to the original reasons for admiring these works—which is not for us to determine—a new and equally important reason. This, through unforeseen byways, merges with the original reasons, namely, their authenticity, which cannot be established by the traditional investigation of sources (the literary appraisal of literature) but is brought out both by this confrontation with the facts and by this incontrovertible numerical proof. The fact that the specialist in social history discovers in *Les Misérables* and *Les Mystères de Paris* an identity of interests and even of techniques—miraculously devised—which in some cases renders these works models of social description supplementing the synthesis already constructed from his own research is surely important for the understanding of literary creation. Still more generally, it is surely true that the specific property of literary sensibility and creation is to reveal by different means the principal and perpetual objective of social research, whether historical or modern: the great mystery of human destinies, an objective essential if we are not to resign ourselves to the conventional description of a disembodied, mutilated, incomplete and artificial society, a mere caricature. "It is the haunting of vast cities, above all, and the intersection and cross-breeding of their innumerable relationships that engender this obsessive ideal," Baudelaire wrote in the Preface to *Le spleen de Paris*; an ideal for the poet, but an ideal, too, for the research worker, who recognizes his own problem and his own aim in Baudelaire's phrase.

Literary Description and Statistical Information

The study of literary creation in the first half of the nineteenth century could no doubt help to throw light on some of the incontrovertible reasons for the matching of contemporary literary description with the statistical description, the ultimate aim of our study. They are not the most important reasons, however; for the main problems of Parisian civilization are everywhere posed in most of the works, or at any rate are usually the background to them, and they are everywhere observed with a numerical accuracy and a precision which cannot but solicit our attention and excite our amazement. We shall observe this care for measurement throughout the *Comédie humaine*. Mortality, fertility, economic situation, social group, criminality: all these problems Balzac defines by estimates or proportions which, though sometimes inconsistent, denote an attention to official or generally accepted numerical data, expressing at the very least the inability of the novelist—like the historian—to describe social developments save by assessing and expressing them in terms of figures. We find this concern again in *Les Misérables*, in which the descriptions of abandoned children and of the sewers are extremely accurate and of a high quality, with many references to the most important official documents. And similar precision of information is to be found in *Les Mystères de Paris*, where some paragraphs are simply a commentary on or illustration of official reports or contemporary surveys. Even the most commonplace, cheapest novelettes pay similar attention to population estimates.

It is evident enough now that this general development of description during the first half of the nineteenth century is not to be accounted for simply by the specific characteristics of literary creation, but rather by the new relations between statistics and opinion. This quite exceptional information is the result simultaneously of a certain state of statistical research and of the dissemination of its results.

This development does not occur until the first half of the nineteenth century and disappears soon after. It is something very unlike the contradictions we find between the social history of Paris during the Second Empire and Zola's depiction of it. The reason is that since the Second Empire was more normal demographically, more prosperous socially and economically, and better balanced statistically, it generated no documentation at all comparable to that which accumulated in the Paris of the July Monarchy, whose unhealthy biological and social conditions were recorded in disquieting statistics. Another reason is that the results of statistical research were not published as widely under the Second Empire as they were during the first half of the nineteenth century and did not arouse anything like the same interest. We must now describe this attitude to statistics, or perhaps we might say this youthful outburst of statistics, as manifested first in research and then in opinion.

Can we speak of a "youthful outburst of statistics" in the sphere of research? Perhaps this is going too far. It was much more of an eager effort to use the new and more potent tools provided by a very much fuller documentation in order to fulfill the eighteenth-century forerunners' great ambition to devise a measurement for the description and prediction of moral, physical and human phenomena.

Such was the ambition of Moheau, whose *Recherches et considérations sur la population de la France* [1778] gave a foretaste of our qualitative demography's entire program; the plan has been revived time after time but never completed. His book contains the first study of the correlations of fertility with regional geographical diversity, urban and rural distribution of the population, year and economic situation, seasons, institutions, customs and laws. Mortality itself is considered in the context of region, place, trade, age and sex. Despite the general inadequacy of the figures and a frequently rudimentary statistical technique, these analyses still stand up as a whole, so potent was the influence on life and death exercised by natural and supernatural factors during the last decades of the Ancien Régime—good and bad harvests, that is to say, rain and shine, sun and moon, which govern the marriage and birth rates and exert an even greater influence perhaps on fertility. Such was the ambition of Buffon, too, in writing his *Essai d'arithmétique morale*, and especially of Condorcet in taking up and perfecting the earlier attempts at a political arithmetic, asserting that "the truths of the social and political sciences can be ascertained with the same certainty as those in the system of the physical sciences." Holding that nature obeys invariable laws, Condorcet advocated a rational observation of facts to reveal those laws. Going further, he founded his social mathematics, an application of the theory of probability to the study of human phenomena, and outlined an ambitious program which it would be presumptuous to regard even now as so much as partially completed.

This at any rate was the program which the statisticians of the first half of the nineteenth century wished to try to revive and carry through with the abundant means now available to them. It was an eighteenth-century program taken over by men who regarded themselves as the inheritors of a grand design and who, in their techniques and interests, in fact were the inheritors. Hence the intransigent and augmented curiosity of their incursion into statistics, and hence their daring use and interpretation of figures.

This determination to obtain figures for everything, to measure everything, to know everything, but to know it by way of number, this encyclopedic hunger, was what inspired the successors of Moheau and Messance, who created the Bureau of General Statistics and first attempted a census, all of them men of the century of Enlightenment and steeped in philosophy. Duquesnoy, born in 1759, the successor of Moheau, Necker and François de Neufchâteau, held that demographic inquiry should be at least as qualitative as quantitative. His curiosity was voracious and the statistical enterprise he launched has the dimensions of a cosmogony.[6] Moreover, certain surveys—that on longevity, for example—aroused great public interest and gave rise to an abundant and often curious correspondence. Thus, the President of the Canton of Saint-Antonin in the Aveyron wrote to the Minister of the Interior on 5 Nivose of the Year II:

I am engaged in making observations on longevity. I believe I have a clue with which all the ideas held on this matter will connect up. I need to collect a great number of facts to make sure of this. I should like to have mortality tables for all the Paris arrondissements, separately and by year, comprising all individuals of both sexes who have died aged seventy and upwards since the mayors were put in charge of the registers of vital statistics.

We talk of statistical ambition; we might equally talk of statistical imperialism. In a curious pamphlet of some fifty pages entitled "*De la statistique et particulièrement de l'opération ordonée en l'an IX sous le nom de Statistique générale de la France*,"[7] Alexandre de Ferrières related that questions as terrifying in number as they were disturbing in nature were sent out to the untutored mayors. A Prefect he consulted on "how to extricate himself from this operation" replied: "I will do it and I would do it ten times over if I were ordered. If the Government asked me the number of birds flying over my department yearly, I would tell it straight off, correct to the last lark."

This effort was, it is true, to become more sensible and, from the Restoration onwards, to comply with more reasonable instructions for regularly and carefully worked out censuses. But even when the statistical torrent had subsided and been induced to flow within well-marked banks, it was still to carry down plenty of debris from those old ambitions. We have only to recall the headings of the first large-scale censuses, and above all to look at those in the *Recherches statistiques de la Ville de Paris*, which were always models for statistical research throughout France. The scope of the facts covered in this first volume, containing the results of the 1817 census and inaugurating this admirable series, is astonishing. The number of inhabitants and the death, birth and marriage rates, of course; but also figures for natural children, stillborn children, accidental and violent deaths, intentional or unintentional suicides, deaths from some of the lung diseases, inmates of old people's homes and general hospitals, with particulars of age and occupation, home-assisted indigent persons, a weather survey and various tables concerning the economy, consumption in particular; in brief, the whole city, with its heights and depths, its work and needs, its climate and seasons.

A glance at the headings alone shows at once that this new statistical documentation, the lack of which had impoverished earlier research and hamstrung earlier ambitions, enabled the new men to embark once more upon the statistical study of the relations between demographic developments and economic and social developments which their great eighteenth-century forerunners had sketched out but been unable to complete.

These ambitious statistics became the stuff of equally ambitious research.

We have here to deal only with the theoretical aspects of this research and the constantly recurring effort to solve the old, the basic, problem to which Moheau, Messance, Turgot, Condorcet and the rest had already addressed themselves, namely, the correlations between the demographic and other facts. Quételet's contribution and influence were inestimable here.[8] We need not go into the way statistics invaded branches of science in which they had hitherto played a minor part; but it is worth noting at least that the subject of the thesis presented by Broussais in 1840 was the application of statistics to pathology.[9]

Administration and action were involved, as well as research. The main point about this statistical activity was the fact that the statistician, the heir in fact and by choice of the eighteenth-century Encyclopedists, was compelled by universal demand to assume the greater responsibility that seemed to be his due by virtue of his new and deeper knowledge, not only in Paris itself but also, by the contagion of example and owing to the capital's influence, in most of the large towns in France during the first half of the nineteenth century.

He was not exactly a population statistician; he should rather be called a demographer raised by public opinion to a sort of magistrate for the general weal; and this is explained in part by the public's sudden alarm at the consequences of its recent discovery of its own growth. He might, indeed, rather be called a population technician, because the basic problem, and the one seen to be basic, was in fact the population problem.

In these years Paris looked around and was unable to recognize itself. Another, larger city had overflowed into the unaltered framework of streets, mansions, houses and passageways, piling man on man and trade on trade, filling every nook and corner, making over the older dwellings of the nobility and gentry into workshops and lodging houses, erecting factories and stockpiles in gardens and courts where carriages had been moldering quietly away, packing the suddenly shrunken streets and the now overpopulated gothic graveyards, too, resurrecting and overloading the forgotten sewers, spreading litter and stench even into the adjacent countryside and besmirching the lovely sky of the Ile-de-France with the vast and universal exhalation recorded in medical topographies and official reports. "Quite apart from the fogs, which are a natural product of the composition of the local atmosphere," wrote Lachaise,[10]

there habitually hangs over Paris a very noticeable haze formed by the exhalations from the prodigious amount of men and animals confined in the city and by the evaporation of the damp and the mud which at all times carpets most of the streets. This habitual haze is clearly visible from the Butte Montmartre and the Butte Chaumont on bright days, and the more populous the districts from which it arises, the denser it is. Thus, it forms a sort of cloud above the towers of Notre-Dame and Saint-Jacques de-la-Boucherie and is less dense in the east over the faubourg Saint-Antoine, where the main streets are so wide that they set up great draughts which disperse it faster. It is barely perceptible to the northwest over the Chaussée d'Antin. The metaphorical expression that one can see Paris breathe is therefore correct.

Similarly, Bruneseau noted in a health report: "There can be no doubt that so much noxious gas affects the health of Paris when it can be seen from afar hanging in a cloud above the city in the finest weather."

This universal exhalation was generally regarded as caused by the increase in population. The city had become unhealthy, both materially and morally. We shall later go on to determine the causes and consequences of this pathological fact; indeed, the pathological aspects of the history of Paris are to be the main theme of this book. Here we must pause to note that the inhabitants were aware of it and expressed their alarm at the consequences of their own growth in a stream of complaints, recriminations and acts of violence which left their traces in the official documentation.

They were alarmed at the material consequences, especially in the eastern districts, where the population had recently become densest and busiest and the kinds of work most liable to create dirt. We can discern the whole drama of these districts by way of the Amelot sewer—a place of stench, terror, prostitution and crime[11]—and by way of the history of Montfaucon, too; the dwellers in the neighboring faubourgs tried on several occasions to settle the problem of this muckheap by force when the Administration failed to do so. The city had become morally pathological, too; and for the same reasons and in nearly the same way, the moral consequences of Paris's population growth coincided with the physical consequences in the same places, at the same periods and in manifestations equally unhealthy and equally feared. The districts with the highest death rates had the highest crime rates, too; and prostitution bedded down over the sewers.

The fears of a population becoming aware of its own growth account for this resort to the men who knew, measured and predicted, the statistical men; hence the constant turning for consultation to specialists in population problems.

This was, of course, nothing new. Certain notable experts in population matters had played a considerable part in actual administration in the eighteenth century and even before that, their skills being held to be those best suited to solving the most varied problems of communal life, even those furthest removed from ordinary demography. In 1762

Deparcieux, the author of the important *Essai sur la probabilité de la vie humaine,* submitted to the Academy of Sciences a report on the city's water supply, its inadequacies and the possibility of conveying 1,200 inches of water to Paris.[12] In 1764 he was looking into ways to prevent Paris floods.

In the early years of the Restoration such exceptional consultation at times of major disasters like floods, epidemics and famines was replaced by a sort of permanent and normal system of consultation. The population expert henceforth played an important part in the city because the facts of population themselves were making an ever-increasing impact. Population statistics became one of the essential documents in the city's management, embracing fields far beyond its own specific scope. Accuracy and continuity of quantitative information were regarded as one of the prerequisites for good city management.[13]

Without going into the details of this system of consultation, what we must stress is this unity of the material and moral consequences of the city's growth. It shows up in the documents of the Board of Health. And it is most clearly apparent in the work of the man who played the leading part in this research and had the greatest influence on opinion, Parent-Duchatelet. He was the first to go into the material consequences of urban growth in his earliest General Reports, and later, after 1825, in his reports to the Board of Health. In 1836 Leuret wrote of Parent-Duchatelet's work:[14]

There are many reports to the Board of Health by Parent. . . . When he had to give a decision whether a manufacturer proposing to operate a factory might do so, he did not confine himself to visiting the workshops in order to judge whether the permit should be granted in accordance with scientific criteria. His duty as a member of the Board of Health required no more of him, but his devotion to science took him much further. He studied every detail of the industry on which he had been consulted, went to see the workmen, conversed with them, asked after their health and gathered information on their longevity and kinds of illnesses. He wrote down his observations and he used figures. The words "in many cases" and "in some cases" never appear in his notes; he demanded figures. When we consider the vast number and importance of the facts with which he enriched the study of health, the vast number of errors of which he rid it and the method he applied to it, we may well say that he inaugurated a new era in this science.

This unity comes out very plainly in the periodical Parent-Duchatelet founded with Esquirol, Marc, Orfila and Villermé, *Les Annales d'hygiène publique et de médecine légale.* Its program, presented in the first issue in 1829, notably extended the definition of health:

Our subjects are in particular the quality and cleanliness of foodstuffs; endemic and epidemic diseases; hospitals, lunatic asylums, lazarets, prisons and cemeteries. But this research opens up further prospects of a moral nature. It deduces from the investigation of habits, occupations and all the variations of social position matter for reflection and advice. . . . Its intention is to enlighten morality and reduce social infirmities. . . . Faults and crimes are diseases of society which we must strive to cure, or at least to alleviate.

Parent-Duchatelet's interest in prostitution reflected this coincidence of the material and the moral consequences of urban growth extremely well. He became the man of the sewer and of prostitution alike by investigating both of them at once, with special reference to the various aspects of a degradation and a gangrene common to both, conducting his inquiry in a cesspool common to both. "The generally accepted opinions on everything that relates to prostitutes," he wrote in the opening pages of his great work, *De la prostitution dans la ville de Paris*,

compel me to make a few comments here. I have found in most minds a peculiar disfavor attaching to the functions of all those who in one way or another have to concern themselves with prostitutes. Several persons, even among the most enlightened, scandalized to find me engaged in investigations so disgusting in their view, were not sparing of charitable comments and counsels. But on reflection I failed to appreciate this excess of delicacy and to concur in these observations. If I have been able to creep into the sewers, handle putrid matter, spend some of my time on muckheaps and in some sort live in the midst of all that is most abject and disgusting in assemblies of human beings without scandalizing anyone at all, why should I blush to approach a sewer of another kind (a sewer, I admit, fouler than the rest) in the well-founded hope of doing some good by examining every possible aspect of it? If I engage in research on prostitutes, must I necessarily be sullied by my contact with these unfortunates?

The attention to crime, regarded by Parent-Duchatelet and his con-temporaries as one of the consequences of urban pathology, was something of a similar sort. The moral and biological aspects coincide in crime just as they do in prostitution. When the cholera epidemic of 1832 broke out, people's first thought was for the prisons; not that they were particularly concerned to protect the prisoners, but because the prisons were regarded as prime sources of infection; and it was there that the first sanitary operations were carried out.[15] This is the real reason for the prominence accorded to crime in the general population statistics. The statistician was merely responding to the general disquiet of people who regarded crime as the expression of a sick society and of many other evils besides criminal ones. Similarly, the importance of statistics and studies of criminality in the United States at the present

time is accounted for by a disquiet summed up by Calvin Schmidt in his
Social Saga of Two Cities: "In our American civilization there are
chronic conditions of criminality which far exceed those in Western
Europe or our British neighbor to the north." It is crime that best
accounts for the pathological nature which urban growth can exhibit,
and which in fact it did in the Paris of the period.

Statistics and Opinion: The first half of the nineteenth century was
the prime age of statistics, not only because of the ambition to know
and measure everything and the continuous consultation demanded of
specialists in population problems by an alarmed public opinion, but
also because of the rapid and widespread dissemination of the figures
showing the results of the most important statistical surveys and because
this information reached the public immediately and informed public
opinion.

If we are to understand the interest with which the public followed
the progress of statistical research, it is not sufficient to stress, as we have
above, the mere fact of the evident importance of this research in the
solution of the day-to-day problems raised by the city's recent and ever-
increasing transformation. We must also describe the development of
opinion with respect to this research; more particularly, with respect
to the censuses. Curiosity and, in some cases, enthusiasm replaced
anxiety and fear.

We must remember the sheer terror in earlier periods aroused by
"these impious censuses, which," Saint-Simon said, "have ever offended
the Creator." It took a violent reversal to embed census-taking in
manners and customs and to overcome the repugnance and fear which
may, at bottom, be found to originate in religion. The Revolutionary
period made matters no easier, for people inevitably—and not always
wrongly—regarded the censuses taken in Paris at the time simply as
police operations to unmask suspects. The mere announcement of the
census unleashed a veritable epidemic of denunciations throughout the
city. The files of the censuses kept at the National Archives—mainly of
the census of July 1791—contain reports by citizens who turned it into
a sort of inquisition, a generalized police drive. The prefects of the
Empire later described the peasants in some backward departments as
standing arms akimbo on their doorstep or clutching their little ones
to them. "M. Fauchelevent," Hugo wrote, "had been unable to escape
the tight meshes of the 1831 census." Riots broke out in certain areas
even as late as 1841.

This fear, was, however, very soon replaced in Paris by a tremendous interest, evinced in the press and in the picturesque literature written for mass consumption to the requirements of the public's taste and curiosity. Censuses and statistical surveys enjoyed a vast circulation, owing to the flood of light they threw on population problems in general and on the problems of the Parisian population in particular.

The scope of the comments and passionate controversies aroused by Malthus's grim description, as reflected in a great many newspaper articles,[16] is striking. Opinion abounded in Malthusian themes and Malthusian images. It is very probable that there is a reminiscence of Malthus's celebrated tirade against banquets in the following poem by Savinien Lapointe entitled *"Entresol et grenier"* and published in *La Ruche populaire* in 1841:

> *Des ris à l'entresol! des coupes jamais vides*
> *Mais dans l'affreux grenier, des visages livides*
> *Qui seront morts demain . . . Grands du jour, prenez garde,*
> *Car Pierre le maçon descend de sa mansarde.*
> *Et le maçon entra pâle comme un linceul . . .*
> *Un valet s'élança tout à coup vers la porte*
> *Pour écraser du pied le monstrueux cloporte*
> *Et le pauvre maçon que la sueur inonde*
> *Est chassé du festin comme une bête immonde.*[17]

Far greater, however, was the interest aroused by statistical surveys concerning the capital. The admirable statistical surveys of the City of Paris published successively by the Prefects Chabrol,[18] Rambuteau and Haussmann were considered by contemporaries as providing a complete revelation of the population of Paris, which greatly interested civil servants but thrilled the public at large as well. They proved a revelation in that they provided material for a critique of former opinion about the city,[19] but also because they gave the public another way of becoming acquainted with their city through facts not images, and through experience, not official statements. Above all was the revelation of an unsuspected increase in the population and its unhealthy consequences. The phenomena of the city's growth rate,[20] and the biologically and socially different and inferior condition of a large percentage of the population, were very soon noted and commented on; they were not incorporated into literary and social description until much later. On November 14, 1824, the *Journal des Débats* published lengthy extracts from the Board of Health report for 1823 on consumption of the lungs, smallpox, suicides and deaths in Paris: "The most curious and most singular observation," it noted,

is the table for differences in the death rate in the various arrondissements. In the IInd arrondissement (Feydeau, Chaussée d'Antin, Palais-Royal and faubourg Montmartre), only 1 in 55 dies yearly, whereas 1 in 36 dies in the VIIIth (Quinze-Vingts, Marais, Popincourt and faubourg Saint-Antoine).

On November 19, 1824, three of the paper's four pages were devoted to this report. On December 10, 1824, a page was given up to a review of Villermé's report, *La Mortalité en France dans la classe aisée, comparée à celle qui a lieu parmi les indigents*; it noted that "there are four and a half times as many deaths in the rue de la Mortellerie as on the quais of the Ile-Saint-Louis, where the inhabitants live in large and well-aired apartments." There was a similar abundance of statistical analyses in 1825 at the time of the smallpox epidemic and a similar emphasis on the biological inequality of the population. The *Globe* and the *Journal des Débats* devoted whole columns to the proceedings of the Academy of Medicine and Villermé's recent report.[21] The third volume of the *Recherches statistiques*, published in 1826, and the very full comments on it in the press supplied a far more general and accurate knowledge of this inequality. All the characteristics of this different and inferior part of the population were therefore assembled and made available to the public years before they became one of the major themes of literary and social description. The problem of urban growth was henceforward raised in its acutest form through the general and the epidemic death rates and the statistics for fertility and illegitimacy, as well as those for suicide and madness,[22] owing to the increasingly pessimistic comments on them, which cast a deeper shadow even on the chronicling of crimes and accidents and the ordinary interpretation of the hundreds of daily incidents and petty dramas of Paris life. Hitherto the problem had been merely guessed at; now it was expressed in figures and known.

The Statistical Description: This knowledge and popularization of the results of statistical research and this interest in figures and the great revelation provided by the censuses together explain why most of the descriptions of Paris in the period are couched in quantitative terms. The picturesque literature, which continued the tradition begun by Mercier in many depictions of manners and customs, but henceforth took most of its effects and the substance of its statements from facts fully supported by figures, was stuffed out with statistics. The second volume of Montigny's *Esquisse des moeurs parisiennes* was simply a commentary on the most recent census.[23] There was a similar use of statistics in *Le Frondeur, ou observations sur les moeurs de Paris*, published in 1829,[24] and in Doin and Charton's *Lettres sur Paris*, published in January 1830. Even *Le Diable à Paris*[25] contained an important chapter of social statistics supplied by the statistician Legoyt.

But, of course, this concern for statistical exactitude and this high quality of quantitative description appeared most plainly in the principal literary documents of the period. There are scores of estimates in Balzac. Hugo never fails to cite his quantitative evidence. Sue gives pride of place in his novels to criminal and police statistics. Even when they did not give actual figures, in all of them the statement and setting of the facts in the description was based on verified data and the description dwelt on the most incontrovertible social facts. It reproduced very closely the development which was to be traced and measured by later statistical research, but was known pretty accurately to contemporaries owing to the wide circulation of statistical information.

The investigation of sources, therefore, is of small moment. There can be no doubt that demographic history has the opportunity and the good luck to reveal the true (or at least probable) source of certain famous descriptions which could not have been identified by purely literary research. It can pertinently point out the appreciable influence of Parent-Duchatelet's work on certain descriptions, where the indubitable borrowing is too carefully concealed. Hugo did not quote Parent-Duchatelet, but it is certain that Parent provided the inspiration for the description of the sewers in *Les Misérables* far more than Bruneseau, whom Hugo did quote, making him into something of an epic hero and conqueror of subterranean empires. Parent-Duchatelet's influence is likewise quite obvious in the chapters in *Les Mystères de Paris* in which Sue in turn explored the sewers which the statistician had measured, and in those passages in which he described population groups whose main characteristics had been irrevocably fixed by quantitative study, such as prostitutes[26] and the savage tribe of stevedores, to whom Parent-Duchatelet had devoted an important study, incarnate in Sue in the horrible Martial family.[27] The influence of Frégier,[28] and of Villermé, who greatly influenced Frégier,[29] is equally evident.

This investigation of sources, many more examples of which could easily be given, seems, however, secondary beside the essential fact of the importance of statistics in forming opinion during a period when the practice of census-taking was becoming a routine affair in France. The accuracy of the literary description is not accounted for merely by the existence of some particular study known to and used by Hugo and Sue, or of some particular report which may be rediscovered by learned research, but was infallibly identified in the contemporary information. One of Sue's correspondents spoke, in a letter of March 28, 1843, of "this heredity of crime whose horrors had already been revealed in the learned works of Parent-Duchatelet and M. Frégier." The accuracy is accounted for by the increase in the general documentation within everyone's reach, which, even without statistical backing, stamped social phenomena with a definite shape that could not be distorted by literary creation.

This is the main reason why the social historian, however distrustful of literary evidence, is compelled in seeking the facts for his quantitative study to pay attention to a literary description which, in the first half of the nineteenth century, was so extraordinarily true to life.

III
The Demographic Approach to Opinion
Concerning the Facts

We have seen that the description of the facts is true to life; so, too, is the description of opinion concerning those facts. Indeed, the description of opinion concerning the facts is as essential as the description of the facts themselves in any essay in research in quantitative social history. The most important demographic and social developments— or at any rate, those revealed as the most important by later research and by the test of statistics—can only be taken as truly relevant if we can also show that their contemporaries found them as significant as we do, were aware of them as something other than just personal experience, assessed them, foresaw them, dreaded them and did not merely experience them passively.

The mortality rate has, of course, to be measured, and the physical consequences of such wholesale slaughter to be defined. The statistical research thus brings out dismal landscapes or sinister eras illuminated by the harsh glare of the figures, dominated and spotlighted, so to speak, by death. But they are dismal and sinister only to the research worker, who attributes to them, after the event and from outside, the sensation of contemporary terrors or terrors engendered in other climes. These are superinduced terrors, nonexistent terrors, as death itself is nonexistent, however severe the mortality, or perhaps because of it, in areas which are as familiar with death as if it were part of the natural environment. They are distorted terrors, too: romantic history is distorted by an indiscrete compassion, more concerned with itself than others, and by a hypocritical attempt at sympathy. But the opinion of others matters more than one's opinion of oneself. This alone can confer upon the facts a real existence. This alone aligns them with the historical reality of what actually happened. It is quite impossible to understand the condition and behavior of the workers in Paris in the nineteenth century unless we know what image of that condition and behavior was held by their contemporaries—what they thought of it. Their behavior was, indeed, partly conditioned by the contemporary judgment. The workers' attitude was in many respects a reaction to others' opinion of them and a reflex of their own opinion of themselves. They were what they were wished to be—on the margin of Paris civilization, excluded from it by a moral condemnation which isolated them and which they appropriated to themselves.

However capable statistics may be of determining facts, they cannot record what opinion was held of those facts or the extent to which contemporaries were aware of them; that is to say, of the actual existence of the facts. The most incontrovertible statistical series have in themselves no historical existence. At the very most, opinion can be deduced from the prevalence of certain series; from the attention accorded to the statistics of criminality, infanticide and suicide in the statistical publications concerning Paris in the first half of the nineteenth century; from the statistician's difficulty in distinguishing the settled from the floating population and from the importance accorded by him to this distinction. These are, however, very inadequate elements for a general and reliable description of contemporary opinion, the lack of which has been sorely felt in history to this day.

One is struck by the contrast with the position of opinion surveys in modern sociological research. With recent well-tried techniques and a documentation immediately at hand or readily established, it is now possible not merely to chart current opinion concerning facts but also, in many cases, to reach the facts through opinion. In historical research, conditions are quite different. The documentation is insufficient and it records facts more often than opinion. Any view that can be gathered must come from documents which merely record, but do not express or transmit it in the form of accessible raw material capable of being worked up by further research—evidence, that is, *on* opinion, but not *of* opinion. This documentation is, moreover, fragmentary. It deals only with such limited aspects as the opinion of a group or the opinion relating to an isolated and usually abnormal fact, such as an economic crisis, a war, a revolution or an epidemic. It is no accident that the documents on and surveys of opinion, like the major studies in social history, and contemporary views on events and ideas become abundant only during great convulsions, when the whole of society flares up. At such moments, the opinion on the facts gives us as full an account of those facts as they themselves do and itself becomes a fact. In normal times, however, opinion never intervenes as a collective and total phenomenon of society as a whole, embracing every aspect and every instant of it. That is to say, opinion never intervenes with a full array of these features; but, without them, it is not opinion.

For opinion is not opinion unless it is universally shared. A group has an opinion only in relation to the opinion of others, by repercussion, by reaction. While the opinions of various groups can be studied separately, in their aggregate they form a collective opinion which, though a compendium of these separate views, differs widely from them and, indeed, acts upon them. This is the compound we need, a compound which differs from its components; for unless we can examine this compound, an examination of its components is meaningless. We require an opinion held by all in common, which must also be an opinion on all of the phenomena, down to the least exceptional and most commonplace, the phenomena of everyday life being quite as essential as the rest. This may seem platitudinous to sociologists, but it is not so to historians, whose surveys of opinion tend to cover everything but opinion.

The use that is generally made of electoral statistics attracts the same criticism as we are leveling at historical research. Undoubtedly, of all surveys of opinion they are the least remote from our purposes. In certain respects they do get at opinion in the aggregate of the groups, in their coexistence and reciprocal influence, perhaps even in the aggregate of the subjects with which they are concerned, since a political judgment may be regarded as a synthesis of all the choices. We may recall that in the absence of a coherent, homogeneous and general description of the social structures of the Paris region in the middle of the nineteenth century, we have suggested in an earlier study[30] that one could derive a tentative picture of these structures from the frequent polls in the period, since contemporary opinion concerning the facts could subsequently be utilized by historical research as a document concerning the facts themselves and as a form of preliminary measurement of them.

It is easy, however, to demonstrate the inadequacy of such documentation and we have done so elsewhere. It is inadequate for the identification of the groups sharing a single opinion. The study of electoral statistics is more useful for describing social structures than opinion, and the fact that we are obliged to derive the elements of a social description from statistics of public opinion emphasizes how greatly the absence of such a preliminary description impairs social identification—which must, however, be attempted—and weakens any conclusions about political opinion itself. It is inadequate, above all, for the description of political opinion. Political judgment imperfectly reproduces the aggregate of other judgments and gives no account of its components as a whole. Even though it is the sum total of them, it places great difficulties in the way of distinguishing and identifying them. It remains basically political, by which we mean that it is sensitive to the political circumstances which distort, fix and immobilize it. It belongs in another universe. It may sometimes even conflict with the aggregate of the judgments which it sums up but which are imperfectly embodied in it; even when they are simply multiplied together, something extraneous is added to the result. Historical research has usually quite rightly confined itself to drawing narrowly political conclusions from political documentation of this sort.

We do not believe that history has been finally frustrated in its effort to describe an opinion, without which any description is incomplete and imperfect. Where we went astray was in seeking a description of opinion in the documents relating specifically to opinion. It is opinion itself that we have to seize—not the texts which purport to record or capture it, to grasp something that eludes grasping, to comprehend something that eludes reasoning.

Yet all aspects of the opinion of the Parisians in the first half of the nineteenth century about themselves and about others—even the most intimate, the most secret and the least consciously held—exist in the vast literary documentation, pregnant with a reality which later historical reconstruction has exhausted itself in seeking or, even more commonly, failing to recognize when it has found it. Such testimony is continuously present; but it must be heard aright, not for what it purports to say but for what it cannot help saying.

Social literature and description in the first half of the nineteenth century assert massive claims to transmit an immortal, total testimony. Literary research has brought these claims into focus. This testimony is of little interest to us, and conventional literary and social historians have gone entirely astray in using these documents for the descriptions they have attempted. They embody the opinion of the few, not of all, even (perhaps especially) when the opinion of the few purports to be identified with the opinion of all. Opinion as such vanishes in this erudite effort to establish a collective viewpoint.

In any event, demographic research generally enables us to discover the sources of this erudition, and this discovery deprives the literary amplification of all historical interest. We should do better to go straight to the sources rather than to their literary transposition. *Les Misérables* is not important to historical research for Hugo's analyses of the social ideology of his time in dozens of heavy-handed passages, for such disquisitions are to be found in most of the contemporary writers, borrowed from the same sources and set out in the same terms with the same arguments and the same examples. This also applies to the major works by the social reformers; their importance for the social history of the nineteenth century is not simply their exposition of systems. Whether these documents partake of social theory or of literature, they are relevant to the conventional history of ideas, but not to the history of opinion which we are attempting to sketch here. The history of ideas and the history of opinion do bear some relation to each other, which we shall go on to discuss; but they do not coincide.

It is not in these documents—even in those which purport to describe opinion—that opinion is recorded. The evidence of opinion transmitted by these authors is to be found not in what they intended to say, but in what they could not help saying. Its traces, barely visible in most cases, elude the conventional literary and social criticism but show up singularly well in the light of quantitative, and more especially demographic, appraisal. They are obtained from the comparison which we cannot fail to establish between the social facts a demographic assessment identifies as having been the most important and the description of them given deliberately, or, far more often, involuntarily.

What is most important are the themes, not as they appear in final form—manipulated, attenuated, with their most significant contradictions smoothed out, almost identical in all the works, illustrated by the same examples, and in brief, stereotyped, barely good enough to be deposited in the grand museum of ideas (dead ideas)—but the themes as they developed. These themes are seen at various uncertain and fluctuating stages in their development, as they imposed themselves, or rather, were imposed, by pressures set up not as a result of the facts but as a result of the progressive experience of those facts by opinion and in new terms exactly fitted to the facts they expressed; or, even more usefully, in the old terms—proletarians, men of the faubourgs, the wretched, *les misérables*—which had recently taken on a new meaning.

CHAPTER TWO

The Picturesque Literature

The transformation of the theme of crime into a social theme in the literature of the first half of the nineteenth century reflects a development in both fact and opinion. The documents and examples of this are common enough and provide material for a literary analysis which we shall not undertake here. We should do better, we think, to pay more attention to the works which created the greatest stir and supply us with the major evidence of this dual development: some because facts of opinion which they rejected or tried to ignore were imposed upon them, enmeshed as they were in literary traditions or prejudices; others because they recorded the experience "passively" and so reconstructed it for us.

The so-called picturesque literature provides us with the prime evidence of how real and immense were the pressures, because its main business was the description and celebration of crime as defined in its most traditional terms.

There is a great bulk of this literature. Mere statistics of the works published would, in the last resort, suffice to show that crime was undoubtedly one of the major preoccupations of the period. It was one of the most constant themes in the literature in the strict sense, as well as in the social literature incorporated in a body of works readily catalogued. This applies particularly to the novel, of which Anne Bignan wrote in a book on "The Scaffold" in 1833 that it "takes serious matters to the furthest extremes of the tragic and the horrible." "All that is abject and foul in the human heart," she added, "has been dissected by our novelists' scalpels. Every bodily infirmity, every moral sore has been laid bare. The Hospital, the Convict Prison, the place de Grève, the Morgue have been exploited for scenes of a revolting realism."

But this is not our main interest here. More important than the sheer number of volumes, chapters or pages is the transformation of the theme of crime in the literature on crime during the period.

I
The Tableaux de Paris

Let us look first at the *Tableaux de Paris*, which, exploiting the vein prospected by Mercier, would have been expected to remain faithful to the older formulas, the traditional and picturesque conception of crime, and to their ingenious precursor's very profitable teaching.

In the description by Mercier and his immediate successors, crime was very different from what it became in books of a similar sort published at the end of the Restoration and during the July Monarchy.

Mercier's *Tableaux de Paris*—the model—certainly depicted criminal groups and districts, and one cannot help thinking that these prodigious little books influenced later descriptions by working up the themes and what might be called the recipes which his successors could not do without; for the public had acquired a taste for them, and here more than elsewhere the public was the great judge. But in these early works very little significance was attached to the theme of crime. The criminal groups were barely noticed amid the swarming mass of a population in which Mercier himself took far more care to distinguish the small picturesque trades. And this criminal world inspired no fear; it was not formidable; there were far more petty thieves than robbers or murderers. If Mercier happened to pass through the criminal districts, he observed characters very different from criminals and settings very different from the settings of crime; even the Cité was not horrible in Mercier. In short, this Paris was unhealthy and brutal, its faubourgs inhabited by a population of primitives, but it was not a Paris threatened by crime and haunted by fear; it was a Paris crowded with unfortunates, but not with criminals. Crime remains an exceptional fact in this description; it exists, but merely on the fringes of the population and the city.

Similarly, the many portraits of Paris published under the Empire and during the early years of the Restoration only dwelt on criminal themes as a matter of curiosity, out of a taste for the picturesque. They were described, as it were, from outside; crime was merely one show amid other Parisian shows, one contrast amid the manifold contrasts of the city in which these writers took a particular delight.

Describing at length the execution of Laumond, the murderer of the dairywoman in the rue de Verneuil in 1813, Jouy was mainly concerned to draw a contrast between the Parisian at the Opera and the Parisian at the place de Grève.[1] He dwelt at length on the bloody ceremonies made illustrious by Ravaillac, Brinvilliers, Damiens and Cartouche, criminals famed by their origin, their story or the rank of their victim, something quite different from the obscure criminals of that proletariat of blood who were to stage their death agonies on the place de Grève in the last years of the Restoration in spectacles in which the actor was to resemble the spectators in many physical and moral traits—plebeian shows for plebeian crowds.

These descriptions were quite different from those in books of the same sort published in the last days of the Restoration and after. Quite new characteristics appear: crime occupies a larger and larger place, readily measurable by the volume of chapters or pages; the descriptions are more serious, more observant and more accurate; and, even more noteworthy, there is a change in the nature of the phenomena, which are, so to speak, transformed. Crime had ceased to be something picturesque and exceptional; it was no longer embodied in some famous highwayman or regicide; it became commonplace, anonymous, impersonal, obscure. It ceased to leave its mark on the districts assigned to it by law or custom and spread over the whole city, no longer expressing itself in a reverberating expiation on the place de Grève— a grandiose and epoch-making spectacle to which crowds flocked as to the King's entry into his city or a victory celebration—but becoming instead no more than a vague threat, everywhere and at all times present, capital execution itself being nothing more than one settlement of scores among others. We can say that crime ceases to be picturesque and becomes social, in the sense that it is brought increasingly into relationship with the changes occurring in the Paris of the period. Beyond crime and the particular behavior of criminal groups it is to this general problem that Montigny, and especially Doin and Charton, refer, the latter writing in their *Lettres sur Paris*:

Paris had 714,596 inhabitants on March 1, 1817; there were 890,431 on March 1, 1827. If circumstances do not change, the population will have doubled fifty years hence; the old native corruption is nourished dangerously from this continuous increase, in turn almost always impregnated with a poison peculiar to itself. The immigration imprudently allowed to flood into the city year after year is by no means wholly pure.

This raises, beyond the limited problem of crime but also by way of it, the problem of the increase in the population of Paris, which is the eventual objective of this study because it governs its entirety. It may even be held that, at this point in the development of the problem viewed through these works of picturesque literature, it is this literature itself which disappears, losing its raison d'être—to entertain— and blending with a far more significant literary documentation in which the problem of crime is merely an expression of the social problem. It is the social criminality, indefinable and elusive, growing up with the city and penetrating it like some pestilent fog or damp coating the walls, that creeps into the *Diable à Paris* and prevents it, despite its author's best efforts, from being amusing. "You made me promise," says George Sand, "to say what I too had to say about Paris. . . . Beware lest you repent of your polite invitation; for, in truth, you could not send it to a worse address. No one knows less of Paris than I. One knows only what one loves, one is almost always ignorant of what one hates; and, I admit, I hate Paris." There follows a description of poverty and crime, of popular crime born of the people's poverty and of the inequalities aggravated by developments in the first half of the ninteenth century: "There are no poor people on the streets any more," she wrote; "you have forbidden them to beg there, and the man without means of support begs by night, knife in hand." This popular criminality was also evoked in Gavarni's sinister portraits of the people of Paris illustrating the book. In the last days of the picturesque literature, the description became more accurate. Figures were given. As we have already seen, at this period statistics invaded literature like everything else and conferred upon it a significance and what one might call a weight which the earlier books, though in the same tradition, did not have.

The development of the theme of crime was the more remarkable in these works in that they were written to suit a public whose wishes and beliefs they passively adopted and inasmuch as they might have been expected to invoke the laws of the genre against any such development. Despite those laws and despite the fact that their sole aim was to entertain the reader, despite their hunt for relatively artificial contrasts, and despite the devices in the handling of which Jouy was a past master, a disquiet grew up which no longer fitted the older framework and indeed altered its entire significance.

Other eminently popular genres later developed in the same way and became subject to similar pressures, notably the melodrama. Jules Janin described in the *Journal des Débats* in April 1833 how Benjamin and Polyanthe's innocent *Auberge des Adrets*, "a well-conducted, fairly rational, fairly moral piece," ended up by becoming a revolting tragedy of crime. "When they begot this masterpiece of the century," he wrote,

they, like many another father, did not know what they were doing. Robert Macaire and Bertrand were two robbers such as you find in any and every melodrama; at the second or third performance Frédérick Lemaître's Robert Macaire was a jovial bandit. But today even this pleasant side has vanished. He had been odious but gay; he has remained odious, but he has become gloomy by his exaggeration of the villainy and even the gaiety. . . .

We should say rather that he became what the public wanted him to be; and far more so than Janin supposed.

II
Jules Janin

But what of Janin himself? He may be classified among the entertainers. What is astonishing is the evidence of the influence of opinion upon the copious, brilliant and superficial productions of an author who repudiated that influence and opposed it, but was nonetheless gradually compelled to give more and more attention in his articles to the subjects which he condemned when he did not refuse to acknowledge their existence. The importance of these subjects and the abnormal and unhealthy nature of the city are just as evident in the attitude of a writer who wished to hear no evil and see no evil as in that of Eugène Sue, who experienced, recorded and transmitted them.

When he added a Preface in 1841 to his first book, *L'âne mort et la femme guillotinée*, published originally in 1829, Janin wrote: "Despite its strange title, the book was anything but a parody; if by some mischance it was a parody, it was a serious parody, an involuntary parody, such as many great writers are producing today without being any more aware of it than I was." A parody, true, but a serious parody, and one far more serious, and serious in a quite different way, than Janin himself supposed.

It was a parody of the horrid literature which flooded in from all sides in those years, for which Janin had a contempt comparable to that he displayed for political attitudes closely akin to the literary fashions of the same period. In his *Histoire de la littérature dramatique*, recalling his early articles in the [*Journal des*] *Débats*, in which he had attacked the Revolutionary parties by demonstrating (in 1829!) the strength of the Monarchy, he said:

"Begin to tremble," I wrote, "before the tribe of the faubourgs when the faubourgs are no more." When the faubourgs are no more was rather a premature way of putting it, I admit; the faubourgs were there and they still are; these armies encamped at our gates will always number such besiegers among them. . . . Happy, crystal-clear years of the Restoration, the mother that nursed us! We were babes and boys in those days; they sheltered us against the pernicious blasts still sweeping out of the recent past, the horrible time of the Empire.

The literature was still swollen with those blasts, the barbaric and crude literature which enjoyed a tremendous public success; and they remained a threat to the insecurely restored civilization of the Ancien Régime comparable to that maintained by an equally barbaric, crude social and political opposition engendered by the same environment. It was this literature that Janin was attacking in his little book, with the intention of "showing that nothing is so easy to concoct as gothic terror. Anne Radcliffe, so decried today, is a true priestess of this genre. . . . All we have done is to dig deeper as our knowledge of anatomy has improved."

Hence the novel's parodic aspects. All the high places of horror and crime are to be found in it: Montfaucon and the adjacent barrière, with its mastiff fights and its orgies; the boulevards crowded at peak hours with the vast throngs of the city's prostitutes; the Morgue; the hospitals, all the hospitals, from the Capucins, refuge of the venereally diseased, to the Salpêtrière and the Bourbe, where the prostitutes lay in; and the place de Grève. And also the most traditional representatives of crime, plus the disguises later familiarized by Vidocq, Balzac and Sue. "One day," Janin wrote in this book,

I saw a man in rags, horrible in aspect, enter the little pothouse in the rue Sainte-Anne; his beard was long, his hair wild, his whole person filthy. A moment later I saw him emerge decently dressed, his chest bristling with crosses of the two Orders, his aspect venerable; he was on his way to dine with a judge. This quick change terrified me and I thought, with a shudder, that it is thus perhaps that extremes meet.

A parody, yes, but a "serious parody." If we did not know beforehand that it was a parody, if Janin had not taken great pains to warn us by piling up grotesque devices, even making the victim himself recount his own execution, if we were to read the descriptions apart from the extravagant connecting plot, we might well suppose that we had here some remarkable documents on the physical and moral misery of the lower classes in Paris, in some cases even more remarkable than those we ordinarily find by historical research. The author's talent is no doubt responsible in part; in imitating certain contemporary descriptions, Janin was not able to avoid giving them the imprint of his more finished art. But the influence of the subjects he selected was more important: the places and scenes he could not avoid selecting and could describe in no other way.

The places were inevitable. It was no accident that, with the choice of so many criminal scenes available, the writers of the time, Janin among them, invariably dwelt on the same settings. Inevitably this book, intended as a parody of the horrid, could emerge nowhere but in the landscape of Montfaucon, assembling as it did in the eyes of all contemporary observers and in documents of every kind all the aspects of urban misery. Not a map but featured it: "The whole terrain between the boulevard, the Meaux turnpike and the Butte Chaumont," we read on Maire's map drawn in 1813, "is covered by the remains of corpses of animals and the ordures of the great city." What horrors piled up around this Butte! Montfaucon, the great sewage dump, the dog fights and the cat fights, the hospitals and even the street names, like Dead Men's Street, the rue des Morts, perpetuated the facts, or at any rate the images, which were no less real and material than the things themselves. By a similar kind of predetermination, the *Mystères de Paris* begins in the heart of the Cité, in the rue aux Fèves, and ends at the barrière Saint-Jacques, drawn along this route by collective forces expressed by Sue himself far better, indeed, than he intended: "The Slasher was carried along willy-nilly by a dense crowd, a torrent rushing down from the pothouses of the faubourg de la Glacière, piling up around the barrière and then flooding over the boulevard Saint-Jacques where the execution was to be held." No place could be more suitable for assembling in a final appearance—but merely by chance—all the characters in the novel at one of the crucial moments of their lives and for bringing together in the narrowest possible space all the mob's violence and all its delights, from Carnival masquerades to the thrills of executions. And, above all, no other place was so implacably imposed by a public opinion as compelling as the crowd which bore the Slasher along with it. Similar imperatives were to drive the characters in *Les Misérables* irresistibly towards the southern barrières, where the persons and places Hugo described, and could not help describing, found their best expression. It is beside the point that these places were not always those where crime was in fact at its worst or poverty most desperate; they were universally regarded as such.

Equally inevitable were the appearances they assumed. *Habent sua fata loci.* Even the witty author who chose to parody them could give them only the character which they themselves imposed, or contemporary opinion imposed upon them, the obligatory colors conferred by the crowd, the reputation attributed to them, the significance assigned to them, the feelings of terror or compassion they were bound to arouse. Thereafter, parody gave way to satire and satire became testimony; thereafter, the facts held sway, facts as detailed as those to be derived from statistical description and just as important for our research. Urban destitution was present in its entirety as certainly as in the works to which the conventional historian resorts for his subject matter, though he is not so certain to find or recognize it there. We must indeed place Janin's description of the southern faubourgs—so deeply dyed with poverty and crime, crushed under the detritus of the city— in the front rank beside the contemporary medical topographies and Parent-Duchatelet's monographs and, too, on a level in this respect with Balzac, Hugo and Sue. Like the doctor, the criminologist and the novelist, the entertainer was compelled to invest these places with the character which was specifically their own.

Literary criticism will no doubt judge the description fairly mediocre; social criticism, too; both of them perhaps discouraged by the banality of the observation. But historical research will not. For in this repetition—the fact that the same places were described by every writer in the same terms and associated with the same images—we detect the expression of the pressure of opinion. The Bourbe, for example,

the last refuge of the poor girl who has become a mother, the young wife whose husband is a gambler, the woman condemned to death, for whom the executioner is waiting at the gate. At the Bourbe misery engenders misery, prostitution engenders prostitution, crime engenders crime. The children who come into the world on those befouled beds can expect no heritage but the convict prison or the scaffold.

Or the Salpêtrière:

the asylum for old women, the outcasts of society whom society no longer wants even as concierges or wardrobe dealers. The Salpêtrière is a whole village, as populous as a town, but, good God! what a population! Wives without husbands, mothers without children, grandmothers without grandchildren. . . . The building rises lofty, like all the buildings inhabited by the poor. Mendicant and mendacious palaces! They are embellished with a gilded dome and a marble face, but beneath that dome the poor are lonely, behind that dressed stone there is nothing to do but die on the cheap. The old folk huddling in this frightful solitude are a pitiful sight. Involuntarily, one counts up all the shattered affections that go to make up a hospital like this!

"Involuntarily." This was an acknowledgment of the author's inability to describe things in any other way. It may be parody, but it is such a successful and serious parody that it brings out by its very success—however much it may be a failure from other points of view—the overwhelming influence of subjects which could not be treated unseriously.

This applies too to Janin's later works, equally hostile to public opinion, but equally stamped with its imprint and expressing that opinion the more authentically because he would rather have repudiated it.

Janin was certainly fully aware of the importance of crime and the place of the criminal population in contemporary society. Like Balzac, however, he would have preferred to see it as something keeping within its own bounds, something alien to the city, specifically a population which was not Parisian, one which differed from it in every respect and lived in different districts. It was these differences that he stressed when he happened, exceptionally, to pay some attention to this exceptional population. "There are in Paris," he wrote of the Stroller,

places known to him alone, horrible passages, labyrinths, ruins, courts inhabited by all the thieves of the Cité. . . . Paris at night is fearsome. This is the hour when the tribe of the underworld sets forth. Darkness reigns, but little by little the gloom lifts in the flickering lantern of the ragpicker going off, basket on back, to seek his fortune amid those foul rags that have no name in any language. At that hour, too, bespattered carts draw up to the door of the sleeping houses to carry off every kind of filth. At the corner of the gloomiest streets through the blood-red curtains the pothouse lamp shines out with funereal gleam. Along the walls slink marauding robbers, ever and anon uttering the cry of some night bird; women come and go seeking the cellar where they are to spend the night; for this abominable population spends its nights in the cellars. So the terror is vast, horrible, formidable. Those steps you hear thudding on the muddy paving are the gray patrol starting out on its voracious prowl. . . . In the hideous lairs which Paris hides away behind its palaces and museums . . . there lurks a swarming and oozing population that beggars comparison. There are crusts and wretched remnants all around. They speak a language spawned in the jails; all their converse is of larceny, murder, prisons and scaffolds. A vile bohemian world, a frightful world, a purulent wart on the face of this great city.[2]

To Janin, as to Balzac, to Vidocq and to all the depicters of old-style criminality, criminal society was a closed society, comprising proletariat and aristocracy, gentry criminals and petty thieves, a society which, moreover, merited scant interest. "If all orders of society are represented in the convict prisons of Toulon and Brest," Janin wrote,

just as they are in the Golden Book of the Legion of Honor, does that mean that the novel and the play may concern themselves with those vile heroes, ever cowering beneath the public's contempt or the warder's truncheon? In his *Histoire de la prostitution publique* M. Parent-Duchatelet, the learned gentleman who, out of pure charity, lived amid filth, that rigid Port-Royal Christian who lived out his whole life in haunts of ill fame out of sheer virtue, tells us that in order to perfect his frightful knowledge of Parisian vice he was once taken to a house where five-score ladies of the night were sleeping promiscuously with thieves on a great pile of rags gathered from all the garbage heaps in the kingdom. M. Parent-Duchatelet saw it; he tells us so; and we must credit him. And yet, merely because the thing exists, does that mean that the novel and the play may pore over this den of vice to dredge up choice morsels? No, no, there are some things from which we should avert our eyes. . . .[3]

"Whoever you may be," he wrote elsewhere, "leave such sordid details to the politicians; let the novelists make their money out of them; let the theaters draw their sensations from them to titillate the mob; but you, if you are wise, must shun these warts and pustules."[4]

However, despite Janin's repugnance, he was himself compelled to give an ever-increasing place in his other works to the facts which he despised and denied, and to describe them in terms and tones which the youthful author of *L'âne mort* would have condemned; but, above all, to present the problem as a form of popular violence.

He was forced to it by the great public tragedies which exacerbated these acts of violence, merging and mingling one with another—the riots and the revolutions.[5] This is particularly true of the 1832 cholera epidemic, of which Janin gave a historically important description in a little book published shortly after the event, *Paris depuis la révolution de 1830*. His account not only equals Heine's or even Hugo's in vividness and the frisson he communicates, but is equally important for the connections he established between disease, destitution and revolt which we have already noted.

Thus, under the pressure of exceptional circumstances, in frivolous works intended to be merely witty, Janin, who disliked any kind of demonstration of mob excitement and detested the noise and dust rising from the city, expressed—and extraordinarily accurately, too—facts measurable by statistical research. "I find it impossible," he wrote, to extend my sympathies to these slow fevers, these hidden fevers, this universal malaise which is neither peace nor war, these political ideas which are neither night nor day. I am above all a man of the time of true tranquility, all passion spent, when one has leisure to set one's mind to fine prose that is both neat and resonant and to the well-made play. I hate with every fiber of my being the brutal drama of violence, disorder and raging mobs. Where are these changes, these disgraces to history, taking us? They are weakening, disturbing, degrading, destroying a great people.

Janin's works may have been written on the whole from a negative standpoint, but they nevertheless succeeded in expressing the "brutal drama" which he obstinately chose to ignore.

CHAPTER THREE

Balzac

I
The Dangerous Classes

Unlike Janin, Balzac certainly saw criminality as an important social fact and in the *Comédie humaine* assigned to it a role for which Janin himself expressed his dislike in his reviews of the work. But his description still kept to the older themes and was full of characters and beliefs stemming from the Ancien Régime. The reason for this is probably the originality of Balzac's creative genius—which lies outside our province—and that he was more interested in social facts of a different sort. Another factor to be borne in mind is the predominance in Balzac's works of the society of the early years of the Restoration, that is, of a period earlier than the one we are dealing with here; and this tended to distort his descriptions of the July Monarchy. In Balzac's novels, as in Janin's articles, the criminal world was a closed world; the relationships between the dangerous classes and the upper classes were far more sharply defined than the contacts between the dangerous classes and the laboring classes. Balzac observed the psychological conditions of crime more often than its material imperatives; evil was picturesque and aroused curiosity rather than terror. This dated it in some respects; Vidocq himself, who embodied these survivals as no one else did, was careful to note this in his book of thieves, faulting Balzac for anachronisms, mistaken identifications and resurrecting the past.[1]

The characteristics of criminals were summed up in one of Balzac's earliest works, the *Code des gens honnêtes*,[2] as follows:

The thieves form a republic with its own law and its own manners and customs . . . they present in the social scene a reflection of those illustrious highwaymen whose courage, character, exploits and eminent qualities will always be admired. Thieves have a language, leaders and a police of their own; and in London, where their association is better organized, they have their own syndics, their own parliament and their own deputies. We have not yet reached this height of perfection in France. Nonetheless it is a patent fact that among us too robbery is a regular profession and honest folk must be constantly on their guard.

There certainly were new features in the description of the criminal classes in this early work. As we have already noted, the description was based on statistics. We must stress this interest in measurement once again. We are not, of course, making Balzac out to be a statistician, and we would certainly not say that his estimates coincide with ours. In this book, as in subsequent ones, he quotes from memory or checks his sources—the same sources as ours—too hastily, and he often goes wrong. His estimates changed from novel to novel, and they deteriorated. In his works as a whole, however, just as in contemporary opinion, a notion of statistics, even a quite rough or totally erroneous one, transformed the nature of the beliefs, if not the facts. Statistics acted as a multiplier of opinion. The measurement of crime, even when the results did not wholly square with the true facts, gave a new depth to the problem, as may be seen from the following estimate:

40,000 rogues, 15,000 petty thieves, 10,000 burglars and 40,000 ingenuous females living at someone else's expense add up to some 110 to 120,000 persons who are a great handicap to efficient administration. If the population of Paris consists of some 1,200,000 souls, you can see that 120,000 crooks account for a ratio of one villain to 10 honest folk.[3]

The new quality that quantification confers on the description is extremely striking wherever the attempt to be accurate deals with the more basic trends, such as fertility, ageing and mortality, which show up in even greater detail in the censuses. It was in terms of statistics— in terms of demography, to be even more precise—that Balzac explained certain characteristics of the dangerous classes unperceived or misinterpreted in the older and less well informed descriptions. For the first time death was the consequence and the measure of everything else,[4] death in all its forms, but particularly suicide, the importance and implications of which were such in this book of his and in the day-by-day history of Paris that it will have to be discussed in a separate section of this book.[5] This might be called a statistical mentality rather than a statistical curiosity. It brought a new rigor and unexpected insights to the description of the older crime and the older notions of contemporary crime; in some respects, it transformed the problem completely. The measurement of crime transformed the very nature of crime.

There can be no doubt, however, that we are still dealing with the older crime here. The dangerous classes are described as groups apart, despite their extension underground into the laboring classes and despite their aristocratic relations; and they never cast the sinister shadows over the landscape of Restoration Paris which shrouded later descriptions, Hugo's and Sue's, for instance, in gloom and were already beginning to invade the lightest picturesque literature. This one, for example:

Paris is ventilated, her streets are broad. . . . She is no longer the old Paris, unpoliced and unlit; true, there are few gas lamps, but the moon and the police make good this municipal parsimony. We must be fair to the new laws: by eschewing the lavish use of capital punishment, they have compelled the criminal to attach some importance to life. Now that thieves are able to enrich themselves by dint of skill without risking their necks, they have come to prefer swindling to murder. In the old days you were suddenly faced with a demand for your money or your life; nowadays, no one dreams of demanding either. Honest folk used to dread the murderer; nowadays, their only enemy is the confidence trickster. We sharpen our wits these days, not our daggers.

There is scarcely anything to cast a shadow on the sunny landscape or strike a note of gloom in the optimistic and good-humored narrative. The performance on the place de Grève itself was scarcely a tragedy; it was a popular fête to which the Paris crowds had become accustomed.[6] As to robbery, Balzac described it by resurrecting many droll stories, some of them borrowed from the most frivolous literature of the eighteenth century. In brief, this sort of crime still made an amusing tale. What would become of literary men if there were no criminals? "The boulevard geniuses owe their daily success solely to these strenuous collaborators."

Lastly, this crime was seldom related to the material changes in society. Entry into the dangerous classes was accounted for naturally if one questioned beggars or prostitutes, as Balzac did:

Have you watched them, have you had the patience to question them, to burrow behind their lowering brows to get at the truth? You will have learned that sudden death, the Bicêtre prison, the police, the jails, the galleys and those disgusting occupations of which you have no inkling make up the sinking fund which, through a thousand secret channels, is fed by this hideous corps of 100,000 villains. But such is the constitution of society, such the force of destitution and imbecility of opulence, that misfortune constantly draws off 100,000 individuals from the 1,200,000 who make up the population of Paris and dooms them to destitution. No system of government can prevent this terrible ebb and flow; and the only state that ever did so in the past was Holland, by means of a vast trade.

A similar demographic and economic determinism is apparent in the following:

Some needs are insuperable, for, after all, society does not provide bread for all who are hungry; and if they have no means of earning their bread, what do you expect them to do? Have the politicians foreseen that on the day when the mass of the unfortunate is greater than that of the wealthy, society will take on some totally different form? At this very moment England is threatened with a revolution of this kind. The Poor Tax will become exorbitant in England, and on the day when 20 million men out of 30 million are dying of hunger, yellow leather breeches, cannon and cavalry will be able to do very little about it.

The influence of Malthus's revelation is surely evident in Balzac's borrowing of these examples from Holland and England. His description and explanation of crime and the links he establishes between poverty and crime denote at least a broad grasp of the system set out in the famous *Essay on the Principle of Population*, if not a perfect familiarity with Malthus's work. Many of Balzac's contemporaries had only a confused idea of this revelation, which gave rise to numerous impassioned discussions under the July Monarchy: "No, sir, I'm no Malthus!" M. Prudhomme snorts in one of Henri Monnier's sketches.[7] "Malthus," the other asks, "what's that?" "I've no idea," M. Prudhomme replies firmly. Not so with Balzac. His information is of a high theoretical and practical quality and his explanation of crime and working-class protest concurs with that expressed in Malthus's eloquent apologue of the banquet. Owing to Malthus, and despite the survival of the older notions of crime, the proliferation of the dangerous classes was related in Balzac and his contemporaries to demographic and economic changes and the unbalanced development of resources and population, and crime was now an aspect of poverty.

The psychological causes are observed far more often than the material causes, however. In particular, Balzac showed less interest in the relationship between poverty and theft than in the general determination to enrich itself by which society at large was actuated, from the lowest to the highest classes. Balzac very obviously preferred to study this universal passion among the highest class.

The *Comédie humaine* as a whole displays similar characteristics and similar survivals. The dangerous classes are still apart from the other classes, forming a separate people wholly isolated by its customs, speech, history, mode of life and death, and the places where it ordinarily lives out and ends its existence.

The description is, however, exact and devoid of any kind of romanticism; terms are always defined by their etymology, habits explained by their reason for being as they are. In short, the very rigor of the account and its very technique confine the dangerous classes yet more securely within the closed world of the criminal class as a class, the *pègre*. The relations between laboring and dangerous classes are more evident in *Les Mystères de Paris* and *Les Misérables* because their description is more dramatic, though more confused. It is hard to distinguish the various categories of the people, the honest workers from the rest, in the obscure mass fighting and dying on the barricade in the rue Saint-Denis, between the Charybdis of the faubourg Saint-Antoine and the Scylla of the faubourg du Temple, in the "intermittent gleams," the shadowed dawn or dim twilight. Such confused, and confusedly described, hordes appear nowhere in Balzac. And this is probably one of the reasons why Balzac's way of describing the lower classes appears to have a slighter sociological impact than the description in *Les Misérables*, which deals with masses rather than individuals. The crowds are broken up in Balzac's description into characters as easily identifiable as if they were to produce their birth and marriage certificates or their identity cards. The honest craftsman really is an honest craftsman, the villain a villain. And there can be no deception, at any rate for readers whom Balzac directs and teaches to read, to see, to understand, to divine the significance of an attitude, a costume, a glance, a wrinkle. Look at the difference between the four bandits in whom Hugo incarnates both the criminality and the destitution of Paris, shrouding them in chiaroscuro, and Balzac's villains, about whom we know every particular, their origins, their kinships, their contacts, where they go and their shady practices.[8] Hugo raises the whole social problem, voluntarily by way of his analysis, starting by etymologically combining *pègre* and poverty, *pégrenne* and hunger, and ending with an evocation of popular revolutions; involuntarily, by a proliferation of images which are no more Hugo's own than the common property of all his contemporaries and, charged as they are with collective emotions, go far beyond what the author intended, communicating to us a message of which neither Hugo nor his contemporaries were fully conscious. Whereas Balzac virtually provides us with a lexicon. Note the great difference between his dry, legal and almost administrative study of the condition of the convict on licence and the tragic story of Jean Valjean, which embodies many forms of woe besides those of the hulks.

Balzac's fidelity to the older themes is the more evident in that that world of evil is incarnate in a few figures larger than life. Especially, of course, Vautrin, a prodigious criminal, who is relevant only to crime as such, and a limited, picturesque and adventurous crime at that, but is quite irrelevant to the confused criminality that rises from the crowd and is engendered by destitution.

Vautrin is Vidocq; this has been demonstrated so often and so well that we need not press it further.[9] But Vautrin is something else again; and this has not been sufficiently demonstrated. He is the culmination of shocking conditions, which became irrelevant in later history but could be observed by Balzac and his contemporaries in the early years of the Restoration, when the old scores of the troubled years of the Revolution and the Empire were being settled. The importance of exceptional crime in Balzac's works and his persistent fidelity to the older notions of it are accounted for, too, by contemporary circumstances which Balzac knew more about than most people because of his personal acquaintance with Vidocq, but which all the Parisians of the period knew tolerably well merely from reading the newspapers. Literary influences and sources, which can be traced easily enough, are of less importance here than these facts of opinion. As Balzac wrote:

One of the duties to which the historian of manners must always remain faithful is not to spoil the true by seemingly dramatic devices, especially when real life itself assumes the form of fiction. Society, particularly in Paris, teems with hazards and capricious tangles of coincidence that surpass the contrivances of imagination at every turn. Real life brings out striking coincidences which art eschews, so improbable or inartistic are they unless the writer tones them down, purifies and chastens them.[10]

Some descriptions and some aspects of Vautrin the character do, of course, express the taste for the superhuman and the fantastic which Balzac shared with his contemporaries. This taste was simply a result of the social upheavals exemplified in the aftermath of Revolution and Empire by the sensational adventures of ex-convicts raised to high public office, such as the self-styled marquis de Chambreuil, Director-General of the Royal Stud in 1815 and chief of the Palace Police, arrested by Vidocq; and Coignard, who turned up as the comte de Pontis de Sainte-Hélène, Knight of the Order of Saint-Louis, battalion commander in the Legion of the Seine, also arrested by Vidocq; as well as Collet, "arrested at Le Mans, where he was passing as a reputable citizen amongst a population which had the utmost esteem for his virtue, and subsequently died in the Rochefort convict prison in 1840";[11] and many others whose arrest was reported in the newspaper[12] or who succeeded in concealing their criminal activity under the most respectable appearances to the very end. "In Paris I knew a ticket-of-leave man from the Lorient prison," Vidocq wrote in *Les Voleurs*,

who wore three decorations on his lapel, the Legion of Honor, the Order of Saint-Louis and the July Cross. In vain I reported him to the police. . . . If he had gone straight, I would not mention him, but he still is what he was in the old days, an incorrigible rogue. . . . So I believe I am rendering my readers an important service by sketching this gentleman's portrait.

These exceptional situations carrying over authentic survivals of the crime of the Ancien Régime into the last years of the Restoration account for certain aspects of the contemporary literature which at first sight strike us as extraordinary. Such social monstrosities led contemporaries to regard as quite probable situations and characters which seem to us to come from the most extravagant fiction. This would later account for Rodolphe in the *Mystères de Paris*, the aristocrat turned bandit, the apparently outlandish inventions in Sue's novel, and Vautrin and the astonishing society around him; and this was the reason for Balzac's interest in the gentry criminals, the *haute pègre* he described in *Splendeurs et misères des courtisanes*. Literary criticism, with its attention to literary influences and sources, is not adequate for charting such facts, which have to be derived from the study of opinion; though simply reading the contemporary newspapers would establish it solidly enough. They are the origin of many of the seeming improbabilities in the *Comédie humaine* and many of the incongruous digressions in the unfolding of the plots, such as the queer pirate episode in the middle of *La femme de trente ans*, which entirely alters the course of the narrative, or the horrible intervention of Madame Nourrisson at the end of *La Cousine Bette*.[13]

II

From the Dangerous Classes to the Laboring Classes

Nevertheless, though the older characteristics predominated in Balzac's society and though he paid more attention to the older forms of crime, the new forms finally made their appearance in the *Comédie humaine*; but only in the background, in incidental descriptions, in observations of detail and in apparently inconsistent contexts, sometimes even inconsistent with the general description, as if Balzac were not wholly aware of this and as if, for once, he had abandoned understanding and explanation and had simply recorded experience.

As the work proceeded, the crime became both darker and more impersonal, moving anonymously into a city that became dangerous throughout. Theft gave way to murder, the existence of which he had denied or treated as a joke in the *Code des gens honnêtes*. When Horace Bianchon meets the comte de Granville in December 1829 after midnight in the purlieus of the rue de Gaillon, he cries, "Aren't you risking the assassins' dagger there?"—"I don't fear them," the comte de Granville replied, gloomily and devil-may-care. "But at least, this is no place to loiter in," said the doctor, leading the lawyer towards the boulevard. "I was beginning to think you want to cheat me of your last illness and die by a hand other than mine."[14] In Balzac's later works, when a bourgeois of Paris is late coming home, his family fear for his life; "Your district gives me the horrors," a character cries in *La Cousine Bette*, speaking of the Vieux Louvre. "You'll be murdered there some day."

But, above all, criminality was now described, though incidentally and often irrespective of the tone of the rest of the book, as no longer merely an appanage of those giants of crime to whom Balzac devoted his main attention, but an emanation from the popular masses as a whole; not something exceptional, but something ordinary and genuinely social.

This popular crime was expressed in the characters themselves, who are exceptional and do not belong to the people at all, though it is not possible to distinguish the element in them that is personal adventure from the element of collective destiny, to say what is crime and what revolt, what savage and what social, so loaded is Balzac's description of them with new and often inconsistent elements at the crises of the dramas, which suddenly swell with a vast discordant menace. Thus, Vautrin suddenly assumes destinies that are not his own; he is an exceptional criminal, but also an "embodiment of the people in revolt against the laws," a people which is not simply the people of crime. The character's significance goes beyond the character itself. It goes even further, inasmuch as the transformation is achieved at the very last moment, breaking with all the other novels, and almost unperceived by Balzac himself. Or it is achieved at any rate by some sort of final discovery—which was never to be wholly expressed—in a confused mass of words that had never yet been uttered, but suddenly burst forth. They demand quotation:

Thus the various interests intertwined in the depths and at the heights of society were all to meet in the Procureur-Général's office, all brought thither by necessity and represented by three men: justice represented by M. de Granville and the family represented by Corentin, face to face with the terrible adversary Jacques Collin, in the shape of the savage force of social evil. What a duel between justice and the arbitrary, both united against the galleys and their cunning! The galleys, the symbol of the audacity which eschews calculation and reflection, knows no scruple, has none of the hypocrisy of the arbitrary and hideously symbolizes the interest of the famished belly, the sudden bloody protest of hunger! Was this not attack and defense? Theft and property? The terrible question of the social condition and the natural condition fought out within the narrowest possible space? In brief, it was a terrible, living, image of those anti-social compromises which the representatives of power enter into with savage rioters when they are not strong enough to quell them.

Here crime takes on an element of popular revolt and is transformed into it.

We must focus on this revolt in order to measure the evolution of the theme of crime in the *Comédie humaine*. In the work as a whole, the social aspects of the problem of crime were stated not so much by the description of the haunts of criminals as by the evocation of the potential criminality secreted both by the masses and by the lower-class districts. Balzac continually described the lower classes as threatening the social order. They threatened it through the lower groups who lived very near the haunts of crime, like the beggars in the opening pages of *Ferragus*:

Situated between crime and charity, they are past remorse and loiter cautiously around the scaffold without falling to it, innocent in the midst of vice and vicious in their innocence. They often make you smile, but they always make you think. One embodies a stunted civilization; he is a compendium of everything, the honor of thieves, patriotism, virtue, and the malignance of vulgar crime combined with the subtlety of an elegant but more atrocious crime as well. Another is uncomplaining, a masterly mimic, but stupid. All of them have vague leanings toward order and work, but they are thrust back into their mud by a society which is quite unwilling to find out what poets, what great men, what intrepid individuals and magnificent constitutions there may be among the beggars, those bohemians of Paris; a people superlatively spiteful, like all masses which have suffered; accustomed to bear unheard-of evils and kept by some fatal power forever down at the level of the mud. All of them have some dream, some hope, some happiness—gambling, the lottery or wine.

The masses threaten the social order as an entity, as they are presented at the beginning of *La fille aux yeux d'or*, in the lowest circles of the Parisian hell, in the depths of the cave where Vulcan reigns and where the proletarians are astir. The characteristics Balzac gives them should be carefully noted, for it is hard to tell whether they are those of crime or of poverty. This intermediate position is summed up in the description in *L'Interdiction* of the poor districts in the XIIth arrondissement, on which the contemporary medical topographies later supplied a detailed commentary:

Further on, an old woman, pale and chilled, displayed the repulsive mask of pauperism in revolt, ready to take its revenge for all its past sufferings on some day of sedition. There was also the young workman, weak and listless, whose intelligent eye bespoke abilities of a high order repressed by needs against which he has struggled, in vain, suffering in silence and near to die for lack of a chance to slip between the bars of the vast animal-pound in which these miseries devour each other and writhe in torment.

Thus, the relationships between the dangerous classes and the laboring classes were indicated in the very book in which the older crime had pride of place. And this despite the persistent mirages of past eras, despite a greater curiosity about other problems, despite the pressures of the story—indeed, inconsistent with that story and the consequence of other pressures which, without the author's knowledge, changed the very meaning of the words he used and the very significance of the facts he observed. These pressures were to act as even stronger determinants when exerted upon works which were more subjective, more permeable to social developments and to opinion concerning those developments.

CHAPTER FOUR

Hugo

The *Mystères de Paris* was originally intended as the book of the dangerous classes but became the book of the people by a process of transformation and under the influence of pressures which we shall describe when we come to study opinion itself, rather than the documents concerning and expressing opinion. It may be called a "passive" work because it records rather than describes. Hugo is even more "passive." The evolution of the definition, meaning, emotion and colors of crime from the early *Dernier jour d'un condamné*, which was still pervaded by the older theme of crime, to *Les Misérables*, the very title of which sums up the whole period we are dealing with and every aspect of our subject—the correlation between the proletarian condition and the criminal condition—was part of that transformation.

I
Le dernier jour d'un condamné

The story of *Le dernier jour d'un condamné*, written in 1828 and published in 1829, to which Hugo added a long Preface in 1832, certainly seems to complicate the description of crime by the introduction of novel characteristics—a subtler form of anguish, a skillful advance into horror, going so far as to let the victim himself recount his last moments on earth. The older theme of crime itself was henceforth to bear this imprint, even in those works which remained most staunchly faithful to it, above all in "the strange language of suffering, an amalgam of somber and funereal words,"[1] never heard before.

But it was still in fact the older theme of crime, that of Mercier and his imitators. The setting was the traditional one; not the wide areas in which crime lived and spawned, that vast, dark and menacing Paris, but the precise places where the last acts in the tragedy of crime occurred, places alien to the city and often external to it, like distant Bicêtre and Clamart, the cemetery of the poor and of the guillotined, "Clamart where the grass grows so green"; places to make excursions to. Victor Hugo, like Mercier and Jouy before him, had to visit them. All these writers, indeed, described these places in almost the same terms— not that his predecessors had any great influence on Hugo, but it was a historical imperative imposed at the time by the places themselves, one which, however, was to be effaced by later developments. Paris appears only from time to time on the way to these places of crime, apart and distant, summed up in brief glimpses: the towers of Notre-Dame suddenly framed in the back window of the cart carrying the condemned man from Bicêtre to the Conciergerie, "blue and half-shrouded in the fog"; the tower of Saint-Jacques de la Boucherie, which the condemned man on the way to the scaffold sees in the distance above the roofs, "black, isolated, with its two stone gargoyles squatting in profile." The contrast between the setting of crime and Paris, different and indifferent, was one of the most effective devices for communicating terror and distress.

The criminal society, the characters expressing it and the scenes evoked were also quite different from those in earlier works. The criminals were still the leading representatives of the tradition of horror, alien to the rest of the population, even the lowest classes, not only because of their sinister renown and even the species of nobility conferred on them by their crimes, but also because of their abnormal and monstrous nature. We have only to look at the signatures carved on the walls of Bicêtre:

From the wall beside the name Papavoine I pulled away an enormous spider's web, clotted with dust and stretching to the far corner. Four or five names were perfectly legible beneath the web: Dautun, 1815; Paulain, 1818; Jean Martin, 1821; Castaing, 1823. I read the names, and sinister memories came back to me. Dautun, who quartered his brother and prowled about Paris by night, throwing the head into a fountain and the torso into a sewer; Paulain, who murdered his wife; Jean Martin, who fired a pistol at his old father as he opened a window; Castaing, the doctor who poisoned his friend and when attending him in his last illness, which he himself had caused, administered poison to him again instead of medicine; and beside them, Papavoine, the horrible madman who killed children by knifing them in the head.

Crime was monstrous, abnormal, in the older tradition. The *Journal des Débats* itself pointed out that this crime did not tally with the new forms, which held a menace of a different sort. "The author," it wrote on February 26, 1829,

should have chosen a setting truer to life. . . . Imagine, for example, a condemned man whose name would have been cried in the streets of Paris; a young man, an unfortunate who had shed blood in a moment of madness, who had been a quiet and honest fellow till then. . . . His grief would take the form of dull apathy rather than subtle disquisitions. . . . As he was carried by in the cart, exhausted and shattered, all thoughts, clear or vacant, would cease. It would be the people itself that rounded off the drama and watched the victim fall, not as bloodthirsty spectators, looking forward a week beforehand to the severing of a head, but as impassioned and compassionate witnesses watching with painful curiosity, who would return home more shaken by the punishment than the crime.

That sort of crime would not appear until later, in the beliefs, at any rate, if not in fact. It was to be incarnate in Ulbach, the workman who, whether by misfortune, chance or passion, was reduced to the criminal condition and was to loom large in the background of crime in *Les Misérables*. Ulbach did not appear yet; he was first actually named in the 1832 Preface, which visibly took developments a great deal further than the stage reached in the book itself. The crime embodied in the structure of *Le dernier jour d'un condamné* was still exceptional crime; not the type of crime represented by Ulbach, which, if not yet entirely normal, was well on the way to becoming so.

There was a similar fidelity to the older themes, which sum up the main phases of the great drama of crime in the book. Note the great contrast between the chain gang in *Les Misérables* and the shackling scene in *Le dernier jour d'un condamné*. Contrast the sinister procession which Jean Valjean and Cosette encounter by chance when strolling near the former barrière du Maine—or rather the confused mass and vast murmur they somehow feel rising and swelling from Paris as if it emanated from the entire city, expressing some part of its horror— with the scene at Bicêtre, which has quite rightly been compared with earlier and contemporary descriptions to show the overwhelming superiority of Hugo's talent and to stress the differences between the accounts. But in fact it is the similarities that we find remarkable;[2] for it is evident that the same settings and the same places evoke the same images and that all these accounts share a common tradition of crime. They are scenes from the Ancien Régime; and Hugo regarded them as such. He said so himself in the 1832 Preface:

In August 1830 there was so much generosity in the air, such a sense of tolerance and civility among the masses . . . that we felt that the death penalty had been abolished automatically, out of hand, by tacit and unanimous consent, like the rest of the evil things which had plagued us. The people had just made a bonfire of the rags of the Ancien Régime. This was the bloodstained rag. We believed that it had been altogether abolished.

Different aspects of the problem, the significance and even the definition of crime, all come to light in the 1832 Preface.

The difference does not lie in the plea for the abolition of the death penalty, so heavily stressed by Victor Hugo himself and by his commentators, critics of literary or social history.[3] Indeed, there is hardly a trace of any such plea in the story itself. "Somber elegy, vain plea," Balzac wrote later. Somber elegy there is, but the vain plea appears only in the 1832 Preface. This is not the main difference between the story and the Preface. It does not lie in the author's ambition to stand in the forefront of those who protested against the death penalty in the early years of the July Monarchy. But it does lie in an evolution in the concept of crime which seems quite obvious to us, but which Hugo and his contemporaries do not seem to have perceived so plainly.

The Setting of Crime

The crime to which the Preface referred was indeed different from that in the story, for it no longer attached only to the districts or localities which were most particularly the peculiar setting of crime in most of the older writings—the place de Grève, Bicêtre, the prisons. Now it extended to the whole of the capital, the description of which was shadowed and, as it were, draped in mourning for its sake; an anonymous crime emanating from the city as a whole, crime of which the city was ashamed and of which it shamefacedly rid itself by moving the performance on the Grève to the barrière Saint-Jacques.

The Removal of the Guillotine and Its Significance: The removal of the guillotine, to which Hugo devoted a good deal of space here, was significant of this transformation of the older picturesque crime into a social form of crime. "In Paris," he wrote,

we are reverting to the age of secret executions. Since they no longer dare after July to behead on the place de Grève, since they are afraid, since they are cowardly, this is what they do. Recently at Bicêtre they took a man, a man condemned to death, one Desandrieux, I believe, and put him in a sort of basket on two wheels, shuttered on all sides, padlocked and bolted; then, with a gendarme before and a gendarme behind, with hardly a sound and with no crowd in attendance, they delivered this parcel at the deserted barrière Saint-Jacques. It was eight in the morning when they got there, barely daylight. There stood a brand-new guillotine and for public only a few dozen small boys clustered on heaps of stones around the unexpected machine. Swiftly they drew the man from the basket, and, giving him no time to draw breath, furtively, slyly, shamefacedly they took off his head. This is what they call a public and solemn act of high justice. What pitiful mockery!

This sums up the whole evolution of the theme of crime in fact and in general belief. Primarily, the removal of the guillotine and the new rites of execution could be accounted for only by an awareness of the new characteristics of a crime which henceforth required a new setting. But, conversely, the choice of the barrière Saint-Jacques was to lend to crime—to what it represented and to the horror it spread— aspects very different from those conferred upon it by the place de Grève. The evolution in crime and the evolution in the opinion of the people of Paris concerning the crime were both cause and effect. It was the evolution in crime that made the place de Grève impossible and demanded a new setting. But it was this setting, in turn, which conferred upon crime aspects which had not been conferred upon it by the old place de Grève. These new characteristics of opinion—an expression of the new characteristics of crime—were very evident in the Preface.

What part did opinion play in the decision to move the guillotine and in the choice of the barrière Saint-Jacques? "Since they no longer dare after July to behead on the place de Grève," says Hugo, "since they are afraid, since they are cowardly . . ." This fear, this cowardice was expressed in the official documents of the time. "In the palmy days of the Empire and the Restoration," the *Journal des Débats* noted, "when an execution was to take place, the windows of the houses along the condemned man's route were booked long beforehand. . . . Purified as it was by the blood of the victims of July, the place de Grève could no longer be used as the stage for the execution of murderers."[4] There were other reasons. "The place de Grève," the Prefect of the Seine wrote on November 16, 1831,

can no longer be used as a place of execution since generous citizens so gloriously shed their blood there for the national cause. But, in addition, traffic difficulties in the confined district adjoining the place de Grève have long brought home the need to set aside some other place for capital executions.[5]

It was true, indeed, that intolerable frenzies of mass hysteria had marked the executions carried out there in the last years of the Restoration and immediately after the July Revolution, causing traffic blocks and disorder in the middle of the afternoon. The execution of Daumas-

Dupin on December 3, 1829, for instance, attended and, as it were, participated in by a huge crowd, despite the efforts of the police to prevent the sentences of the criminal court being cried in the streets.[6] Or, yet more horrible, that of the three murderers of the concierge of the Hotel Vaucanson in the rue de Charonne.[7] "It is important," wrote the Prefect of the Seine on November 16, 1831,

preferably to select select places far from the center of Paris but as close as possible to the prison in which the condemned prisoners are confined. The place Vauban, behind the Invalides, with excellent means of access, seems very suitable. If executions were carried out there, the class which usually attends them would lose the habit and by these means alone we would bring about an appreciable amelioration in manners.

This proposal met with opposition from the Minister of War, who, on January 2, 1832, proposed the place de Breteuil, near the Grenelle slaughterhouses. The square at the end of the faubourg Saint-Jacques was finally chosen, on January 20, 1832. It was inaugurated by Desandrieux on February 3, 1832. Moreover, executions now took place at dawn instead of at four in the afternoon.

Les Misérables gave the reasons for the choice of the place Saint-Jacques much more clearly than the 1832 Preface. It was, Hugo wrote, "as if predestined; for it had always been horrible." When we come on to *Les Misérables*, we shall discuss the main aspects of this predestination and this horror. Some appeared as early as the 1832 Preface.

The place was predestined because it was associated with the memory of so many crimes. Above all with Ulbach's—mentioned here for the first time by Hugo, with the remark that he started writing the book "to the best of his belief on the day after Ulbach's execution." As a matter of fact, Ulbach was executed on September 11, 1827, not in 1828. The crime and the execution had made such an impact that it never occurred to Hugo that he need check the date; but no more than the rest of the people of Paris had he forgotten the details of the case.

The place also evoked other crimes, very different from those which bloodied the capital. It was at the barrières, and more particularly the barrière Saint-Jacques and the neighboring barrières, close to the poorest districts in Paris, that working-class violence—to which we shall revert—was most intense and most frequent. It was there that the most primitive, worst-paid and least stable population engaged in the bloodiest settlements of scores, in which workers themselves were the victims far more often than bourgeois. The bourgeois hardly ever ventured into these purlieus; the assaults on them occurred in the central districts, along the communication lines of trade and business which can be traced so easily in the *Comédie humaine*. The great battles of the journeymen [*compagnons*] were fought out at the barrières. And, above all, the crimes among the migrant workers, who lay in wait for, robbed and murdered each other.[8]

The place was predestined, lastly, by its proximity to the faubourgs most deeply stamped with destitution and crime, especially the faubourg Saint-Marcel, "the sick faubourg," where, between the boulevard and the city whose domes and belfries were silhouetted against the far horizon, a backward, brutish and miserable population huddled together, a faubourg long doomed to the dirtiest and most degrading work, a disinherited zone of tanners, skin-dressers, curriers and ragpickers, of which Lachaise wrote in 1822[9] that "it is very like a fifth- or sixth-class town, a district entirely apart from the other districts of the capital." A faubourg damned both in fact and in Parisian opinion. This opinion is curiously expressed by Parent-Duchatelet in a medical topography of the banks of the Bièvre in 1822:

The first glance at such a focus of infection, flowing through a district inhabited by thirty thousand persons, most of them reduced to indigence and packed together, would convince anyone that it would cause people to contract serious illness or at least make them constitutionally listless and weak. Such, at any rate, is the notion generally held in Paris about this part of the faubourg Saint-Marceau; such was the opinion we ourselves held when we undertook last year, for purely philanthropic reasons, to make the survey we are now publishing. . . . There is a tradition at the Hôtel-Dieu that patients from the faubourg Saint-Marceau and the neighborhood of the Bièvre are much more seriously affected than others and usually find it harder to recover.

But the whole southern banlieue was in a similar plight; reduced to rendering to the city as a whole the most necessary but least decent, least remunerative and, frankly, the most degrading services. The least enlightened, the least skilled and least demanding laborers fetched up there, Parisian workmen driven out by more profitable business, laid off even from the workshops in the neighboring faubourgs; as well as migrant workers, far more of them in these parts than in the northern banlieue. It was a sort of world's end, a strange country to which for years there was no access save by dirt paths; and it was terrifying. The more vehemently the bourgeois of Charenton refused to have a police station which they would have to pay for, the more vigorously the bourgeois of Ivry and Montrouge demanded one. It is not surprising, in short, that the Paris Administration, seeking a new place for its guillotine, should have dumped it on these lowlands on which it had acquired a habit of dumping many other things of a similar sort.

If this place was predestined to receive the guillotine, it conferred new aspects on crime in return. "The illustrious criminals—sometimes innocent—of the place de Grève, the successor of Montfaucon, are often cited, and there is a long list of them," Delvau wrote in 1865 in his *Histoire anecdotique des barrières de Paris*.

The heretic Marguerite Porette opened the procession in 1310. After her came famous men and women, judges and warriors, philosophers and poets, fanatics and dreamers. People like Desrues and Brinvilliers abound—as well as Ravaillac and Damiens—and, too, Etienne Dolet! Not to mention the Sergeants of La Rochelle. The famous names of the barrière Saint-Jacques— the *abbaye de monte à regret* [the scaffold] of the reign of Louis-Philippe are of two sorts only: villains and madmen, murderers and conspirators— people like Lacenaire, Alibaud, Poulmann and Fieschi.

And others, too, representing an obscure criminality meriting a punishment as obscure as themselves.

For here there was nothing in common with the expiation on the place de Grève, in the full light of afternoon, amid the great roar of the city only for a moment interrupted, at the center of work and business, in a historical setting dominated by the Hôtel-de-Ville, Notre-Dame, the Tour Saint-Jacques, in the symbolic neighborhood of the Palais de Justice. Execution now became a sort of foul blow, shameful, shady, comparable in every way with the very act to which society wished to respond—without glory, without meaning, without utility. "Do you seriously believe you are making an example," Hugo wrote,

when you miserably cut the throat of some poor fellow at the most deserted spot on the outer boulevards? On the place de Grève, in the full light of day, maybe; but at the barrière Saint-Jacques! at eight in the morning! Who on earth ever goes there? Who has any idea that you are making an example? An example to whom? To the trees on the boulevard, apparently.

Henceforth, the whole city appeared guilty, and crime, at this stage in its development, became nothing but a sort of by-product, just one more bit of garbage among others. Ordure and crime already blended here as two necessary and barely separable aspects of urban living. They blended in the sick faubourgs which attracted the guillotine.

They blended in the same way in the landscape of Montfaucon, which summed up more thoroughly than any other setting the past and present horrors of the city. "Give us back Montfaucon," Hugo cried,

its sixteen stone pillars, its squatting beasts, its cellars of bones, its beams, its hooks, its chains, its skewered skeletons, its mound of lime pocked with crows, its lesser gibbets and the smell of corpse which it wafts in great gusts all over the faubourg du Temple when the wind is in the northeast.

Note this corpse smell. All the unhealthy consequences of the city's growth in the past and the present blended in it and were expressed by it, as they were expressed and blended in the landscape of Montfaucon. This mound was a high place of criminal history and by this fact alone aroused horror and disgust. But to the horror at crime there was later added a further horror at the degrading labor which—no doubt because of this older horror and this ancestral character of infamy— settled in there, the older horror henceforth becoming indistinguishable from the present one. It was this fact of collective opinion that was so well reflected in the 1832 Preface, in the probably involuntary passage from the past to the present and the more or less unconscious play on words about "the smell of corpse which it wafts in great gusts all over the faubourg du Temple when the wind is in the northeast."

Old corpses marked with the old criminality, vanished, but spreading a pestilential and ever-present stench, just as the building materials of the former gibbet contrived to survive in the foundations of the reservoirs into which the fecal matter of Paris flowed and in the walls of the horse butchers' yards. Their stench still spread in great gusts over the faubourg du Temple, mingled with the powerful stench of the carcasses of more recent times, the carrion which the city dumped in these places.

Both the setting and the theme of crime evolved in this way between the narrative of *Le dernier jour d'un condamné* and the 1832 Preface in which crime was regarded as a sort of necessary, though deplorable, by-product of urban living.

The Criminal Groups

The description of the criminal groups was no less significant. Ulbach appeared in these pages and, through him, popular, daily and what might be called normal crime. We must particularly stress the new sense in which Hugo used—for the first time—the word "*misérables.*" In the story itself, Hugo used "*misérable*" to mean a man who had committed a crime. Finding the name of one of the Four Sergeants of

La Rochelle[10] on the wall at Bicêtre, the man condemned to death cries: "Poor young man! How many so-called political necessities are hideous! The horrible reality they call the guillotine is the fate of an idea, a dream, an abstraction! And I was feeling sorry for myself, I, a wretch who have committed a real crime, who have shed blood!" "Every Sunday after Mass," he wrote, "they let me out into the exercise yard! There I chat with the prisoners; and so I should. They are good people, the *misérables*." After 1830, in *Feuilles d'automne*, the term denoted the destitution which engenders crime, the thought of which "seethes in silence in the heart of the *misérable*"; but no longer crime alone. It denoted destitution, too, in the long passage in the 1832 Preface in which it was first given the wider significance which it was to assume in *Les Misérables*.[11]

II
Les Misérables*

The Importance and Limitations of the Testimony

The way in which crime invades and pervades the Parisian landscape and population; the transformation of a picturesque, exceptional, grandiose fact peculiar to certain groups, attached to certain settings, and restricted to certain districts, into a general and collective fact important at all times and places, as characteristic of the form of urban living as housing or working conditions or the rhythm of existence itself; and the new meaning of the word *"misérables"*—the various aspects of one and the same evolution observed in the development from the narrative of *Le dernier jour d'un condamné* to the 1832 Preface— all these factors come to full fruition and assume their full significance in *Les Misérables*, whose subject is identical with our own.

This is true especially of the period described. Jean Valjean enters Paris with Cosette by the barrière de Monceaux at nightfall at the end of 1823. The capital is henceforth the main scene of the story and the principal incidents take place during the period from the end of the Restoration to the early years of the July Monarchy, in which evolve all the economic, social, political and biological forms of the malaise we are discussing. The varied aspects of this crisis, combining

* Though Hugo published *Les Misérables* only in 1862, he began it before 1850. Hence he had a considerable number of years in which to rework his initial concepts, while his exile steadily heightened his desire to condemn the injustices of the social order.—Trans.

"the political sickness and the social sickness," have never been so powerfully related as in this book, in which the account of the insurrection begins with a description of the cholera epidemic. And, above all, crime had never been so closely and so consciously identified as the city's major problem as it was here.

Crime fills the book just as it fills the Paris described in it. It was there at the barrières and it imbues the solitary stretches near the faubourgs with something of the distress and dreary foreboding which the writer powerfully felt, but wholly failed to account for; he did, however, provide valuable clues to their interpretation. Crime was in the central districts, where the walls of old prisons like La Force merged with those of old mansions and bourgeois houses. Crime was in the maze of quarries and sewers, in the underground Paris which summoned up terrors, whose traces linger in the novel as they did in contemporary news items—strange noises from cellars or abandoned quarries disturbing the inhabitants of a district and investigated by the police.[12] But, above all, it spread through the whole population attracted or threatened by it, or at least that large part of the Paris population whose unity and diversity Hugo stressed in the closing passage of his description of Gavroche:

. . . that indigent class which begins with the last small tradesman in difficulties and sinks from wretchedness to wretchedness down into the lowest depths of society, to those two beings to whom all the material things of civilization descend, the scavenger who sweeps the mud and the ragpicker who collects the rags.

Crime is most certainly the book's dominant theme. Almost at the start, Hugo raised "the three problems of the century, the degradation of man by proletarianization, the downfall of woman by hunger, the atrophy of the child by the dark." This was indeed the sickness from which Paris suffered.

We are not, however, so much concerned with the crime in *Les Misérables*, or at least the criminality described in it, since this has often been studied and, though important for literary historical research, has little relevance to social history. For the predominant place given to crime in the novel, which has so frequently been discussed, is not in itself sufficient authority for maintaining that crime held a similar place in daily life. It is probable, but by no means evident, that this literary description tallied with a set of social facts. A literary document is not necessarily a historical document and cannot be classed as genuine historical material without more ado. Literary comment certainly cannot be regarded as proof that a testimony is authentic. What we have to study is not the place given to crime, the criminal groups and criminal localities in the general drama of the Paris described in the book, on the prior assumption that the literary description tallies with contemporary facts, by simply listing the chapters dealing with crime; but rather, the pressure exerted by the facts upon the description. We are not concerned with the deliberate and conscious description, but with the "passive" description; not with the book Hugo intended to write, but with the book he was compelled to write; not with the situations he observed, but with those which he recorded more or less passively; not with the finished and structured accounts he gives in many famous passages, but with the details, corrections, erasures— the traces of contemporary circumstances confirmed by historical research, but not always clearly perceived by their contemporaries.

The first thing to observe here is that there are a striking number of obsolete situations and unconscious anachronisms in the book, and that the description of criminal life in Paris under the July Monarchy is still marked by a great many characteristics dating from the old crime of the palmy days of the Restoration, of the Empire and even of the Ancien Régime before the great Revolutionary upheaval; that there are all too many annoying and incongruous reminiscences and quotations which somewhat impair the dominating impression of authenticity and undermine one's initial belief that here at last we have a genuine eyewitness account.

The crime of the Ancien Régime pervades the book. In the important chapter on the language of criminals, the history of thieves' slang is dwelt on at far greater length than contemporary examples of it. This restricts its scope; antiquarian erudition weakens observation, and what is derived from the Paris Hugo knew is diminished by what he took from the books he may have read; for we too have read them. The portrait of Gavroche gains nothing from being placed in the portrait gallery of Paris *gamins*—*gamins* of the older Paris—which Hugo sees fit to display, those sent to the galleys by Louis XIV, those whom Louis XV kidnapped for "some mysterious employment or other." "This lad may be traced in Poquelin, a son of Les Halles, and again in Beaumarchais." No doubt, but what is that to our purpose? As a citizen of Paris Hugo knew his city, but knew a great deal more from all those who had written about it, from Barbier and Restif, in whose tatters Hugo's characters are still clothed. He takes a plan of Paris of 1727 to trace Jean Valjean's route and places the cul-de-sac Genrot in the Petit Picpus.

There are even more unfortunate survivals, however, though closer in time. The influence of the crime of the Empire and the first decade of the Restoration, so obvious in *Le dernier jour d'un condamné*—and in the 1832 Preface itself, despite the development we have described—is still evident in *Les Misérables*. How much the story of Jean Valjean and Javert owes to Vidocq, whom Hugo quotes several times—he was the model for several traits in both Valjean and Javert, the convict and the policeman—has been very rightly pointed out. The survival of these old forms, of what Hugo had learned from others, from books and especially from Vidocq's Memoirs, probably accounts for the astonishing contrast between the authenticity of the crime Hugo did not intend to describe and the artificiality of the crime he did mean to describe, embodied in Babet, Gueulemer, Claquesous and Montparnasse. In all the crime literature of the July Monarchy, even the clumsiest and most melodramatic, it would be hard to find bandits less convincing and less impressive than this quartet who, Hugo claims, "governed the lower depths of Paris from 1830 to 1835." A most improbable government. It is hardly possible to take these small fry seriously and to believe that "owing to their ramifications and the subjacent network of their relations they had the general direction of all the villainies in the department of the Seine." The horror with which Hugo invested them does not impress us, though he added details and corrections, which are to be found on the original manuscript of *Les Misérables*. He first wrote of Montparnasse: "at the age of nineteen he had several corpses behind him." This he corrected to: "at the age of eighteen he had several corpses behind him," and added: "More than one wayfarer lay in the shadow of this villain, with outstretched arms, his face in a pool of blood." They are small fry as villains, expressing only, and badly at that, their own criminality or a form of criminality abundantly illustrated in Vidocq's Memoirs. Indeed, Hugo tried to give an additional turn of the screw by referring to Vidocq and by bringing him in in person: "These four bandits formed a sort of Proteus, winding through the ranks of the police and striving to escape Vidocq's uncanny penetration under cover of various disguises."

Admittedly, these survivals of a former or immediately prior criminality are a small matter compared with the description of the social criminality which germinated in the Preface to *Le dernier jour d'un condamné* and came to full fruition here. But simply to note this as a fact is not wholly satisfactory. The most important pieces of evidence are not, on the whole, those which Hugo meant to put forward or thought he had. An antiquarian view of social matters is of no more help than an academic view of crime. What we have to seek, beyond this social or criminal antiquarianism, by reading beyond this fabricated description, is the trace of the facts themselves in the book, both in its final form and at its various stages—visible enough in the manuscript[13] —of a work which became "*Les Misérables*" only after it had been "*Les Misères.*" Erasures, corrections and interpolations, which can be dated fairly accurately, enable us both to follow the development of Hugo himself and his contemporaries and to describe how the text was invaded, as it were, by certain facts which were not there at the start. It is this involuntary and "passive" testimony that counts. It is not enough to say that *Les Misérables* gives us the most complete description of the social criminality characteristic of the July Monarchy. The novel in itself is a testimony and a document at least as much for the impress of the facts embedded in it as for the description which it gives of those facts.

The Vocabulary

This influence can be observed with most certainty perhaps in Hugo's choice of words to denote the popular classes and in the evolution of the meaning of those words. The content of the descriptions was subject to other pressures and reflected other requirements, most obviously those of literary creation—internal devices peculiar to the author with which we are not concerned here. What is important is rather those words which Hugo used in conformity with the common usage, words which expressed social changes by remaining current so long and coinciding with realities, deriving their vitality from the changes as assuredly as they denoted them.

Some words disappear because the situations or beliefs they denote have ceased to exist or because they no longer fit new beliefs or new situations. The life and death of words is the sum of slow developments and is as significant of those developments as the most detailed description or the most accurate statistical measurement.

One striking point is that in the very last years of the July Monarchy, and definitively after the Revolution of 1848, the popular classes of

Paris were no longer called "populace" or mob, but became the "people." Daniel Stern recorded the end product of this evolution:

The people and the bourgeoisie; I am afraid I must use these two terms in the narrow and inaccurate sense given them in 1848, since I do not think that they could be replaced by more precise terms without losing the characteristic accent of the time when they were in every mouth.[14]

Hugo's novel bears the trace of this evolution no less than the contemporary language, and in a similar way. He spoke of "populace" in his *Discours de réception à l'Académie*, provoking a vigorous protest from Vinçard in *La Ruche populaire*.[15] His reply to Vinçard was embarrassed and confused:

I did not say "*la populace*," but "*les populaces*"; to my way of thinking, the plural is important. There is a gilded mob just as there is a ragged mob; there is a mob of the salons just as there is a mob of the streets . . . at all levels of society . . . all that is deliberately idle, all that is lazily ignorant, all that does evil intentionally is mob, *populace*. At the top, selfishness and idleness; below, envy and slacking; these are the vices of the mob.

This was to use reasoning against what was still only reasoning. In using the term "populace" spontaneously and naturally Hugo was conforming to usage, and the protest against it was still based solely on theory. It was the populace that was still in existence, rather than the people, both in the vernacular and in actual fact, as the opinion concerning the facts and the words sum up.

Hugo was probably thinking of this terminological dispute when he wrote in the second draft of the Gavroche section:

The Parisian race, we say again, is found most truly in the faubourg; there it is pure-blooded, there we find the real physiognomy, there the people work and suffer; and toil and suffering are the two faces of man. There are these immense numbers of unknown beings, among whom may be found the strangest types, from the docker of la Rapée to the horse butcher of Montfaucon. *Faex urbis*, Cicero exclaims; Mob, Burke adds, indignantly; a crowd, a multitude, a population, these words are quickly uttered.

"These words are quickly uttered," certainly, but it is precisely when they are uttered quickly that they are most valuable. Hugo's spontaneous use of the word "populace," commonly employed by the bourgeois of his time, is of far greater interest than the distinctions he afterwards tried to draw between "people" and "populace." Or rather, the distinctions at the beginning of the story of the insurrection of June 1848 are of interest only because they express both the former meaning of the word "populace" and the new meaning of the word "people"; that is to say, they express the facts and the awareness of the facts acquired both by the narrator and by his contemporaries equally slowly and equally passively, by habit and usage, not by thinking about them.

This passive subjection to the facts is even more evident when new developments are designated not by new words, but by a gradual change in the meaning of the older ones. For instance, the word "*bas-fonds*," the lower depths, seemed in some chapters of the novel to be about to shed its depreciatory implications and now came to mean not simply the dangerous classes, but the lower strata of society in general—though this development remained incomplete.[16]

The major example of this is the word "*misérables*," which carries on the development we have already noted throughout the writing of the book and completes it in expressing fully and simply that complex relationship between the laboring classes and the dangerous classes which poses one of the most important problems in the social history of Paris, just as those problems are the real subject of the novel. At the final stage in this development, the word "*misérables*" did not even denote, as at earlier periods, one or another of the social categories distinguished as sharply as at the Last Judgment or in Littré's definitions—the criminal on the one hand, the unfortunate on the other. It was to apply more and more often and more and more entirely to those who were simultaneously, or at any rate to some degree, both unfortunate and criminal; to those on the uncertain and continually changing borderline between poverty and crime. It was no longer to denote two different conditions but the passage from one to the other, the social deterioration we are discussing: an intermediary and fluctuating situation rather than a status. It is the internal development of the word which, though itself remaining unchanged, reflects a development of the facts and of opinion concerning them as precisely as any detailed description of the phenomenon itself. The development has its difficulties, however, because of an inherent contradiction: whereas the author was more and more sharply aware of a social development for which he had to use the traditional and necessary terminology, that terminology became steadily more and more inappropriate owing to the older usage.

Without in the least meaning to do so, the manuscript of *Les Misérables* provides proof both that no other term can possibly be used for the condition of the lower classes in the first half of the nineteenth century and that the older word is incapable of summing up that very elusive condition. It was only much later that the word came to tally with the reality, with something, however, which Hugo had previously described—or rather, had experienced himself throughout the writing of an account on which the reality had stamped its own imprint. It was only late and unconsciously that the word "*misérables*" exerted the full force of its impact, not merely in details and haphazardly in descriptions, but at the very head of the work, finally becoming its title, somewhat reluctantly and by a sort of revelation to which we can in fact put a date. Only in this sense is the book a historical document; not because of what Hugo intended to describe, but because he could not help describing it owing to the pressure of facts and the violence done to the words.

It is clear that in works before, or even after, 1848 Hugo did not habitually use the word "*misérables*" in the sense which he was nevertheless beginning to give it. The chapters dating from this first period enable the historian to experience the condition of the *misérables* far more precisely than Hugo himself supposed; indeed, the more precisely and usefully in that such was not his intention. There is a very great contrast between the importance of the evidence concerning the condition of the "*misérables*" and the continuing ambiguity of a word by which Hugo had not yet succeeded in denoting a condition he had nevertheless already described. The "*misérables*" were still criminal more often than unfortunate.

Though they were sharply conceived—described and passively recorded, perhaps, rather than conceived—the relationships between the laboring classes and the criminal classes were viewed far more often from the viewpoint of the latter than from that of the laboring or unfortunate classes. Admittedly, the Thénardiers embodied poverty as well as crime, "the most miserable of all those dwelling in the Gorbeau tenement"; but the stress was on crime rather than poverty. More, the book's title was still "*Les Misères*." "You tell me, finish your book on *Les Misères*," Hugo wrote in *Toute la lyre* in 1850. "*Les Misères*," not yet "*Les Misérables*," for the word "*misères*" seemed to denote misfortune at least as much, if not more, than crime and the content of the word "*misérables*" still seemed to be criminal only.

We have more definite evidence of Hugo's difficulty in realizing social developments which he had in fact described and had even named by the word that best suited them. At the sitting of the Legislative Assembly on July 9, 1849, Hugo had to abandon his notes and improvise, and he was quite unable to define exactly what he meant by "*misère*":

the *"misère"* of the last years of the July Monarchy, of which, nevertheless, he provides us, after the event, in the chapters he had already written, with an experience for which there is no substitute. It was a curious sitting, because the author of *Les Misères* was totally unable to explain that *"misère"* did not denote solely the condition of the unfortunate classes, but the far more complex relationships between those classes and other classes, as well as much more far-reaching physical and moral disturbances. The official record has retained the traces of the poet's confusion, which he removed from the version he later published, after thinking it over:[17] What, then, is *"misère"*? "Certainly," said Gustave de Beaumont, "there are *'misères'* that can be abolished. But you cannot abolish *'la misère.'* That is reckless talk. Disappointment makes for revolution." To which Hugo replied: " *'La misère'* will vanish as leprosy has vanished. *'La misère'* is not suffering; *'la misère'* is not poverty itself *(murmurs)*; *'la misère'* is a nameless thing *(protests)* which I have tried to describe." "But it has a name," it was objected, "surely it has a name if it's called *'misère'*?" "The honorable M. Hugo," Benoist d'Azy replied, "has explained the word *'misère'* as the lowest form of *'misère,'* if I may venture to call it so, as the extreme degree of *'misère.'* "

It was a curious but important sitting because of its testimony to the lag between the development of the facts and the general awareness of them, on the one hand, and the development of the words, on the other; because of the experience it provided of the way in which new and peremptory facts had to be cast in the mold of old words and how hard it was to do this; and because the facts, dominating and finally annexing the words, ultimately won out, as may be seen in Hugo's reply, a final improvisation in which the word *"misérables"* takes on its full meaning: "Suffering cannot disappear; *'la misère'* must disappear. There will always be some unfortunates, but it is possible that there may not always be *'misérables.'* " Here the official record noted: "Hear, hear! on the left. Ironical laughter elsewhere in the House."

The fact takes possession of the word and, conversely, the existence of the word makes for total awareness of the fact summed up and illustrated by it. *"Les Misérables"* was henceforth the title of the work which Hugo announced in 1854 as forthcoming. But the word was still used to denote the criminal classes in the chapters drafted in 1860 and after: "More than one wayfarer lay in the shadow of this villain [*misérable*], with outstretched arms, his face in a pool of blood," Hugo wrote of the bandit Montparnasse. But the term was increasingly used for the laboring and unfortunate classes, and when it happened to denote the dangerous classes, it was used to stress their pitiable rather than their formidable aspects. Jean Valjean was the *"misérable"* par excellence. This is even plainer in the manuscript than in the work as printed, especially in the scene where the ex-convict, strolling at daybreak with Cosette on the boulevard de l'Hôpital, sees the chain gang from Bicêtre emerge from the shadows: "Cosette, trembling in every limb, added: 'Father, are they still men?'—'Sometimes,' the wretched man [*misérable*] replied." In the printed version the account goes straight on, on the same page: "It was in fact the chain gang . . ." But in the manuscript Jean Valjean's reply is by itself at the top of a page, the remainder of which is blank, as if in the first draft it was the wholly adequate finale to a description completed and summed up by the word *"misérable"* and as if the next sentence, which is quite separate and on a fresh page, began a new line of thought. "It was the chain gang which, leaving Bicêtre before daybreak, was taking the Le Mans road to Fontainebleau, where the King was then in residence." In this sentence the subdued murmur of the convict prison, and an entire criminality which is not present in the physical layout of the manuscript, pervade the description.

Thus, the development in the meaning of the word, Hugo's long hesitation about its predominating significance, and his inability to explain clearly what he meant by *"misère"* and *"misérable"* when he had already written much of his novel, all stress the fact that the problem is not to seek out and classify the various aspects of crime in the novel, but to see how a social development external to the book and its author's creative effort finally imprinted itself on the work, so much so that it changed the meaning of the words. This is not literary, but historical, research, the trace of history being the more evident in that it was not intended. And we have every reason to believe—the sitting of the Legislative Assembly seems to prove it—that Hugo was not fully aware of it himself. It is a "passive" testimony inherent in the evolution of the meaning of a word and, even more plainly, in the transformation of the districts and population of the criminal Paris it records.

The Description

The description of the criminal districts and criminal groups in *Les Misérables* is as important to social history, and important in the same way, as the development or coincidence of words, not because of its antiquarian and contrived elements but because of the traces of contemporary social facts, however involuntary and however insignificant from the literary point of view they may be. Hugo, in spite of the special nature of literary creation, conceived, registered and expressed these in precisely the same way as most of his contemporaries. His testimony stemmed from common opinion far more than from his own genius. His genius, indeed, in many cases merely impaired the authenticity of the original description by what he added to it in the second draft of *Les Misérables*.

The criminal landscape: To begin with the setting. The criminal topography was no longer the same. Crime no longer adhered to the traditional localities peculiar to it in the early years of the Restoration and assigned to it in most of the literary documents, as, indeed, in Hugo's own earlier narratives. It moved away from the Grève; the former characteristics and almost the memory of the Grève—despite its ancient repute, the accumulation of so many seemingly unforgettable horrors and images—faded out of *Les Misérables*, just as they died out of the Parisians' memories at the same period, quite as rapidly and for the same reasons.

This is a very good illustration of the operation of the collective memory concerning the images attaching to a given place, to which Halbwachs has devoted an interesting study.[18] The problem posed by the disappearance of the Grève and made specific in *Les Misérables* is especially important in the history of Paris, because the city's material frame evolved very slowly. The very obvious and strangely long-lasting social characteristics of certain districts, the behavior of their inhabitants and the surprising survival of longstanding attitudes probably bore some relation to the occupational structures determined by the material frame itself and some relation, too, to habits which were the result of that material frame and were no less definitely determined by it. The inhabitants of these districts moved into other trades, streets and dwellings but still adhered to the traditions attached to the places. These traditions were not, perhaps, absolutely determinant, for living in a formerly criminal district does not necessarily make a man a criminal nor does living in a district of barricades necessarily make a man a revolutionary. But they do posit possibilities, offer incentives, make things easier, in short. While the persistence of the former frame— old monuments, old housefronts, old streets, old cafés, old tenements, old theaters—ensured that the moral, political and social traditions we are observing would last, conversely the disappearance of the old stones and mortar led to the total disappearance of those traditions and of the images transmitted and imposed by them. In destroying the old district of the Cité so thoroughly as to wipe it off the map of Paris, Haussmann destroyed far more than a tangle of slums and thieves' kitchens. He did much more than eliminate and scatter a criminal population to the four corners of the city and out to the farthest banlieue; he destroyed the very images evoked and provoked by the district, the images attaching to it in the memory of the people of Paris. These images passed from this collective memory into another sort of memory, the picturesque tradition of the antiquarian, one of the most certain forms of oblivion. There are, however, cases intermediate between these extremes—between the persistence of the older frame, which ensures that traditions will last, and the complete disappearance of the frame, with the annihilation of the traditions—the Grève, for instance.

"Its former name, stained with memories of blood, is already being rejected," a writer in *La Ruche populaire* stated in 1841. "The place de Grève has disappeared and has now been replaced with the place de l'Hôtel-de-Ville."[19] The Grève had not disappeared and, despite the change of name in 1830, the place de l'Hôtel-de-Ville took a long time to displace the place de Grève; until indeed the physical rebuilding, which played as great a part here as in the Cité, but was not carried out until 1853, when Haussmann quadrupled the area of the square by tearing down the neighboring tenements. Throughout the July Monarchy and even during the Second Empire, the Grève continued despite the rebuilding. But it is quite true that it no longer necessarily evoked images, as it had in earlier periods, of criminal spectacles, the memory of which died out very quickly. Its name was thenceforth associated with other facts and images; it denoted the place where the unemployed gathered. It is the place de Grève that Proudhon and Martin Nadaud[20] mention when speaking of the early years of the July Monarchy, which were so hard for part of the working population, especially the masons: "After March 1834 many kicked their heels on the place de Grève, which was thronged with haggard men in shabby coats stamping to keep warm in the last cold days of the winter." The "place de l'Hôtel-de-Ville" rooted itself in the bourgeois literature faster than the "place de Grève" disappeared from the popular literature.[21]

We can, however, watch this disappearance in Hugo's novel. The Grève fades out from the criminal setting in the description in *Les*

Misérables, as it did in fact and in the Parisians' memory, at the same rate and for the same reasons. Admittedly, the old Grève of capital executions still appears in a few scenes which take place in the closing years of the Restoration. It is one of Gavroche's pleasures: "No fun like the Grève!" Gavroche promises the pleasures of the Grève to the urchins he harbors in the belly of the elephant at the Bastille: "And then we'll go and see a man guillotined and I'll point out the executioner to you; he lives in the rue des Marais, and his name's Sanson. He's got a letterbox on his door. We'll have a lot of fun!" But though the name "place de Grève" is used in the remainder of the book in preference to "place de l'Hôtel-de-Ville," it no longer arouses such sinister images. Some characters in *Les Misérables* still went to or passed by the place de Grève, but Hugo no longer felt obliged to refer to the bloody spectacles of a former age.

Most of the older localities of earlier crime faded out of the narrative in much the same way. The prisons themselves are barely mentioned in the book, though their habitual inmates play such a large part in it. Hugo hardly describes the prison of La Force from which Thénardier escaped, though it was mentioned so often in the picturesque and crime literature of the time. It was probably no accident that the building merged with the general Parisian landscape in reality and in Hugo's description; so much so that it is impossible to say whether the horror of the district left its mark on the prison or the horror of the prison on the district.[22]

The Paris of the barrières and sewers: Henceforth, criminal fact, detached from these traditional localities, was not peculiar to any one district rather than another. Some haunts, to be sure, were favored by criminals over others, but not by them alone. Crime now filled the whole of the city without distinction: the old central Paris, "the old miserable Paris which is vanishing"; but the rest of Paris too. The extension and transformation became particularly evident in the fact that the dominant setting of crime was no longer the city but the places which reflected the fundamentally dangerous nature of urban society better than that society itself could, especially the barrières and the sewers. This marginal aspect of the setting of crime best expresses the pervasion of the whole of the Parisian landscape by a criminality so total and so generalized that we have henceforth to get at it not through a detailed description of the city's districts, but through the places which best summed it up and provided an image of it in the most simplified terms, which may be said to give it its cue, as it were, the barrières circumscribing it and the sewers revealing it. "The history of men is reflected in the history of the sewers," Hugo wrote. The importance of the description of the barrières and the sewers in *Les Misérables* was a response to the need—not wholly conscious, perhaps—to find some means of expressing this development of crime other than by the habitual description of the traditional criminal districts. Hence, at a second stage, the expansion of the theme of the lower depths, the *bas-fonds*, and the description of the lower depths par excellence—the sewer.

Hugo first sought this expression of the aggregate of Paris criminality in the barrières surrounding the city, especially those in the south marking out the boulevard de l'Hôpital, the boulevard des Gobelins and the boulevard Saint-Jacques, the barrière d'Italie or de Fontainebleau, the barrière de Croulebarbe, the barrière de l'Oursine, the barrière Saint-Jacques and the barrière d'Enfer.

These barrières and the adjoining districts bulk large in the general description of Paris. Jean Valjean did not enter Paris by one of the barrières, but he went there at once: "The pair of them, in the black of night, by the deserted streets neighboring l'Oursine and la Glacière, went on towards the boulevard de l'Hôpital." The Gorbeau tenement stood there. It was there, on the Champ de l'Alouette, that Marius loved to stroll; it was there that Jean Valjean and Cosette saw the chain gang go by. The characters in *Les Misérables*, try as they may to move into other districts, fall back to this barrière as if weighted towards it by a species of gravity. Gavroche preferred to frequent the neighborhood of the Château d'Eau, where the waifs and strays crowded at the time.

Still, abandoned as this child was, it happened every two or three months that he said—"Well, I'll go and see Ma." Then he quitted the boulevard, the Circus, the Porte Saint-Martin, went along the quais, crossed the bridge, reached the Salpêtrière, and arrived, where? Exactly at that double no. 50–52 with which the reader is already familiar, the Gorbeau tenement.

Quite obviously, the barrières, especially the southern barrières, meant something important to Hugo. What was it?

There was one barrière which had already embodied the displacement of the setting of crime in *Le dernier jour d'un condamné* and especially in the 1832 Preface, but which expressed it far more clearly in *Les Misérables*, more particularly in the important chapter on the Gorbeau tenement, a basic text which demands reproduction in full:

Under the Empire and the Restoration, men condemned to death returned to Paris through it on the day of their execution. Here was committed, about the year 1829, that mysterious murder known as "the murder of the barrière de Fontainebleau," whose perpetrators remain unknown to the police, a sinister problem which has never been elucidated, a frightful enigma never solved. A few steps further on you come to the fatal rue Croulebarbe, where Ulbach stabbed the goatwoman of Ivry amid peals of thunder, as in a melodrama. A few more steps and you reach the abominable pollard elms of the barrière Saint-Jacques, that philanthropic expedient concealing the scaffold, the paltry, disgraceful place de Grève of a shopkeeping society which has recoiled before the death penalty, but has not dared to abolish it with grandeur or maintain it with authority. Thirty-seven years ago—and leaving aside this place Saint-Jacques, which was, as it were, predestined; it has always been horrible—the gloomiest point perhaps of all this gloomy boulevard was that where the Gorbeau tenement stood. Tradespeople did not begin to sprout there till twenty-five years later. . . . But at nightfall, at the hour when the light has waned, especially in winter, at the hour when the chilly evening breeze is tearing the last rusty leaves from the elms; when the darkness is profound and starless, and when the moon and the wind make rents in the clouds, this boulevard became suddenly terrifying. The straight lines plunged into the gloom and were lost in it like sections of the infinite. The passer-by could not refrain from thinking of the countless gallows traditions of the spot. This solitude in which so many crimes had been committed had something awful in it.

Note the words, "this place Saint-Jacques, which was, as it were, predestined; it has always been horrible." Note, too, the allusion to "the countless gallows traditions of the spot." These southern barrières bulk large in *Les Misérables* because they sum up the city's criminality in a book devoted to criminality, but more especially, both in the Paris of the period and in the novel as a whole, a criminality of the people which is simply a by-product of poverty, an accident of the proletarian destiny. Ulbach, whose image is evoked several times, embodied this new criminality of sheer chance, youth and misfortune, and effaced the memory of the old, exceptional and monstrous criminals. Ulbach, whose memory was recalled so clearly by a small mound raised to the memory of his "good girl," still to be seen on the boulevard des Gobelins in the early years of the Second Empire, that Hugo did not even feel he need verify the date of the crime and execution for the Preface to *Le dernier jour d'un condamné* in 1832. No more than his contemporaries had he forgotten the details of the story, if only the thunder that accompanied the crime; it turned up in the street ballads, too:

> *Au même instant que tomba la victime*
> *Sous quatre coups de poignard inhumains*
> *Du haut des cieux le maître magnanime*
> *De son tonnerre effraya l'assassin.*[23]

The image of these great crimes is supplemented by that of other crimes very different from those in the capital itself, the proletarian crimes we have mentioned, one of the forms of working-class violence which we shall discuss later. And in the background to the account, if only through the smell of copperas, "gusts of it rising from the roofs of a nearby factory," there is the hint of the vast poverty of the faubourgs and of the adjacent banlieue, with its potential for crime.

While the volume and the transformation of these images of crime account for the preoccupation with the southern barrières in the novel, the revisions in the manuscript are even more significant. In the first draft the predestined nature of the spot was merely stated, but no examples of crimes were yet given—the crime of the barrière de Fontainebleau or Ulbach's crime. Describing this district for the first time, Hugo simply referred to its criminal and fatal character, but gave no details of its criminality, which he presented as wholly contemporary. The details came in later—but only a little later, though the interpolations cannot be dated. The appearance of the manuscript and the handwriting show only that the additional details belong to the early period, before the 1848 Revolution. The interpolations concerning Bicêtre and Ulbach's crime were noted—in the margin—at that period. They were additions that did not seem essential in the first burst of inspiration, so powerfully and simply did Hugo feel the impression of horror and the certainty that crime was there.

Thus, the old and new correlations between these places and crime in the Paris of the first half of the nineteenth century would suffice in the last resort to account for the preoccupation with these southern barrières and fatal boulevards in a novel in which crime plays so great a part. Indeed, the point most strongly made about them is their association with crime. The four symbolic bandits hold their confabulations there: "They generally met at nightfall, the hour at which they awoke, on the steppes that border the Salpêtrière. There they conferred, and as they had twelve hours of darkness before them, they settled their employment." It was there, too, in the Gorbeau tenement, that the Thénardier household laid the trap for Jean Valjean: several new details were superadded to fill out the description of the place's character:

Jondrette's den was, if the reader will recall what has been said of the Gorbeau tenement, admirably chosen for the scene of a violent and somber deed and the setting for a crime. It was the innermost room of the most isolated house on the most deserted boulevard in Paris. If the trap had not existed, it would have been invented. The whole bulk of the house and a series of empty rooms separated this den from the boulevard, and its only window gave onto vast stretches of waste land enclosed by high walls and fences.

This extraordinary night scene must be borne in mind; it is found again in the street ballads, the refrains and the *chansons réalistes*:

And now the reader, in order to form an idea of the scene which is about to be acted, will be good enough to imagine the freezing night, the snow-covered solitudes of the Salpêtrière, stark white in the moonlight like an immense winding sheet, and the light of the lamps casting a red glow here and there over these fatal boulevards, and the long rows of black elms; not a passer-by for a quarter of a league round, and the Gorbeau tenement at its highest point of impressive horror and night. In this tenement, amid this solitude and darkness, sprawls Jondrette's candle-lit garret.

The correlations between these places and crime do not suffice, however, to account for the large place they are given in the general description of Paris. Hugo was seeking something else in the footsteps of Jean Valjean over by the boulevard Saint-Jacques and the boulevard de l'Hôpital. These places sum up the city in a different way. Themes other than that of crime fill the pages and inspire the descriptions.

We have to look for these themes in the passages in the book mainly describing these districts. But we must first emphasize the contrast between Balzac's description and interpretation of these places and Hugo's. These districts were not, of course, accorded a weight in the *Comédie humaine* and in Balzac's landscape at all comparable to their place in *Les Misérables* and in Hugo's Paris. But the fact remains that there is a vast contrast between Balzac's description at the end of *Ferragus* and the many descriptions in *Les Misérables*. In Balzac's account we find a detailed topography, an accurate nomenclature of places and buildings, but also, immediately following, a virtually impersonal and almost administrative interpretation and observation of the social significance of things, inseparable from the description and blending with it. ". . . A space without gender, a neuter space in Paris," wrote Balzac.

For, here, it is no longer Paris; and, here, it is still Paris. This place conveys at one and the same time something of the square, the street, the boulevard, the fortification, the garden, the avenue, the highway, the provinces, the capital; true, there is something of all of them in it; but it is not any of them: it is a desert. Around this nameless spot rise the Foundlings Hospital, the Bourbe, the Hôpital Cochin, the Capucins, the La Rochefoucauld almshouse, the Sourds-Muets, the Val-de-Grâce hospital; indeed, all the vices and all the misfortunes of Paris find asylum here. And, to ensure that nothing shall be lacking to this philanthropical precinct, science here studies the tides and the longitudes; M. de Châteaubriand placed the Marie-Thérèse infirmary here, and the Carmelites founded a convent. The ceremonials of life are represented by the bells incessantly tolling in this desert for the mother who gives birth and the child who is born, for vice that expires and the worker who dies, the virgin who prays and the old man who shivers, and for genius astray. Then, a couple of paces further on, there is the Montparnasse cemetery, attracting from hour to hour the scanty funeral processions of the faubourg Saint-Marceau.

Hugo's approach is very different: he passes straight from reality to reverie, from image to philosophical musing: "All aspects of things are God's thoughts."

It is true that in both of them the observation is the same, inevitable in a description of the banlieue. "For, here, it is no longer Paris; and, here, it is still Paris . . .", says Balzac. And Hugo: "It was not the country . . . it was not the town . . .", and he added: "The place where a plain makes its junction with a town is always imprinted with a species of penetrating melancholy." But whereas Balzac feels a similar melancholy yet gives the reasons for it plainly and directly, Hugo tries to do so in vain. He does not succeed in giving us an explanation of the melancholy he several times asserts, an uneasiness he does not feel when viewing other Paris districts and which expresses the special significance of these barrières in the total landscape of Paris; or at least the only explanation he does give is of a state of mind, a matter for the literary critic but not for the critical historian. We can, however, deduce the explanation from the elements which go to make up his account.

This uneasiness arises from the way in which the banlieue sums up totally the contrast between the city and what is no longer the city, and from the fact that this can be taken in at a glance.

In the chapter on Gavroche, Hugo wrote:

Paris is the center, the banlieue the circumference—that is, the whole earth for these children. They never venture further, and no more leave the Parisian atmosphere than fish can live out of water. For them there is nothing beyond two leagues from the barrière; Ivry, Gentilly, Arcueil, Belleville, Aubervilliers, Ménilmontant, Choisy-le-Roi, Billancourt, Meudon, Issy, Vanves, Sèvres, Puteaux, Neuilly, Gennevilliers, Colombes, Romainville, Chatou, Asnières, Bougival, Nanterre, Enghien, Noisy-le-Sec, Nogent, Gournay, Drancy, Gonesse—with these their universe ends.

There is a similar idea in:

To wander in a reverie, that is, to stroll, is a good way for a philosopher to pass the time; especially in this species of countryside—rather ambiguous, fairly ugly, but queer and having two natures—which surrounds certain large towns, notably Paris. To observe the banlieue is to observe the amphibious. End of the trees, beginning of the roofs; end of the grass, beginning of the paved road; end of the furrows, beginning of the shops; end of the rut, beginning of passion; end of the divine murmur, beginning of the human growl; hence, it is of extraordinary interest. Hence the dreamer's seemingly aimless walks in these rather unattractive places, forever marked by the passer-by with the adjective "sad."

A district expressed nothing but itself. The banlieue, delimiting the city, sharpened its contours and defined it. It expressed the city better than the city itself, just as the population of the faubourgs expressed the Parisian population better than the latter could express itself.

Another setting was, however, to afford Hugo an even more significant experience: the basic poverty of the city into which its criminality progressively became transformed found its final and most perfect expression in the sewers. But not all at once; it is the stages in this development that are important.

In the seventh book of *Les Misérables*, entitled "*Patron-Minette*," in which the sewers were described for the first time, they still denoted only city crime, the lowest depths, "*la troisième dessous*," of human societies and the "great cavern of Evil." Their darkest dark was the refuge of the quartet of bandits who embodied this circumscribed form of criminality.

These beings, who were very cautious about showing their faces, were not the sort of people one normally sees on the streets. By day, wearied by their wild nights, they went to sleep sometimes in the lime kilns, sometimes in the abandoned quarries of Montmartre or Montrouge and sometimes in the sewers.

They went to earth in places "far away from other places," bearing no relation whatever to the upper levels, wholly alien to the city—threatening it, indeed, but different from it.

The sewers in the second book of the fifth part of *Les Misérables*, entitled "*L'Intestin de Léviathan*," have a quite different significance. They are no longer described as a threat to the city but as a replica of it, the most faithful, the most complete and yet the simplest imaginable.

This document is important in many respects, both for social history in general and for the history of the Paris of the period in particular. Hugo's approach, expressed in a wealth of important observations, leaps to the eye as he rediscovers—though he believed he invented it— the most fertile of all techniques for the study and description of social facts, by relating the highest to the lowest, the normal to the abnormal, and—what is of even greater value—by penetrating to the biological bases, normal or abnormal, of social development. The imperatives of literary creation coincided with those of research; and, albeit under the stress of vaster ambitions and using different methods, literary creation spontaneously and by other routes finally came to apply the methods which are inevitable in such research. In reality, literary creation had less to do with this discovery than the fact that neither a writer nor a research worker could possibly approach the social facts in any other way. The compulsion lay in the things themselves, not in those studying or describing them. It would be quite wrong to assert that these observations and images, in which the social historian finds a perfect expression of his own rules, were merely literary embroidery.

The history of man is reflected in the history of the sewers. The Gemoniae narrated the story of Rome. . . . The drain is a cynic. It tells all. This sincerity of uncleanliness pleases us and reposes the mind. . . . As we said just now, history passes through the drain. . . . The ghostly brooms can be heard under these vaults. The enormous fetor of social catastrophes is breathed there. . . . The social observer should enter these shadows, for they are part of his laboratory. Philosophy is the microscope of thought. Everything strives to flee from it, but nothing escapes it. Tergiversation is useless, for what aspect of himself does a man show in tergiversating? The one of which he is ashamed. Philosophy bends its righteous gaze upon evil and will not permit it to escape into the void. It sees all in the effacement of disappearing things and in the diminution of vanishing things. It reconstructs the purple from the tatters and the woman from the rags. With the sewer it remakes the city; from the mud it recreates morals. It decides whether the potsherd was an amphora or a pitcher.

This approach is inescapable in social history and description at all periods, but more especially in the darker days of the July Monarchy. Never was it so essential—and so feasible—to approach the better through the worse, to find that the most reliable expression and measurement of social facts are the rates for morbidity, mortality and criminality. The sewers never summed up the city so well. And, above all, the pathological aspects of urban life were never studied so often and so accurately. Though Hugo arrived at this conception magnificently, he did so very tardily, using documents which had expounded and identified the sewers' social significance long before him.

Some of these documents he quoted, especially the reports by Bruneseau, the Inspector-General of Health under the Empire. Bruneseau's first exploration of the sewers between 1805 and 1812 became in *Les Misérables* an extraordinary epic of the underground.[24]

The lanterns would scarce burn in the mephitic atmosphere. From time to time a sewerman was carried away unconscious. At certain spots there was a precipice; the soil had given way, the tiling had crumbled, the drain had become a cesspool; nothing solid could be found. A man vanished suddenly from sight and they had much ado to drag him out.

Bruneseau's original account was hardly less dramatic:

I have traversed the sewers of Paris several times, very often crouching, my nose in the mud; and even more often I was so choked by the mephitic vapors that I was compelled to have myself pulled out to breathe; that is how I realized how urgent is the need to renew the foul air one breathes there frequently in order to counteract the dangers to which the workmen scouring them are exposed.[25]

These official documents certainly contained a record of the material and moral consequences of the city's growth which was to be so magnificently expanded in this chapter of *Les Misérables*. In a report to the Prefect Frochot on the garbage dump of Montfaucon, Bruneseau gave many examples of the correlation between biological and moral facts, which will be the principle topic in this chapter, as it was in most of the Paris medical topographies and almost all the contemporary social literature: "Health of body reflects cleanliness of soul," Bruneseau wrote.

The cleanliness of a city reflects the purity of its inhabitants' morals. . . . It should not be thought that from the viewpoint of public health the plague alone is to be feared. . . . Learned physicians recognize and assess the stages in the onset of that listlessness and inertia to which the most robust persons are far more prone in Paris than elsewhere.

There was, however, another writer whom Hugo did not mention, though he probably borrowed the greater part of his documentation from him and though, like most of his contemporaries, he was directly or indirectly influenced by him: Parent-Duchatelet. It is a really surprising omission, since Hugo's description of the sewers went beyond Bruneseau's period into the early years of the July Monarchy, when the sewers had become part of everyday Paris life and the inhabitants' day-to-day concerns, as is clear from articles in the press and tales in the picturesque literature.

The sewers of Paris in 1832 were far from being what they are now. Bruneseau gave the impulse, but it needed the cholera to determine the vast reconstruction which has taken place since. It is surprising, for instance, that in 1821 a portion of the outer-circle sewer called the Grand Canal, as at Venice, still stagnated in the open air in the rue des Gourdes. It was not until 1823 that the city of Paris fumbled in its waistcoat pocket and found the 266,080 francs 6 centimes needed finally to lock this skeleton into the cupboard.

No doubt, but that stage in the history of the sewers was closely bound up with the publication in 1824 of Parent-Duchatelet's important report, *Essai sur les cloaques ou égouts de la ville de Paris, envisagés sous le rapport de l'hygiène publique et de la topographie médicale de cette ville*, a document of great significance for the history of the sewers and the study of *Les Misérables* alike, since Hugo quite certainly borrowed a great deal from it. It would be easy, in fact, to demonstrate the relationship between this—and other—works by Parent-Duchatelet and Hugo's description. It was probably no accident that the latter begins with a chapter entitled "*La terre appauvrie par la mer.*" "Science," wrote Hugo, "now knows that the most fertilizing and effective of manures is human excrement." One of Parent-Duchatelet's earliest reports, written when nearly the whole crew of a ship was poisoned by a cargo of dried excrement carried from Montfaucon to Guadeloupe, was devoted to this problem.[26] Nor, probably, was it an accident that the specific sewers which Hugo described most terrifyingly were precisely those which Parent-Duchatelet had explored and described at length. The most famous was

the great opening of the Marais drain, which remained yawning until 1833 in rue Saint-Louis nearly opposite the sign of the *Messager Galant*. The mouth of the drain in the rue de la Mortellerie was celebrated for the pestilences which issued from it; with its iron pointed grating that resembled a row of teeth, it yawned in this fatal street like the jaws of a dragon breathing hell on mankind. The popular imagination seasoned the gloomy Parisian sewer with some hideous savor of infinitude.

It was no accident, lastly, that Hugo found a far more impressive topography of the crime and poverty of Paris in a description of the sewers than in the criminal districts. Parent-Duchatelet had in fact already stressed the common factor linking the sewers with prostitution, but he was merely reproducing a widely held opinion, the generally accepted assumption that crime was identical with poverty as a result of the co-existence of extreme poverty and extreme criminality. This was the opinion most notably expressed in *Les Misérables*, albeit somewhat tardily.

The criminal society: The characteristics of the development in the description of the criminal groups were much the same. Crime was no longer closely tied to the dangerous classes, but changed its significance and extended to broad masses of the population, to the greater part of the laboring classes. The word "*misérables*" less and less frequently denoted criminals and more and more often the unfortunate, whether criminal or no.

The strictly criminal groups were those who dwelt in the lower depths, the *bas-fonds*, the *troisième-dessous*, "the great cavern of Evil" to which Hugo devoted the book in *Les Misérables* entitled "*Patron-Minette*." The anachronisms, the clumsiness, the bogus antiquarianism, the highly improbable details in this evocation of the criminal groups, all contrast strongly with the authenticity and beauty of the description of the diffused criminality that pervades the paragraphs and chapters devoted to the lower classes. We can interpret this contrast as yet another proof of the transformation of a picturesque criminality, of which Hugo knew very little—and that only from books—into a social criminality, which he knew well but only in exactly the same way as any of his contemporaries, since it was one of the most obvious aspects of contemporary city life in Paris.

The description of the criminal groups appears lifelike or at any rate conveys horror only when it deals with masses or crowds, that is to say, when it compounds men with things, and when it uses the procedures whose efficacy we noted when investigating the description of things by way of an approach to the description of men. Thénardier on his way to the place de la Bastille or going up the rue Mouffetard was merely a petty criminal. He did not terrify Marius until he reached the deserted district near the Salpêtrière and the boulevard de l'Hôpital, when he merged with that vast landscape of crime, absorbing from the inexpressible horror of the place the total horror which he henceforth exuded. It was then, and only then, that Marius shuddered, as Thénardier straddled over a gate and vanished into the night. It is then, and only then, that Hugo speaks of terror. It is then, and only then, that he obtains an effect of terror. In the same way, the slow and monstrous progress of the chain gang looming out of the fog and, as it were, mounting from Paris, calls forth a horror that is not aroused by the convicts described individually. As soon as the description attempts to individualize any particular character, it loses both efficacy and probability. Note the contrast between the great criminals in Balzac, who are formidable and really horrible, and Hugo's petty loafers of the outer boulevards, whose criminal enterprises are always paltry exploits; they can easily be gulled by an urchin like Gavroche.

The more lifelike and historically important the descriptions of the criminal districts, because they were significant of a criminality that surpassed their bounds, the harder it was for the description of the criminal groups to do what it set out to do. It is upon the districts that the city's criminality as a whole and the social problem as a whole leave their mark, whereas the bandits do not even succeed in conveying to us their criminality as such and the specific problem they constitute. Indeed, the more Hugo tries by using the documentation on crime too obviously and employing contrivances which are all too apparent and all too unconvincing, the less he succeeds.

What Hugo does is effective only when he deals with the kind of crime which is earlier than and different from that in *Les Misérables*, the grand picturesque crime whose characteristics we have already defined and whose importance in the collective psychology of the people of Paris we have already stressed. Hugo borrowed from the popular memory of terror the roll of names which in themselves called forth a horror due to the vast publicity by which they were surrounded. The roll of honor is as complete in the novel as it was on the wall at Bicêtre in *Le dernier jour d'un condamné*:

In the urchin's realm Voltaire is unknown but Papavoine is famous. . . . Traditions exist about the last garment they wore. It is known that Tolleron was wearing a bandit cap, Avril a cap of fur, Louvel a round hat and that old Delaporte was bare-headed and bald, that Castaing was rosy-cheeked and a pretty fellow, that Bories had a Romantic beard, that Jean-Martin was in his braces and Lecouffé and his mother kept shouting abuse at each other.

These were, of course, the most notorious names in the criminal history of the Restoration, the names most calculated to arouse memories of terror in readers, to extract such memories from the reader's inmost depths, the unforgettable details set down in this as in preceding works, and as alive in the writer's memory as they were in that of his contemporaries. "I recall," Hugo wrote in the notes on 1846–1847–1848 published in *Choses vues*,

that in my very early youth I saw Louvel cross the Pont-au-Change the day he was being taken to the place de Grève. It was in June, I think. It was bright sunshine. Louvel was in a cart, his hands tied behind his back, a blue frockcoat flung around his shoulders, a round hat on his head. He was pale. I saw him in profile. His whole demeanor was redolent of a sort of serious ferocity and violent resolution. There was something severe and cold about him.[27]

The writer's recollection here was simply an expression of the collective memory. The names and details existed in his memory, as they did in everyone's, with such precision that he had only to write them down to make the shudder of the Grève palpable in his narrative.

But when the crime was the crime of the July Monarchy, contemporary with the action of *Les Misérables*, and when Hugo tried to connect the story he was telling and the groups he was describing with this general criminality, his antiquarianism miscarried. It not only weakened the effect of horror generated by the story as a matter of course, but, curiously, emphasized the artifice and improbabilities in the picture. Hugo vainly rushed to succor a quartet whom he himself probably considered to be rather thin by giving them a reinforcement of accomplices with whom Moreau-Christophe, the Inspector of Prisons, declared in his book *Le Monde des coquins* (1863) that he was well acquainted.[28] As belonging merely to information on crime, but not to the popular tradition, these petty criminals add little to the major criminals in the story. Thus, on several occasions Hugo brings in the most famous of them all, Lacenaire: "When the President of the Criminal Court visited Lacenaire in prison, he questioned him about a crime which the murderer denied. 'Who committed it?' the President asked, and Lacenaire gave an answer which was an enigma to the judge but plain enough to the police: 'Patron-Minette, perhaps.' " Lacenaire had a sinister fame, of course, on which we need not dwell since it is obvious enough in the contemporary literature and in the evidence of popular opinion. The Minister of Justice even felt it necessary to ask the editor of the *Gazette des tribunaux* to spread the impression that Lacenaire had died a coward's death.[29] But bringing in Lacenaire himself does not manage to confer upon Hugo's petty criminals any part of the terror that Lacenaire inspired. It fails because the contrast between the crime embodied in him and the paltry plotting of the four bandits is too great, but above all because the kind of crime he represents does not tally with the concept Hugo arrived at in *Les Misérables* by a route we have already observed. Lacenaire was still part of the older, exceptional, monstrous crime, represented it and would continue to conjure it up. The *Histoire de l'échafaud en France*, or "*Livre rouge*," a collection published in 1863, classified him as one of the "legendary brigands, with the Marshal de Rais, Guillery, Ravaillac, Mandrin, Cartouche, Damiens, Louvel and Fieschi." He was alien to the diffused collective and social criminality which is the basic theme of *Les Misérables*. Indeed, the contradiction between the person of Lacenaire and Hugo's description of crime stresses even more clearly the extent to which the development in the theme of crime, the blending of the dangerous with the laboring classes and the transformation of crime in *Les Misérables* are accounted for not solely by the operation of literary creation but by the influence of the general evolution of public opinion, far more than by any sustained subjective meditation. The most important pieces of evidence relating to this transformation are those which Hugo simply could not help introducing, and even more often those which he did not realize he was introducing. Conversely, there are flagrant inconsistencies in Hugo's elaborated, finished and documented descriptions. When he wrote: "What crawls in the lowest depths is no longer the stifled demand of the absolute, but the protest of matter . . . Lacenaire issued from this cave," Moreau-Christophe, anticipating our criticism, promptly retorted that

this conclusion stands in flagrant contradiction with its premises; for if it is true that Lacenaire issued from this cave—and he certainly did—it is definitely not true that "its vault is built of ignorance, it knows no philosophy, its dagger never made a pen and its blackness bears no relation to the sublime blackness of the inkwell."

Few criminals have attached so much importance to the accoutrements of culture as Lacenaire.

The less convincing this description of the criminal groups as such, owing to its too bookish and too obvious documentation, its borrowed and incomplete information, and the survival of older characteristics tacked onto newer characteristics (Dautun rubbing elbows with Lacenaire), the more important for historical research is the description of the social criminality whose image embraces a large part of the working-class population, all those who are termed "*misérables*." Through most of the book, and as the story unfolds, criminality ceases to characterize criminal groups in the strict sense; henceforth it exists potentially in those other categories of the population, which share the mark of poverty with the criminal groups and are differentiated from them only by imperceptible gradations.

This shared plight of the "*misérables*" is brought out in the novel far less by the actual descriptions than by the habitual use of certain words and the development of some themes rather than others. Such traces of opinion are more important for our investigation than the happy accidents of literary creation.

One instance is the way in which the word "*bas-fonds*," the lower depths, no longer denotes simply the criminal groups, but far larger entities. Similarly, Hugo does not use "*faubourien de Paris*" to mean the inhabitant of the faubourgs, or even of the faubourg Saint-Antoine, the faubourg par excellence, but to designate part of the capital's working-class population. "The Parisian race, we say again," he wrote in the section on Gavroche,

is found most truly in the faubourg; there it is pure-blooded, there we find the real physiognomy, there the people work and suffer; and toil and suffering are the two faces of man. There there are immense numbers of unknown beings, including the strangest types, from the docker of la Rapée to the horse butcher of Montfaucon.

The faubourg means all the working-class districts of Paris. Thus, commenting on the Prefect Anglès's report on the small stature of Parisians, Hugo said:

Take care. He will make Caudine forks of the first rue Grenéta to hand. If the hour strikes, this man of the faubourg will grow big, this small man will arise and look terrible, and from this poor narrow chest a breath will swell strong enough to unfold the Alps themselves. It is thanks to the man of the Paris faubourg that revolution, pervading armies, conquers Europe.

We have already described the meaning of the faubourg in the strict sense, all that it summed up in the way of degrading, insecure and underpaid jobs and poverty and crime. The people of the faubourg were different from those of the city. The old term "*faubourien*" connoted those differences and kept them alive. Its application to the greater part of the Paris working class reflected a development similar to that in the word "*misérables*," for the characteristics formerly ascribed only to the lowest strata now, like the word itself, spread to the rest of the population.

This shared plight is most evident in the description of the children of the common people in the section in *Les Misérables* on Gavroche.

The blending of destitution with crime and the assertion of an intermediate and indeterminate situation could hardly be kept consistent with "*misérables*" of the species and age of Thénadier, for instance, or the men of the faubourgs, sweating, toiling and fighting in confused masses, as the description of the capital required. This does not hold good when it comes to the children, "*misérables*" at an age when evil can barely be distinguished from misfortune and both arouse nothing but compassion. The best example of what Hugo and his contemporaries meant by "*misérables*" is the character of Gavroche. Gavroche represented the final stage in this development of the concept of crime.

But not the Gavroche of the legend, a legend already present in the facts and in the popular imagination when Hugo took it over and fixed it forever.[30] Describing the insurrection of 1832, Canler, a former Prefect of Police, noted in his Memoirs:

An urchin aged about twelve, dressed in a colored Auvergnat waistcoat, had willy-nilly slipped into the front rank. Everyone knows the race of Paris urchins, who have always raised the cry of sedition in our meetings, carried the first paving stone to the barricade in our riots and fired the first shot.

In his epic account of the riot at the Cloître Saint-Merri, Rey-Dusseuil depicted them dragging along guns bigger than themselves:

These children, saucy, ardent and brave, true types of what people call the Paris urchin, children who give promise of providing France with a generation of heroes, cradled amid the clamor of the glories of the Empire, brought up on the love of liberty and contempt for death. They go into combat as we at their age went out to play.[31]

"It is the Paris urchins who usually start insurrections," Tocqueville wrote in his account of the Days of February 1848, "and they usually do so merrily, like schoolboys on holiday."[32]

Hugo's description is important to our study not for the commonplaces of literature and opinion which he used, for the situations he embroidered and the examples he dragged out to an inordinate length, but for the details and apparently incidental observations: though, indeed, there are not very many of them and they are barely noticeable, being as it were muted in the tumult of battle, swept away in the epic outburst. But they are present in the book as they were in news items and police court records, bringing out one of the great contemporary problems, that of abandoned and vagrant children, the waifs and strays. This may be regarded as a comparatively constant element in the economic and social diagnosis, at least as constant as the problem of poverty or the reiterated impact of political or economic crises. Nearly all the quantitative and qualitative elements of this problem are charted in detail in this context.

First, the number of children wandering over the Paris landscape:

At the almost contemporary period when this story happened there was not, as at the present day, a policeman at every street corner (a blessing which we have no time to discuss) and wandering children abounded in Paris. Statistics give us an average of 260 shelterless children picked up yearly by the police patrols on unfenced lots, in houses under construction and beneath the arches of the bridges. One of these nests, which has remained famous, produced the "swallows of the Arcole Bridge." This, incidentally, is the most disastrous of social symptoms, for all the crimes of the man begin in the vagrancy of the child. . . .

We should carefully note both the statistical precision and the concision of this observation and others like it, incidental and virtually parenthetical as they are. The problem summed up in them was so evident and so characteristic of the Paris of the Restoration and the July Monarchy—not so much of the Ancien Régime—that Hugo did not think it necessary to comment on it more fully.[33]

There were certainly vagrant children in the older Paris, for there is evidence in the statistics and in the picturesque descriptions; but they were fewer in proportion to the city's total child population than they were to be later. They remained on the margin of the city, its population and its trades; their interest was picturesque, not general. There were the little chimney sweeps who so touched Voltaire:

> . . . *Ces honnêtes enfans*
> *Qui de Savoie arrivent tous les ans,*
> *Et dont la main légèrement essuie*
> *Ces longs canaux engorgés par la suie.*[34]

Mercier too gave them some space, noting that

they form a sort of confederation in Paris with its own laws. The elder ones have a right of supervision over the younger; there are punishments for those who step out of line; they have been seen giving short shrift to one of their number who had stolen something; they tried him and hanged him. They deprive themselves of bare necessities to send something home to their poor parents every year. These models of filial love are to be found in rags while fine raiment clothes unnatural children. They run through the streets from morning to night, their faces smeared with soot, their teeth gleaming, simple and gay; their call is long drawn out, plaintive and mournful.[35]

After the beginning of the nineteenth century they were no longer, or no longer only, little chimney sweeps; a large child population appeared swarming in the heart of the capital, mentioned in all the documents. This provides at least as reliable an index as a particular fertility rate, death rate or standard of living to a particular stage in the demographic and social development of Paris and the rest of France,[36] just as it was to do in other capitals and other regions at later periods.

And the causes of these conditions—namely, the demographic, economic and social state of the whole country, not merely the capital—are equally evident. The problem of the waifs and strays connects up here with the general problem of begging and demonstrates the transformation we have already discussed of an exceptional and picturesque phenomenon into a social and general one, at the same rate and accompanied by the same symptoms. Child vagrancy ceased to be a curiosity and became a social fact in the same way and for the same reason as begging, of which child vagrancy was merely one aspect. In the eighteenth century beggars, in fact and in the description of them, remained on the city's fringe, interesting but hardly formidable, an obstruction but not a nuisance. They obviously reflected a demographic and social condition and constituted a surplus population, but this fact was not plainly seen. The attitude of the authorities and the ruling classes toward them hardly differed from what it had been in the past, simply to try to thrust them back into the productive sector. Innumerable administrative measures were taken to curb begging, all of them apparently effective for the time being, such as the committal of the poor described by Sauval:

It was given out that the General Hospital would be open on May 7, 1657, to all the poor who were willing to be admitted of their own free will and through the magistrates. By public cry the beggars were solemnly forbidden to ask for alms at Paris; never was an order so well executed. On the thirteenth a solemn mass of the Holy Spirit was sung at the Church of la Pitié and on May 14 the poor were committed without the least trouble. The whole of Paris changed its appearance that day; most of the beggars retired to the provinces. . . . The most prudent of them decided to earn their living without begging and the frailest committed themselves of their own accord.

The measure had to be repeated over and over again, however, owing to the permanent imbalance between population and resources. The ignorance of the demographic and economic causes of mendicity and the indifference toward beggars were particularly noteworthy. Throughout the eighteenth century the philosophers and politicians who worked out plans for expelling the beggars or sending the parasites encumbering the towns back to the land consistently favored the growth of population; they remained populationists in the face of all the obvious facts.

From the first half of the nineteenth century onwards, however, new factors entered the situation: firstly, an increase in the old imbalance—an early effect, paradoxically enough, of technological progress—and, secondly, a growing awareness of a situation which, we can say, was now regarded as one of structure rather than conjuncture and gave the impression that administrative measures could not cope with it, but that more far-reaching and complex decisions would be required. Malthus is credited with this discovery, but it was in fact the response to a far more general psychological development. The aim was no longer merely to shut up the poor and the beggars or to expel them from the towns, but to curb their dangerous fertility and, more generally, the fertility of the lower classes. Thus, begging was no longer regarded as exceptional and circumscribed, but increasingly assumed a social significance.

The most obvious sign of this transformation of opinion was probably the greater interest taken by most writers henceforth in waifs and strays and children in general. Children had received scant attention in earlier descriptions. Sauval visiting a *Cour des Miracles*[37] saw "a half-buried mud hut, tottering with age and rot, less than six fathoms square, in which there nevertheless lived fifty or more households with an innumerable swarm of small children, legitimate, natural or stolen"— stolen children whose parents, we learn in the last act of the melodrama, were precisely those honest burghers or benevolent noblemen who came on in tears at the rise of the curtain.

Children were barely mentioned in the chapters on begging in the writings of authors like Mirabeau and Necker. Their growing importance in the first half of the nineteenth century denoted an awakening to the demographic causes of the problem.

"Wandering children abounded in Paris," Hugo wrote. They did indeed; opinion realized this fact and, in contrast to previous periods, related it to demographic conditions, traces of which are to be found in *Les Misérables*. First, to the growing fertility of the lower classes—the whole of contemporary literature stressed this, and this general assertion was quite certainly the result of the recent publication of statistics on the birth rate;[38] secondly, to the reduction of infant mortality, due to vaccination;[39] and thirdly, to the fragility of family ties among the poor classes and to illegitimacy, factors themselves related to the high fertility rate. Gavroche's family was a good example. "The reader will recall," Hugo wrote,

the great croup epidemic which afflicted the districts adjoining the Seine in Paris thirty-five years ago, of which science took advantage to experiment on a large scale with the efficacy of alum sprays, so usefully replaced today by the external application of tincture of iodine. In this epidemic the Magnon woman lost her two very young boys on the same day, one in the morning, the other in the evening. It was a blow. The children were precious to their mother, for they represented 80 francs a month. The 80 francs were paid very punctually on behalf of M. de Gillenormand by his agent, M. Barge, a retired writ server dwelling in the rue du Roi-de-Sicile. The children dead, the income was buried. The woman Magnon had recourse to an expedient. Everyone knows everything in the shady freemasonry of evil of which she was a member, mum is the word and mutual aid the order of the day. Magnon needed two children; the woman Thénardier had two, of the same sex and the same age. A fine settlement for the one and a fine investment for the other. The little Thénardiers became the little Magnons. The woman Magnon left the quai des Célestins and went to live in the rue Clocheperce. In Paris the tie of identity binding a person to himself is broken from one street to the next. The registry office was not informed and so did not object and the substitution took place in the simplest possible way.

An uncertain civil status was a feature of the lower-class family. The traffic in children, the substitution of children and the exploitation of children were current practices, and Hugo's story is supported by many items in the press.[40] The exploitation of children for criminal acts was one of the commonest topics in the police court news.[41] Demographic conditions also account for the cruelty to children which is such a feature of the book and was so common at the time.[42]

It is this element in the description of Gavroche and the urchins of Paris that is of interest to historical research, rather than the description as a whole. Not the trappings which Hugo bequeathed to the legend or borrowed and supplemented from a legend that was still in formation, but rather the commonplace and virtually incidental observations and the words he could not help using. These observations and words, by very reason of their commonplaceness and general usage, throw a flood of light on the causes and effects of one of the most important social facts in the history of Paris in this period.

Crime, inseparable from poverty and fostered by it, is the main effect of this state of affairs. The description of the correlations between poverty and crime is one of the main themes in the description of children in *Les Misérables*, as it was in the contemporary literature on the children of the lower classes. The observations we find scattered through Hugo's novel are brought together in certain works which had an influence upon the literature of the period, notably Frégier's book, *Les classes dangéreuses*, for which he took a great deal of his material from the police court records which he was in a very good position to investigate. This work is a close study of the process by which the course of the lower-class child's life was shaped toward crime.[43]

The operation of this process is present in Hugo's book but in a different way. Not in the finished description, in which the combination of the imaginary with the real, of reflection with observation and literature with history, serves purposes which are not our concern; but in the use of themes and words imposed by contemporary circumstances rather than by the purely personal imperatives of artistic creation. Not in the images, which become more and more frequent as the manuscript changes, and which change both its meaning and its historic interest:[44] "The urchin of Paris is the dwarf of the giantess," or

Paris has a child and a forest has a bird; the bird is called a sparrow, the child is called an urchin. Couple these two ideas, the one which is all fiery furnace, the other all dawn; bring the two sparks, Paris and childhood, into collision, and a little being is produced, a *homuncio,* as Plautus would call him.

These images only appear in the second stage of the draft. The first draft begins—far more satisfactorily, so far as history is concerned:

The Paris urchin is a very joyous being who does not eat every day and goes to the theater every night it suits him; the Paris urchin has no shirt to his back, no shoes to his feet, no roof over his head; he is like the birds which have none of these things. He is from seven to thirteen years of age and he lives in gangs. . . .

"Gangs of children, gangs of thieves," the saying went, because the child criminals operated in gangs, as Frégier observed, giving similar details and ages,[45] and as the contemporary police court records also showed.[46] But the term "gangs" had not yet acquired its full criminal content. "Gangs of children" certainly seems to connote "gangs of thieves," but it is impossible to tell just when and how far this meaning attached to the word "gangs." It remained indeterminate, like *"bas-fonds"* and *"misérables,"* its ambiguity due to the imperceptible gradations. It did not quite fit its new significance, yet it was the only possible term. Like *"misère,"* it connoted a situation somewhere between misfortune and crime, or rather the transition from the one to the other. Like *"misère,"* it described a situation of which we may say, as Hugo said about *"misère,"* that it is "a nameless thing."

The evolution of themes and words in *Les Misérables* very closely reflects the problem of the relations between the dangerous classes and the laboring classes, one of the most serious problems in the history of Paris in the first half of the nineteenth century and one that was in fact regarded as such. It is not reflected in the description of the facts, but in the traces left on it by opinion concerning those facts, which is expressed in Hugo's novel precisely as it developed, with its slow adaptation to things, its imperfect perception of new phenomena, its fidelity to former beliefs and earlier attitudes fostered by the survival of the old images and more especially by the persistence of the old words. The trace of this gradual, reluctant and imperfect perception at which Hugo arrived at the same rate as his contemporaries, as confusedly and, indeed, as passively as they, is to be sought in the manuscript rather than in the version finally published.

If we scrutinize the chapters in the manuscript which have the most direct bearing on our subject, we find that everything is already there in the first state of the text and the first burst of inspiration: the most accurate and greatest wealth of observation, which tallies most closely with what we ourselves know, and the most appropriate use of terms. It was, in fact, all there in Hugo's seemingly fumbling reply to his colleagues' ironic questions in the Assembly in 1849: " '*Misère*' is a nameless thing . . . There will always be some unfortunates, but it is possible that there may not always be '*misérables*.' " It was all there in the speaker's words uttered spontaneously, just as it was in the sentences and words that flowed straight from his pen. The reason is that, whether in speaking or writing, Hugo in his initial improvisation was using terms or setting forth themes which were no more peculiar to him than to any of his contemporaries, because he was obeying an imperative of language and because his oratory, like his manuscript, was recording facts with far wider implications—indeed, the major social facts of his time.

Additional matter and new details, a display of erudition concerning crime and society, that often merely weakened the first impression and impaired its authenticity, were inserted later—though still in the first stage of composition and in the same handwriting; but as corrections or additions on the margin of the original text. Still later, however, at a second stage, that is to say, after 1861, Hugo made further corrections and interpolations of a different kind.

In the first place, he had to fit the narrative to the period. At the top of the first page of the chapter on the Gorbeau tenement (we have already stressed its importance), Hugo penciled: "Perhaps a note here saying that this was written twelve years ago when the old Paris with its twelve arrondissements was still in existence and before all the building was started in 1852." Actually, this note comes a little further on, not at the beginning of the chapter on the Gorbeau tenement, but at the beginning of that entitled "*Les zigzags de la stratégie*." Hugo warns the reader:

An observation is necessary about the pages here and some of our later ones. The author of this work, who regrets that he must speak of himself, has been absent from Paris for many years now; and since he left it, that city has been transformed and a new city has sprung up which is to some extent unknown to him. He need not say that he is fond of Paris, for his mind was formed there. Owing to demolition and rebuilding, the Paris of his youth, the Paris which he religiously carried away in his memory, is now a Paris of the past. Permit him, then, to speak of that Paris as if it still existed. It is possible that at the present day there is neither street nor house at the spot whither the author proposes to lead the reader, saying, "In such-and-such a street there is such-and-such a house." Readers may well verify this. He himself does not know the new Paris and writes with the old Paris before his eyes in an illusion which is precious to him.

His most difficult problems in fitting his scenes to the period are set down in this paragraph and in the description of the Petit-Picpus convent.

But, in the second place, Hugo had to interpret these initial descriptions and impressions fifteen years later, deepen them, explain them and make them sharper in this very different sort of correction and interpolation, in a quite different handwriting; and the recastings are not usually well conceived, at any rate from the point of view of historical research. He deleted some sentences which we have already pointed to as significant and important. "The solitary stroller coming to places where it might be said that Paris disappeared, even though he was still in Paris," was in the first draft. "Even though he was still in Paris," a most important phrase for the description of the banlieue, was subsequently dropped. But the main point is that the recasting made for far too sharp a delineation of the problem of the dangerous and the laboring classes and this weakened it, for two reasons. Firstly, despite Hugo's increasing emphasis on the link between poverty and evil, the more heightened the description of misfortune and crime, the more sharply the two became dissociated. The description of *"misère"* and the meditations on it were inflated with the philosophical elucubrations which constitute the chief difference between the post-1860 and pre-1848 texts. Even in the chapter on the Gorbeau tenement, the greater part of which comes from the first state of the manuscript, he slipped in the phrase, "the guillotine, that expedient of philosophers to conceal the scaffold," which adds nothing to the purpose. But apart from these philosophical meditations, the many details supplementing the description of crime add little to the evocation of horror in the first draft. One good example is Part III, Book VII, entitled *"Patron-Minette."* The whole of this book comes from the second draft. It was written straight off, with very few erasures. There are a few additional details, such as we noted in the portrait of Montparnasse; and the sentences about Vidocq and Lacenaire are also inserted. In fact, the description of Patron-Minette is merely a reflection, dragged in as an afterthought at the second stage in the composition of *Les Misérables*, on a form of criminality of which we and Hugo himself had become aware as early as the first state of the manuscript. By heightening the criminal element and complicating it with examples which entail real inconsistencies within the description, Hugo dissociated crime from poverty. So far as the historian is concerned, he toned down his original testimony, the affirmation of social deterioration presented—though involuntarily—in the first manuscript draft and in what remains of it in the final text. And he toned it down precisely because he was now describing, after the event and from the outside, facts which he had previously merely experienced passively and expressed immediately. The problem of the relationship between poverty and crime, which he had simply sensed and experienced in the first improvisation, was now posed, defined and supported by documents taken from the contemporary literature, a social literature which itself adduced its evidence—and most incomplete evidence at that—very tardily concerning the social developments it nevertheless purported to describe and explain.

CHAPTER FIVE

The Social Literature

I

Characteristics and Implications of the Testimony

In a period when most of the major social systems were being worked out, it would have been strange if these social developments and their contemporaries' opinion of them had not left a corresponding imprint on the works which chiefly claimed to describe them, and if the social literature, with its evident connections with literature proper, had not expressed the transformation of picturesque crime into social crime in a similar way, but even more obviously.

The works of the social reformers did in fact bear important testimony to this transformation. They did provide a complete description of this problem of the dangerous classes and the laboring classes and its causes, specifics and solutions; but with a considerable time lag. The social reformers did not really describe, did not really explain—we might even say did not really feel—the developments we find bulking larger and larger throughout the social literature until the closing years of the July Monarchy. The fact is that their descriptions are less relevant to our type of research than the purely literary evidence. We do find a development in the ideas, but we do not find the traces of collective opinion that we can gather from a study of literature proper. The systems were curiously remote from the facts they purported to be investigating. Theory predominated over observation, book learning over experience, the subjective imperatives of personal logic over the collective imperatives of opinion—the only imperatives that can really concern the historian. These social ideas were of course to pass into general opinion by some process which has yet to be adequately investigated. But they were to do so very tardily and they were to acquire historical importance only in 1848, on the eve of the February Revolution and during the grand climax of the Revolutionary June Days.

It was then that social themes ceased to be the province of the schools and of small groups of enlightened workmen and became a universal concern. Thereafter, the proletariat could never again be assessed and described as it had been in the past. During the June Days the workingman assumed, both in his own eyes and in the eyes of others, a new identity, a new value, a new significance, and even a new appearance. It was then that social systems developed into facts, became embodied in opinion and dictated attitudes. It was then that, from the historical point of view, they became a reality and warranted description because they merged their own identity with, or rather attained bulk in, a collective mode of thought—which constituted a historical fact. But not before. Until then they are dead to history; their study is more relevant to the branches of philosophy which describe the autonomous development of ideas than to history as a discipline, which takes no interest in ideas until those of the few become the ideas of the many or bear the imprint of ideas held in common.

Ideas do not of course exist in a vacuum, and economic and social developments strongly influence the development of systems of ideas; indeed, the influence is the stronger precisely because these systems deal with these developments. No one would argue that economic and social developments in the first half of the nineteenth century were not one of the principal reasons for the social research so characteristic of the period. This is such a familiar and evident fact that there is no need to dwell on it. What we must rather do is to point out that these influences were neither immediate nor direct. There is a vast contrast between the literature, which recorded social facts immediately, passively and far more accurately than it intended; and the social analysis purporting to describe and explain social facts, which was not, however, subjected to their pressure precisely because the intention was to describe and explain them. It provided indirect evidence about them, but it did not reconstruct them. In these works the social facts showed up only through the medium of the documentation recording them after the event, and did so less relevantly; for what we are seeking is the fully authenticated facts themselves, not the interpretation of them given by writers, which in many cases was distorted by the inevitable time lag between the developments themselves and the recording of them. The lessons drawn from them were always incomplete, always after the actual event and, by very reason of this time lag, nearly always inaccurate. For the striking point is how tardily, and how incorrectly in some cases, the authors of some of the important social investigations carried out during the Restoration and the early days of the July Monarchy drew the most unrealistic—or at any rate the least relevant—conclusions from the most evident and striking quantitative documentation; how they used the magnificent work of the statisticians of the period to bolster up obsolete systems or antiquated concepts; and how they read the studies by writers such as Guerry, Villermé and Quételet like men of another age, hidebound by ancient attitudes and ancient disciplines, clinging to the older meaning of terms and to survivals of facts which had already become antiquated. The literary description tallied and merged with the statistical description because it returned —via different routes—both to the facts measured by the statistics and to the statistical documentation itself, reaching them by way of the course we have already described in connection with opinion, and is thus relevant in the highest degree to historical research. It checks against the statistics, supplements them and confers upon them not merely significance, but actuality. What is more, it produced these fruits of literary observation and creation (whose inner operation is no business of our present study, but does not seem to have been uncovered to any great extent by literary research itself) a good fifteen years before the social documentation, which attained this form of historical existence only about 1840 as the result of many different influences—one of them being, it should not be forgotten, that of the literature itself.

In many cases, indeed, the literary description provided the social description with its first experience of the developments which were its principal subject matter. In many cases, the literary sources came as a revelation to the social reformers themselves. It is patent that, despite appearances, the Fourierists had less influence on Eugène Sue than Sue had on them. The Fourierists recognized in Sue's stories themes which they had believed to be their own and they sent Sue documentation, traces of which are to be found in the latter parts of the first edition of the *Mystères de Paris* and throughout the work in the form it assumed in the later editions. But these passages had far more to do with possible solutions of the social problem—solutions patently Fourierist—than with its actual components, which Sue discovered for himself without Fourierist influence of any kind, merely by a sort of compliance with the opinion we shall discuss later. To many social reformers, a reading of the *Mystères de Paris* was a revelation of facts about which, however, they had believed that they themselves were the specialists. It was as much of a revelation to them as it was to the artisan or worker, whom the portraits of the artisan Morel, of Rigolette or the Slasher aroused to a consciousness of their own plight, who became aware of it because they found in the book the images, or perhaps merely the words, which were henceforth to enable them to articulate facts they had not fully grasped before because they had been unable to define or put a name to them.

II
The Social Reformers
The Emergence and Development of the Theme of Crime

The social reformers' major works illuminated this evolution in fact and in public opinion, however, by the importance they attributed to the problem of crime and by placing crime at the center of systems in which it had not appeared previously—which, indeed, had been almost completely indifferent to the problem. This development gains added interest from the existence of the time lag and from the obstacles in its way.

The precursors: The problem of crime was barely considered by the great precursors. Saint-Simon scarcely regarded it as a problem at all, hardly thought of criminality as a social problem. His various definitions of the proletariat showed fairly convincingly that he could perceive no relationship between the dangerous classes, in which he took no interest, and the laboring classes. For instance, in defining the differences between English and French proletarians, he wrote that the former thought only of the struggle of the poor against the rich, whereas "the latter in general display an attachment and goodwill towards the opulent manufacturers."[1]

Fourier was a visionary. Of him, Hugo wrote that "in the year 1817 there was at the Academy of Sciences a celebrated Fourier whom posterity has forgotten and in a garret an obscure Fourier whom the future will remember." Fourier's system was constructed with a minimum of documentation and based upon a minimum of specific facts. His experience as the head of the statistical office of the Prefecture of the Rhône in 1814–15, during the Hundred Days, left hardly a trace. Moreover, the system was erected very early, in 1820, that is, at a period when the problem we are studying was not yet clearly defined; and it developed very little thereafter. Fourier remained shut in with his discovery that the face of the world would be changed as soon as he could construct his first phalanstery. Further, in his critique of capitalism the problems of exchange and reflections on trade were more important than the problems of production. He knew very little about the proletariat, which he disliked and regarded with the terror of a small shopkeeper ruined in 1793.[2] Hostile to the Revolutionary spirit and to democratic illusions, he abominated the memory of the Revolution. He knew the workers of Lyon, where he had resided, better than those of Paris, where he lived as a recluse with his cat and his cup of milk in a room on Montmartre and died in the winter of 1836–37. He did make a striking analysis of poverty, reproduced by his successors, and he did stress the "misfortune of the industrious" and the "slow starvation" of the proletarians. But he never established the correlation between physiological and social conditions and crime, or at any rate he failed to draw conclusions from profound observation, as Proudhon did later.[3] It can be said of Fourier, as of all the first generation of social reformers, that their works are not much use to the type of research which deals with facts and opinion rather than with the development of ideology. This is accounted for by certain internal aspects of these doctrines, which have been satisfactorily explained by authors specializing in the subject and, too, by the fact that they did not regard crime as a social problem; and in truth, it was not a social problem, that is to say, a problem of society as a whole at the time.

The successors: Crime was, however, given great importance in the writing of those who continued and deepened the major systems during the July Monarchy, especially in its later years, or who worked out original systems of their own.

Thus while crime was almost entirely absent from Fourier's work, it assumed a large, if not the cardinal, place in that of Considérant, his successor. The following quotation from Fourier was inset at the head of the first part of the *Destinée sociale*, published in 1848:

Can a more fearful disorder be conceived than that which reigns over the entire globe? Half of the earth is overrun by beasts, wild or ferocious—which is the same thing. As for the other half, the cultivated half, we see three-quarters of it occupied by head hunters or barbarians who enslave the farmers and the women and are in every sense the converse of reason. There remains, therefore, one-eighth of the globe for the knaves or the civilized, who boast of perfection in raising indigence or corruption to the highest degree.

Considérant, however, did not construe this disorder in the same way as his master. In his critique of disorder, it was not crime that Fourier was thinking of. Yet in quoting Fourier, it was crime—at least as much as the other forms of disorder—which Considérant had in mind. Reviewing the vices of the industrial system, he put crime first[4] and social antagonisms second. Crime was, indeed, only one of the forms of a social antagonism which was displayed in other forms of violence. "Must we not wonder at the stupidity of those people," he wrote,

who go about declaiming, even before the tribunal of the nation, against those who observe that the nation is divided into classes; good people who imagine that a few words uttered by them will close eyes and ears, will lull the people to sleep, will prevent proletarian bellies from feeling hunger, proletarian mouths from exclaiming against poverty? Yet division and war are here, and the bourgeoisie was well aware of that when it cried out in an agony of fear: "The barbarian is at the gates!"

As a matter of course he referred to the riots, which necessarily occurred "so long as you keep legions of workers huddled up in great agglomerations, living from day to day on a fluctuating wage, constrained by their hard lot to repugnant labor"; and, concluding the first part, he quoted the Preface to Auguste Barbier's *Oeuvres*: "Look at Paris as an observer and measure how much mud there is in this sewer of the world, how many savage races amidst its bustling, witty, elegant, polite inhabitants; you will be terrified." Through Considérant's work we can see how a system which otherwise remains extremely faithful to its origins and to Fourier's basic ideas was, so to speak, compelled—by recent experience—to afford a place to social facts which the system had not originally contemplated.

The works written in the second half of the July Monarchy also bore the imprint of this pressure, despite their theoretical and doctrinal concerns and requirements. A preoccupation with crime and the transformation of exceptional, picturesque crime into general, social crime developed in them to the point where crime, previously ignored, became the very symbol of poverty and social disorder. It even invaded the studies least apt to admit it. Proudhon himself, sturdy, generous, optimistic, the least mawkish writer conceivable, impervious to baseless terrors, asserting his own certainties against the influence of collective opinions, paid more and more heed to crime from his first work, *Qu'est-ce que la propriété?*, in which he depicted "the working class, part of which regularly perishes on the highways, in the hospitals, the prisons and the hulks," to his *Systèmes des contradictions économiques*, in which he made crime the main theme of his social criticism and one of the main characteristics of the proletarian condition.

Thus, alienated as he is from nature by monopoly, cut off from humanity by poverty—the mother of crime and punishment—what refuge remains for the plebeian who cannot be fed by his work and is not strong enough to grab? . . . O people of workers—people disinherited, harassed, proscribed! People imprisoned, condemned and slain! People flouted and branded!

Crime in this book, which he probably began writing at Lyon in 1844, was an essential element of "monopoly" and "the property system," one of the forms of the social order.

It is important to recognize the place of such considerations in Proudhon's social criticism, but it is no less important to note the use he made of crime statistics. Louis Blanc, too, recorded eyewitness evidence and juxtaposed statistics, often without noticing their contradictions or interpreting them incorrectly. Proudhon sometimes fell into similar errors, but used the figures, compared them, went beyond them and frequently extracted from the statistics far more than they could give. Thus, noting the regularity of the crime rate and its constant relation to a certain numerical composition of the population—on which Quételet, Benoiston de Châteauneuf and, after them, Moreau-Christophe also dwelt—he deduced from the crime statistics themselves the fact that crime was far more widespread than those statistics showed, and tried to give exact figures.[5] Statistics other than those for crime need to be taken into account, those for illegitimacy, suicide and mortality, as well as other, deeper-seated phenomena. "I have mentioned elsewhere," wrote Proudhon,

the reduction of the average stature of persons observed by writers on economics. This fact, which can no longer be questioned, is evidence not of some incidental distress such as arises all of a sudden after a bad harvest that brings work to a standstill and causes a dearth of victuals, but of a constitutional and chronic poverty, afflicting the whole species and deeply infecting all parts of the social body. . . . To this fact some people oppose the lengthening of the average span of life which subtle statisticians claim to have discovered. I have shown how deceptive this is in relation to the people at large.

But it was probably in the books of Louis Blanc—the least structured, least systematic, most "passive" of all the social reformers' writings, perhaps the least noteworthy, but at any rate the works most sensitive to the development of opinion—that crime occupied the largest place.

Crime obsessed Louis Blanc to such an extent that it became the initial theme, the starting point, of all his social studies. The *Organisation du travail*, first published in 1830, the successive editions till 1848 being supplemented with fresh considerations and fresh statistics concerning crime, began with a description of crime:

When a man who asks to live serving society is inevitably reduced to attacking it or dying, his alleged aggression is a state of legitimate self-defense, and the society which strikes him down does not judge; it murders. The question, then, is this: Is competition a means of ensuring work for the poor? But to pose the question in this way is to resolve it. What is competition in relation to the workers? It is work put up to auction. A manufacturer needs a worker; three appear.—How much for your work?—Three francs; I have a wife and children.—Good! And you?—Two and a half francs; I have a wife but no children.—Splendid! And you?—Two francs will be enough for me; I have no dependants.—The job goes to you. That's all; the bargain is sealed. What will become of the two proletarians who were shut out? They will resign themselves to dying of hunger, we must hope. But supposing they go off and become robbers? Have no fear, we have the police. Or murderers? We have the executioner. And as for the luckiest of the three, his triumph is but temporary. If a fourth worker comes along sturdy enough to fast one day in two, the downward path will run to the full; yet another outcast, yet another recruit for the galleys perhaps![6]

The Social Reformers and Social History

The fact remains that the problem of crime as we find it posed in the works of the social reformers is not comparable in importance for historical research to what we find in the literary works, from the most noteworthy to the most insignificant.

Personal experience: The traces of personal experience, so numerous and so valuable in most of the novels of the time, are seldom to be found in these works. Can the recollection of the emotions felt by Louis Blanc on reading some particular article in the *Gazette des tribunaux* truly be called a personal experience?[7] And such traces are even rarer in the works of a writer like Proudhon, preoccupied as he was by textual criticism and logical imperatives, and barely influenced by opinion save to criticize it and confront it with its own contradictions or even turn it to ridicule, and that only in his correspondence.[8]

Borrowings from British research: In the social reformers' works, system took precedence over observation. Society and the economic situation were visualized as a whole, and the interest was far more commonly focused upon their general operation than their physical structure or geographical location. Precisely because the concern for theory predominated, whenever such physical or geographic aspects were brought in incidentally, the examples were borrowed for preference from countries in which the baneful consequences of capitalist and liberal economics were most evident or had been studied most often.

Especially England. The social literature and with it literature in general in France approached the French problem of poverty essentially by way of the social and moral consequences of demographic and economic developments in England. It was in England that urban distress produced its earliest and most devastating results, and it was in England that it was most fully described. This description did a great deal toward helping to reveal certain aspects of French distress which had been less evident—because possibly less violent in France and depicted in colors less somber—slower in developing, more familiar and so less noticeable. When Flora Tristan[9] in 1842 published a second edition of her *Promenades dans Londres* (first published in 1840) entitled *La Ville monstre*, the Fourierist paper the *Nouveau monde* wrote: "Mme Tristan has deserved well of the English people by stripping the veil from poverty and all the social sores which corrode the capital of Great Britain. We are hoping that some English lady will, by way of gratitude, render the French people a similar service by publishing a *Walks in Paris*." London far more than Paris was the monstrous city, the city of poverty and crime. And in many cases the choice of colors and words, of subjects, and the description of poverty and crime in Paris originated in a knowledge of a state of affairs which probably was worse in London than in Paris, or at any rate had been more fully studied, measured and known. The poverty of other towns was evaluated by reference to the scenes and statistics of poverty in London. When Flora Tristan visited Lyon, she wrote that "the cold, damp, muddy alleys" reminded her of the English towns, "except that here there are no sidewalks and the streets are narrower." Wisps of London fog trailed thereafter over the Parisian landscape in novels and melodramas. Proudhon, Louis Blanc and Considérant immediately thought of London, like Hugo, who referred to English statistics in *Les Misérables*, "which show that the direct cause of four robberies out of five in London is hunger."

By a literary study of the subjects, colors and words it would be a simple matter to identify the main aspects of this transference, the interest being as much historical and sociological as literary. The picture of London spread by newspaper serials and illustrations, and by plays, led the Parisians to discover certain aspects of their own daily life. *The Mysteries of London*, in short, made it easier to appreciate the *Mystères de Paris*. The contemporary popular literature, Sue's novel especially, shows this transference more clearly than any of the other documents. It has been said that Sue drew his inspiration for the *Mystères de Paris* from [Félix] Pyat's *Les deux serruriers*, which was set in London. According to Legouvé, Sue's reading of an illustrated edition of *The Mysteries of London* was the origin of his novel, a publisher having asked him to do something of the same sort for Paris. It would be easy to pick out the colors and devices Sue borrowed from the descriptions of London in his own descriptions of crime, not so much because of the direct and evident influence of any particular book as because Parisian brutality readily assumed the aspects of London brutality at this period.

But the British revelation was still plainer in the sphere of social research. "We resolved," [Eugéne] Buret wrote in the Preface to his book *De la misère des classes laborieuses en Angleterre et en France* (1840),

> to confine our research to our own country and to England, the prime country for social studies, the country from which we had more to learn than from the whole of the rest of the world. In our project England was the central point of our research, for it is there that recent surveys and the application of new laws to pauperism have enabled an intelligent curiosity to grasp the social mystery we are trying to solve.

It was in England that the burden of overpopulation first appeared, permanent, irreducible and overwhelming; and it was there that a new attitude and policy embodying the Malthusian analysis, or rather revelation, were adopted to cope with the surplus and irremediably poverty-stricken population. The aim was no longer to relieve the poor, whose numbers had not been regarded as an evil in itself during the greater part of the eighteenth century, but to prevent the proliferation of the fertile lower orders, which presented a threat to the common weal. Statistics and descriptions of poverty abounded in connection with the successive amendments of the Poor Law, culminating in the Act of 1834; and European economists and philanthropists, more especially the French, drew on them for the essentials of their own studies.

Borrowing from social surveys: The works of the social reformers are less important than the literary documents for a description of the dangerous and the laboring classes in the Parisian environment. They are also less useful because, for lack of personal and original experience, they merely borrowed their examples from the main contemporary research, [Bigot de] Morogues's *Du paupérisme, de la mendicité et des moyens d'en prévenir les funestes effets* (1834), Buret's *De la misère et des classes laborieuses en Angleterre et en France* (1840), Villermé's survey, *Tableau de l'état physique et moral des ouvriers* (1840) and

Frégier's *Des classes dangereuses de la population dans les grandes villes* (1840).

Certainly, one could not wish for fuller documentation. The problem of the relationships between crime and poverty is all there. From the viewpoint of historical research, however, there is little point in digging out of the social reformers' works figures, cases and experiences ten years out of date, which could just as conveniently be taken from the original surveys. The surveys themselves are only important to historical research in the original form they assumed at the time they were carried out; important, that is, for the traces of contemporary social circumstances and for their "passive" testimony rather than for whatever they purported to demonstrate. This initial authenticity is dissipated by later use, because such use transforms and distorts it or, to put it even more simply, perhaps, because of the mere fact that it is later.

These were the works which Proudhon used and from which he drew his inspiration; but he interpreted them, incorporated them into his system and transformed them into a solid and coherent Proudhonian substance. Louis Blanc pillaged them, but merely juxtaposed the basic elements and composed an unoriginal, often incoherent, whole from chapters in which fragments and passages could easily be traced to their source, if social history had any particular interest in doing so. We should note, however, that though laboring classes and dangerous classes were juxtaposed in *L'organisation du travail*, the connection between them was not demonstrated.

Even worse, Louis Blanc selected from Frégier's book and from the contemporary documentation of crime what was most characteristic of what we have called "picturesque" crime, what Moreau-Christophe was to call "the world of villains," what, in short, was least suited to a description of the consequences of poverty.[10]

The social reformers' borrowings from the major social surveys are of little historical interest precisely because the surveys themselves were slow to recognize the correlation between crime and poverty and found such great difficulty in doing so.

III

The Social Surveys

The Surveys Before 1840

The surveys before 1840 are no use whatever to our historical research, some because they dealt merely with theories about the general problem of resources and population, which they took from Malthus and did not even attempt to apply to the distress of the French people, especially those in the towns; others because their observation of contemporary social developments was based solely on interests, concepts and methods dating from a former age; in short, either because they were too modern but over-theoretical or because they were not modern enough.

One group of surveys of poverty was directly based on the Malthusian revelation and British post-Malthusian research, and on systems and surveys carried out in connection with the amendments of the Poor Law.

The spread of concepts of this kind in France could be observed during the competition on "Charity as Related to Social Economy," which was set by the French Academy in 1827 and again in 1829 for the special prizes offered by the Montyon Foundation. Fourteen essays were submitted. Three shared the prize, including that by Tanneguy-Duchâtel, who had already introduced into France the teachings of Dr. Chalmers, one of Malthus's chief successors, in articles in the *Globe*. Gérando said very rightly of Tanneguy-Duchâtel's work, *De la charité dans ses rapports avec l'état moral et le bien-être des classes inférieures de la société* (1829), that "one might have wished that he had not observed France through the spectacles of English institutions and theories." The work was in fact a very academic exposition of Malthus's theories.

The main impression we derive from Tanneguy-Duchâtel and writers like him is that at no time did they attempt to discover in contemporary France facts tallying with those they borrowed from the British descriptions; they neither checked nor applied nor even transposed them. While both contemporary statistical material and everyday experience of the social malaise, or indeed, merely reading the newspapers would have enabled them to draw up an equivalent description of the poverty of certain French population groups, especially in the working-class and urban groups, they simply blended the most antiquated themes of the problem of French poverty, and such obsolete commonplaces as foundlings and beggars, with the exposition of British theories. In short, the imbalance between population growth and economic expansion —the subject of Malthusian alarm—still seemed far off. The Malthusian illumination, which lit up the rural and urban landscape of England with a truly apocalyptic glare (especially the enormous huddle of London) here quite uselessly lit up only conventional and comforting scenes from the most antiquated literature of poverty.

Even worse, the same traditional settings and the same traditional concerns were given much space in the surveys before 1840, which, opposing the Malthusian ideas, not only failed to ask whether the system applied to France, but rejected both its data and its conclusions. This applies to Villeneuve-Bargemont and particularly to Morogues and Gérando.

The Baron de Morogues's book *Du paupérisme, de la mendicité et des moyens d'en prévenir les funestes effets* (1834) is of far less interest for its statistical material or even its descriptions—which we shall beware of using—than for the quite involuntary and rather strange juxtaposition of new characteristics with old. One would suppose it was something by the marquis de Mirabeau, but a Mirabeau who still clung to his former ideas about economic development, large towns, begging and poverty.

Morogues did regard the population increase in the large towns, Paris especially, as the main cause of a malaise engendering poverty, crime, begging and a widespread social and political unrest, the demographic causes of which he clearly identified. But his appreciations of that increase and of a development he regarded as harmful are worthy of a man of the eighteenth century. His descriptions of this population, which he considered to be too large, were even more anachronistic. The terms he used, the colors and the cases come straight out of Sauval. According to Morogues, Paris was full of beggars as such, corrupted and debauched, and a working-class population which was merely a monstrously developed form of beggary. He called the population "*misérable*," extending his definition and evaluation of beggary to cover almost the whole of the working masses. "It may be roughly estimated," he wrote,

that there are no less than 300,000 persons in Paris who receive yearly, on one pretext or another, free relief amounting to no less than 50 francs per head, either from philanthropic or political or religious individual charities, or from private mutual funds, or from the public funds. Though there are proportionately more poor in Paris than elsewhere, they receive more assistance in Paris.

The poor and the beggars mingled, according to him, in one and the same mode of life, equally dangerous and equally distressed. "Let us remove the poor from the towns," he said, "where they are reared in idleness and grow perverse in debauchery when they have work and corrupted by begging and rapine when they are unemployed." The solution he advocated was the outright "transfer" already envisaged by the marquis de Mirabeau, described here in terms differing only slightly from those used by "the Friend of Man."

Gérando shared this traditional position. In his *De la bienfaisance publique* (1839) he gave the same account of contemporary destitution as his charitable predecessors had given of the destitution of a former age. It was a striking example of the survival of the older outlook. Neither Gérando nor Morogues, of course, ignored the mass migrations of their time or shut their eyes to the increase in the capital's population, and both of them needless to say were aware of the economic causes of poverty. But, invincibly, they were driven by older beliefs and older ideas, by the determination of terms, to give an ever-increasing place within the problem of poverty to the ancient problem of beggary, and finally to merge the two. In Gérando's descriptions and estimates, as in Morogues's, a large section of the working population of Paris was transformed into a population of beggars. And in their writings, the problem of the proletariat was related to the old problem of the *Cour des Miracles*, except where, by a reverse process—from definition to definition and distinction to distinction—the problem of poverty came to relate only to an infinitesimal number of persons and was thus stripped of all its gravity and horror. "The largest number of the truly indigent," said Gérando,

belong to the class of the aged, the infirm, the sick and children, all of them in the circumstances of age or health least productive of crimes and felonies. The largest number of crimes are committed precisely at the age at which indigence is least common and easiest to avoid, that is to say, between the ages of twenty-five and thirty.

The cities were being accused falsely. They had great evils, admittedly:

Is it not within the walls of the cities that the most abundant, the most hideous poverty is displayed? Is it not the corrupting poison of the cities which extinguishes the bodily and mental strength of so many unfortunates by its insidious operation? Is it not there that harlotry and gambling insolently reign? . . . Look at London, they tell us, with its 118,000 thieves and fences, its 75,000 whores, its 16,000 beggars, its 20,000 persons without visible means of support.

Gérando did not deny this. "But," he added, "besides these drawbacks there are three great advantages, namely, a more assured protection for the weak, the existence of a middle class between the poor and the rich, and the resources of a more liberal and more enlightened charity." So far as Paris was concerned, the problem of real indigence affected only a few persons, those included in the successive enumerations of the capital's indigent, each more reassuring than the last.

Thus attenuated, and despite the increase in the population of Paris, the problem could obviously be solved in the old way. In this literature on poverty, all the themes of the older books reappeared. Gérando and his like, friends of benevolence, as they called themselves, philanthropists accustomed to climb the staircases of the poor, to visit the hospitals, to carry on the traditions of the ancestral urban charity, friends to benevolence and to the industrious and deserving poor, and always certain (by virtue of this reciprocal benevolence) of succeeding in all their undertakings and of solving all the problems, were almost wholly blind to the demographic and social changes around them, imprisoned as they were in their branch of study and their professional charity.

But around 1840 these busybodies, these experts in charity, with their comfortable clientele of honest artisans, old folk, widows and nursing babes, vanished, or at any rate gradually faded away. With them vanished, too, the old Paris of the deserving poor and of charity, the old Paris of the neat garret and the hospital. Another form of poverty began to spread. It had long existed in fact and most people had long been aware of it; most people, but not the experts, by very reason of their distant and hidebound professionalism.

The Surveys After 1840

The successive surveys after 1840 brought a real revelation. Misery was no longer a marginal fact; it was central. It was no longer innocuous, nor did it have the species of utility attributed to it; it became large, a public nuisance and a danger. In short, it existed. "Misery exists," said Buret, bringing together in the following passage the main elements of this revelation,

and we shall shortly place before the reader the evidence for its existence. In England and France there is to be found side by side with extreme opulence extreme destitution, whole populations, like that of Ireland, reduced to the slow agony of starvation, to the extremes of physical and moral distress. In the very heart of the busiest centers of industry and trade, you see thousands of human beings reduced to a state of barbarism by vice and destitution. Humanity is afflicted by this evil, whose existence it still merely suspects, for we do not yet at all know its full extent. The governments are rightly apprehensive. They fear lest formidable dangers may some day burst forth from amid these degraded and corrupted people; yet political economy, the so-called social science, remains almost indifferent and regards misery only as something regrettably exceptional, the cause of which lies wholly with the poor themselves. . . . But it is here that, with the help of time, experience is using facts to test the theories of the new science. Many unforeseen effects, the reverse of those expected, are occurring daily. Physical and mental misery, the so-called trade crises, so frequent that they are becoming, it may be said, the permanent state of industry; frauds and the falsification of goods, which have infected almost all branches of business; the disastrous fluctuations in the demand for labor; the growth and agglomeration of classes of person who have no means of existence except wages, often inadequate, always insecure, who have no industry except sheer strength; and, as an inevitable result, the ravages of vice and crime. This ever-growing accumulation of social distresses has caused the governments serious alarm and has sadly disconcerted the optimism of the science of wealth.[11]

Why was social research so slow in becoming aware of social phenomena when the literary documentation had been producing incontrovertible evidence of it for some fifteen years past? And why did it finally accept facts which were perfectly evident from other sources, indeed, very well known? First, there was the rise of statistics and their interpretation, which had been going on for some time, and to which we need not revert. Secondly, there was the competition on distress organized at the time by the Academy of Moral Sciences.[12] The chief experts on poverty—Gérando and others—could not enter this precisely because of their eminence, and so it was reserved for the scarcely known and the unknown; we should add that the rapporteur was Villermé, whose statistical research is the most noteworthy document on distress. Such was the quite incidental reason accounting for the contrast between works which were nevertheless virtually contemporaneous. Gérando's major book, *De la bienfaisance publique*, appeared in 1839; Buret's in 1840—only one year between them, but far more in effect. But this lucky circumstance—the admission of unprejudiced persons to the competition—should probably not be given precedence over another reason; or, at any rate, it only operated as a consequence of it, namely, the great volume of distress and crime which already existed in fact, in the statistics and even in the literary description, and which could no longer be ignored in social description.

These surveys, especially the two most important, those by Frégier and Buret, are relevant to our research far more for their progressive discovery of this state of affairs than for their quantitative documentation, which cannot be regarded as historical material without some prior criticism. To be more precise, their interest is of two kinds. The value of their quantitative documentation can be tested, and it does enable us to describe the facts more accurately. But, more importantly, they bear, in the same way as the literature proper and the social literature, the imprint of contemporary preoccupations. This may perhaps raise the question whether their findings tallied with the realities, but it is no less useful to recognize them as existing in themselves and in the same way as the realities themselves. Though the surveys recorded these preoccupations some ten years later than the literature, they did so far more clearly and far more lucidly. The social disquiet we have felt spontaneously arising in Balzac's and Hugo's descriptions at last found its full expression and justification in these surveys. Here it completed the difficult transition from the dangerous to the laboring classes. The old themes of crime disappeared with the appearance of these surveys, and in them the development of the notion of *"misérables"* reached its final phase.

Frégier's book, *Des classes dangereuses de la population dans les grandes villes*,[13] reflected this effort, which is apparent even in his uncertain use of terms. Frégier, a departmental head at the Prefecture of the Seine, proposed mainly to describe evildoers of all sorts, whether of the working class or not, crooks, thieves and prostitutes, and tried to identify them by means of statistics while situating them in their actual setting in Paris. It should be noted, however, that in doing so he had to take a breakdown of the laboring classes as his starting point. His study of the dangerous classes covered a large part of the working classes, owing to the statistics he used, the facts he observed and his very terms; but he did not finally succeed in even roughly determining the frontier between the two groups. "The poor and the vicious classes," he wrote,

have always been and will always be the most productive breeding ground of evildoers of all sorts; it is they whom we shall designate as the dangerous classes. For even when vice is not accompanied by perversity, by the very fact that it allies itself with poverty in the same person, he is a proper object of fear to society, he is dangerous.

The imprecision of the terms and the confused syntax reflect the complexity of the subject no less than the imprecision and confusion of thought. The survey, Frégier stated, "is to deal with the vicious and poor classes which swarm in the city of Paris." Vice and poverty are thus confused both in word and fact. "The social danger," he went on, "increases and becomes more and more pressing as pauperism deteriorates through vice and, worse, through idleness." And:

What we have just said about the inroads of audacious and maleficent vice among that part of the working class which has already been spoiled is all too true. . . . These unfortunates, who were still seemingly attached to the mass of honest and industrious workers by the practice of their trade, gradually shed their remaining habits of industry under the malign influence of their companions in disorder and ended by embracing their idle and criminal life.

Frégier analyzed this contagion by describing daily life in the workshops, the course of the worker's life, and child vagrancy, all of them scenes which literature and social literature were to repeat and use so often. What chiefly strikes us in this book is how Frégier was quite unable to find any way out of the confusion between dangerous classes and working classes, despite his stated subject matter, the dangerous classes. The time was long past when the world of crime could be described as a world apart. The danger lay not in crime, but in the relationships between the underworld and the world of labor, relationships upon which Buret threw light at the same period but in a totally different way, taking the laboring classes rather than the dangerous classes as his starting point and finally stripping the notion of *"misérables"* of all anachronistic vestiges of the older criminality.

The development of ideas concerning the correlations between crime and poverty culminated in Buret's survey, *La misère des classes laborieuses en France et en Angleterre*. The subject was truly poverty, not crime; the laboring classes, not the dangerous classes.

Nevertheless, poverty and the laboring classes still exhibited most of the characteristics which were the property of the criminal world; the social terror they roused was still stamped with the specific horror formerly attaching to crime.

Distress (*la misère*) had never before been analyzed in such detail. The importance of this analysis has been pointed out so often that we need not revert to it here. We should, however, note the emphasis on the psychological and moral aspects. *"La misère,"* Buret wrote,

is poverty felt morally. The recognition of evil is not adequately sustained solely by the injury to the physical sensibility; it affects something higher, something more sensitive even than skin and flesh; its pain penetrates to the moral sense. As distinct from poverty, which, as we shall see, is often merely a physical affliction, distress—and this is its constant characteristic— afflicts the whole man, soul and body alike. Distress is a phenomenon of civilization; it presupposes the awakening, even the higher development, of the human consciousness. We need not go back to barbarism or the state of savagery for we can find classes of individuals, or even of peoples, in our own societies who are destitute, but still lack that consciousness of it which brings the real effects of physical suffering home to the inmost feelings. Certain classes of mankind suffer the most extreme poverty, but not distress in our sense. The Picardy peasant, with his sordid hut of mud and straw, is as poor as a man can be, but he practically never importunes public charity; he is not distressed. The same may be said of all the groups which have remained in their primitive indigence, such as the people of lower Brittany and the Corsicans.[14]

Hence, distress was the state of people in the cities, those more sensitively conscious of suffering. The distressed were essentially workers in the cities, particularly in the capital, where civilization was furthest advanced. And the more lucid the consciousness of distress, the stronger and more formidable its effects.

In proportion to the extent that the enlightened parts of the working class become aware of their distress, the more restless, the less resigned they become. They begin to reason, to seek out its causes with a passion for investigation. The poor have already engendered their theoreticians, who maintain that political institutions are the cause of the people's sufferings. Let governments beware!

The most important point to be noted here is that with Buret "*la misère*" became the central theme of demographic and economic research. Buret made distress the cardinal subject—or rather, the cardinal discovery—in a system of economic research. The effort to reintroduce the human element necessarily entailed the introduction of the distressed, the "*misérable*," who thus became the measure of man. The approach was fitting for a period during which the rates of destitution and death became the preferred tools of social study. It marked a return to the tradition of the eighteenth-century economists, who had held that the theory of wealth was the science of man, not of things; but now in a new form and with new interests: a rediscovery of man, but of nineteenth-century man. The cardinal subject of economic and social research and the main instrument of measurement were not only the birth and death rates, but also the varied forms of distress. "J. B. Say felt some scruples about calling the science he practiced political economy," Buret wrote,

and would have preferred to call it social economy—which would not have been appropriate either. The physiology of society comprises many phenomena besides those of the production and distribution of wealth. If in your studies you isolate the values of the people who produce and consume, you fall back into the science dealing solely with money, which the ancients called chrematistics. . . . Is not the study of distress an integral and necessary part of political or social economy, or of the physiology of society, as it may better be called? We do not consider that the statement that the picture of the wealth of nations must be confronted with the picture of the distress of nations is merely a play on words. The latter part of the science does more than supplement the former; it provides a test, a critique and a means of verifying it.

Nevertheless, though every aspect and every cause of distress was thus defined, and distress presented as the essential characteristic of the working-class condition, it was still stamped with the outward marks of criminality. The description of laboring classes is, it is true, entirely severed from the description of the dangerous classes in this book, but it still bears the mark of the former confusion. Crime was the property of the lower classes. It was so by reason of their criminality as such, in the older sense of the term. "The crime statistics of a country," wrote Buret, "are one means of obtaining an approximate knowledge of the moral state of the lower classes, because the great majority of crimes are committed by those degraded groups which form the residue and lees of societies." It was so, above all, because of the varied characteristics possessed by, or attributed to, these groups, which were those of the older criminality. It was so because of their marginal existence, the chief aspects of which Buret summed up in the section he entitled *"L'extrême misère est une rechute en sauvagerie."* "The lower classes," he wrote,

are gradually expelled from the usage and laws of civilized life and are reduced to the state of barbarism through the sufferings and privations of destitution. Pauperism is tantamount to exclusion from society. The destitute resemble the bands of Anglo-Saxons who took to a nomadic life in the forests to escape the Norman yoke. They are outside society, outside the law, outlaws; and almost all criminals come from their ranks. Once distress has brought its weight to bear on a man, it gradually presses him down, degrades his character, strips him of all the benefits of civilized life one after another and imposes upon him the vices of the slave and the barbarian.

Thus, regardless of quantitative research into the demographic, economic and social development of Paris at this period, the progressive transformation of the criminal theme into the social theme in most of the contemporary descriptions of the capital must necessarily be considered as an expression of a material and moral transformation of the human beings concerned. The city's social degradation imprinted its mark more and more deeply upon these documents. A criminal city? Yes, but crime was not its only sickness. A sick city? Yes, but sick for reasons and with symptoms which, after this long detour, we have now to observe directly.

BOOK II

Crime

The Expression of a
Pathological State: Its Causes

Introduction:
The Contemporary Diagnosis

A change in the composition of the population is the principal reason for the pathological state we are discussing. In our initial approach there is no need to go to the abundant evidence in the quantitative documentation, for all the qualitative documentation goes to support this contention.

I

From the End of the Ancien Régime to the
Last Years of the Restoration

During the eighteenth century, Félibien, Sauval[1] and Delamare emphasized the ill effects of the city's growth on the physical and moral health of its inhabitants. Delamare summed up the material conditions: "The air ought not to be so polluted, water and food ought not to be thus infected." They were problems, but they were solved more effectively in eighteenth-century Paris than they had been in earlier periods and they could have been completely solved, had the royal power, the Administration and the citizens really tried. Eighteenth-century writers, it is true, never lost an opportunity of dwelling on the city's dirt and stench, Mercier in particular. In a famous passage which sums up the main features of the insanitary condition of Paris, easily visible in the prospect from the towers of Notre-Dame, he wrote of: "The perpetual smoke rising from countless chimneys. . . . You can see a haze forming above the mass of houses and the city's transpiration, as it were, becomes perceptible."[2] It was a filthy, stinking, badly kept city, hard to keep clean, but not unhealthy; or so it was described in the principal literary, official and medical documents.

But no one yet perceived any connection between the growth of the population and the general conditions of health and cleanliness. Mercier spoke of "the fearful consequences of great numbers to a society," but the consequences were not so fearful as to be unamenable to improvement by good administration, a better knowledge of discoveries in chemistry, vigilant and enlightened inspection and the inhabitants' cooperation. The city's dirt, indeed, sometimes had some advantages of a sort for health.[3] The consequences of geographical and topographical factors were very commonly considered to be at least as great as that of population. "The healthiest district," Mercier noted, "is the faubourg Saint-Jacques, inhabited by small shopkeepers and artisans, and the unhealthiest is the Cité. Why is this splendid city not situated where Tours is? The fine climate of Touraine would suit it better." But these insalubrious conditions were never described as irremediable. In these eighteenth-century descriptions Paris might have its feet in the mud, but its skyline was a magnificent array of domes, palaces and spires. The splendor of monumental Paris predominated over the other aspects, admiration over criticism. Even the districts which were soon to be depicted as the dirtiest and unhealthiest were pictured quite differently in the eighteenth century. Sauval considered that the district of Les Halles was the busiest and wealthiest in Paris.

It has an abundance of everything, vegetables, market-garden produce and orchard fruit, sea and fresh-water fish, all that contributes to the comforts and luxuries of life, all that is most excellent, most exquisite, most rare in the air and on earth is assembled here when it reaches Paris. A market, a fair that never closes and a storehouse, garden and fishpool, and the royal furniture repository. It is the most bustling and the wealthiest district on earth.

He even gives pleasing architectural details, such as "a bas-relief on the pillars representing infants dancing to the flute." Sauval described Montfaucon as "the most ancient, the most superb and the most famous gibbet in the kingdom." When the burghers of Paris or the monarch opposed the capital's growth, they did so only for political reasons. The evil came, or probably came, from some source which was not the city itself or its inhabitants. If the city was sometimes unhealthy and was periodically ravaged by epidemics—which seemed in any event to be becoming rarer[4]—that was no fault of the urban environment itself, but was due to circumstances extraneous to the city or else to persons unknown and to the fact that the city adjoined backward and ignorant rural areas. But the main source was the presence of, or invasion by, types of people foreign to the city (but in some cases actually of the city), who were regarded as inferior, alien and not really part of the city: beggars driven from time to time by poverty and disease from the famished countryside, who were turned back at the first signs of an epidemic;[5] inhabitants of the faubourgs, who lived on the outskirts of the city and its trades, regulations and civilization, or in the oldest districts in the heart of the city itself; and inferior trades such as that of the ragpickers, who brought into the city manners and customs which were not truly its own, and the inmates of the hospitals and prisons, often so packed and intermingled in the same places that the horror they inspired fell on both and both were treated alike when some contagious disease struck the city.

These themes predominate almost unchanged in the literary descriptions and medical and official surveys of Paris during the early years of the Restoration.

It is not surprising then that the picturesque literature, whose aim was to amuse and entertain, should be full of them. More specialized works, such as the curious and important *Mémorial d'un Parisien* published by Dufey in 1821, have, however, to be taken seriously. One passage is worth quoting in full:

Who could now recognize Paris in the well-known descriptions by Sainte-Foix, Piganiol de la Force and Mercier himself? They were true enough in their time, but not in ours. Everything in Paris has changed, even the air we breathe. The masses of buildings that obstructed the traffic no longer exist. Spacious quais adorn both banks of the Seine from end to end. New bridges make for speedier and easier communications. Ancient buildings, the inner and outer avenues, have been embellished in a way that our fathers who admired them would never have conceived possible. Wide and solid arcades, well aired and artfully laid out, have replaced the narrow, insanitary and muddy crossings where the daily provisions for 200,000 families piled up without order or taste. The privilege of insulting the helpless buyer has vanished with the gothic booths. The one flaw is that they still speak the dialects of Vadé and l'Ecluse, but self-help will eradicate this last remnant of ignorance and barbarism. Paris is no longer an abyss in which the country produce and the manufactures of the provinces were engulfed and nothing sent out in return. Paris has become a manufacturing city and the warehouse for all the manufacturers of France. Establishments of all kinds employ a multitude of craftsmen and mechanics. There is no part of France which is not now in contact with Paris at every hour of the day and night.

It is a really extraordinary point in the history of a city when both an improvement in urban living conditions and public health and a boom in manufacturing (which at other periods was described precisely as responsible in part for bad living conditions) can be thus related to each other, or at least coupled in a single account. Dufey described the living conditions of the people of Paris in these terms:

> . . . the multitude of obscure but useful workers who people the faubourg Saint-Antoine. Everything there is eloquent of the contented tranquility of industrious mediocrity, regular manners, attachment to work and the public peace, simple and clean clothing and united families. They know neither vice nor debauchery and there are no places of prostitution and profligate idleness. I saw only two pothouses beyond the barrière. There are very few inside it. Those outside are crowded only on holidays, and I observed none but families refreshing themselves together cheerfully and quietly after their occasional outings to the Bois de Vincennes. In a district where the inhabitants are so sober and industrious there are naturally very few sick or indigent persons. So I was pleased rather than surprised to observe that the number of beds in the Saint-Antoine hospital was not proportionate to the size of the building and that the few beds were sufficient for the needs of a fairly large population.[6]

It is more remarkable that these themes are also to be found in the medical topographies, notably that of Lachaise. Like his predecessors, Lachaise placed his main emphasis on conditions extraneous to the city, chiefly geographical circumstances.[7] The perpetual haze on which he commented—as Mercier had commented before him in nearly the same terms—was due less than it had been in the past to natural fog and was more charged with the city's immense respiration and transpiration; but it is certainly curious that Mercier's description could be thus reproduced, almost word for word, twenty years later. The reason was that, on the whole and despite human and economic changes, the natural conditions—the site, exposure to sun, composition of the atmosphere, prevailing winds—were of greater moment than the demographic conditions, or at least were thought to be so.

Similarly, "the causes pertaining to the city itself which may affect its salubrity" were described by Lachaise in almost the same way as they had been at earlier periods, the same themes arranged in the same order, the same optimism and the same belief in the possibility of an improvement in urban living conditions simply by progress. This caused Lachaise to examine the two facts with which he summed up the general problem of the influence of the urban environment upon the inhabitants: the crowding of a large number of individuals into a limited space and the effects of trades and crafts upon health.

The dense population was admittedly responsible in part for bad living conditions, both material and moral. It is worth noting that Lachaise observed this almost exclusively from a material point of view;

the important point was density in the geographical sense—the ratio of individuals to area—not economic, social and biological density. It is also noteworthy that his survey bears the imprint of older and strictly geographical factors, such as exposure, sunlight, ventilation, contour and slope, and humidity. It is an important passage which calls for quotation almost in full:

The inevitable result of the congestion of the houses and their excessive height is that the sun shines for a short time only in some of the streets, hardly at all in others and never in most of them, and that the people living on the ground floor are still in the dark when the sun is far up the horizon. This lack of sunlight may be regarded as one of the true causes of the city's humidity and of the prodigious amount of mud that carpets its streets, two essential reasons for its insalubrity. Not a doctor practicing in the larger towns but must have observed that persons who are compelled by their occupation to live in low-lying and dark places, such as porters, certain workmen, even persons who, though well enough off, live on the ground floor in dark, narrow streets, fall prey to the so-called intermittent fevers, scrofula, scurvy, dropsies, arthritis and rheumatism and the like, and to a multitude of other illnesses similar to the wilting of plants. This perpetual dusk, and the damp that always accompanies it, are the main causes in Paris of the scrofulous complaints, the rickets, scab and white swellings which are so common among children of all classes, especially those of persons who pack them pell-mell into what are called back shops, in defiance of purely instinctive hygiene. The observations I had collected in various districts had long convinced me of the truth of this, so much so that I thought they might be carried a good deal further, and I chose it as the subject of my inaugural thesis.

We cannot fail to note that not long after this, and despite greater attention to more recent phenomena, which we shall discuss later, Balzac, describing the oldest quarters of Paris, stressed the aspect and slope of streets, damp, sunlight and shade in similar terms. Lastly, we should note that the population densities studied by Lachaise were not regarded as so formidable nor their consequences so irremediable as to be beyond the possibility of improvement.

Similar characteristics are to be found in the study of "the influence of trades and crafts upon the city's health." The observations are similar to those made in previous periods, as are the examples and the use of terms. They are summed up in what Moheau had already written at the end of his study of the death rate in the various classes: "This study would give an idea of the healthiness of each trade and the extent of the sacrifices involved in engaging in certain occupations."[8] What we find, from the Ancien Régime to the early years of the nineteenth century, is Old Paris unchanged, with its ancient trades and the ancient death rate that attaches to them.

II

From the Last Years of the Restoration to the Early Years of the Second Empire

In the period from the last years of the Restoration to the early years of the Second Empire the characteristics of the descriptions of the capital, from the most insignificant to the best known, are very different and so sharply defined that it is impossible not to grant them at least as much significance as we would grant to a rise in the quantitative data in the death or illegitimacy rates. Just as a rise in such rates sums up demographic and economic, social and moral developments, which could not be discovered in any other way, so the progressive transformation of the qualitative documentation and the coincidence of the most subjective data reflect—at any rate if we assemble a large enough number and a varied enough assortment of texts—a change in opinion through which it is possible to discern a change in the facts, a complete revolution in, and worsening of, the conditions of urban living.

In the first place, these descriptions both as a whole and in all the forms in which they are embodied (the picturesque literature designed for entertainment as well as the administrative and medical reports) became more serious and more somber, as if the old characteristics of filth, stench and damp had worsened and now spread all over the city, constituting a very real threat to it and a threat of a new sort. Paris seems suddenly to become darker and unhealthier, crushed by its mass, stifled by its own respiration, transpiration and excreta.

Such was the city described by the vicomte de Launay in 1838:

How ugly Paris seems after one has been away for a year. . . . How one stifles in these dark, damp, narrow corridors which you are pleased to call the streets of Paris! One would think one was in an underground city, so sluggish is the air, so profound the obscurity. . . . And thousands of people live, bustle, throng in the liquid darkness, like reptiles in a marsh; and the foul, mean noise of steps splashing in the mud pursues one on all sides; one carries no lantern on one's travels, simply because one assumes that as it is high noon, one will be able to see one's way.

Such, too, was the city described by Balzac, just as subterranean, dark, dank and muddy—both the city as a whole and the individual districts. He wrote of the central districts, those containing the Grève and the Hôtel-de-Ville, summed up in the rue du Tourniquet-Saint Jean:

The broadest part of the rue du Tourniquet was its junction with the rue de la Tixeranderie, where it was only five feet wide. So in rainy weather the blackish waters promptly washed against the base of the old houses on this street, carrying down the garbage deposited by each household beside the corner posts. As the garbage carts could not get by, the inhabitants counted on the thunderstorms to clean their street, which was always muddy—for how could it have been clean? When the sun darted its rays perpendicularly on Paris in summer, a sheet of gold, sharp-edged as the blade of a saber, momentarily lighted up the darkness of this street, but could not dry the perpetual damp which pervaded those black and silent houses from the ground floor to the first floor. The inhabitants lit their lamps at five in the afternoon in June and never extinguished them in winter. Even today any daring pedestrian who ventures to walk from the Marais to the quais, turning at the end of the rue du Chaume into the rue de l'Homme-Armé, the rue des Billettes and the rue des Deux-Portes which lead to the rue du Tourniquet-Saint-Jean, will have the feeling that he has been groping through cellars all the way.

And particularly Les Halles, with the Cour Batave: "This unhealthy pile hemmed in on all sides by tall houses is the center of the black passages which meet here and join the quartier des Halles to the quartier Saint-Martin by the notorious rue Quincampoix, damp thoroughfares on which the thronging people are stricken with rheumatics." But even the districts with the most bourgeois population, the Marais, for example, with the rue de Normandie, "one of those old streets with broken paving, in which the Paris Municipality has not yet placed drinking fountains and in which the black gutter laboriously rolls down the slops from every house so that they seep under the paving stones and produce the mud peculiar to the city of Paris." Such was the city in all the descriptions of the period, even the most obscure; it was depicted everywhere in similar colors and described in similar terms.[9]

The correlations commonly established between the urban environment and unhealthy material and moral conditions are even more remarkable than the general darkening of the description. Unlike the earlier literature, nearly all these portraits of Paris relate the death rate to damp and dirt. In connection with plans for opening a rue Louis-Philippe from the Louvre to the Bastille, the *Edile de Paris*, "the houseowners' journal," wrote in its issue of March 5, 1833:

The Administration has better things to do. Yes, indeed, a street running from the Louvre to the Bastille would be a fine thing . . . but it would be better postponed. With the funds set aside for this scheme the Administration might widen several of the present impassable streets to which the inhabitants are relegated like pariahs: their looks are haggard and cadaverous. There are more than a hundred of these streets. Properties are valueless, the owners are as poor as the tenants, and yet a genuine wealth is there, the land. For all these narrow streets are in the very center of Paris, in the part of the city where land is of immense value owing to trade's general need for centralization. We would remind the Administration that, according to the table of mortality we published in our first issue, over one-fifth more people die in Paris than in the entire kingdom, and that if the number of deaths per calendar year amounts to 24,000, more than 4,000 persons per year could be saved if the city were cleaned up and purged of the foul hovels which people still have the audacity to call houses. The Administration would, therefore, do better to set up financing companies for the purpose of widening these stinking and lethal streets.

But the main point is that these unhealthy conditions were related in these descriptions to the increase in population; no longer to such limited and marginal groups as ragpickers, beggars and inhabitants of the faubourgs, who had been held responsible at earlier periods for every ill and could easily be confined in the hospitals or expelled to the outskirts of the city, but to nearly the whole population, many estimates of which are to be found even in the picturesque literature.

This population was held directly responsible for every ill at once as a population and because of its occupational and social composition. It undoubtedly included large numbers of bourgeois (which we shall estimate in due course), but they were less important both in reality and in the opinion of contemporary Parisians. Moreover, they were less visible in the urban setting than the lower-class groups, who thronged the streets, noisy, ragged, ill-fed and often unemployed, and were generally regarded as a vast proliferation of the beggars of former times. This population was held responsible for every ill, especially because by very reason of its numbers it burdened the other categories and the city as a whole with its bad living conditions, its primitive way of life, its vices and even its stench and bad breath.

It was in such beliefs that the idea of contagion, still shrouded in mystery and confusion, found expression in opinion during the 1832 cholera epidemic. These beliefs were reflected in the vicomte de Launay's description of the Paris fog: "It is a foul medley of all the miasmas we fear, it is the concatenation of vapors and smoke which links the street to the roofs, it is the monstrous and fatal union of the exhalations from the chimney and the breath of the sewers." These were beliefs which Considérant expressed even more remarkably in 1848, in his book *Description du phalanstère et considérations sociales sur l'architectonique.* All the aspects of contagion were brought together in this work; it demands quotation:

Look at Paris: all these windows, doors and apertures are mouths which need to breathe—and above it all you can see, when the wind is not blowing, a leaden, heavy, gray-and-blueish atmosphere composed of all the foul exhalations of this great sink. This atmosphere is the crown on the great capital's brow; this is the atmosphere that Paris breathes; beneath it Paris stifles. . . . Paris is a great manufactory of putrefaction, in which poverty, plague and disease labor in concert, and air and sunlight barely enter. Paris is a foul hole where plants wilt and perish and four out of seven children die within the year. The doctors who treated their patients at their homes during the cholera epidemic and ventured into the dens of the poor gave accounts at the time to make one shudder; but the rich have already forgotten. The cholera will not come to Paris, they said, or at least it will hardly be noticed; it will get no grip on this center of Civilization, this center of enlightenment. The rich did speak of the misery of the poor, but it was as a thing for pity, not fear; they had had no notion of this frightful, contagious poverty; the cholera starkly revealed it.

Lastly, these descriptions differed from the earlier because they presented the situation as irremediable. It was no longer, as in Mercier's *Tableaux* and the portraits by his genial imitators in the early years of the Restoration, a case of distressing circumstances to be put right by a far-sighted and enlightened Administration, but an evil with no remedy. The splendor of the city's buildings gave way to horror and disgust. There had never been such anathemas of the city in every sort of publication. Witness Doin and Charton, writing in 1830:

Those who have something to hide come to Paris. They see the labyrinths of its streets and the depravity of its morals, and they plunge into it as into a forest. Paris must change. Its present composition is an unmitigated evil. The crime statistics show that it has twice as many thieves as any of the other royal residences in France. The nearly 900,000 persons thronging it are prey to a corruption twice as bad as that of the 31 millions surrounding them.

And Lecouturier in 1848, in a little book with a very characteristic title, *Paris incompatible avec la République*:

If you contemplate from the summit of Montmartre or any other hill in the neighborhood the congestion of houses piled up at every point of a vast horizon, what do you observe? Above, a sky that is always overcast, even on the finest day. Clouds of smoke, like a vast floating curtain, hide it from view. A forest of chimneys with black or yellowish chimneypots renders the sight singularly monotonous. . . . Looking at it, one is tempted to wonder whether this is Paris; and, seized with sudden fear, one is reluctant to venture into this vast maze, in which a million beings jostle each other, where the air, vitiated by unhealthy effluvia, rising in a poisonous cloud, almost obscures the sun. Most of the streets in this wonderful Paris are nothing but filthy alleys forever damp from a reeking flood. Hemmed in between two rows of tall houses, they never get the sun; it reaches only the tops of the chimneys dominating them. To catch a glimpse of the sky you have to look straight up above your head. A haggard and sickly crowd perpetually throngs these streets, their feet in the gutter, their noses in infection, their eyes outraged by the most repulsive garbage at every street corner. The best-paid workmen live in these streets. There are alleys, too, in which two cannot walk abreast, sewers of ordure and mud, in which the stunted and withered dwellers daily inhale death. These are the streets of Old Paris, still intact. The cholera had scourged them so sorely as it passed that it expected they would no longer be there if it returned; but most of them are still there, they are still in the same state, and the disease may still return.

Between 1830 and 1848 innumerable anathemas of Paris appeared in every sort of publication. The *Fous de Paris*, dropping its jesting, wrote in 1842:

> *L'air est froid et pesant, la nuit n'a point d'étoiles*
> *Les flots sont tout bourbeux . . .*
> *On coudoie en marchant un peuple au regard noir . . .*
> *Restez chez vous, enfants, on souffre trop ici.*
> *A Paris, voyez-vous, tout est luxe ou misère.*
> *Oh! n'y venez pas, pour vous, pour votre mère!*
> *Car la nuit du départ un bon ange vous dit*
> *Que Paris est maudit!*[10]

Proudhon, too, in a letter dated April 11, 1839:[11]

I shall never be able to write again save on the banks of the Doubs, the Ognon and the Loue. The people of Paris simply cannot understand words of truth, of justice. . . . I find that it is more than I can do to live in this vast cesspool, this place of masters and lackeys, thieves and prostitutes. One day the *Dies irae* will sound over Paris; it will come from the provinces.

This universal view that the growth of Paris was the main reason for the general malaise is the more striking because it is reflected just as strongly in many other ways and in many other documents, such as the municipal and police reports, which give a vivid picture, complete to the most commonplace detail, of the invasion of houses, blocks, streets and districts by newcomers, whose way of life, of working or not working, manners and customs, clothing, speech, even smell, whose very presence were intolerable to the older inhabitants; problems of coexistence which racial changes in the population composition in the great American cities have greatly accentuated in modern times, so that we can now experience them continuously. And it is most evident in the demographic documents, which by confronting us with the actual fact make it abundantly clear that an increase in population on so large a scale must inevitably have had material and moral results and have been at least one basic cause of the phenomena recorded in descriptions of the most varied sort.

This is what we must now discuss. The increase in the population of Paris during the first half of the nineteenth century was the major fact in the social history of Paris; first, the population's growth rate, and, secondly, the change in that population's demographic characteristics; overpopulation on the one hand and a new population on the other.

PART I

The Increase in Population

From Theoretical Analysis to the Description of the Facts: Population, Economic Factors and the Urban Environment

When an excessive and over-rapid increase in population occurs on such a scale, demographic fact is of more weight than economic fact. But we still have to make a preliminary analysis in order to account for and justify an unusual historical approach which pays little attention to economic structures and factors. The reasons are that, first, we have already studied the economic development of Paris in another book,[1] and secondly and more particularly, that economic developments weigh less in the general history of Paris than this sudden human invasion.

The size and rate of population increase in great cities are two of the most important factors in their social development; that is to say, in the material and moral changes which occur within groups and in their reciprocal relationships in all great cities at all periods. This was even more true of the Paris of the first half of the nineteenth century, when immigration accelerated and the composition of the population definitely changed at the same time; when an old society, slowly matured in the course of ages, was replaced with a new and suddenly altered society with strangely different characteristics. This fact is so obvious that it is very curious that the historians of Paris have not perceived it as clearly as the inhabitants of the old bourgeois Paris, hostile as they were to rejuvenation and proletarianization when their habits were thrown into disarray by it. The fact was patent to its contemporaries, though it has not been obvious to the historians. Hence the need to pose the problem in general and somewhat theoretical terms before looking at it in the context of the Paris of the period; in the first instance, solely from the point of view of the numbers and the human overload, leaving aside the whole question of the changes in that population.

I

The General Problem of Population and Resources

Recent demographic studies have shown that the economic and social development of populations is conditioned in all countries and at all periods at least as much by numbers, growth rate and age composition as by the traditional economic factors. The cardinal problem in both economic and social research is that of population and resources— not considered separately and as a branch of demography and a branch of economics, alien and indifferent, if not hostile, to one another, but in the light of their interrelationships and the continually interrupted and continually restored equilibrium between the increase in the number of human beings and increase in wealth. A demography concerned only with changes in the composition of a population would be useless; an economics taking within its purview only the production, exchange and consumption of goods, with man entering the cycle merely as one thing among other things, would be unrealistic.

This sort of approach is essential for descriptions covering long periods, owing to the apparent predominance of the demographic phenomena over the economic. It is equally essential for descriptions covering short periods, and even recessions, despite the apparent predominance of the economic phenomena over the demographic. For in these crises the economic phenomena appear to predominate so strongly only because they can be dated incontrovertibly at both ends of the period concerned; because of the influence they exert upon everyone and of which everyone is conscious; and because the poverty they spread and the maledictions they attract cause everyone, contemporaries and historians alike, to overlook the very existence of the demographic phenomena, which do not appear on the scene, or appear only indirectly in the form of a rise in the death rate, and as a subsidiary element in casting up the balance of the results but never of the causes.

We cannot fail, however, to discern in these crises themselves the influence of the kinds of changes involved in the composition of the population, both in purely traditional crises (despite the determining factor of bad harvests or plague) and in crises of which we have some modern experience in those vast areas that still linger at an archaic economic and social stage or are making great efforts to emerge from it, or even in areas with modern economic and social structures into which war reintroduces (together with famine and epidemics) ordeals and reactions which might have been supposed to be peculiar to other countries and other periods. In all these traditional types of crises, natural or man-made disasters, famines, epidemics and wars have such immediate or widespread effects only because they are the sequel to a comparatively ancient imbalance between resources and population, an ancient decline and an ancient poverty precipitated by them, the harvest of which they suddenly reap. But among the factors in the more recent crises in countries with a Western civilization, preceding monetary disasters, preparing the way for them and perhaps providing a partial explanation for them, there are older demographic changes—a slow ageing of the population, for example—without which these disasters would not have occurred, or would not have had such large repercussions.

II
The Problem Related to the Urban Environment

The measurement of changes in population composition is far more important, however, for the economic and social descriptions of great metropolises than for other environments, whether rural or even urban.

In the countryside and in medium-sized towns, the increase in population is usually so slow and coincides so nearly (at any rate so far as the birth and death rates are concerned) with the development of the country as a whole that it is perfectly feasible to neglect the demographic data and merely to take the occupational and economic characteristics and circumstances of production, exchange and consumption and the growth of wealth. Even here, of course, the social description should go further and is likely to be consistent and accurate only if it uses the demographic documentation. This is not true of the economic description; the quantitative data on economic structures and conditions are quite adequate for charting a population's standards of living and even, in part, its modes of life and the behavior of social groups to each other. Even political history has until recently been able to live with an almost total lack of demographic identification and measurement. It must be acknowledged that political history and economic history have frequently kept house tolerably comfortably together without ever finding it necessary, when visited by demographic history, to set up a *ménage à trois*.

But demographic estimates are a basic prerequisite for any general history of great metropolises. They are essential to the study of problems for which a new precision and new quantitative data will undoubtedly be found in the demographic documentation, and found nowhere else; essential also to political problems, because the estimate of groups, with specifics of their distribution by age, sex and provincial origin, is of such value and because it is in many respects impossible to account for political developments in a metropolis in its entirety and its districts in detail, without such estimates; and to social problems, because the demographic estimate of the various groups is equally valuable here and because here too it is just as impossible to obtain this estimate from any other source, not to mention the social significance of marriage, fertility and death rates. Demographic estimates are essential for the study of those very facts which most plainly fall within the sphere of conventional economic research, especially the study of standards of living, the figures for which hold the secret of economic and social peace or war and of upward and downward social mobility —which can be fully accounted for only by means of a prior measurement of the rate at which a population increases.

The Phenomenon in Vitro: *Experience and Theory*

The phenomenon is not so well known or so obvious, however, that it does not have to be explained. It should first be observed in its pure state, so to speak, in the metropolises, where it has the largest and most incontrovertible impact. Not in the ancient metropolises, where it must certainly have obtained (but that is a matter for another branch of history), but far more usefully in the great modern metropolises in economically backward countries, whose demographic, economic and social characteristics are so simple and archaic, despite modern accretions, that they can be observed in two ways. First, as providing a modern experience of what could have happened elsewhere at some other period; and second, as providing the equivalent, despite their differing colors and forms and despite all the differences in space and time, of a kind of theoretical model set up outside space and time, and so schematizing the influence of population increase upon the economic and social development of a population within the imaginary frame of a metropolis. It is then seen that urban expansion develops irrespective of whether the economic trend is upward or downward, and that the growth incentive is the same in either phase. This does not mean that urban increase from immigration is not the result of a particular economic situation and that adequate and satisfactory reasons for it are not to be found in that economic situation. It simply means that in studying a metropolis at least as much attention must be paid to this purely demographic fact—the rate of increase in the population —as to an economic situation, whose trend is almost always expansive and does not necessarily drive social groups upward or downward in accordance with recession or prosperity. A downward trend in the economic situation operating simultaneously on country and town promotes a population movement from the country to the metropolis because of the existence of a margin, even at periods of general recession, between rural and urban poverty, as well as the abundance of welfare and charity organizations subsidized by the cities or the authorities for the benefit of their own proletariat. Conversely, when the trend is upward, though rural prosperity is an appreciable impediment to migration to the cities and curbs the exodus, the margin between rural prosperity and an urban prosperity which is usually at a higher level maintains a flow of immigration that is hardly likely ever to dwindle, at any rate in theory, if it is agreed that people under the guidance of economic criteria always obstinately go where it is in their interest to go.

The chief consequence of this mode of growth is that the figure for such metropolises is never precisely in line with the figure to be deduced from the existing economic structures; and that, irrespective of the economic situation, part of the population remains on the margin of the economic structure. The city exercises a permanent attraction exceeding its capacity. The population is too large in periods of prosperity and even more so in periods of recession. Economic recession only partly accounts—in respect of only a part of the population—for an urban poverty perpetually maintained by an immigration promoted by slump and prosperity alike. This is a theoretical model which will be considered as applying only to the imaginary capital of an imaginary country. But it does reproduce the mechanics of the growth of the great African and Asian metropolises. Its main purpose is to present in simplified and elementary form a mechanism that operates equally, though less plainly and subject to different influences, on metropolises with a more advanced economy and civilization.

The Western Metropolises

Although the mode of population growth is less dominant and less apparent in great cities, and although it no longer takes the form of the vast concourses of nomads who camp at the gates of African and

Asian cities, is there any reason to suppose that it is not equally applicable and at least as important as economic factors proper for the economic and social description of urban or recently urbanized populations or those living on the fringes of urban civilization? Let us look, first, at the economic and demographic aspects of the growth mechanism; and secondly, at the resulting urban equilibrium from the economic and demographic points of view.

The Factors in the Growth of Metropolises

As to the mechanics of growth, a rise or fall in the economic situation is certainly an essential factor in the increase of an urban population by immigration, in addition to the individual or collective psychological factors which can never be ignored. But it is equally certain that a rise and a fall alike promote a constant migration to the metropolis, though this is less pronounced and less constant than with the great primitive cities; and it is inevitable. As Simiand has shown in the case of France in the nineteenth century,[2] the curve for migration to Paris does not coincide with the wage curve which plots the trend of migration in the country as a whole. Whereas the peaks of migration in France as a whole show up at periods of falling wages and migration slows down when wages rise, migration to Paris and the growth of Paris do not follow this pattern and seem to be subject to more complex laws. We shall investigate these laws at a later stage, only observing here that both a rise and a fall in economic movement promote a constant migration, which, though perhaps not involving the same social groups in both phases, does contribute to an urban growth varying in rate at different periods, but remaining constant overall. Recession and prosperity alike work in this direction and both operate in excess of the city's capacities. We would put it rather that recession and prosperity alike set in motion a demographic mechanism which goes beyond what would normally be expected from the recession or the prosperity. And it reaches such proportions that this demographic phenomenon, though engendered and set in motion by the economic one, now assumes an independent existence as a demographic phenomenon and operates as such, so that it need no longer be related to the economic phenomenon which engendered it.

The effect of recession is so evident that it hardly requires further comment. Slumps give rise to a population movement from the countryside and the small towns toward an urban center which enjoys the benefit of better protection and housing, private and public liquid resources that enable it to make better arrangements for its defense, and perhaps, too, stronger pressure to organize this defense in the interests of public policy. Nevertheless, by definition, since the large city is affected just as strongly by recession as the rest of the country, and though recession affects one particular group rather than another at one period rather than another, this migration develops immediately and totally in excess of what the overstrained economic structures can bear. And it moves beyond the capacity of the urban equipment and the public facilities, which are themselves unable to expand since they are compelled by the recession itself to divert progressively diminishing liquid funds to other purposes. In times of crisis this new population, engendered by the recession and composed of social groups further impoverished in proportion to its severity, becomes immediately and totally supernumerary.

Though less immediately and less totally, the comparatively recent immigrants also become an excess population in periods of prosperity. Prosperity—regardless of whether it is enjoyed simultaneously by the great city and the rest of the country or by one of them rather than the other—attracts social groups very different from those set in motion by recession. It is an immigration of conquerors—of people bent on exploiting the favorable circumstances and what resources they have in hand in order to try their luck or push it further—which moves in beside the earlier immigration of the poor and defeated, a free and voluntary immigration supplementing the former passive one. But this prosperous immigration grows in excess of what the economy can tolerate in precisely the same way as the recession-induced immigration and, for the same reason, beyond what the urban structures can bear— whether the economic structures or the urban environment in general, and every aspect of it, material and moral, housing, streets and public facilities as well as social contacts. Engendered by the economic phenomenon, the demographic phenomenon develops autonomously. It is henceforth so completely severed from the economic phenomenon and bulks so large in itself that it operates as a cause and warrants at least as much, if not more, attention than the economic phenomenon. Not only does the earlier immigration of the poor continue in periods of prosperity, although on a smaller scale relative to the total immigration, in excess of what is justified by this prosperity and in excess of what can be tolerated; but the other immigration itself—that of the victors, which is distinguished from the immigration of the defeated by a whole range of intermediate situations, some of them hard to identify—although at certain periods, at least, it may not exceed what was justified by the favorable economic situation at the start, is certain eventually to overtax the capacity of the urban environment, however much it may benefit from the general prosperity and however capable it may itself be of expansion and adjustment. We find that this immigration of bourgeois or artisans (the extent of which we shall be able to estimate from the newcomers' distribution by age and residence) not only does not prosper as a whole, but adds to the other immigration in every sphere and in every way, affecting air and water, supplies and over-crowding, central markets, street markets, streets, hospitals and drains, and even the prisons, which, prisons though they are, are nonetheless inhabited by bourgeois; and in terms of the economy, too, which does not develop at an even rate, since some sectors of it become over-burdened. Furthermore, to trace the influence of the economic situation upon the increase in the urban population at different periods, and to describe the phases of acceleration and deceleration of immigration at times of prosperity or recession, is not all that is needed. Even if the phases of recession coincide with an acceleration of immigration (an immigration of the poor) and even if the phases of prosperity coincide with a deceleration of the total immigration (a large proportion of it being accounted for by the "immigration of conquerors"), we should not overlook the fact that the numbers accumulate, irrespective of whether they were attracted by prosperity or recession. The period at which these groups were formed, the economic motive that prompted them and even their slow or rapid growth rate are hardly relevant. There they are and there they stay; and this is what counts in the present and for the future.

The Factors Making for Perpetuation

Not only are these groups immediately supernumerary, owing to the way in which they were formed and settled into the city, but they continue to be permanently supernumerary in the balance between the urban environment and the population. While the demographic phenomenon predominates over the economic in any consideration of the process of migration, this applies with even greater force to the consideration of the urban environment, that is to say, of the subject with which we are presently engaged. This population is definitively supernumerary.

It is supernumerary in periods of recession, and in many ways. In the first place, the labor market contracts because of the slump. We have only to remark here that, from the demographic point of view, the labor market usually reacts to recession as it reacts to prosperity, going in either direction further than what would be regarded as normal in the way of adjustment to the economic situation. In slump and prosperity alike the classical conjuncture analysis is inadequate, in that it takes the determinant and virtually automatic action of the economic situation for granted and holds that its effects should be precisely commensurate with the cause, as they would be in the case of a trajectory whose span or speed should be accurately calculable by measuring the motive force or initial thrust. Just as the expansion of employment in periods of prosperity exceeds the capacity for employment, so the contraction of employment in periods of recession is far greater than would be expected from measuring the recession. The excess population formed by the effects of the slump over and above the number justified by it is supplemented in periods of recession by an excess population already existing in periods of prosperity; the crisis simply gives a rather clearer idea of its size and helps to define its contours more sharply.

In great cities even periods of prosperity are marked by what might be called a demographically supernumerary population. The economic causes and characteristics of the changes in the composition of this supernumerary population certainly warrant consideration. We must not overlook the fact that the special conditions of employment, the extreme mobility of demand, and the perpetual changes in manufacturing processes in the great modern metropolises in the most advanced countries leave by the wayside quite large groups of workers who are unable to adjust: and not always the oldest, least skilled or least industrious workers; a temporary defeat for some—but their number mounts up; a final defeat for others, pregnant with the sort of total failure we shall discuss in due course.

These groups are demographically supernumerary in that their demographic characteristics are the main reason for their inability to adapt to the internal economic mobility of great cities. Age is one of the worst handicaps, primarily the ageing which drives the workers destroyed by urban life and no longer welcome in the close-knit urban family to pack into hospital and garret on the fringes of the city and its work and families. It is a fact, too, that the physical and occupational effects of this ageing become manifest in the city far earlier than in any other environment. It is all very well for a young worker in the Paris of

today to indulge his whims and change bosses every month; but he had
best settle down well before thirty into the job, good or bad, which he
has been lucky enough to find. The effects of ageing showed up far
earlier in the inhuman Paris we are describing. We have to look at
family circumstances, too, the few or many children who made for or
against success, the happiness or misery of a couple—the pale urban
happiness, precarious and threatened from all sides. But it was primarily
because of the total number of individuals that this popuation was demographically supernumerary, irrespective of age or civil status, on the
well-founded assumption that this total summed up the whole. Even
in periods of prosperity the part of the population which might be regarded as integrated in the urban economy and as enjoying advantages
in the general economy of the urban environment suffered from drawbacks in some of its subdivisions, such as housing, urban facilities and
sanitation. It is even possible that in some respects the dominance of
these groups which enjoyed certain advantages tended to limit the
privileges of other groups and to lower their standards of living.

III
From Theory to History

Thus the rate of population growth in great cities provides at least
as good an account of that population's living conditions as the economic situation, even if seen from the economic point of view alone.

The demographic phenomenon can be ranked on a level with the
economic situation as a causative factor. But to account for developments in the standards of living of urban populations we have to do
more than observe the curves charting the development of an economy.
We must also study its growth rate, in order to find out how far it
corresponds with observed economic progress and what proportion of
the population is involved.

The Phases of Adjustment

Even if in highly developed countries the greater part of a demographically expanding population shares in a movement at periods of
advanced development and adjusts itself closely to them, the fact
remains that the rate of population growth is also a factor in other
aspects of city life relating to other details of administration. In the
history of Paris during the few decades of the nineteenth and twentieth
centuries in which the growth of the population was concomitant with

economic expansion, just as in the modern American cities, the adjustment of the population to the economic situation cannot obscure the fact that newcomers found it hard to adjust to certain other conditions of urban life. And these conditions, though not economic, still warrant examination as equally important phenomena in the history of cities— social conditions which nevertheless themselves have economic aspects in the consequential difficulties of employment and living and in the burdens they impose on municipal budgets.

The Phases of Nonadjustment

This applies with even greater force to phases in which the changes in population composition are more rapid, in which the imbalance of the sexes is more pronounced and changes more frequently, in which the incidence of the death rate is heavier and more unjust and the illegitimacy rate higher, and in which these major demographic facts are accompanied by an impressive train of minor demographic events such as infanticide and suicide and a very high crime rate.

The fact that the description of these phases is not confined within narrow chronological limits as it would be in modern research, but covers long stretches of time, seeks the manifold correlations between phenomena, and records similarities and differences, rises and falls, makes it even more significant.

It is easy to see in Paris that, proportionately to the population, the death, illegitimacy and crime rates rose to a peak in periods of rapid population increase, due to an influx of migrants, even if the economic situation was favorable; but slackened off in the intermediate periods, when the proportionate increase declined, even if economic factors (in periods of recession and prosperity alike) did not have an incontrovertible influence. But, as we demonstrated earlier, this influence was not so great as that of an excess of population, which, even in periods of prosperity, far exceeded the housing, employment and general capacities of the urban environment, such as houses and streets, hospitals and prisons, water supply and drainage, the very purity of the air, the volume of silence or noise, or even the relations (harder to perceive) established at all hours and places between a very large number of people, the collective fever that rose from the crowd.

Thus there were successive periods in Paris, almost all of which shared a common characteristic, in that a phase of expanding population, expanding economy and prosperity was followed by a phase of recession marked by social, political and, in some cases, biological disturbances. It was as if the development of Paris was constantly exceeding some of its economic and social capacities and must ineluctably exceed them, upset a certain equilibrium or fail to create conditions for a new equilibrium soon enough before a world crisis, a domestic crisis or some disaster precipitated a breakdown already potentially in existence.

The Paris of the Popular Front: The influence of the acceleration in growth and change in composition of large sectors of the Paris population during the years following the First World War upon a social development where political and economic description, abundant and detailed though it is, does not wholly account for the fact that it was truly revolutionary (far more revolutionary than has been thought, and revolutionary in a different way) is particularly striking. This was the Paris of the depression and the Popular Front, transformed economically and occupationally by the heavy iron, steel and chemical industries of the banlieue, which welded the capital tighter and tighter to the European economy and the world economy as a whole, making it more powerful but also more fragile; and transformed especially by an immigration which had for some years reverted to its earlier style, attracting new ethnic groups not only from France but from other countries as well.

The end of the nineteenth century: The history of Paris from the last years of the nineteenth century to the years immediately preceding the First World War was more disturbed, however, and certainly more somber. Jules Romains and Martin du Gard have left an unforgettable large-scale portrait of those years, but our statistical investigations reveal, behind the economic, social and political appearances, unappreciated yet potent demographic facts. This was the Paris of 1914, the sultry summer of 1914 described at the end of *Les Thibault*, racked with nationalist and revolutionary passions clashing and mingling in all the great centers of collective life, and especially in the heart of the city and on the Grands Boulevards crowded with demonstrators, swept by thunderstorms, not far from the rue du Croissant, where Jaurès was felled. It must not be forgotten, however, that the population as a whole, with all the variety of its occupations and standards of living, the population of this feverish and tragic Paris was no longer that of the Paris which had grown up in the course of the nineteenth century owing to the exceptional circumstances we shall discuss later.

Rather, it was a Paris whose growth rate had become more and more rapid, reaching its climax between 1872 and 1881, but maintaining up to the war some of the highest proportionate increases in its history, except for the first half of the nineteenth century; a Paris augmented by an immigration in which every region in France, however distant, increasingly participated, so that the physical type of the Parisian was no longer the same. It was a Paris in which the occupational and social distribution had changed and had in certain respects been simplified, a Paris surrounded by factories and enveloped in fumes which corroded its buildings and dramatized its skies, a Paris upon which a proletarian banlieue, drawing closer and closer and spreading further and further, acted to exert a manifold influence. But it was a Paris, too, in which— coincident with social conflicts and violences of every kind—there was an increase in the demographic events which reflected the city's malaise, such as illegitimate births, infant mortality, and infanticide; and a free- dom and anarchy of sexual relationships which could be found in the statistical data even if we could not (as we can) observe the preoccu- pation of the literary documentation with such topics as venereal diseases and the curious terror caused by them, and crime, bulking so large in the facts and in opinion that Tarde had no hesitation in basing part of his social description on their measurement. We cannot fail to perceive in all this, together with the unfavorable economic and political circumstances, "this rising tide of danger," the consequence of an immi- gration too rapid and too large for the economic and material capacities of the urban environment.

This period was the more somber and the more disturbed in that it followed on that of the Second Empire and the beginnings of the Third Republic, when a less abrupt and more regular demographic development adjusted more easily to an urban environment which, from the economic point of view and that of the physical setting, was in full spate of transformation and even at times ahead of population pressure. The disease, death and crime rates were lower then, and quantitative demographic history cannot recognize the relatively tranquil, prosperous and relaxed climate of the Second Empire in the somber and vengeful description conceived by Zola after the event.

Actually, the Second Empire merely remedied—whether intentionally or by chance, by executive fiat or simply by taking advantage of favor- able economic circumstances—the unhealthy state of the Paris of the first half of the nineteenth century, whose main characteristics we have already reconnoitered, but only from outside; and whose causes were noted by contemporary witnesses, namely, the increase in the population, to which we return at last after this long detour, for we now have a better understanding of its operation and consequences.

The Ancien Régime

Before embarking upon this period, however, we must refer to the more distant past. The increase and the change in the population in the first half of the nineteenth century followed centuries of slow growth and—at some periods—stagnation. Their effects were the more remarkable in that they concerned an ancient city, a bourgeois city, in which a native demographic and economic development had for centuries implanted social, family and moral structures, a hierarchy of values and relationships of mutual dependence and respect, the alterations in which were merely apparent, or so gradual that what strikes us most is their continuity rather than their change.

CHAPTER TWO

The Population: From Stagnation to Increase

I
The Ancien Régime

We shall have little to say of the stagnation of the population in earlier periods, for this is only relevant insofar as it bears upon the new increase in the population with which we are concerned. The history of the Paris population under the Ancien Régime has no place in this book. The history of a population in any period, but especially pre-statistical periods, can only be attempted with any likelihood of success by specialists in those periods, even though they may not be demographers.

It so happens, however, that demographic research provides specialists in the seventeenth and eighteenth centuries with certain fairly precise data which take the political and economic history further, so that they become relevant to the history of societies; not a picturesque and literary type of history, but the total, homogeneous and numerate history for which demographic research, for the first time, supplies a first-rate tool. A use of the older demographic documentation and the new demographic techniques, as well as a knowledge of societies at a stage of development today comparable to that of Paris under the Ancien Régime, make it possible to draw some reasonably likely conclusions about the rate of increase in the Paris population prior to the nineteenth century and about the original characteristics of economic and social conditions in the Paris of that period. The demographic approach gives some guidance to the economic, social and even moral description. It enables us to use the qualitative documentation in a new way, wherein any descriptions which tally with previously recognized and measured economic and demographic facts will be retained and considered as likely to be accurate. What this amounts to is merely a statistical framework, with a margin of uncertainty which cannot of course be neglected but is not so wide as it is in the traditional, and conflicting, estimates of the Paris population by contemporaries, who put it indiscriminately at 500,000, 800,000 and sometimes even higher,[1] depending on national arrogance, pride or hate.

Techniques for Estimating

There are two sorts of operation for obtaining an estimate of population in general and the Paris population in particular; or rather, two methods of estimating coincide, namely, the census and the procedure of relating population to other demographic facts such as the birth rate, the death rate and even the marriage rate.

1. *The census*: The technique of numbering people, which writers like Bodin and Montchrestien described as modeled on the principle of the Roman census, is as old as man and is the more usual method. An attribute of power, whose military, fiscal, police and even moral interests it expresses, it entails an encroachment upon both the public and the private domain. For ages it was a terror to the people concerned, as we have already seen.

In the many attempts to take a census in Paris under the Ancien Régime one contrast stands out, the fact that while those in the early decades of the seventeenth century provide useful material, those at the end of that century and in the eighteenth, although more spectacular, reach conclusions suspect to their most enlightened contemporaries and even more so, of course, to us.

The former—without going as far back as the beginning of the Absolute Monarchy—were strictly utilitarian, whether military or fiscal, taken for the sole purpose of making it easier to raise supplies. Ordered by a monarchy in the flower of youth, they readily obtained the cooperation of a bourgeoisie which was itself interested in the results. They show no trace of the political polemics which distorted the later censuses.

This is true of the "Enumeration of the population of Paris and the state of annual consumption carried out by order of Cardinal Richelieu by the Commissioners appointed in the year 1637," according to which Paris had 20,000 to 30,000 houses and 412,000 to 415,000 inhabitants. Though the survey of 1663–65 was incomplete, the census of 1684, conducted with much care and accuracy, is well worth our attention. This put the population of Paris at between 400,000 and 450,000.

On the other hand, from the end of the seventeenth century onward the censuses, undertaken in less favorable political and administrative circumstances, were subject to conflicting political trends, like the 1695 census, which was carried out only in some parishes. The Intendants' survey, which estimated the Paris population at 720,000, was equally unsatisfactory and was criticized by Vauban: "I cannot conceive that Paris is so densely populated as is made out." The 1762 census, which brought in a total of 600,000, was equally unsatisfactory. Such great differences within such a short space of time show that something went wrong with the procedure as the result of a looser control over the census-taking, but also of the existence of another more refined and attractive technique which the experts tended to prefer.

2. *Estimates derived from births and deaths*: Two circumstances had induced contemporary statisticians to conceive and desire a method of estimating other than the census: the publication, ordered by Colbert, of monthly returns of baptisms, marriages and deaths, parish by parish; and the sudden alarm summed up by Messance in his *Nouvelles recherches sur la population de la France*: "The book *L'ami des hommes* appeared in 1756 and almost everyone believed in the depopulation of France simply because the author announced it."

It was thought that it would be possible with the help of the registrar's returns to check the accuracy of the facts, using a procedure first perfected by Messance and very frequently employed thereafter, summed up well by Necker: "It was not possible to take a general census of so large a country; it was even less feasible to repeat it every year. But after partial censuses were ordered at various places, the result was compared with the number of births, deaths and marriages; and these relations, confirmed to some extent by the experience of other countries, established a standard of comparison which may be considered to be reasonably reliable." If the choice of this relation posed great problems with respect to the regions of France, the problem with respect to Paris was even greater. "The population of Paris is hard to determine by ordinary computation," wrote Necker,

since of a total of 20,500 or 20,000 births yearly about one-quarter is made up of foundlings born in Paris; and a generation of this kind, a terrifying proportion of which dies very young, does not provide an accurate basis for a survey of the population. A large number of foreigners and provincials, too, come to Paris for pleasure or on business. . . . The ratio of the number of births to that of the inhabitants is 1 to 23, and 1 to 24 in places where nature is unkind. In the greater part of France it is 25, 25½ or 26. In the towns, depending on their trade and size, each birth corresponds to 27, 28, 29 or even 30 inhabitants, and even more in the capital.

The Estimates

These statistical enterprises—censuses and the search for a relation to births and deaths—would themselves warrant a lengthy analysis if we were proposing to study Paris in the seventeenth and eighteenth centuries. As we are only concerned with observing the contrast between the city's rates of growth under the Ancien Régime and in the nineteenth century, however, we may confine ourselves to describing the trends without going on to attempt precise estimates.

Firstly, whatever method of evaluation or whatever coefficient we take, the growth of the Paris population in the seventeenth and eighteenth centuries seems to have been slow and slight. Such is the conclusion to be drawn from all the statistical research of the period, used, summarized and blended by Buffon:

> More children are sent out to nurse in the country from Paris than from London, and as fewer move to London than to Paris, fewer also die at between two and five years of age and even between five and ten and ten and twenty. But between twenty and sixty the number of deaths in London greatly exceeds that in Paris, particularly between twenty and forty. This shows that a very large number of adults go to London from the provinces and that the city's own fertility is not sufficient to maintain its population without large additions from outside. This is confirmed by comparing the birth certificates with the death certificates. In the nine years from 1728 to 1736, there were 154,957 baptisms and 239,327 deaths in London. Hence London needs to supplement the number of its births by more than half in order to maintain itself, whereas Paris is self-sufficient to about one-seventy-fifth.[2]

A basic text, which would not, however, exempt us from making more precise estimates if we intended to trace the history of Old Paris; but it does mark the contrast between the eighteenth and the nineteenth centuries well enough to meet our needs. Before the first decades of the nineteenth century, Paris maintained its level and grew far more by the balance between its births and deaths than by immigration; from within rather than from without. From Buffon we gain a better insight into the many descriptions of the capital, in which there is no trace whatever of the preoccupation with immigration and the uneasiness that were to mark most of the later descriptions. Deparcieux, it is true, wrote that "cities grow only by what comes in from the country," and Messance: "Male deaths exceed female by one-sixth. Hence it appears that there are more males than females in Paris, the reason being the large number of male foreigners who come to Paris to engage in professions and trades or to work as domestic servants, besides the officers and officials daily drawn to Paris from the provinces."[3] This is purely a demographer's viewpoint, his work being complicated by this floating population. Messance himself added later:

It has been said that the towns depopulate the countryside, and been said by the most authoritative writers. I shall not follow them in their reasoning. The population of the country and the small towns in northern France is larger than in central and southern France because there are more towns in the north of France. And until it has been demonstrated that northern France owes its large population to some other cause, the larger number of towns there, which account for a larger number of consumers, may be regarded as one of the principal causes, if not the sole cause; and, in that case, the towns would populate the country, which is just the reverse of what has been said.

The Intendants' survey did not even mention the capital's attraction as one of the causes of the decline in the population of France as a whole. The marquis de Mirabeau himself, so eager to decry the large towns, considered that Paris was ruining France economically by its luxury and waste, but not demographically. As to the literature, it treats the subject as a jest. Thus, Voltaire wrote:

> *Le fils de mon valet, en ma ferme élevé*
> *A d'utiles travaux qui me fut enlevé,*
> *Des laquais de Paris s'en va grossir l'armée.*[4]

The second point to note is that not only did Paris grow slowly, but most of the authors of works on statistical research, whatever the results of their calculations, considered that the population was probably smaller than their own estimates.

Epilly alone, whose estimates are on the high side, saw no contradiction between his figures and the Paris setting:

There are various opinions; some estimate the population at 1 million, others at 700,000 to 800,000: on the basis of the 1694 census we had always supposed that it was 720,000. But, in accordance with the procedure we shall use, we are compelled to recognize that the population is not so large. . . . It is not that it formerly was larger and has fallen in the last seventy years. We believe, on the contrary, that it is now greater, the city having been enlarged since then and none of the new districts having been populated at the expense of the old.

On the other hand, Messance stated:

The many new buildings north of the boulevard from the porte Saint-Antoine to the porte Saint-Honoré, at the Palais-Royal and at the Quinze-Vingts have increased the number of houses and mansions proportionately far more than the increase in the population, so that, if there are no empty houses, this means that people have more accommodation than they had formerly.

Similarly, Buffon wrote:

This table seems to show that the population does not grow as fast as one might suppose from the extent of the buildings prolonging the faubourgs. If we take the first ten and the last ten years of the forty-six from 1721 to 1766, we find 181,590 births in the first ten and 186,813 births in the last ten, the difference, 5,223, amounting only to 1/36th. But Paris has grown in area since 1721 by more than 1/18th. Half this increase must be put down to greater accommodation.

And Moheau:

One of the cities in the kingdom in which growth is most probable is the capital. We shall not seek to prove this by the prodigious increase in the number of houses, because the same buildings today contain fewer people than they formerly did; but, apart from dwellings, it is obvious that there is an annual and appreciable increase in the number of the city's inhabitants. It has been observed, however, that the number of births and the consumption of bread and meat have remained practically the same for the past twenty or thirty years; and the last ten years, as compared with the previous ten years, subtracting wartime, give almost the same figure for production and losses and almost the same number of marriages. It is true that in the last period the absence of the Parlement left a considerable void in the city, and the proof is to be found in the fewer births in 1771, 1772 and 1773. But the most cogent reason is that for some time past the inhabitants of Paris have acquired a taste for the country, and these absences explain why consumption and the number of births and deaths are not increasing, though probably more people than ever before are domiciled in the city.[5]

II
The Revolutionary Period

Just as we had no intention of studying the growth of the Paris population under the Ancien Régime, so we cannot embark here upon a demographic description of Paris under the Revolution, since that is a matter for the specialist in the history of the Revolution—who is far better equipped than we are to interpret the statistics—and also since we are not dealing at this stage in our discussion with demographic factors such as changes in the distribution of the population by age, sex and origin, but only with the rate of population increase. The history of the Revolution is, however, more noteworthy in the general history of Paris for such changes than for the increase in the population. The population underwent profound changes, but did not become larger; it probably even declined at times. This seems to be the probable inference from the successive censuses, allowing for the exaggerations of the 1793 census:

1789	524,186
1793	640,504
1795	551,347.

It becomes very clear if we compare the Revolutionary censuses with a later census known to have been carefully taken, that of 1801, which gave the population as 547,756.

With respect simply to the size of the population, the history of the Revolution blends with previous history. The age-old stagnation continued until developments in the first decades of the nineteenth century interrupted it abruptly. This long, slow development over centuries makes it easier to measure the ensuing acceleration of the increase in population.

III
The First Half of the Nineteenth Century

After the centuries of slow growth, the first half of the nineteenth century brought a tremendous increase in population. This fact is noteworthy in relation both to the past and the future. The Paris population never rose in similar proportion in the ensuing period, except in 1856. It is a definite fact that a new Paris came into being between 1800 and 1850. The later additions were large, but merely supplémented the numbers which accumulated mainly during this perod; the effects lasted—as can easily be deduced from the age pyramids—until quite recently.

Since we have studied the growth of the Paris population during this period in a previous book, we shall merely summarize here the main conclusions drawn from our earlier research and note what is most relevant to the present study, the proportionate extent of this increase and its autonomy relative to contemporary political and economic facts; that is, the leading part played by demographic fact, a point which we had not fully appreciated hitherto.

The Rate of Population Increase

Our point of departure must be the statistical table overpage with, first, the official figures and, second, the corrections to be made to them.

2. *The corrected figures:* A closer study of the categories of population enumerated makes it necessary to correct the results of the 1836 census and the percentage increase commonly reproduced, both as we ourselves had copied them in our earlier study of Paris and in the

1. *The official figures*

Year of census	City of Paris						Arrondissements of Saint-Denis and Sceaux		Department of the Seine	
	Districts within the limits prior to consolidation in 1860		Communes of petite banlieue annexed in 1860		Total population of the city of Paris and former petite banlieue					
	Census results	Increase (%)	Census results	Increase (%)	Census results	Increase (%)	Census results	Increase (%)	Census results	Increase (%)
1801	546,856									
1811	622,636	13.88								
1817	713,966	14.67								
1831	785,866	10.07	75,574		861,436					
1836	899,313	14.44	103,320	36.71	1,002,633	16.39				
1841	936,261	4.1	124,564	20.56	1,059,825	5.70	259,342		1,194,603	
1846	1,053,897	12.56	173,083	38.95	1,226,980	15.77	310,570	19.75	1,364,467	14.22
1851	1,053,261	0.06	223,802	29.30	1,277,064	4.08	368,803	18.75	1,422,065	4.2
1856	1,174,346	11.50	364,257	62.75	1,538,613	20.48			1,727,419	21.47
1861					1,696,141	10.24	257,519		1,953,660	13.10
1866					1,825,274	7.61	325,642	26.45	2,150,916	10.10
1872					1,851,792	1.45	368,268	13.09	2,220,060	3.2
1876					1,988,800	7.40	422,043	14.60	2,410,849	8.59
1881					2,269,023	14.09	530,306	25.65	2,799,329	16.11
1886					2,344,550	3.33	626,539	16.24	2,961,089	5.78
1891					2,477,957	4.86	693,638		3,141,595	6.10
1896					2,536,834	3.63	803,680		3,340,514	6.33
1901					2,714,068	6.99	955,862		3,669,930	9.86

foregoing table. There were 866,438 inhabitants (not 899,313) and a percentage increase of 10.25 (not 14.44). The following table for the absolute and percentage increases in the Paris population should be substituted for the foregoing official table:

		%
1801	547,756	–
1807	580,609:	5.66
1817	713,966:	22.97
1831	785,862:	10.07
1836	866,438:	10.25
1841	936,261:	8.06
1846	1,053,897:	12.56
1851	1,053,261:	– 0.06

Population Increase and Events

The extent, consistency and drive of this population explosion will appear more clearly if we try to analyze the percentages in relation to each other and to date them, that is, to interpret them in the light of contemporary events.

Let us first make clear the limitations of this commentary. Obviously, the percentage increases that can be established merely by looking at the census results presuppose the occurrence of phases. But it is not possible by means of the statistics alone accurately to date the beginning and end of the movements deduced from them, since they spread over the whole period between two successive censuses. The dating that is of historical relevance will in some cases be suggested by specific economic, political or biological circumstances of a certain magnitude—major public works, revolutions, wars and epidemics—which may have had some effect in attracting or repelling labor and may also have acted on the natural population movement by increasing the birth rate or, more often, the death rate. Nevertheless, it would be rash to comment forthwith on the proportionate increases that emerge from the censuses by reference to events of this kind, or rather to establish any close causal relationship between proportionate increases and events.

A few comments can, however, be made forthwith. The increases were extremely large from the beginning of the nineteenth century to the census of 1836; indeed, if they are brought into the same chronological framework, they become larger and larger. The increase was very great during the Empire in spite of the wars, though we cannot date the exact moment of increase from the statistics alone. Peace had reigned for two years and many Frenchmen had come or returned to Paris when the 1817 census was taken. The increase seems to have slowed down between 1817 and 1831, but actually it remained very high and the slowdown was more apparent than real. "It is probable," the editor of the 1841 census wrote, "that if the census had been taken in 1830 before the July Revolution, it would have produced a different result. In 1831 many circumstances had induced a large number of the inhabitants to leave Paris and had deterred many others from going there." The percentage increase between 1831 and 1836 was 10.25, despite generally unfavorable circumstances, despite the outbreak of cholera in 1832, despite the Revolutionary upheavals in the early years of the July Monarchy and despite the combination of biological and political circumstances in a general convulsion reflected in Part IV of *Les Misérables* in the epic of the rue Saint-Denis. The expansion nevertheless continued, as if its causes were so constant and compelling that obstacles were of little account and the fear of the cholera itself was less effectual than the fear of political perils. This is no doubt accounted for by the memories left by the Great Revolution, but also by the fact that it was futile to try to escape an epidemic which affected town and country alike. It is interesting that the commentator on the 1851 census, which for the first time recorded a fall in the population of Paris, attributed this partly to a recurrence of the cholera, but even more to political circumstances. Thus it was stated in Volume VI of the *Recherches statistiques*:

A new fact in the annals of our statistics appeared in 1851: the figure for the Paris population fell. This result should occasion no surprise if it is related to the circumstances accompanying and following the events of 1848. The immense void which then occurred in all classes of society had not been filled by 1851.

The Consequences of the Population Increase as Such

From these two points of view—the numbers themselves and their speed of increase—the demographic fact emerges as so important and decisive that it would in the last resort fully warrant us in seeking for or even reconstructing the economic, social and moral consequences directly without reference to the events, simply from a glance at the figures.

In many respects, indeed, these figures suffice or in themselves provide incontrovertible evidence. In the course of this period Paris became a tremendous concourse of human beings, and many situations, material and other, can be inferred from the mere fact that especially in Paris hundreds of thousands of people had to live together. All the differences between Paris and other towns and between the nineteenth-century capital and the capital of the Ancien Régime—in which fewer people lived, linked in an entirely different way by closer, more frequent and more widely recognized and accepted interrelationships, in a social environment more homogeneous in origin and more limited in dimensions —are expressed and assembled in these figures. Without going further in our quantitative research and without, moreover, seeking to verify and draw conclusions, it would be perfectly legitimate to assume that the most original characteristics of Parisian civilization are summed up in the following figures: Paris had between 400,000 and 450,000 inhabitants in the seventeenth century, between 525,000 and 550,000 on the eve of the Revolution, over 700,000 immediately after the Empire and more than a million in mid-century. A scrutiny of the census results is like a traveler's discovery of this huge concourse of human beings. The figures and the image have one and the same social significance. There is no reason whatever why the one should not reveal the same consequences as the other and why the statistician should be blinder or less venturesome than a newcomer to the city like Balabine, when he recounts in his *Journal* his discovery of "monstrous Paris" and deduces simply from the spectacle of the crowd a voracious and violent way of living which could only be how the crowd in fact behaved; there was no need to go and verify it on the spot. The evidence of the figures is much the same; the very size of a society may suffice to account for its characteristics.

Not only had the population vastly increased in the space of a few years, but the increase had occurred in an old city which had not changed at the same rate; which, indeed, had been unable to do so. The city had twice as many inhabitants in 1851 as in 1801. Even if we knew nothing of the history of Paris during the period, even if we had not already listened to this vast hubbub in the literary documents, even if we decided to continue acting like a blind and deaf theoretician, we should be able to decide that an increase of this magnitude—by its mass alone, leaving aside the ethnic changes necessarily involved—must inevitably have come up against intractable problems. All the more so if we now go on to examine the material setting in which this increase occurred.

CHAPTER THREE

The Population and the City: Housing

The city which concerns us here is the city of stones, what Mercier called "the physical mass of Paris,"[1] that is, the buildings, too few of which were erected; and the facilities, that is, the streets, drains, water supply, schools, hospitals, cemeteries and even the cesspools and butchers' yards, which did not grow at the same rate as the population— in short, the material setting, which was no longer commensurate with the number of inhabitants.

The material setting must, of course, be understood as including the setting of labor, not so much the actual factories, workshops and work sites—the study of which merges with that of the buildings and facilities —as employment itself, the development of which must be discussed if we are to find out whether it was commensurate with the supply of labor. Human overcrowding is not so vital a matter if its ill effects are offset by jobs in plenty, as in the great modern cities, in which high wages often coexist with slums. In the Paris of the first half of the nineteenth century, however, the economic situation was not capable of providing any appreciable correctives for a state of affairs which, it is evident simply from a theoretical analysis of the population and resources, must inevitably have been difficult and was bound to become even more so as the population increased. Irrespective of purely economic circumstances such as the level of employment and wages, we shall find that the disparity between the increase in population and the rigidity of the urban setting in itself indicated a social condition fraught with problems.

I
The Housing

Building in Paris in the first half of the nineteenth century did not increase at the same rate as the population. Of this very broad subject, which has a bearing upon the history of capital in Paris, upon the history of daily life and upon the history of architecture, we shall discuss and summarize here only what is relevant to this study; in the first place, housing.

The Restoration

The Restoration was plainly a great period of building in Paris. A number of facts testify to this, such as the importation of building materials, the large immigration of masons, the speculations described by Balzac and his contemporaries, the building fever and the mania for construction mentioned by Montigny in 1825 in his *Provincial à Paris*, various statistics, in particular those for building permits,[2] and the building crisis in the last years of the Restoration, which led contemporaries to wonder whether there had not been some over-building.

As a matter of fact, the statistical investigations carried out precisely because of the crisis produced an entirely different conclusion. "In 1817 the number of dwellings, including lodging houses, was 27,493; in 1827 it was 30,000. The population increased by 25% during these ten years, the number of dwellings by 10%. It is obvious, therefore, that too many dwellings were not built." Such was Daubenton's conclusion. He noted that the population was far more cramped in 1826 than in 1804 or 1817 and that building had been very unevenly distributed.[3] In the affluent districts it exceeded the population's requirements. In the Ist arrondissement, for example, there were 52,421 persons and 1,984 dwellings in 1817, or 26.42 persons per dwelling. In 1820 there were 72,101 inhabitants, or 19,630 more; "as to dwellings, 509 have been built since 1817, which, at the rate of 40 persons per dwelling, provides accommodation for 21,160 persons; as the population has increased by only 19,680, it may be said that too many houses were built." In the IInd arrondissement, too, "new building has exceeded the population's requirements. Similarly, in the Xth arrondissement there is accommodation for 15,240 persons and, since the population has grown only by 9,490, the requirements have been exceeded."

On the outskirts of the old city there grew up a new aristocratic and bourgeois city, in which the inhabitants had plenty of elbow room. It was the region of the building sites vaunted by contemporary authors, such as Montigny, who wrote of

. . . the new Athens and what is being built on the Champs-Elysées and the new quartier Poissonnière; and Tivoli, the magnificent and delightful Tivoli, will soon be undergoing a similar transformation. This building mania is attributed to the present scarcity of openings for capital and to our cheese-paring treatment of foreigners. The mania may also have its source in a prodigious desire for luxury and the conveniences of living. People are no longer satisfied with their fathers' modest dwelling. Everyone in Paris wants a full set of chambers. Except for a few streets whose inhabitants are wholly devoted to trade and are not yet thinking of retiring for good, we now find delightful, large and spacious houses in every district of the capital, and any house in the Marais; the Marais, which is still cited out of habit as far behind the other districts, could compete on favorable terms with the most splendid mansion on the Chausée d'Antin. The rage for building has risen to such heights that there will soon be no gardens to be seen. Paris will shortly be nothing but an immense pile of stones. The most notable new buildings are those in the rue de Rivoli, rue de Castiglione and rue de la Paix. The new quartier Poissonnière (between the faubourg Poissonnière and the faubourg Saint-Denis) and the private mansions being erected between the faubourg Saint-Martin and the faubourg du Temple are noteworthy.

The situation was different in the old districts. "In the IInd arrondissement," wrote Daubenton,

the ratio between the number of dwellings and the number of inhabitants was undesirable as early as 1817, that is 42,932 persons to 1,435 dwellings, or 32 persons per dwelling; in 1826, 54,167 persons, an increase of 9,235, and 114 new dwellings with capacity for 4,500 persons. Similarly, in the IVth arrondissement, the smallest in Paris, lacking squares and public walks, the streets have increased many times over since 1817, but they are narrow, winding and dirty. No new avenue has been or could be opened, for there is no space free; only 63 new dwellings have been built since 1817, or 6 yearly; 26 buildings have had several storeys added, making the equivalent of 9 new dwellings. Taking demolitions (for the big market) into account, there were 43 new dwellings, with capacity for 1,720 persons. But the population has risen by 5,169 persons. Accommodation therefore is far more cramped than it was in 1817.

The July Monarchy

The affluent districts continued to grow during the July Monarchy, notably the quartier Poissonnière and the quartier des Champs-Elysées. Immediately after the cholera epidemic there was some demolition in the old districts. In Old Paris the characteristic of the régime's administrative activity was the revision of all the building lines planned under the Directory and the Empire because of the traffic and the growing number of carriages.[4] There were few new thoroughfares, some thirty between 1833 and 1847, the chief being the rue Rambuteau.

In fact, this policy of destruction and construction worsened the housing conditions of the poorest classes. The main demolitions were in the districts in which they lived, such as those for the opening of the rue Rambuteau in 1838, for clearing the approaches to the Hôtel-de-Ville after 1836 and for planning the Cité after 1833. In theory this was to relieve congestion in the center for the benefit of the new districts. "It would, in our opinion, be wrong to find fault with the building of the new districts which are rising on the outskirts of the capital," the *Journal des Débats* stated.

By attracting people there they will rid the center of excess population and then there will be an opportunity to open up in the old districts the communications and enlargements demanded by public health. The trend towards the outskirts is already apparent. Trade has been concentrated too long in a few streets but is now following the trend; people are beginning to leave the Palais-Royal itself, brilliant meeting place of every manufacture and every pleasure, for the boulevards.

But the people moving into the new districts were not the working population. No one cared what the working class was doing and what was to become of it. "The population of Paris, formerly crowded in the center of the city, tends to move to the outskirts," the writer presenting the results of the 1846 census noted in Volume VI of the *Recherches sur la Ville de Paris*. "The population of Old Paris will later be accommodated in healthier conditions as the result of rebuilding, but it will hardly be able to increase"; an optimistic remark, to which the census results gave the lie.

II
The Inhabitants

The censuses revealed the crowding in those districts customarily inhabited by the laboring-class population in the figures for the increase in numbers and the increase in densities alike.

The Population in Numbers

To observe the population increase by arrondissement and district in absolute figures is not satisfactory, because the highest percentages are to be found in the districts which had previously been least populated, the new districts where, by definition, housing grew at the same rate as the population, or was considerably ahead of it. Nevertheless, the charts showing the percentage population increases from census to census stress the continuous overcrowding in the oldest districts themselves and the persistence of old modes of settlement.

The percentage population increases in 1817 as compared with 1801: Between the censuses of 1801 and 1817, and unlike what is to be seen in the later censuses, the very appreciable population increase occurred throughout the city, except in the XIth arrondissement. It is already plain, however, that the Right Bank was being more densely populated than the Left. On the Right Bank itself the arrondissements which had previously been the most densely populated were those with the largest accretions; first, the VIIth (Arcis, Mont-de-Piété, Sainte-Avoye, Marché Saint-Jean) with 48%; then, with 40%, the IXth, the distribution of its inhabitants in 1817 being:

> 12,561: quartier de l'Hôtel-de-Ville
> 11,554: quartier de la Cité
> 10,908: quartier de l'Arsenal
> 5,691: Ile Saint-Louis.

Second came the IInd arrondissement with 44.5%. Thirdly, we should stress the high percentage increase in the VIIIth arrondissement, namely, 36.5%, distributed as follows:

Quinze-Vingts	53.57
faubourg Saint-Antoine	51.63
Popincourt	33.13
Marais	18.57.

1831 as compared with 1817:   Between 1817 and 1831 the percentage increases were not so high as they had been previously. The distribution over the city as a whole, too, was less uniform; the contrast between Right and Left Bank, already evident in the preceding analysis, sharpened. The increase occurred almost entirely on the Right Bank and the decrease on the Left. On the Right, the population of the old arrondissements in the center remained almost stationary, and the IVth, containing Les Halles, fell, whereas the peripheral arrondissements continued to grow, though not so much as in the past. Too much significance should not, however, be accorded to the decrease in the IXth and VIIth arrondissements. The census was held in 1831 and bears the traces of a period of troubles. It is probable that part of the migrant lower-class population which had been counted in 1817 was not counted in 1831. The districts with a decrease are those like the Cité and the Hôtel-de-Ville, usually inhabited seasonally by masons. The movement of this type of labor is quite different from that observed in the VIIIth arrondissement. The VIIIth arrondissement grew by 17.7%. The distribution by district was:

District	1817	1831	%
Quinze-Vingts	18,254	16,607	− 9.02
faubourg Saint-Antoine	11,051	19,123	+73.04
Popincourt	14,178	18,828	+32.79
Marais	18,353	18,242	− 0.60

It is noteworthy that the increase in the faubourg Saint-Antoine continued despite economic and political circumstances which led to a decrease in districts inhabited by other categories of the working class.

1836 as compared with 1831: Between 1831 and 1836 we observe the general distribution of a population increase of less than 20% overall, a lag on the Left Bank once again, and comparatively slight differences between the arrondissements on the Right Bank. The consistency of the figures for the arrondissements in the center, in spite of unfavorable circumstances, notably the cholera epidemic, is remarkable. The VIIth arrondissement increased by 11%; but it contained streets sorely ravaged by cholera, in particular the rue de la Cour du Maure, the rue du Renard and the rue Brise-Miche in the quartier Sainte-Avoye. The same is true of the IXth arrondissement and the quartier de l'Hôtel-de-Ville, where the mortality was so severe: 64 deaths per thousand in the rue de la Mortellerie, 136 per thousand on the quai de la Grève.

1841 as compared with 1836: In 1841 the new fact, as compared with 1836, was the decrease in the depressed districts, into which, according to the previous censuses, the population continued to crowd nonetheless. The Cité district had had 12,481 inhabitants at the 1836 census: it had only 11,928 in 1841; the quartier de l'Hôtel-de-Ville, with 14,807 inhabitants in the 1836 census, now had only 12,215. The decrease was the result of the demolition of houses considered unfit for habitation and of improvements, such as the clearing around the Hôtel-de-Ville, the opening of the rue Lobau and the rue du Pont Louis-Philippe, and of a thoroughfare connecting the back of the Hôtel-de-Ville with Saint Gervais; on the Ile de la Cité the opening of a broad street connecting the parvis Notre-Dame with the Hôtel-de-Ville via the pont d'Arcole, and, starting from the Palais de Justice, another even broader street, the rue de Constantine, joining the former at right angles; and the widening of the rue de la Cité, formerly the rue de la Juiverie. The decrease in population, however, remained slight. The population of the IVth arrondissement fell from 48,729 in 1836 to 46,430 in 1841, a reduction of 4.71%; and that of the IXth from 46,143 in 1836 to 45,822 in 1841, a reduction of 0.69%.

1846 as compared with 1841: The salient feature of the percentage increases between 1841 and 1846 is that they were particularly high in the IXth arrondissement, amounting to 11.3%. This increase was, of course, not so high as that in other arrondissements such as the Ist, but it is far more significant. A smaller increase in an already over-crowded arrondissement like the IXth is of much greater social significance.

1846 as compared with 1801: The following conclusions emerge from the comparison of the percentage increases by arrondissement in 1846 with those in 1801.

First, the Right Bank continuously developed at the expense of the Left. This involves the general problem of the geographical orientation of Paris, which lies outside our particular scope; the development of the Right Bank during this period was simply the result of much older history, a history with which this book is not concerned. It is worth mentioning, however, that the Commission on Les Halles, noting this fact, seems to have explained the reasons in 1843—they were not the topographical circumstances on which Husson placed such emphasis, but were due rather to the sites of the oldest Paris markets. Secondly, despite age-old overcrowding, the rates of increase in the districts of

	1800	1817	%	1831	%	1836	%	1841	1846
viith									
Mont-de-Piété	7,631	13,179	72.7	14,885	12.9	17,268	16		10.8
Sainte-Avoye	12,623	17,680	40.1	18,787	6.3	19,804	5.4		14.2
Marché Saint-Jean	8,865	14,068	58.7	15,141	7.6	17,044	2.6		43.3
Arcis	8,741	11,166	27.7	10,602		11,887	2.1		9
			48		6.03		11.08	0.81	9.64
ixth									
Hôtel-de-Ville	8,221	12,587	53.1	12,598		13,761	9.2		17.9
Arsenal	6,611	11,163	68.8	11,960		13,429	12.3	8.3	18
Cité	10,550	12,574	19.2	11,925		12,405	4		1.6
Ile Saint-Louis	4,703	5,778	22.8	6,078		6,548	7.7	9.1	
			39.9		−4.05		8.41	−0.6	11.3
ivth									
Marchés	8,861	11,173	26.1	10,766		11,125	3.3		
Banque	8,842	11,635	31.6	11,747		13,897	18		
Louvre	10,310	12,151	17.8	11,215		11,359			
Saint-Honoré	9,764	11,665	19.5	11,000		12,348	12.2		
			23.4		1.09		8.93	−4.71	3.88

Old Paris call for attention. The charts showing population size which we took as our starting point are certainly less significant socially than those showing the densities. The highest percentage increases naturally appear in the new districts, and this may well distract our attention from the old quarters, in which the percentage increases were lower. For our social study, however, the percentage increases in the central arrondissements, though lower than those in the Ist and IInd, are of far greater significance. It was there, particularly in the VIIth and IXth arrondissements, that the increase in 1817 was largest in all Paris; the population of the VIIth rose from 37,860 to 56,088. Though the percentage increases in these arrondissements remained at a lower level after 1817, they grew constantly, except for a very slight decrease in 1841.

The Population in Densities

Population densities give a far better idea of the way in which the population settled into the urban environment than do numbers of inhabitants, and they establish certain assumptions concerning the influence exercised by the urban environment; they are therefore far more significant. We are not speaking of overall population densities, for their percentage increases differ only slightly from the percentage increases in population size; thus

Density (inhabitants per hectare)		Percentage increase: densities	Percentage increase: population size
1800:	159	–	–
1817:	208	30.8	–
1831:	229	10.1	10.07
1836:	253	10.5	10.25
1841:	272	7.5	8.06
1846:	307	12.9	12.56

What we are speaking of is density by district. High densities and their persistent increase in the same districts indicate a certain social condition, or at the least conduce to the inference that serious problems, both material and moral, existed there. It is no accident that a constant relation is found between these densities and such phenomena as normal mortality, abnormal mortality, illegitimate fertility and crime. The charts for increases in density between 1801 and 1846 stress their constant growth in the old central districts, which had been noted in

1801 as the most overcrowded. In 1801 there were over 150,000 inhabitants per square kilometer in the quartier des Arcis, bounded by the place de la Grève, the place du Châtelet and Saint-Jacques de la Boucherie, and crossed by the rue de la Coutellerie, the rue de la Tixeranderie and the rue de la Verrerie; 100 to 150,000 in the quartier des Marchés and in the quartier des Lombards, the narrow, dense mass of houses hemmed in between the rue Saint-Denis and the rue Saint-Martin, between the rue aux Ours and the rue Saint-Jacques de la Boucherie, and in the quartier Montorgueil. These were the districts that became even more densely populated in 1831; les Arcis rose into a higher category. Remaining in the same category, Marchés and Lombards became still denser, Marchés increasing from 107,000 to 134,000 and Lombards from 82,000 to 106,000. Next in this category now came the quartier Montorgueil, situated immediately north of the wholesale market, its main arteries being the rue du Renard, the rue de la Cygne and the rue de la Grande Truanderie.

The same districts show increased densities in 1846:

	per square kilometer		per square kilometer
Arcis	243,000	Saint-Honoré	91,000
Marchés	136,000	Saint-Martin-	
Lombards	120,000	des-Champs	91,000
Montorgueil	113,000	Saint-Eustache	90,000
Banque	110,000	Marché Saint-Jean	89,000
Sainte-Avoye	108,000	Mail	82,000
Porte Saint-Denis	103,000	Palais-Royal	82,000
Bonne-Nouvelle	100,000	Mont-de-Piété	76,000
Hôtel-de-Ville	96,000	Montmartre	75,000

A calculation of the number of square meters per inhabitant leads to a similar conclusion. In 1831, for example:

Roule	82	Saint-Honoré	12
Champs-Elysées	190	Louvre	20
Place Vendôme	31	Marchés	8
Tuileries	59	Banque	10
Chaussée d'Antin	53	fbg Saint-Denis	39
Palais-Royal	15	Porte Saint-Martin	61
Feydeau	21	Bonne-Nouvelle	12
fbg Montmartre	36	Montorgueil	10
fbg Poissonnière	46	Porte Saint-Denis	11
Montmartre	15	Saint-Martin des Champs	13
Saint-Eustache	13	Lombards	10
Mail	13	Temple	44
Sainte-Avoye	11	Monnaie	16
Mont-de-Piété	10	Saint-Thomas	52

Marché Saint-Jean	13	Invalides	18
Arcis	7	fbg Saint-Germain	43
Marais	26	Luxembourg	77
Popincourt	99	Ecole de Médecine	18
fbg Saint-Antoine	55	Sorbonne	19
Quinze-Vingts	152	Palais de Justice	29
Ile Saint-Louis	18	Saint-Jacques	15
Hôtel-de-Ville	12	Saint-Marcel	19
Cité	13	Jardin du Roi	49
Arsenal	29	Observatoire	53

It is quite clear, however, that—in view of the extent of Les Halles—the inhabitants of the quartier des Marchés had nothing like the 8 square meters attributed to them by the statistics. The charts showing the number of inhabitants per dwelling are equally significant. In 1846, for example, the districts for which the figures were highest were not those in the center (except Hôtel-de-Ville), but the quartier Saint-Denis and especially the Porte Saint-Martin. On the other hand, the districts with the lowest figures were the central districts and two districts on the Left Bank, Saint-Jacques and Saint-Marcel. The charts of course, mainly show differences between types of dwelling. Nonetheless, there are districts in which they confirm our earlier conclusions: the Hôtel-de-Ville in particular, which had not only the highest percentage increases but also the highest densities and the largest number of inhabitants per dwelling.

The Workers' Housing

The worsening of housing conditions for the poorest groups was primarily due to the fact—and this shows up plainly in the statistics—that the numbers in the oldest districts even when they did not rise, fell but slightly.

Reconstruction caused some movement to neighboring districts such as the Ile Saint-Louis, "which had such a reputable population formerly," as the Commission on Les Halles observed in 1842, "but where there are no longer any well-to-do tenants except in the houses along the quais. Nowhere are rents cheaper than in the streets on this island. So the undesirable population driven out by the demolitions on the Cité and round the Hôtel-de-Ville is moving there, replacing a less poverty-stricken population which is leaving the district." Similarly, a new influx of this "undesirable population" reinforced the poverty-stricken and dangerous population frequenting the purlieus of the place Maubert.

It also contributed to the development of suburban communes such as Belleville, whose demographic, economic and social characteristics were beginning to change in the last years of the July Monarchy.

The largest numbers, however, stayed where they were, clinging to the very districts in which there was most demolition, merely moving from one street to another or settling into the extra storeys or the garrets which house owners piled onto the old buildings.[5]

In his book *Les voies publiques et les habitations particulières à Paris*, Charles Gourlier noted that

the very strict regulations[6] concerning the height of buildings are legally applicable only to street frontages and there are no legal provisions concerning the buildings erected within properties away from the street. In the present state of the law, the aforesaid regulations (the letters patent of 1783 supplemented by the ministerial decision of 1825) still govern the Paris streets. In general, they permit streets narrower than those under the London regulations, but, on the other hand, in no case do they permit such high building. In London, however, buildings are erected on land which is in most cases not owned by the builders but is rented on a ninety-nine-year lease, so that the buildings are less grandiose and less durable. In Paris one and the same person almost always owns both the land and the building and so tends to build for strength and duration; but this stands in the way of change. Moreover, the Municipality has sometimes required extra strength —and outlay—which induces the owner-builder to exercise his rights to the full and even beyond in order to get an equivalent return on his heavier outlay. Hence there are hardly any buildings in London which reach the height or nearly the height permitted, whereas in Paris there are very few which are not built up to the maximum height permitted for frontages. Further, as there are no legal provisions either for the number and height of storeys or for the height of buildings other than the frontage, for the size of the interior rooms, for the courts or other open spaces for ventilation or for sanitary arrangements, too many defective, inconvenient and unhealthy buildings have been erected owing to the owners' greed and the builders' inventive genius.

In addition, the exodus of the bourgeois to the new quarters worsened material conditions in the central districts, where only the poorest classes still lived, abandoned to their sorry plight in buildings no one was prepared to maintain, in the twilight and dirt of streets where the shops that had once been so brilliantly lit up were now dark.[7]

Haussmann's buildings and the opening of broad, well-laid-out and ventilated avenues later put a stop to this exodus and brought bourgeois and shopkeepers back into the center. But the very last days of the July Monarchy saw the beginnings of a totally different development. In and after 1842–43 the wealthy population and shopkeepers began to leave the IVth, VIIth and IXth arrondissements for the outskirts of Paris and even to move outside the city walls. All the administrative documents noted this fact with alarm, for example, the tax reports, which stated that "the number of licenses has greatly increased in the IInd and IIIrd arrondissements, where there has been the greatest reduction in the indigent population, and has remained almost stationary in the IVth, IXth and XIIth arrondissements, which are the only ones where the indigent population has increased"; and the electoral reports, which noted that

of the 347 electors who changed arrondissement for any reason whatever, 147 from the IVth, Vth, VIth, VIIth, VIIIth, IXth, Xth, XIth and XIIth arrondissements moved to the Ist, IInd and IIIrd arrondissements as a result of the movement of the population towards the northwest; a shopkeeper who does not set up in the neighboring arrondissement when he leaves his own settles for preference in the IInd or IIIrd electoral district.

Such was the conclusion in 1843 in the report of the Commission on Les Halles explaining both this exodus and its effects on the arrondissements in central Paris. On the IVth arrondissement:

It is the smallest in area. Its only communications are narrow thoroughfares running between old buildings without light or air. The provisions market causes traffic blocks. The part of the arrondissement between the Pont-Neuf, the Marché des Prouvaires, the Louvre and the Bank is still a business center, though it is tending to move away. The part between the quai de la Mégisserie and Les Halles used to contain wholesale and semi-wholesale trade, notably that in cloths and fabrics, but is beginning to desert it. It is only too true that the affluent population has moved away from the market and has taken with it the prosperous establishments founded to serve it. What has become of the great silk merchants in the quartier des Bourdonnais and the flourishing passementerie industry in the rue aux Fers? They have been attracted to sites better suited to modern civilization.

On the VIIth arrondissement:

There are districts in it with poor, badly built and unhealthy streets tenanted by undesirables. The poorest is the quartier des Arcis, which, except for the quai Pelletier, is largely occupied by tenants of lodging houses which let out rooms by the month or by the day and by the sort of people attracted to this type of establishment. The opening up of the rue Rambuteau will bring a little sunlight into the quartier Beaubourg, which has been in equally sorry plight. The main streets in this arrondissement are shopping streets and would become busier if only they were further widened. The rue de la Verrerie, the rue Barre-du-Bec, the rue Saint-Merry and the rue Sainte-Avoye are still occupied by the wholesale and semi-wholesale trade in groceries and oils. This important trade is well situated in these districts close to the center of Paris and since communications with the business center have been improved, it will establish itself there and spread to the quartier du Marais instead of moving away. But something must be done to keep it there, since it is the principal and almost the sole resource of the VIIth arrondissement. The only public buildings are the Market and the butchery of Blancs-Manteaux, the La Force prison, which is to be demolished, the Mont-de-Piété and the Archives. The only connections between this arrondissement and the business center pass through narrow, congested streets. But the opening up of the rue Rambuteau will make for easier and more direct communication with the rue Montmartre which runs through the business center.

And on the IXth arrondissement (the quartier de l'Hôtel-de-Ville had been rebuilt):

Before the rue du Pont Louis-Philippe was opened up and the Hôtel-de-Ville cleared, the part between the place de Grève and the rue Saint-Paul was one of the unhealthiest districts in Paris. The main business was lodging masons and laborers in furnished rooms in the rue de la Mortellerie, the rue du Grenier-sur-l'eau, the rue de Longpont, the rue Pernelle, the rue de la Levrette and the rue des Haudrettes. The quai, the rue des Nonaindières, the rue de Jouy Saint-Antoine, the rue du Monceau Saint-Gervais and rue du Martroy alone had a few retail shops with a dull trade. There were no large manufacturers, no wholesale trade, in short, no resources. The rue du Pont Louis-Philippe has at last been cut through the old houses in this wretched district. New building has brought in a less poverty-stricken population and a few shopkeepers have tried to establish themselves along this busy thoroughfare. But the quartier de la Cité is still what the quartier de l'Hôtel-de-Ville was ten years ago; its alleys and dead-ends are still the haunts of most of the released convicts who flock to Paris. The demolition of the Archbishop's Palace has deprived this wretched district of the few advantages it may once have derived from the neighborhood of the Archbishop's residence. It is true that the Municipality has given an earnest of its concern for this district by opening up the rue d'Arcole and declaring the opening of the rue de Constantine of public interest. Unfortunately, the delay in opening up the rue de Constantine has merely added to the troubles of the owners of the houses affected by it by keeping them in a state of uncertainty which has prevented them from letting them, and the shopkeepers who are trying to set up in the rue d'Arcole cannot hope to earn a living there until the street is given an outlet by clearing the access to the pont d'Arcole.

The social and moral consequences of this segregation have often been described. It is worth recalling that the first study of it was made in June 1855, in a "Report by the Paris Chamber of Commerce and by the Prefect of Police on the question of workers' wages and the increase in rents and the price of food":[8]

The circumstances which compel workers to move out of the center of Paris have generally, it is pointed out, had deplorable effects on their behavior and morality. In the old days they used to live on the upper floors of buildings whose lower floors were occupied by the families of businessmen and other fairly well-to-do persons. A species of solidarity grew up among the tenants of a single building. Neighbors helped each other in small ways. When sick or unemployed, the workers might find a great deal of help, while, on the other hand, a sort of human respect imbued working-class habits with a certain regularity. Having moved north of the Saint-Martin canal or even beyond the barrières, the workers now live where there are no bourgeois families and are thus deprived of this assistance at the same time as they are emancipated from the curb on them previously exercised by neighbors of this kind.

Thus, as we look at the facts to find reasons for the growing shadow over the descriptions of Paris in and after the last days of the Restoration and for the growing awareness on the part of the population as a whole of the disastrous results of its own growth—the way in which the whole city was stigmatized as dangerous and unhealthy—we discover an initial measurement and an initial explanation in the numbers and the densities. The urban environment was hostile because building lagged behind population. The newcomers were the chief sufferers, those who accounted for the highest proportion of the total population increase and had no alternative but to crowd into the districts in which densities already were highest. But the older inhabitants themselves were affected by the repercussions, all of them, not merely the most underprivileged, owing to the generalized malaise of the larger part of them (as noted by Considérant) and to the feverish daily life in Paris, life in the workshop, traffic in the streets and even the feverish social attitudes engendered by the disparity between the urban setting—here observed through housing—and the population.

There was, however, another way in which this disparity exercised a tremendous effect on the population of the city as a whole, irrespective of social category or place of residence, namely, as a result of the urban facilities generally rather than housing alone. Whereas the disparity between housing and population affected the poorest social groups most strongly, the disparity between the city's facilities and the population brought the effects of the increase in the city's population home to every person in it.

CHAPTER FOUR

The Population and the City:
The Basic Facilities

Urban facilities had improved during the period. We are not concerned here with describing the changes in the city; this has often been done in histories of Paris and its architecture, a fact that in itself goes to support our conclusion. City planning continued, but on the basis of architectural rather than demographic and social concepts, with a view to greater aristocratic and bourgeois convenience and with no regard to the daily life of the masses. The trend of both public and private ambition, and of capital and interest, lay in a quite different direction. It was easier to build palaces, churches, mansions, theaters, markets and bridges than waterworks, sewers and cesspools, easier to adorn or even light the city than to clean it, easier to embellish its face than to sound its depths.

And it was all the more easy to do this when the population increase had not yet made its effects felt by upsetting the building programs and posing problems for which no preparations whatever had been made. This is the main reason for the great contrast between urban policy under the Restoration and under the July Monarchy, which has often been noted but never adequately defined and explained. It is not enough to contrast the volume and splendor of the buildings erected under the former with the timidity and mediocre quality of performance under the latter. Both shared a single program of improvement and city planning, which was fairly well suited to the needs of the population in the earlier period; but from the end of the Restoration onward, the main items which had become customary in that program were endangered. It was still directed chiefly toward creating beauty and convenience, whereas the essential aim should have been immediate utility, a policy of the lesser evil and coping with poverty; it was still concerned with the affluent districts, when the pressing problem was the sewers and the slums.

I

The Restoration

The Traditional Tasks

The Restoration continued to develop the old program based on the old concepts, the old budget allocations and the old lavish expenditure. Commenting on the statistics of the receipts and expenditures of the City of Paris between 1797 and 1830, Martin-Saint-Léon wrote:

It would be easy to calculate what sums out of the eleven hundred millions spent were used in increasing the city's capital in properties and buildings which brought in public revenue or were destined for public use. The central and local markets, the Bourse, the warehouses, the slaughterhouses, the barracks, the grammar schools, the churches built, acquired or restored, the main cemeteries, the progressive widening of streets and squares, the completion of the city gates, walls and sentry walks, as well as the ownership of several large buildings such as local town halls and the bare ownership of the Ourcq and Saint-Martin canals and of bridges and the like acquired by the granting of advances and long-term concessions, are all so many additions to the increase in Paris's real estate assets. These are quite certainly capital investments rather than true expenditures.[1]

This sound management of the public monies continued undisturbed. The hospitals and almshouses and the distribution of relief to the indigent placed a heavy burden on this budget, it is true; they entailed the heaviest of all the communal outlays and echoed withal the city's poverty; but they barely increased from year to year,[2] and Martin-Saint-Léon himself presented them as traditional expenditures rather than an adjustment to a new demographic and social situation.

The old program included the building program described by contemporaries as "brilliant": new churches, new mansions, new palaces, new theaters, and luxurious shopping galleries in the main business districts. The city was planned for convenience, luxury and beauty, both by order of the authorities and by a purse-proud and spendthrift bourgeoisie with a mania for ostentation. "Paris would be Venice ten times over today," wrote Balzac,

if the retired shopkeepers had the instinct for the grand gesture which distinguishes the Italians. Even today a Milanese businessman may well bequeath 500,000 francs to the Duomo for gilding the colossal Virgin on the roof. . . . Would a bourgeois of Paris even contemplate building the missing bell-towers on Notre-Dame? Count up the sums the State comes into from estates with no heirs. The entire embellishment of Paris could have been completed for the price of these follies of papier-mâché stone, gilded putty and sham sculptures.

Many useful public works were also included in the old program, such as bridges, market buildings, sidewalks, new public fountains, the earliest gas lighting, canals[3] and, in and after 1828, the initial preparations for piping water for domestic supply.

The New Tasks

In the last years of the Restoration, however, a wider and wider gap appeared between these public works and those urgently required by the increase in the city's population.

This gap is evident from the way in which the items in the city's budget were allocated; those connected directly or indirectly with the increase in population were not increased commensurately. The allocation of expenditures remained practically the same and most still went to the traditional items.

The streets: The gap is evident in many other ways as well. It is quite clear that most building—except canal work—benefited the affluent districts more than the others, and a growing volume of documents, such as official reports, articles in the press and literary descriptions, stressed the contradiction between the steady pace of the old program and the complexity of the problems posed by the human influx, by infection, poverty and death. "Never within the memory of the oldest inhabitants," wrote the *Journal des Débats* on November 1, 1826, "has the city been so filthy, and everybody is wondering desperately how anyone will be able to get across a gutter three years hence unless some means be found by then to dry up and remove the torrents of mud that are flooding and infecting our streets." Street-paving and sidewalk construction proceeded very slowly; the sidewalks encroached on the carriageway and made the traffic blocks even worse; and work of this kind presupposed habits of cleanliness which were alien to the Parisians.[4]

The garbage dumps: Another problem connected with the population increase makes its appearance in the documents, that of the cesspools. These were originally on the outskirts of the city, but the city caught up with and surrounded them. We shall discuss the cesspool at Montfaucon later; its horrors were to haunt the programs of the July Monarchy. Here we are dealing with those mentioned by Parent-

Duchatelet in 1831 in his *Recherches sur l'influence des émanations putrides sur l'altération des substances alimentaires*:

. . . The huge cesspool known as the Poland pool backing onto the Pépinière barracks; houses have been built on the edges of it and are inhabited by a great many poor persons and by many workers from the district; the cesspool at Ménilmontant which, under M. Delvau's administration, caused a riot in part of the faubourg Saint-Antoine, when the tenants of the houses which had been built around it, finding that their complaints were ignored, ejected the dung carts; their complaints were backed by the commanding officers of the 7th regiment stationed in the nearby barracks. I shall not go into detail about the alarm spread in Paris by this incident; people believed for a moment that the plague was upon them. The Ménilmontant cesspools being overloaded by this slush, it was drained off into the Montreuil pit, which was soon so blocked that the ordure rose 4 or 5 meters above the road level. With the intense heat and the thunderstorms, the fermentation inconveniences the many restaurant, cookshop and pothouse keepers in the neighborhood.

The sewers: And, lastly, the sewers. The authorities and public opinion did not awaken to this problem until the cholera epidemic broke out. "Enlightened by the cholera epidemic," said Emmery in his *Statistique des égouts* in 1837, "people have come to realize since 1832 how important it is to clean up the cities." But Parent-Duchatelet had published an *Essai sur les cloaques ou égouts de la ville de Paris, envisagés sous le rapport de l'hygiène publique et de la topographie médicale de cette ville* as early as 1824. "Paris," he wrote, "situated as it is in an almost flat valley from which the waters can barely drain off, needed a well-conceived system of sewers more than any other town. The prodigious increase in the population made it necessary to construct several sewers, one after another, their course being governed more by chance than calculation."

The spread and layout of the sewers were no longer adequate for the population's requirements.[5] Both the main encircling sewer—which took the rainwater and household slops of all the districts between it and the banks of the Seine at one end and the drainage of the northern faubourgs at the other—and the sewers on the southern slopes—which were entirely separate from the main sewer and flowed into the river through twenty-one outlets, the chief being the Amelot sewer, the sewer at the Popincourt slaughterhouse and those at Petit Musc, the Grève and the rue de la Tannerie—were overtaxed, especially the Amelot. "The sludge carried down by the rainwater and the houeshold slops," Parent-Duchatelet noted, accumulated in the Amelot sewer. The infection to which the inhabitants of the district were thereby exposed was all the worse because many animal breeders lived in the neighborhood. If you lingered a few moments where the sewer disembogued into the ditches at the Bastille, you got a whiff of cow dung and animal urine. All previous attempts to unchoke the sewer had failed. Most of the workmen were stifled; some died. The sewer had consequently been left alone and had gained such a reputation among the workmen that whenever they wanted to give an idea of a dangerous sewer they likened it to the sewer in the rue Amelot. But the sewer soon overflowed; the waters stayed on the streets and seeped into the courts and cellars of the houses. They flowed back through the culvert in the rue Saint-Pierre, which lay at the bottom of the slope, and flooded it in a trice. The apprehensions of the inhabitants of this crowded district added to the Administration's perplexities.

On June 24, 1826, the Prefect decided that the Amelot sewer and its branches should be cleaned out, as well as the sewer into the Saint-Martin canal. Though the plan of the newly built sewers and the upper part of the Amelot sewer was known, that of the lower part and the La Roquette branch was not, for they had been neglected so long that no one knew their course or even their real layout. "No detailed plan of the sewers was known before 1833," Emmery wrote. "So, naturally, no survey existed, not even a partial one. A preliminary investigation had, however, been made by Bruneseau and Nargaud (between 1805 and 1812) and a nomenclature had been drawn up; but these concise notes, however valuable as statistical documents, were not accompanied by any plan, cross-section or survey." So the undertaking was a hazardous venture.

Similarly, when the lowest part of the main sewer was tackled on July 14, 1826, that is, at the point where it flowed into the river opposite the sharp end of Louviers Island, many workmen fell sick and it took six months to complete the work. On July 7, 1827, the *Journal des Débats* reported that on the previous day, a Sunday, a rumor had spread around the faubourg Saint-Antoine:

At about eight in the morning several stretchers were seen, some of them laden with corpses and proceeding towards the Morgue, others towards the Saint-Antoine hospital, to which they were carrying the dying. These unfortunates, to the number of ten or twelve, had just been asphyxiated while cleaning out the sewer at the porte Saint-Antoine. Two years before, seven persons had fallen victim to the same putrid stench.

Thus, during the last years of the Restoration new requirements for utilities arose in addition to the old, no longer determined by the harmonious continuation of the old programs but imposed by the human

influx; no longer planned but improvised; no longer conceived to promote greater wellbeing but designed for a policy of the lesser evil. These
tasks were to complicate the July Monarchy's building programs even
further, for they were far more urgently needed and far more difficult
to execute.

II

The July Monarchy

The New Tasks and the Old

The July Monarchy faced new tasks—that is, tasks relating to the
changes in the Paris population—imposed first by the facts, and secondly by opinion.

The facts: The realization that the city was highly unhealthy and
that the traditional programs which still lingered on were in strong
contrast with the new ones to which the authorities were unable to
resign themselves and which, indeed, they were incapable of conceiving
if left to themselves, was brought home realistically by the cholera
epidemic of 1832. So the people of Paris concluded, to judge by comments published in the press as the epidemic took its course. "One advantage at least of the disease which is ravaging Paris," wrote the
Journal des Débats on July 24, 1832, "will be that it will compel the
Administration to decide to clean up the city." The conclusion in the
official report, too, was:

The epidemic has passed, but it is surely the counsel of caution to support
the Administration in measures calculated to mitigate its effects should it ever
recur; and among them the Commission would still urge, despite the examples to the contrary observed in a few places, everything calculated to contribute to public health and sanitation, to make streets cleaner and buildings
healthier and to improve the living conditions of their inhabitants.

This emphasizes, together with the economic and social circumstances of a wretched population decimated by the epidemic, the extent
of the city's insanitary state, aggravated as it was by the increase in its
population. And it does so in such detail that the statistics of the cholera
epidemic constitute the best document we have concerning the effects
of the material framework on the population and the most accurate
illustration of the foregoing analyses:

Of the 48 districts of Paris, 28 situated in the center make up only one-fifth
of its area, but contain one-half of the population. In 35 of these districts,

180 streets have 146,430 inhabitants; in one of these districts, the quartier des Arcis, there are only 7 square meters per person; and of these streets there are 73 in which there are, on an average, 30, 40 or 60 persons per building. It is in these streets, without exception, that there were 45 deaths per thousand, or double the average; it is in these buildings, most of them 5 storeys in height and 6 to 7 meters in breadth, without open courts, that there were 4, 6 and up to 10 or 11 deaths, because nowhere else is the space more confined, the population more crowded, the air more unhealthy, dwelling more perilous and the inhabitants more wretched.

There follow comments to the same effect on the narrow and congested streets, the excessive height of the new buildings which made the streets dark, dirty and damp, the inefficient street-cleaning system, the equally inefficient methods of draining the household slops, the inadequate provision of street taps, which meant that the Parisian received barely 7 liters of water when the Londoner had 62, and the inadequacy of the sewers.

A whole new program of urban facilities was thus defined; it could no longer be ignored. And the press repeated this. "The most urgent task is to clean up Paris," the *Journal des Débats* wrote in 1833.

To this end a general reconstruction of the sewers has been undertaken at many places. But defective drainage is not the only reason why Paris is unhealthy. There is also the crowding and height of the buildings and the constriction of streets deprived of air and light. It will be seen from the official report on the cholera epidemic that the disease was most destructive in the darkest streets.

From now on, this was the main theme of treatises on health.

Opinion: All this demonstrates the existence of a climate of opinion; inadequately, however. It is still more noteworthy that through this general and detailed problem the city's population began to see itself as a danger and became alarmed at its own growth. As we have already noted, Paris was described as a sick city, an impossible city, an accursed city; and much of the denunciation was directed against the sewers, drains and hospitals, all the places where the refuse of daily living piled up. And this for purely physical reasons. At that period of rudimentary technology, when everything depended on human labor, on human strength, skill and health, some tasks seemed monstrously hard, all the harder in that they had long been neglected or even forgotten. But for moral reasons, too. Correlations which, as we shall see, were not always imaginary, were established both in fact and in public belief between the places involved and such social dangers as sickness, poverty, crime and prostitution; and riots and revolutions too.

The Inadequacies of the Urban Facilities

But these public works, so urgent and so formidable, could scarcely be incorporated into the old programs. While they hindered the execution of current work, they could not themselves be carried out on a large enough scale. Hence the timidity of the July Monarchy's town planning, which has often been noted but never adequately explained. To the régime's credit there were the Hôtel-de-Ville, the rue Rambuteau, two road bridges and three foot bridges, the boulevards laid out and the quais built. While the authorities and the Municipality were hesitant in undertaking major enterprises, such as reconstructing or moving Les Halles, they did not even provide the necessary resources for the completion of current projects such as the Bourse or the river wharfs at Saint-Germain. The reason may have been shortsightedness or pennypinching, but it was more probably that the old program could not be adapted to the new requirements. The new tasks, growing as the city grew, were ineluctable and costly and so brought the old tasks to a halt even as they were brought to a halt by them.

This is shown in the city's budget by the levels of allocation for the traditional expenditures, as compared with those which can be related to the economic, social and moral problems posed by the increase in population. Thus the funds allocated for poor relief remain surprisingly stable and, so to speak, ritually ordered[6] as compared to those allocated for what may be called the human equipment, which remained far below what was required by the excess population.[7]

This disquieting state of affairs is reflected in other documents besides the budget, especially in the various documents relating to the sectors of urban facilities in which the inadequacies were particularly evident in relation to the increase in population. Two items in particular were greatly overburdened and were so far behind that this had a serious effect upon the most ordinary circumstances of existence: the water supply and the sewers.

Work progressed on the water supply and new piping was laid to draw off the water from the Ourcq.[8] But, allowing for consumption by workshops, each inhabitant had no more than 6 or 7 liters of water per day.[9] Piping water to the streets and carrying it to the upper floors of buildings also created difficulties, described by Mrs. Trollope in 1835 as follows:

Very nearly every family in Paris receives this precious gift of nature doled out by two buckets at a time, laboriously brought to them by porters clambering [up the stairs] in sabots; it can hardly be supposed that the use of it is as liberal and unrestrained as with us. Much as I admire the Church of the Madeleine, I conceive that the city of Paris would have been infinitely more benefited, had the sums expended on it been used for the purpose of constructing pipes for the conveyance of water to private dwellings. . . . The patient endurance [of filth] by men and women of the year one thousand eight hundred and thirty-five is a mystery difficult to understand. [Letters XV and XXVI.]

It was not so much a matter of patient endurance as of long-standing habits, whose persistence could be amply documented. There was an obstinate prejudice against using the waters of the Ourcq. "It is said that their quality is bad," wrote Emmery in 1840.

As a matter of fact, they are preferable to all the old Paris spring waters and even to the waters of Arcueil which look so fine and clear. Filtered at the Boule Rouge, faubourg Montmartre, they have furnished half the domestic supply to one of the wealthiest districts in Paris for the past twelve years. The facts cannot ever be repeated too often to the poor, the class which is naturally mistrustful as a result of its miseries; it is likely to be shortsighted enough to reject the immense benefits from drawing its water from the street taps if it believes that it is not being supplied, so far as quality is concerned, with water in the same way as bread, that is, with the same care for quality as the more privileged classes get.[10]

In 1840 only one of the thirteen commercial taps—those at which water was sold by the barrel or bucket—was supplied solely with Ourcq water.

Between 1817 and 1831 thirty-seven public bath houses supplied by Ourcq water were opened, and twenty-three between 1831 and 1840; and though this was regarded in administrative and other reports as an improvement in habits of cleanliness, we are, on the contrary, more inclined to measure the persistent habits of dirt by baths taken as compared with population of districts,[11] the decline in their business in winter and the many bankruptcies at periods of social disturbance and revolution. Cleanliness was still a luxury to which only the bourgeois had access. Surveying the distribution of bath houses by district and the number of baths taken in them or supplied to homes in 1839, Emmery wrote: "One notes the differences between districts. An analysis of them would provide material for almost a page on the manners and customs of the various groups of the population."

While there was a sharp increase in work on the sewers immediately after the 1832 cholera epidemic, the advance in construction and outlay fell off during the last years of the July Monarchy, whereas the population was increasing at the rate we have described.[12]

The lag in public facilities was especially patent in the districts in which the population had increased most, or on which the consequences of the general replanning of the city bore most heavily. Local circumstances of population—the increase in numbers and densities we have measured—were of far less account than the new burdens laid upon certain economically essential districts by the expansion of the city as a whole. It would be worth looking into the consequences of the local and the overall population increase to each district. Local circumstances alone were of importance in some districts, whereas in others which were economically important to the city as a whole the material frame proved capable of absorbing the new population and the new tasks. This was probably so in the faubourg Saint-Antoine, where a growing population fitted its housing and work into the old frame. "The faubourg Saint-Antoine," Luchet wrote in 1830, "is very large; the houses are in general well built and almost always clean, because of the slope of the land. It is the biggest manufacturing district in Paris. This faubourg is inhabited by the most industrious and sturdiest population, but also the most turbulent and the most formidable when roused."[13]

On other districts, however, the city's demographic and economic growth laid new burdens and aggravated their former difficulties. This was probably so in the districts on the Left Bank and in the communes of the inner banlieue to which the city relegated its dirtiest trades. Parent-Duchatelet noted some local consequences of this general economic development in 1831:

The lower stretch of the Bièvre stream, into which the sewers of a whole district flow as it crosses Paris and, in addition, the refuse of a multitude of skin-dressers, tanners, wool washers and the like, is nothing but a foul sewer giving off a miasma of putrefaction so intense that it tarnishes and blackens the kitchen utensils in all the houses on the banks.

The report of the Health Committee of the XIIth arrondissement noted in 1832 that "the streets on the Bièvre and the Champ de l'Alouette, unmade and unpaved, are simply sewers."[14]

The local consequences of the general development were most evident, however, in the quartier des Halles. Owing to the links between this district's economy and that of the city as a whole, and also to the constricted material frame, all the older characteristics of Les Halles became progressively more pronounced—the overcrowded dwellings, workshops, mews, shops and streets, and the overcrowding of the markets themselves, with dirt, crime and prostitution and the mortality that sums and totals up the whole. Evidence of this aggravation of the problem of Les Halles and the Municipality's difficulties when it tried to solve it appears in many documents, especially the reports of succeeding commissions, all of them equally alarmed and equally impotent. It is a vast subject as regards both the historical and the contemporary data, and we intend to tackle it some day. Here we shall confine ourselves to noting the repercussions and the accumulation of all the city's material and moral problems at that particular spot. "What has to be done," Lanquetin, the spokesman for the Commission on Les Halles, wrote in April 1840, "is to open up the traffic which has become so difficult and dangerous in some streets, clean up and improve certain wretched and unhealthy districts and make safety precautions easier, more effective and less perilous." But it was elsewhere that the aggravation of the problems was summed up most strikingly, without any of the brutal merriment and animal spirits characteristic of Les Halles: at Montfaucon, the setting of horror par excellence.

Montfaucon[15]

The problem of the cesspits—the deposits of the city's excrement—and of the horse butchers' yards—the places to which dead horses and other dead animals were carted—summed up this general problem of the inadequacy of the urban equipment better than any other. And Montfaucon presented all the material and moral aspects in the highest degree.

The material aspects: The problem of Montfaucon arose from the increase in the capital's population. "Two causes have been engendered by this increase in the population," Parent-Duchatelet wrote in 1833,

and, acting concurrently, have ruined all the amenities procured for the city by our ancestors and produced a state of affairs now approaching barbarism, which, both within Paris and in the surrounding villages, has become intolerable to more than 100,000 persons. The two causes are, first, the growth of Paris and, secondly, the increase in the accumulation of stuff giving off noxious effluvia. The reservoirs of this cesspool cover an area of 32,000 square meters, not to speak of 12 acres given over to dry refuse and horse butchers' yards; some 230 to 244 square meters of human excreta are carted there daily and most of the corpses of 12,000 horses and 25,000 to 30,000 smaller animals are left to rot on the ground.

The place was horrible because of the charnel house on permanent display. The offal rotted on the spot in heaps 4 or 5 feet high until the plowing season, when the peasants came in to fetch their fertilizer; the bones were burned, and were used in the old days in building walls in the faubourg Saint-Marceau, the faubourg du Temple and beside the barrière des Fourneaux, near which horse butchers' yards were situated; the hides were carried off every two or three days by the tanners of the Bièvre. But gut-dressing works and chemical factories were established nearby, and the discharge from them ran through the marshes and flowed in the open beside the rue Grange-aux-Belles to the city sewer in the rue des Marais near the rue de Lancry. Around the charnel house were the rats, in such swarms that if carcasses of quartered horses were left in any corner of a yard during the day, they were completely stripped by the next; they burrowed under the neighboring hills and brought down whole houses in ruins. The comments by Fourcroy, Hallé and Thouret in 1788 had lost none of their pertinence: "You have to visit these places of infection to get some idea of the residues and refuse that may be called the excrementa of a great city and to conceive the true physical extent of the immeasurable increase of filth, stench and corruption that comes from assembling people in a densely populated city."

The place was horrible, too, for the stench it spread over the neighborhood and, when the wind was in the right quarter, to the furthest confines of the city. "If you conceive what can be produced by the putrid decay of piles of meat and guts exposed in the open for weeks and months on end to the full glare of the sun and left to swell and rot," wrote Parent-Duchatelet,

and if you then imagine the kind of gases likely to be given off by piles of carcasses with much of the offal still clinging to them, as well as the emanations generated from a soil soaked for years with blood and animal sweat and urine, and from the blood itself left to clot in some yard or other with no drain, and from the waste matter from the gut-dressing works and skin dryers' shops nearby; if you multiply the degrees of stench indefinitely by comparing them with the stink that all of us have smelled sometimes when passing the decaying carcass of a dead animal we may have happened upon, you will get only a faint idea of the truly repugnant reek from this sewer, the foulest imaginable.

The attractions of the banlieue and the Parisians' customary outing to Belleville, the Pré-Saint-Gervais and the banks of the Ourcq were ruined. The town council of Belleville was not the only one to lodge protest upon protest; Pantin and Romainville, the communes affected by the prevailing winds to the detriment of property values, also protested. The malodorous winds usually passed high above the Paris houses, but in summer, when the weather was sultry or thundery and the air still, the stench of Montfaucon sometimes spread beyond the boulevard du Temple into the streets of the Marais running into it, and as far as the Tuileries Gardens themselves, where it was worst after sundown.

Hence Parent-Duchatelet's conclusion in his *Rapport sur les améliorations à introduire dans les fosses d'aisance*: "Montfaucon must be abolished; it is repugnant to the population of Paris and the surrounding country and public opinion is running too strongly against it; it plagues Paris, and visiting foreigners hold it as a reproach against us." But where could the charnel house and cesspool be moved to? The vain efforts to find a satisfactory solution and choose a suitable spot close to Paris— a long administrative story which we need not go into here—no less than the actual appearance of the place was an expression of the gravity of the problem posed by the increase in the city's population, one of whose aspects was summed up by Montfaucon.

The moral aspects: There were, however, other horrors which combined with these physical horrors. "The gibbet was abolished many years ago," Eugène de Monglave wrote in the *Livre des 101*. "Its site is covered by a cesspool where the excrements of Paris are deposited and where the horse butchers work. What was a place of horror in the old days is a place of disgust today; once they hanged men there, now they slaughter horses." Images blended of filth and crime are thus evoked here as two aspects of one and the same discharge from the city.

Such images were ancient ones because of the traditional coupling of the gibbet and the cesspool. The first gibbet, situated somewhat lower down the hill, adjoined a site on which stuff from the drains and the corpses of animals had been deposited since 1595. In 1761 the remnants of this gibbet, which had gone out of use in about 1627, and the adjoining cesspool were moved to behind La Villette. As if the destiny of one was bound up with destiny of the other, it was decided that the four sandstone pillars, the sign of the Royal High Court of Justice, should be set up near the new cesspool. When the gibbet was demolished during the Revolution, the huge blocks of which it was made were sold to a certain Fessard, a plasterer, and were used some time later in the construction of the upper outfall reservoir for fecal matter, forming the embankment along which the dung carts drew up.

But the images were still contemporary, both because the ancient images and all the crime of the past persisted, transmitted by the place and by the name Montfaucon, and because they were rejuvenated by contemporary facts, charged though they were with poverty and crime of another sort. Laboring class and dangerous class blended in Mont-faucon, or at any rate blended in the contemporary opinion, which regarded as one and the same the criminals and the poor wretches who sought refuge in the quarries of the Buttes-Chaumont, the workers in the horse butchers' yards who—like the Slasher in the *Mystères de Paris*—were doomed by their occupation to the bloodiest violence, the brutal inhabitants of the barrières and the faubourgs drawn there by the vilest kinds of work or by the combats between bulls and mastiffs, and the poor who, at times of utmost destitution, came there to fetch (and to fight dogs for) the meat of the slaughtered animals, despite all the regulations and despite the danger of infection.[16]

Many other aspects and consequences of the increase in population and the disparity between the urban setting and the population deserve mention in this study; but it has been kept to the essentials, that is to say, to the numbers of people and to everything pertaining to their mass and weight, everything consequent upon their physical presence, their crowding and contacts, their breathing and evacuation, everything that attaches to the simplest aspects of their lives. We must also pay some attention to their industry, to the workshops that increase commensurately with the workers, the inconveniences of which were pointed out in report after report by the Board of Health,[17] such as the steam, smells and noise. They had, of course, already been mentioned in earlier reports; in those by Bruneseau, for example, who wrote:[18]

Most of the smaller streets in this great city are not ventilated; the sun and air hardly enter them, the filthy ground fills the atmosphere with too many noxious exhalations, rotting matter continuously piles up and constant effluvia arise from vegetable and animal matter. In order to remedy the evils inseparable from insalubrity, a most careful supervision should be exercised over workshops of all kinds, such as foundries and furnaces, the sewers, putrefaction in cesspools, drains and ponds, the emanations from dead bodies in the cemeteries and the noxious evacuations from hospitals and prisons, and over the city's dirt in general, both in the streets and inside the houses.

Similar comments are to be found in Lachaise's description, but couched in graver and more somber terms. They grow even more somber in the Board of Health's later reports.

The cloud over the city has grown denser. The time was past when the Englishman Lister had been able to say, describing his visit to Paris in 1698, "The chief contrast between London and Paris comes from the climate. Though Paris is built on a dirty and spongy soil along a muddy river, the air there is drier than in London and the sunlight brighter." The time was past when Sauval had been able to describe in sharp detail the wide landscape he descried from the tower of Saint-Jacques-la-Boucherie. A perpetual fog seemed henceforth to brood over the city, darkening the prospect, corroding the buildings and corrupting the inhabitants.

PART II

The Composition of the Population

The city had fallen sick as the result of the vast and rapid increase in its population and the failure of the urban frame to adjust to over-population, and as the result, too, of the equally rapid change in the composition of the population. The population was not only excessive, but new; the city was not only overburdened, but invaded and, so to speak, conquered.

CHAPTER ONE

The Earlier Demographic Characteristics

I

The Ancien Régime

The foregoing study of developments in the Paris population in earlier periods does not, of course, exclude the part played by immigration. At all times there was an influx into the capital of people from outside it. If we were to make a detailed demographic analysis of this immigration and re-examine the abundant qualitative documentation, we could probably establish, if not the actual numbers of this immigration, at least its major phases and salient characteristics. Many eighteenth-century writers deplored the migration from the provinces to Paris and adduced historical material that should by no means be ignored. But this immigration could not cause any appreciable change in ancient and stable characteristics. The newcomers were few in relation to the total population. The place they occupied in the picturesque literature and in the streets, in Mercier's descriptions and in police reports, is not particularly relevant. The city grew mainly by the surplus of births over deaths. The only thing that does matter is the demographic fact we have already identified, in relation to which the historian has to reread and reassess the qualitative documentation in order to seek out everything that does not tally with this basic criterion. This would restore meaning to the many contemporary observations which pay hardly any heed to immigration. There is the further consideration that this immigration seems to have come from the areas nearest Paris and that, regardless of its origins and the initial distance from Paris, it remained closely attached to its traditional routes and habits. Auvergnats and Gascons were part of the Paris landscape, with their own occupations, their own dress and their familiar manners and customs, whether appreciated or distrusted; everyone deduced all their other characteristics from their name alone.

Only a small part of this immigration became fully integrated in a city which grew slowly and spontaneously by the natural growth of its native aristocratic, bourgeois and artisan families. A high proportion of the immigrants remained nomads, and were known as such, or settled in inferior occupations and inferior districts on the margin of the capital and its business and civilization.

These immigrants differed from the population as a whole in every way. Demographically, their distribution by sex was different; it can be reconstructed approximately. The distribution of the population by sex is the result of the ratio between the sexes at birth and of the death rate by sex at various ages, and what is now known of these phenomena makes it possible to reconstruct what they probably were in earlier periods. While it is likely that there were more females among the native population—but not as many more as in the nineteenth century because of the greater frequency of epidemics which struck down men and women at the same or nearly the same rate[1]—it seems very probable that the sheer physical facts of immigration, the long journey and fatigue involved, as well as the kind of work they engaged in, made for a predominance of males. "It is noteworthy," Moheau wrote, "that the greater the demand for labor due to the great number of factories, to trade or to proximity to the sea, the larger is the proportion of males in the towns." The division of labor by sex that was to develop later did not, of course, yet exist in the old France. "One should be surprised and indignant," to quote Moheau, "to find some tall sturdy fellow wielding comb or needle or busy tailoring clothes while one sees women plowing the hills with the animals or hoeing vines."[2] Arthur Young later expressed a similar indignation at the sight of women working in the fields like beasts of burden. Even in Paris, especially at Les Halles, women did men's work under the Ancien Régime and during the first half of the nineteenth century. Most of the immigrants, however, engaged in the heavy work for which the Parisians were unfitted. They worked, for example, as water carriers, 20,000 of them, who from morning to night carried pails of water up to the seventh floor, according to Mercier.[3] There was a high proportion of men even in domestic service, a fact abundantly confirmed by the available statistics.

A different distribution by age and sex means a different marriage and fertility rate and a different death rate, with all the differences of occupation and social status disclosed by them. A different mode of living can be discerned through a different way of dying, both of them so stable that medical topographies copied each other for a century. Patissier merely reproduced Cadet de Gassicourt's comments on the death rate and the characteristics of the various trades, repeating his observations on the seditious proclivities of masons, the miserliness of tinkers and the quarrelsomeness of tailors, especially those from Flanders and the Low Countries.[4]

This demographic and social stability overlay a similar stability of manners and customs, feelings and expression. A part of the population of Paris remained on the fringe of its civilization as an entity endowed with physical and moral characteristics, the originality and relative stability of which can be identified in an abundant, though inconsistent, literature when viewed in the demographic perspective. This was the brutal, violent and primitive population described by Mercier and Restif de la Bretonne. It had a language of its own, a mode of life of its own and its own attitude to women.

This population was not only different, but was seen to be so. There were the Parisians and the rest—those who were not born, did not live or interact in the same way, did not have the same conditions of living and the same mode of life, did not live in the same districts and the same streets, whose dwellings had a different exposure to the sun and the healthy breezes blowing down the Seine, who were even then described in contemporary documents (treatises on the policing of towns, miscellaneous descriptions, even population studies) in terms suggestive of a population different racially. Sauval asserted in his *Histoire et recherches des antiquités de la Ville de Paris* (1724) that "the Parisians are friendly people, sweet-tempered and very civil. . . . Robberies and murders, insolence, blasphemies and similar disorders are far less common in Paris than is said and are usually perpetrated by soldiers or the dregs of the people, who are not Parisians." Mercier said of the quartier Saint-Marcel in 1781:

The people of the faubourg are more ill-disposed, quicker to take offense, more quarrelsome and more unruly than people in other districts. The police are afraid to bear down on them too hard; they are treated circumspectly, for they are capable of the worst excesses. These people have nothing in common with the Parisians, those polite dwellers on the banks of the Seine.

II

The Revolution

In the years immediately preceding and during the Revolution the changes in the composition of the population upset the numerical relationship between these two different groups. The total population rose very slightly, or perhaps even fell a little, as we noted in our initial analysis: 547,756 in 1801 as against between 525,000 and 550,000 in 1789. It is not the total that is important, but the composition. "But where are the Parisians I used to know?" asked Meister, Grimm's ex-secretary and the friend of Diderot, in his little book, *Souvenirs de mon dernier voyage à Paris vers la fin de 1795.* A change had taken place in the population as a result of immigration, the extent of which will only become evident if we first try to determine what part the balance between births and deaths played in the change in the population's composition.

Births and Deaths

During the Revolutionary period, the number of births was slightly higher than in the last years of the Ancien Régime.[5] Even allowing for the fact that the population increased very little, or probably even decreased, and especially for the fact that the Revolutionary armies drew heavily upon the age groups old enough to beget children, it looks as if the fertility of the Parisian population rose appreciably.[6]

Other statistics, especially those for foundlings, even seem to show a changed attitude towards the family. As Peuchet commented in his *Dictionnaire universel*, published in the Year VIII: "Despite the extreme poverty of people in all classes in Paris, despite the tolerance and protection of secret unions and informal marriages, nevertheless the number of babies taken to the Foundlings Hospital is nowhere near so large as might have been feared. In M. Necker's time it was nearly 6,000; today it does not exceed 4,000." Peuchet gave the following reasons for this change:

The fact that the status of natural children is safeguarded by law means that the mothers feel less shame and have fewer difficulties; but, more importantly, there has now grown up a species of attachment to the domestic state and to bringing up children, which has been engendered by misfortune itself, by the persecutions for differences of opinion and the cruelties of every sort that have fallen on great and small families alike. It is also true that the frightful state of penury in which the Foundlings Hospital continued so long deterred mothers from sending their babes to it, as they were quite sure that the children would inevitably perish there.[7]

But the death rate largely canceled out the results of the increase in fertility. The balance between births and deaths, if taken by itself, would indicate a decrease in the population.[8]

Migration

It is obvious that migration was responsible for maintaining the relative stability of the Paris population we have described, and this constitutes an important and novel fact, with serious social implications. Whereas in previous periods, and as far back as quantitative historical research can go, Paris maintained and developed its population rate by its natural growth rather than by immigration, "being nearly 1/75th self-sufficient," as Buffon wrote,[9] in the Revolutionary period, and for the first time, immigration became the main factor in the maintenance of its numbers rather than merely its growth, indeed in its very survival.

Emigration: Immigration was the more important in that the losses by emigration have to be added to those due to deaths. The Paris population was reduced by the emigration of aristocrats and bourgeois.[10] One has only to leaf through the documents on the Public Assistance Department during the Revolution published by Tuety to note the traces of this emigration and its consequences. "During the sitting of the National Assembly on April 15, 1790, the curé of Chaillot, at the head of a deputation, expounded the sufferings of Paris with its wealthiest citizens absent, its workshops deserted, in short 120,000 inhabitants in the depths of destitution, and besides them the poor and beggars who were strangers in the city." Mercier had predicted this. "One-quarter of Paris," he had written,

does not know from one day to the next whether its labors will bring in enough to live on on the morrow. If luxury is to be less lethal . . . it must permit no interruption of work. Whenever a branch of industry falls or breaks, you find unemployed and needy from one moment to the next. It is very certain that if the wealthy were to interrupt the course of their heedless spending for the space of a year, half the capital would not be able to exist.[11]

It is hard to see what there was to induce any number of wealthy persons, most of whom owned provincial estates not far from the capital, to stay in Paris.

In addition to this bourgeois emigration there was the void left by those who joined the colors, either as volunteers at the start or after 1793 as conscripts. No estimate of their number has been made, and it is not for us to make one. "It is estimated," Meister wrote in 1795, "that the city of Paris alone has been able to supply the armies with more than 150,000 men in four years." The figure seems high; though it is true that many citizens called to the colors in Paris were not

Parisians. And lastly, allowance has to be made for war losses, which have not been estimated either. In default of a reliable estimate, we may consider that, at the lowest, if the bourgeois emigrants accounted for 50,000 persons and the armies for 100,000, at least 150,000 has to be subtracted from the numbers in 1789; that is, 524,000 minus 150,000 = 374,000. Since the population in 1795 was about 551,000, the immigrants at that date could not have amounted to less than 177,000.

Immigration: The historian of the Revolution will attach qualifications to this conclusion and identify the peaks and troughs of this immigration. Any statistics he compiles are, however, unlikely to conflict with the aggregate statistics which enable us to infer that the composition of the population changed, if only because of the new influx, homogenous in most of its demographic and social characteristics, an immigration of male laborers from new and more distant provinces as well as from the traditional areas. The workers who reached the capital in such unaccustomed numbers on the eve of the Revolution were of this kind, like those of whom a statistical study might perhaps be derived for the Revolutionary period from the documents of the charity workshops. The Montmartre workshop, for example, had 2,000 workmen at the beginning of 1789, nearly 20,000 in August 1789 and 22,000 at the end of August. Many of these workmen came from outside Paris, and when the workshop closed down on August 31, they were given an allowance to return to their province. The workshop was re-opened early that winter. Further, the system of allowances swelled the immigration. Speaking of the 3 sous per league given to the workmen to assist them in leaving, Bailly wrote on April 12, 1790: "The workmen who left Paris assisted with 3 sous per league not only return in the hopes of obtaining another gratuity, but induce people from their provinces to come and share it . . ." Many left Paris; the archives containing the files on the repayment of the monies advanced to workmen by the municipalities in 1790 might disclose how many.[12] But this emigration was undoubtedly very much smaller than the immigration which the very fact of the Revolution kept permanently in being and which must be taken into account if certain aspects of Revolutionary violence are to be intelligible.

For in certain respects the Revolution looks like a settlement of scores between two groups of the population, the old Paris bourgeoisie and the rest—those who used to be called savages, barbarians or vagrants, of whom it was stated in a petition put forward by some bourgeois in 1789 concerning the Montmartre charity workshops: "They were truly a horde of savages within reach of the most civilized city in existence." With the Revolution, the savages entered and remained in the city.

They were to be far more apparent in the first decades of the nineteenth century, for it was they who then accounted for the change and increase in the composition of the Paris population and imposed upon the community the rate of their own increase, fashioning it in their own image.

CHAPTER TWO

The New Demographic Characteristics

I

Migration and Urban Growth

The New Population

The history of the formation of the Paris population in the first half of the nineteenth century is the history of immigration into Paris. Its novelty lies not in the distribution of the areas from which the immigrants originally came, for, as in the past, they came mainly from northern France, but rather in their increased numbers, which were so large that their very magnitude makes it easier to assess them.

The differential immigration: Before the census of 1861, which was the first to give the distribution of the Paris population by department of origin, the immigration into Paris posed complex problems which we have discussed in another book. We shall merely outline them here. Theoretically, the method is simple enough, for all we have to do is to deduct the increase due to the surplus of births over deaths from the increase in population between two censuses. If we note, for instance, that the population increased by 69,823 units between 1836 and 1841, and if we know that births exceeded deaths by 16,864, we can attribute the difference between the two, namely, 52,858, to migration. We say migration deliberately, that is, the balance between immigration and emigration, not simply immigration. Here, indeed, lies the chief difficulty. A study of migration from the censuses only gives the result of migration at any given moment; it does not give a specific notion either of its size at various periods or of its chronological development. Emigration and immigration may be equally large, but may offset each other and so fail to show up in the tables at all.

Though immigration into Paris was fairly considerable, emigration was also of some size and has to be deducted from the figure for evident immigration. This emigration consisted very largely of children put out to nurse in the suburbs or the provinces: "The number of infants in the 0–5 age group," the commentary to the 1817 census noted, amounting only to 48,824, is far lower than one would expect from the total population of Paris if the known proportions are observed. A great many infants are put out to nurse in neighboring towns either by their parents or by public institutions. It is not possible at present to give the average number of children absent and the average duration of their absence with any certainty; the estimates of the inroads made on the 0–5 age group are too imprecise. It is probably that the number of children between five and ten is also reduced by this emigration, at any rate among the bourgeoisie.

"Shortly after she is born," Léon Gozlan wrote of the Parisian woman in *Le diable à Paris*,

she is bundled up, confided to the mercy of Providence and sent as far away as possible to a nurse who hangs her up on a nail somewhere. One fine day eighteen months or two years later, the father says, "Surely we have a daughter out to nurse?"—"The darling child," the mother answers, "it is really high time to get her back!" The next week a peasant woman comes in with her arms full of a wild little girl, a bunch of wild flowers and a round of cheese.

But there are many examples in the picturesque literature of children returning to Paris at a much later age.

Among the adults who left the city we should not overlook the journeymen workers leaving for the Tour de France and merchants going to seek their fortune elsewhere in France or abroad. Paris was one of the main areas of migration charted in nineteenth-century France. Estimating the number of immigrants over sixty years of age is still further complicated by other circumstances whose effects are contradictory. There was an immigration of soldiers to become pensioners at the Invalides, and of old men, large numbers of whom were attracted to Paris by the hope of qualifying for indoor relief or admission to the hostels for the aged. Conversely, there was an emigration of indigent males, formerly part of the Paris population, who were afterwards admitted to the home for the aged at Bicêtre *extra muros*. The number of those who went into retirement in the provinces, whether prematurely or after reaching the retiring age, is harder to estimate. "Forever nostalgic for their mountains," La Bédollière wrote of the water carriers from the Cantal and the Aveyron,

they go back as often as they can. They are so eager to see their native village again that they often sell their business, with the idea of buying it back or setting up another when they return to Paris. Thus, before they retire for good at the age of about fifty, they make several journeys home and invest their savings in real estate there, play skittles, dance jigs and take the waters at Cransac or Mont-d'Or for the rheumatism they claim to have contracted while plying their trade.[1]

On the other hand, the bankruptcy files show that many Paris tradesmen never retired completely; bakers and butchers kept their interest in the business which they transferred to one of their assistants. Literature is full of instances of tradesmen living in certain streets in the center of Paris, keeping an eye on their former stores. "The rue Quincampoix, that silent street between the rue Saint-Denis and the rue Saint-Martin, inhabited by uncles who have handed over their business to their nephews; a place of semi-retirement."[2]

Thus, the immigration shown up in the tables by the balance between births and deaths from one census to another is merely a differential immigration. A considerable figure has to be added for the deficit carved out by emigration, which, as is shown by a document of 1817, was very large in the age groups up to fifteen;[3] but we know that other age groups are also involved, though to a lesser extent.

If we were to take this differential immigration by itself, we should conclude that in the periods between censuses the following totals were involved:

1817–1831	71,896
1831–1836	82,047
1836–1841	52,858
1841–1846	97,119
1846–1851	no apparent immigration.

From these figures alone it appears on the face of it that the two biggest phases of immigration were those between 1831 and 1836 and between 1841 and 1846.

The real immigration: It is worth trying, however, to replace this evaluation with an evaluation of the gross immigration, or at least to attempt to approximate to it as closely as possible. It is true that we know nothing of the adult and aged emigrants away from Paris, except in the homes for the aged, which were part of Paris socially but administratively and statistically outside it. At least we know that we have to add to the immigration the figure to be deducted for the emigration of newborn babies. We do not have exact figures for every period, but the calculation made on the basis of the 1817 census shows that it was very considerable. In 1817 the emigration was 36,473 in the 0–5 age group, 29,455 in the 5–10 group and 21,873 in the 10–15 group. Taking only the immigration in the 0–5 age group and the estimate most unfavorable to our thesis, it seems very probable that we would be far below the true figure in assuming that the figure for the differential immigration can be increased by 30,000 units. In other words, we replace the foregoing table with the following:

1831–1836	112,047
1836–1841	82,858
1841–1846	127,119
1846–1851	30,000.

Annually this immigration amounts at least to:

1831–1836	22,000
1836–1841	16,000
1841–1846	25,000.

The Lodging-house Population

Though we cannot at this stage specify what proportion of this mass of immigrants is accounted for by those who lived in lodging houses, this part of the population, comprising mainly seasonal immigrants but with some permanent immigrants, must be examined separately. The seasonal immigration declined in the last years of the July Monarchy, to be replaced by permanent immigration. Special attention is paid in the statistics to this part of the population, regardless of whether it comprised seasonal workers or workmen resolved to settle in Paris. The censuses place it in a separate classification and the material circumstances of its housing and existence likewise isolate it in the Paris setting. It seems very likely that it was regarded within the newly immigrated population and in relation to the old Paris population as most representative of the nomadic elements, with which the new population was assimilated both in the censuses and in public opinion. Though the lodging-house population was not wholly responsible for the growth of the city, people generally believed that it was.

The specificity of the classifications: An examination of the lodging houses is specially interesting because it provides specific figures. It might be supposed that the statistics included traveling salesmen and tourists staying at hotels as well as workmen, but most of the censuses specifically stated that casual travelers were not included. Even in the furnished lodgings in the affluent districts only domestic servants were included. The lodging-house population covered that portion of the working population which was least stable or had come to Paris most recently. It can be identified from an abundant documentation by the Prefecture of Police, used by Frégier, who made a threefold classification of workmen's accommodation. First, lodging houses proper, sub-

ject to inspection by the police, which was carried out so efficiently
that "the figures obtained from the weekly returns drawn up by the
municipal police must be regarded as absolutely accurate." Secondly,

the lodging houses also contain communal rooms; but these rooms, the furniture being owned by the landlord, should not be confused with the communal rooms in private houses where workers club together to acquire the
furniture and which for this reason are not subject to inspection of any sort
by the police. Thirdly, the workers who set up independent communal rooms
or live in private dwellings, either alone or with their family, account for a
population about twice as large as that living in the lodging houses.[4]

Many contemporary descriptions, the most noteworthy being those by
Eugène Sue and Martin Nadaud,[5] might be used to illustrate this. The
lodging houses were frequented by such seasonal workers as the masons
from the Massif Central, but there were workmen in other trades as
well who had finally settled in Paris, and also families. The *Nouveaux
tableaux de Paris* (1828) observed:

Only in Paris can you find a species of hostel for which the very poor pay
dearly to those horrible bonifaces known as lodging-house keepers. For 10
francs a month a whole household, composed of husband, wife and a brood
of children, crowds into a room 8 feet square, in which there is one ram-
shackle bed with covers of pack-cloth. A bachelor or solitary pays 6 francs
a month for the use of one of the thirty or forty beds in the common dormi-
tory. A small locker of bed height serves him as trunk and cupboard, but
he almost never dares to keep what is left of his week's pay in it, for theft
in lodging houses is too common. . . . If he fails to pay his rent, the owner
seizes any clothes in the locker and the poor lodger is evicted forthwith
without legal formalities. He then has no alternative to renting a room by
the night; 50 or 60 centimes is the price of a refuge which the police may
visit at all hours. Not a minute passes in these hovels but a lantern shines
into some face, and for good cause.

The more suspect these lodgers were and the more closely watched by
the police,[6] the more accurately their numbers were measured. As to
foreigners, especially the less well-to-do, the Prefecture of Police reports on passports and houses letting furnished rooms would provide
an accurate guide to their immigration into Paris.[7]

Developments in the classification: While the lodging-house population constituted a well-defined category within the censuses, the position in which the category was placed at various periods is of no less
interest. "It is essential," it was stated in Volume IV of the *Recherches
statistiques* (1829), "to distinguish the sedentary population, composed
of persons who have established residence in Paris, from the variable
and mobile population, which merely happens to be visiting the capital;

for the movement in and out must be quite considerable." Similarly, in Volume VI the commentator on the censuses of 1841 and 1846 wrote:

It would be very hard, impossible perhaps, to give precise figures for the share of each of the causes of the growth of Paris; for the ebb and flow of this tide of humanity leaves few traces on the composition of the successive waves that roll in unceasingly. After the 1851 census has been taken, we shall, however, try to give some idea of the causes of the larger or smaller increase in the population of each arrondissement and district.

The main problem was whether the lodging-house population was to be classified with the population counted by name in the censuses and known as the normal population, or with the population counted by totals alone, which was called the collective population.[8]

In 1817,

the foreigners and Frenchmen present in Paris at the time, but not domiciled permanently there, such as travelers and soldiers, were very carefully identified. This distinction between the sedentary population and the population that can be regarded as mobile and very variable required the most careful supervision on the part of the Administration because of the many different situations involved. It was essential to draw a distinction between hotels in the strict sense and houses kept by lodging-house keepers and inhabited by a section of the population made up of workmen who could be regarded as inhabitants of Paris and were therefore enumerated individually.

The lodging-house population was therefore classified with the normal population and persons in hotels with the population counted collectively. In 1831, however, persons resident in Paris for less than six months and living in hotels, furnished rooms and houses managed by innkeepers and lodging-house keepers were classified with the individually enumerated population. This was also done in 1836, 1841, 1846 and 1851. The commentator on the 1851 census, indeed, gave the following reasons for this procedure in Volume VI of the *Recherches statistiques*:

The collective population does not represent the general run of the floating population, that is, the population comprising all individuals who live in the territory of a commune but have not established residence there. For, in accordance with the Ministry's instructions, persons in lodging houses are classified with the normal population because, since they almost always stay in Paris for an indefinite period, they should rightly be included in the part of the population which forms the basis for allotting the public charges; but they are in fact part of the floating population.

Developments in population totals: The evolution of the lodging-house population cannot be studied in 1817; for in the 1817 statistics furnished hotels meant hotels in the strict sense, as distinct from lodging houses inhabited by a part of the population made up of workmen who could be regarded as inhabitants and were enumerated individually. The census showed 692 furnished hotels, housing 9,484 persons. But a glance at the number of persons in lodging houses in each district makes it obvious that the working-class population was included in that classification only by oversight or error.

The following table can be compiled, however, from the censuses for 1831 to 1851:

	Lodging-house population	Men	Women	Percentage increase (lodging-house population)	Percentage increase (total population)
1831	23,150				
1836	34,905	29,742	5,164	50.8	10.25
1841	40,304	33,758	6,726	15.5	8.06
1846	50,007	41,580	8,427	24.1	12.56
1851	47,216	37,410	9,803	−5.6	−0.06

Thus, the lodging-house population increased continuously from 1831 to 1846; the increase was greatest between 1831 and 1836 and between 1841 and 1846; in each period it was larger than the general increase in the population; and its fall in 1851 was greater than that in the total population. It is noteworthy that three-quarters of this population was male; but the number of females increased steadily.

As regards locations, this population was largest in the central and eastern districts. The 1851 census calls for closer scrutiny. Part of the lodging-house population had left Paris, but the percentages remained highest in certain districts in central and eastern Paris, according to an initial chart; in the east, in the faubourg Saint-Antoine and the faubourg Saint-Jacques, and in the center, in the quartier de l'Hôtel-de-Ville, the quartier de la Cité and the quartier des Arcis, according to a second chart. Within the lodging-house population, there were more women in the western districts. In the central districts, in which men predominated, the largest concentration of women was in the quartier Sainte-Avoye and especially in the quartier de la Cité—a fact which could easily be illustrated from Eugène Sue's or Parent-Duchatelet's description of the number of prostitutes in those localities.

If we examine the evolution between two censuses, between those of 1841 and 1846, for instance, we find that the increase was larger in the new districts, but also in districts in the east and center which already had an excess of working-class population. The only central districts which showed a decrease were those in which the main clearances were being carried out; and this magnifies the image of the central districts both by throwing light on the decrease in the Cité and by simultaneously emphasizing the steady growth of the Marché Saint-Jean district.

The population of Paris was greatly increased by immigration, but the lodging-house population, which we know to have consisted mainly of itinerant and mobile workmen with no settled domicile, increased even more. Even at times of crisis there were 50,000 persons living in Paris for varying periods, sometimes six months, sometimes longer, without establishing a residence; or even if they did, nevertheless in a very precarious situation. This huge increase in the Paris population by immigration can be determined from its numbers alone. But many of the individuals involved did not settle in; they may rather be said to have camped out.

II
Immigration and Age Distribution

This immigration altered the age distribution of the Paris population, and we are able to say that, even if we cannot estimate the immigration itself with any precision, the developments in this age distribution during the first half of the nineteenth century constitute conclusive enough evidence of the preponderant influence of immigration both upon the total population and upon the groups within it. Accurate statistics do exist for the city's total population and for the population broken down by arrondissement and district.

The Documents

We can say at once that the statistical documents enable us to trace the development of the age distribution in the population of Paris. The statistics are not fully comparable as they stand, but they can easily be made comparable by using certain adjustments which statisticians in the first half of the nineteenth century, and Bertillon after them, did in fact make. The main documents bearing upon the age distribution are the censuses of 1817, certain estimates compiled at the time of the 1832 cholera epidemic and the censuses of 1836 and 1851. The comparison between these documents presumes that the data they present for both the enumerated population and the total institutional population can be computed on the same basis.

The 1817 census was the first to compile a series for age distribution in the individually enumerated population (657,172 persons). It was, however, thought necessary also to compile a second table for the collective population, that is, of inhabitants who had not stated their age or civil status, namely, persons in the prisons, hospitals, homes for the aged and miscellaneous institutions, 56,794 in all, bringing the total population up to 713,966. In order to compile this second table, "it was thought necessary," the compilers of the census wrote,

to assemble all information which might serve to give an accurate estimate of the age of the 56,794 persons included in the collective census; to them were added the inmates in the homes for the aged at Bicêtre and Montrouge, who are manifestly part of the Paris population. The two institutions situated *extra muros* should not have been included in the census of the inner city, but it was essential to ascertain their population separately and to classify it by age.

Bertillon adjusted the 1836 census to that of 1817 in a statistical study published in the Yearbook for 1903.[9]

We assumed that the population of the hospitals and municipal homes for the aged and its age composition were approximately the same as in 1817 (12,596 in 1817; 12,055 in 1836), and for the military population we made a similar assumption about the ages of the cadets and those at other military schools. There remained 14,838 inhabitants whom we had to classify as "age unknown."

The censuses of 1831, 1841 and 1846 did not include a classification by age. But the 1851 census contained data readily comparable with those for 1817 and 1836. One difficulty, however, remained, and was very evident in the 1851 census: "The ages were compiled in accordance with statements made by the persons counted, not on presentation of authentic documents, and in some series the statements were not, perhaps, invariably truthful."[10] Hence, up to the census of 1901 there was a tendency to go for round numbers, a study of which was carried out later by Léon Tabah, who made the requisite corrections by estimating the number of survivors of the successive generations, using the annual numbers of births and the appropriate tables of mortality and then comparing his findings with the data shown in the census and cross-checking the age groups against the round figure.[11]

Age Distribution: Total Population

If we take the comparable data in the censuses of 1817, 1836 and 1851 and leave aside the population counted collectively, we note a reduction in the population under fifteen and over fifty-nine years of age in the first half of the nineteenth century.

The major groups: This fact is obvious if we confine ourselves to three age groups, namely, 0–15, 15–60 and over 60. Between 1817 and 1856, the evolution of the figures in each group per thousand inhabitants shows that:

(i) the proportion of adults (15–60) was on the increase, thus:

1817	694
1836	713
1851	742
1856	758

(ii) the proportion of persons over 60 decreased until 1856, thus:

1817	103
1836	78
1851	62
1856	71

(iii) the proportion in the 0–15 age group also decreased, but less regularly and a slight increase occurred in 1836, thus:

1817	207
1836	209
1851	196
1856	171.

The minor groups: This fact is still more obvious if the population is classified in five- and ten-year age groups, with particular attention to the 15–60 age group. The figures per thousand inhabitants for 1817, 1836, 1851 and 1856 were:

Age	1817	1836	1851	1856
0–4	68	72	57.3	52.4
5–9	64	67	60.6	56.7
10–14	70	70	63.9	62.2
15–19	100	90	79.9	85.2
20–24	103	107	108.9	106.7
25–29	98	106	120.3	124.1
30–39	163	204	196.5	205.7
40–49	127	127	142.8	142.3
50–59	103	78	96.4	93.8
60–69	70	50	48.7	47.5
70–79	27	24	20.2	19.1
80 and over	6	5	4.5	4.2

Thus the general increase in numbers in the 15–60 age group did not apply to every age group.

It did not apply either to the lower or the higher segments, thus:

15–19:	1817	100
	1836	90
	1851	79.9
	1856	85.2
50–59:	1817	103
	1836	78
	1851	96.4
	1856	93.8

It applied to the intermediate categories, but unevenly, thus:

(i) the smallest increase was in the 20–24 age group:

1817	103
1836	107
1851	108.9
1856	106.7

(ii) the most regular increase was in the 25–29 age group:

1817	98
1836	106
1851	120.3
1856	124.1

(iii) the increase in the 30–39 group was:

1817	163
1836	204
1851	196.5
1856	205.7

(iv) the increase in the 40–49 age group was:

1817	127
1836	127
1851	142.8
1856	142.3

The evolution of these latter age groups is of special importance for immigration.

To sum up:

(i) in 1836, as compared with 1817, the development by age group was:

20–24	+4
25–29	+8
30–39	+41

(ii) in 1851, as compared with 1836, the development by age group was:

20–24	+1
25–29	+14
30–39	−8
40–49	+15
50–59	+18.

Let us consider these two phases in the development of the Paris population, and, first of all, the composition of the population in 1836 as compared with that in 1817. The age distribution shows a larger immigration of persons between thirty and thirty-nine than of persons under thirty. It would, of course, be an exaggeration to say that any immigration between twenty and thirty was more likely to be mostly working-class and between thirty and forty mostly bourgeois. For instance, we know that the young masons from the Creuse were accompanied by older and more experienced masons to look after them. However, if we only go by the statistics, it is probable that the fact that there were more immigrants between thirty and thirty-nine than between twenty and twenty-nine does show that alongside the working-class immigration there was another immigration, which we cannot definitely call bourgeois but can only say was composed of other occupational groups.

The statistical data should be handled in the following way. Initially, we should approach the statistical information as if we possessed no other documentation. Our next approach should be to use that other documentation; it is not adequate in itself, but we may use whatever part of it is consistent with the incontrovertible and determinant evidence in the aggregate statistics. This documentation consists, in the main, of the vast qualitative material, which is far more concerned with the description of the bourgeois than with the working-class immigration into Paris and has been adopted by qualitative social history as a ground for overestimating the bourgeois immigration. But the documentation also includes a quantitative documentation, which, however, only involves limited numbers and is itself meaningful only in the light of the aggregate statistics, such as a statistcial examination of the bankruptcy files, which we have made in an earlier work.[12]

The age distribution in 1851 as compared with that in 1836 definitely confirms these observations. We know that various circumstances brought the growth of Paris to a halt and that the political and economic crisis slowed down the working-class immigration. Nevertheless, the large increases in the 25–29 age group shows that the youthful immigration into Paris after 1836—which is highly likely to have been mainly working-class—was a larger factor than it had been before 1836.[13]

Now let us assemble the conclusions that can be drawn from this initial analysis of the changes in the age distribution of the Paris population which took place during the first half of the nineteenth century. While it is true that the general development of the Paris population in the nineteenth century showed a constant decrease in the 0–15 and the over-60 age groups and an increase in the intermediate 15–60 age group, this development was certainly more clear-cut and more rapid during the first half of the century; after 1860 it definitely slowed down. Secondly, we can perceive in this phenomenon the results of an immigration which was very large during the first half of the nineteenth century, larger than it had ever been before and larger than it was to be again, at any rate until the last two decades of the nineteenth century. The development in the 15–60 age group, however, shows that there were several types of immigration: a youthful immigration, probably of workmen and artisans, and an older immigration, which we may assume, pending the discovery of further statistics, to have been bourgeois.

The City and the Age Groups

The population of the arrondissements and districts was just as much affected by the age distribution among the immigrants as the aggregate population, but unevenly; the differences in age by arrondissement and district provide a valid measurement of the immigrants' settlement into the Paris setting and of their comparative density when they occupied certain localities. Before we examine this uneven conquest, however, we must note that, unlike what we see in the second half of the nineteenth century, the examination of the age distribution in the Paris arrondissements in our period relates only to immigration, and not to such factors as the death, marriage and fertility rates.

Age distribution and population movement: It was generally held, after the end of the nineteenth century, at any rate, that age distribution must necessarily have a great effect on the fertility, marriage and death rates by district. In theory, the districts in which the population is most youthful should be the districts with the lowest death rate and the highest marriage and fertility rates. While this relationship between age and population holds good for a city as a whole, it is not absolutely clear in the individual districts. There very probably is a relationship, and a close one, between these phenomena, but it cannot be substantiated by a study of the statistical documents alone. And, secondly, although such causal relationships may have emerged after the end of the nineteenth century, they were far less evident in the period we are considering.

Let us take the ages at which it seems easiest to perceive a relationship between age and the death rate. If we pass beyond the ages of heavy infant mortality and take only the fortunate age at which a man has escaped the perils of childhood and is not yet experiencing the dangers in store for him when he grows older, we should assume theoretically that, at all events, the lightest death rate lies between the ages of twenty and thirty and—whether normal or exceptional—in the arrondissements with the largest population between these age limits.

In actual fact, many factors intervene to upset this assumption. There are social factors which originate in the unequal conditions of living and modes of life. There are also psychological and moral factors, as can be seen from this comment by Quételet on the 1832 cholera epidemic:

The violence of the passions seems to have a great influence in shortening human life. Thus, when a man has attained his full physical development after the age of twenty and one would suppose that he would develop his full energies to counter all the forces of destruction, his vital force is apparently subject to a "minimum" degree of resistance. This undue liability to death, which does not at all apply to women, lasts until he reaches the age of thirty, when the fire of the passions has already begun to die down. The influence of morale on the number of deaths becomes very apparent during epidemics. We were able to observe, especially during the ravages of the heat wave in Europe, how fatal intemperance was to those addicted to it.[14]

Age distribution has considerable relevance, therefore, to both the quantitative and the qualitative study of the death rate. A district with a predominantly youthful population is not necessarily one in which the death rate is lowest, either in normal times or during epidemics.

Similarly, the relationship between age and the marriage rate, which holds good for a city as a whole, does not necessarily apply to the districts. A district is not isolated like a village.

In the second half of the nineteenth century, the urban unit broke up into widely differing social areas. In 1876, for instance, there was a great contrast between the poor districts, which were younger, and the wealthy districts, which were older. The wealthy arrondissements had the fewest children in the 0–5 age group, notably the VIIIth (397 per 10,000) and the IXth (472), while the XIIIth (957 per 10,000) and the XIXth (990) had the most; the difference was twice as large. When the ratio was 1,310 per 100,000 for the city as a whole in the 5–15 age group, it was again the VIIIth (900) and the IXth (880) which had fewest and the XIVth (1,830) and the XXth (1,720) which had the most. These differences had a great influence on the marriage, fertility and death rates.

In the Paris of the first half of the nineteenth century, however, we can assume at this stage in our study that it will be harder to establish a relationship between age distribution and the marriage and fertility rates by district. Quite obviously, in a smaller Paris with a proportionately larger population a great variety of contrasts will show up within a single district and these contrasts will not merge in large blocks of districts or arrondissements differing from each other so widely as they did later in the century.

Great contrasts certainly existed, and were vividly described in the picturesque literature already discussed, but they were less marked at the end of the Restoration and during the July Monarchy than at the beginning of the century. "I've just conceived a wild and extravagant idea," a young fop cries in the *Voyage aux faubourgs Saint-Marcel et Saint-Jacques par deux habitants de la Chaussée d'Antin* (1806). "You barely surmise the existence of another half of Paris. . . . Do you feel up to embarking upon a journey through the dirty smoky streets of the faubourgs? Personally I adore contrasts, and methinks 'twill be a pleasure to observe the manners and customs of an almost savage tribe." Of the many descriptions, Dufey's *Mémorial de Paris* and the *Voyage aux cimetières de Paris*[15] perhaps best contrast the most affluent with the most poverty-stricken districts and, among the working-class districts, the more civilized faubourg Saint-Antoine with the faubourg Saint-Jacques and the faubourg Saint-Marcel, which, as Lachaise remarked, seemed to belong to some other city.

However, though there were great differences between certain marginal districts, certain faubourgs and the rest of Paris, and though these differences were still evident at the beginning of the century, they vanished in face of the new influx into the heart of the old city. Before the great segregation, which was just beginning to crystallize in the last years of the July Monarchy, the greater part of the Parisian population mingled in the same districts and streets regardless of social differences. Neither the contrasts in age distribution nor the relationship between age distribution and the fertility and marriage rates, therefore, were so pronounced at that time. Whereas some conclusions about the fertility rate and the death rate can be derived from an examination of age distribution at the end of the nineteenth century, in the first half of the century the immigration aspect of the population movement is all that we are concerned with—the differences in immigration by arrondissement and district disclosed by the evolution of the age distribution within them. From this point of view, the great contrast between the Paris of 1817 and the Paris of 1851 is the only really relevant point.

Age distribution in 1817:   In the age distribution in 1817 the contrasts between arrondissements were not so great as those in the second half of the nineteenth century.

This greater uniformity is characteristic of every age group, but perhaps most particularly the youngest group.

In the 0–5 age group, for example, if we except the XIth arrondissement, which included the Latin Quarter, and the Xth, which included the Invalides, and also the IInd (Chaussée d'Antin, Palais-Royal, Feydeau) and the IIIrd (faubourg Poissonnière, Montmartre, Saint-Eustache, Mail), rich and poor arrondissements showed much the same proportions.

In the 5–10 age group, the distribution was also fairly uniform, though it was largest in the VIIIth (Marais, Popincourt, Saint-Antoine, Quinze-Vingts) and the XIIth (Saint-Jacques, Saint-Marcel, Jardin du Roi, Observatoire), an anomaly explained by the existence of the Foundlings Hospital in the VIIIth and similar institutions in the XIIth.

The distribution of the 20–30 age group brings out a contrast between a younger and an older Paris. This group predominated, firstly in the IIIrd, IVth and Vth arrondissements and, secondly, in the Ist, VIth and VIIth, that is, in the central districts, in which the heavy work at Les Halles set the standard; but also in the luxury and business districts, extolled in scores of descriptions from which we select that by Lanfranchi:

The faubourg du Roule, the Chaussée d'Antin, the faubourg Montmartre, the faubourg Poissonnière and part of the faubourg Saint-Denis, the quartier de la Halle, the quartier du Palais-Royal and the quartier de la place Vendôme are the districts where we find the notabilities of banking and every-

Age group	Arrondissement (per 10,000 inhabitants)											
	Ist	IInd	IIIrd	IVth	Vth	VIth	VIIth	VIIIth	IXth	Xth	XIth	XIIth
0–5	758	632	658	632	743	763	722	759	729	604	522	749
5–10	654	597	583	600	670	691	654	800	669	647	584	711
10–15	704	672	671	635	749	814	725	810	718	651	664	779
15–20	1,040	1,102	1,085	1,053	966	1,143	1,083	1,002	996	926	981	972
20–25	928	1,063	1,039	1,104	1,090	953	967	898	864	899	993	920
25–30	1,023	1,092	1,116	1,065	1,008	965	983	838	879	891	844	871
30–40	1,691	1,760	1,708	1,766	1,624	1,588	1,605	1,523	1,542	1,614	1,568	1,489
40–50	1,339	1,341	1,380	1,274	1,262	1,266	1,288	1,296	1,339	1,389	1,369	1,280
50–60	1,011	985	1,008	991	1,025	990	1,047	1,046	1,156	1,151	1,190	1,090
60–70	588	543	569	645	641	616	678	759	783	862	890	814
70–80	194	178	187	207	195	185	229	278	281	305	329	297
80–90	34	33	38	28	26	25	37	49	41	58	64	55
90–100	2	2	1		1	1	2	2	3	3	2	3
TOTAL	10,000	10,000	10,000	10,000	10,000	10,000	10,000	10,000	10,000	10,000	10,000	10,000

thing connected with the Stock Exchange; those who frequent public places, the theaters, the Ministries and the Court; courtesans of high and low degree; actors and men of letters. Wherever you stroll there are resplendent shops. It is the land of the elegants of trade, of pretty shopkeepers, of "morality" and virtue as a stock-in-trade.[16]

On the other hand, the arrondissements with the lowest proportions were:

the VIIIth:	Marais, Popincourt, Saint-Antoine, Quinze-Vingts	1,736
the IXth:	Ile Saint-Louis, Hôtel-de-Ville, Cité, Arsenal	1,743
the Xth:	Monnaie, Saint-Thomas d'Aquin, Invalides, faubourg Saint-Germain	1,790
the XIIth:	Saint-Jacques, Saint-Marcel, Jardin du Roi, Observatoire	1,791.

There are, of course, arrondissements where in some districts the age distribution was weighted by homes for the aged or hospitals, the Invalides in the Xth, the Cité with the Hôtel-Dieu in the IXth; and even more obviously, the faubourg Saint-Antoine in the VIIIth with the Saint-Antoine Hospital and the Quinze-Vingts Hospital for the Blind; and the Salpêtrière and the numerous hospitals and homes for the aged in the faubourg Saint-Jacques and the faubourg Saint-Marcel. We should not overlook other public institutions, which, conversely, made the population younger, such as the many barracks in the faubourg Saint-Antoine and the Foundlings Hospital; but these youthful groups failed to counterbalance the generally older level due to the relative paucity of the 20–30 age group.

This age distribution puts us on the track of an important social fact. It is true that there was a youthful population of workers and artisans in the IXth and VIIIth, containing the Marais and the quartier Saint-Antoine, but this working-class and artisan population was not so youthful as the population of the luxury districts. The wealthy, rather than the other, districts were pre-eminently the haunt of youth.

The attraction exercised on the young by the most profitable, the best paid and least onerous occupations—those demanding versatility and adaptability rather than physical labor, those concentrated by economic development in the Paris of the luxury trades, banking, business and entertainment—and the relegation to the east and south of Paris of the most arduous and least attractive work—the obscure artisan toil which wrought in the back shop, in thousands of back shops, every kind of article which became the delight and fame of luxurious and resplendent store windows—were manifest facts as early as 1817, though still on a very small scale; but developments during the nineteenth century were to reinforce this trend. In the last decades of the century the banlieue became even more sharply defined. Economically, it began where the undertaking—factory, workshop or warehouse—ceased to serve the customer direct, but worked for one or more enterprises with direct exchange relations with trading. This industrial belt became a place where raw materials were processed for working up at a later technical stage, for using up by-products and waste and for preliminary or marginal work; unlike the districts inside the city, it had to deal with things rather than men. Socially, this division of labor became reflected in a corresponding segregation of men. The least youthful and least skilled made their way to the southern suburbs; and it was there that integration with the Paris environment was longest delayed and that survivals of provincial manners and customs lingered longest.

These differences, however, could be deduced from the age distribution as early as 1817. We can see from the 1851 census how they became wider during the first half of the nineteenth century.

Age distribution in 1851:   As we have already shown, the population under twenty and over sixty decreased between 1817 and 1851, while the adult population increased, the youngest age groups even more than the rest. We shall now see how this evolution was distributed among the arrondissements and how the contrast between a younger Paris and an older Paris crystallized.

I. THE CHILDREN. In all the arrondissements there was a decline in the child population; this occurred in rich and poor arrondissements, old and new districts alike.

The proportionate decrease in the 0–5 age group was general. While it was roughly the same in every arrondissement, it was slightly more marked in the IXth (-1.71) and XIIth (-1.71), as well as in the Ist (-1.51) and IInd (-1.52). We should note that a very slight rise or fall in this general and almost uniform decline catches the eye and seems to highlight differences which are more apparent than real, reflecting particular and exceptional phenomena far more than actual differences in the distribution. It is manifest, for example, that the VIIIth and XIth were exceptions to the general decline because they contained institutions sheltering children in these age groups, the Foundlings in the VIIIth, and in the XIth the Deaf-Mutes, an infants' institution and a maternity home in the former Port-Royal.

In the 5–10 age group the development was much the same and

applied to the same arrondissements, except that the proportions fell in the VIIIth itself. Only the Ist and XIth rose slightly. It is very probable that the foregoing remarks about the purely local significance of marked rises and falls apply in full here also. It was not the distribution of children that caused the greatest differences in the age distribution in 1851.

2. THE ADULTS. In fact, it was among the adults that the general increase in proportions was most unevenly distributed—more particularly in the 20–30 age group—and the contrasts between arrondissements greatest. The size of the 20–30 age group rose everywhere, but notably in certain arrondissements. We should not attach too much importance to the Xth, in which the large increase (+8.3) was due to the growth of a military population, or the XIth (+6.4), in which many more schools had been built. On the other hand, we cannot fail to note the appreciable increase in the IXth (+7), an already overcrowded working-class arrondissement, and in the VIth (+3.4), the IIIrd (+3.6) and especially the Ist (+6.3), to which more profitable economic developments had attracted a more youthful population.

The distribution of the population between the ages of twenty and thirty by arrondissement in 1817 and in 1851 is even more significant. The distribution in 1817 already showed some differences, which we have stressed and commented upon earlier (see p. 240), but they were not as yet very sharp; the general profile was barely indented. In 1851 the indentations were very marked, showing greater differences. The arrondissements in which the population between twenty and thirty was smallest show deeper troughs. Here was the less youthful Paris we have already seen, but here the slightest trace of youth becomes more obvious, especially in the three artisan arrondissements, the XIIth (Saint-Jacques and Saint-Marcel), the VIIIth (Marais, Popincourt, Saint-Antoine, Quinze-Vingts) and the VIIth (Sainte-Avoye, Arcis, Mont-de-Piété, Marché Saint-Jean). But some arrondissements tower up, crushing the older Paris with their youth; on the one hand, the Ist (Roule, Champs-Elysées, place Vendôme, Tuileries) and the IIIrd (faubourg Poissonnière, faubourg Montmartre, Saint-Eustache, Mail) and, on the other, the IXth.

We should carefully note this contrast and the two kinds of youth shown up by these peaks. The most youthful population occupied the quartier des Halles and the quartier de l'Hôtel-de-Ville, where we know that a population of masons and laborers crowded the lodging houses near the place de Grève. But there was also a large youthful population in the Ist arrondissement (Roule, Champs-Elysées, place Vendôme, Tuileries) and the IIIrd (faubourg Poissonnière, faubourg Montmartre, Saint-Eustache, Mail). These contrasts stressed, even more clearly than in 1817, the attraction exerted upon the young by the most profitable and least arduous occupations, those assembled by economic development in the business, luxury and entertainment districts, while the districts in the east and south were abandoned to the more taxing occupations and to other age groups. The study of the age distribution of the population thus provides us with statistical material for social descriptions and enables us to single out the usable evidence in an inconsistent qualitative documentation.

III
Migration and Distribution by Sex

Even larger social consequences were entailed by the combination of the change in the distribution by sex with the lowering of the distribution by age in the composition of the Paris population. Studies of modern capitals, and of Paris in particular, have shown that the proportion of women to men in the population of almost all large cities is higher and have stressed the economic and social significance of this predominance of women both in the total population of capital cities and in that of their most affluent districts. As J. Daric has shown, the suburban districts and communes of Paris with the largest proportion of women are also those in which the average income per taxpayer, the number of dwellings with bathrooms and the stature of both servicemen and newborn babies are highest and the Communist vote lowest.[17] This diagnosis of the population throws light on the earlier development of Paris as well as on urban economics and sociology in the modern period.

The distribution of the Paris population changed radically during the first half of the nineteenth century. Though the female population before the Revolution cannot be estimated at all accurately, it was probably slightly larger than the male. The lower-class social groups which migrated temporarily or permanently to Paris were predominantly male, whereas the composition of the native population was normal, that is to say, it had a higher proportion of women, as in all capital cities.

Women predominated in 1817, the year at which this study starts. The census for that year was the first to show distribution by age and sex. In a population totaling 657,172 individually enumerated persons, there were 305,247 men and 351,925 women. After 1817, immigration radically changed this distribution; the proportion of females fell constantly both in relation to the total population and, even more steeply, in relation to the population of certain districts.

Distribution by Sex in the Total Population

A sharp fall in the female population can be seen between the censuses of 1817 and 1836, followed by a slow decline between 1836 and the end of our period, with a rise only in 1851.

This development is very apparent when the proportion of women is computed in relation to the total population, that is to say, the population comprising both the individually enumerated and the population counted collectively in the hospitals and homes for the aged, prisons, military establishments and miscellaneous institutions. The percentage figures for the female population computed on this basis were:

1817	54
1836	48.61
1841	49.60
1846	49.39
1851	50.98.

Despite the difficulties and uncertainties necessarily involved, we have now to delimit the categories of the population in which this increase occurred. Eliminating the collective population and taking only the "normal" population, and being careful to include in this only the same groups, we obtain the following percentage figures:

1817	53
1836	49.40
1841	51.27
1846	51.16
1851	52.58.

The percentage decline is quite large between 1817 and 1836 and shows the effect of a predominantly male immigration; the conclusions to be drawn from an examination of the established population confirm those drawn from our examination of the aggregate population in this respect. On the other hand, the rise in the total population between 1836 and 1841 is seen to have been larger in the "normal" population, within which women had been in the majority even before this. While there was a slight fall between 1841 and 1846, the percentage increase became far more pronounced between 1846 and 1851. The 1841 and 1846 censuses take us further and disclose, in part at least, the origin of this rise in the female population. They give percentages for the individually enumerated population, first with and then without the domestic service category, thus:

	Including domestic service	Excluding domestic service
1836	49.40	–
1841	51.27	49.81
1846	51.16	49.65

This shows that if domestic servants are excluded from the "normal" population, the proportion of women was a good deal lower. The ratio of women per hundred men within the "normal" population in 1846 was 104.80; but in the domestic service category it was 242.57 and in other occupations 98.65.

Distribution by Sex and Age

A change also took place in the distribution by sex and age, with economic and social consequences quite as important as the changes in the aggregate distribution. A balance between the sexes in the groups which make up the adult age group is important for its demographic effects—the marriage and fertility rates—as well as for its social effects; it is likely that the imbalance of the sexes between the ages of twenty and forty in the marginal Paris groups in the last years of the Ancien Régime had a good deal to do with the brutalities described by Restif, the women-hunts he tells about with such a pretense of naïveté.

The sex distribution of the population counted at home in the 1817 and 1836 censuses was:

Age group	Men (per 100)		Women (per 100)	
	1817	1836	1817	1836
0–5	34	37	35	37
5–10	32	32	34	34
10–15	35	35	37	34
15–20	50	51	54	39
20–25	40	54	56	48
25–30	41	53	55	52
30–40	73	108	89	97
40–50	59	65	72	67
50–60	53	39	53	41
60–70	35	22	35	28
70–80	11	10	13	12
80–90	2	2	3	3

Thus, in 1817 women predominated both in the total count and in every age group except the 50–70 groups. This predominance was very strongly marked in the 20–50 groups owing to the accumulated effects of the drafts and wars; in the 20–25 group there were 56 women to 40 men, in the 25–30 group 55 women to 41 men. In 1836, though the total for women was lower—49 to 51—the fall was particularly marked in the 30–40 age group, in which there were 97 women to 108 men. Women were fewer, and therefore scarce and sought after. It is easy enough to find scores of illustrations of this in the romantic literature, Eugène Sue's *grisettes* and *lorettes*, for instance; and in the less famous novelists we see women not at all reluctant to find themselves protectors or lovers, or even, gaining wisdom as they grew older, husbands. It is just as easy to see the consequences in the feminist literature that sprang up at this period, culminating at the Revolution of 1848. The principal feature of a development most marked in districts with a large working-class population was that it necessarily affected every aspect of urban life.

Paris in the first half of the nineteenth century was a city with more men than women.

An inquiry conducted by the Chamber of Commerce in 1846 estimated the working-class population at 342,530, with 204,925 men, 112,891 women and 24,714 children and young persons. Thus men outnumbered women in that group. It is true that this conclusion needs some qualification in the light of the percentages calculated solely within the population counted at home, but these percentages, with domestic servants excluded, bring out the importance of domestic service in the female population. The least debatable is the evolution that appears in the percentages within the total population.

It makes little difference whether or not one takes the population counted at home, for this was in any event a population counted in Paris, a population which was there and in which males predominated over females, and to a still larger extent in the age groups in which such an imbalance between the sexes affects every aspect of social life.

Distribution by Sex and the City

The censuses from 1836 onward show the increase in the male population and the decrease in the female population in the arrondissements and districts. We shall examine them, first, in relation to the total population and, secondly, in relation to the domiciled population.

Relation of the sexes to the total population: In 1836, men predominated in all arrondissements except the IInd (Chaussée d'Antin, Palais-Royal, Feyreau, faubourg Montmartre), the wealthiest and the most elegant. The predominance of males is most marked in the IXth (Cité, Ile Saint-Louis, Arsenal, Hôtel-de-Ville), the VIIIth (Marais, Popincourt, faubourg Saint-Antoine, Quinze-Vingts) and the IVth (Marchés, Banque, Louvre, Saint-Honoré).

Three divisions of Paris were taking shape: a western Paris in which women predominated, an eastern Paris with rather more men than women, and a central Paris with a very high proportion of males.

The 1841 census reinforced this development. Firstly, though there still were more men, the percentage increase in the female population in relation to total population was evident and continued from census to census. Secondly, however, this increase did not occur in all parts of the city. A western Paris acquired a personality; the proportion of women in it rose, and they increased even more notably in the regions in which contemporary novelists situated the ambitions of their young adventurers, such as Rastignac, of whom Balzac wrote: "His eyes fastened almost greedily on the region between the place Vendôme and the dome of the Invalides, the haunt of that fashionable society which he had proposed to invade." In all the literature of the period it was there that the largest number of young, lovely—and wealthy—women were to be found; and it was there that the bourgeoisie from other districts dreamed of living and finding a species of ennoblement.[18] They were districts in which women gained their conquests, though often only ephemerally: "There are women who pass through Paris like the sons of the Virgin in the upper air," wrote Balzac in his little book on women. "One has no idea where they come from or where they are going, queens one day and slaves the next."

Where did they go? To districts for whose description we must turn to authors other than Balzac, Esquiros, for example, who best described the fate of the aged women of the people in inhuman mid-nineteenth-century Paris.[19] They went mostly to the districts with the highest proportion of men. Describing the poverty of the working classes in the XIIth arrondissement, Buret noted that "here there are proportionately more indigent women than men. Women are not completely workers in the industrial sense. If a man does not add what he earns to his companion's inadequate wages, her sex alone will doom her to poverty."[20] This lays the correct emphasis on the main difference reflected in the relative predominance of women in the affluent districts, but not in the other districts. In the former we find a civilization based upon a preponderance of women; in the latter the women are not only fewer and older, but exist only as adjuncts to the men.

This development culminated in 1846, when the individuality of the three divisions of Paris was delineated more sharply than ever before or after: the western Paris, in which the proportion of women rose, especially in the IInd arrondissement; the eastern Paris, which annexed even the XIIth arrondissement; and the central Paris, which grouped the IVth, VIIth and IXth arrondissements in a single block in which men predominated by far.

In 1851, this pattern began to break up and give way to a different distribution, which was carried further under the Second Empire. The general increase in the female population was marked by a proportionate increase in the affluent western districts. This predominantly female region began to encroach upon eastern Paris, annexing the Vth and even the XIIth arrondissements. The decrease in the male population was revealed by a shrinkage of the areas in which it had predominated. Even in the male block in central Paris, the proportion of males in the IXth fell, and only the VIIIth (Mont-de-Piété, Sainte-Avoye, Marché Saint-Jean, Arcis) kept its former ascendancy.

Relation of the sexes to the domiciled population: Eliminating the institutional population and taking only the domiciled population in which, as we have shown, there was a large proportion of females, we note that the distribution by sex observed earlier remained practically the same.

In 1836, the elimination of the institutional population increased the female proportion in some arrondissements in which the institutional population was predominantly male, as it was in the barracks and in the hospitals and homes for the aged intended solely for men, provided, of course, that the numbers were of some significance in any case. In the institutional count of the Xth arrondissement, for example, there were 4,263 soldiers in the Ecole Militaire barracks and 2,929 in the Invalides hospital. There were 2,933 men in the military establishments in the Ist, including 1,569 in the quartier du Roule. Their elimination appreciably raised the proportion of women.

In other arrondissements, however, eliminating the institutional population affects both the men and the women and is not, therefore, so clear-cut. In the XIIth it reduces the male population to some extent by eliminating the men in the barracks in the quartier de l'Observatoire (1,801); but it likewise eliminates the 5,243 women in the homes for old women and the 4,679 in the Salpêtrière, the old women's home in the quartier Saint-Marcel. Nevertheless, there still were more men than women relative to the total population, and the proportion would be even higher without these institutions. In the VIIIth the elimination of the institutional population affects large numbers of men (the 2,224 soldiers in the quartier Popincourt), but the population in the hospitals and homes for the aged in this arrondissement was almost equally divided between men and women (677 persons in the Quinze-Vingts, 284 women and 393 men). Relative to the total population the preponderance of men was still such that its proportion of the domiciled population corresponds almost exactly to that of its proportion to the total population. In the IInd, the elimination of the institutional population affects the 1,492 soldiers in the faubourg Poissonnière, but also the 733 women in the Saint-Lazare prison.

By thus taking the individually enumerated population separately—but bearing in mind that that population includes migrant workmen as well as Parisians—we obtain a distribution by arrondissement which resembles the distribution of the total population, except that as early as 1836 it reveals the contrast (which showed up in the total distribution only in 1846) between the three divisions of Paris already described.

In 1841, the distribution of the female population relative to the domiciled population alone brings out clearly an increase in the number of women in all arrondissements. After 1841, there were more women than men in all parts of Paris except the center, the IXth, VIIth and IVth arrondissements.

Nevertheless, the differences already noted between the three divisions of Paris continued, except that the female proportion of the population was higher. But—and this is very important—the statistics in the census reveal the share of female domestic service in the new proportion of the female population relative to the domiciled population alone. If we eliminate domestic servants from this female population, we find that the female proportion drops everywhere and that the decrease is no larger in western than in eastern Paris. This fact needs stressing. The differences with regard to the proportionate female population between the affluent arrondissements (Ist, IInd and Xth) and the poor arrondissements (VIIIth, VIth and XIIth) are accounted for not so much by domestic servants—most of whom were female—as by the size of the domiciled population. It is true that the elimination of domestic servants reduces the proportionate female population in the affluent districts to a greater extent than in the other districts, but the reduction is not much larger in one than in the other.[21] Only in two arrondissements does the elimination of domestic service cause a real collapse in the proportionate female population; these are the VIIth (Mont-de-Piété, Sainte-Avoye, Marché Saint-Jean, Arcis), with a drop from 48.80 to 42.56%, and the Vth (faubourg Saint-Denis, Bonne-Nouvelle, Montorgueil, porte Saint-Martin), with a drop from 50.96 to 45.92%.

Again, if domestic servants are eliminated, the proportion of men in these arrondissements becomes even higher than it was.

In 1846, the statistics for the female population relative to the domiciled population alone restore the contrast between western Paris, with the highest proportion of female population, and eastern Paris, with which central Paris now merged.

The districts: A scrutiny of the distribution of the male and female population by district not only confirms the contrast noted between the three major Paris groupings, but reveals in detail the particular districts which weight the arrondissements in one direction rather than the other.

In 1836, for instance, it is obvious that the constant high proportion of males in the IXth arrondissement was accounted for by the quartier de l'Hôtel-de-Ville; the Ile Saint-Louis had a higher proportion of women. In the VIIth arrondissement, the explanation for the almost constantly high male proportion is the quartier Popincourt and the faubourg Saint-Antoine; the quartier du Marais had a larger female population. Contemporary descriptions amply confirm this statistical observation, that by Lanfranchi, for example, with his distinction between the Marais and the neighboring districts in his *Voyage à Paris* (1830):

We must except the Marais in its narrower limits, that is to say, the parts around the place Royale, inhabited only by the melancholy and peaceable nation of rentiers. In this dim recess all is calm, all is monotony, all is dead, while, not far off, trade with its myriad arms everywhere displays its fertile and industrious strength to the full.

Other groupings occur; the districts, breaking out of their administrative bounds, form far more realistic units. The Paris of the center ob-

viously takes in a larger area than it does in the map of the arrondissements, and the size of the proportionate male population becomes more
evident; Cité and Arcis, Sainte-Avoye and Lombards, Saint-Honoré
and Banque in the heart of Paris have the highest proportionate male
population of the whole capital. And in eastern Paris the quartier
Popincourt, the faubourg Saint-Antoine and the Quinze-Vingts stand
out sharper.

The census of 1851 takes us beyond the foregoing analysis by district and reveals the very streets which had the larger proportion of
men or women in each district. The main finding is that in the districts where women predominated they were distributed almost equally
in the principal and secondary streets. In the Ist arrondissement, for
example, the preponderance of women was general and uniform in the
quartier du Roule, the Champs-Elysées and the place Vendôme.

On the other hand, in the predominantly male arrondissements this
preponderance was not general; it varied a great deal. In the IXth
arrondissement, for example, in which men were in an overwhelming
majority (6,305 men to 4,794 women), men predominated in most of
the streets, but there were more women on the quais and in the rue
Saint-Antoine.[22]

In the VIIth arrondissement, though men predominated in every
street in the quartier Sainte-Avoye, totaling 11,196 as against 10,194
women, there were more women than men in the rue Saint-Martin.
There was a similar contrast in the VIth arrondissement: though the
porte Saint-Denis district had 9,998 men to 9,521 women and there
were more men than women in most of its streets, there were more
women than men on the boulevard Saint-Denis and in the rue Saint-
Denis.

Such was the distribution by sex of the Paris population. And it
emerges even more clearly in that we are dealing only with the city,
not with the banlieue, where the distribution by sex was more evenly
balanced and remained so throughout the period. Except in a very few
communes in which the preponderance of men reflects a demographic,
economic and social situation closely resembling that of the capital,
there were more women than men in the banlieue.[23]

"There are arrondissements in which there are not enough women
as compared with men," Bertillon wrote in 1880. "They are the arrondissements inhabited mainly by the poor."[24] This comment is far more

applicable to the Paris of the first half of the nineteenth century, in which the totals were much more out of balance and the contrasts even more pronounced, though gathered within a smaller space. One recalls the many instances of this lack of balance in the descriptive literature, in which the bourgeois are presented not only as over-privileged, but as seducers of the daughters of the people, like Ferrand the notary in the *Mystères de Paris*: "Nothing is commoner than the corruption of servant by master, more or less by force," Rodolphe mused. "Sometimes by terror or stealth, sometimes by the sheer imperatives of the servant's situation." One cannot help feeling that this aspect of social antagonism must have represented at least one contribution towards inflaming the great settlement of scores.

Another problem is posed here, the consequences of this trend in the population. The growth and change in the capital's population reflected the causes of an unhealthy situation. They likewise reflected the effects of an unhealthy situation, the city's malaise, the economic, political and social aspects of which have often been described, but have still to be analyzed demographically.

A. *Distribution by sex in relation to total population*

	Arrondissement: Sceaux				Arrondissement: Saint-Denis		
	Total population	Females	%		Total population	Females	%
1836	78,463	40,154	51.17	1836	104,414	52,533	50.31
1841	87,217	44,465	50.98	1841	125,475	65,323	52.06
1846	104,089	53,426	51.33	1846	170,137	87,758	51.58
1851	119,047	60,296	50.65	1851	222,039	111,986	50.43

B. *Distribution by sex in the communes later annexed*

	1836			1841			1846			1851		
	Total population	Females	%	Total population	Females	%	Total population	Females	%	Total population	Females	%
Arrondissement: Saint-Denis												
Batignolles	10,681	5,606	52.48	13,076	6,965	53.26	19,380	10,241	52.84	28,185	14,709	52.49
Belleville	9,858	5,365	54.42	17,839	9,460	53.03	25,736	13,375	51.97	34,146	16,965	49.68
La Chapelle	3,417	1,643	48.08	8,202	4,125	50.29	12,911	6,301	48.80	18,679	9,096	48.70
La Villette	6,416	3,227	50.30	8,251	4,072	49.35	12,180	5,627	46.20	18,650	8,662	46.44
Montmartre	5,884	3,006	51.09	7,241	3,727	51.47	14,234	7,382	51.86	23,110	11,474	49.65
Neuilly	7,537	4,003	53.11	8,806	4,815	54.68	12,200	6,486	53.16	15,735	8,245	52.40
Arrondissement: Sceaux												
Bercy	6,145	3,034	49.37	7,308	3,582	49.01	8,641	4,199	48.59	10,654	5,009	47.01
Grenelle	2,809	1,419	50.52	3,689	1,936	52.48	4,853	2,502	51.55	7,705	3,989	51.77
Vaugirard	8,237	4,177	50.71	9,377	4,722	50.36	12,978	6,611	50.94	14,880	7,434	49.96

BOOK III

Crime

The Expression of a
Pathological State:
Its Effects

Introduction

Rate of population increase is one of the essential elements in any social description. At all periods and in all great cities it is at least as important as, sometimes indeed more important than, the economic situation, so much so that demography becomes the measure of social facts, which it sums and totals up. This applies with even greater force to the Paris of the first half of the nineteenth century, when the increase in population was more rapid and less immediately dependent on the economic situation, when the characteristics of the population changed more radically and when the demographic facts were more heavily loaded with social significance than in any other city or in Paris at any other period.

All the demographic facts; that is to say not merely the normal facts, but more particularly the abnormal facts, which henceforward came to represent basic categories so broad in scope, so constant in duration and so comprehensive in number that they may be regarded as the normal expression of the abnormal nature of life in the great city— the demographic facts embodied in the statistics for infant mortality, illegitimacy, infanticide, suicide and, finally, crime. The significance of crime both to contemporary Parisians and to ourselves thus becomes evident and we can now see more clearly why it was one of their basic preoccupations at that period and why we are wholly justified in taking crime as the major theme in a social description of Paris during this time. Our justification lies both in the contemporary accounts and in the statistics. The crime statistics are so large numerically and so closely related to those for other pathological facts that they may be regarded as registering the very pulse-beats of the city's life just as closely, perhaps more palpably, and even more reliably than the statistics for illegitimacy localized in space and time; and indeed they were identified socially with greater precision.

Crime is the major theme because it transcends these social facts taken in themselves and sums up the whole of the major problem of the social development of Paris in the period: that of the dangerous classes and the laboring classes, which is really the subject of this entire book. The problem is not crime as such; our intention is not to give much space to a detailed description of crime and criminals. What we are really concerned with are the three major aspects of a problem which is placed in its true perspective by crime.

These aspects are, first, the fact that the rate and mode of increase and change in the Paris population were such that the city's inability to readapt itself to its new population relegated a large part of the working-class population not actually to a criminal condition perhaps, but at any rate to the furthest confines of the economy, of society and almost of existence itself, in material, moral and, basically, biological circumstances conducive to crime, of which crime itself was a possible consequence. Secondly, this population not only lived in fact on the very edge of the city and virtually on the verge of the criminal condition but was, besides, relegated to that condition by public opinion on the facts, which in itself constituted a fact. And, thirdly, these were the reasons why this population adopted in all respects, in its mode of life, its attitude to politics and religion and its private and public existence a behavior which conformed to the opinion of it held by others, with what others expected of it and with what it actively or passively acknowledged itself to be, precisely owing to the pressure of this collective opinion upon it and its own acquiescence in this universal reprobation.

The facts, the opinion about the facts, and the behavior in conformity with both facts and opinions were the three major aspects of the fate of the Paris population during the first half of the nineteenth century. The history of this fate has often been written; but demographic analysis—to which our own study will be restricted—invests that history with a greater precision, a greater continuity and a graver tone.

PART I
The Facts

CHAPTER ONE

Social History and Historical Sociology

I
Social History

Conventional economic and social history does perhaps give us an adequate account of an excess population, a change in the population, and a relegation of part of that population to the margin of the city owing precisely to this excess of and change in the population as a whole. If we simply review the principal accounts and documents, we can detect the biological effects of this social development with which we as demographers are mainly, indeed almost exclusively, concerned. Conventional history makes it abundantly clear that throughout the entire period and irrespective of the economic situation, large numbers of people remained on the fringes of the city economically—that is to say, remained unemployed or virtually unemployed on the fringes of its trades and employment—and biologically—that is to say, in the utmost extremes of poverty and destitution. This distinction, drawn by Fourier in his *Création de l'ordre*[1] and later taken up by Proudhon, applied more aptly to the Paris of this period than to any other city. Proudhon wrote: "Where a civilized people does not die of 'immediate starvation' it dies of 'slow' starvation through privation or of 'imminent' starvation through overwork, being compelled by its needs to engage in dangerous or exhausting kinds of work which engender fevers and infirmities." Everything we are trying to demonstrate and everything we are trying to identify comes out clearly in these accounts and documents and in these facts. Historical research has already thrown sufficient light on them. We shall have to return to them before we embark upon a further analysis, within the frame of historical sociology rather than social history; but we shall deviate from conventional history only to lay down new tracks for a kind of history that has yet to be written.

The Biological Aspects of the Economic Situation

The study of the economic situation in Paris during our period and the many works dealing with it, Simiand's being perhaps the most brilliant of them,[2] plainly demonstrates that a large part of the Paris working class was permanently racked with hunger owing to unemployment or the price of bread, either the one or both at once—immediate hunger during the great crises, imminent hunger during the brief periods of a prosperity which never spread far and was always precarious.

The price of bread: The price of bread was of the utmost importance; its curve followed the curve of all the ills that Paris was heir to. All the police reports agreed that when the price of the 4-pound loaf rose above 12 or 13 sous, most of the working-class population was undernourished. "It is imperative to see that the price of bread does not go higher than 3 sous the pound," the Prefect of Police wrote on October 27, 1827.[3] We have only to check this with the list of market prices.[4]

There was "imminent hunger" during the early years of the Restoration. "The bakers complain that flour is too dear," the superintendent of the faubourg Saint-Antoine police wrote on November 30, 1815. "They want an increase in the price of bread, or else, they say, they will be ruined. But they agree with me that the slightest increase, especially in the present harsh season, would be dangerous. There is a rumor abroad in the Lenoir market in the faubourg Saint-Antoine that the 4-pound loaf is about to rise from 13 to 15 sous."[5] There were other ills, too. "This class is suffering as it has never suffered yet," the superintendent wrote on May 12, 1817. "Most of the workers had their daily wages cut long ago and the rest are out of work; you can imagine that they found it hard enough even before this to afford bread at 18 sous."

After a slow decline in price, reaching its lowest point, 11½ sous for the 4-pound loaf, between February 1 and August 15, 1826, the rise set in again, implacably, terrifying, until—after an initial reduction to 13½ sous in October 1832—a municipal order of November 1832 placarded on the walls of Paris, which caused a terrific sensation,[6] fixed the price at 11½ sous. In the interval there had been six years of destitution, a fearful destitution, for each increase in the price spread the disaster to fresh groups of the population and was everywhere received as tantamount to a death sentence, especially the rise in the autumn of 1828. "At the end of 1828," the *Journal des Débats* wrote later, the price of the 4-pound loaf rose to 19 sous at the bakers'. Even before that it had been more than could be borne not merely by the wholly indigent population, but by a fairly large part of the Paris working class, and people were desperately afraid that the price would stay at that level.[7]

In October 1828 the superintendent of the faubourg Saint-Antoine police wrote:

The increase in the price of bread in the faubourg Saint-Antoine has not given rise to disturbances of any sort in the faubourg, only to bitter complaints. But the approach of winter rightly terrifies the working people; they are wretched enough as it is. Soon fathers of families will not be earning enough to buy bread, and how will they be able to clothe their children and pay their rent? Employment is not recovering.

All the police reports during the terrible early years of the July Monarchy stress the importance of the price of bread and the dreaded effects of the slightest increase. On November 6, 1832, the Prefect of Police described

the crowd which stormed into the police stations and charity centers demanding bread tickets for a reduction of 1 sous on 16. More than 200,000 persons stretched out their hands for this public alms. Some of them used up a fortnight's supply in one day, and if it was impressed upon them that they were encroaching on the following days, they said: at least we shall eat today.

Hunger: The price of 12 or 13 sous the 4-pound loaf was a true physiological limit. Above, but only just above it, lay hunger. The contemporary statistical analyses give glimpses of this hunger. In *Les consommations de la Ville de Paris en 1817 par rapport à ce qu'elles étaient en 1789* Benoiston de Châteauneuf wrote: `

The Parisian gets only 4 ounces of butcher's meat daily, whereas he ate nearly 5 ounces in 1789, at a time when Lent and fast days were still observed. If these calculations are correct, they are saddening. They show that the working class, the class which most needs a really nourishing diet, a good strong broth and a nourishing soup, has nearly always gone without it.

Commenting on this book, the *Journal des Débats* said on November 8, 1829:

The people of Paris makes up for this lack of sound nourishment with unhealthy foods. Pork is the main substitute for butchers' meat, which is priced too high for workmen, artisans and day laborers. M. de Châteauneuf notes that when butchers' meat is scarce, either because it is too dear or for any other reason, the price of pork immediately rises, as if the one was always fated to replace the other.

They also made up with the crumbs from the tables of the rich, the "*arlequins*" Sue mentioned, or even the carrion from Montfaucon.[8] And, too, they made up with spirits and wine. The *Journal des Débats* asserted that

> spirits and wine most certainly form a large part of the people's diet. In the old days pharmacists were the sole distillers and there were no more than 10 houses in Paris which dealt in spirits. Today there are over 200, which proves that spirits are widely used and shows the species of revolution which has taken place in the people's diet.[9]

Wine was a form of nourishment whose consumption varied with the consumption and price of other foodstuffs. "The excessively high price of wine has reduced its consumption," a report on provision supplies in Paris stated in 1816. "The working class needs all the more bread in order to feed itself."[10] "How are you raising your son?" the judge asked Old Christy, whose son had been arrested for theft, in 1828. "Your Worship, I just provide him with drink, food and work, that's the lot."[11] Drink first, be it noted.

We find hunger frequently mentioned in the qualitative documents of the period too. People die of hunger in *Les Misérables* and the *Mystères de Paris*.[12] "Near the Porte Saint-Martin," Heinrich Heine noted on March 25, 1832, "a man pale as death and with a ghastly rattle in his throat sprawled on the damp pavingstones. The idlers gathered round him asserted that he was dying of hunger. But my companion assured me that the fellow died of hunger every day on one street or another; it was his living." Remarking, however, that it was a very lifelike imitation, Heine went on: "There is this particular point about this dying of hunger, that you would see several thousand people doing it every day if they were able to hold out longer. But the poor usually die after three days without food; they are buried without a word, for no one takes much notice."[13] The *Journal des Débats* of December 12, 1832, reported that "the King visited the Museum in street clothes. When he came out, a child aged about ten flung himself down before His Majesty and cried: 'Sire, my father and mother are frightfully poor; there are six of us children and we have no bread.' "

The police reports confirm all this testimony, some of which might seem suspect. In 1831, for instance, one of the worst years of all, the Prefect of Police wrote to the Minister of the Interior on September 11: "I cannot repeat too often that destitution is at its worst and it is impossible to suppose that its victims will not cause the Administration a great deal of trouble if they come to feel that they have to resort to the most violent means to make their situation less frightful."[14] He attached reports from local superintendents giving preliminary detailed statistics by district of this extreme destitution; the cholera epidemic was to supply further details very shortly. Indeed, these reports may be regarded as something of a foretaste of the fuller description which can be constructed from the statistics for the epidemic.

The Hungry Paris: The hungry Paris was the Paris of the central districts in which shop and workshop, trade and crafts shared a common plight—the Porte Saint-Denis and the faubourg Saint-Denis, for example, where

the depression in which trade has been languishing for a year is growing even worse. . . . It is to be feared that there will be great distress this winter. The manufacturers' situation will soon be as difficult as the workers'; those who used to provide a livelihood for many fathers of families are now in a most alarming situation themselves. . . . We have been informed that some National Guards who are shopkeepers or industrialists were obviously reluctant to bring their weapons during the disturbances this week because, they said, they could only pity unfortunate workers driven to despair by their poverty.

In the quartier du Mail, "the meetings in the rue du Croissant have left the unfortunate idea in everyone's mind that such riotous scenes are likely to recur frequently this winter. Nine shops have closed down in the rue des Fossés-Montmartre alone. Many of the persons arrested in the past few days do not seem at all to mind going to prison." In the quartier du Louvre: "The workers are totally destitute; they now have no bed or clothes and will not have any blankets or firewood this winter. . . . People are very worried about how they are going to get through the winter." And in the quartier de la Cité, inhabited by building workers, with whom we are well acquainted from Nadaud, "the discontent caused by the prevailing poverty is driving people to look to innovations in the hope of better things. The continuance of these flagrant proclivities to subversion makes any idea of a return to lasting order and tranquility in the near future problematic." A large number of workers lived in the quartier de l'Arsenal: "Most of them have large families and lack all means of support. . . . Their constant cry is, let the Government give us work or hunger will bring the wolves out of the forest! Many single workers are living in lodging houses, and they are the ones most to be feared."

Feared, closely watched, the faubourg Saint-Antoine was well equipped with police patrols and soup kitchens. Hunger played a very large part in the political agitation in the faubourg during the last years of the Restoration and on the days of revolution. A police report of October 21, 1828, stated:

A handwritten placard has been put up at the corner of the rue Saint-Nicolas in the quartier des Quinze-Vingts: "Long live Napoleon! War to the death against Charles X and the priests who are starving us to death!" Several workers cheered, saying that "they would make an end of it, if die they must, since there was no work for them. . . ." Similar leaflets have been distributed in the rue de Charenton and the rue de Charonne in the faubourg Saint-Marceau and the faubourg Saint-Martin. . . . People are saying in the wine shops and workshops that the people must assemble and march on the Tuileries to demand work and bread and that they do not fear the soldiery, since many of them have been won over. This exasperation on the part of the workers has been noted ever since the recent rise in prices, and professional agitators (there are plenty of them in the faubourgs) are trying to exploit it to incite the workers to indulge in excesses. Circumstances are favorable. A great many workers have been suffering for a long time and the price of bread is driving them to utter despair. . . . I have begged the Prefect of Police to get some digging and similar work started from which they can earn at least a pittance.[15]

Recent memories of this sort account for the special measures taken in the faubourg immediately after the 1830 Revolution. "The workers in this district," the police superintendent wrote on September 6, 1831, "have so far displayed great devotion to the King and the law. But those acquainted with their utter poverty consider that their sensible behavior poses a problem. Their patience is at an end, and I believe we could not count upon them if their distress continues much longer."

The most conclusive documents are those concerning the quartier Popincourt (in the VIIIth) and the XIIth arrondissement:

In the quartier Popincourt alone 7,000 workers, who, with their families, make up four-fifths of the population, live in overcrowded rooms and great masses of them are exposed to every sort of misery. Their distress is inconceivable. They have sold or pawned everything they have, even the tools of their trade; having parted with their furniture for practically a song, they have taken refuge in low, filthy inns, where they are horribly overcrowded. They have fallen deep into debt and exhausted their credit.

In the XIIth arrondissement the superintendent of the quartier du Jardin du Roi police wrote on March 30, 1831:

The district is still perfectly quiet, but the poverty of the working class, where those of them who were still in employment have been given notice for the end of the month, is equaled only by their despair. I visited some of the artisans in my district yesterday. I saw unfortunate fathers of families, with their four or five children around them, without bread and with no notion how they were going to be able to support them next day. To make matters worse, the soup kitchen in the rue Mouffetard is closing down on Friday by order of the Mayor of the XIIth arrondissement just at the time when the bread allowance we had been authorized to distribute has been canceled, so that unless another soup kitchen is opened, half these unfortunates will have no food at all that day.

The Biological Aspects of Urban Pathology

These documents, which are of the kind used by conventional history, throw light not only on the biological aspects of the economic situation but also on the biological aspects of all the ills that afflicted Paris during the period and on all its political convulsions.

We shall not go into the political upheavals, which have been adequately studied elsewhere.[16] All we need note here is that they present the biological characteristics mentioned in the contemporary accounts which were not, however, fully utilized in later studies. "Every revolution," Proudhon wrote in his *Idée générale de la Révolution au XIX*^{e} *siècle* in 1851, "first takes the form of a protest by the people against a vicious state of affairs in which the poorest are the first to suffer. It is not in the nature of the masses to revolt except against what afflicts them physically and morally." All the contemporary reports echo this protest, the protest of hunger. "Hitherto," the Prefect of Police wrote in September 1831,

this population has been very patient . . . but its patience is becoming exhausted. It is moving from complaints to murmuring, and in these murmurs it keeps going back to recollections of our recent Revolution. Hunger is an ill counsellor and some people do not scruple to assert that the Revolution was made by some only to be exploited by others, giving it to be understood that they may be none too averse to starting all over again in order to get more out of it. Alarming symptoms testify to this imminent peril. In the past few days groups have been seen gathering around the bakers' shops. Yesterday there was an attempt at machine-wrecking. Disturbances engendered by want are far more serious than those instigated by politics.

But the main interest in these documents is the part played by other pathological facts with which we are more concerned and will discuss in detail later, facts such as those mentioned in a report on the public temper, dated June 4, 1828, summarizing a course of action for the police:[17] "(1) Put a stop to usury, which is becoming excessive; (2) Curb the bailiff's rapacity; (3) Expel five-sixths of the beggars still here; (4) Clear Paris of a crowd of vagrants who do nothing but spread theft and crime; (5) Halt the proliferation of common prostitutes." This program was drawn up by the Prefect of Police, who wrote in his report of September 6, 1831:

On every hand destitution rears its ugly head. The number of beggars is growing daily. Were we to arrest the lot, the jails could not hold them. When people complain of their importunity, their answer is that they are racked with hunger and, unfortunately, this excuse is all too true. There are also far more vagrants around. Our night patrols and our police on the beat in the daytime arrest them, and hunger, hunger and its horrible pangs, is again their excuse. Ordinarily, there are few robberies in summer; this year they have been more frequent. Despair has been the sole reason for several suicides. In a district as small as Chaillot three persons have done themselves to death in a single week. They had come to the end of their tether. An event of this kind has never been witnessed in this part of the city. Prostitution has also increased. The number of applications for the registration required by the police in the interests of health and public safety is growing.[18]

Beggars swarmed in the city. "Beggars are displaying themselves in Paris and the adjacent communes in every hideous and distressing guise," the *Journal des Débats* wrote on November 27, 1828. "They pursue passers-by in the streets, besiege the doors of churches, creep into houses, hold the shopkeepers to ransom, and everywhere present a shocking contrast of abject poverty in the midst of wealth and plenty, of idleness and vagrancy amid the most thriving industry and the most polished civilization." The Prefect of Belleyme issued an order on September 20, 1828, in vain.[19] In vain, the beggars, old and young, were hunted down.[20] Further measures had soon to be envisaged.[21] Crime and prostitution foisoned as starvation grew, linked to it by a chain of cause and effect commented upon in an abundant specialist literature.

This adds up to the fact that conventional history possesses material in plenty for describing the pathological aspects of the life in Paris we are examining and even for digging down to its biological foundations. The account it gives and the use it makes, after the event, of the archival material which constitutes the principal documentation tend, however, to be incomplete, even though in these documents it has all the material it needs for a complete study. A historical study closely following the chronological development of the facts would find no difficulty in pinpointing the development of the correlations between the various pathological forms of a common destitution which are so very evident during this long crisis and equally so during the last ten years of the July Monarchy.

II
Historical Sociology

What we propose to do here is something entirely different. As we consider that the conventional historical accounts throw sufficient light on this course of developments—often more than they suppose—we shall devote most of our attention to the mechanics of urban poverty, examining its various elements separately and not necessarily chronologically. The method is in fact an exercise in historical sociology rather than in the history of societies.

Destitution in Paris during the first half of the nineteenth century provides a monstrous experience of the physical and moral destitution secreted by great cities in every age. The study of the dark Paris of that period is relevant to the study of modern Paris, just as modern urban sociology illuminates many aspects of the old Paris. For our purposes, crime is simply an expression of a biological determinism, which we are here concerned with singling out and examining.

Our study is concerned less with crime itself than with one of the major aspects and probabilities of working-class life in the Paris of the period, summed up by crime. For crime reveals the downward course of working-class life at that period and throws light on the major factors involved. We are not concerned with crime in itself, save to the extent that it was for some, was likely to be for many and was considered by most to be the final possibility, the last act in an existence which everything combined to drive in that, rather than any other, direction. The problem of crime is important because it was the major problem of working-class life in this period. Proudhon summed this up in 1851 in his *Idée générale de la Révolution*:

And just as if evil, like good, must have its sanction, so pauperism, thus foreseen, prepared and organized by economic anarchy, has found its own sanction in the crime stastistics. . . . When the worker has been stupefied by the fragmentary division of labor, by serving machines, by obscurantist education; when he has been discouraged by low wages, demoralized by unemployment and starved by monopoly; when he finally has neither bread nor cake, neither farthing nor groat, neither hearth nor home, then he begs, he filches, he cheats, he robs, he murders. After passing through the hands of the exploiters, he falls into the hands of justice. Is that clear?

The advantage of taking crime as our theme is that it sums up the problem of the course of working-class life in an extreme form and reduces it to its simplest and most striking expression. It supplies a basis for studying social deterioration in the working classes during this period—a fundamental aspect of the general study of social mobility in an urban environment—which may be almost as precise as the study being carried out today in the great modern metropolises. It is true that modern research has a number of advantages, such as a fuller, more varied and more readily renewable quantitative documentation; the permanent accessibility of experimentation of every sort; and the results of the general advances in psychology and biology. Nevertheless, and apart from any question of the precision of the study, the demographic conditions of social mobility in an urban environment emphasize the fact that the phenomenon of social deterioration was more evident in the first half of the nineteenth century than it is today, and is therefore easier to study, even though the quantitative documentation of social deterioration itself may be less abundant.

This phenomenon was more evident then than now because the evolution of the population has driven it in opposite directions in the two periods: in modern times toward success, during the first half of the nineteenth century toward failure. Of this irresistible, simplifying and determinant demographic drive we have to examine both the mechanics and the major aspects. Part of the Paris population was doomed to failure. Firstly, because of the way in which it had assembled —no matter whether we look at the over-rapid and over-large immigration, which kept the part of the population concerned on the fringes of the city by its weight alone, or whether we take the fertility rate, the proportion of illegitimacy within it enabling us to calculate how large the criminal classes were likely to become. Secondly, it was doomed to failure by its living conditions and by its mode of life, as expressed and summed up in the statistics of mortality.

CHAPTER TWO

Population Increase and Social Deterioration: The Problems in General

The rate at which a population increases provides a criterion of social mobility everywhere and at every period, but more especially in Paris in the first half of the nineteenth century, when its speed and extent were such that the population statistics alone supply ample material for its study.

I
Population Increase and Social Mobility

The study of social mobility—that is, the passage not from one occupation to another, but from one social level to another either in the course of a lifetime or from one generation to another and within a single family—is fraught with difficulties. The main difficulty is to define at the start what is meant by social level. There is a correlation between certain occupations and certain social categories, such as those of doctor or notary, but as a general rule social categories are not so clear-cut as occupational categories and cannot be so incontrovertibly ranked in order. The distinction is less objective; it is created by the groups themselves and by the attitudes of acceptance or rejection, of friendship or hostility they adopt among themselves. Although important, capital and income are only one criterion among many. In the absence of an authentic social documentation, however, and owing to the difficulty of defining exactly what is meant by social category, demographic documentation and demographic development supply a number of criteria.

The Modern Period

This is also true of the modern period. In spite of the lack—at present, at least—of French sociological research at all comparable with the

American, especially that of the Chicago sociologists, we should be able to show simply from the demographic and economic character-istics of great cities, and of Paris in particular, that the course of work-ing-class life in modern times is quite different from the historical course we are examining, particularly since demographic and economic devel-opment now direct, or will most likely direct, social mobility upward, not downward, regardless of individual case histories.

We have only to look at the demographic structures of Paris to see why social mobility must inevitably be greater in the capital than elsewhere and more likely to trend upward rather than downward. It is hardly necessary to emphasize again the obvious fact that a city like Paris was, until recently at any rate, incapable of renewing and increas-ing its own population simply by its surplus of births over deaths. For this reason alone, immigration—provided that it does not exceed the economic capacity, as it has at certain periods—reflects and promotes social mobility just as much as demographic and geographic mobility; that is to say, it expresses a social promotion which could neither exist nor even be conceivable without it. Besides the migration from the countryside and smaller towns to Paris there was an internal social migration due to the varying fertility of the groups, a demographic phenomenon which in theory should inevitably promote upward mobility because, as has been proved, the middle and upper social groups have, until recently, been less fertile than the lower groups.

The part played by these demographic phenomena is all the greater inasmuch as the economic structures of modern Paris themselves pro-mote social mobility still further. While the size of immigration and the factor of differential fertility are not peculiar to great cities but are found in most towns regardless of their size, this is not equally true of the economic structures, which make capital cities, and Paris in particular, the privileged territory of social mobility. The rapid changes in these structures, the diversity of occupations and the perpetual renewal of types of employment create constant incentives and a vast number of varied opportunities. We should add that these effects are, by and large, relatively independent of the economic situation.

The First Half of the Nineteenth Century

During the first half of the nineteenth century, however, the demo-graphic and economic circumstances could not fail (whatever contem-porary observers may have said) to stand in the way of success so far as the great majority of the people were concerned, that is to say, the great mass of the working class, which alone concerns us here; nor could it fail to direct social mobility toward failure rather than success.

Admittedly, the contemporary literature and the historical documentation itself seem to testify to just the opposite. The careers of craftsmen and shopkeepers in the *Comédie humaine* present social promotion as one of the most obvious characteristics of the society of the Restoration and the July Monarchy, as shown by César Birotteau, the son of a smallholder near Chinon, whose history is traced in such detail. His arrival in Paris: "After César had learned to read, write and count, at the age of fourteen he left the country and went to Paris on foot to seek his fortune with one louis in his pocket." His start as shop assistant; his marriage with Constance Pillerault, the lady floor-walker in a linen draper's called *Le Petit Matelot*—the shop which we learn from a placard nailed to the wall of a building site at the corner of the rue des Deux-Ponts and the quai Bourbon had recently been pulled down and had moved to another district—and his various speculative ventures. There are stories like those of Remonencq, the second-hand dealer, and Cadenet, the wineseller, and many others.

Balzac's testimony is the more convincing in that it corresponds with the descriptions that can be derived from the bankruptcy files in the archives of the department of the Seine. These check in some respects with the court files, but are convincing in other respects too because they imitate the historical documents so perfectly that he seems to be providing quantitative social study with the guarantee of authenticity and the verification which, in fact, social history should be conferring on him. The oft-quoted testimony of Le Play is of the same kind; in his monographs on owners of small businesses and craftsmen he pays far more attention to successes than failures. "In the occupations in which a worker needs only a few inexpensive tools to set himself up," Vinçard wrote in 1863,[1] "he has a chance of becoming the head of a business. It is not the same in the industries, in which setting up costs too much." There was no possible chance of rising in status in most of the food industries except by marrying the boss's daughter or his wife after she was widowed; the baker's assistant, the pastrycook's assistant and the butcher's boy could hardly hope to set up on their own. There was no chance of rising in the building and clothing industries and especially the furniture industry, where the workmen hawked their own goods around, as described in the Inquiry of 1847.

Social history has concluded that the Restoration and the July Monarchy were periods of social success, with all the more probability in that the economic situation was favorable at some periods. We ourselves have noted in a previous work that in the first half of the nineteenth century, as in our own times, exceptional conditions of employment promoted a constant immigration into the city, but that the graph of this immigration bore no relation to the graph for wages, and that it fostered a social mobility which contrasted in periods of crisis with the stagnation of the countryside and other towns. Besides, in that period as in our own, economic conditions in Paris were particularly favorable, and the population of great cities, Paris in particular, is well fitted for the exploitation of such conditions owing to the selection of the fittest, as revealed by migration at all periods.

In spite of this evidence, however, and in spite of the examples of success, always the same ones, to be found in the literature and in contemporary social analysis,[2] and in spite of incontrovertible promotion in some privileged occupational and social sectors, one cannot help observing that, without even going as far as the total description we are to undertake, and holding provisionally to the methods of conventional history, it would be easy enough to find plenty of examples of mobility in the opposite direction. One has only to take the literature of the Left instead of the Right. "It is correct, therefore, to postulate," Considérant, for example, wrote in his *Principes du socialisme* in 1847, "that, apart from a comparatively very few individuals who come from the lower classes and rise through quite exceptional circumstances or talents to the higher ranks, the classes become established in their relative status of superiority and inferiority at birth," a pessimistic assertion which would be of no more interest to social history than the assertions of optimistic contemporaries mentioned previously if it did not correspond more accurately to the major trends shown clearly enough in the demographic and economic development of the period.

Indeed, and for reasons we have already given, the extent and rate of immigration in Paris in this period are such that, no matter what examples of success one finds or what evidence one collects, most of the recent or older immigrants, as well as some part of the native working population—owing to competition from both the newer and the older immigrants—were inevitably and permanently thrust aside away from the road to success immediately or very soon after their first contact with the urban environment. Or else they were doomed by the sheer process of growing older to failure, failure in every form, and were irresistibly driven down the slope at whose bottom was crime: crime in actual fact for some and crime as a distinct possibility for the great majority.

II
Social Deterioration: The Phenomena

These differences between the population trends in the two periods account for the fact that, despite the lack of detailed documentation, social deterioration is easier to trace during the first half of the nineteenth century than it is today and therefore easier to examine. This is so, to begin with, because the phenomena summed up in social deterioration are more sharply delimited today. Each of them exists independently and has specific characteristics instead of blending, as they did in the first half of the nineteenth century, with the major phenomena of urban life; they are truly exceptional and abnormal, not commonplace, normal and social in the full sense of the word. To take only the extreme forms of urban pathology, this is true of infanticide, prostitution and madness, which in the earlier period were closely bound up with the general conditions of working-class existence and fully representative of it, though we do not find so many examples or such adequate statistical documentation for them as for the major phenomena. The city's poverty, more particularly that of the working classes, shows up strongly in such basic statistics as the general or exceptional death rate and the illegitimate birth rate. But it is equally accessible in other statistics, those for crime, infanticide, prostitution and mental disorders, which, though they embrace fewer units, are none the less meaningful for that and were used by contemporary statisticians on a par with the general statistics. They are not marginal statistics concerning merely exceptional and abnormal phenomena, since they reproduce, though in miniature, the occupational and economic correlations which can be derived from the general statistics.

The General Significance of Certain Limited Phenomena

Infanticide: In Paris during the first half of the nineteenth century the correlation between infanticide and the general increase in the population was close and indubitable.

This correlation was reflected first of all in the facts: in the extent of infanticide, as measured by the number of indictments and convictions, and (noted in the reports of the Board of Health[3]) as a form of criminality expressed in the definite correlation both between the increase in infanticide and in population and between this type of crime and economic, political and biological crises. It was reflected, secondly, in the distribution by occupation and locality, where the highest proportionate figures are found in the working-class districts and in the lower-class groups. And finally, it was reflected in the many accounts indicating that the practice was far more widespread than appears from the judicial and other statistics and was a very common form of behavior in certain social environments. The abolition in 1838 of the *tours*[4] doubled the cases of infanticide registered by the Morgue. This Parisian practice had been reported from the earliest times; under the Ancien Régime the Commissioners of the court of justice known as the Châtelet used to collect numbers of corpses of newborn babies from the sewers every day. Furthermore, infanticide was freely practiced in most large towns: "At Lyon infanticide is a common practice," we find in a report to the Board of Health of the Rhône department.[5]

Recent research on infanticide goes to show that these correlations have now disappeared, together with the social significance of infanticide, if social significance means the expression of a general phenomenon of society as a whole. The number of cases is smaller, so small, indeed, that for statistical purposes its distribution by age, family situation and the victim's position in the age ranking of the guilty mother's children has no absolute significance, any more than its distribution by town and country gives any certain indication whether it is an urban rather than a rural phenomenon or even explains the influence of town or country upon it. It is even harder to establish a correlation between infanticide and demographic and social development today. Infanticide may now be said to be an obsolescent crime, which has lost its former social significance and has become an expression of the individual pathological case, material for psychiatry or medicine rather than an expression of the general pathological state that supplies the material for social research.

Prostitution: There are other phenomena, too, which while they cannot be regarded as significant of the general social development, undoubtedly bear some relation to it. Prostitution is probably one of them.

Prostitution was a basic phenomenon of urban life, more particularly of working-class life, during the first half of the nineteenth century. The general importance and significance of prostitution were plain enough in Parent-Duchatelet's description of it and in the rough but adequate correlations he established between the number of prostitutes and the size of the Paris population; between the prostitutes' and the inhabitants' provincial origins; between the prostitutes' occupational origins and the occupational distribution of the lower groups in the working class; and between the economic situation and the increase or decrease in prostitution. Its social importance is brought out even more clearly by general phenomena which Parent-Duchatelet was unable to perceive: the relations we are going on to establish between working-class cohabitation, illegitimacy and prostitution, and the description we shall have to try to construct of the workers' general behavior and, indeed, of their generally morality, manners and customs, of which prostitution is simply one aspect.

The position of prostitution in modern urban society is very different. It is of course possible, even pending the findings of statistical surveys, to detect probable correlations between prostitution and certain general phenomena; the obvious correlation between prostitution and the break-up of the family, for one, is probably evidence of a general phenomenon. But there is no correlation between it and the economic situation. Prostitution does bear some relation to population growth and occupational distribution, but this is hard to establish, except that an apparently high proportion of prostitutes have never engaged in any trade or profession, which is as good a way as any of putting them in an occupational category. Other determining factors which are harder to detect and measure come in here; they are material rather for biological, psychological, psychiatric or psychoanalytic research. It is far from simple. The nineteenth-century descriptions, admittedly general but significant and adequate nonetheless, are no longer relevant.

Madness: When we note the number of cases during this period of workers arrested as mentally deranged by the gendarmerie of the department of the Seine or by the municipal police on day or night patrol, we cannot but ask ourselves whether madness too may not be regarded as a phenomenon just as characteristic of urban pathology as these we have already mentioned and whether it does not differ in some respects from mental disorder today.

It must be acknowledged that the documents, though numerous and couched in statistical terms, are of little help. This should not be surprising in the light of the modern difficulties involved in attempting a quantitative study of insanity. The definition of madness differed from one contemporary alienist to another, like the definition and list of the causes, which they regarded as either physical or mental. The most eminent appear more concerned to derive confirmation of their preconceived ideas from the statistics than to use them for a description and explanation of the facts. Writers like Esquirol and Brière de Boismont, for example, convinced beforehand of the influence of what they call moral causes, had no trouble in establishing a correlation between political disturbances and the evolution of madness. "In 1830," Esquirol wrote in his "*Histoire et statistique de Charenton*,"[6]

social apprehensions and social disturbances exercised a certain influence upon madness. This conclusion confirms what we first published in 1805, namely, that the ideas prevailing in every century, the state of society and the political upheavals exercise a great influence upon the incidence and nature of insanity. I could compile the history of our country between 1789 and our own time from an observation of mentally deranged persons who attributed the cause or nature of their madness to some outstanding political event during this long period of our history. And if I had to account for the large number of suicides noted in 1834 and the reasons for their frequency, I would simply refer to a well-conceived history of the mental and moral state of society in France. We should see that the disease was long-seated, but aggravated by new circumstances.

Brière de Boismont, noting in his study, *L'influence de la civilisation sur le développement de la folie*, the relation between the main crises in the first half of the century and the growth of madness, had no difficulty in finding confirmation of his thesis in the figures. Almost anything up to a visit to Paris by the Pope, according to him, would bring on a vast access of religious mania. "In his report on the insane," he wrote, "Desportes notes that 3,222 persons were committed to the Salpêtrière and Bicêtre between 1831 and 1833, one-sixth more than in previous years; this was due to the Revolution and the epidemic."[7] Some—like Moreau de Jonès—classified destitution as a physical cause; others as a mental cause. In any case, what was destitution, *la misère*? "To cite destitution as a cause of madness is to use a very vague term," a contributor to the *Annales d'Hygiène* objected against Jonès. "In my opinion, it means the worry caused by privation and the anxieties attaching to poverty. *La misère* is, I believe, a mental, not a physical, cause."

To add to this confusion there was a belief in a part-madness for which at the beginning of the century Esquirol coined the lasting name "monomania," the term being used to designate states in which the patient retained the use of almost all his faculties and was insane only on one subject or a few subjects, but otherwise felt, acted and reasoned as he had before he fell sick.[8] "Everybody knows what monomania is;

you are seized with a desire to kill or rob. It overpowers you, but that does not mean that you are a dangerous criminal. The patient needs cold baths, plenty of cold baths," declares Simon, the doctor in *Le Monomane*, a melodrama by Charles Duveyrier first performed at the Porte Saint-Martin Theater on April 13, 1835. Monomania was invoked time after time by lawyers defending hopeless cases, quoting Pinel, Esquirol, Gall, Foderé, Marc and Georget, and relying on Article 64 of the Criminal Code, which laid down that an act is not a crime or felony if the accused was of unsound mind at the time. So did novelists; Sue represented the Slasher's urge to kill and the erotic mania of the notary Ferrand as cases of monomania. Indeed, the *Annales d'Hygiène* was much read by Sue; it carried many articles on erotic monomania,[9] and we find traces of these in Sue's novel, as well as of the crime news from the press.

The statistical study of madness, particularly madness among the workers in Paris during the period, is inevitably obscured by this cloud of beliefs exploiting rather than using the statistics, falling upon them in rather the same way as destitution fell upon the poor. Such a study would, however, be feasible. Its findings would be of great interest, even if they proved negative; but even more interesting would be the intriguing methodological problem of using a relatively small body of statistical material for quantitative history. While one can easily see what history can derive from massive statistics such as the censuses or the figures for births and deaths, even if they are only approximate, it is a fascinating question whether it is equally able to use statistics covering only a few cases for the study of such phenomena as madness. The accuracy of the statistics is of no great importance in measuring the major and normal phenomena, for the errors cancel out; it is quite easy to apply a refined technique to deduce what is impossible and what is certain in the doubtful statistics for backward countries or distant ages. But is this true of abnormal phenomena which are not precisely defined, where measurements must be meticulously exact just because they record only a few cases?

We shall reserve such methodic analysis for another problem, that of workers' suicides. We take the opportunity to note here that in the specific case of madness a statistical study itself is not as important as the two facts on which some light is thrown by even approximate statistics, namely, the occupations of the workers afflicted with mental disorders and the districts in which they lived.

The occupations are, as a general rule, the lowest, the hardest and the most despised, those, in fact, in which there was the heaviest death rate from cholera. "The dockers at the port at Bercy," Parent-Duchatelet wrote,

are particularly prone to mental disorders and insanity: eight dockers there were stricken in 1827. Why there and not at other ports? While in some yards they drink red wine and spirits to excess, the workmen at Bercy are exceptional in that they drink nothing but white wine, 5 to 6 liters a day. Almost all these white wines come from Anjou and are often blended with perry to give them extra strength and bite. Since these wines are the headiest known, we should not be at all surprised if they were the cause of the disease. But why the difference? It is solely due to the municipal duty on wines, which makes for great variations in the price of wines and leads to innumerable adulterations, themselves varying with the competition and the location of the retailers' shops.

In the files of the Paris police and the gendarmerie of the department of the Seine and in articles in the *Annales médico-psychologiques* there are, however, many more cases of the insanity of day laborers and workers described as "itinerants" or "nomads." Most of them were from the provinces and were arrested at the barrières or in the central districts where these lower-class groups were densest, such as the Cité, the Hôtel-de-Ville and the market districts. This seems to confirm the correlation between mental disorders and the failure to adjust to the urban environment which was to be studied in detail by later sociologists. There is good reason to believe that madness among the workers was, like the other phenomena we have examined, a fundamental element in the pathology of the Paris of the period.

This is also true of workers' suicides. But here we must stress even more strongly than we have in connection with madness the difficulties involved in attempting any historical examination of the abnormal facts, because the relevant statistical material is so scanty.

An Example: Workers' Suicides

1. The assertion of the fact: One assertion found constantly throughout the descriptions of the Paris population in the first half of the nineteenth century is that the suicides of proletarians accounted for the general increase in suicides and that they were a reflection of the misery of the working class. We must start with this belief before we go on to discuss its validity and significance. Even if we later find that it does not square with the truth, it is nevertheless significant that the belief did exist as a fact of opinion throughout the period, quite patent in the most diverse documents, but most notably in the picturesque literature we have already discussed, which here as in other ways carried on the tradition of Mercier.

As early as 1782 Mercier wrote:

Why have so many people killed themselves in Paris during the past twenty-five years? What is the reason for so many suicides when one hardly ever heard of them in the old days? People have tried to blame modern philosophy for what I venture to say is simply the work of the Government. Those who kill themselves when they have no notion how they are to survive next day are anything but philosophers; they are the indigent, the wearied, those worn out by life because merely to subsist has become so difficult, nay, sometimes impossible. The number of suicides in Paris may amount in the calendar year to 150, or about one-third of their present number. The police take care to ensure that the public hears nothing of these suicides. When someone kills himself, a superintendent of police presents himself in plain clothes, draws up a report without more ado and compels the priest to bury the body hugger-mugger. Those who used to be prosecuted after their death under an absurd statute are no longer carted to the scaffold. Indeed, that was a horrible and disgusting spectacle calculated to have dangerous consequences in a city teeming with pregnant women. This kind of death is nowhere recorded on paper, and those who compile history from such papers a thousand years hence may well cast doubt on what I am advancing. But it is all too true that suicide is commoner in Paris today than in any other city in the known world.[10]

There are many similar allusions to workers' suicides in the *Tableaux de Paris* under the Empire and the Restoration. "Every day one hears talk of suicides and murders among the people and the petty bourgeoisie," wrote Reichardt in *Un hiver à Paris* in 1802.[11]

We find the most definite assertion, however, in Lachaise's *Topographie médicale* (1822), and the most important, because it was based upon the many and varied daily observations of a Paris doctor and because he used the earliest quantitative research on the subject and in this work reflected what we described in an earlier chapter as the statistical revelation. In Lachaise's description, as in the *Recherches statistiques sur Paris*, the figures for suicide were part of the normal statistical material and the study of suicide an indispensable feature of urban demography. Süssmilch had written as early as 1742 in the first and most remarkable demographic compilation, *Die göttliche Ordnung*:

We leave this life by three gates: the first is that immense gate of colossal dimensions through which an ever-growing multitude passes, the gate of disease; the second is smaller and seems gradually to be narrowing, old age; and the third, gloomy, of sinister aspect, blood-bespattered and widening daily, is the gate of death by violence, especially by suicide.

Lachaise believed that there were more suicides than were recorded in the statistics:

One of the reflections that strike us when we examine the mortality tables for the two sexes, and one which deserves more thought, is the suicide rate. Many unfortunates in Paris despair of happiness, devise their own destruction and lay violent hands upon themselves. The average arrived at by sifting the recorded deaths is between 300 and 350; in 1817, it was 351, 235 men and 116 women; in 1819, 376, 250 men and 126 women. This number, though alarming as it stands, may, however, be thought to fall far short of the true average, for two reasons. The first is that the relatives of some suicides try, and in many cases succeed, to have deaths of this kind recorded as the outcome of delirious fever and accordingly to have the phrase "while of unsound mind" substituted for "suicide" on the death certificate in order to avoid the stain on the family honor. The second is that the death registers carry no mention of the many persons who had not the resolution to consummate their deed or cases where the deliberate attempt to put an end to themselves was frustrated by prompt and unexpected rescue.

As to the distribution of suicide, "experience shows," says Lachaise,

that it is by far the most frequent in Paris among the class of proletarians. The mortality tables in London show exactly the opposite; whence it might be concluded that suicides in Paris are caused very largely by poverty and among our neighbors across the Channel by idleness, drunkenness, debauchery and the gloomy prospect that faces them at an early age of the impossibility of finding fresh sources of debauch. In the one case, it is an aversion from life, a real hatred of it; in the other, it is a disgust, a mere boredom with life, in short, the spleen.

The comparison between Paris and London is of no great relevance; it reflects not so much the statistical data as ancient beliefs, very evident as early as Mercier's *Tableaux*, where it was stated that there were more suicides in Paris than London, "here mainly among the poor and there mainly among the rich." Many eighteenth-century writers called England the classic country of the spleen and suicide,[12] and it is possible that the poor tax may have contributed by reducing the number of those who, having fallen into extreme destitution, found a last resort in suicide. In Lachaise's analysis the only point of importance is his assertion of the frequency of workers' suicides: "Let us all hope that the people may recognize how very useful are the various savings funds and well-managed tontines under the direct protection of the Government."

The further one goes into the nineteenth century, the more numerous the assertions about the frequency of workers' suicides. There were a great many in the principal descriptions of the manners and customs of the period, though the chief emphasis was placed on political and literary suicides, and less on poverty than on the fashion mentioned by Balzac: "Suicide was all the rage in Paris at the time." In his lectures on literature, *Du suicide et de la haine de la vie*, Saint-Marc-Girandin said in 1843: "If the very craftsmen are now, alas, infected with the malady of suicide, the reason is that their minds are constantly irritated and soured by modern science and civilization." Perhaps; but the real point is "the very craftsmen are . . . infected with the malady of suicide." We have only to look at the number of craftsmen's suicides in the descriptive[13] and social literature, not to speak of the works actually devoted to the subject which became very common during the last ten years of the July Monarchy.[14]

Suicide was on the increase, more in Paris than elsewhere and among the working class more than among other classes. This assertion we find in the medical literature, the moralist literature, the picturesque literature and—during and after the last ten years of the July Monarchy —the working-class literature, including the working-class press, the popular novels and the writings of the social reformers.

2. *The nature of public opinion*: This aspect of public opinion must be examined as such, being itself a fact. The belief in the large number of workers' suicides must inevitably have been a factor in their increase, just as opinion concerning suicide in general contributed to the general increase in suicides. It seems very probable that the many sensational suicides during the Revolution and the Empire familiarized people with the idea of self-slaughter. The contagious effects of suicide were often noted.[15] Suicide had its own favored spots in the city, and popular belief soon came to decide that they attracted suicides; not necessarily heights—the towers of Notre-Dame very seldom, but the July Column and the Vendôme Column, which had to be equipped with a balustrade in 1843. Different spots were preferred at the end of the nineteenth century and in the twentieth. "The newspapers," the *Annales d'Hygiène* wrote in 1829, "ought to refrain from reporting any suicides whatever. We have good reason to believe that such publicity has on more than one occasion decided people already in a desperate frame of mind to hasten the ending of their lives."

It is likely that the workers were just as much affected by the influence of the contemporary fashionable despair, for which material circumstances do not adequately account. The influence of literature on bourgeois suicides was often noted. "If I seek the source of these extravagant ideas, is it not to be found in Romanticism, in these anti-social books, in these plays which lead the imagination astray?" cried the defender of Dr. Bancal, to whom the double suicide of Indiana and Ralph in George Sand's novel had suggested the idea of killing himself together with his mistress. There were even queerer cases, such as that reported by Jules Janin of the Courbevoie hairdresser, named Molard, whose head had been turned by the Preface to [Hugo's] *Cromwell*. He gassed himself, leaving this note: "Farewell, my friends in politics and literature. . . . Farewell, all my good neighbors. . . . Down with *The Sicilian Vespers* and hurrah for *Cromwell!*" We could find many documents to show, if we had not already suspected it, that the workers were just as subject to these influences as the other classes. We have only to look at the novels of Sue or Frédéric Soulié, the Porte Saint-Martin melodramas and the street ballads. We have, too, only to read the crime news in the papers,[16] or, even more to the point, the suicides' letters used by Guerry in his *Statistique morale de France*, some of which were published in the press. These reveal how the contagion worked. They contain references to recent suicides and friendly and affectionate messages, as if, on the point of quitting a society in which he no longer can, or no longer wishes to, live, the suicide, rejecting the solitude in which he is living, and even denouncing and denying the apparent solitude to which death dooms him, were taking refuge in another society in the Beyond, whose existence he asserts and indeed proposes to prove by his act itself. It is a classless society, as we can see from the case of the worker who, on the point of flinging himself from his garret under the eaves of a tall house in the rue Saint-Denis, mentions the suicide of a peer of the realm in his farewell letter. A species of fraternity of suicides grew up, similar to the fraternity of the guillotined imagined by Hugo in the *Dernier jour d'un condamné*, with its stress on the fatal attraction of the Grève:

More than one who goes there for my sake will go there for his own. For these doomed beings there is a certain place on the place de Grève, a fatal spot, a pole of attraction, a snare. They linger around it until they are caught. . . . It may well be, too, that on a certain date the dead of the Grève may gather on black winter nights on the square that is theirs. It will be a livid and bleeding crowd, and I shall not fail to be among them. There will be no moon and the talk will be low. The Hôtel-de-Ville will be there, and its clock, which once struck pitilessly for all of them.

A kindred society of suicides takes form in these letters and in the popular literature, in which the street ballads have pride of place.

3. The fact itself: Although there is a good deal to be said for observing this evidence as revealed in opinion concerning the frequency of workers' suicides, we still have to see how far this belief was justified by the facts. The problem is whether the number of suicides in general did increase, more especially amongst the lower classes, and whether the increase can be regarded, like the increases in prostitution, madness and crime, as expressing pathological conditions of urban living. Death by suicide was only a small component of the general death rate.[17] Is its significance comparable to that of the general rate, or is it merely a sum of individual cases, each differing from the other, each due to different causes and to a long private history irrelevant to the kind of history we are concerned with here?

A PROBLEM FOR SOCIOLOGY RATHER THAN HISTORY   The suicide statistics and the comments on them—both at this period by Quételet in particular and later by Durkheim in particular—seem to show that while suicide was commoner in Paris than elsewhere and while it was perhaps more frequent in the first half of the nineteenth century than at any earlier or later period, it is a phenomenon whose interest is not confined merely to Paris and to the particular period. It concerns other great cities besides Paris and a study of it is thus far more relevant to the description of urban civilizations in general than to one of Paris alone. It is relevant, too, to the general development of societies up to the present day as well as specifically in the first half of the nineteenth century. It is, basically, a social rather than a historical phenomenon, material for sociology rather than history, since it can be studied in itself, and not necessarily as it developed chronologically.

The increase in the figures for suicide is constant and regular in all countries for which statistics are available all through the nineteenth century and beyond it, as if there were a constant and stable correlation between the course of suicide and the course of other demographic, economic and social phenomena.[18]

Moreover, this increase is greatest in the cities, both in Paris and in the other European capitals for which statistics are available.

The stability of the other characteristics is even more patent and even more surprising; the demographic characteristics to begin with. A similar distribution by sex is observable almost everywhere.[19] "The tables show over ten years," the *Annales d'Hygiène* stated in 1829, "that women are able to bear the vicissitudes of life better than men, since they account for barely one-third of the suicides." Distribution by age is similar.[20] "Suicides in France," wrote Quételet, "are infrequent at an early age; their number increases with age and the rule applies in practically the same way to men and to women. But rather more women commit suicide before twenty or twenty-five, presumably for the same reasons as they commit infanticide." He noted, too, that the distribution in Paris was much the same as that in Geneva, Berlin and London, and that there were more unmarried than married suicides.

The distribution by season, day of the week and time of day is equally general and equally surprising. Spring and summer seem to be the periods in which most suicides occur, while they are least frequent in winter and autumn.[21] "Summer," Quételet noted, "has a greater influence on the number of suicides than the other seasons, as it has on the number of cases of mental disorder and crimes against the person." And Esquirol noted the effects of a very hot summer followed by a wet autumn in his articles on suicide in the *Grand Dictionnaire des Sciences médicales.*

Most suicides occur early in the week and early in the morning.[22] The methods of suicide are also just as stable and general. Concluding a statistical study of suicide in Paris, Guerry wrote:

Nothing would seem more arbitrary and to leave a wider freedom of choice than the method of killing oneself. But this choice is unconsciously influenced by age, sex, social status and a variety of other circumstances often very hard to assess. Chance has no more to do with it than with the distribution of crime or any other statistical fact; and, provided that enough observations are made, certain well-tested criteria can be used to work out some of the other factors. One remarkable example is that man chooses a particular method of killing himself at each age; in youth he takes to hanging, but soon drops this for firearms. As his strength declines, he goes back to the earlier method; and an old man putting an end to his life usually resorts to hanging.[23]

Factors other than occupation have a determining influence. As Legoyt demonstrated,[24] Esquirol's assertion that suicides as a general rule prefer the tools they use in their trade was mistaken, though it was actually true of laundrymen and especially washerwomen, who took poison, or rather substances containing poison, such as Prussian blue for whitening laundry.

The surprising regularity of all the statistics for suicide—including the numbers involved and the distribution by age, sex and season, day of the week and time of day or night—is the reason why the analysis of suicide by the statisticians and sociologists is relevant to general social behavior (even though it may show no specific relation to time, place or almost to the facts themselves) but cannot really be used for the social description of a particular city at a particular period: in this case, Paris in the first half of the nineteenth century.

Quételet noted this, pointing out the remarkable regularity with which certain social phenomena repeat themselves during identical periods of time. His explanation was his theory of the average man. On suicide he wrote:

As a general rule everything a man does, he does with great regularity. He always seems to be acting under the influence of predetermined causes situated outside the sphere of his free will, whether in marrying, begetting, killing himself or laying violent hands on his fellow men's property or life. What, then, are we to conclude? Must we believe in a depressing fatality that drives us to crime and every excess, and that no human power can deliver us from it? No, certainly not. Man within the scope of his free will can muster all the energies of his reason to obey or resist extraneous suggestions, but experience teaches us that where one triumphs, another succumbs.

One can see, therefore, that it is just as feasible to estimate suicide as any other demographic event and that it is just as possible to construct tables of the suicide rate as of the death rate.

Durkheim pointed out the fallacy of this theory of the average man, both in general and in its application to suicide. "However the preponderance of the average man is explained," he wrote,

this conception could never account for the regularity of the reproduction of the social suicide rate. Actually, by definition, the only possible characteristics of this type are those found in the major part of the population. But suicide is the act of a minority. In the countries where it is most common, 300 or 400 cases per million inhabitants at most are found. It is radically excluded by the average man's instinct of self-preservation; the average man does not kill himself. But in that case, if the inclination to self-destruction is rare and anomalous, it is wholly foreign to the average type, and so even a profound knowledge of the type could not explain the source of suicides, let alone help us understand the stability of the number of suicides in a given society.[25]

If it does remain stable, this is owing to another phenomenon, namely, a collective force which tends to drive individuals in a particular direction and is expressed in the way in which they are attached to society and governed by it. Durkheim held that suicide varied in inverse proportion to the degree of integration with religious society—religion is a protection—in inverse proportion to the degree of integration with domestic society—marriage is a protection—and in inverse proportion to the degree of integration in political society—the city is a protection.

Although he corrected and supplemented Quételet, Durkheim lifted suicide out of the diversity of historical facts and set it in the context of the immutability of sociological space just as much as Quételet did.

So the suicide statistics, and such analyses of them as Quételet's and Durkheim's, relate to a pathological phenomenon less relevant to our study than those we have already examined. The statistics establish a constant relation between suicide and population and its demographic characteristics, and great stability and uniformity in the methods of suicide throughout the entire course of a century and in most of the great cities in which a quantitative study can be made. Unlike the other pathological phenomena—which are specifically Parisian and specifically of the Paris of the period, and reveal the unhealthy state of the city even when broken down into the detail of district, occupation and year—suicide seems to have had much the same characteristics in Paris as it had elsewhere. The tragic situation was no more typical of Paris than any other city nor of our period than of any other period. It was one factor in Paris, just as it was in similar or even quite different cities. In any quantitative description of Paris or any statistical quest for it, the material to be derived from an examination of suicide is meager indeed for the purposes of description or, for that matter, of history in general.

The same could be said of Quételet's and Durkheim's interpretations. Their analysis of suicide takes it into a realm with which we are not concerned. Their conclusions cannot be used for a description of Paris during a single restricted period in its development.

But this is only apparently so. This sociological description, especially Durkheim's, is in fact relevant to our form of social history both where it is incontrovertible and where it is inadequate.

THE SOCIOLOGY AND HISTORY OF SUICIDE   Though Durkheim moved his study of suicide outside our area and period, his basic conclusion is relevant: that there are no individual suicides and that personal motives, such as poverty, sickness or frustrated love, are significant only insofar as they are related to collective pressures or prohibitions. However unfortunate individuals might be, suicide would not be endemic in a society strongly integrated in respect of politics, economics, religion and the family. The thing to be noted is the degree of a society's integration, not the individual factors.

The term "social integration" was new, but not the idea. We find that the conclusion which Durkheim reached at the close of lengthy surveys was similar to that reached by all who dealt with suicide throughout the nineteenth century, moralists and churchmen,[26] alienists and criminologists alike.[27] "If a man has not fortified his soul, education aiding, with religious ideas," Esquirol wrote in *Maladies mentales* (1839),

with the precepts of morality and with orderly habits and regular conduct, if he has not learned to obey the law, to fulfill his duties to society and to bear the vicissitudes of life, if he has learned to despise his fellow men, to disdain the parents who bore him and to give full rein to his desires and whims, it is certain that, other things being equal, he will be more prone than others to put an end to his life as soon as he meets with disappointment or adversity. Man needs an authority to direct his passions and govern his actions. Left to his own weakness, he falls into indifference and then into doubt; he has nothing to bolster up his courage, he is defenseless against the sufferings of life's mental anguish.[28]

The fact remains that the advantage of the new term coined by the sociologists is that it defines a concept used very vaguely and inconsistently in the nineteenth-century studies. Adopting both the concept and the terminology, we may say that the weaker the material and moral integration, the higher the number of suicides. It is very high, therefore, in large cities, "which often entail the torments of passion and interest," as Esquirol wrote in his article on suicide; and this was especially so in Paris during the first half of the nineteenth century when, as we have already pointed out, the increase in its population relegated part of its working class to the margin of the material and human environment.

Though sociological analysis does point to social nonintegration as an important factor in the increase in suicide, and though this generalized conclusion does throw a certain amount of light even on a study narrowly bounded in space and time, it does not satisfactorily account for the particularized aspects of suicide at one specific place and in one specific period.

The reasons for this inadequacy are statistical. The prerequisite for a statistical study of suicide is a numerical count of the facts; it must be extremely precise, simply because death by suicide is far less frequent than death in general. A statistical study of the general death rate need not be absolutely accurate in detail, but a study of suicide must be, since only a few cases more or a few less may well throw the conclusions completely out of kilter. Lachaise, it will be recalled, warned that doctors ascribed many cases of suicide to illness or accident in order to spare the family's honor.[29] As to attempted suicide, Esquirol wrote: "Not 40 of 100 attempted suicides are successful." And hundreds of attempted suicides were never recorded. It hardly seems feasible, therefore, to compile statistics of suicide by age, sex and cause.

We can, however, set this objection aside. A constant relation may be assumed between suicides recorded and suicides concealed; since the number of recorded suicides remained fairly constant, the total number of attempted and successful suicides very probably remained constant too.

Our main criticism is directed not so much to this point as to the notion of some sort of constant or invariable rate of suicide. This idea will do well enough when applied over long periods of time in which the peaks and discontinuities level out. But while both the sociologist and the historian deal in averages, the historian is bound, once the averages have been established, to look more closely at the annual totals from which these averages are derived, but which they conceal. Admittedly, the rate levels out over a period of a hundred or even fifty years; but from year to year the differences come to the fore. It is here that there emerges in the background to the series for suicide in general, about which there is no disagreement, a particular kind of suicide, or rather kinds of suicide, as evidenced in a particular city, in particular districts, in particular methods, for particular reasons, in particular social groups and in particular years. And it is here that the history of suicide parts company with the sociology of suicide.

First, it becomes clear that the increase in suicide is greater than the increase in the population. To take only suicides consummated in death, these rose from 285 in 1817 to 357 in 1826 and 477 in 1835; the number of suicides in 1835 was 250% above that of 1817 and 350% above the average annual rate for the period 1794–1804. "This increase," a criminologist wrote in 1836, "cannot be due to the population increase, since it did not multiply by three in forty years."[30]

Secondly, it is clear that there were many more suicides at particular periods and even in particular years. The peaks did not occur at the time of the great Revolutionary upheavals; in 1830, suicides in Paris fell by 13%, as compared with 1829, from 307 to 269; in 1848, by 32%, as compared with 1847, from 698 to 481. "The great social disturbances," said Durkheim, "stimulate the sense of community and promote integration with society; people come closer to each other; the individual thinks less of himself than of the common weal." But suicides increased in the years of gross poverty preceding and preparing the final political upheavals before, as it were, finding an outlet in them, as in the last years of the Restoration, notably 1826, and in 1840 and 1841 and the last years of the July Monarchy.[31]

In these years, too, suicides increased at the same rate as other acts of violence, notably homicide. Guerry observed in 1833 that there were twice as many crimes against the person in the southern provinces as in the northern, whereas the reverse held good as regards suicide. He concluded that to some extent suicide did not parallel homicide, and here he was followed by the principal Italian criminologists of the second half of the nineteenth century, who held that since suicide and homicide were two manifestations of the same state, they would express themselves now in one form, now in the other. Lombroso believed that the psychological constitution predisposing to one or the other form of violence was likely to be an identical decay of the organism which put the person at a disadvantage in the struggle of life. Both the murderer and the suicide accordingly were degenerate and impotent; equally unable to play a useful part in society, they were consequently doomed to defeat. The only difference between them was that one person killed other people and another killed himself, depending on the social environment and the period. In actual fact, there were periods in Paris in which there was a great deal of murder and an equal amount of self-slaughter; in the last years of the Restoration and between 1840 and 1850, suicide and homicide ran parallel. In this respect, suicide was clearly one of the forms of urban pathology.

The cause was identical: poverty. It is true that, without nonintegration with the city, poverty would not in itself have been sufficient to cause suicide, since at other places and in other periods poverty acted as a protection against suicide. But actually, in Paris and at this period, it was poverty that caused a large proportion of the suicides shown in the statistics, whatever category we take.[32] All the commentators agree on this.[33] "Since the beginning of this summer," the *Journal de Débats* wrote on July 9, 1847,

suicides have been increasing at an alarming rate, not only in Paris but in the neighboring communes too. Within the space of a month and a half there have been eight in the commune of Batignolles. The reports from the criminal courts show that the number of suicides is on the increase, but never before at this year's rate. Why? You can easily account for it if you look at the ever-growing poverty of the working classes.

The working classes were mainly affected. But which in particular? In the last decades of the century the official statistics for France divided suicides into ten occupational categories, the last headed "Persons without occupation or occupation unknown"; the highest proportion of suicides fell into this category.[34] Commenting on these statistics, but extending his conclusions to cover the whole century, Legoyt wrote in 1881: "Persons with no known occupation and therefore with a very precarious social position account for by far the most suicides. We might well call this category that of the *misérables*."[35]

The *misérables*: the term conjures up a myriad memories and throws a flood of light on the history of suicide. Let us look at our statistics once again, especially those of the Morgue, which were very accurate. Not all suicides went to the Morgue, only those who died on the public highway or in places of public resort; deaths by drowning account for about two-thirds of them. Whereas at the end of the nineteenth century only a very small proportion of the suicides laid out at the Morgue remained unknown and unidentified by their family, between 1830 and 1835 almost two-thirds of them were not claimed or identified—an anonymous mass, without civil status in death as in life. The rest, whose identity and residence were known, had had the worst jobs and had come from the districts with the largest nomadic population.[36]

CHAPTER THREE

Population Increase and Social Deterioration:
Social Groups and the Urban Environment

Social groups considered as one of the pathological aspects of urban life are also easier to examine in the Paris of the first half of the nineteenth century than they would be in the modern period because, unlike today, they were then so large that a quantitative approximation will suffice even if it is not entirely accurate. Another advantage is that most of the data were assembled in Paris itself and were expressed in the Parisian environment. We shall first take the groups separately, then together with the environment.

I
The Groups

It would, of course, be quite wrong, despite the lack of detailed studies, to say that the general trend as regards the greater part of the working-class population of Paris at the present day is towards success. The French population as a whole is not so socially mobile as that of the United States,[1] and everything goes to show that in normal times, and even more, of course, in times of crisis, hardly any of the individuals who make up the working-class population of Paris has any real likelihood of success.

They are not, however, irremediably doomed by imperative demographic and economic determinants to the social and occupational failure which inevitably attended the course of working-class life during the first half of the nineteenth century. Indeed, they have solid defenses, especially social legislation which protects them against the extremes of misfortune and safeguards the great majority of them against total destitution.

This means that far fewer people are now relegated to the margin of economic and social life, or have less protection than the majority, or none at all, than in the period under study. It is hardly correct to speak of a social deterioration in connection with the kind of people encompassed by a modern investigation of social deterioration comparable with our sketch of conditions under the Restoration and the July Monarchy, for the term cannot now be applied with propriety to the condition and course of life of the groups we have in mind. The vagueness of the terminology itself reflects the development of the problem. It is not at all clear that we can properly speak of social deterioration today in connection with the criminal groups, which, unlike those during the earlier period, seem to move straight to the margin of the whole course of social development at the start. These dangerous classes differ at all times and in almost every respect from the laboring classes, to which they apparently bear no relation whatever. Nor is it clear that we can properly speak today of social deterioration in connection with social groups as a whole, such as those we are examining historically in this survey. Whereas social degradation in the sense of the degradation of large numbers of workers to the most appalling conditions is definitely the correct term to use in dealing with the first half of the nineteenth century, in modern times the only persons who would constitute the material of such a survey are the marginal groups, in our special sense, and the merely underprivileged—those who do not have a social protection which was originally won by the demands of a majority and is enjoyed only by a majority, that is, by the very young and by the best organized and most cohesive groups. These marginal groups are made up of those in whom no one takes an interest because there are so few of them and because as groups they are so heterogeneous and dispersed, the aged poor of both sexes, the decrepit and sick, the ever-present but numerically insignificant refuse of city life.

A modern investigation would also include those who do enjoy these benefits but yet remain on the lowest rungs of the ladder, in the worst districts and the least remunerative, hardest and most dangerous occupations, who rate high in the tables of morbidity and mortality— for they are the most liable to tuberculosis and the venereal diseases— as also in the statistics for madness and crime. Two ethnic groups in modern France stand out in sharper relief than any similar groups in the first half of the nineteenth century: the Bretons and the North Africans. In them all the after effects of the older misery seem to combine and linger on.

It is difficult to study them because their problems do not blend with the general problems of the Paris proletariat; a separate statistical documentation would have to be established especially for them. The principal difficulty—at least so far as research in Paris itself is concerned—is that attention has to be focused on the characteristics of the point of origin rather than on those of the receiving area.

II
Out-migration Environment and In-migration Environment
Research on the Modern Problem:
The Out-migration Environment as Determinant

The focus of interest in a study of the modern problem shifts from the characteristics of the receiving area to those of the place of origin. The effects of living in the city are not the determinants here.

Not that they can be wholly ignored. Some description of them is, indeed, required at the first stage in a study of the circumstances of this immigration. The economic structures and economic situation may help, hinder or even entirely prevent the immigrants' economic and social integration. It is very probable that the greatest misfortune of the Breton immigration into Paris was that it did not start until the end of the nineteenth and the beginning of the twentieth century. At that period an economic structure was growing up far less conducive to upward mobility than the more varied, flexible and remunerative structure in the best years of the nineteenth century, which had provided opportunities that could be grasped even by the workers from the Massif Central, who at last managed to achieve a decent competence after vegetating so long at the bottom of the scale. Thus, batch after batch from the provinces took it in turns to replace one another in Paris in tune with economic changes and developments, starting wretchedly poor and engaging in the most despised jobs until they in turn were replaced by fresh batches, the Bretons in the last three decades of the century taking the place formerly occupied by the immigrants from the Massif Central and by a rural, semi-rural and urban proletariat drawn from most of the provinces close to Paris. The new immigrants differed from their predecessors, however, in forming more cohesive provincial groups, in retaining their countrified outlook and in their total lack of training for their new jobs. A more decisive factor was the difference between the new economic environment and the old. The suburbs now took precedence over the city and large-scale industry over small factories and crafts. The Bretons arrived just at the moment when industry was becoming concentrated and centralized. This mass immigration was unfortuante enough to settle into a mass economy, the best suited to using the immigrants' brute strength but the least capable of enhancing its value. This ill-luck was even more disastrous to the ethnic groups which immigrated still later into even worse districts and in even worse circumstances, notably the North Africans.

It may be, however, that even here in these restricted areas the urban phenomenon only exerted its influence consequentially to that of other far more complex but far more significant phenomena, namely, conditions in the areas of out-migration, the study of which has so far been entirely neglected. Here we shall simply list those conditions to serve as a program for future research rather than as an index to the investigations already completed. First, the economic and occupational conditions, including the older and more recent traditions of emigration; next, the moral and psychological conditions; and lastly, the biological conditions. These should be studied separately at first and the separate studies should then be collated and related.

All these problems emphasize the extreme difficulty of investigating social mobility in the modern period, despite the apparent advantages of the fact that documentation is already in existence and that further documentation can be established as the need arises.

The First Half of the Nineteenth Century: The Predominance of the In-migration Environment

Despite the scarcity of quantitative documentation, the unreliability of the qualitative documentation and the impossibility of establishing further documentation, the study of social deterioration is easier in the first half of the nineteenth century than in the modern period, chiefly because the principal data were assembled within Paris itself.

Ethnic influence and survivals: The study of the out-migration environment cannot, of course, be neglected in this period any more than in the modern one, for its traces remain very evident, especially in the qualitative documentation, which is so well known and has been used so much as a matter of course that there is no need to dwell on it here. Nothing was more familiar to the Parisians of the time than the regional origin of large groups of workers. They could always be recognized at sight by their dress, dialect, general behavior and, even more easily, by the trades they plied and the districts and streets they lived in. The characteristics attributed to them remain invariable in every official report throughout the period, especially in the reports by the Prefects of the Empire compiled in compliance with a circular by the Minister of the Interior of May 10, 1808, concerning emigration and immigration in the provinces, and in the documents of the Paris Administration on seasonal immigration to the capital. The migrations of the people from the Massif Central in particular were described, accounted for and estimated here, with their causes, development and the very varied local habits connected with their special trades, together with the seasonal rates of flow, their age distribution and their morality. These admirable reports have often been used and commented on; they will not detain us here.[2]

We have no such detailed sources for the Restoration and the July Monarchy, it is true. But in default of quantitative documents, there is the fact that the Imperial Prefects' reports on special regional traits were reproduced in a vast literature and in many official reports without any essential change, showing how the same regional occupations and habits persisted in Paris. The petty trades were invariably described in the same terms in the portraits of manners we have mentioned, as well as in Gavarni's sketches and the *Comédie humaine* and *Les Misérables*,[3] and even more notably in the scores of news items reporting street incidents which as a matter of course ascribed to the immigrants the trade, dress, vices and virtues peculiar to them. Both at work and play the regional groups were described as closed circles, what would now be called "isolates." "On Sundays," La Bédollière wrote,

the Auvergnat water carriers go to the Auvergnat *musette* to dance, never to the French *bal*, for they adopt neither Parisian manners nor Parisian ways of speech or amusements. They keep to themselves like the Hebrews in Babylon amid a vast population which threatens to absorb them. We may say that, happier in this than the savages, they carry their native land with them on the soles of their shoes.[4]

Le Play, as we know, tried to correlate the course of working-class life in Paris with the survival of the manners and customs of the provinces from which the workers came. In his opinion, their success or failure was accounted for by their retention of, or failure to retain, their propensity to thrift, their regular habits of work, their strong feeling for keeping the family together, and even by their birth rate and other demographic characteristics.

These influences would show up even more plainly if we were to attempt to use a wide-ranging quantitative exposition deriving its chief raw material from the civil registers of the villages of origin in order to fill out, verify and explain a qualitative documentation already exploited so thoroughly that there is hardly anything more to be extracted from it. To reconstruct family histories and their demographic evolution over several generations, and to identify demographically and by occupation those who emigrated and those who stayed behind, would undoubtedly make a valuable contribution to the study of social mobility.

In our period, however, the characteristics of the point of origin were less influential than they would be today. While the contemporary writers stressed the persistence of provincial habits in Paris, even in the literature which was most eager to emphasize local color these habits were treated as precarious survivals, as they were in social surveys such as Le Play's. Le Play observed that the manners and customs of such "seasonal migrants" as the masons "contrast strikingly with those of the established population"; he added, however,

they have been tending to change in the past few years as a result of events which have interrupted former habits of work and have set all at sixes and sevens. A young mason is now less reluctant than he used to be to contract an illegitimate union, spend money on his clothes and attend meetings and entertainments during his sojourn in Paris. Now that he has less chance of becoming a property owner in his own right, he is becoming increasingly envious of the classes above him in society. Where this form of depravation is contracted far away from family influences by men who have retained all their native rusticity, and where their greed has grown uncurbed by religious sentiment, this sometimes produces a boorish nature quite unlike that of the established Parisian workman, even though he may be in less easy circumstances than they. If these budding tendencies should come to fruition, the system of periodic migration would no longer ensure that desirable balance it ensured in the past, but would continually inject disturbing elements into French society.

We have discussed the deterioration of provincial habits elsewhere. First, its causes; they were the disturbance of seasonal migrations by economic crises, but even more by the construction of the railways; the decline of the *compagnonnage* trade guilds, those sturdy upholders of ancient customs, which, however, never had the influence in Paris that they had in other towns and regions in France; and the competition between the newly arrived ethnic groups and the older groups who possessed the same skills, so that the newer groups broke down ethnic diversity precisely by means of ethnic diversity.[5] Secondly, its main characteristics, particularly the immigrants' rejection by various environments. We shall not go over this again. Although we are very well aware that there is a great deal more to be said on this subject, we prefer to go straight to essentials. These ethnic differences and the explanations for them that could be drawn from a study of the places of origin are of no great importance here. What really matters is the environment of the receiving areas; most of the data required for an understanding of both success and—far more frequent at this period— failure are to be found here. Provincial origin and ethnic persistence or resistance ran into, broke against or became blunted on the unyielding city environment, made up of the stones of the city no less than manners and customs as unyielding as the stones, because they were backed by them and lent them their significance.

"The stones of the city": *some general remarks*: The difficult problem of the influence of the city viewed materially and morally on the behavior of the inhabitants (also viewed materially and morally) could hardly be better summed up than by the title of one of the most enthralling chapters in Halbwachs's *Mémoire collective*. "It is not the stones and mortar that will resist you," Halbwachs said,

but the groups; in them it is the very real resistance, perhaps not of the stones themselves but of their incorporation in buildings in the distant past that you will come up against. They were, of course, once erected by a group, and what one group made another can unmake. But this human planning of old was embodied in a material setting, that is to say, in a thing, and the strength of local tradition is derived from the thing which was the image of that setting. For there is no doubt that a powerful characteristic of the group is its imitation of the passivity of inert matter.

Here we have an attempt to define the relations between men and things. Men create things, but at the very moment of creation they are subjected to their influence and remain subject to it even when the things are not there or even after they have disappeared, and give expression to it in a form of behavior that prolongs the influence of ancient situations and determinants which have apparently lost their reason for existence.

But this was also one way of posing and solving in general terms, through long meditation on insights and intuitions, a problem which could only be posed in the first instance by combining modern experience with historical observation.

This, however, is to exaggerate both the influence of things and the durability of traditions, the resistance of stones and human beings alike.

While human behavior may persist after the disappearance of the material environment which prepared and in some sort shaped it, these traditions, attitudes and beliefs far more often than not disappear too. In destroying whole districts of Old Paris Haussmann destroyed far more than slums, thieves' dens and churches. So total was the destruction that it is not surprising that nothing survived of the squalid setting in the Cité district depicted by Eugène Sue, Parent-Duchatelet and Frégier. But it is equally a fact that no further traces of it are to be found in the memory of the people of Paris either, nor in the images evoked by the old sites—though one would have thought that they would still cling perhaps to the towers of Notre-Dame—nor of the physical and moral horror on which contemporary narratives under the July Monarchy dwelt so insistently. And we find evidence of their disappearance in the picturesque literature and official records under the Second Empire and in the early years of the Third Republic. The districts destroyed in the War disappeared both from the landscape and from memory in the same way; they are already evoking different memories and preparing other attitudes and forms of behavior. The pulverized cities too have disappeared. The capitals have been rebuilt, it is true, and invariably just where they stood before, partly for immediate material reasons, but also for moral reasons reflecting the determinants of the old physical layout. But they are different cities and they have already become a setting for different human adventures. "Happy the cities which, like people, have not yet grown their wrinkles," wrote Mercier long ago in the 1783 Preface to his *Tableaux de Paris*, thus coining the neat metaphor later immortalized by Baudelaire in "*Dans les plis sinueux des vieilles capitales.*" We may suppose that the recent destruction of condemned slums in certain Paris districts, Belleville, for example, and modern urban renewal will lead to similar changes both in the district itself and its local legend and in the opinion of it held by the people of Paris. This, too, will have to be studied some day.

AN EXAMPLE: THE PORTE SAINT-DENIS These examples are too facile, however. They are less useful for our purpose and for the adjustments we shall have to make to Halbwachs's thesis than those we can derive from districts still intact in which the ancient but everpresent stones and traditions still impose their laws, though we cannot tell for certain what part of these laws is old and what new because of the way in which they buttress and support one another, blend together and reflect each other's influence.

The relationship between the quartier de la Porte Saint-Denis, for example—not the whole district as an administrative unit, but the far narrower limits of the blocks of houses surrounding the famous intersection—and crime poses a large and complex problem. It may be objected that this is an extreme example, but in the present state of social research in France, especially where Paris is concerned, the easiest and most rewarding examples are those involving phenomena of this kind and districts of this sort, not solely for their relevance to the phenomena and the districts themselves but also for their relevance to the most normal phenomena of urban life and even to districts in which these phenomena do not occur. The happy have no history—nor do honest folk; or not much. The first approach to the study of social phenomena should be through the sectors and groups in which these phenomena are most sharply defined, present extreme cases, and accordingly accumulate the largest body of statistical material and are most accessible to social inquiry. This general technique of social inquiry holds good for all periods and all countries and is particularly valid for the Paris of the first half of the nineteenth century. We have already given a sufficient description of its malaise; the sole purpose of the analysis of modern conditions set out below is to throw additional light on the older characteristics.

Is the Porte Saint-Denis a center of crime today? Let us first observe the criminal nature of this district both present and past and, to be more precise, the permanent existence here, at every period, of the same type of criminality, under the July Monarchy and in modern times alike. We do not mean that more crimes are committed in this than in any other district, though more crimes have indeed been committed here than in most of the Parisian districts in every age—and perhaps most frequently during the first half of the nineteenth century. We do not even mean that more crimes are planned here than elsewhere. But it is the district in which the largest and most lastingly recurrent number of criminals has always congregated, that is, actual or potential criminals whose characteristics, evident enough from the beginning of the nineteenth century down to our own days, differ appreciably from these of the criminal population in districts such as Pigalle. The criminals of the Porte Saint-Denis are petty criminals, the mere riffraff of crime, unorganized and poverty-stricken, with no money and no plans, criminals not by choice but drifting into it out of laziness, stupidity or bad luck. It is the district in which the correlations between laboring classes and dangerous classes which we are investigating became most clearly evident during the mid-nineteenth century. But it is here too that even today there still linger the last traces of that ancient community of interest, or at any rate of fate, at the lowest levels of the working class and the criminal condition alike.

At this intersection of streets and boulevards—the great crossroads of the city—petty criminals recently discharged from jail or turned back from Pigalle, on the lookout for a new job, mingle with, take stock of and often recognize the unemployed workers coming in from other districts or newly arrived in Paris at the nearby stations in confident search of a job, or at any rate some adventure, amid all the bustle and attractions and city lights assembled here, in the cheap hotels and restaurants close at hand or in some chance meeting in the crowd, and in the promise of adventure enhanced by the throng, almost indistinguishable from each other in age, appearance and, sometimes, in what lies in store for them. Such was the Porte Saint-Denis in the old days and such is Strasbourg-Saint-Denis today. This is the criminal setting from which we have to start if we are to find out why it has lasted and to use this modern example perhaps not actually to solve the problem of urban determinism—the stones of the city—facing us at this stage in our historical survey, but at any rate to clarify some of its data. What we can gather from a modern example is more help toward putting our ideas into some sort of order than what can be derived from a historical example; and that is all we are attempting to do here.

Even if we did not already know from an abundance of historical evidence that the district has always sheltered crime and criminals of the same type, the reasons for the existence of a modern criminal population, whose size and characteristics can easily be charted, are not far to seek; or, if not the actual reasons, at any rate the conditions which are conducive to its existence and persistence. They are patent enough and we can list them rapidly here.

In the first place, the district's location in the setting of the city as a whole, right in the heart, whether of the modern city or the city of the past. In the heart of the city means at a place where the main lines of communication meet, the busiest, the largest, those connecting the most distant, most diverse districts and the districts which complement each other best, the communications which necessarily ensure the economic and social unity of the city and carry along best and worst alike.

It is no accident that the district is now usually known by the name of a Métro station; today it is no longer Porte Saint-Denis, but Strasbourg-Saint-Denis.

In the heart of the city also means the place where the city's most essential and characteristic activities congregate, where all that is most necessary to it and all that best expresses and sums it up is gathered together in the smallest possible space. Leaving aside the modern industrial and proletarian economy, with its great workshops and its labor situated elsewhere, the highest and most significant proportion of all the activities and phenomena of Parisian economic and social life are discovered here. It is a capital in miniature, with the most complete, most varied and very often the densest samplings of the city's activities—all its activities, the most normal and most abnormal alike. The whole of Paris is perceived here, far more than in any other district, in all that is most expressive of it—workshops, stores, cafés, theaters and cinemas, even its monuments in the shape of the lofty triumphal arch; in its criminals, too, the largest numbers of whom congregate here in a sort of intense and excessive life, just as all the other phenomena do and for the same reasons.

But it is impossible to ignore the dominating element in the relation between geographic location and crime, both of them viewed in the modern setting: the factor of the vicinity of Les Halles, a very evident factor if we single out one of its aspects from criminality in general for the sake of greater clarity, namely, prostitution.

We observe the obvious fact that the prostitutes, who as a general rule swarm densely between the Porte Saint-Denis and Les Halles, throng more densely as one approaches Les Halles, until in certain streets and in the activities of the louche hotels, the cafés, shops and mews, depending on the time of day or night and the location, the activities of the sidewalk leading to Les Halles and of its main hall can hardly be told apart; whereas there are hardly any prostitutes on the other side of the boulevard and beyond the gate, although the alleys, courts, hotels and slums are just as shrouded in twilight. Pending a full statistical study of this phenomenon some day, it is easy to see at once that its causes lie in the demographic and occupational characteristics of work at Les Halles. The workers are mainly men and young men at that, but this labor force is also unstable, vagrant and occupationally, socially and morally underprivileged, finding jobs here that it could not find elsewhere, crowding in from all the working-class districts in the city. Most of the work is biologically abnormal because it has to be done mainly at night, because all the implications of work and all the impressions of night combine in a state of mental and bodily confusion, and because it leaves the whole vast daytime free, for rest maybe, but far more probably for pleasure once again, providing an unrewarding but necessary clientele for the prostitutes who find their best customers among the workers of Les Halles.

All these reasons would probably account adequately for the Porte Saint-Denis's share in the general criminality of modern Paris and for the role of physical setting as a determinant which we are trying to define. It is not, of course, that physical setting in itself is the determinant, but it does provide the conditions in which a determinant can operate.

But other districts which would seem to provide equally or almost equally favorable conditions today are not places of similar current crime nor centers of a similar contagion. If the Bastille district were a haunt of crime, its geographic, economic and social circumstances, which are not so very different from those we have just listed for the Porte Saint-Denis, would readily account for it. But the Bastille is not a particularly criminal district and is not regarded as such, though the square is one of the great meeting places of proletarian traffic, though it is closely hemmed in by working-class districts, back streets and courts crowded with workshops, hotels, cafés and dancing places, and though a huge open-air fair is held there almost continuously. The Bastille is not even a place of prostitution, except for one side street, the rue Jean-Beausire, which is thronged with prostitutes. But it is impossible to see the reason for this, at any rate the contemporary reason, and there seems to be no accounting for the data as they stand; it may be that the many hotels in the street and its dim lighting recommend it, but circumstances are just as propitious in the neighboring streets.

It is very probable that circumstances other than those of the present must be exercising some influence here, or rather that the modern physical setting acts so strongly as a determinant only because of the permanence of things, the perdurability of the stones. And even if these things, these stones do not in themselves adequately account for it, they do prolong certain imperatives into our own time, the imperatives of interests, habits and beliefs, particularly if these habits and beliefs are evil ones, which—it surely can be demonstrated by psychological analysis—are more ineradicable than good ones.

This assumption does seem to be borne out by the rue Jean-Beausire. There had once been a *Cour des Miracles* there, the historians of Old Paris tell us, that is to say, a very ancient haunt of beggars, criminals and whores. How very interesting it would be to make a study that would not try to trace the historically difficult and dubious course from the distant past to the present in order to describe and account for the permanence of criminal habits, but would start instead from a modern moral and especially physical description and try to go as far back as possible into the nineteenth century, to the major rebuilding of the district and the laying out of the place de la Bastille, and to find out, if only for a single house or hotel, the permanent characteristics of the building, its ownership and the uses to which it has been put. One would undoubtedly find that the existing physical conditions act so strongly as a determinant simply because they reflect habits and interests (if only in the arrangement and equipment of the building—such as the disposition of rooms, staircases and floors, and conveniences such as running water, gas and electricity) better than those in neighboring buildings or streets, habits and interests which are so firmly established only because they are enjoying benefits bestowed by older habits and are keeping them in being.

It is the influence exercised today by older phenomena, both material and nonmaterial, that determines the present importance of crime and criminals in the Porte Saint-Denis district, to which we now return in order better to define, by means of rapid modern analyses, the operation of the old determinants. It is very probable that modern material and moral conditions, such as places, interests, habits and beliefs, act so strongly as determinants only because they carry on the influence of older material and moral determinants without interruption, blending with them to such a degree that it is hard to distinguish one from the other. Let us, however, so distinguish them before we blend them again in our analysis, just as they are blended in fact.

There is no need here to trace things to the distant past and chart the continuity of the material determinants. We should simply note that the favorable material conditions which we can very easily detect in the modern setting are the same as those present in the first half of the nineteenth century. The intersection of roads is just as important; it must then have had an even more decisive effect since, before Haussmann's rebuilding, it concentrated a heavier traffic on a single artery, the rue Saint-Denis extending into the rue du faubourg Saint-Denis. Les

Halles was just as important for the same reasons and in the same way; the same type of population, the same work, except that the abnormal characteristics we observe today were even more in evidence at that period. The presence of Les Halles in that precise location had consequences in this and many other respects, even in the spread of the city in one direction rather than another, which Les Halles's present position in Paris [at the time this work was originally published] does not sufficiently bring out. The present material conditions are so favorable simply because they always were favorable, or rather because they became so ultimately; not all at once, it is true, but at any rate, though progressively, within a brief period and then decisively. It is these few years that really count and their study is of the utmost importance to the study of subsequent crime and of crime today. These are the years which require far more attention than our period as a whole and they are, regardless of our own investigations, the years during which the somber god of Evil established himself here and wove his web. After that, the whole situation was there, the use to which places were put and the interests, beliefs, habits and reputation attaching to them. Unless some total destruction occurs—some visitation of divine or administrative wrath like Haussmann's setting up his offices on the very site of the rue aux Fèvres—there will be nothing to be done about it. No local rebuilding or alterations will be the least good; tear down a thieves' den, it will spring up again ten yards further on.

It is the beginnings which count, which must be observed and grasped, whether from the viewpoint of a distant age or that of modern times. There are districts in the city today into which crime is settling before our eyes, taking advantage of apparently favorable material conditions, which, however, had exerted no such influence in the past; for instance, the case—an exceptional one, admittedly—of the recent settlement of an exclusively North African criminal population in the quartier de la Chapelle. The setting is hardly different from that described by Zola in the early pages of *L'Assommoir*, the scene which Gervaise observed from the hotel window on the boulevard de la Chapelle, of poverty, violence and drink, but not prostitution and crime. We need not describe the recent transformation here nor try to account for it. We shall simply observe that something is beginning here before our eyes, calling for a study involving both modern and historical research. Similarly, the establishment and migration of crime in the great American cities coinciding with their material changes has enabled

American sociologists to observe the circumstances in which the phenomenon comes into being, the gradual criminalization of districts, that is to say, from the viewpoint which concerns us and which is not that of crime alone: the use and enhancement of material conditions by certain groups, the social transmutation of things, which take on a significance they did not previously have and will retain until they are totally destroyed.

Similarly, it is the establishment of crime in the Porte Saint-Denis district that is important to the study of crime, not in our period only, but in the modern one. We ourselves cannot, of course, embark upon that study now. But we may observe at least that crime apparently settled into that district in the closing years of the Restoration and in the years of the July Monarchy with which we are dealing. It is probable that the district even then had certain quite evident criminal characteristics—places and traditions of past crime which the historians of Old Paris could enumerate in far greater detail than we can. Not far away, where the place du Caire was created in 1799, there had been situated one of the last of the *Cours des Miracles* in Paris, closed down by La Reynie in 1667. Many other less ancient circumstances must also have had some influence. The main point is that it was during this period that they seem suddenly to have borne fruit, that scattered circumstances suddenly coalesced, that things which were virtually anachronisms suddenly became up to date. A vast criminal landscape replaced the isolated localities. A social problem replaced the problem of picturesque crime; and this is our own special problem, encountered once more after this long digression.

THE FACTOR OF PARIS ITSELF   Some stronger determinant must have been at work. The effects did not manifest themselves in this district alone, and they operated on many other phenomena besides crime. This determinant was the city itself, as well as the demographic, physical and moral conditions already described. All that need be said of them now is that it was no accident that they found their plainest expression in this district and its link with crime. The repercussions of the excessive increase in the population were felt most strongly here, and its most abnormal consequences. Urban determinism, expressed most clearly at this particular place in the closer relationships between crime and poverty, between laboring class and the criminal class and by the invitation to a criminal course of life extended on every hand, was simply the expression of a general determinant, stronger than all the determinants of the immigrants' place of origin; it can be observed in many other ways too.

Regional origin, attachment to traditions and old habits and even the customary levels of health of the place of origin were hardly relevant in the period of the Restoration and the July Monarchy. In every respect it was the city that shaped, or rather mis-shaped. Demographic documentation exists by which we can accurately measure the operation of this process on the human body itself; we have already noted its social significance. On these bodies the city imposed—together with puberty at an earlier age and a more intense and irregular sexual behavior, the effects of which were observed by Quételet—a particular fertility rate of its own, which very soon replaced that of the place of origin; and a particular appearance, rate of growth, weight and height, even a special pallor remarked on by all contemporary observers. There was also a sickness and death rate on which it imprinted its characteristics so indelibly that the statistics for them, especially the cholera statistics, supply precise details of their social group, level of living and mode of life; they even reflect the detail of working-class habits, for instance in the rise in admissions to hospital on Tuesdays and Wednesdays after the traditional Sunday and Monday debauch.

The determinants are certainly moral, hard though they are to distinguish from the physical. And the moral determinants exercise just as great an influence as the physical in pushing large numbers of people toward social deterioration. Paris not only infected, withered and killed them; for the same reasons and at the same rate, it drove them to total ruin by the moral effects of physical change, the ill-health, the nerves on edge, the perpetual presence of death, which gave an added savor to the pleasures of life. The process was helped on by the persistence of the ancient setting, which superimposed the whole weight of ancient causes on the immediate causes; and by the ancient dwellings, forever contaminated and criminal, the old districts instigating crime, perpetuating and imposing a tradition of crime, summed up by Balzac better than anyone else. At the beginning of *Ferragus* he wrote:

The streets of Paris have human qualities and imprint upon us by their very aspect certain ideas against which we are defenseless. Isn't the rue Traversière Saint-Honoré an infamous street? There are tumbledown two-windowed houses on it packed from top to bottom with vices, crimes and poverty. The narrow streets with a northern exposure into which the sunlight penetrates no more than three or four times a year are murderers which kill and go unpunished.

Such was the determinism of the city, brought out and measured by the facts. It was patent in scores of testimonies in the picturesque literature and court reports. And it was summed up in the exclamation of an old woman who had hastened to Paris from a village in Lorraine to attend the trial of her fourteen-year-old son: "It's Paris that's to blame; I'm taking my son out of it and I'll make sure he never sets eyes on it again."[6]

CHAPTER FOUR

Fertility and Social Deterioration

Doomed to failure by its sheer mass and by the general demographic trend toward social deterioration, this population was also doomed to failure, though in a different way, by a specific aspect of this trend—in addition to that of immigration: its fertility. "One bastard in three babies. Paris does not reproduce, it recruits," said Lecouturier in 1848.[1] How could these workers be anything but savages, large numbers of whom (we shall later estimate how many) displayed the first and most essential characteristic of savages, an existence in fact but not in law? They lived on the margin of the law because they were born, mated, procreated and sometimes even died unrecognized and unregistered by it. Outlaws they should rather be called, but far less on account of their incidental criminality—which might indeed be regarded as a benefit in a certain sense in that it brought some of them under the law, if only by subjecting them to its yoke—than on account of a mode of life which was criminal by definition and criminal in some sort biologically.

I

Working-Class Cohabitation

The two results of working-class cohabitation—that form of savage life which can be measured by the illegitimacy statistics—were to keep many of them on the margin of the law and to drive some of them eventually to rise against the law.

An attempt at an estimate

The extent to which working-class concubinage bulked large in Paris during the first half of the nineteenth century first becomes apparent from the fact that the estimating technique used by Bertillon in the last decades of the century cannot be applied to this period. When he investigated the illegitimacy rate in 1880, Bertillon could very effectively use as a means of measurement simply the statistics for illegitimate children recognized by their father at birth or subsequently by their parents' marriage, instead of the aggregate illegitimacy statistics.[2] In the first half of the nineteenth century, however, it does not seem possible to distinguish nonrecognized illegitimate children, born in hospital or taken to the Foundlings Hospital immediately after birth (probably the issue of sexual relations so casual that they could not be called cohabitation) from subsequently recognized illegitimate children, who were born at their parents' home and were probably the issue of stable cohabitation, which can therefore be evaluated. A high proportion of illegitimate children were born at their parents' residence but not recognized.[3] If recognition was very likely to indicate stable cohabitation or at any rate a fairly durable union, this also applied to rather less than one-half of the nonrecognized children.

Hence, the estimate for cohabitation is less accurate than it was at the end of the century, but there is every reason to believe that the figures were far higher, since the number of recognized illegitimate children was combined with nearly half the nonrecognized. Though the proportion of illegitimate births fell slightly in the last years of the July Monarchy,[4] it still accounted for one-third of total births. It is, of course, more difficult to estimate cohabitation by the total figure for illegitimacy than by the statistics of recognized natural children alone. As the commentator on the Municipal Statistics for 1837–46 remarked, "It should not be inferred that one-third of all children born in Paris during these ten years were born out of wedlock, for the figure 99,952 includes babies whose mothers were not part of the Paris population." In fact, the relevant statistics for foundlings and abandoned babies, which were kept in considerable detail, show that even in this category there were less immigrants from the provinces than might be supposed.[5] Most of these births were due to the fertility of Paris itself. Taking the proportion of children of provincial origin recorded in the statistics for foundlings and abandoned babies, and extending to the total of illegitimate births the method Bertillon used for recognized illegitimate births alone, we may conclude that a population of some 100,000 to 110,000 lived in illicit unions with a degree of stability which obviously cannot be evaluated, but should not be confounded with casual sexual relations. This estimate cannot be regarded as exaggerated in view of the fact that the illegitimacy statistics do not cover illicit unions which remained sterile either by choice or necessity. How many of these there were proportionately can be estimated on the basis of modern research on sterility.

We cannot maintain that this population living normally in concubinage was wholly working-class in the face of all the accusations in the picturesque and social literature that the bourgeois seduced workers' wives and daughters—an essential aspect of social antagonism to which we shall return later. Quite certainly half the illicit unions were working-class, that is, so far as the women in the statistics of the aggregate rate were concerned. Almost certainly more, for if we look as carefully at the social literature as at the picturesque, we find this popular custom widely recognized and very frequently described; and if we bear in mind, too, that since in all probability the temporary or lasting unions between bourgeois and working girls came under the head of prostitution rather than cohabitation, they left barely a trace on the birth statistics.

So we can say that almost all such unions were working-class; but this did not apply to every occupational and social category of the working class to the same degree. A distinction into which we shall go more thoroughly later shows up in the illegitimacy statistics at this point. While it is probable that nearly all the illegitimate births can be attributed to the working class and while this does provide a basis for an estimate, it can hardly be said that the distribution of illegitimate births by district provides an equally valid basis for drawing conclusions as to the topographical and social distribution of cohabitation. We do not know to which districts illegitimate births in hospital, especially the lying-in hospital in the XIIth arrondissement, should be attributed.[6] The lying-in hospital in the rue de la Bourbe and the home for nursing mothers in the rue d'Enfer were intimately linked with this arrondissement; they were brought into being by it and its poverty and grew up with it. "At the downfall of the religious orders which had covered the southern plateau of Paris with gardens and churches," Esquiros wrote, "the working class moved to the quartier Saint-Marceau and the far end of the faubourg Saint-Jacques. The two lying-in hospitals and the home for nursing mothers followed the migration of the lower class, which moved away from the center to one of the outlying parts of the city."[7] Very probably, the illegitimacy rate in these two faubourgs was heavily weighted by the statistics for these hospitals, which were part of the faubourgs before they became part of the city. It is even possible that their convenient location was a contributing factor.

The fact remains, however, that, except for illegitimate births in hospitals, the distribution of illegitimate births and recognition of illegitimate children by district suggests that cohabitation was less common in the major artisan faubourgs, the faubourg Saint-Antoine and even the faubourg Saint-Jacques and the faubourg Saint-Marcel (despite the difficulty of identifying the share of the two last-named faubourgs in the figure for births of illegitimate children at the lying-in hospital) than in the central arrondissements, more particularly those containing or adjoining Les Halles.[8] The proportion of illegitimate births to total births is lower and the proportion of illegitimate children recognized at birth and legitimized by the parents' subsequent marriage is higher.[9] This distribution of illegitimacy brings out the differences between two categories of workers: first, a more stable population with a greater propensity to the moral habits of the city in general, situated in the faubourgs (the faubourg Saint-Antoine probably to a greater extent than the faubourgs Saint-Jacques and Saint-Marcel). And secondly a population with different demographic characteristics, situated in the central districts (especially around Les Halles), with a different distribution by age and sex, with more single men and women both doing the same sort of work, a more recent immigration and, precisely for this reason, with most of the characteristics which were attributed to almost the whole of the working-class population by a public opinion to be described later. We find an echo of this opinion in the municipal statistician's comment that "the number of illegitimate births in Paris is distressing but not surprising, considering that the capital is the center of the movement of a huge population which is not composed of inhabitants of the city." This implies that the illegitimacy was mainly provincial in origin. One cannot help thinking, however, that a more extensive illegitimacy was meant, for the terms used here recall those we have so often encountered and commented on, an illegitimacy with its origins in those "who are not truly Parisian," as Sauval put it, people who camped out in the city like vagrants rather than inhabited it.

It is far more significant that the illegitimacy statistics show not only that large numbers of the working class lived in concubinage, but also that this was a working-class custom. This is, of course, suggested by a great deal of the picturesque and social literature and even more clearly by a great many stories in the newspapers. We must be struck by the language used by workers prosecuted for assault or crimes to which these irregular unions were particularly propitious, such, for example, as the term "child of friendship," used by an old woman at a police court hearing reported in the *Journal des Débats* of September 29, 1829, when she asked for the discharge of a man aged about forty up on a vagrancy charge. "Is this man your son?" the magistrate asked. "Yes, sir," the old lady replied with a sob, "he is my child of friendship, a child I had before the Revolution out of friendship for a man. He had settled down with a wife and children whom he left in my charge." "You are asking the court for him, then?" "I'm not asking for anything," the poor old mother replied, "I'm only begging Your Worship to give him a good kick up the —— and discharge him." And the dialogue reported in the *Journal des Débats* of November 1, 1828, in connection with a brawl about a woman in a Belleville *guinguette;* the workman whose mistress the woman was having spoken of her as his legitimate wife, the judge observed that the term "wife" was improper. "But, sir," the workman replied, "I am a widower and it's quite natural I should have someone to look after my family." "Well, marry the girl." "She's not my wife, it's true, but she's no one else's wife either; anyway, I'll call her whatever you please."

That this was a working-class custom is even more evident from the illegitimacy statistics. The statistics for nonrecognized natural children rose steeply in relation to those for total illegitimate children in periods of crisis, in the last years of the Restoration, the early years of the July Monarchy and especially the last ten years.[10] A closer scrutiny restricted to the illegitimacy rate by year and month would show that the proportion of natural children not recognized at birth was higher at periods of dearth, unemployment and severe cold.[11] But certainly not a great deal higher, nor in every such period, nor even in the category of nonrecognized illegitimate children upon whom a bad economic situation would be expected to have the most direct and greatest effect, the foundlings, of whom Terme and Monfalcon wrote:

The average price of bread in Paris during the first twenty years of the century was 69 centimes 81 for 2 kilograms and the average number of abandoned babies was not more than 4,616. In 1815, bread cost 59 centimes 53 and 5,080 babies were taken into the Foundlings Hospital; the figure did not rise in 1816, when bread cost 82 centimes 25. In 1817, 5,467 newborn babies were left at the Foundlings and the price of bread rose to 96 centimes 40. It has also been said that more newborn babies are abandoned in Paris in winter than in summer and especially when there is no work or work is badly paid. In 1803, the number of foundlings in the three winter months amounted to one-half of the figure for the whole year. It has also been stated that more babies are abandoned in the last month of the year when the workers have exhausted all their resources. So, 1817 was a disastrous year; the number of abandoned babies suddenly rose by 800 in Paris, 5,000 in the whole of France and 900 in Belgium. We do not believe that it is possible to establish any logical relation between the increase either in abandoned babies or foundlings and the high cost of living.[12]

This is an oversimplified way of blaming the immorality of the working class. All we need say here is that the lack of correlation between the demographic and economic statistics indicates that cohabitation was one of the forms of working-class civilization. Frégier appears to have expressed one of its main aspects very well:

Habits, whether good or bad, are all-powerful among the people; the people act by imitation, and though they know that an illicit union is contrary to the precepts of morality and the customs of society, they will not hesitate to incur the shame of this state if their comrades are also involved in illicit unions. If you represent to them the impropriety of an illicit union as a deterrent, they will quote in reply many examples among their own comrades; for these examples ought, in their opinion, to acquit them of the reproach of immorality because it applies to too many people.[13]

The Consequences

The illicit union placed a whole population on the margin of the law; often, too, it drove them outside it. The scores of news items reporting working-class brawls undoubtedly covered many instances of such unions breaking up. But the high proportion of single men[14] brought before the criminal courts—as shown in the statistics issued by the administration of criminal justice in France, in the age distribution of the accused[15] and in the number of breakdowns of illicit unions accompanied by violence —provide even more conclusive confirmation. Crimes of this sort were by far the commonest in the department of the Seine. What is very striking is the tremendous repercussions of these dramatic incidents upon contemporary opinion, and the extent of the collective pity and terror evoked by such crime and the contemporary interpretation of it. "Two young men scarcely twenty years of age, Sureau and Ulbach," the *Journal des Débats* of January 30, 1828, wrote,

have paid the penalty, the former hard labor for life and the latter the capital penalty, for murders to which they were instigated by love and unbridled jealousy. Another young man, also of the working class, will be up before the court tomorrow, but his victim, luckier than the unfortunate goatwoman of Ivry, is still breathing.

Ulbach and Sureau sum up working-class criminality. We have already drawn attention to Ulbach's place in the criminal setting of *Les Misérables* and we shall not revert to it. Sureau's crime left no such notable traces; the victim was no shepherdess and he was not sentenced to death. But Sureau too belonged to the lower classes and everything indicates—the newspaper reports and the street ballads—that his deed was just as sensational. Born at Marles, in the Seine-et-Marne, aged twenty-one, residing at No. 16, rue des Deux-Ponts on the Ile Saint-Louis, he worked as a barber's assistant with Mahy the hairdresser at No. 79, rue de Charenton. At 7.30 P.M. on September 14, 1826, he stabbed a young girl, Henriette Coulon, on the rue de la Bucherie. He had been living with her and she had left him; he attempted suicide after killing her. He was a criminal, true, but, like Ulbach, he won a great deal of popular sympathy because he was a victim of the savage condition which compelled a great many workers to live on the margin of the law and drove some of them to rise against it.

II
Illegitimacy and the Renewal of the Criminal Population

Working-class concubinage is one of the best documented of the biological forms of this savage condition and one of those most easily expressed in figures. And it contributed to the renewal of a dangerous, if not actually criminal, population to a degree that can be equally easily identified through the illegitimacy statistics, which, by definition, we can relate to illegitimacy itself before taking them further to estimate cohabitation. Illegitimacy provided a permanent source of replacements in a population which, though not necessarily wedded to crime, was from the first, and biologically, situated outside the city, on the margin of the law, we must repeat, and therefore more liable to come into conflict with the law.

It would, of course, be possible to investigate the relationship between illegitimacy and the criminal condition by reversing the procedure we used with regard to cohabitation. One cannot help thinking that illegitimacy contributed to a renewal of the criminal population when the crime statistics show that a large proportion of criminals had been illegitimate children. This conclusion can be drawn from the statistics of the courts, and was so drawn by Guerry in his *Essai sur la statistique morale de la France,* by Villermé, by Quételet, and by Parent-Duchatelet in his investigation of the civil status of prostitutes born in Paris.

The conclusions were incontrovertible, and they are confirmed by modern investigations; but their drawback is that they relate only to crimes actually committed. We are more concerned with the dangerous condition, which is not the same thing as the criminal condition. It is a larger group; and the illegitimacy statistics provide an approximate enough measurement of it.

Illegitimacy and the Criminal Propensity: An Initial Hypothesis

To attempt this estimate obviously means assuming at the start that "Children who are the issue of illegitimate unions," as Frégier wrote,

are predestined by their birth to every stroke of misfortune. At an early age they are set on the downward slope to vice, surrounded by bad examples, a prey to precocious passions, and they are lost almost before they know the difference between right and wrong. It is from their ranks that those who instigate begging, vagrancy and theft recruit their adepts. The material to be found in the annual reports of the Paris society for the protection of discharged juvenile convicts is both interesting and conclusive.

Modern criminologicial and sociological research, especially in the United States, with its emphasis on the influence of the environment in which a child grows up upon the formation of its attitudes, shows how the compulsion towards crime operates.[16]

We ought really to reread the whole of the medical literature of the first half of the nineteenth century at this point, not in order to analyze and assess it—that is not our concern here—but simply to observe how extremely familiar it is with the notion of the influence of environment upon the formation of personality. Cabanis had had much to say about this in his time. Esquiros reminded his readers in his article on foundlings in the *Revue des Deux Mondes* in 1846 that Cabanis had thought he detected a physical and mental inferiority in these children; when the ballot for conscripts was drawn, only half of them were found fit for military service. "Cabanis," he added, "regarded these children as extraordinary beings lacking all moral and ordinary feelings. Popular tradition attributes to illegitimate children a character and vices all their own." He went on to say that Cabanis found the reason for this in the infant's earliest impressions. Villermé and Frégier said much the same. "What perseverance, what obstinate courage are needed by children born into this condition and raised amid vicious example if they are to rise above this abject state!", Dr. Henri Bayard wrote in his *Topographie médicale du IVe arrondissement et Description du quartier des Marchés.* "Very few of them, therefore, ever achieve a decent and honest life." And the commentators on the *Statistique de la Chambre de commerce de Paris en 1847*: "Some individuals are unfortunately the victims of an ineluctable fate. The circumstances of their birth are unpromising; they are cursed with a kind of flaw *ab initio*, a bad start in life, and very few of them are able to rid themselves of it." The flaw *ab initio* is the family environment, and this leads to breach of the family contract, breach of the employment contract and breach of the social contract by a train of events here described in masterly fashion.[17]

Illegitimacy and the Criminal Propensity: An Estimate

The inference to be drawn from these observations is that though illegitimate children may not be doomed irremediably to crime, they are fated at least to a dangerous condition, a situation outside the law in a group continuously renewed by the illegitimate, whose numbers can be estimated by means of the illegitimacy statistics.

This estimate will gain in probability if we are careful at the outset to discount as far as possible anything which seems to militate in favor of the thesis we believe we have demonstrated. We shall, therefore, first eliminate the statistics for foundlings from the statistics for illegitimate children, on the assumption that they could not contribute in any way to the renewal of the dangerous groups we are trying to estimate, either because of their very high mortality immediately on entering the Foundlings Hospital or because they were sent to the provinces, where their mortality still was higher than that of other children, and on the assumption that they all stayed in the provinces, despite the considerable contemporary evidence to the contrary. Another precaution we shall take is to consider only the age groups in which we know the crime rate to be the highest, that is the 18–35 age group, although we are trying to measure a population far larger than the criminal population as such.[18]

We shall confine our initial estimate to the years for which very detailed illegitimacy statistics were published, 1817 and after. Those born in 1817 theoretically reached the age of criminality, eighteen, in 1839. If we eliminate foundlings, apply the relevant death rate by age to the children who remained in Paris and estimate their number at 2,000, we arrive at the conclusion that in 1847—to take only the year in which those born in 1817 reached the age of thirty—the total was 13 generations of new criminals, or 26,000 individuals.

Let us rather say a minimum of 26,000. If we construe criminality to mean not only criminals brought before the courts for serious criminal offenses but also minor offenders brought before the police courts, we find that much older groups are also involved. The upper limit is 60, not 35. We have therefore to add 25 more generations to the previous 13 criminal generations. Taking into account the fact that the proportion of illegitimate children before 1817, though not so accurately counted, must have been much the same, and taking into account, too, the higher death rate for the age groups, we arrive at a total of 37,500 individuals to be added to the previous total. We may therefore conclude that at least 63,500 individuals must be placed in the dangerous category in 1847 simply by reason of illegitimacy. But we may also conclude that the share of illegitimacy in the renewal of the dangerous category could hardly have been less than this in each year throughout the first half of the nineteenth century.

CHAPTER FIVE

Death Draws the Balance

Doomed to failure, finally, by their life, a life whose balance was drawn and summed up by death. This is the vital inference from the statistics for mortality, at any rate in the Paris of the first half of the nineteenth century. They show a way of dying rather than a way of living, for which very few other sources of information can be found. This, indeed, is the main significance of two facts: first, that the aggregate total of deaths increased and changed; and, secondly, that the differences in age, sex and place revealed major social differences. This is true of the normal mortality, but even more so of the two abnormal death rates for the cholera epidemics of 1832 and 1849, which enabled the contemporary statisticians to grasp and measure, as never before, the inequality before life by way of the inequality before death.

I

Normal Mortality

The growth and change in the statistics for normal mortality reveal that the living conditions of a large part of the Paris population grew worse. At the same time, they enable us to identify and isolate the components most affected, by observing the unequal incidence of this mortality.

The mortality increased and changed in this period. For the sake of greater accuracy, before we try to measure this increase and change we shall have to give some account of the death rate in Paris at an earlier period, before the great massacres of the Revolution. This would be extremely laborious if we did not have a guide, Buffon, who summarized the work of his predecessors and used the Paris registers of vital statistics to good purpose in the second volume of his *Histoire naturelle*.

Calculating the average annual death rate for all years of the eighteenth century in his initial approach, Buffon placed it at between 18,000 and 19,000. But there were irregularities due to abnormal mortality which had to be eliminated. Buffon thought that

we shall approximate more closely to the true figure for the average death rate if we only use the registers of deaths since 1745, for it was only in that year that male and female infants were recorded separately in the registers of baptisms and men and women in the registers of deaths; which shows that these registers were then kept more accurately than in previous years. The figure for total deaths from 1745 to 1766 was 414,777, which, divided by 22, the number of years from 1745 to 1766, gives 18,853, a figure which is not far from the 18,881 given by Messance; so that I believe we can establish the average annual death rate in Paris at 18,800 without going far wrong.

This rate was higher in any event than that for the surrounding districts in the countryside ten, fifteen or twenty leagues distant from Paris, for which Buffon established mortality tables comparable with those for the capital. It was not, however, so much higher as to cancel out the effects of fertility and make the renewal of the population dependent on the influx of a new immigrant population. Indeed, a comparison of the Paris death rate with that of the countryside from the age of forty to the end of life "shows that more people constantly die in Paris than in the countryside and the rate of death increases with age; which seems to indicate that the commodities of life contribute greatly to its length and that those rural people who are most exhausted and worst fed generally die much earlier than townspeople." Furthermore, Buffon's comparison of mortality by age in Paris and London showed fairly clearly that before the nineteenth century the great unhealthy man-eating city was London rather than Paris. The death rate was higher in Paris than London up to the age of twenty, including the first two years of life, where the Paris statistics, unlike those for London, did not record the deaths of infants put out to nurse. As to other age groups, the number of deaths

is lower in Paris and in London from 20 to 50, nearly the same from 50 to 60 and much higher in Paris than in London from 60 to the end of life. This seems to show, by and large, that people reach old age far less often in London than Paris, since of 13,189 persons, 2,799 die after the age of 60 in Paris, whereas only 1,820 out of the same number, 13,189, die after the age of 60 in London; so that there is one-third more chance of achieving old age in Paris than London.

This situation changed in the first half of the nineteenth century. It was no longer London but Paris that was the unhealthy and lethal city.

Assertions by contemporaries and in the picturesque literature on which we have already commented would carry conviction even if we had no other evidence. But not complete conviction. It cannot be taken on trust that the greater significance accorded to death, and the way in which the problems and terrors of death entered the preoccupations of contemporaries, may be accepted as evidence of a rise in the death rate. On the contrary, modern experience in territories in which the statistics situate the highest death rates shows that a higher death rate may well be accompanied by complete indifference to life and death. It is even possible that death only begins to acquire significance once the death rate begins to fall. The preoccupation with death in the literature of the first half of the nineteenth century and in the contemporary news items might reasonably be interpreted as evidence of a fall in the death rate and as a sign of a greater interest in living because new means were available to reduce it still further.

We must go to the figures, as Buffon did, following both his example and his method. Despite the existence of a large body of statistics, the study of the evolution of mortality in Paris from the beginning of the nineteenth century onwards calls for an approach in successive stages comparable in every respect to the approach taken so assiduously by our great predecessor.

It is the total number of deaths that is important in the first instance, regardless of the size of the population to which the deaths have to be related, regardless of its age distribution and regardless of the demographic inadequacy of such an evolution. Admittedly, the real death rate does not show up in the aggregate statistics giving each year its weight of deaths. Though the figures may rise, there need not necessarily be an absolute increase in the death rate. But large differences in any year show up, and the historian perforce has to pay attention to them. We may go so far as to say that even the aggregate figures are of interest precisely on account of their increase and that their historical significance —even though their demographic value is nil—is undeniable. A larger number of deaths does not denote a higher death rate if the rise is accounted for by a larger population. So far as the demographer is concerned, that is. Not to contemporaries and to the historian attentive to such facts as the publicity given these deaths by the statistics and their dissemination by the press, and especially the preoccupation with death and its shows in a Paris where, as we have seen, the material setting had not changed—ancient, cluttered cemeteries, overcrowded hospitals, streets blocked by funeral processions, reported in all the papers. It was the continual contact between the living and the dead that was stressed by the aggregate statistics, which show that this increased from year to year, thus:

1780	21,391	1807	20,587	1832	44,463
1781	20,180	1808	17,352	1833	25,095
1782	18,953	1809	16,718	1834	22,991
1783	20,010	1810	17,705	1835	24,792
1784	21,778	1811	16,029	1836	24,057
1785	20,365	1812	19,952	1837	28,134
1786	18,665	1813	19,761	1838	25,797
1787	18,139	1814	33,116	1839	25,324
1788	19,959	Hundred		1840	28,294
1789	19,962	Days	5,247	1841	26,028
1790	19,947	1815	20,429	1842	28,676
1791	17,952	1816	19,124	1843	27,967
1792	17,416	1817	21,124	1844	27,360
1793	21,167	1818	22,421	1845	26,156
1794	30,388	1819	22,671	1846	28,595
1795	26,978	1820	22,464	1847	30,920
1796	27,779	1821	22,648	1848	30,088
1797	20,381	1822	23,282	1849	48,122
1798	20,287	1823	24,600	1850	25,852
1799	22,932	1824	22,617	1851	27,585
1800	19,872	1825	26,892	1852	27,980
1801	20,767	1826	25,341	1853	33,262
1802	20,582	1827	22,534	1854	40,968
1803	25,791	1828	24,557	1855	36,016
1804	20,870	1829	25,600	1856	29,951
1805	18,469	1830	27,464	1857	33,251
1806	19,752	1831	25,996	1858	32,262

It appears that the number of deaths diminished during the last years of the Ancien Régime and the early years of the Revolution, until the three terrible years 1793, 1794 and 1795, and ran in the same direction during the Empire until the disaster of 1814. From 1815 to 1821, it remained at a high but stable level at between 21,000 and 22,000. These were difficult years owing to food shortages and harsh winters. Quételet in his study of the relationship between bad harvests, the high price of bread and the death rate called them "deadly," and Balzac mentioned them several times. It was during the winter of 1819 that the drama Balzac related in *La Vendetta* came to its climax: "Poverty appeared suddenly, not hideous, but simply clad and almost tolerable; then came destitution in all its horror, uncaring in its rags and trampling on every human feeling." The years of dearth did not, however, result in any very considerable increase in the number of deaths in Paris. "The average rate for the ten years ending in 1817," Lachaise wrote,

was 21,350; for the four years 1816, 1817, 1818 and 1819 it was 21,344. The average mortality for the 40 years ending in 1763 was, according to M. Messance's observations,[1] 18,881. An increase of only 2,463 in deaths in relation to an increase of 163,116 in the population leaves no doubt as to the more confident attitude and more regular application of medicine following the revival of the physical sciences.[2]

He went on to say that the effects of the dearth could be seen only in the fact that "the incidence of mortality fell more heavily on women and children."

On the other hand, from 1822 to the cholera epidemic of 1832 the annual average was higher; while the trend was upward, larger differences appeared in some years. These two features also marked the period from the cholera epidemic of 1832 to that of 1849, namely, a similar upward trend and similar differences in certain years.

Mortality: While the register of crude mortality concerns the historian immediately and directly, but not the demographer, since he regards it as only a preliminary approach—necessary but inadequate—to his research, the study of real mortality—i.e., relative to the population—concerns the historian and the demographer alike. To what extent was the increase in deaths due to an increase in the population and to what extent did the death rate rise in Paris in these years?

Mortality can be computed only if the number of inhabitants is known; hence the difficulty with the earlier periods. Furthermore, with these periods not only is it difficult to compute a death rate by relating a yearly figure for deaths to the total population, but the total population itself was estimated by the contemporary writers precisely from the annual figures for deaths. Here we run into a problem comparable with that which arises today in countries where the number of births and deaths is fairly accurately known but the size of the population to which those births and deaths have to be related is not. That is why the normal death rate in Paris can only be estimated by reference to the general death rate for France, which can in fact be computed.[3] In the light of this general death rate, we may consider that the annual number of deaths in Paris per thousand inhabitants was probably:

1781–1785	39	Year IV–Year VIII	41
1786–1791	36	Year IX–Year XIII	37
Year I–Year II	49	1806–1810	30.

The ratio of deaths to population during the first half of the nineteenth century was as follows:

Year	Population	Increase (%)	Deaths	Number of deaths per 1,000	
1807 to 1817		22.97			
1817	713,966		21,124	29.5	
1818	719,101		22,421	31.5	
1819	724,236		22,671	31.3	
1820	729,371		22,464	30.8	
1821	734,506		22,917	31.2	
1822	739,641				
1823	744,776		23,282	31.5	smallpox
1824	749,911	10.07	24,600	33.3	smallpox
1825	755,046		22,617	30.1	
1826	760,082		26,893	35.6	smallpox
1827	765,318		25,341	33.3	
1828	770,454		22,534	29.4	
1829	775,590		24,557	32.0	
1830	780,726		25,600	33.1	
1831	785,862		27,464	35.2	
1832	808,552		25,996	33.7	
1833	831,242		44,463	55.0	cholera
1834	853,932	10.25	25,096	30.2	cholera
1835	876,623		22,991	27.0	
1836	899,313		24,792	28.3	
1837	906,501		24,057	26.7	
1838	913,691		28,134	31.0	
1839	920,881	8.06	25,797	28.2	
1840	928,071		25,324	27.5	
1841	935,261		28,294	30.5	
1842	958,986		26,028	27.8	
1843	982,715		28,676	30.0	
1844	1,006,442	12.56	27,967	28.4	
1845	1,030,169		27,360	27.2	
1846	1,053,897		26,156	25.4	
1847	1,053,770		28,595	27.1	
1848	1,053,643		30,920	29.3	
1849	1,053,516	−0.06	30,088	28.5	
1850	1,053,389		48,122	45.6	cholera
1851	1,053,262		25,852	24.5	
1852	1,077,478		27,585	26.2	
1853			27,890	26.0	
1854			33,262	30.2	
1855			40,968	36.5	cholera

From this table we can draw the following conclusions: first, that for all years in the first half of the nineteenth century and—apart from the years of the cholera epidemics—even for those years which show the highest death rate, the death rate remained lower than we may assume it to have been in the eighteenth century. The decline in the death rate which apparently occurred under the Empire continued. Whereas the death rate was 39 per thousand from 1781 to 1785 and 30 from 1806 to 1810, the average in the earlier years of our period—1817 to 1820—was 31. This statistical estimate would seem to tally with the impression of improvement, relief and convalescence in a large number of descriptions of life in Paris during the early years of the Restoration. This is also the impression to be derived from the commentaries in the first volume of the *Recherches statistiques sur la Ville de Paris*: "Abnormal death rates are beginning to disappear and the rates are also becoming more stable. The series for annual mortality have become less variable." In the ensuing decades, however, the death rate rose, more steeply during the second half of the Restoration as may be seen from the following rates for five-year periods:

1817–1820	31.0	1836–1840	29.3
1821–1825	32.3	1841–1845	27.4
1826–1830	32.8	1846–1851	31.1.
1831–1835	34.0		

Note, however, that in computing a death rate the number of deaths per year has to be related to the figure for population given by the census nearest to the year for which the death rate is to be worked out. Everything goes to show that the population increased between one census and the next, so that an accurate death rate can be obtained with any certainty only for the actual census year. A first census was taken in 1817; there was an estimate in 1826, but it subsequently proved to be wrong; censuses were taken in a regular manner in 1831, 1836, 1846 and 1851, when the death rate developed as follows:

1817	29.5	1841	27.8
1831	33.7	1846	27.1
1836	26.7	1851	26.2.

Thus, no matter whether we take the annual rate or the rate in the census year, we find that the death rate was higher during the Restoration than during the July Monarchy; but that under both régimes it rose between the earlier and later years, though less steeply during the July Monarchy than during the Restoration. Moreover, the mortality in Paris was higher than it was in the rest of France and—to take only one comparison—higher than that in a metropolis like London.

It is nonetheless true that the conclusions drawn from this preliminary statistical analysis hardly tally with a great deal of the contemporary evidence, all of which, as we have already seen, concurs in stressing that living conditions grew worse and that poverty and death were the outstanding feature of Paris at this time. Are we to accept the judgment of the statistician of 1846, who simply took the figures at their face value and wrote, in Volume VI of the *Recherches statistiques*: "One death in 36.39 in Paris is a figure more favorable than any of those for earlier periods; it is accounted for by the spread of orderly habits and welfare, better sanitation for the city and its inhabitants and the progress of medical science and hygiene," thereby flatly contradicting contemporary opinion? As a matter of fact, our statistical analysis is inadequate; it lacks an element, the distribution by age.

Mortality by age group: In computing mortality rates we have to take into account the rejuvenation of the population by immigration, which, as we have shown, was very large. From 1817 onward, the number of children and the aged diminished constantly, whereas the number of adults rose. Most deaths occurred in the youngest and oldest age groups, and since the adult 15 to 60 age groups were the largest in Paris and the least subject to serious illnesses, the absolute figure for the death rate in them should be very much lower; consequently, the general death rate should be lower too. The important factor is the death rate by age, not the death rate for the total population.

In our period and the years immediately ensuing, the number of deaths per year per thousand inhabitants in each age group was as follows:

	0–4 years	5–9	10–14	15–19	20–24	25–29	30–39	40–49	50–59	60–69	Total
1817–1820	147	18	9	11	17	12	13	17	26	49	31.0
1821–1825	157	21	9	11	19	15	12	17	27	51	32.3
1826–1830	155	19	8	10	17	17	14	18	28	52	32.8
1831–1835	140	21	8	10	21	18	17	18	35	63	34.0
1836–1840	126	18	9	12	19	15	13	19	28	52	29.3
1841–1845	130	17	8	14	19	14	12	18	23	45	27.4
1846–1850	160	19	9	13	19	16	15	20	27	54	31.1
1851–1855	167	18	8	15	20	14	13	17	28	51	29.8
1856–1860	158	13	7	12	15	11	11	15	24	49	26.5
1861–1865	134	11	5	9	12	11	12	16	26	50	25.7
1866–1870	128	10									27.0
1871–1875	101	9									22.4
	108										23.7
	114										24.4

Now let us eliminate two age groups in which the death rate recorded in the tables was certainly lower than it was in reality, although there is no way of estimating it more precisely. As regards the highest age group, 60–69, we have to take into account the indigent males, who were formerly part of the Paris population but were admitted to the Bicêtre almshouse *extra muros,* and whose mortality does not appear in the tables. In 1817 there were 3,100 persons at Bicêtre, 3,056 of them men. As regards the lowest age group, we have to take into account the infants put out to nurse. How many they were was not known until the closing years of the nineteenth century, when they accounted for one-third of the newborn babies in Paris; but in the early decades of the century Lachaise estimated them at two-thirds, noting that "those who remain in the city belong to families in easy circumstances."[4] It is possible that the rejuvenation of the Paris population in the ensuing decades and the consequent rise in the number of births may have made this practice commoner and may have inflated the death rate for children, which was in fact part of the Paris death rate, but did not appear in the statistics for it. Even if we take only the deaths in the lowest age group which were registered, we cannot fail to observe that they increased regularly during the Restoration and until the 1832 cholera epidemic; after a deep trough due to the great cholera massacre and the selection that occurred in consequence, the movement resumed, reaching its highest level between 1851 and 1855.

Though it was smaller, the rise on which we have to focus our attention is that which affected the intermediate levels, containing those groups responsible for the increase in the Paris population. The death rate per thousand between 20 and 39 years of age developed as follows:

1817–1820	42	1846–1850	50
1821–1825	46	1851–1855	47
1826–1830	48	1856–1860	37
1831–1835	56	1861–1865	35
1836–1840	47	1866–1870	41.
1841–1845	45		

If we eliminate the substantial irregularities due to the cholera epidemics in the periods 1831–35 and 1846–50, we find that the death rate rose during the Restoration and that, though it fell during the July Monarchy—if we allow for the crisis of the cholera epidemic—it remained at a level hardly lower than it had been in the worst years of the preceding régime.

The general increase in mortality in Paris is of little relevance here. What is important is the fact that the largest and most constant rise in the rate affected the age groups containing the very groups which were most responsible for the city's population increase, whose youth and physical strength might have been expected to protect them most effectually from the onset of mortality.

Another aspect of mortality in this period shows up here: its inequality. The mortality statistics were progressively weighted down by the poverty of the majority and, moreover, pointed to and singled out the groups whose conditions of living and way of life burdened the general death rate most heavily.

Inequality Before Death

The leading contemporary statisticians, especially Villermé, devoted the major part of their research and their most noteworthy works to studying, observing and measuring the fact of inequality before death; so much so, indeed, that this may be regarded as the predominant concern of the period. And they studied it so thoroughly that we have nothing to add; all we need do is summarize the conclusions set out by Villermé himself in the *Annales d'Hygiène*,[5] in a table classifying the arrondissements by order of deaths at home and in untaxed residences, that is to say, by order of poverty.

| | Untaxed residences as % of total | Deaths at home | |
Arrondissement	residences	1817–21	1822–26
IIIrd	7	1 per 62 residences	1 per 71 residences
IInd	11	60	67
Ist	11	58	66
IVth	15	58	62
XIth	19	51	61
VIth	21	54	58
Vth	22	53	64
VIIth	22	52	59
Xth	23	50	49
IXth	31	44	50
VIIIth	32	43	46
XIIth	38	43	44

One very striking result of ranging the arrondissements of the City of Paris in accordance with the increase in the number of rented accommodations not liable to tax, that is to say, of their poor, is that they too fall into line very clearly one after another, with perhaps a single exception in each period, in the order of the increase in mortality. Thus, wealth, easy circumstances and poverty are, as things now stand and because of the situations in which they place the inhabitants of the Paris arrondissements, the main causes (I do not say the sole causes) to which the great differences in mortality must be attributed. All that need be said of this truth is that I have established it.

The inequally before life was undeniable, total. And it was summed up, and the balance of all its aspects drawn, in the inequality before death.

Inequality Before Life

It is life, not death, that is of interest to history. The measurement of death is of interest only insofar as it is, in many respects, the sole and most incontrovertible means of measuring life.

This view was not shared by the statisticians of the first half of the century, for they went no further than this final balance and, though they did not neglect the problem of its causes—living conditions and modes of life—they invariably looked at it only in terms of mortality. "It would no doubt be very interesting," wrote Villermé,

to determine, as we have done, in all cases from observation, the mortality of each class of those which make up the Paris population, the mortality peculiar to each particular mode of life, to each particular habit, to residence on each particular storey, and so on. But the *Recherches statistiques sur Paris* do not provide the data for solving any of these problems; they simply show that in Paris, in present circumstances and with the existing health regulations, the only conditions with an appreciable influence upon the death rate are those necessarily attached to easy circumstances or poverty.

But these are precisely the conditions which interest the historian, who is less concerned with death than with the traces on death of the vicissitudes of life. Beyond the inequality before death and through it there appears the inequality before life, the latter being the more incontrovertible as the former is the more certain, the more manifest as the diversity of economic and social facts themselves and their vast uncertainties are stamped upon it in irrefutable signs as legible as the scars on a body. This history is pitched at body level; while it is not indifferent to work and customs, it holds that work and customs have never left so deep an imprint on the body and that economic and social inequality has never been reduced to terms of biological inequality so simply as in the period we are studying.

The biological inequality existed from the start. Deparcieux said the final word on this subject in his description of the results of the Parisians' custom of putting their children out to nurse in the country, that is, both a higher death rate and a higher fertility rate, "the mothers becoming pregnant again much sooner." Hence the birth of ill-favored individuals who themselves engendered ill-favored individuals:

Some of those who escape the mortality caused by their sickly constitution or by lack of care on the part of their nurses become semi-paralyzed, rickety, hunchbacked or are afflicted with some other infirmity. When they reach a certain age, however, they do not hesitate to marry, and the children born to them inherit their enfeebled constitution, which will thus go on perpetuating itself so long as mothers entrust the suckling of their children to others.

This custom was characteristic mainly of the poor. "I have observed," Deparcieux commented,

that fewer children of rich parents or parents in easy circumstances die in Paris than children of the lower classes. The former take nurses in Paris or in the neighboring villages and live near enough to visit their children every day and supervise their nurses' care of them, whereas the lower classes cannot pay high fees and can only take nurses far away. The fathers and mothers only see their children when they are brought back; and in general rather more than half of them die while out at nurse, which is largely due to these women's lack of care, either because their milk is stale, or because they do not have enough of it, or because they suckle them incorrectly or not long enough, or because they cut down their share by suckling their own children from time to time to the detriment of those for whom they are paid, the parents being too far away to keep an eye on them.[6]

We should take special note of Deparcieux's observation concerning "constitutions":

Everything depends on the start in life; a person who has been nursed in this way and lives to seventy or eighty might have lived to ninety or a hundred, had he had all the milk nature had appointed for him. There are, therefore, far more aged persons in the distant provinces than in Paris; there the men are strong and vigorous and commonly work as hard and assiduously at the age of seventy or eighty as men do around Paris at fifty or sixty; tall and well-made men are as common in the provinces as small and weakly men around Paris.

These observations by an eighteenth-century precursor concerning this basic inequality, the consequences of which were to last throughout life, surely apply to our period as well.

The mortality of lower-class children: More lower-class children died, to begin with. Though the statistics are hard to interpret, most contemporary analyses agreed that the increase in infanticide and stillbirths in Paris during this period could only be ascribed to the increase in the numbers of the lower classes.[7] Most stillbirths, indeed, occurred in the main lower-class arrondissements. As to premature births, which were classified in a different group, Trébuchet noted that "they mostly meet the same fate, since their precarious life cannot tolerate the least disturbance. There were 5,215 in Paris during the period 1840–1844, or 1 in 30 births"; the largest number also occurred in the lower-class arrondissements. Not to speak of the thousands of deserted babies, legitimate or illegitimate, almost all of them belonging to the lower classes, put out to nurse or apprenticeship by the hospital administration in regions where they were decimated, such as the marshy and backward Sologne, where the death rate for Paris children was all the higher because, if we are to believe Villermé, "places which are very unhealthy owing to marshes are inhabited by few except poor peasants who, wrapped in fatalism and imbecile apathy, watch their children die, without realizing that they could keep them alive at some other place."[8] If we simply observe the mortality at home, we note sharp contrasts in child mortality in each age group in both the wealthy and the poor districts.[9] From 1817 to 1823, taking deaths in all age groups together, the proportion of deaths in the first ten years of life in the rue Mouffetard was almost twice that in the rue Saint-Honoré and the rue du Roule, and, of a given total of deaths (all at home), infants under one year alone accounted for as many deaths in the rue Mouffetard as all the children in the 0–10 age groups in the other two streets.

While the inequality shown in the mortality of lower-class children brings out many aspects of the physical and moral condition of the working class, this is to be seen even more plainly in one form of this mortality, death by smallpox, where an abundant archival material supplies what we might describe as a running commentary on the statistical data.

Smallpox was the cause of nearly 30% of deaths in the 1–4 age group before 1789; this percentage diminished thereafter owing to vaccination, which began to spread after 1795. As early as 1800, the death rate in the 1–4 group fell sharply as a result of the almost total disappearance of smallpox, while it remained practically without change in the 14– or 15–24 age group. Epidemics again broke out in Paris in 1822, 1823 and 1825, however, and there were more deaths by smallpox in Paris than in the rest of France in each subsequent year to the end of our period. This is accounted for by the heavier smallpox mortality in the poorest arrondissements.[10]

There were a number of reasons for this. To begin with, the mass immigration into these arrondissements by workers who had not been vaccinated because they came from areas in the Massif Central where, as we know from other sources, there was a great deal of resistance to vaccination. Describing the ravages of the 1822 epidemic, the Prefect of the Seine wrote:

The epidemic appeared early in the year in the VIIth, VIIIth, IXth and Xth arrondissements, and it went on to invade all the arrondissements. The IVth and the XIIth have suffered most severely, and no less than 17 persons were affected in a single house in the faubourg Saint-Jacques. Doctors have definitely established that the first persons to contract smallpox were workmen who had recently arrived in Paris carrying the disease with them. The smallpox has, in fact, claimed most victims in the faubourg Saint-Morceau and the quartier des Halles, which are working-class districts. The way to avert this danger is to compel all workers carrying *livrets*[11] who come to work in Paris and have not had the smallpox or have not been vaccinated either to be vaccinated at once or to leave Paris.[12]

But the contagion brought in by these immigrants spread in these districts only because the workers permanently resident there themselves did not trouble or refused to have their children vaccinated. In a "Warning to the Laboring Classes" the Prefect Chabrol stated:

The smallpox has appeared in several Paris districts. . . . The Administration must address its warning especially to the laboring class. Its members know with what solicitude the Prefect of Police regards their work; he is entitled to their confidence; he has no intention of giving them any advice that is not useful to their families. In recommending the use of the vaccine to parents he is indicating to them the most effective means of protecting their children from the consequences of the smallpox.

Much the same occurred in the 1825 epidemic: "Carried by the workers who flocked in from the provinces to take advantage of the high price for labor in consequence of a large competitive tender," Trébuchet wrote, "it spread rapidly among a population which had refused the benefits of the vaccine out of indifference or prejudice."[13]

The administrative reports laid stress on these popular prejudices and tried to combat them. In contrast to what was observed in the rural areas, such prejudices were seldom described as having a religious flavor in Paris.[14] The Prefect of the Seine stated on December 18, 1817: "We cannot deny that the reason for many people's repugnance to the new method is the mistaken fear of failing to comply with the precepts of religion. I have written to the Archbishop of Paris asking him to send instructions to the parish priests."[15] Such observations were rare, and popular prejudices were of a different sort in Paris, or at any rate so it was supposed. In a letter to the Minister of the Interior in 1818, a doctor in the rue Haute-Ville stressed

the completely false but generally accepted idea that all the inhabitants have the germ of smallpox pre-existing in them; for, if that were so, it would be hard, or even impossible, to suppose that a single atom of vaccine fluid injected into our humors can, by its action, neutralize a germ so potent and so fertile in its effects that it is able to cover the body with a disgusting suppuration. That, at any rate, is the objection I have most often heard used against the vaccine.[16]

Some people actually believed, in Paris and elsewhere, that "smallpox is a natural disease and one ought to have had it,"[17] and often even that "smallpox serves to purify the body and fortify the health."[18] In many works of the picturesque literature and in melodramas, in *Les Mystères de Paris* and in Gavarni's *Masques et visages,* pockmarked faces and ravaged snouts signified brute force and violence rather than physical inferiority or blemish. References to disfigurement were very little emphasized as compared with other arguments in the pleas in favor of vaccination. Though Dr. Bergeron, a member of an arrondissement Charity Center,[19] and Dr. Menuret, the author of a well-known *Topographie médicale,* mentioned the risks of disfigurement, they laid far more stress on the exemplary behavior of the Paris bourgeoisie and the spectacular vaccination of H.R.H. the Duke of Bordeaux on November 13, 1820. There were few allusions to disfigurement in the posters by the Prefect of Police.

The attitude was perhaps resignation or indifference rather than prejudice, an attitude toward sickness which itself can be accounted for only by the attitude toward life and death to which we have already referred. As Dr. Bergeron wrote in 1821: "This horrible disease seems virtually endemic in some districts in Paris and in several departments; the reason is the neglect of the vaccine."[20] And Dr. Menuret wrote to the Minister of the Interior in 1810:

Lower-class children are too carelessly vaccinated, too carelessly observed thereafter and too carelessly followed up until the vaccination has been completely effective. They are not visited; no one knows whether the scab has formed or whether it has gone through its specific and distinctive stages. Doctors certify correctly enough that the child has been vaccinated, but it is not always true that the result has in every case been what it should have been in order to ensure the proper effect. If it should so happen that a child who has been vaccinated contracts the smallpox afterwards, this gives rise to a strange rumor in the house and district, and the gossips do not fail to grasp the opportunity to use this as backing for their diatribes against the vaccine.[21]

Whether it was prejudice or lack of interest made little difference. Such lower-class attitudes were hard to combat. The campaign continued from one end of our period to the other, more intensively during the Empire and the early years of the Restoration. On March 18, 1811, the Prefect of the Seine wrote:

The ever-recurring dangers of the smallpox and the continuing difficulties encountered in establishing the useful method in Paris itself have prompted me to issue the following order: "In addition to the free vaccinations given at all times at the Central Vaccination Hospital in the rue du Battoir Saint-André, vaccination shall be provided at fixed periods in May and September each year in each of the twelve municipal arrondissements. At the beginning of April and August each mayor, accompanied by one of the doctors attached to the Welfare Office in his arrondissement, shall proceed to all the schools in it and require the masters to submit to them a list of their pupils who have not had the smallpox and have not been vaccinated. It is hereby decided that notices shall be sent to the parents listing the persons who have died in the arrondissement since the beginning of the year and that special assistance shall be granted to indigent parents whose children have been vaccinated.

A fresh effort was made during the early years of the Restoration which were so marked by "the smallpox epidemics, the deplorable results of the people's obstinate resistance to the progress of vaccination," mentioned by Lachaise in 1822.[22] It was decided in December 1817 that in Paris "one of the surest methods of persuading the indigent to have their children vaccinated would be to distribute 5 francs for each child vaccinated, as is customary at the yearly vaccinations."

By Prefect's Order in 1818 a vaccination certificate was issued and parents had to produce it to obtain public assistance. The Minister of the Interior wrote on October 30, 1822, that "the course of persuasion, the only course that has been followed so far, seems inadequate so far as the poorer class is concerned." Other means had to be devised, such as visits of inspection by the police superintendents and especially an appeal to the clergy. As early as October 1810, "the vaccination committee having informed the Prefect of Police that children were often to be encountered in churches with their face and hands covered with smallpox scabs ready to fall, which is the moment when the contagion is most liable to spread, the bishops are requested to see to it that the parish priests refuse them admission to the churches."[23] From the Restoration on, the clergy were increasingly used. "I am counting particularly on warnings and exhortations by the clergy of the capital," the Minister of the Interior wrote, "and I have just written to the Archbishop of Paris on this subject." In actual fact, the unequal social distribution of deaths by smallpox during the greater part of our period stressed a fact which

Villermé summed up in 1833 in his study of epidemics: "In every society it is found that it is the educated and comfortable classes which have their children vaccinated and the lower classes which refuse; Jenner's fortunate discovery mainly benefits those who have drawn the best ticket in the lottery of life."[24]

The basic inequality: "Everything depends on the start in life." To this basic biological inequality which Deparcieux had asserted in terms that tally with our statistical commentary[25] the lower-class children in Paris were to be subjected for the whole of their lives, or at any rate to seem as if they were.

Unfortunate from the start was how Lachaise described them in 1821. He noted that even for those who remained in Paris, the benefits of being suckled by their mother were soon canceled out by "the species of wilting in narrow, dark and often dirty lodgings to which the majority of those who belong to the class of workers are subject," particularly those in the central districts, and especially Les Halles; doomed to grow up in the damp and dark.[26]

This basic inequality was also asserted in all the evidence in the literature on which we have commented; thus, there were different ways of ageing, which brought it about that "two girls born on the same day, one on the first floor and the other under the eaves," very soon no longer appeared to be the same age[27] and that Esther's maid in *Splendeurs et misères des courtisanes* could say: "I am twenty-three, the same age as Madame, and yet I look ten years older." We have to wait until the Second Empire to find the Paris worker's physical appearance described in any other way; for the first time perhaps by Dr. Véron in his *Mémoires d'un bourgeois de Paris*:

The rich man has to look after himself more carefully and from the point of view of health is not so well circumstanced as the worker. This is no paradox; compare the young workers with this generation of wealthy young men who now enjoy fortunes amassed under the Empire, the Restoration and the July Monarchy. The young worker who does not indulge in drink is strong, elegantly lithe, free in his motion, supple of gait; his hair is thick; his head is well set on his shoulders. The limbs are well developed mainly by the swell of the muscular frame. The teeth, the primary digestive apparatus, are healthy, strong, deeply rooted and, for the worker, a formidable and powerful weapon. The chest is broad; the pectoral muscles stand out; the walls of the stomach are not thickened by cell tissue nor overloaded with fat; the spine is very flexible and the muscles attached to it well developed and very powerful. How few wealthy young men resemble these athletes of labor!

We must make some allowances, of course, for Dr. Véron's comfortable optimism, as in these further observations: "Weak stomachs, bad digestions and stomach aches are rare among the working class. The worker's stomach laughs at the coarsest foods, those which put the most strain on the digestive apparatus; it even laughs at the most adulterated, the most spurious, the least fortifying wines." It is nonetheless true, though, that it would be hard to find any observations of this sort in the literature of the July Monarchy and that—whatever the value of these observations— it is a striking fact that they appear at some periods and not at others.

The many assertions would not, however, have any but an anecdotal significance if important contemporary statistical research did not confirm them, notably that by Villermé, who first measured the inequality of stature by arrondissement.[28] This measurement is important not only for the date at which it was made—in response, we might say, to contemporary preoccupations—but for its results. Examining the statistics of recruits published in the *Recherches statistiques sur la Ville*,[29] and arranging the arrondissements in decreasing order of average stature, Villermé noted in the first place that, with the sole exception of the XIth arrondissement, all of them came in the same order as that of the decrease in the proportion of rented accommodation liable to the personal tax alone; that is to say, the proportion of fairly well-to-do inhabitants who lived solely on their income or on earnings from an industry not liable to the licensing fee. "We therefore see," he concluded,

that stature depends on wealth, or rather, is in inverse proportion to the heavy labor, fatigue and privations undergone in childhood and youth. The exception in the XIth—Luxembourg, Ecole de Médecine, Sorbonne, Palais-de-Justice—may perhaps be raised in objection to this inductive reasoning. But when we find that the well-to-do population in that arrondissement is composed of a very large number of persons who have retired from business in their declining years, generally with a very moderate competence acquired late in life, the objection falls of its own weight.

Secondly, comparing by arrondissement the number of young men found fit for military service with the number excused, he observed that the latter were more numerous in the poor arrondissements, while the reverse held good in the wealthy arrondissements. The two rural arrondissements were similar to the poor arrondissements in this respect.

The resultant inequality: Underprivileged at the start, the working class was even more underprivileged thereafter, and in such a way that the inequality of its economic and social condition was reflected in a definitive biological inequality extending and aggravating the initial biological one, the effects of the course of working life and the effects of birth being imprinted on the body in precisely the same way. This fact was stressed in most of the contemporary documents relating to highly detailed investigations of the working-class condition or assembling contemporary observations.

It is the subsequent inequality of this frail and wasted class considered in its physical consequences and reflected in its physical characteristics that Lachaise described:

The muscular system is usually only slightly developed, so that the forms are somewhat feminine in appearance. In the working class the motor system is sometimes developed, but in almost every case irregularly or incompletely. . . . The number of rachitics, popularly known as the rickety, is fairly large, as well as the narrow-chested, lanky and weedy.[30]

Villermé's conclusions were very similar; he summed them up as follows:

In the light of all these very numerous, positive and concurrent indications, we shall conclude (whatever may be said in fashionable quarters) that the health of the poor is always precarious, their stature is slighter and their mortality excessive in comparison with the development of the body and health and with the mortality of persons better treated by fortune; or, in other words, that affluence and wealth, that is to say, the circumstances in which those who enjoy them are situated, are indeed the prerequisites for health.

In an earlier work he had written: "I have established that once illnesses have taken hold, they are more often fatal to the indigent than to the well-to-do."[31] Parent-Duchatelet noted in connection with the workers in the faubourg Saint-Marceau and around the Bièvre that it was believed at the Hôtel-Dieu that if they contracted a serious illness, they had far less chance of recovery than others.[32]

Industrialists, employers and civil engineers badly in need of labor shared this view and considered the Paris workers unfit for work requiring a certain degree of physical strength. Observations of this sort on the physical inferiority of the people of Paris are in fact to be found earlier than our period. A report of April 16, 1791, published by Tuéty, stated:

The Government was compelled by imperative circumstances at the end of May last year to set up charity workshops in Paris; the industrious class of the people of Paris is the one that is the neediest. But the persons composing it, accustomed as they are to sedentary work, are not able to endure the sun's glare and withdraw from the workshop at the slightest sign of rain.

In the correspondence relating to the workers employed on public works in Paris, the Highway Department engineers often noted that though crowds of Paris workers flocked for hire, they were very soon forced to give up for lack of physical stamina.[33] In the history of the labor market in Paris during the first half of the nineteenth century, a close reading of the major journeymen's literature alone, besides the well-known facts of economic history, would bring out the extent to which the inequality of physical strength among the workers determined both employment and the situation at the work place. The Paris worker was excluded from certain kinds of work and certain work sites because he was not up to the labor, or so it was believed.

OCCUPATIONAL MORBIDITY AND MORTALITY   Though the biological inequality summed up all the rest, so that inequality before death is the most reliable measurement of inequality before life, and though the conditions of existence and the course of working life aggravated the conditions of birth and childhood, it would nevertheless be of interest to identify the main reasons for this deterioration, or at any rate to isolate the reason which appears to have been the most important, namely, occupation.

The problem presents great difficulties at all periods. As subsequent studies on occupational mortality were to show, one factor that has to be taken into account is the relative influence upon the computed mortality exercised by recruitment into an occupation. Certain occupations requiring intense physical effort attracted strong men. Other trades —tailoring, for example—requiring only a minimum of physical effort provided a refuge for frailer persons.

In addition to these difficulties, which are common to all countries and all periods, there are others peculiar to the period we are examining, arising from the vagueness and variety of the nomenclature.

Nevertheless, the difficulties of interpretation are greater in modern times than they were in the period under review. This is to be ascribed far less to greater scruple in statistical research than to a more incontrovertible influence of occupation. The difficulties stem from the evident relationship between occupation and mortality, which was asserted in identical terms from the end of the eighteenth to the middle of the nineteenth century both by population statisticians and by physicians. It is this identity of observations, and even of terms, that calls for major emphasis.

Referring in 1778 to the value of specifying what he called the order of mortality in the various estates, Moheau wrote that "it would give a notion of the healthiness of each trade and the magnitude of the sacrifices undertaken in adopting certain occupations or régimes."[34] Lachaise also alluded to this notion of regarding the choice of a trade as equivalent to a species of sacrifice at the beginning of the nineteenth century in a chapter entitled *"De l'influence des arts et métiers sur la salubrité de la ville"*:

The feelings of the philosopher who reflects on the price at which we have purchased the benefits of social life and considers how many thousands of lives are sacrificed daily to our simplest enjoyments must surely be painful. When one sees that most of the workers who operate certain branches of industry do not live out more than half the span of an ordinary life, does it not seem that man is destined to find his destruction in the very causes of his existence?

Balzac expressed the same idea in almost identical terms.

While the study of occupational mortality seemed to be very much more complex in the closing years of the July Monarchy—as appeared plainly in the later research by Villermé and his contemporaries,[35] reflecting as it did the more complex state of the economy itself—it was very simple and very stable in their earlier works and in the works published at the end of the eighteenth century and in the first three decades of the nineteenth. They affirmed the close and in every case identical relationships between trades and mortality; this was a reflection of a stable economy, an immobile, stratified and compartmented society in which everyone assumed the dress of his estate and the disease and death of that estate. The analyses of occupational mortality among the people of Paris differed very little, we find, in successive works, which appear to copy one another. The *Essai sur l'histoire médico-topographique de Paris* by Menuret, published in 1786 and reprinted in 1804 virtually unchanged; the *Essai sur la topographie physique et médicale de Paris* by Audin-Rouvière, a medical officer, published in Year II of the Republic; the *Traité des maladies des artisans* by Patissier, published in 1822, which is simply an updated version, barely adapted to the Paris scene, of Ramazzini's classic work *De Morbis artificum diatriba,* published at Padua in 1713 and translated into French in 1778 by Fourcroy, who himself merely added a few passages to the original text, adding the Seine dockers to the occupations that caused ulcers; and Lachaise's medical topography and the earlier articles of Villermé himself. Through all these works, despite the time lapse, the relationships between occupation and mortality appeared so constant that Ramazzini's analyses were still authoritative and the classification of the divine Hippocrates himself was the necessary frame for all research, to all eternity.

These relationships were indubitable and constant particularly in the artisanal trades, which occupied so much of the Paris population that the observations concerning them could be interpreted by their authors as representative of the morbidity and mortality of the city as a whole. This was the Paris *fabrique*—the craft production sector—huge and varied, but invariably assembling in damp, dark workshops and a foul, reeking atmosphere men and women crouched over their work, all doomed to the same diseases, those most commonly cited being consumption and ulcers of the lower limbs. Parent-Duchatelet compiled impressive statistics of them in 1830:[36] tailors in the quartier des Halles and the quartier du Palais-Royal, particularly numerous behind Saint-Germain-l'Auxerrois and in the alleys which received all the garbage of the markets since they led down to the Seine; hatters in the quartier des Arcis and the quartier de Sainte-Avoye; gilders and mirror-cutters and printers. All the specialty trades of the central districts would have to be cited, with emphasis on the extent to which all the medical topographies describing them bring out the same relationship between working conditions and health. This relationship was even more evident in the case of the roofers, amounting to some 400 in Paris, whose trade was so dangerous that many mutual benefit societies formed by the Paris workers refused to have them as members; and of the laundrymen and dyers who lived along the Gobelins River, breathed in the miasmas from its stagnant waters and suffered from the fevers so familiar to the people of Paris. There is no need to refer once again to the abundant literature inspired by the mortality among the workers in the two white-lead factories, one at Ivry, the other at Clichy in the environs of Paris.

There can be no doubt about these relationships either, if we study certain grave diseases which, though not specific to the workers, were more fatal to the working class than to any other; in particular, the various diseases which can be classed together as diseases of the pulmonary system. As compared with the other commonest diseases, these were responsible for the most deaths in every year throughout the period, in particular consumption of the lungs, the deaths from which increased to such an extent in the closing years of the Restoration that a separate monthly register of them was kept at the Paris hospitals from 1831 onward.

Contemporary statistical research demonstrated irrefutably the influence of occupation upon lung consumption. Benoiston de Châteauneuf's studies were not at all convincing. Comparing the number of patients from each occupation in the Paris hospitals with the number of deaths from lung disease in each occupation, he had observed that 745 out of 26,074 male working-class patients died of consumption and 259 out of 17,447 female patients.[37] In reality, as Dr. Lombard of Geneva remarked, "to know that only 1 of 98 starch makers admitted to hospital died of consumption is hardly enlightening. What would be important to know is the ratio of deaths from consumption to all deaths in each occupation, and this the hospital reports cannot show." This ratio was established by Dr. Lombard from the register of deaths in the Geneva registry of vital statistics, which recorded all deaths of workers in the same occupation, as well as the deaths of consumptives in the more affluent classes of society who were wealthy enough to avoid going to hospital.[38]

By using these records and comparing them with the records of the hospitals in Hamburg and Vienna as well as in Paris, Dr. Lombard found that certain occupations everywhere and in all cases came above the average and others below it. He could easily demonstrate, moreover, by comparing the position of these occupations in the list, that this depended on the influence of occupations upon the health of those engaged in them rather than upon the workers' mode of living in a particular country. With regard to Paris, the comparison between the number of deaths in the hospitals from all diseases and the number of deaths from consumption enabled him to determine the influence of occupation upon consumption. Above the average were jewelers, cabinetmakers, printers, polishers, barmen, turners, weavers, house painters, pit-sawyers, wig makers, porters, tailors, millers and cobblers; below it came day laborers, blacksmiths, shoesmiths, masons, unskilled laborers, saddlers, joiners, bakers, cooks, inlayers, carters, coopers, roofers, concierges, wheelwrights, butchers, navvies, gardeners, water carriers, quarrymen, founders, porters and casual laborers at markets, and winesellers. As to female workers, above the average were polishers, weavers, shoemakers, binders and casemakers, knitters, gauze workers, glovers, embroiderers and sempstresses; below it came menders, dailies, charwomen, sick-nurses, concierges, tailors, gardeners and shop assistants.

By and large, the Paris classification coincided with the general classification, and in Paris, as everywhere else, death from consumption was closely related to such occupational characteristics as a sedentary life—which produced more consumptives than an active life owing to the cramped posture, very evident with tailors, cobblers and copyists, and owing to the atmosphere, with a great difference between outdoor and indoor work. Here, however, Paris differed from other cities: "Some occupations," Dr. Lombard wrote,

can only be carried on in a wet atmosphere, such as those of tanners, laundrymen and laundresses, watermen, weavers, water carriers and washerwomen. And of all these occupations there is not one which comes below the average, or, in other words, among those in which consumptives are comparatively rare. This invariable observation is the more remarkable in that in theory we should have expected to find precisely the reverse. Workers exposed to steam are very rarely consumptive in Geneva. M. Benoiston de Châteauneuf reached a contrary conclusion as regards Paris, but this was based only on the large number of laundresses who die of consumption in the Paris hospitals; there are very many contributing factors apart from humidity making Paris laundresses more liable than others to contract lung diseases.

This brought out very well the fact that, besides the strictly occupational conditions, there were others which, though connected with occupation, were equally closely connected with other living conditions and modes of life not wholly bound up with occupation. The biological inequality of the people of Paris was not merely the consequence of their occupations but also of their mode of living, as a study of the normal mortality suggests but does not specify in sufficient detail.

We have now to consider not normal mortality, but abnormal mortality, especially the cholera epidemic of 1832, which confirms and carries further the conclusions in the contemporary studies, supplements them with additional conclusions concerning living conditions and modes of life and for the first time reveals both occupation and mode of life as a weight in the scales of death.

II
Abnormal Mortality

We decided to begin this whole book with the experience of the cholera epidemic, wholly disregarding the chronological sequence, in order to make our ultimate target quite clear: the biological structures neglected by conventional history in its preoccupation with political, economic and social facts, but rediscovered in this catastrophe, exposed at its very feet, so to speak, like a canyon on whose sides the traces of subterranean upheavals are plain for all to read after the eruption has died down.

This understanding is indebted to the successive advances in statistical research, which, by observing the unequal distribution of deaths from cholera by districts, attempt to relate this to every kind of fact that could have had some effect. By eliminating those to which most importance had usually been attached—the topographical and geographical factors of exposure, lie of the land and humidity, besides the densities of population—the statistical approach manages to identify irrefutably the economic and social conditions of the population, a population which had never yet been described so accurately or in such detail by occupation and working conditions, levels of living, and especially by its manners and customs. The statistical report on the 1832 cholera epidemic not only described the biological bases of social inequality in both physical and moral detail, but delineated the contours and characteristics of those groups which, though belonging to the city, were relegated in every respect to its outskirts, differing from the rest in their death as in their life.

The Material Facts

The statistics of the cholera epidemic give us the actual numbers of people with which this study must be concerned and also one of the most useful breakdowns of the Paris population by occupation that we possess. We shall have to look more closely at this distribution. It is relevant not only for the categories established by the contemporary statisticians, but also for the specifics and corrections by which the death rate enables us finally to delineate the groups by manner of their death.

The population was broken down into four categories. First and second came the liberal professions and the commercial category, which need not detain us here. Third, the artisanal occupations, or, in other words, "all the trades carried on by using some tool," which necessitated apprenticeship and specialized skills. They constituted all the various crafts which made up the Paris *fabrique*, such as the tailors, modistes, sempstresses, florists, dressmakers and cabinetmakers, all the people who milled around in the lowest circle of Balzac's Hell in *La fille aux yeux d'or*: "The workman, the proletarian, the man who uses his feet, his hands, his tongue, his back, his arm alone, his five fingers in order to live; the very man who should be the first to hoard up the main source of his livelihood works beyond his strength and harnesses his wife to some tool." Masons were included in this category, for many reasons. This third category included, too, all those who received wages for services rendered. Cab drivers and domestic servants were placed in a separate subdivision.

But by far the largest number comprised those whose sole capital was their native strength, day laborers, water carriers, porters and all those employed in the markets, charcoal sellers, watermen and bargees. This category would include Bourgeat, the lowly water carrier in *La messe de l'athée*; and the freshwater pirates in *Les Mystères de Paris* and the Slasher, the docker on the quai Saint-Paul: "And what do you earn a day?" Rodolphe asked him. "Thirty-five sous. That will last as long as my arms do; when they fail, I shall take to a hook and wicker basket, like the old ragpicker I see in the mists of my childhood." In this lowest category we find at length the workers placed on the lowest rung of the social ladder, not merely by the nature of their work but also by the general disgust aroused by it, the ragpickers in particular.

The distribution of deaths from cholera among these groups, and the comparison with the normal mortality in them, led to the following conclusions, as expressed in the text of the report itself:

(1) The first category (liberal professions) seems to have been less affected by deaths from cholera than by the normal mortality. In accordance with the figure for deaths in 1831, it should have been 2,651 out of 14,592; but only 2,073 died; thus the deficit was 578, or 218 per thousand. In the first category, property owners and rentiers stand out; in 1832, they alone accounted for 67 per thousand deaths from cholera, whereas clerical and nonmanual workers accounted for only 32 per thousand and among the latter 36 per thousand normal deaths. Thus the higher social categories were less severely affected by the cholera than by the normal mortality. The greater difference favored the highest subdivision of this upper social category, that of property owners and rentiers. In reality, we lack one figure essential for the statistical interpretation of a difference which had such large social and political consequences, the figure for those who fled from Paris.

(2) The second category (commercial), on the other hand, was harder hit by the epidemic than by the normal mortality. For to go by the deaths in 1831, its cholera mortality in 1832 should have been only 1,422; but the figure was 1,816. The surplus was 394, or 207 per thousand. Closer examination of this category shows that this was due to the fact that the various occupations carried on indoors, thus imply-

ing a certain affluence, accounted for few deaths, whereas the reverse occurred in occupations involving selling goods either in damp and unhealthy places, or out of doors, or by displaying them on the public highway.

(3) The third category (mechanic occupations) seems to have had a less disastrous experience, since proportionately to the 4,328 deaths in 831, the number in 1832 should have been 7,066, but was only 6,523, the difference being 543, or 77 per thousand. But two subdivisions must be noted:

(a) Three occupations which had a far greater number proportionately of deaths from cholera than normal deaths were carried on out of doors:

	1832 Deaths from cholera		1831 Normal deaths	
	number	% of total in occupational category	number	% of total in occupational category
Laundrymen	533	3.7	227	2.5
Masons[39]	351	2.4	140	1.6
Mattress-pickers	80	.6	26	.3

(b) On the other hand, some occupations which suffered far less from the cholera mortality were carried on indoors:

	1832 Deaths from cholera		1831 Normal deaths	
	number	% of total in occupational category	number	% of total in occupational category
Jewelers	141	1.0	115	1.3
Cabinetmakers	111	.8	109	1.2
Carpenters	291	2.0	206	2.3
Cobblers	459	3.2	344	3.8
Dressmakers	665	4.6	491	5.5
Florists	21	.1	24	.3
Sempstresses	99	.7	149	1.5
Modistes	10	.1	44	.5
Tailors	305	2.1	278	3.1

(4) Lastly, the effect of the cholera epidemic on the fourth category (wageearners) seems to have been more severe than the normal mortality. The number of deaths in this category in 1831 should have produced a death rate of only 3,451 in 1832; it was in fact 4,180. The surplus was 729, or 211 per thousand of deaths in 1831. The occupations in which the rate was highest were:

	1832 Deaths from cholera		1831 Normal deaths	
	number	% of total in occupational category	number	% of total in occupational category
Sweepers	37	.3	10	.1
Watermen	28	.2	9	.1
Charcoal sellers	74	.5	31	.3
Scavengers	62	.4	9	.1
Porters	194	1.3	90	1.0
Cooks	295	2.0	153	1.7
Market laborers	48	.3	4	.04
Children's helps	29	.2	6	.06
Sick-nurses	77	.5	35	.4
Male nurses	38	.3	14	.2
Day laborers	1,171	8.0	588	6.6
Water carriers	89	.6	49	.5
Concierges	496	3.4	231	2.6
Knife grinders	9	.06	1	.01
Navvies	54	.4	20	.2

The Moral Facts

While this inequality in the cholera mortality denoted a physical inequality, it also pointed to moral facts. It is noteworthy that the statisticians of 1832 paid a great deal of attention to studying the relationships between the cholera mortality and what they called "the emotions of the soul" or "the passions," to use the terms of the eighteenth-century demographers, Moheau in particular. It is true that a study of this sort was doomed to failure, given the state of statistics at that period and for a long time thereafter. We may think that the demographers of the first half of the nineteenth century went little further than the author of *Recherches et considérations*. But have we ourselves done better?

Nevertheless, where this preliminary statistical research is restricted to a few specific facts, it does indubitably throw light on some aspects of working-class life about which we know nothing specific, despite an abundant literature. For one thing, it stresses the effects of the working-class excesses on Sundays and Mondays upon cholera morbidity and mortality. "It is well known," the statistician observed,

that on these two days and even thereafter there is a deplorable custom of transforming a necessary period of rest into a blameworthy idleness, and that the worker, improvident as he is and unheeding of the fact that he will pay for his prodigality of one day by utter destitution on the next, squanders a week's wages in a couple of days and acknowledges no end to his lavish spending but the complete exhaustion of the money to pay for it.

An analysis of the number of cholera patients admitted daily to the hospitals throughout the epidemic provides an indirect means of measuring the possible effect of intemperance on the patients admitted. The influence of the excesses of Sunday and the beginning of the week upon working-class patients admitted to the hospitals was indicated by the rise in admissions on Mondays, Wednesdays and Thursdays, the fall in Tuesday admissions apparently being due to the large rise on Mondays. The contemporary statisticians and moralists tried to descry some other more recondite and less accessible facts by means of this unusual statistical documentation. The statistician of 1832 was alluding to one of the most complex themes of the old program of qualitative demography when he wrote:

The lively emotions of the soul have been held to be liable to aggravate the state of sick persons in many cases; thus, overwork, outbursts of anger, unexpected afflictions, all the moral ailments, and above all fear have been mentioned as some of the causes of the cholera. The Board most certainly believes in the powerful and rapid action of the passions of the soul upon our organs and in the disturbances and disorders of all kinds that this may cause; it by no means disregards the close alliance between the physical and the moral which has been proclaimed down the ages without ever being contested.

On the other hand, we are bound to remark that the 1832 statistician's effort to ascertain the influence of political passions on cholera mortality was doomed to failure from the start. It will be recalled that the events of June 1832 occurred between the first and second periods of severe cholera mortality precisely in the quartier Sainte-Avoye and the streets adjoining Saint-Merri in which the cholera mortality in March and April 1832 had been one of the highest in Paris. "If there is one thing calculated to spread terror among a large population in the highest degree," the statistician remarked, "it is a hard-fought struggle waged in their very midst; guns firing in the streets; bullets, cannon balls, shot and grapeshot plowing through them in every direction; the sight of the dead, the dying and the wounded; the fear of arson, looting and violence; and all these horrors combined." As a matter of fact, though the Board traced the progress of the cholera in the very places which were the scene of the events of June 5 and 6, it found no increase whatever in the disease at that time or in deaths in houses in the rue Saint-Merri and the cloître Saint-Merri. As might have been expected. The 1832 statistical document is certainly important, but its importance does not lie nearly so much in this investigation into the influence of political facts upon the cholera mortality as in the obvious relationships shown up between cholera mortality and political violence. The mortality was most fearful in these old streets, alleys and courts, some of which —the passage de la Réunion, the rue du Maure and the impasse Beaubourg—still exist, enabling us to reconstruct the older Paris as it must have been.[40] But it was in these streets too that the most desperate combats were fought. It is very hard to refrain from assuming a relationship between the violence of the mortality and the violence of the struggle. The statistics alone would have been enough to suggest it, even if contemporaries had not provided us with their testimony.[41]

But here we approach quite a different subject. Death summed up life, and the inequality before death the inequality of everything else. It emphasized reality. Over and above the fact of inequality, however, mortality begins to throw some light on the behavior determined by such inequality, which arose from this biological inequality but also had its own biological characteristics imprinted upon it, practicing violence against a situation that was itself one of violence.

Conclusion: An Estimate

An account of the attitudes of various social groups towards this inequality is of no great value, however, unless we first estimate their size. This estimate does not relate only to a study of the laboring classes, for, though the size of the groups which may be called bourgeois cannot be accurately measured simply by deducting the number of the poor from the total population, we can at least derive from it a specific notion of the size of that part of the population whose mobility was not downwards and whose course of life might move upwards—or at any rate had some chance of doing so.

I
Two Contradictory Estimates

The social reformers rightly criticized the official statistics for poverty assembled in the *Renseignements statistiques sur la population indigente de Paris, d'après les recensements opérés depuis l'an X*. These statistics dealt with only a small fraction of the indigent. The welfare offices gave periodic relief to registered indigents and temporary relief in sickness to those who applied for it "and whose situation is truly interesting." The qualifications for admission to the list of indigents were restrictive in the extreme.[42] These enumerations reflected the Administration's attitude and the way in which it varied from time to time far more than the way in which poverty rose and fell. As Buret said,

facts like poverty are not subject to such abrupt changes as those we note in the official figures. Unless some great public disaster, such as the cholera epidemic, occurs, poverty on one day is much what it was the day before; the changes one way or the other operate imperceptibly. So that when we observe any fairly abrupt change from one year to another, we shall generally have simply to conclude that the administrative rules have been changed, nothing more.

We can quite see why another estimate was preferred to these incomplete statistics, one which gave a more accurate notion of the total poverty: the statistics of mortality in the hospitals. "Complaints are made that admission to hospital is granted too easily," wrote Buret, "but our conviction is that the mere fact of applying for admission to hospital provides a sufficient presumption of poverty."[43]

The People and the Hospital

This presumption was very likely to be correct, inasmuch as the people feared the hospital and were very reluctant to resign themselves to entering it. "The popular classes' obstinacy in this respect is such," Balzac wrote in *Le cousin Pons*,

that sick people's repugnance to going to hospital comes from the fact that they believe they kill people there by giving them nothing to eat. So many deaths occurred from the victuals which wives took to their husbands in secret that the doctors established an extremely strict body search on the days when relatives visited the patients.

"Oh to be sure of not dying in hospital . . . above all, not to die there!" Fleur-de-Marie cried out in *Les Mystères de Paris*. "Alas for us poor people! . . . It is not poverty that is so distressing. . . . But afterwards, when you are dead. Don't you know what they do to you afterwards, Monsieur Rodolphe? There's a girl I knew in prison. . . . She died in hospital. . . . They handed her body over to the surgeons." Nadaud told how his father refused to let him be taken to hospital after a fall from a scaffolding: "He shall not go if I have to spend my last penny to prevent it." Every administrative report on the management of the hospitals stressed this fear.[44]

It is true that other evidence contradicts this. "There is more than one master of the art of healing," Horace Say wrote in *L'Administration de la Ville de Paris* in 1846,

who, being unable to accept responsibility for those who apply to him, advises the sick to go to hospital . . . where they will receive free of charge the same advice as that for which he charges high fees in his own consulting room. People thus get into the habit of considering the hospital as the place where it is natural to go for treatment and the almshouse as the home to which they will retire when they are no longer able to earn the wages they now spend heedlessly, without thought of the future. There is nothing more distressing to a friend of the industrious classes than the cynicism with which some improvident workman believes that he has had the last word in reply to the best advice one ventures to give him by repeating, like many many others, that the hospitals were not made for dogs, meaning that he will be entitled to go there one day and that he will be able to demand proper treatment as of right when he falls sick or destitute.

An article on the aged in Paris published in the *Annales d'Hygiène* in 1832[45] took much the same line:

The working-class population in Paris has been accustomed from time immemorial to regard the Bicêtre, Salpêtrière and Incurables homes as its own domain. It is a retirement to which they are entitled in their old age and they take full advantage of it. So long as these institutions exist, they have no anxiety about the future and see no necessity for thrift.

It was a bourgeois theme,[46] which contradicted much lower-class evidence and was easily refuted by Buret:

The charity of the homes and hospitals, however fine it may appear, is not so enticing that it attracts any great number of persons who could do without it. I know that in the very large towns, Paris especially, they are not so bitterly disliked. People easily grow seasoned to dangers that they foresee and have already experienced; the soul very quickly grows hardened against the feeling of a shame that is inevitable. The intelligent poor do not long harbor prejudices which wound their self-respect, and this is why the sentiment which keeps all those who are able to do without it away from charity, so pronounced elsewhere, is not so strong in Paris. But is not this lack of strong feeling on the part of the poor, this readiness to leave home and family at the onset of sickness, in itself proof of great poverty?

Hospital Statistics and Estimating Poverty

Thus it was from the statistics of deaths in hospital that Buret derived an estimate of poverty in 1836, by means of a procedure which we shall apply to the period as a whole:

We cannot agree with the Prefect of the Seine that the average ratio of the indigent to the population of Paris is only 1 in 12.32 when we see that of 24,057 deaths, the official figure for the death rate in Paris in 1836, 9,034 deaths (1 in less than 3) occurred in hospital. These 9,000 deaths in hospital correspond to over one-third of the Paris population. The average ratio of mortality to population is 1 in 36; the figure obtained by multiplying the deaths in hospital by the figure for this ratio would be a number corresponding to almost one-half of the inhabitants of Paris; but this would be too high. The population on the hospitals' registers of deaths die faster than the rest of the inhabitants; in the poorest districts death carries off 1 human being in 22 each year. Pursuant to this well-known law, we shall take the figure 26 to express the ratio of the mortality of the poor, and if we multiply total deaths by this ratio, which is almost one-third lower than the average, we obtain the figure of 237,484 inhabitants of Paris who supply the hospitals with their quota of corpses. This calculation seems to us more likely to give the real number of indigents than a calculation based upon indoor assistance. It is true that by this method of estimation the ratio of indigent persons comes to as much as 1 in 4.20 instead of only 1 in 12.32.

If we apply Buret's method to the period as a whole, we obtain a figure appreciably higher than the figure in the statistics for the indigent, 238,000 in a population of 900,000 in 1836. But in the last years of the Restoration it was nearly 350,000 in a population of 750,000; and in 1830 and 1831, that is, before the cholera mortality, 420,000 in a population which was 755,000 in 1831. Though the figures fell from 1840 to 1846 to one-quarter of the population, they rose again to one-third after 1846. A monstrous and permanent poverty, in brief, becoming intolerable at the peak of crises and bringing hunger, sickness and death to nearly one-half of the Paris population, or, in other words, almost the entire working-class population. But it was rampant in normal periods too, and never fell much below one-quarter of the total population, or, in other words, still affected a large proportion of the working class.

II

Two Complementary Estimates

Were the estimates contradictory? No; they were complementary. Each of them related to one and the same population of the poor, but described it at different depths and in forms which were given unequal emphasis. The hospital death rate measured the normal totals of the poor, irrespective of crisis or prosperity. The statistics of the indigent measured only the marginal totals of these poor, but their characteristics coincided with those of the general population of the poor and rendered them more specific.

The two sets of statistics related to a single population of the poor and to the same people, despite their very different totals. The aggregate and permanent number of the poor was given by the hospital death rate, a mass which never fell below one-quarter of the population of Paris and rose to one-half in times of crisis, or, in other words, included nearly the whole working-class population. These statistics project a vast structural poverty, a fundamental poverty, onto the background of the history of Paris, like a funereal curtain before which the drama was played out and on which the statistics of the indigent spotlighted some groups which were not exceptional but were significant of all the rest.

It was, indeed, the ultimate limit of the general poverty that was defined in the official statistics, a poverty which was one and the same poverty, but here reached its extreme point of suffering and resistance, a physiological limit beyond which there was nothing but death. "If one judged the extent of indigence in 1836 by the amount of indoor relief," Buret wrote,

one would be almost entitled to doubt its existence, since a grant of a bare 22 francs 35 centimes per registered indigent person suffices for his official relief. Does a sum of 22 francs 35 centimes represent an amount of privation large enough to arouse public charity? If these 62,329 persons are really so poverty-stricken that it is a public duty to assist them, must it not be that before they are placed on the list they are in a habitual state of distress which in itself deserves the name of destitution, in the frightful condition in which one more privation, however slight, exceeds the ordinary bounds of human endurance and of moral endurance too?

We are bound to think, surely, that the two sets of statistics relate to the same poverty-stricken groups, but at different depths of affliction, when we find that the figures for the number of indigent persons in receipt of relief and the number of deaths at home were distributed in precisely the same arrondissements,[47] and especially that the statistics of indigent persons developed in parallel with the statistics derived from the mortality in the hospitals. The fact that the relevant numbers are infinitely lower is beside the point, for the curve is identical and the peaks occur in precisely the same years. The tightening up of the administrative rules is quite irrelevant; and though, as the social reformers demonstrated, the reduction in the numbers of indigent persons in receipt of relief was due to a tightening up of the regulations rather than to a real reduction in the numbers of the poor, poverty set in with such violence in some years that the figures rose very abruptly.[48] Moreover, in these years the statistics of indigent persons again coincided with the estimates to be derived from the statistics of the mortality in the hospitals; that is, not the statistics of the indigent persons habitually in receipt of relief, but of those who had to be relieved because, though they were not on the lists of the indigent, they were in fact driven to the physiological limits established in the official statistics as permanent. "The number of persons in receipt of relief," the *Journal des Débats* wrote on November 2, 1830, "began at 100,129 and, increasing from month to month, had risen by July to 227,399. It was the time of the harvest. From that date no new applicant for the distribution of tickets was accepted." In 1830 those protected from utter destitution by a miserably small pittance in relief amounted to 227,399.

Admittedly, this figure is lower than the figure of 420,000 out of a population of 755,000 derived from the mortality in the hospitals. We can see, however, that it does not conflict with it if we keep in mind the fact that many of the workers refused to apply for a bread ticket, "since most of them regard the formalities they have to go through as humiliating,"[49] and if we note, too, that it measured the marginal totals of the poor, the crowd of those for whom a hunk of bread was a matter of life or death, not merely the old, the infirm and the sick, but also the workers burdened with a family, as well as the young and the single, and even the masons from the Creuse, whom Nadaud depicted in the lodging houses of the Cité district fighting each other for crusts to dip in the soup.

The population of the poor that was measured by the two sets of statistics was the same. We should by no means ignore the official statistics of indigent persons, but should rather regard them as contributing specific elements to the description of poverty which cannot be gained from the statistics of mortality in the hospitals. The estimate from the mortality in the hospitals gives the total. The statistics of the indigent supply the detail: the distribution by sex, which reveals that women were even more poverty-stricken than men; the distribution by occupation, which coincides with that for the cholera epidemic;[50] the distribution by provincial origin, which emphasizes the preponderance of immigrants;[51] and the distribution by district, which places the districts with the largest working-class population—the faubourg Saint-Jacques, the faubourg Saint-Marcel, the faubourg Saint-Antoine, the quartier de l'Hôtel-de-Ville and the quartier de la Cité—at the head of the list, irrespective of the period or the origin of the statistics, and within these districts, places the population born outside Paris ahead of the native population.[52]

These were the component elements of this people of poverty. A poverty that recovers its true characteristics from demographic research, which restores to it the biological bases neglected by history despite their prominence in the contemporary testimony. "The poverty which is crushing a large proportion of the population of our arrondissement goes very deep," Leuret wrote in his report to the Welfare Office of the XIIth arrondissement in 1836. "For many of the poor it is one of the misfortunes due to their birth, to illnesses untreated for lack of resources, to the excessive burden of family, to unemployment and to inadequate wages." This observation clearly identified and brought to the fore the biological determinants we have already discussed, which placed under a curse a section of the population we now know to have contained at all times, even in the most prosperous periods, nearly one-third of the total population of Paris.

PART II
Opinion

CHAPTER ONE

Bourgeois Opinion

The fact is important, but so is what contemporaries thought of it and the conclusions they drew, especially the conclusion that this population was doomed by its increase, its fertility, even by its very existence to certain ruin, on the extreme edge of the city, differing from the inhabitants of the city and dangerous to it.

It should be noted that Buret, the author who presented the best estimate of the size of this ill-fated and dangerous population, also presented the best evidence for, and the best interpretation of, this fact of opinion, in a passage which has never been properly appreciated. In it he likened the condition of the Paris proletarian to that of the savage, summing up in that word (which will keynote the whole of the rest of this survey, just as it keynoted the whole history of the period) the fact he had already measured, opinion on that fact and the behavior dictated by both fact and opinion. The workers were savages by reason of their precarious existence: "the first point of likeness between the poor man and the savage. The life of the industrial proletarian and the savage alike is at the mercy of the hazards of life, the whims of chance; one day good hunting or wages, the next day no game or unemployment; plenty one day, famine the next." They were alike, too, in their perpetual roving, which started with the waifs and strays and later characterized "the floating population of great cities, that human mass which industry summons to attend on it but cannot keep in continuous employment and constantly holds in reserve at its good pleasure. It is from the ranks of this population, which is far larger than is supposed, that the paupers are recruited, the enemies who threaten our civilization." This working-class and truly primitive population displayed every feature of the savage condition.

If you venture into those accursed districts in which they live, wherever you go you will see men and women branded with the marks of vice and destitution, and half-naked children rotting in filth and stifling in airless, lightless dens. Here, in the very home of civilization, you will encounter thousands of men reduced by sheer besottedness to a life of savagery; here you will perceive destitution in a guise so horrible that it will fill you with disgust rather than pity and you will be tempted to regard it as the condign punishment for a crime.

This horrid spectacle was to be seen in all great cities, but more especially in Paris.

If you make your way into the old districts now relegated far from the center, into the Cité, into the narrow crowded streets of the IXth, VIIIth and XIIth arrondissements, wherever you go you will encounter the image of poverty, even of utter destitution. Indigence in the great cities has a far more disturbing mien than poverty in the country; it inspires disgust and horror, for it assails all the senses at once.

Particularly drunkenness:

Savages alone take to drink with the fervor displayed by the most degraded part of the poor classes, like the Negro on the African coast, who sells his children and himself for a bottle of spirits. Drunkenness did more to exterminate the natives of North America than famine and systematic massacres by the whites. To the savage, intoxication is supreme felicity; to the destitute of the great cities it is an invincible passion, an indulgence which they cannot do without and purchase regardless of its price at the expense of health and life itself. A gloomy comparison indeed! What a depressing picture this is, these people who are our compatriots and brothers deliberately plunging into the most bestial inebriety, of malice aforethought, inoculating themselves with the ferocity of wild beasts by means of alcohol and indulging in ignoble orgies, with their accompaniment of brawls and blood!

The workers' condition and mode of life were described by analogy to the condition of savages, but the various aspects of working-class revolt and the class struggle were couched in terms of race:

The workers are as lacking in a sense of duty to their masters as their masters to them; they regard them as men of a different class, quite unlike, and even hostile to, them. Isolated from the nation, outlawed from the social and political community, alone with their needs and miseries, they struggle to extricate themselves from this terrifying solitude and, like the barbarians to whom they have been compared, they are perhaps meditating invasion.

The use of the terms "barbarians" and "savages" identifies and sums up the main aspects of the workers' condition and the workers' behavior remarkably well; this condition and behavior are reduced to biological traits and physical characteristics. The whole substance of the ensuing chapters in this book is condensed in the foregoing passage: the emphasis upon differences which were believed to be racial, and the behavior—and in particular the violence—justified and accounted for by that belief. Buret's account, however, is so logical and lucid that the comparison of proletarian to savage has been regarded as an academic exercise, and it has in general attracted too little attention. It may well be an academic exercise, but it was based on beliefs which, as is evident from other contemporary documentation, were certainly held as a fact both by the bourgeois classes and by the lower classes themselves.

So far as the Paris bourgeois were concerned, the laboring classes were and remained on the edge of the city in precisely the same way as those population groups which were confused with the criminal groups at earlier periods.

I

Confusion About the Recruitment of the Dangerous Classes and the Laboring Classes

The same sort of people came to swell the ranks of both the dangerous and the laboring classes—such, at any rate, was the general opinion and thus it was expressed in print. At this point the facts and the increase in the Paris population as a whole and in its occupational categories are irrelevant. Here we are dealing exclusively with the opinion, very plainly expressed in an abundance of documents, which are at one in their assessment and in the terms they used to describe it. When the great influx of immigrants we have already measured began during the second half of the Restoration, the newcomers were universally described in terms of what we should nowadays call racial or ethnic differentiation, the very same terms which, as we have already seen, were used in earlier periods to designate groups alien to the city, differing from it and dangerous to it. The immigrants, alien as they were to the manners, customs, morality and laws of the community, were more than ever "*misérables*," wretches, barbarians, savages, nomads. That is how they appeared in the picturesque literature and the press under the Restoration and increasingly so as events moved towards the final crisis, in Luchet's book,[1] for example. They were thus described in the great volume of literary, official and newspaper records during the 1830 Revolution and the ominous early years of the July Monarchy. The "invasion of the new barbarians" supplied the theme of a sensational article in the *Journal des Débats*.[2] This distinction between the old-established Parisians and the rest was the keynote at the sitting of the Chamber on August 26, 1830, called to discuss a bill to authorize the Minister of the Interior to spend 5 million on public works in Paris.[3] They were thus described throughout the July régime and particularly during the crises when social antagonisms were intensified. Especially so in the great upheaval of 1848. Referring to "the difficult social situation" in Paris during the closing years of the July régime, Daniel Stern wrote that

it was produced by the excessive growth of a large section of the popular classes which had come to form a separate class, as it were, a nation within the nation, by a concatenation of circumstances which was to some extent inevitable. People are beginning to use a new term for them, the industrial proletariat.[4]

This well sums up the most general view of the causes of the crisis. In his *Souvenirs*, Tocqueville registered a protest against "the industrial revolution which has for the past thirty years made Paris the leading manufacturing city in France; it first attracted within its walls an entire new population of workers and then the work on the fortifications drew in a further population of farmers, who are now out of work." He blamed "the greed for material enjoyment which, stimulated by the Government itself, increasingly inflamed this multitude, the democratic disease of envy which surreptitiously leavened it." Both opponents and proponents of the 1848 Revolution agreed in making these precariously established new arrivals mainly responsible for the difficulties and disturbances.[5]

Nomads and Proletarians

The evolution in the content of the terms is a striking reflection of the evolution of the ideas underlying them. "A nation within the nation," for whom people were beginning to use a new term: "the industrial proletariat," as Daniel Stern had written.

The industrial proletariat; the term was certainly new and was to become the one more and more commonly used to designate the working class both in Paris and elsewhere. It henceforth connoted strictly economic and occupational characteristics; social characteristics became no more than a secondary aspect of the economic one. The term was stripped of all ethnic associations and no longer bore any traces of the former biological differentiation save those reflecting and recording economic differences. It was simple and straightforward, neither equivocal nor blurred, as incontrovertible and imperative as the statistics themselves which measured the social groups to which it applied; imposed by the facts, acknowledged and virtually authenticated by the people, above all by the workers—some of whom entered themselves on the electoral rolls of the Second Empire as "proletarians"—who wished to be proletarians, and to be known as proletarians. A term with a future—stern and inexorable.

What is really remarkable, however, is how dilatory the guardians and watchdogs of the French language were in accepting the word in its full and final sense, the guardians of that language, which, according to the author of the Preface to the sixth edition of the Dictionary of the Academy (1835), is "the apparent and visible form of a people's spiritual essence." "Proletarian" was included in that edition only as a noun and was defined as follows: "Word used in Ancient Rome for those composing the sixth and lowest class of the people who, being very poor and exempt from taxation, were only of use to the Republic for the offspring they produced. By extension, in modern states, those without capital or sufficiently lucrative occupation." "Proletariat" first appeared in the 1862 edition and was defined as "The class of proletarians. Condition of proletariat. The modern proletariat." In 1869 Littré first referred to the Roman proletariat[6] and then went on: "In modern authors, members of the most indigent class," giving as examples a quotation from the *Contrat social*, which applied only to the urban proletariat,[7] and an opinion of the Conseil d'Etat of 1806 relating to estovers, which therefore quite definitely meant the rural proletariat in contradistinction to the class of large landowners. As late as 1892 the terms "proletarian" and "proletariat" were not mentioned in Léon Say's *Nouveau dictionnaire*, not even in the long article on socialism nor, amazingly, in the summary of Marx's writings. Right at the end of the nineteenth century, when hundreds of documents of every sort showed that if there was one thing about which the entire urban working class was perfectly clear it was the notion of proletariat, the Academy of Moral Sciences, of which Léon Say was the very embodiment, had still got no further than "pauperism." This it presented as the perfect expression of the economic and social development of the second half of the nineteenth century and the quintessence of economic thinking,[8] an academic term—as construed by the academic at any rate—with a larger content of erudition than fact, hardly to be distinguished from the old terms "poverty," "indigence" and "destitution," and colored even further with all the associations of the far more ancient mendicity.

In the first half of the nineteenth century the associations of the term "proletariat," as envisaged not in the dictionaries—in which it had not yet appeared—but in the contemporary literary and social documents and in the facts, still of course conjured up characteristics which were not yet economic. It had not yet been purged of the ethnic and physical antagonisms we are discussing, and it still had to compete with other terms and images more expressive of the biological characteristics of social antagonisms. It is used in this latter way in Balzac, where the proletariat is a race rather than a class and the word connotes a savage and barbarous way of living and dying rather than an occupational distribution or economic characteristic. This is also true of Frégier; classifying the ragpicker in the dangerous classes, he wrote—but with some hesitation and confusion, which should be carefully noted:

When the proletarian—for we are wholly justified in using this term in speaking of the ragpicker and the nomad—when the proletarian, I repeat, aspires to quaff the cup of pleasure reserved for the wealthy and well-to-do class instead of mitigating his poverty by sobriety and thrift, when he seeks not merely to moisten his lips at this cup but to slake his thirst from it to the point of intoxication in an access of foolish pride, his degradation is the deeper for his desire to rise above himself.[9]

Other terms still predominated, for instance those used by Lecouturier in 1848: "There is no such thing as a Parisian society, there are no such persons as Parisians. Paris is nothing but a nomads' camp";[10] or Jules Breynat in *Les socialistes modernes* (1849): "The victim of these barbarians was to be the bourgeoisie, or rather those who had earned their affluence by dint of order and work. . . . Intoxicated with disorder and carnage, this populace disowned by the people laid siege to power." But even more significant are the terms used in final judgment and as final insult by people like Thiers and Haussmann. "There are a large number of vagabonds who earn high wages," Thiers said in his speech on May 24, 1850,

and others who earn enough by unlawful means to have a domicile, but refuse to do so. These are the men who form not the bottom, but the dangerous part, of great congested masses; these are the men who deserve the name, one of the worst stigmatized in history, mark you, of mob. The vile mob which brought every Republic down in ruin. It is the mob, not the people, that we wish to exclude; it is this heterogeneous mob, this mob of vagabonds with no avowed family and no known domicile, a mob of persons so mobile that they can nowhere be pinned down and have not succeeded in establishing any regular home for their family. This is the mob which the law proposes to expel.

Haussmann, too, designated this mob, these vagabonds, nomads, in a speech for which he incurred a good deal of unpopularity. It is noteworthy that Haussmann was the last to employ the term "nomad" under the Second Empire in a speech which part of the Paris working-class population resented as an insult, for the nomads had finally settled into Paris and henceforth merged with the authentically Parisian population. "I have said it and repeated it time and again," Haussmann wrote in his *Mémoires*,

Paris belongs to France, not to the Parisians by birth or choice who live there and especially not to the mobile population in its lodging houses, which distorts the meaning of the polls by the pressure of unintelligent votes; this "mob of nomads," to use an expression for which I have been reproached, but which I maintain is correct, the best of whom move to the great city in search of fairly regular work, but with the intention of returning in due course to their place of origin where their true ties persist.

To which Cochin retorted in an article in *Revue des Deux Mondes* in 1871:

Haussmann held the view that there were no such persons as Parisians; the city was a mere hostelry for wealthy and worker alike. . . . The Siege has given M. Haussmann his reply. The foreigners, the notables, the bureaucrats, the pleasure seekers, the nomads have left. The real inhabitants of Paris have stayed on by themselves. They were isolated, separated, driven from district to district, deprived of all rights for twenty years. But municipal life had not dried up and it has emerged from our ordeal like wine from the press.

It might be said that the terms "barbarians" and "nomads" were merely images or metaphors, not current words in everyday speech. Metaphors they may well have been in these speeches, but they were so frequent that they merit attention even here and have a significance in their own right. In attempting to detect, however, what part the population described as "nomadic" or "nonestablished" played in the growth of Paris one cannot but see something more than metaphor in these terms, since they are also to be found in the news items and even in the statistics.

Most of the characteristics of the bourgeois population's attitude to the laboring classes were thus borrowed from an older attitude to a population which had been regarded as not belonging to the city, as suspect of all the crimes, all the evils, all the epidemics and all the violence, not merely because of its own characteristics, but on account of its origins outside the city and of the immigration which had incontinently been put down to a proliferation of the beggars of old. We may well cite in evidence the astonishing report by a Prefect of the Seine quoted by Morogues,[11] in which the growth of manufacturing in Paris was described as having peopled the city, not with workmen, as one might have thought, much to the employers' advantage, but with beggars engaged in sponging on the bourgeoisie.

II
Laboring Classes and Dangerous Classes with Similar Characteristics

It is very hard to distinguish the laboring and the dangerous classes from each other because it is so difficult to discern the frontiers between the groups gathered within these categories, and also because of the existence of intermediate groups all along these uncertain frontiers; it is very difficult to tell whether these have more in common with one or the other. How can we distinguish them when both seem to depend so closely on economic, political and biological circumstances which blend them and shift them from one category to the other, depending on year and season, on revolutions, crises and epidemics?

Indeed, how could contemporary opinion, badly informed and sensitive to appearances, colors, smells and acts of violence as it was, find its way when even someone like Frégier, an expert on the subject and one so scrupulous in drawing distinctions, measuring and comprehending, failed to do so? He resigned himself to charting a common condition and fate, and to determining only approximately a social entity embracing a broad section of the working-class population, within which existed close contacts and many interchanges between the laboring and the dangerous classes and an intense mobility in both directions. For there were social groups between the laboring classes and the dangerous classes, or rather along a wavering and variable frontier, which brought them together far more than it separated them, and it was hard to assign these to one class or the other. They certainly were part of the laboring classes, but their jobs were degrading, or were regarded as such. Most of the contemporary criminal descriptions had no hesitation in taking them as their commonest illustrations of the criminal classes.

The Ragpickers

The ragpickers are one example. The literature had not yet transformed them into great social liquidators, supreme righters of wrongs.

On the contrary, they still seemed to embody most of the characteristics which bourgeois opinion attributed indiscriminately to workers and criminals. Savages, barbarians, nomads, they were called, and they were summed up and judged as such. By Le Play, for instance:

At the beginning of their career they have, all unwittingly, the charm, irresistible until it wears off, of the young of races tolerably close to the savage state, who subsist mainly by hunting, fishing and fruit gathering. Obeying the instincts of savage life, they have a pronounced repugnance to the effort required to raise themselves to the wellbeing concomitant with a settled life. They do not willingly obey any master.[12]

And Frégier, describing the quartier Saint-Jacques and the quartier Saint-Marceau, and in particular the rue de l'Oursine and the neighboring streets:

A fair number of the ragpickers who live in the lodging houses sleep in the fields during the fine weather to save money. A ragpicker's daily earnings amount to from 15 to 20 sous and his children's to about 10 sous. Some of these children abandon their parents' home at a very early age and set to scavenging in order to live. Their way of life is wholly nomadic and almost savage. They are remarkable for their boldness and the asperity of their manners.[13]

Characteristic of the savage way of life was their lack of identity and civil status and their indifference to it, for which much evidence is to be found in the literature and in the newspaper reports.[14] They retained the hideous characteristics of savage life, of which Frégier, like most of the contemporary official reports, gives many examples. Frégier wrote:

Of all the poor classes the ragpickers are those who live in the foulest and most disgusting places. . . . The better off occupy one or two small rooms which they rent for themselves and their family. The others possess a straw mattress which serves them as a bed in the common room, but this possession is more often collective than personal and, though shared, it is still coveted by the poor wretches who sleep in a species of trough on rags or a few handfuls of the straw scattered on the stone floor. The police responsible for the supervision of lodging houses or furnished rooms set aside for the ragpickers paint an incredible picture of them. Each lodger keeps his basket beside him, sometimes full of filth, and what filth! These savages do not shrink from including dead animals in their harvest and spending the night beside their stinking haul.

River Dockers and "Freebooters"

Similarly, did the workers on the Seine, the river dockers and "freebooters" whom Eugène Sue most significantly took as some of the chief characters in the *Mystères de Paris* belong, or rather were they considered as belonging, to the laboring or to the dangerous classes? Like the Slasher, docker on the quai Saint-Paul, a criminal in the first book, an honest man in the last; or the Martial family, freshwater pirates, established not far from the Asnières Bridge at the point of a small island known as Freebooters' Island, whom Sue endowed with savage characteristics identical with those which Parent-Duchatelet recognized and measured at the same period and in the same terms in an important statistical report Sue very probably used. They were themselves close to the ragpickers and, with the onset of age and bad luck, very often became ragpickers in their turn.

Other Occupational Categories

Some categories of the working class which contemporaries would not have hesitated to classify as such also have certain criminal characteristics, such as the white-lead workers at the factory at Clichy-la-Garenne. They were loathed and shunned because they bore within them misfortune, death and crime, though it is hard to tell which of these was the reason for the horror they inspired. This blending of death with crime was mentioned by Vidocq:

During the twenty years and more that I spent as head of the criminal police, I employed released convicts and often even escaped convicts almost exclusively. I gave preference to those who had acquired a certain notoriety from their criminal record. When I left the police and the Government refused to keep them in its employ, several of them went to work at the white-lead factory; they died martyrs to the horror they had conceived of crime. The local people draw back and move off at the approach of a worker from this factory; no one would take a pinch from their snuffbox and no one would allow them to take a pinch from his. They are plague carriers and everybody shuns their contagion. There are many pothouses where they are not admitted. . . . The cry of "Lead!" is raised when they approach.[15]

Crime and death are blended, too, in a letter from two Clichy workers published in *La Ruche populaire*.[16]

Men who are utterly without resources, without work, struggling for bare necessities so as not to cast a stain on their families by turning to theft, are compelled to go to Clichy-la-Garenne as a last resort. . . . There are 60 of us in this slaughterhouse. . . . Men whose constitution is too feeble for other work and old men thrown out of the workshops or turned away from the work on the fortifications are reduced to this white-lead factory, where they are looked upon as if they were workers spewed up by the jails.

Whole sections of the laboring classes gradually came to be stigmatized in this way. "The great manufacturing industry," Le Play wrote, "draws into the midst of the older and relatively sound population the needy and the failures from all over Europe. . . . Some of these aliens live like nomads; they are reduced to the degraded condition of a gang of navvies."

An even greater difficulty in drawing a distinction between the laboring and the dangerous classes is that some of these intermediate groups, or those regarded as such, did not work and live in distant workshops or building sites in the banlieue, but in the center of the city, cluttering the streets and squares with their trade, their rags and their noise. They thus forced everyone in Paris personally and concretely to be daily aware of the existence of a nomadic way of life in the very heart of the city; like the petty industries, met with as frequently in the picturesque literature and caricatures as at every crossroad, and for the same reasons—reasons not of picturesque tradition, but of fact.

III
Laboring Classes and Dangerous Classes Governed by Similar Imperatives

And how, finally, could opinion distinguish between the laboring classes and the dangerous classes, mingling as they did in their social contacts, both of them merged together in the Paris setting, when they both seemed to be governed at the same points of time and in the same violent, unlawful and, in a word, savage way by the same economic, political and biological imperatives? Crises, riots and epidemics suddenly filled the ranks of the dangerous masses with new recruits, or rather mustered criminals and workmen, people and populace into a single mob bent on the same sort of acts of public or private violence.

The facts are not so relevant here as the belief that destitution, sickness and riot, which contemporaries were prone to put down to the same causes and to view in the same light, gave rise to acts of violence that were regarded as outgrowths of crime and were invariably attributed to the criminal classes.

Doin and Charton referred to this combination of biological, economic, political and criminal themes in their *Lettres sur Paris* in January 1830: "The laborer's indigence will never be as terrifying, as desperate as that of the miserable families living on this side of the Bièvre, sick and shuddering at the very thought of the hospitals, prisons and the Morgue." And Luchet describing the faubourg Saint-Antoine in 1830 in his *Esquisses dédiées au peuple parisien*:

The people were illiterate in 1789. . . . Today they can write. So the workers' fury is expressed in censure and anathema nowadays, whereas in those days it would have led to fire and slaughter. The sufferings of most of them are beyond description, now that the destitution is so vast and industry lacks resources. . . . The 4-pound loaf costs 22 sous (which they often cannot earn by a whole day's labor) and yet they have not taken vengeance, they have as yet done no more than groan and grumble. . . . They are waiting for the last straw. . . . The last straw will be the death of a wife or child by starvation and destitution. Beware lest that terrible moment come at last!

And Mrs. Trollope, who wondered after a visit to the streets near the Porte Saint-Martin, still heady with riot, how "to wave off to a safe distance some of those reckless spirits who are ready to lay down their lives on the scaffold—or in a gutter—or over a pan of charcoal, rather than 'live peaceably in that state of life unto which it has pleased God to call them.' "[17] Most contemporary eyewitnesses took a similar view. The origin of the disturbances might be more specifically economic, political or biological; but it was everywhere presented as the same abnormal phenomenon, leading to the same abnormal results, unanimously described as manifestations of criminality.

The Economic Crises

The correlations that can be established between economic crises and crime, and the parallel between the rise in the price of bread and the increase in the number of assaults, are not so relevant here as that the fact could not have been more potent, more frequently asserted and more dreaded. When crisis came, the bourgeois barricaded himself in and the passer-by hurried homeward. It was no accident that Frégier identified economic crisis as one of the chief causes of working-class crime.

The Winters

The great killer winters, their consequences often blending with the crises, were equally dreaded and equally determinant. Balabine wrote of the winter of 1845:

A terrible scourge here, for there are an immense number of people, thousands of families, with no means of coping with it. Huddled up there in garrets under the leaking tiles, packed together, pent up between dripping, freezing walls, with no fire and no means of getting one, innumerable families, throngs of workmen, with nothing but sordid rags to clothe them, are suffering unto death in this Babylon of pleasure and luxury. As the cold came on, dense fogs shrouded Paris in an impenetrable and mysterious winding sheet. It was all that was needed to bring crime, the offspring of destitution, down into the streets and freeze the soul of the late walker with dread. In dark and lonely districts unknown even by name to the opulent inhabitant of the wealthy districts flooded with the light of innumerable lamp posts, the cutthroats, the *"escarpes,"* as this plague is called, crept closer and closer, and emboldened by the success of their nightly ventures, finally fell upon our districts. In the rue de Castiglione, at nine o'clock in the evening, at the door of the Hôtel Clarendon, right opposite the sentry outside the Ministry of Finance, a young man was very nearly murdered. . . . These dark deeds soon came up before the criminal court.

The Political Crises

The political crises, which were often hardly distinguished from the economic ones, were generally thought to be the direct cause of fresh outbreaks of crime, even when the crises themselves were not attributed simply to the criminal classes.

This opinion was reflected by Frégier, who wondered whether "those who stir up popular seditions should be classified in the dangerous classes." Most of the contemporary bourgeois accounts took the same view when describing the major disturbances during the Restoration and the July Monarchy; they held that the criminal classes, or the popular classes infected by a sort of contagion of crime, were solely responsible for them. Richerand, for example, describing the Revolution of 1830 in his *Population dans ses rapports avec la nature des gouvernements* (1837):

The ragged mob milled around the Palace gates . . . and though they soon covered their hideous nakedness with hastily contrived blue cloaks, they remained sinister of aspect. A great number of released jailbirds, the pick of the line in riots, swarmed in the streets; already overburdened with the loot of the Royal Palace and some of the museums, they coveted yet richer spoils.

"Populace"—mob—was the word most commonly used to designate the popular and criminal groups combining in enterprises which were at once political and criminal. It entered the bourgeois vocabulary, alongside "barbarians," "savages" and "vagrants" or "nomads." Richerand spoke of "populace." So did the son of a wine grower in Auxerre in a letter telling his father about the July Days in 1830.[18] Hugo used "populace" in his speech on his admission to the French Academy, rousing Vinçard to vigorous protest and giving rise to a controversy, traces of which are to be found, as we have already seen, in the description of the barricades in *Les Misérables*. We shall not revert to it here, but merely observe that in the last years of the July Monarchy and quite definitely after the June Days of 1848, the popular classes in Paris were no longer called "populace," but became "the people," and the terms "savages," "barbarians" and "vagrants" were no longer used to describe them. "Two things in particular struck me about the Revolution of 1848," Tocqueville wrote in his *Souvenirs*. "The first was the popular—and I would say exclusively, and not mainly, popular—character of the revolution which has just taken place, the complete power over all others it conferred on the people in the strict sense of the word, that is to say, the people who work with their hands. . . ."

CHAPTER TWO

Bourgeois Opinion: Balzac

The works of Balzac may be regarded as the outstanding documentation of bourgeois opinion, in particular because they reflect two facts: firstly, the confusion between the laboring and the dangerous classes, the proletariat and the mob, poverty and crime; and, secondly, the conflict between two categories of population in the ordinary settlement of scores, of which crime is one aspect, and in the exceptional settlement of scores, expressed in riots and revolutions.

Balzac's testimony is the more valuable in that he himself was not primarily concerned with the events it describes. The lower classes play a very small part in Balzacian society. But whenever they do appear or are mentioned, even if only in parenthesis, in a few lines, in the course of a casual stroll, through some doorway or at some street crossing, glimpsed by the light of a candle end on a marketwoman's stall, they always have the accurate characteristics and are described in the specific terms we expect, as if Balzac could not possibly see or describe them otherwise, however rapidly he passed them by. The diagnosis is brief, but it is plain, inexorable, ineluctable, as if it came not from the author himself, but from some collective pressure of opinion working upon him. These works are presented to us as a monument of bourgeois literature, in which the bourgeois classes are described almost exclusively, in their essence, and, as it were, spotlighted. But the people of Paris is certainly there, though in the background of the great personal dramas, on the fringes of Balzacian society and its individual histories, with their specific chronology of success and failure, the very street numbers of their addresses, their impeccable genealogies and their vital statistics. The people is there, with its physical and moral characteristics, etched in a few lines far more deeply than in any lengthy description; in an anonymous growl and a shadow; in an absence, or a form of absence, which have a significance all their own.

I

The City

A Bourgeois Paris

The working-class districts appear only incidentally in Balzac's Paris, in no way comparable to the privileged districts such as the faubourg Saint-Germain, the Chaussée d'Antin and the Marais. In any case, in the Paris of the first half of the nineteenth century and in Balzac's Paris it is not the districts that are important, but the streets, which, regardless whether a district is predominantly working-class or bourgeois, shelter a bourgeois or a working-class population owing to historical or geographical circumstances or to their exposure to sun or wind. The streets inhabited by rentiers or tradesmen are the most frequently mentioned, such as the rue Saint-Honoré, in which César Birotteau lived; the rue des Bourdonnais, in which Camusot sold his silks; and, above all, the rue Saint-Denis. It was the description of the rue Saint-Denis in the *Dictionnaire des enseignes de Paris* (1826) that virtually inaugurated the general description of the city: "And now say there is no genius in the rue Saint-Denis," Balzac wrote. This genius was to be one of the themes of the *Comédie humaine*. Working-class streets and districts are mentioned only because in this ancient city they happened to be "on the route necessarily taken by hurrying tradesmen." Balzac no more lingered in them than his characters did.

The city itself as a whole, summed up in the broad urban landscapes whose dominant traits and colors express Balzac's own vision of it, never has that proletarian aspect that it had in most contemporary descriptions. In Balzac it never shows the traits attributed to it by writers like Lecouturier, who wrote in 1849:

If you contemplate from the summit of Montmartre the congestion of houses piled up at every point of a vast horizon, what do you observe? Above, a sky that is always overcast, even on the finest day. Clouds of smoke, like a vast floating curtain, hide it from view. A forest of chimneys with black or yellowish chimneypots. . . . One is tempted to wonder whether this is Paris; and, seized with a sudden fear, one is reluctant to venture into this vast maze, in which a million beings jostle one another, where the air, vitiated by unhealthy effluvia, rising in a poisonous cloud, almost obscures the sun.

The passage seems to prefigure Zola's immense hopelessness. It is a foretaste of the landscape of grief and ruin that spread before the abbé Froment as he went to say Mass one January morning at the Sacré-Coeur on Montmartre: "A Paris of mystery, veiled in cloud, as if buried under the ashes from some catastrophe, half-vanished in the suffering and the shame for what lay hidden within its immensity." Balzac's landscape is totally different. The huddle of houses and the sordid proletarian encampment, "this illustrious valley of crumbling bricks and mortar and black gutters of mud," fade into a brilliant mist silhouetting spires and domes. With Rastignac on the last page of *Père Goriot* Balzac faces a different Paris, and, like Rastignac, challenges it.

True, the horror of Paris unanimously expressed in many books throughout these years impregnates the *Comédie humaine* too. But it is a horror that clings far less to the physical characteristics of the city or to the customs of the people than to the moral characteristics, the vices, betrayals and treacheries characteristic of high society, as expressed by the solicitor Derville as he looks at the setting of Bicêtre at the end of *Le Colonel Chabert*:

I have watched a father die in a garret without a farthing, deserted by two daughters whom he had presented with 40,000 livres in the Funds. I have seen mothers stripping their children of their last penny. . . . In short, all the horrors that novelists believe they are inventing always fall far short of the truth. That's the nice life you'll be getting to know; as for me, I am going away to live with my wife in the country; Paris horrifies me.

And again:

When Blücher reached the heights of Montmartre in 1814 with Saacken, if you will forgive me, gentlemen, for taking you back to that day of ill-omen, Saacken, who was a brute, said: "Now we'll burn Paris!"—"Do nothing of the sort; France will die of that alone!" Blücher replied, indicating the great ulcer gaping below them in fire and fume in the valley of the Seine.

A Proletarian Paris

The proletarian Paris certainly exists in Balzac's works, though on the fringes of the description, exactly as would be expected from contemporary and later statistical research.

It was the existence of a vast working-class population that gave the city the material and moral characteristics stressed by Balzac and most of his contemporaries. It filled the streets; and its presence, numbers, life, death, its work and movement, its very breath imprinted certain dominant characteristics upon the city. As we have shown, if inequality before life is a major fact of the history of the Paris of this period, inequality before death is no less so, owing to the influence of the environment on all the city's inhabitants. This despite the differences in their levels of living, in the air they all breathed, the water they drank, the noise, the feverish rhythm of their days, of all the physical and moral conditions which bore the stamp of the masses and impressed upon the privileged classes the crowd's permanent vengeance. The Paris of the *Comédie humaine* is damp, dark, unhealthy and the color of mud, even more so in the working-class districts. The quartier de la Grève, for example, which Balzac observed in *Une double famille*, as Lachaise also did; and Les Halles, in *César Birotteau*, very like what is reported in most of the contemporary medical and administrative descriptions; the faubourg Saint-Marceau, in *Le Colonel Chabert*; and, even more noteworthy, the rue du Fourarre, in describing which Balzac assembled all the biological and social facts whose importance and relationships we are studying:

Today it is one of the dirtiest streets in the XIIth arrondissement, the poorest district in Paris, in which two-thirds of the inhabitants lack firewood in winter, the district which sends the most brats to the Foundlings Hospital, the most sick to the Hôtel-Dieu, the most beggars onto the streets, the most ragpickers to the garbage dumps at the corner, the most sick old men to lean against the walls in the sun, the most unemployed workers to the squares, the most indictments to the police courts.[1]

II

The Population

The characteristics of Balzac's description of the lower classes are similar to those of his description of the city.

It is an incomplete description; often begun, never finished. The best example is the promising opening of *Facino Cane*:

I used to go and study the manners and customs of the faubourg, its inhabitants and their characters. As badly dressed as a workingman, taking no heed of convention, I aroused no suspicion. I was able to mingle with them, watch them bargaining and disputing as they left work. My observation had become intuitive; it penetrated the soul, though not neglecting the body, or rather it grasped external details so well that it at once pierced beyond them. It endowed me with the faculty of living the life of the person I was observing and enabled me to take his place, as the dervish in the *Arabian Nights* assumed the body and soul of the persons over whom he murmured a spell. When I met a workman and his wife on their way back from the Ambigu-Comique between eleven and midnight, I used to amuse myself by following them from the boulevard du Pont-aux-Choux to the boulevard Beaumarchais. The good people began by discussing the play they had seen and little by little went on to discussing their affairs; the mother dragged the child along by the hand without listening to its complaints and questions; the couple reckoned up the money they would be paid next day and spent it in a score of different ways. Then came household details, groans about potatoes costing far too much or how long the winter seemed and the way peat had gone up and fierce diatribes about the baker's bill. The discussion would grow hot at last, and each of them displayed their character in picturesque turns of speech. Listening to them I could make their life my own, I felt their rags on my back, I walked in their battered shoes; their desires, their needs, every part of them entered my spirit or my spirit entered theirs. It was a waking dream. I grew hot with them against the workshop foreman who browbeat them or against the rotten habit of making them go back time after time and then not get paid. To slough off one's habits, to become something other than oneself by an intoxication of the mental faculties and to play this game at will was my distraction. To what do I owe this gift? Is it second sight? Is it one of those qualities whose abuse might lead to madness? I have never investigated the source of this power; I simply possess it and use it.

Balzac used it. But to do what? As we know, the story turns into an absurd Venetian extravaganza which takes us far away from Paris and its working-class population. Similarly, the description of the working-class population appears in Balzac simply on the occasion of a chance meeting or encountered incidentally in passing. The story of Ferragus's assault on M. de Maulincourt produces the following passage:

At that period everyone was building and demolishing something or other, anything at all. There were very few streets without their scaffoldings on long poles, planks on balks clamped from floor to floor, shaky erections swaying under the Limousin masons, but strengthened with ropes, whitened by plaster, seldom protected against danger from carriages by the plank fence which must by law enclose monuments that are not in fact being erected. There is something maritime about the masts, ladders, ropes and the masons' shouts.

Or this hastily noted observation in *La fille aux yeux d'or*:

He found himself on the boulevard Montmartre in the dawn, gazed dully at the carriage as it sped away, took a couple of cigars out of his pocket, lighted one at the flare where an old woman was selling eau-de-vie and coffee to the workmen, urchins, market gardeners, to that whole Paris population which begins its life before dawn. Then he went off, smoking his cigar, lounging along, hands in trouser pockets, with a positively disgraceful insouciance.

Dr. Bianchon's visit to his uncle the judge supplies, purely incidentally, a survey of the poverty of the XIIth arrondissement. A similar chance reveals, in parenthesis, the population of Little Poland, in *La cousine Bette*.

Something of the same sort happens in sketching a career. The description of working-class life is often simply a recollection of a brief, rapid and more or less forgotten phase in a lifetime, like the account in *Gobseck* of the industrious and honest life of Fanny Malvault, the working girl who later became the wife of Derville the solicitor. Like the districts where it lived, the working class only appears incidentally on routes linking shopkeepers', bourgeois or aristocratic streets; or else it is one of the "illogical" routes Balzac's characters so often take[2]—brief meetings, dictated by the hazards of a street, the whim of a recollection.

But Balzac was interested only in certain types in this working-class population, which, fundamentally, he disliked:[3] "You must know," he wrote in *Facino Cane,*

that I had then broken down the elements of the homogeneous mass called the people. I had analyzed it so that I could appraise its good and bad qualities. I already knew the use that could be made of its faubourg, this seedbed of revolutions, which contains heroes, inventors, applied scientists, villains, rogues, virtues and vices, all of them hemmed in by poverty, stifled by need, steeped in wine, ravaged by strong waters. You can't imagine the number of frustrated ventures and hidden dramas there are in this city of grief! The number of splendid, the number of ghastly things!

He singled out of the mass of the working class certain characters who are not always most representative of the working-class condition, but present the moral or physical monstrosities which he took such an interest in collecting; and, above all, "the original characteristics of the Parisian," about which he wrote at the beginning of *Ferragus* and which he pinned down fairly often "in the unfortunates whom Charlet depicted at times with a rare trick of happy observation." These were the characters Balzac preferred to select, in line with a tradition of descriptive literature which is a historical no less than a literary fact.

A Tradition of Picturesque Literature

The main lower-class characteristics in Balzac's description of the Paris population are those which had always been a feature of the picturesque literature from its earliest beginnings. At every period, or at any rate until the last decades of the nineteenth century, the people of Paris was incarnated in a few types chosen for their picturesqueness who seem impervious to the lapse of time. The ragpicker always appears, always with the same rags; and the beggar, the female matchseller, the little sweep. How long this tradition lasted and how continuous it was could easily be demonstrated by literary research. A better way of putting

it perhaps is that a concern which was both literary and artistic reinforced an ancient literary tradition at this period.

The characters on whom Balzac dwells are those already to be found
in Mercier's *Tableaux de Paris* and Restif's novels. What was the reason
for going back so far? One of the literary fashions in the early decades
of the nineteenth century was the taste for depictions of manners and
customs. The first five volumes of Joseph-Etienne de Jouy's *L'Hermite
de la Chaussée d'Antin, ou Observations sur les moeurs et les usages
parisiens au commencement du XIXe siècle* appeared in 1815–16 and
immediately became a best-seller. The types Jouy observed and selected
for description are those already observed by Mercier. For the lower
classes he describes only the most picturesque occupations, whether at
work or at leisure. He gives more space to the description of the di-
versions than the labor of the working class in his essays, as did all
the descriptions of this kind. He prefers to describe the artisan at La
Courtille. What is especially striking is his devotion to the picturesque,
in the etymological sense of the term. In Volume III Jouy wrote:

One of our most famous painters, who combines a special talent for the
kind of sketch which has rightly been called the epigram of design with the
superior talent required for grand compositions, was telling me the other
day of his project to compose a series of caricatures in the manner of Hogarth
to show the development of some moral idea. A preliminary sketch he sent
me I thought as intriguing as it was ingenious; in this series of small pictures, which might be called "contrasts," the painter proposes to show the
various classes of society contrasted with each other, so that the antithesis
brings out the customs, the foibles, the defects and the qualities of each.

His own observation is governed by this purely pictorial search for
contrasts. "My study and my delight," he wrote,

has been to observe the manners and customs of my time. Hence I have to
dine alternately in the salons of Beauvilliers and the pothouses of La Courtille,
to visit the balcony of the Opéra one evening and the gallery of the Ambigu
the next. This diversity of dress, speech and behavior blends into what I
may call a moral panorama, which, under the brush of a skilful painter,
would turn out to embrace the entire population of Paris. . . . The whole
science of observation, I believe, can be summarized in two points, namely,
to listen to the rich talking and to get the poor to talk. That is why I chat
with the cab driver, the water carrier, the old-clothes dealer, all of them
people who have much to tell because they have seen a great deal.

During the last years of the Restoration the artists enhanced this
literary tradition. Writers and artists competed in their search for the
picturesque.

There were a great many collections of drawings representing *grisettes*,

porters and members of the *claque*. How strongly Balzac was influenced
by these sketches in his descriptions of the lower classes, or rather
lower-class types, is well known; his relations with the contributors to
La Silhouette and *La Caricature*—Henri Monnier, Travies, Daumier
and Gavarni—have often been studied. Literary men and artists collab-
orated on the same books and on literary descriptions containing the
same types, notably *La physiologie du rentier*, published by Balzac in
1841 with illustrations by Monnier, Daumier and Meissonnier, and above
all *Le diable à Paris*. In the latter book the popular types were derived
from a picturesque tradition going back long before Mercier: concierges,
beggars and ragpickers. Gavarni drew them and Balzac described them
in a chapter entitled "*Ce qui disparaît de Paris*." But it was going too
far to call these types "vanishing," so solid and unchanging do the
characters appear, although invariably presented as threatened survivals. Balzac described them in the past tense: "The lamplighter who
used to sleep all day, family with no home but the contractor's shop,
all of whom used to do their bit in the business, the wife cleaning the
panes, the husband filling up with oil, the children polishing the reflec-
tors." So far from vanishing, they, or their like, are found at every
turn in Balzac's itineraries, the nail collector whose business he assessed
in *Un grand homme de province à Paris*, or those whom de Rubempré
watched,

the stinking squadron of *claqueurs* and ticket sellers, all of them fellows in
caps, with trousers which had seen better days, shabby frock coats, hang-
dog, blueish, greenish, muddy, scraggy visages, long beards, eyes at once
fierce and wistful, a horrible mob which lives and swarms on the Paris boulevards, sells safety chains and gold-mounted jewels for 25 sous in the morning
and swells the *claque* under the chandeliers at night; and, in brief, lends
itself to all the dirty work in Paris.

Not vanished at all, but very much alive in Balzac's work, as in the
street and in most contemporary descriptions, the most noteworthy
being perhaps Janin's in *Le livre des 101*:

Paris is full of a crowd of "industrialists" who belong only to the great city
and are quite meaningless outside its walls. The industry of sewer and street
corner, of garret and gutter; the industry of hazard, which has its hopes,
its craft mastery, its central department; the industry of rags, old nails, and
broken glass. The petty trade prevails in this great city. It costs so much to
buy a licensed job, even a bailiff's man's. It takes so much money to open
the tiniest shop at a time when no shop but has its mirrors on the walls and
mahogany counter! The Paris landlords are so harsh, bills so hard to discount! But one has to live, one has to avoid dissipation and the hospital!

So long live the petty trade, without shop, without licence, without landlord, without bills of exchange, without profit, the petty trade in the open air, afoot, hands in pockets, basket on back, or lounging on the porter's hooks at the street corner, waiting for a customer! . . . The petty trades begin at Les Halles. . . .

The relations between writing and drawing are equally apparent in their influence on each other. The Paris society described by Balzac was illustrated in the sketchbooks published by Henri Monnier towards the close of the Restoration. Besides drawing, Monnier went on to description in words, thus expressing the basic relation between the picturesque literature and the sketch.[4] "In the past," he wrote in the Preface to *Scènes populaires*, "we have seen very few literary men take to painting and very few painters take up literature. Why not try both mediums, since the studies and observations are the same?"

Such are the literary reasons which account for the limitations of the description of the lower classes in Balzac's works and for the search for the picturesque which impairs the impression of authenticity.

A Historical Necessity

There are, however, some further reasons, on which history throws some light.

The prominence given to certain trades in the many portraits of Paris and in the *Comédie humaine* was partly accounted for, admittedly, by literary or artistic circumstances; but even more certainly by their prominence in daily life and in the urban landscape. It was not only in the literature that they, and the characters embodying them, took up so much space. Though they represented only a very small proportion of the Parisian lower classes and were in no way typical of their working or living conditions or their human aspect, they filled the official archives in the same way as they filled the streets, jostling, splashing and spattering the passers-by, disturbing the silence of the night, waking the bourgeois before dawn, uttering the cries of their trade or occupation at all hours.

The picturesque literature's passion for these loud characters expresses a certain state of the streets, itself the result of a certain economic and social state of the city as a whole. Similarly, their disappearance from the contemporary streets, where indeed, they hardly existed any more, but also from the contemporary literature, to which they seemed to owe a curious sort of survival, reflected and expressed another stage in the city's economic and social development. Today, any would-be picturesque literature has to go at least as far afield as tramps. Nowadays, too, such types no longer exist in the literary description of most great cities. In the first half of the nineteenth century, however, as in yet earlier periods, the people of Paris—consistently with the picturesque literature but equally consistently with the city itself—was the people engaged in these loud trades, who ruled the streets just as they filled the literature and the official reports. The ragpickers foisoned in Mercier's *Tableaux* as they did in the administrative archives of the seventeenth and eighteenth century. Innumerable police orders were issued concerning them, such as that of 1701

against the ragpickers of the rue Neuve-Saint-Martin and thereabouts who make it their business to traffic in dogs, and to feed them they make provision of horsemeat which infects the district, which said dogs, to the number of more than 200, they loose night and day in the streets so that passers-by have been sorely bitten. Furthermore, notwithstanding the police orders and regulations forbidding ragpickers to go and pass on the streets of this city and its faubourgs before dawn, some of them have practiced the custom these several years of leaving their lodgings at midnight and walking the streets on pretext of gathering rags, which may be the cause of most robberies which occur.

These ragpickers and their dogs filled the official documents of the nineteenth century, and for the same reasons, for the same offenses, denounced in the same terms, just as they appeared in Travies's *Tableaux de Paris*, men and dogs fighting each other, practically cannibalistic. There are a remarkable number of water carriers in the literature of the eighteenth and the first half of the nineteenth centuries. This was because the health of part of the Paris population depended for its cleanliness on the labor of these "industrialists." It was not merely the picturesque that was involved. True, the Countess Foedera, the heartless woman in the *Peau de chagrin*, presents a little Savoyard with 5 francs "because he has such pretty rags." But this is not the main interest of these characters, which lies rather in the services they rendered, those essential to urban life. They interested the novelist, the artist and the administrator alike. When the cholera epidemic broke out, they were the first people anyone thought of. Water carriers, street porters, crockery menders, shoemenders and sweeps—whose yearly migration to Paris was so familiar and has so often been described— filled the police reports, some of which give us a more specific commentary on the literary descriptions than we could make ourselves, and, in a way, account for them.[5]

Despite these limitations, the working-class population was part of the description of the Paris population, as it was of the Paris landscape, no matter whether we take the general description of Paris or a certain quality in the air or water, certain colors, the noise by day or the silence by night, or the description of lower-class districts. It is ever-present in the *Comédie humaine*; but, more importantly, it reflects the economic, physical and moral characteristics, the conditions of life and the modes of living, the kinds of work, and the behavior, speech and dress we expect. That is to say, set apart from the rest of the population, differing from it, universally so regarded and reacting in accordance with those differences, both in its daily life and in the great manifestations of the city's economic, social and political existence. This is precisely how it appears in many passages in the *Comédie humaine*, most particularly in the early pages of *La fille aux yeux d'or*—written between the spring of 1834 and the spring of 1835—from which we shall be taking most of our quotations.

A Different People

A different people. This was the "ugly and sturdy nation" for which Balzac gave actual figures. "This people is made up of 300,000 individuals." There were two reasons for its difference, a biological inequality and an economic and social inequailty.

A biological inequality: Inequality before life and before death, the major inequality, was the consequence, and also the measure, of all the other forms of inequality in Balzac's work as in most contemporary descriptions. This was itself merely one aspect of the fundamental biological inequality which made this people different even in bodily appearance, and doomed it for that very reason to every sort of ugliness and degradation.

All these aspects of biological inequality are brought together in the early part of *La fille aux yeux d'or*, especially in the opening passage, any analysis of which could be no more than a commentary on it:

One of the most horrifying sights is certainly the general aspect of the Parisian population, a people of ghastly mien, gaunt, sallow, weather-beaten. Should we not compare Paris to a vast field incessantly swayed by storm of interests, beneath which a crop of human beings tosses, scythed by death more often than elsewhere, yet forever springing up again as densely packed as before, whose contorted, twisted faces exude at every pore of the spirit the desires and poisons teeming in their brain; masks, not faces; masks of weakness, masks of strength, masks of misery, masks of joy; all wearied unto death, all stamped with the indelible marks of voracious greed? What is it they want? Gold or pleasure? A few observations on the soul of Paris may explain the reasons for its cadaverous physiognomy, which has only two ages, youth or senility, a wan and colorless youth, a senility bedizened in an attempt to look young. At the sight of this exhumed people, foreigners, who have no obligation to look into the causes, at once experience a feeling of aversion to this capital, this vast sweatshop of pleasure, but soon they are incapable of quitting it again and stay on, deliberately settling down to their perversion. A word or two will suffice to account physiologically for the almost hellish complexion of Parisian countenances, for it is not merely in jest that Paris has been called a hell.

This was to take first things first—life and, above all, death, which, to Balzac and his contemporaries, summed up everything else. There are, for instance, frequent observations about the health of the Auvergnats, of whom Balzac was truly as fond as Desplein, who, he tells us in *La messe de l'athée*, had experienced the protection and devotion of Bourgeat, a poor water carrier, when he was a poor and homeless young student:

One day, Bianchon told Desplein that a poor water carrier in the quartier Saint-Jacques had contracted a horrible disease from overwork and poverty; this poor Auvergnat had eaten nothing but potatoes in the desperate winter of 1821. Desplein left all his patients. At risk of foundering his horse, he rushed to the poor man's lodging, followed by Bianchon, and personally saw that he was carried to the nursing home established by the famous Dubois in the faubourg Saint-Denis.

A remark by Gazonal, when showing a cousin from the Midi the sights of Paris in *Les comédiens sans le savoir*, is really noteworthy here: "Paris industry has made even more fantastic efforts. There are the workers. . . . You who exhibit them don't know all the products of industry. Our industry fights the continent's industry by throwing in misfortune after misfortune, just as, during the Empire, Napoleon fought Europe by throwing in regiment after regiment." And Lachaise said something of the same sort in his *Topographie médicale*:

The feelings of the philosopher who reflects on the price at which we have purchased the benefits of social life and considers how many thousands of lives are sacrificed daily to our simplest enjoyments must surely be painful. When one sees that most of the workers who operate certain branches of industry do not live out more than half the span of an ordinary life, does it not seem that man is destined to find his destruction in the very causes of his existence?

Disease and death are, however, merely the consequences of a profounder biological inequality, a basic inferiority or degeneration.

Degeneration is an ancient belief; there are many traces of it in the literature of the Ancien Régime. Mercier described the physical and moral degeneration of the people of Paris:

The people are flabby, pale, short, stunted; one sees at first glance that these are no republicans. It is only the republican who displays the bluntness, the peremptory gesture, the lively glance that denote a militant spirit and sustain patriotism. . . . Any citizen who does not stride down middle of the street, head high, ready for fisticuffs, will lose his true worth, for the proud virtues of states greatly depend on more than a touch of bluntness! The nerve and, we venture to say, the insolence of the people will always be an earnest of their forthright nature, their probity, their devotion to duty. Once the people abandon rusticity and rant, they become pompous, vain, debauched, poor and therefore debased. I prefer to see them using their fists and getting blind drunk in the pubs, as in London, than careworn, uneasy, trembling, downtrodden, not daring to raise their heads, as in Paris.

In the very aspect of the streets Mercier finds the most evident sign of this lack of manliness:

One has only to walk down the street to see clearly enough that the people does not make the laws; no concern for the pedestrian; no footways. The people seems to be a body set apart from the other orders of the State; the great and the wealthy who keep their carriage enjoy the barbarous right to run down and mutilate people on the streets; a hundred die beneath the carriage wheels every year.[6]

In 1787, at about the same period, Arthur Young made similar observations and drew similar conclusions:

This great city appears to be in many respects the most ineligible and inconvenient for the residence of a person of small fortune of any that I have ever seen; and vastly inferior to London. The streets are very narrow, and many of them crowded, nine-tenths dirty, and all of them without foot pavements. . . . There are an infinity of one-horse cabriolets, which are driven by young men of fashion and their imitators, alike fools, with such rapidity as to be real nuisances, and render the streets exceedingly dangerous, without an incessant caution. I saw a poor child run over and probably killed, and have been myself many times blackened with the mud of the kennels. This beggarly practice, of driving a one horse booby hutch about the streets of a great capital, flows either from poverty or a wretched and despicable economy; nor is it possible to speak of it with too much severity. If young noblemen at London were to drive their chaises in streets without footways, as their brethren do at Paris, they would speedily and justly get very well thrashed, or rolled in the kennel.[7]

Compare the Prefect Anglès's remarks on the decline in the Parisians' physique since the Revolution and the moral and political conclusions he drew from it.

Such observations became commoner and more detailed in the early nineteenth century and in proportion as statistical research developed. They were a favorite theme in the medical topographies of Paris. Audin-Rouvière thus described the people of Paris in the years preceding the Revolution:

Light, frivolous, taking nothing seriously, they were quick to forget; weak in character, servile by habit, gentle, humane, it seemed that nothing could familiarize them with the sight of blood nor inspire them with the courage needed to break the bonds which held them enslaved. The people could not have cared less and were perfectly unconcerned about their political interests; manifestly, they were not republican.[8]

Lachaise's analysis, which we used earlier when studying the physical characteristics of the Paris working-class population not in opinion but in the facts, in no way tallied with this.

We should note that there already appear in these descriptions some hints of the relationships between the physical and the moral which give a foretaste of the major investigations that came later. Lachaise, for instance, noted the physical effects as well as the physical causes of the over-precocious intellectual development of Paris children. There were a great many papers on bad health and bad morals in the *Annales d'Hygiène*, the importance of which we have already stressed, and on the relationships between working-class physique and working-class behavior. The circumstances which led to the making of these inquiries are irrelevant here, namely, the changes in the composition of the Parisian population and its physical transformation, which we attempted in an earlier book to measure and account for by the new geographical and economic circumstances of immigration into Paris. The relative value of these inquiries is equally irrelevant. We need merely note that they expressed very evident and very disturbing facts and that, when widely disseminated by the daily press, they rapidly became food for opinion, an opinion which avidly seized upon them, but exaggerated and distorted them.

It is the traces of this contemporary opinion that we note in many apparently subsidiary details in Balzac's description, as, for example, the merciless details in the passage in *La fille aux yeux d'or* already quoted: "A people of ghastly mien, gaunt, sallow, weather-beaten . . . cadaverous physiognomy . . . exhumed people . . . hellish complexion of Parisian countenances . . . contorted, twisted faces exude at every pore of the spirit the desires and poisons teeming in their brain; masks, not faces . . ."

These physical characteristics are those of the whole Paris population, but especially of the working-class population, this ugliness being a property peculiar to it. It is the ugliness of the working-class population that accounts for the horror of the whole population of Paris which Balzac felt. "Hence the exorbitant mobility of the proletarians," he wrote in *La fille aux yeux d'or*, "hence the depravation of the interests which crush the two bourgeoisies, hence the cruelties of the artist's imagination and the exaggerated search for pleasure by the wealthy account for the normal ugliness of the Paris countenance." Few of Balzac's portraits of workmen are not stamped with this premature ageing, the failure to be as handsome as they might have been: "These men, certainly born to be beautiful, for everything created has some pretensions to beauty, enlisted from childhood under the orders of force, the domination of the hammer, became Vulcans." The pallor already described by Lachaise in similar terms, giving similar reasons and similar analogies, is the dominant trait:

If there is anyone who doubts the prime cause of the deterioration of the constitutions of persons who live in constant darkness and damp, let him examine by analogy the change in plants that grow in shadow; their stalks are long, tapering, flimsy and knotty, their cortex is spongy and uneven, their leaves pale green, their flowers faded and scentless, their fruits, when they produce any, are watery, taste sour or insipid and never become wholly ripe. Is there anyone, indeed, who has never noticed how the complexion of people who leave the provinces to live in the capital suddenly pales?

Balzac also alludes to

some people's custom of decorating their windows with the plants called ramblers; others raise shrubs in pots which are brought indoors every night. It is well known that plants absorb oxygen at night instead of giving it off, as they do by day, thus producing carbonic acid and infecting the air of rooms in which they are kept at night; several doctors who have practiced in Paris for many years have assured me that they have often encountered cases in which doing so has proved fatal.

A similar view and similar comparisons are found in a description of the rue du Tourniquet-Saint-Jean:

The window bars were bent out, so that the girl had managed to cover the window sill with a long wooden box filled with earth, in which there grew sweet peas, nasturtiums, a small sickly woodbine and some convolvulus whose weak tendrils climbed the bars. These washed-out plants produced pale flowers, a harmony in which something sad and gentle mingled in the picture of this window, which made such a suitable frame for the two faces. Happening to glance up at this domestic scene, the most self-centered passer-by carried away a complete picture of the life led by the working class in Paris, for the embroideress seemed to come alive only in her needle.

Few people reached the turnstile without wondering how a girl could keep her complexion when she lived in that hole.

Zola described a similar pallor, but as characteristic of another sort of population; not the proletariat—which now had a quite different aspect—but the small shopkeepers. Over against the *Bonheur des Dames*, dazzlingly illuminated, was the back shop in which the Baudus were wasting away; Geneviève Baudu on her deathbed, with her ravaged face, "in which the final degeneration of an old family thrust into the dark in this cellar of the ancient Paris retail trades was breathing its last."

This physical inferiority and this ugliness were simply the expression of a moral inferiority summed up in the Paris urchin, Barbier's for example:

> La race de Paris, c'est le pâle voyou
> Au corps chétif, au teint jaune comme un vieux sou:
> C'est cet enfant criard que l'on voit à toute heure,
> Paresseux et flânant et loin de sa demeure,
> Battant les maigres chiens et le long des grands murs,
> Charbonnant en sifflant mille croquis impurs.
> Cet enfant ne croit pas, il crache sur sa mère.
> Le nom du ciel pour lui n'est qu'une farce amère.
> C'est le libertinage enfin en raccourci
> Par un front de quinze ans. C'est le vice endurci.[9]

It was in Balzac's urchins too, like Cerizet, in *Eve et David*, whom David Séchard brought in to help him with his printing press at Angoulême: "Cerizet inwardly set himself up as his opponent and said to himself: 'You suspect me, I'll have my revenge!' The Paris urchin is like that." At the end of the book, when Cerizet's ambition and hatred seem about to succeed owing to his pact with Petit-Claud the solicitor: " 'One must succeed,' said the solicitor drily—'I shall succeed,' said Cerizet . . . 'But if you have deceived me, sir,' said the Parisian, catching an expression that displeased him on the solicitor's face. 'Well, you'll leave a young widow,' the Paris urchin added beneath his breath, looking daggers at him." And a whole destiny of poverty and crime is implicit in this glimpse in *L'Interdiction*:

A young woman was suckling her latest baby to keep it quiet, holding another, aged about five, between her knees. The white breast gleaming amid the rags, the baby with his blue-veined flesh, and his brother, whose attitude denoted the urchin-to-be, were strangely moving owing to the almost graceful contrast they formed to the long line of faces reddened by the cold, among which this family stood out.

An economic and social inequality: We shall say little about the strictly economic inequality, since it has often been studied—by others so far as the economic characteristics of Balzacian society are concerned and by ourselves with respect to the occupational mobility analyzed in an earlier chapter. Social inequality was the major problem of working-class life, and it was well summed up in the following passage in *La fille aux yeux d'or*:

Chance has made a workman thrifty, chance has endowed him with an idea, he has been able to look to the future, he has met and married a woman, he has become a father and, after some years of severe privations, he starts up a small drapery trade and rents a shop. If neither disease nor vice stop him short, if he prospers, this gives you an idea of a normal life.

Vice and disease are indeed the essential criteria for all social descriptions of the working class in this period. Proudhon wrote in *La guerre et la paix*: "A family of four can live on 3 francs 50 a day. But obviously it will enjoy no luxuries, the father will not go to the café; should unemployment, illness or accident supervene, should vice enter the household, they will not be able to make ends meet and will soon be destitute." Deploring the failure to publish the figures for the death rate in 1824 and 1825, Trébuchet commented in the *Annales d'Hygiène*: "The effect of the diet and the moral behavior of the inhabitants of Paris on their state of health could have been assessed and to some extent charted." These were also the two major criteria for working-class life in Balzac.

Working-class life could be successful. There are striking instances in the *Comédie humaine*: "Paris is a city which collects all the energetic people who grow like wildfire on French soil," Crevel says in *La cousine Bette*, "and there are a whole lot of talents there without hearth or home, bold spirits fit for anything, even for making their pile." It would be a mistake, however, to imitate conventional history and use these examples, which, of course, are relatively frequent in the *Comédie humaine*, to present Balzac's description as the main evidence for upward social mobility during the first half of the nineteenth century. This would be to ignore how exceptional such success was and to fail to note the far more important, but virtually unnoticed, incidental passages which show that, quite to the contrary, the essential problem in the period—for Balzac, as for all the other writers—was not that of working-class success but working-class failure. The essential elements of the problem are summed up early in *La fille aux yeux d'or*, in which the workers' way of life is thus described. "Trusting to their muscles as a painter trusts to his palette, lords for a day, on Mondays they fling their money around the pothouses which enclose the city within a girdle of mud. . . . Their relaxation is a wearisome debauch. . . . As ferocious in pleasure as he is calm at work."

The major problems of working-class life in Paris are posed in Balzac's work precisely in this manner. Not, of course, in the main scenes, nor in the pre-eminent characters, whose exceptional nature and limited significance we have already stressed; but in his hurried glimpses of collective life, in the confused swarm, at street corners, in the half-shadow of dawn or twilight, barely sketched, it is true. Yet in these hasty notes, quantitative history discovers the characteristics which it knows were in fact the most important.

We may go further. The impression, so manifest in particular at the beginning of *Facino Cane*, that the great tragedies of working-class life were actually part of the intended scheme of the *Comédie humaine* is almost irresistible; although the scheme was never completed, the outlines are visible throughout the whole work as it stands.

The novel of the lower class suggested above was perhaps *L'hôpital et le peuple*, a work barely sketched out; a few fragments were published in *Le diable à Paris* in 1846. It is true that the descripion of the petty Paris trades in it is in line with the picturesque literature already analyzed. And the subject is still apparently social success, not failure.

The itinerant re-soler of shoes has a shop, pays for his licence and, no less than his neighbor the dairyman, who sells on a marble slab goods that used to be sold from a cart, is qualified to be elector, candidate, deputy and minister, just like any manufacturer. He is one of those infantry who will one day be the hero of a democratic novel. He makes the traditional journeyman tour of France, crying "Shoon! Soler!," carrying his factory and his store in a basket on his back. A *gniaf* [cobbler]—that is the people's term for them—straight out of apprenticeship in Paris, started out from Paris in 1832 . . . on his way to his native Auvergne.

In this sketch, as in the other novels, the description of Paris breaks off; the story moves to Auvergne with Jean-François Tauleron returning to his native province to draw a lucky number in the draft. But we cannot fail to note the title, *L'hôpital et le peuple*, which certainly fits the description of the people of Paris we were expecting. It is hard not to believe that, if the work had been finished, we should have had a development of the themes and a fulfilment of the promises which are so clearly visible in the *Comédie humaine*.

A Hostile Population

Similarly, the description of the lower classes, incomplete and continually broken off though it is, presents another characteristic which quantitative historical research shows to be of the essence. This is the struggle between two populations, an antagonism whose forms are biological and moral as well as economic, occupational and political, expressed not only in strikes, riots and revolutions, but also in a certain aspect of everyday relationships and social relationships at work or in the street, culminating in the extreme form of violence—crime.

This description, too, has its limitations. We have already demonstrated the precise, but restricted, significance of a form of crime which in Balzac very soon and very often ceases to be a consequence of a general evolution and is confined to the reflection of a small class of criminals embodied in a few exceptional characters such as Vautrin.

It is noteworthy that the supreme form of working-class violence, revolution, is barely mentioned in the *Comédie humaine*. This omission is the more surprising in that the work took shape precisely at a period when the workers' tragedy—as Hugo realized—was at once material, moral, biological and political, the political fact being the result and expression of the other facts. Balzac only occasionally refers to the social aspects of these upheavals. The successive revolutions in those years interested him in quite a different way. The personal drama of the young republicans was more important to him than the popular upheavals. The Revolution of 1830 and what he called "the Saint-Merri affairs" he linked mainly to the story of Michel Chrestien. It is not the historical event which brings the character to life by dating him, but the human event—the personal drama of one of his favorite characters—that brings the historical event to life. The 1830 Revolution; but only in connection with Michel Chrestien's love for the princesse de Cadignan.[10] The riot at Saint-Merri; but only in connection with Michel Chrestien's death.[11]

Thus, the general significance of the successive political disturbances of the period—so evident in *Les Misérables*—does not appear in the *Comédie humaine*, or is merely the occasion for hurried observations, swiftly effaced, swept away by a narrative less concerned with collective affairs than personal histories.

Nevertheless, these collective phenomena themselves are present in the work, and with the characteristics we expect. The revolt of a population regarded as different is described, and in the light of these differences.

The savages—a literary influence: Balzac does not give the term "savages" the specific meaning we have already discussed. Traces of the fusion between the old term and the images engendered by Fenimore Cooper's books that took place at this period are very evident in his work. To Balzac the savages were the savages of Mercier, Sauval, and scores of works of the eighteenth century and the Revolutionary period, but they are also characters from *The Prairie*, *The Last of the Mohicans* and *The Trapper*. Cooper's influence is very evident in the early part of the *Mystères de Paris*, but images of the prairie soon fade out before the spectacle of the Parisian jungle. Cooper's images are more tenacious in Balzac's description, but whereas Hugo and Sue construed them as covering not criminals only, but a large part of the working-class population, to Balzac the "savages" were criminals. Thus, reverting in *Splendeurs et misères des courtisanes* to a statistical improvisation he had already attempted in the *Code des gens honnêtes*, he wrote: "In twenty years Paris will be besieged by an army of 40,000 discharged convicts. As the department of the Seine, with its 1,500,000 inhabitants, is the only place in France where these unfortunates can hide, Paris is to them what the virgin forest is to wild animals." In the same book he thus described criminals:

Terrifyingly energetic in their conceptions, they are like children once they have brought off their coup. Theirs is, in short, the nature of wild animals, easily slain when replete. In prison these singular men are men through dissimulation and through their discretion, which gives way only at the last moment, after they have been broken, tormented nearly to death, by long confinement.

The savages—a social fact: The working classes are savages, however, in the behavior Balzac ascribes to them. He describes them as threatening the socal order. In *La physiologie du rentier*, referring to "the offensive of the Producers, the Economists, those Tribes created by Saint-Simon and Fourier against the rentiers," he wrote: "If these insensate innovators were to succeed, Paris would soon feel the absence of rentiers. The rentier constitutes an admirable transition between the dangerous family of proletarians and the very curious families of industrialists and property owners."

The family of proletarians was dangerous because of its situation on the margin of the city. All the characteristics of the savage condition—

the complex relationships between poverty and bad morals, irreligion and crime—appear in the description of Little Poland in *La cousine Bette*, a commentary on which could be derived from contemporary statistical research; but perhaps even more plainly in the description of the place Maubert and the rue du Fouarre. Especially in the following passage, which sums up all the aspects of working-class revolt:

Most of them were women; their husbands had gone off to work, leaving them, of course, to plead the household's case with the wit characteristic of the woman of the people, almost always the queen of her hovel. You would have seen tattered shawls on every head, dresses embroidered with mud, kerchiefs in rags, dirty, ragged jackets, but on every side eyes blazing like leaping flames. A horrible assembly, which at the first sight inspired repulsion; but this gave way to terror as soon as one perceived that, by sheer chance, the resignation of these souls, struggling with all the needs of life, was really a device to exploit charity. The two candles lighting the waiting room wavered in a sort of fog given off by the stinking atmosphere of the ill-ventilated room.

These few examples are enough to show the precision with which Balzac described, however briefly, the relationships between poverty and social revolt, the profound kinship between the laboring and the dangerous classes.[12]

CHAPTER THREE

Popular Opinion

There is no doubt that "savages," "barbarians" and "vagrants" were intended as terms of abuse, but they were not really insults since the laboring classes themselves accepted the terms and acquiesced in the opinion implied in them; their opinion of themselves was not so very different. To the bourgeois classes they were indelibly stamped with vice, akin to the criminal classes; their condition and their revolt was often confused with that of the criminal classes; but so they were in their own eyes.

What is involved here is not merely the survival of old attitudes and the persistance of the belief in what Proudhon called "the drop of bad blood," nor of the strength of the prejudices Corbon later analyzed in the early years of the Second Empire, giving many examples of great relevance to our study.[1] What we have in mind is rather the contemporary form that these beliefs and attitudes of the Ancien Régime assumed under the pressure of new circumstances. Everything goes to show that large numbers of the lower classes—numbers we have already estimated —if not the working class as a whole accepted and shared the other classes' opinion of them and recognized the condition attributed, or rather assigned, to them, a condition not merely inferior and humiliated but virtually criminal. The great reversal of the working-class position, which gradually came to prevail in fact and in idea in the second half of the century—the new and triumphant concept of the worker, suddenly endowed with every virtue, miraculously rejuvenated and, as it were, sublimated, the notion of the "sublime" worker in which even bourgeois opinion was to acquiesce and was indeed to promote with deep respect —would be quite impossible to account for if we fail to realize the full extent to which the lower classes themselves shared the old bourgeois conviction.

This lower-class conviction is expressed in many qualitative documents, especially those brought together in the popular press and literature. We shall have to examine these documents, not for the deliberate description in them, for that is familiar enough from other surveys, but for the traces of contemporary popular beliefs involuntarily preserved in them. The popular press and the popular literature are not relevant for the descriptions they give of the phenomena we are studying, but for their involuntary and "passive" recording and communication of them; not for their testimony concerning the workers, but for the testimony by the workers concerning themselves and their own condition.

I

The Working-Class Press

La Ruche populaire, which claimed to be written by workers for workers, supplies the testimony by the working class: "The author," the paper stated in the very first issue, "is mainly the class of plebians, of proletarians, of workers, since class it is; the author is 'the echo of the workshops,' the workshops under a roof or under the sky; he is our responsible editor, a lens grinder, my neighbor Simon the carpenter; he is you, if you have nothing but your muscles and no private income." But what sort of testimony?

La Ruche protested, indeed, against the usual depiction of the worker, against the bourgeois opinion we have described, and especially against the customary confusion of the laboring with the dangerous classes.[2] But in defending the working classes the paper maintained in essentials, as we shall see, confirmed and very largely accepted the very description it claimed to be refuting. The refutation itself was tantamount to acceptance.

This was shown by an extreme touchiness about any criticism of the working-class way of life.[3] It was shown, above all, by the terms "savages," "barbarians" and "civilized people," which it borrowed from the common vocabulary, thereby recognizing and confirming it. "The worker is ashamed of the degradation into which he is plunged," Varin wrote,

and also wants to prove that he is an intelligent mechanic, more receptive than "civilized people" themselves to noble and generous feelings. . . . We wish to win our right to equal citizenship by peaceful means. It is distressing to read so many infamous parodies, to contemplate the ignoble aspect under which we are presented in the *Gazette des tribunaux*.

But the artisans and workmen who contributed to *La Ruche populaire* not only recognized and acknowledged these physical and moral characteristics of the laboring classes, identical with those commonly attributed to the dangerous classes, a common appearance and behavior, when they protested against the descripion of them; they also confirmed and proclaimed them themselves even more definitely and passionately when their pity went out to embrace dangerous classes and laboring classes alike, the poor and the criminal alike, in dozens of articles and poems. One might almost say in an identical poetic strain, so strongly was this community of feeling brought out in the relationships between the favorite subjects of working-class songs and the criminal themes of the street ballads, in almost the same words, meters and tunes.[4]

Regardless whether the subject was the dangerous classes or the laboring classes, attention focused on social deterioration. Hence the attention to crime, which was simply one form of working-class failure, when it was not an expression of working-class revenge. Petty criminals such as the cobbler in the rue des Vertus Saint-Martin, who was never paid by the woman he worked for and was therefore driven to take what was owed to him by force in order to feed his children; arrested and condemned to five years imprisonment, he returned and killed her. Great criminals and true instruments of popular vengeance such as Lauber, whose execution at the barrière Saint-Jacques was reported by Duquenne:

Aged twenty-seven, this thick-necked, broad-shouldered man appeared to be of a very sanguine complexion, one of those natures which alone are capable of terrible or criminal protest and avenge themselves to the last detail, often by murder, for the equally lethal and criminal desertion of which the so-called "social welfare service" has been guilty by default towards them in the first place. . . . So he refused to have his sentence commuted; he preferred death to stifling imprisonment, that is to say, the end of the struggle, as he called it.

Balzac described Jacques Colin's last combat in much the same terms: "This image of the people in revolt against the law."

Hence the interest taken by *La Ruche* in all works on crime, especially the most violent, and hence its interpretation of them, such as Régis Allier's and Moreau-Christophe's books on the prisons,[5] and in these remarks by the vicomte de Bretignières, to which we must pay special attention:

The poor and the criminals are mustering their adepts today; the former complain and murmur; the latter ply their trade and recruit. And to combat this army of unfortunates (or rather this unarmed crowd) which is setting its battalions in motion, crying "I am cold!", which stands agape, muttering,

"I am hungry!", what have you got to appease this legitimate clamor? To these legions of living ghosts you fling the alms of the welfare offices and private charity, that is to say, a crumb of bread every week or every month, leaving it to despair and death to alleviate devouring hunger the rest of the time by robbery or the grave. . . . No one is there to save the poor girl; no one to save the father and daughter. One of them dies a few days later in hospital . . . the other at the home for incurables. . . . Pity, my God, for so much poverty and so many crimes! The hospital, the prison or the Morgue, that is the lot of the poor man and the discharged convict! And you want to discourage the least or the most courageous of these men, those who insist on living, from revolting against society!

It is very hard to tell whether this is a description of the criminal classes or the dangerous classes, whether it deals with poverty or crime, whether it is condemnatory or approving.

At the periods of the worst working-class distress, poverty and crime filled the paper without distinction, as if they were giving expression to the same phenomenon. During the autumn of 1840–41 *La Ruche* wrote: "The working class is in a ferment. Poverty is growing worse and worse. Young workmen, exhausted by work beyond their strength and too badly paid, are succumbing under it. Heavier work and smaller wages are having a simultaneous effect." Crimes and suicides multiplied and pre-empted the news items in the paper, arousing similar comments and a similar pity.[6] Introducing the statistics of the Welfare Office of the XIIth arrondissement, *La Ruche* wrote:

M. Gisquet, the former Prefect of Police, says in his *Mémoires* that there is a crowd of men so famished and so utterly destitute that they seize the putrid meat confiscated from butchers and thrown out at Montfaucon. He goes on to say that there are 10,000 robbers in Paris, 6,000 of whom are always ready to massacre all that stand in their way.

Here the distinction between laboring and dangerous classes disappears. This press, which carries the workers' opinion of themselves, differing little from the bourgeois classes' opinion of them, was heedless of such distinctions and cared little for such definitions. It recorded a genuine fraternity of fate, described and celebrated in verse.

II
The Popular Literature

A popular literaure, with certain characteristics in common with the working-class press, supplies testimony of a similar kind; we must first examine these common features.

The Reality of Fiction

To say that this common fate was described in the popular press and commented on simply as a piece of police news is, indeed, to fall short of the facts. To say that it was sung and balladed would be more correct; it was expressed in a form quite other than that of the modern press, in a language which one would certainly describe as that of fiction rather than reality, once we have discovered that there is such a thing as a reality of fiction.

The working-class papers revealed, voluntarily or involuntarily, the working classes' conviction that they constituted, on the edge of the city and its civilization, a different, alien and hostile society; and they did so in a way to which we must devote some attention, for this preliminary outline of working-class opinion would be incomplete otherwise.

The first thing we observe is the amount of space devoted to literature, and more particularly poetry, in this press and especially in *La Ruche populaire*, which introduced itself in the first issue as "a medley of prose and verse." This interest in literature and poetry was reflected in the first place in the choice of language. Prose and verse were used without distinction in dealing with general problems of the workers' condition, or incidents at work and in the streets, or imaginary tales. Prose, indeed, was more commonly used for imaginary events and poetry for facts, as if verse were a more accurate means of expressing popular realities and represented an ordinary form of popular culture and even language.[7]

The importance accorded to literature and poetry was also reflected by the interest in fiction, as shown by the large amount of space devoted to the contemporary novels which staged the daily dramas of working-class life, or by turning such dramas into fiction. In some respects and on some occasions the distinction between reality and fiction disappeared. Fiction expressed reality better than a news item; it was reality. It took on a strange kind of existence, comparable to that of some of Frédéric Soulié's characters, but even more obviously to the great popular heroes of *Les Mystères de Paris*. Rodolphe existed. "For the past three weeks," a passamenterie maker wrote in a letter published by *La Ruche populaire* on March 5, 1844,

the workers in many of our factories have been unemployed owing to the flooding of the Seine and the Marne. I live at the top of the rue de Charenton, and an honest family—the husband, who is employed at a mechanical sawmill, his wife and two children—lives in a single room on my landing. The shutdown caused by the flooding of the Marne has temporarily plunged this family into poverty. . . . This morning I asked the wife if her husband had any work. "No, not yet," she replied, "but we have hopes of being happier next winter"—"How is that?" I asked—"Because the gentleman who wrote *Les Mystères de Paris,* I don't know his name, is to protect us; and Philippe says that he will go on writing in order to get the poor worker's wages raised. So we have good hopes; though this winter is hard, the next, he says, will be better."

A woman shopkeeper wrote on May 2, 1844: "I am on the point of losing confidence and honor. I have but one resource left. . . . I was reading in *Les Mystères de Paris* that several persons at Bordeaux and Lyon are setting up a bank to provide unemployed workers with loans free of interest." Not only did Rodolphe exist, dealing out justice and aid, but *La Ruche populaire* became Rodolphe. "The role that M. Eugène Sue gives Rodolphe in *Les Mystères de Paris,*" *La Ruche* wrote, "has inspired us with the idea of inquiring after honest and unfortunate families. . . . We are making an earnest appeal to the humanity of wealthy persons." And thenceforth *La Ruche* reported the neediest cases in each issue; it stated it would shortly open a column of "Mysteries of the Workshop." Fiction became reality. Eugène Sue himself, a tireless purveyor of inventions, wrote to the editor of *La Ruche* in January 1844:

You ask my opinion on the line that the editors of *La Ruche populaire* should take. . . . You can prove with figures that wages are too low . . . by comparing the wage rate with the amount needed for a worker's necessities of life. The straightforward statement of receipts and expenditures, a sort of balance sheet of the deplorable situation of the working classes, would, by its painful simplicity, have a cogent and irrefutable authority, that of fact. . . . In some industries women earn only 8 sous a day and on that they have to dress, pay their rent and buy food. I believe that it is a matter of urgency that the situation of the working classes should be demonstrated with facts and incontrovertible figures.[8]

Quite obviously, this is something other than a literary phenomenon or one that could be adequately accounted for by literary criticism. There were, it is true, certain literary circumstances, which have often been studied, particularly the development of social romanticism, the increasing interest accorded in the contemporary literature to the problems of working-class life and the rise of a new generation of worker-poets. These are, however, circumstances less important than the facts, which are the material of social history, but to which conventional social history has not paid sufficient attention, namely, the influence of literature, ranging from the most distinguished to the most mediocre, from the most lasting to the most ephemeral, upon lower-class opinion, within which this literature bulks large. Without some knowledge of this, a description of the lower-class mentality from every point of view —political, economic, religious and moral—remains incomplete and inaccurate. Whether in the form of poems, songs or ballads, of novels or melodramas, written material or, most often, dramatic performances —at a time when reading called for an apprenticeship and an effort that were not within everyone's reach—this literature was an essential element in the popular culture, the culture which the people adopted, whether in street, theater or workshop. Indeed, it should be termed a civilization rather than a culture; for to the lower classes, this literature had an importance and a significance for their mentality and their behavior which it did not have for the other classes. To the bourgeois classes it was an object of culture; to the lower classes, one of the forms of their civilization.[9]

It brought to the lower classes what it could not bring (to the same degree at any rate) to the other classes, and something which it alone could bring them: ideas and sentiments all the more important perhaps in that this literature chose to take a greater interest in the lower classes and described, sang of, staged and inspired them. It made the lower classes more clearly aware of their own condition and attitudes; and, above all, it gave them a language, sentences, words; for the lack or rarity of such words has a vast influence on the workers' mentality and behavior. We ourselves found this in investigating the working-class population of modern Paris and, more particularly, in observing workers and students participating in the same exercises in mass observation, where workers in identical age groups, and exposed to the identical extremely limited and specific subjects of conversation as students, demonstrated a far poorer vocabulary. May not the oath, the blow, be by way of compensation necessary modes of expression, and may not working-class violence be in certain respects simply the result of an inadequate vocabulary?

This certainly applies even more strongly to the Paris population in the first half of the nineteenth century, when illiteracy was widespread, and to the population which had recently migrated to Paris from regions in which illiteracy was even commoner. The popular literature brought to these populations the means of expression they lacked, the more effectively in that, unlike the modern period—in which cinema and broadcasting, which convey images, sounds and rhythms rather than words, compete with such literature—the popular theater and popular novels dominated the workers' leisure time without competition. There are innumerable examples of the influence of this literature, displayed in letters from workers published in the working-class newspapers and in the judiciary reports in the ordinary newspapers. This is the reason for the working classes' avid interest in this literature; and the lower the social category and the more recently the readers had migrated to Paris, the greater the interest. This, too, explains why this literature is so important for our historical investigation: it reconstitutes a lower-class civilization, whose main means of expression it is. Novels, street ballads and melodramas—or at any rate, the most popular of them— all document this lower-class civilization; but, even more importantly, they actually are the lower-class civilization which they reconstitute so accurately. They transmit a forgotten record, a kind of musical score, as it were, of contemporary beliefs and ideas which formal history seems to have left lying by the wayside or perhaps can no longer decipher; without them we would only be able to get at those beliefs and ideas indirectly by way of descriptions, analyses and eyewitness evidence.

One Example: The Popular Theater

It is in this way that the popular theater lives on; and its study is a matter for historical rather than literary criticism. To literary criticism these melodramas are irremediably mediocre and dead, but not to history; for they reconstitute in all fidelity and in all their native crudity a lower-class attitude which can be recovered only indirectly and uncertainly from the political, economic and social documentation. They live with a life well described by Janin in scores of disgruntled reviews in the *Journal des Débats*—later collected in his *Histoire de la littérature dramatique*—which themselves may be regarded as genuine historical documents owing to the terms he uses: "Rereading today these dead, worthless things, feverish dreams of embittered minds," he wrote of Pyat's *Les deux serruriers*, which probably inspired *Les Mystères de Paris*, "one is amazed to find that the doctrines which once brought France within inches of slavery and so cruelly justified Tacitus's admirable expression when speaking of the mob's propensity to plunge into absolute slavery, *ruere in servitutem*, come precisely from these fine dramas composed for the people and by the people."

They were indeed manufactured for the people by skilled craftsmen to the measure of its wishes and its speech. They simply applied the method of that old master craftsman, Restif, "who speaks as they speak in the furious market places. Even the paper and ink he uses to compose his rude volumes resemble a savage art, a literature of brutes," as Pixérécourt commented. And Ducange observed:

Thinking only of pleasing the lowest type of audience, untutored imaginations. . . . What he [Restif] lacked in style, poetry and wit he made up with something more potent in the theater, passion, fanaticism and especially declamation, which he handled like a true tribune of the faubourg Saint-Antoine. A strange person who kept himself up to the level of the most enlightened imaginations by sheer audacity, savage energy and resolution. His success in securing the emotion, the interest, the pity of the ignorant crowd was the inevitable result of the most diligent and arduous study, not of books and literary theories, which have never been concerned with this base part of dramatic literature, but by dint of observing and divining how the people listens to and grasps a dramatic action, how it weeps, why it weeps and the exact moment of tension at which the drama must halt in order to stop neither this side of grief nor the other. He knew that the people does not like or understand long sentences, that it abhors flowery phrases, that it goes for a sharp, short, clear, brutal, insolent turn of speech, and that is why he went straight to his goal, eschewing the subordinate, like a straight left. He also knew that the people is the most outrageous egoist in the world, and he spoke to his people of nothing but its own miseries, virtues, hatreds and loves, beliefs and superstitions. He was the people's apostle; he was its assiduous flatterer, its indefatigable courtier. The scene of all his plays is the hut rather than the palace, the highroad rather than the domestic hearth; in his dramas he wore out more workmen's blouses than frock coats, more homespun than velvet, more clogs than slippers. His dramas had the smell of the barricade; they gave a glimpse of the implicit struggle of poor against rich, strong against weak, oldcomers against newcomers. He was, without meaning it, indeed perhaps without knowing it, a leveler.[10]

Implicit in this whole passage, over and over again, there are surely echoes of the terms "savages," "barbarians," "brutes."

Restif's plays were made for the people. But it would be more correct to say made by the people; and this would bring out more clearly the historical importance of these crude documents. They were not only manufactured to suit popular wishes; they adapted themselves to them and were transformed with them. Thus Frédéric Lemaître was to make *L'Auberge des Adrets*, originally a conventional melodrama with an essentially moral ending, into an irreverent satire, until there came the day when Robert Macaire, disguised as a ragpicker, pulled the crown of France out of the basket on his back.

Such is the social significance of these documents, and it is really surprising that conventional social history has failed to grasp their importance. "Of all cheap melodramas," Janin wrote,

you can say: there is the socialists' cradle! There is the beginning of the right to work, these are the plays which fostered all these terrifying hatreds and ferocious instincts of vengeance unappeased. . . . No, it is not M. Proudhon and his famous formula, of which no one had ever heard before 1848, nor the philosophers—concocters of books and mob orators in diamond type— who have instilled the corruption into overimpressionable minds. It is the cheap dramas and melodramas, the thing enacted in flesh and blood, in action, barely clothed in a few rags, hoarsely gasping of hunger, cold, winter, injustice, horror, cells, the executioner!

Another example: Les Mystères de Paris

For similar reasons and in a similar way, *Les Mystères de Paris* may be regarded as one of the most important documents we possess concerning this lower-class mentality, which we would have no means and no chance of penetrating otherwise. Yet this is not so much because of the deliberate, organized and documented description found in *Les Mystères*—the picture of the laboring classes in themselves and in their relations with the dangerous classes, which expert demographic investigation confirms as precisely accurate—but far more because of the work's success, the common people's enthusiastic reception of a description that was not concerned with them but in which they readily recognized themselves. And so they gradually reshaped it until they rendered it, by means of their collective pressure, a most faithful portrait, transforming this book of the dangerous classes into a book of the laboring classes who, however, retained most of the physical and moral characteristics of the dangerous classes.

Eugène Sue certainly started out with the intention of describing the dangerous classes: "Everyone," he wrote,

has read the admirable pages in which Cooper, the American Walter Scott, depicted the ferocious customs of the savages, their picturesque and poetic speech, the thousand ruses whereby they flee or pursue their foes. We have trembled for the colonists and the town dwellers, to think that so near them there lived and roamed those barbaric tribes sundered so far from civilization by their sanguinary customs. We shall try to place before our readers some episodes in the life of other barbarians as remote from civilization as the savage hordes so well depicted by Cooper. Only, the barbarians of whom we are speaking are in our midst; we can brush elbows with them if we venture into the dens in which they live, where they meet to plot murder and robbery and to share out their victims' spoils. These men have manners of their own, women of their own, a language of their own, a mysterious language replete with baleful images, metaphors dripping blood. Like the savages, these people usually address each other by nicknames borrowed from their energy, their cruelty or certain physical qualities or defects.

Dangerous classes, certainly; but the lower-class public immediately recognized itself, assimilating its own condition to this savage condition, especially to that of the characters who belong to those groups (already described) halfway between poverty and crime. The Slasher at once attracted the lower-class readers' avid attention, as shown in scores of press reports and even in the correspondence received by Sue, approving, correcting, supplementing and protesting. The docker of the quai Saint-Paul, the villain of the rue aux Fèves, became the main character in the book. Sue was forbidden to take him out of the story until the final scene, in which he at last killed him nonetheless.

It was a book of the laboring classes from the start, despite Sue's intention to write a book of the dangerous classes. But it became a book of the laboring classes increasingly as it proceeded, far less as a result of any decision on Sue's part to alter his earlier intention than owing to a collective pressure which imposed this transformation more and more strongly with every instalment.

It matters little what Sue intended: the social conversion (on which everything has been said that can be said), the documentation he compiled, which was compiled for him, with which he was overburdened and with which he overburdened his readers. His increasingly close relations with the Fourierists and the workers of *L'Atelier* undoubtedly account for certain details in the book and for the overloading of the narrative, the last two-thirds of which are cluttered up with social references and social diatribes, a lot of futile antiquarianism which is of no interest to us, and which, so far from strengthening the book's social evidence, merely weakens it. *Les Mystères de Paris* has become outdated by passages such as these, at any rate so far as our type of social history is concerned. Unless we mean to confine ourselves to the conventional exegesis of social literature, to studying ideas and their derivations rather than the facts, there is meager profit to be gained from going through the book to find the attenuated and often distorted echoes of potent systems that can more usefully be approached direct. We know from Sue's correspondence that his readers, especially his lower-class readers, stormed at these lengthy philanthropic digressions, which devoured space and kept readers on tenterhooks at the end of the instalment, wondering whether the She-Wolf would arrive in time to save her lover Martial, or whether the unhappy Fleur-de-Marie would once again escape from the trap set for her. It was no use Sue's saying: "The reader will excuse us from abandoning one of our heroines in such a critical situation at the most interesting moment; we shall in due course reveal what happened next." The book's most important social testimony did not lie there, either for its contemporaries or for us.

The importance of *Les Mystères de Paris* for the investigation of social history lies in the fact that the novel enables us to become acquainted, through this potent popular intervention and the collective pressures to which the author passively submitted, with the physical and moral features which the lower classes attributed to themselves. The deliberate, documented and undoubtedly able description of the lower classes presented by Sue is of small importance. What does count is the description he could not help giving, for reasons which have not been sufficiently appreciated.

This pressure was exerted in the first instance by the effect of popular opinion, which singled out his characters, directed their fate, decided the plot and intervened daily in the shaping of the narrative, either through threatening or admiring letters, which have been preserved, or by the great subterranean wave of popular demand, of which the whole contemporary press has handed down the evidence: protesting against the premature disappearance of the Slasher, refusing to have a half-witted old woman in the artisan Morel's garret,[11] deploring the inaccuracy of some trait of manners, deprecating some particular solution.[12] Though the lower classes immediately recognized themselves in the book from the opening pages on, from as it were, the first bars of the overture, the surprising collective phenomenon of popular success broke all bounds at length only with the story of the misfortunes of the artisan Morel. It was then that most letters were sent to Sue.[13] It was then that there emerged most clearly this intrusive collaboration and this twisting of a story which, though still the book of the dangerous classes, was transformed from instalment to instalment into a book of the laboring classes by the will of the laboring classes themselves as conclusively and surely as if the workmen and artisans of Paris had taken it in turns each day to guide Sue's pen—and a very fertile pen it was. This intervention could easily be traced in detail by making a chronological study of the correspondence and the serial and by comparing the successive editions of the novel.

It is more important to stress another fact, one so obvious that it is astonishing it has not yet been appreciated. The social importance of this novel, like that of other important novels of the period, is due to the fact that in each case the authors were describing a society and a period of which they were part. What is the use of looking for sources, which are usually nothing of the sort, and finding connections which may be no more than coincidences between one particular book and other books, or between one particular narrative and newspaper items? If we use sources other than those generally employed in literary exploration, we shall have no difficulty at all in discovering other works and other circumstances which might equally be thought to have had an influence. Such erudite games are of little interest in comparison with the verification to which expert demographic research gives us access, designating the cause quite simply and in the most commonplace manner. The extraordinary authenticity of *Les Mystères de Paris*, like that of *Les Misérables*, is due to the fact that both these works passively recorded the demographic and economic developments we have already described. They were of their time and could not do otherwise than attribute to the society they were describing characteristics with which their authors were as familiar as their most untutored contemporaries. Hence the physical and moral appearances which could only be what they were; hence, especially, the immense material and moral misery which to our novelists, as to all Parisians of the period, reflected the formidable urban expansion we have already identified as the major cause of the pathological state of the capital. So the deliberate descriptions, and the literary or historical explanations that may be given of them, hardly matter. What does interest us are the involuntary traces left on these works—in details which are of little significance from the literary point of view— by these compelling developments. The only service that literary criticism can render both to history and to literature is to find out why the literature of this period was more permeable to such general circumstances than that of other periods.

It is, indeed, this permeability which makes Sue's testimony so important. Not the voluntary testimony he labors to give us, but the accord between his description and the description we should expect on the basis of demographic and economic investigation, the testimony concerning the facts, but especially the testimony—far more valuable and unobtainable elsewhere—concerning contemporary opinion on those facts. "Despite all its defects," Dumas wrote later, "*Les Mystères de Paris* was a terrific book; the people played its part in it, a leading part."

It was a book of the people, indeed, because it was, to some degree, written by the people and, moreover, was recognized by the people as its own book. It impresses us too as such because of its terrific popular success. Prudish contemporary criticism and a mendacious tradition went far astray in affecting to see it as the book of crime. Most contemporaries were not deceived; they detected the face of poverty beneath the mask of crime. Balabine, for example, noted in his diary for July 31, 1843:

Although not very productive in general, the literary year has been marked by a number of publications which rightly deserve the attention accorded them by the public and the press. In the popular novel the first place correctly belongs to *Les Mystères de Paris,* in which, often behind the exaggerated depictions of imaginary and fantastic characters, you find lifelike portraits drawn by the hand of a master, boldly sketched and vigorously colored. The author's talent is undeniable; the only thing in his work that might be arguable is the moral tone. For my part, I believe it is moral; at all events, it is certainly nature taken in the act in this terrifying abyss called Paris, where on July 27, the anniversary of the Glorious Revolution of 1830, the mayors of the twelve arrondissements distributed aid in cash to nearly 70,000 poor. Poverty breeds prostitution and prostitution gives birth to poverty, a doubly vicious and deadly circle, around which a vast population revolves, for these 70,000 indigents are only the registered and licensed poor, the patented poor, as it were. Talking of patents, I will quote yet another figure, to wit, the figure for the patents of every sort distributed among the industrial class of Paris, amounting to the staggering total of 80,000! So much for glut and competition, for what is a patent but the hope of a refuge against competition? Eugène Sue has cast his net into the muddy springs of poverty, and that is the reason for the really fabulous popularity of his book; in it the poor have been able to see their reflection and the rich have found something new.

In July 1843, too, a contributor to *La Ruche populaire* wrote:

The extraordinary pleasure and the emotion the workers feel when reading *Les Mystères de Paris* are well known; it is assuredly one of the most novel and remarkable works that have ever appeared on the literary scene. It is a bold and poetic picture of the dangers, the traps, the hellish duplicity and the frightful poverty that assail and destroy the proletarians, or workers lacking all resources, all security, and with no one to act as their protector.

This summed up the working classes' judgment of the book, but also of themselves, extremely well. This work of the dangerous classes had become the work of the laboring classes by popular demand; but of laboring classes which had retained many of the physical and even moral features of the dangerous classes, the same rags, the same ugliness, the same violence, blending with the dangerous classes in a common fate.

"Barbarians," "savages," "nomads": such were the terms used by the lower and by other classes to designate the lower classes, summing up facts and reflecting an opinion on those facts. Buret used them; so did Proudhon in many of his works, in which the distinction between laboring and dangerous classes was eliminated and both were merged in a brotherhood of poverty, described in the same terms. "These barbarians," Proudhon wrote, "whom we have agreed to call proletarians";[14] and: "This multitude, indigent, unlettered and barbarous, granted, but not vile."[15] But it is Hugo's description of working-class revolt in *Les Misérables* that stands out.

"The faubourg Saint-Antoine," Hugo wrote,

is a human reservoir. The Revolutionary earthquake made cracks in it through which popular sovereignty is flowing. This sovereignty may do evil; it may go astray, like any other; but, even when it is on the wrong tack, it is still great. In '93, according as the idea in the air was good or bad, whether fanaticism or enthusiasm was the order of the day, there sometimes went out from the faubourg Saint-Antoine savage legions, sometimes bands of heroes. Savage. Let us be clear about this word. What did these shaggy men want, who, ragged, howling, ferocious, with bludgeon upraised, pike a-tilt, rushed on the old Paris as it gazed astounded on the days pregnant with Revolutionary chaos? They wanted the end of oppression, the end of tyranny, the end of the sword, work for the husband, education for the child, social tolerance for the wife, liberty, equality, fraternity, bread for all, progress. It was this progress, this holy, good and sweet thing, for which they clamored, driven to the end of their tether, beside themselves. Yes, they clamored for it, terrible, half-naked, cudgel in fist, yells issuing from their throats. They were savages, true enough; but the savages of civilization.

This coincidence of descriptions, and especially the choice of the same terms, cannot be due merely to chance or literary device. The identification of the workers of the faubourg Saint-Antoine with savages was something more than a bold simile. It simply expressed a fact of opinion. Savages, barbarians, nomads, the laboring classes were considered as such and for reasons we have specified, namely, that the terms commonly used and recurring so constantly in these works expressed the truly racial character of social antagonism in the Paris of this period. The social groups considered each other, judged each other and confronted each other in terms of race.

CHAPTER FOUR

The Preoccupation with Physical Characteristics and Its Significance

Let us take this further. The judgments which each group passed on the other involved physical characteristics considered to be peculiarly its own and as specific and permanent as racial characteristics, but signifying moral qualities too. Historical observation coincides here with contemporary sociological observation. The violence of the social struggles in Paris during the period cannot be understood unless it is realized that it was based upon physical and, even more specifically, morphological, foundations. The groups considered each other, judged each other and confronted each other physically. It will not do, of course, to minimize the ideological conflicts and to ignore the large number of works dealing with them. But for the simple reason that they have often been surveyed, and well surveyed at that, all we need do here is to add a few touches and a few shadows to the picture. Bourgeois opinion on the lower-class physique summed up the proletarian threat better than all the treatises by eminent economists and articles in the conservative press, and betrayed the secret of the contemporary fear of them: "It was an extraordinary thing," Tocqueville wrote of the aftermath of February 1848, "to see this whole huge city crammed with wealth, and indeed this great nation, wholly in the hands of those who owned nothing. . . . Many people expected acts of unheard-of violence."[1] Similarly, the working-class judgment of bourgeois physique summed up better than any ideological assertion what the people thought of the various aspects of bourgeois power. Not only did the physical characteristics in each camp sum up all the rest, but their part in the political and social history of the period, on the barricades and in the day-to-day history of the streets, was at least as important as the clash of ideas, by reason of the phenomena of attraction and repulsion, of love and disgust they expressed and reflected in hundreds of random and savage tussles.

I

The Origins of the Preoccupation with Physical Characteristics

What we are in fact doing here is simply availing ourselves of the results of modern research. Sociology, especially in the United States, has revealed the effects of such judgments on individual and collective relationships. These problems, first measured by modern sociology, were, as a matter of fact, some of those that most engaged the attention of those moralists, philosophers and physicians of the end of the eighteenth century and during the first decades of the nineteenth century whose work attracted the widest interest in the period we are examining. "Moral sympathy too," Cabanis wrote in 1797,

produces noteworthy effects. By virtue of their signs alone, impressions can be transmitted from one sensitive being, or being who is considered to be sensitive, to other beings, who then seem to identify themselves with him in order to share these impressions. We observe persons attracting or repelling one another. Their ideas and impressions at one time respond to each other by means of a secret speech as rapid as the impressions themselves and attain perfect harmony; at another, this speech is a blast of discord. And every hostile passion, terror, anger, indignation, vengeance may suddenly inflame a vast multitude at hearing, or even at the mere sight of, some person, either because he excites them by expressing these passions or because he rouses them against himself by his very appearance.[2]

Maine de Biran in his *Mémoire sur les perceptions obscures*, written in 1807, referred to "moral sympathy, the sentiments of the soul and the commingled passions based upon communication between one man and another in the complex relationships engendered by the social state."

A fact of science

It would be beside the point here to describe the stages in the research on these physical and moral relationships of man—to borrow the title of a work by Cabanis published in 1802, in which he assembled all the ancient and contemporary knowledge and beliefs relating to his subject. "The ancients," Cabanis stated,

held that certain particular outward appearances, that is to say, a particular physiognomy, figure, proportion of limbs, color of skin, bodily habit and condition of the blood vessels, had a fairly close and constant correspondence with certain intellectual proclivities or particular passions. The moderns have supplemented this doctrine, have eliminated erroneous views and have perceived that it could be placed upon sounder foundations, more consistent with the present state of enlightenment.

It is evident, in particular, that despite corrections, differences of emphasis and complications, research in the early years of the nineteenth century centered on the same facts as the older research and attempted, as in the past, to attribute ascertained moral correspondences to physical characteristics visible to the naked eye. At that stage in medical knowledge, outward appearances were more important than the study of internal reactions, which could not yet be investigated. Internals had to be assessed physically and morally from externals.

It is well known that the writings which enjoyed the greatest renown at that period were the earlier works of Lavater and the more recent work of Gall. Lavater[3] believed that every man resembled, to a greater or lesser degree, some animal, whose primitive character exerted an influence on his "to such an extent that, if souls were physically visible, one would distinctly see a strange phenomenon, namely, that each individual of the human species corresponds to one of the species of the animal creation." Gall, whose system[4] had already been worked out when he arrived in Paris in 1807, held that the brain was the organ of all proclivities and that the form of the head and skull suggested a way to detect the basic qualities and faculties. The influence of these theories on the major writers of the period is equally well known. If Balzac is to be credited, they inspired the *Comédie humaine*. Eugène Sue's criminals present all the characteristics which Lavater and Gall attributed to degenerates.[5]

A fact of opinion

From systems to beliefs: It is more important to stress that Balzac and Sue were simply expressing the influence that these systems—transformed into popular beliefs—had upon contemporary opinion.

In some respects, nothing is simpler than Gall's theory. Gall himself related his earlier experiments at Vienna:

I assembled a number of persons at my house, drawn from the lowest classes and engaged in various occupations, such as fiacre driver, street porter and so on. I gained their confidence and induced them to speak frankly by giving them money and having wine and beer distributed to them. When I saw that they were favorably disposed, I urged them to tell me everything they knew about one another, both their good and their bad qualities, and I carefully examined their heads. This was the origin of the craniological chart which was seized upon so avidly by the public; even artists took it over and distributed a large number among the public in the form of masks of all kinds.

The propagation of these beliefs was encouraged by the conversion of eminent physicians, notably Broussais, whose consultations and lectures[6] popularized the system. The influence of the press was even greater; papers from the *Journal de la Société phrénologique de Paris* were widely published, mainly in the crime press. Equipped with the hypotheses of Gall and Lavater, doctors in hospitals and convict prisons found no difficulty in discovering wolf-men and lion-men among their clientele.[7] The journalists followed suit. Every major crime and execution was commented upon along these lines. Certain spectacular arrests were presented as victories of phrenology, the Saint-Clair and Daumas-Dupin case, for example, as reported by Moreau-Christophe:

In 1829, a young couple had had their throats cut at Attenville, in the forest of Montmorency, by two travelers whom they had lodged at their inn, the Auberge de la Croix-Verte. The murderers were two convicts who had escaped from the Rochefort prison. One of them, Daumas-Dupin, was arrested and executed. Despite a vigorous search, Saint-Clair could not be found. However, one day in 1830, the conversation at table at a hotel in a small town in the Dauphiné turned on Gall and Lavater. A man dressed in black, a Lyon doctor famous for his studies in phrenology, as it became known later, was displaying expert knowledge of their theories. Another guest sitting fairly close to him was skeptical, a pale man to whom no one except the man in black had paid much attention. The pale man suddenly declared: "If everything this gentleman has said is true, any sorcerer who taught the law such secrets ought to be burned alive." Thereupon the man in black scrutinized the pale man more closely and recognized all the features of a robber and murderer in his face. It was Saint-Clair, who was arrested on the spot and guillotined at Versailles in 1831.

From beliefs to systems: It is highly probable that these theories influenced contemporary opinion because they ran along the same lines as it did and merely contributed an apparent scientific justification backed by eminent opinion; the theories were not transformed into popular beliefs, but rather reinforced beliefs held previously.

Nothing is commoner in popular psychology at all places and in all periods than this attention to physical characteristics, which are taken at sight to signify moral characteristics and are crystallized in nicknames, which, however, differ in country and town, as research in folklore has shown. The village nicknames, hereditary in each family, are due to the need to select a physical characteristic which may very well die out, to distinguish people who intermarry and bear the same surnames; whereas urban nicknames are attached to one particular person and relate to physical or moral characteristics peculiar to himself.

This goes back to the beginning of history, but is more frequent at certain periods and in certain overcrowded environments. It then extends to all everyday relationships and to relationships among groups, the sum of social facts, to bodily appearances, to physical details or, even more simply, to mere impressions of a good-looking or ill-favored appearance. "The members of the rival associations," Perdiguier wrote of the *compagnonnages*, "young men traveling to gain skills and learn their trade, look upon each other as repulsive, hideous, frightful, unworthy to see the light of day."[8] The stamp of the *compagnonnage* on this feature of working-class behavior is evident. "I do not know yet if I am the father of a wolf, a fox, a he-goat or a dog," Père Huguenin said in George Sand's novel [*Le Compagnon du Tour de France*]. Parisian nicknames were adapted by opposition to or in imitation of the nicknames of the *compagnonnages*. "The Parisians," Nadaud wrote, "called us yokels and we called them 'cherry sellers,' by which we meant that they were good for nothing but selling baskets of cherries in the streets." But here we are dealing with something wider than the *compagnonnage*. The physical characteristics of individuals and groups have never, perhaps, been so strongly emphasized as in these years of social upheaval; they were used as weapons both by the bourgeoisie and by the common people.

II
The Working-Class Physique

To note that the Paris working class was ugly in most of the contemporary documents is not enough. It must also be noted that the physical appearance of the laboring classes was the same as that attributed to the dangerous classes in the reports of street incidents in the newspapers; in the picturesque literature—except for a few sentimental tales for romantic ladies to dream about, painting such unrealistic portraits of ordinary people as the story of Fleur-de-Marie in the illustrated edition of *Les Mystères de Paris*; and even in the social literature, as shown in Flora Tristan's diary for April 11, 1843, where she speaks of "this brutal, ignorant, vain people, so disagreeable to rub shoulders with, so repulsive when seen close up"; and in the iconography, especially in caricature, which has often been studied, though attention to the demographic facts reveals fresh merits in it.

The whole of the lower-class revolt is present in Daumier, the man of the crowd and its wrath. But it is stamped with such evident biological characteristics that Daumier's drawings become—at least as much as *Les Misérables*—a document for the history of the period, both for the conventional history of political struggles in Paris (as has often been demonstrated), and for the type of history in which we descry, far below the surface, the biological effects of the growth in the population of Paris: hunger, crime and death. This is the significance of Daumier's earliest sketches, contemporary with the Revolution of 1830, and especially of his illustrations to Fabre's *La Nemesis médicale* in 1840, in which the cholera epidemic of 1832 is recalled with horrid clarity. "Daumier was commissioned to illustrate a cheap poetico-medical publication," Baudelaire wrote,

and made some marvelous drawings. One of them, relating to the cholera, shows a public square flooded, riddled, with light and heat. The Paris sky, faithful to its ironic habit in the great scourges and the great political hubbubs, is splendid; it is white, blazing, incandescent. The shadows are black and sharp. A corpse lies across a doorway. A woman rushes into the house, stopping her nose and mouth. The square lies deserted under the glare, more desolate than a crowded square of which a riot has made a solitude. In the background the silhouettes of two or three small hearses harnessed to comic old crocks, and in the midst of this forum of desolation, a poor strayed dog, with nowhere to go and nothing to think of, bone-lean, sniffs at the parched flagstones, his tail wedged between his legs.

What one mainly notices in the representation of the various aspects of popular revolt is the appearance of the people. The sturdy working printer—in the flower of strength, health and virile splendor, embodying the Freedom of the Press, drawn from a trade which made up a working-class élite and transfigured by the beauty of the symbol—is quite an exception. In most of the other drawings the lower classes, even in their hours of glory, are desperately ugly, especially in the drawing relating to the Revolutionary Days of 1830, in which a band of half-naked sweepers passes along the Seine in front of the Assembly, a strong contrast visible between the beauty of their muscular frame and the bestiality of their faces, a contrast to be found in many other contemporary documents. Balzac wrote of a proletarian awaiting his turn in Judge Popinot's anteroom in the rue du Fouarre. "His chest, half-bare, displayed swelling muscles, the index of a temperament of brass which had helped him to bear a vast epic of misfortunes."

Daumier's people is even more hideous and repulsive when depicted in its daily life, away from the great public demonstrations of its existence. Not merely the Parisian "freebooters," whom Daumier rigs out in bourgeois disguise, who plunder the bourgeois as bourgeoisly as you please, but also, and especially, the social groups which *Le Rivarol de 1842*[9] described as follows:

Daumier and Travies are two caricaturists who have had a lot of fun sketching poor human nature in Paris. Old concierges, drunks, ragpickers and the whole race whose privilege it is to arouse hearty laughter in those whose hearts find refreshment not only in everything ridiculous, but in everything ugly and every social misery, these can be seen illustrated in the windows of Aubert and Martinet.

Beside Daumier, who was chosen to depict some of the most hideous characters in *Les Mystères de Paris* in the first illustrated edition, Travies was probably the artist who depicted the people as most repulsive and sometimes most ferocious. Though the leading character in Travies's series around 1830 was Mayeux, the lecherous hunchback with a monkey's face who represented every aspect of the triumphant bourgeoisie—Mayeux as shopkeeper, Mayeux as national guard, a huge bearskin on his head, Mayeux up the greasy pole—until he was eclipsed by M. Prudhomme; yet the street as sketched by Travies was peopled mainly with such characters as the woman selling phosphorous matches, the safety-chain seller, the gutter scraper and the ragpicker, sometimes as Liard, the philosophical ragpicker, but more often as the wretches who frequented the barrières, living with their dogs, spending their time fighting, men against dogs. The people were never to be depicted as such savages as in Travies's drawings; in *Les Mystères de Paris* he gave the Schoolmaster and his frightful offspring faces which really are those of wild beasts.

Despite differences which are a matter for art criticism rather than historical criticism, Gavarni endowed the people with similar characteristics in the series in *Le Diable à Paris* and in the collection devoted to the police courts,[10] in which women stallkeepers from Les Halles, mattress-pickers and the old women drunks from the quartier Maubert invade the court. So too Monnier, in a little book, *Scènes populaires*, of which he wrote in the 1862 reprint that he had "dramatized what Parent-Duchatelet described; it is in a way a book of social medicine." Two facts in *Scènes populaires* stand out particularly: the choice of the savage spectacle on the place de Grève, and the anonymous condition of top-floor lodgers, those who do not even have a name and are identified merely as " a clear voice, a hoarse voice, a person."

Ugly to others, the people was perhaps ugly in its own eyes too; at any rate, it had little connection with the criteria to which George Sand referred in *Le Compagnon du Tour de France* in 1851:

At that time, some dozen years ago, society people who had no direct contact with the people of the workshop might have found that I had made my character Pierre Huguenin too handsome. A well-bred female, as the expression goes, can love beauty in a man of no family; that's often happened! This so-called inferiority of race or sex is a prejudice which now no longer even has the excuse of being harbored in good faith. . . . What will seem strange, and what can be said with certainty, is that Pierre Huguenin had no inkling of his own beauty and that neither the men nor the women in his village had much more notion of his beauty than he had. It is not that man is born in any class without a feeling for beauty, but this feeling needs to be developed by the study of art and the habit of comparison.

Until famous popular books—George Sand's among them—had developed this feeling for beauty and until literature, going from one extreme to the other, came to confer every moral and physical quality upon the proletarian, "the sublime," the fact remains that during our period the same standards were not applied to the proletarian as to others, or else he was simply regarded as most significantly ugly.

III
The Bourgeois Physique

It must be borne in mind that this bourgeois disgust was matched by a lower-class disgust and that the physical appearance which the common people saw in, or attributed to, the bourgeoisie is equally important for the study of social relationships. It was in the work of Daumier, of whom Champfleury said that "he was chosen by the people to express its wrath and hatred," that the features attributed by the working classes to the bourgeois classes were depicted in the most exact detail, the physical appearances borrowed by the caricaturist from the people's way of seeing things, but restored to and imposed upon the people's view.[11] The bourgeoisie in Philipon's *La Caricature*, as embodied in the new political personnel, the ministers, the bankers and the King, grotesque and adipose,[12] was greasy, pot-bellied, lecherous, hypocritical, selfish, irremediably ugly and absolutely repulsive. The bourgeoisie represented in every kind of disguise by Robert Macaire, by turns banker, commercial traveler, broker, stockholder and philanthropist in the 100 plates published by *Le Charivari*,[13] was mendacious, sensual, enemy to the lower classes and invariably ugly, though marked with the wrinkles suited to its various occupations. Writing in 1852, Menche de Loisne stressed both the significance and the repercussions of this series: "Robert Macaire," he wrote, came to typify modern society. This rogue and murderer was appointed to represent the bourgeoisie. In the winter of 1847 a minister died in Paris, and we happened to be strolling on the boulevards at the precise moment when the funeral procession passed by. Deputations from all the public corporations walked in the procession; solicitors, barristers, notaries, deputies, peers of the realm filed slowly past the crowd. Then came the hearse; the tassels were held by ministers. The people laughed and joked. Not a man took off his hat. Suddenly, just as the coffin was passing us, a voice shouted contemptuously: "What a crew of Robert Macaires!" The people clapped and laughed. . . . This happened in 1847, one year before the February Revolution, fifteen months before the fatal June days.[14]

Indeed, certain outbreaks of working-class violence are barely intelligible unless we take account of the physical facts as expressed in the major political crises, but also in daily incidents in the streets, bourgeois ugliness inevitably provoking the rough word or the blow. In the files of the municipal police there are scores of examples of protests by bourgeois who were thrashed, had stones dropped on their head when passing under a scaffolding or were splashed all over, for no known reason—or at any rate no reason known to them.[15]

It is behavior, not simply opinion, with which we have now to deal. The opinion which the lower classes held of the bourgeoisie, but also the opinion which the bourgeoisie held of the lower classes and imposed upon them, together account for working-class behavior; not only in its solemn manifestations, to which conventional history devotes a great deal of attention, but also in the settlement of scores in detail and from one day to the next. The great public disturbances are unintelligible unless these are examined. Regarded as they were by others and by themselves as relegated to the very edge of urban civilization, to the very borders of the domain of evil, it is not surprising that the working classes should have behaved in accordance with that opinion and that verdict. Savages they were called, savages they must be. Savages they would be, therefore, in every way and at every moment of their existence.

PART III

Behavior

Savage this population was above all for the brutality and the cult of strength that distinguished it from the rest of the population; it claimed brutality for itself as, so to speak, its own particular mode of expression.

Manners and customs have changed a great deal. They had already changed when Emile Souvestre, recalling his youth and the workers' cult of sheer strength, wrote in *Confessions d'un ouvrier* at the close of the nineteenth century: "In this regard we had the notions of savages; like them we took brutality and pugnacity for courage." They are even more different nowadays, for the workers in the great cities are no longer addicted to violence nor regard it as the best way of asserting their existence, their distinct character or their superiority. A study of working-class demands, as observed during disputes with employers, for example, or even a description of daily life in the workshop, or of workers and sport, or of workers' frequenting physical culture institutes, would show that the workers now express themselves quite differently and use a quite different language, and that physical strength in itself is no longer so highly regarded nor has the same significance.

Things were different in the first half of the nineteenth century, when a great many workers had no means of asserting an existence which was virtually denied them save by violence, their fists, brutality—the law of working-class life; but a law, like the workers themselves, set apart from the law of the city, foreign to it, likely to clash with it some day and to lead those who abandoned themselves to it into the consequence inherent in the savage life: criminality.

I

The Violence of the Compagnonnages

At certain periods, in particular during the first ten years of the Restoration, in certain trades and in certain districts in Paris, working-class violence undoubtedly had characteristics which were foreign to the city and were simply an extension into the heart of the city of *compagnonnage* disputes, the main feature of which was that they were distinctively provincial and rural. The workmen's riots which broke out on certain evenings on the Ile Saint-Louis or near the Grève or in the faubourg Saint-Denis or at the barrières, filling the city jails with workers otherwise conscientious, industrious and sober, were simply the urban expression of quarrels between the *compagnonnages* which flourished vigorously at that time; Agricol Perdiguier, recalling those years, later wrote: "The *compagnonnages* were hostile armies, rival associations."[1]

These acts of violence were purely the affair of the *compagnonnages*, and they broke out in Paris in precisely the same way as they did elsewhere along the traditional routes of the Tour de France, which was one long battle, for violence flared haphazard at work sites, inns or byways from which "those garlanded *coursières*, so well known to the journeymen workers, which traverse France as the bird flies," as George Sand put it, debouched onto the highway. Clashes occurred especially at certain places which seemed to generate perpetual violence and battles simply because they had previously been the scene of ancient memorable encounters. They invariably broke out at unavoidable intersections or where rivers had to be crossed; at Nantes, where, the local white wine aiding, violence was endemic; at Blois, where the epic battle occurred in 1827, from which George Sand took her description of the fight between *gavots* and *drilles*; and particularly in the lands of the Midi, which, according to Perdiguier, "witnessed real wars between workers. The plain of the Crau was a place of carnage in the old days. Vergèze and Mus, near Lunel, and the village of Ners, not far from Alais, have seen blood redden their fields; great numbers of journeymen were hurt there and others left for dead." Paris was a place of *compagnonnage* violence because it was one of the main crossroads of the Tour de France.

These were purely *compagnonnage* acts of violence, too, because they conformed to traditions of fighting which were foreign to the urban traditions. The technique of combat was not the same; it was reduced to a grapple with bare hands, simply a struggle between two strong men, many examples of which were given by Agricol Perdiguier.[2] No weapons but fists, staves and cudgels. "In those days," said Perdiguier,

the journeymen, chiefly the blacksmiths, farriers, joiners, stonemasons, cobblers, bakers and tanners, could wield the cudgel and often attacked with it. A soldier would have had to give ground to a journeyman, for his saber would have bent or broken under the cudgel; it was a formidable weapon. After serving six or seven years, a soldier could return home as fencing master or assistant fencing master; a journeyman went home as master or assistant master of cudgels.

The technique differed, too, in that individual fights were exceptional unless the fighters were acting as champions of their groups to settle collective scores. And the places were different, though some battles were fought in the central districts near workshops and work sites: "The *compagnonnage* spirit, which has penetrated the hatters, as well as other workers," the *Journal des Débats* noted on November 9, 1825, "is producing the most deplorable results. The hatters are divided into two corporations, one called the companions of duty, or 'the destroyers [*dévorants*],' the other the good lads, or 'the druggists [*droguistes*].' On October 7 members of these two corporations engaged in a bloody battle." And again on June 16, 1827:

About noon the day before yesterday, several groups of hatters, known as the "watered-silk pursemakers of the good lads," formed in the rue des Rosiers and the streets adjacent. Other hatters, known as "*compagnons* of duty," came up and a savage battle ensued. That evening the "good lads" again attacked the "*compagnons* of duty" who had assembled "*chez la mère*" [at the "mother house"] in the rue de Charonne. Another battle with cudgels broke out. Twenty workmen were arrested and taken to the Prefecture of Police.

But the older *compagnonnage* associations more usually met and fought elsewhere, some way out of Paris and away from the Parisians, the gendarmes and sightseers, mostly at the barrière de Monceau or over by Bercy.[3]

These acts of violence were purely affairs of the *compagnonnages*, in that they were the expression of problems solely of concern to the rival associations, mostly having no connection with events in Paris. This made them more conspicuous; but what at the same time made them more mysterious to the authorities, who recorded them without understanding them, was that the economic situation had improved and that there was nothing in the labor market or the wage rates to explain what drove workmen to try to murder each other like this.

Obviously it was often purely a matter of the interests of the craft. "On May 23, 1833, 50 joiners, armed with the staves known as journeymen's staves, went to the market at Sceaux to prevent comrades of theirs who had become the owners of a joinery, thus contravening their association's statutes, from continuing work. One of them was thrown off a wall and was hit on the head with a staff."[4] But even more often the reason was ancient matters of honor, and this is fairly evident since the period was more tranquil and labor seemed to have fewer causes for complaint. "On November 5, 1836," states a gendarmerie report, "groups of joiners and bakers came from different directions to the plain of Neuilly to settle an old *compagnonnage* quarrel between them. The joiners were 500, their adversaries 100. Three of the latter who came forward to parley were ill-treated in a cruel and cowardly fashion."[5]

Some forms of violence thus stood out among the Parisian violence, quite different from it, very evident and easy to identify, stemming from a tradition which was not that of Paris.

II
Parisian Violence

These *compagnonnage* traditions of violence, however, were concurrent with other, truly Parisian traditions of violence and blended with them in a behavior which was no longer that of the *compagnonnages*, but Parisian. They were clearly expressed in the brutality displayed by the Paris working class, regardless of origin, during the second half of the July Monarchy.

The Paris working class was no less brutal than the *compagnonnages*, but brutal in a different way.

It is true that biological pressures did not necessarily lead to violence. Urban levels of living and modes of life tamed the body, attenuated the strength and directed a vigor, which in any case was less energetic than that of journeymen, in other directions. One of the many contemporary testimonies to urban degeneration was that by Corbon who, in *Le secret du peuple de Paris*, subdivided the lower classes into three groups: "the first inoffensive, the second merely vicious, the third aggressive." Of the first he wrote: "Its way of subsisting and its general hygiene are as ill-conceived as may well be. This section of the population is in general native to Paris and usually the greatly impoverished scion of several Parisian generations." He went on:

The three categories of the lower class account for hardly more than one-fifth of the total mass of the proletarian population. If you asked the first group for its secret, and if it could put it into words, it would confess that it has no great ambition; that its enfeebled temper and blood are not in themselves such as to engender violent passions; that its imagination cannot reach out to an ideal; that it takes things as they come, does the best it can; and its highest felicity is the gallery of a popular theater.

It was, however, a violent people, particularly in some trades. In all contemporary descriptions the butchers were associated with scenes of brutality, both at work and at recreation at their favorite shows—the animal fights at the barrière du Combat, of which they were the most assiduous frequenters. But the population as a whole was violent, though in a different way; not with the muscular violence of the robust journeymen, accustomed as they were to walking, to working the fields and to the physical labor of digging, but with the high-strung violence of ill-fed people over-addicted to strong liquor; not the collective violence codified and governed by the special rules of the great *compagnonnage* encounters, unleashed in the open fields beyond the barrières, but the violence of the settling of individual scores at the factory gate, at a street corner, at a dance or during the great days of debauch at La Courtille, which to all contemporaries summed up working-class manners. "If you want to know about the temper of the workers of the faubourg Saint-Antoine," said Luchet, "you must study them on Monday, for that is their holiday. You must enter the taverns at the place du Trône with them and watch how they settle their scores by the *savate*."[6]

The practice of the *savate* did, indeed, best sum up the special characteristics of working-class violence in the Paris of the period. It was born, grew up and was practiced in the low-life districts of the city and at the barrières, at the barrière de la Courtille especially, the worst of the lot, where it had its first theoretician in a former bakery hand, once the terror of the place, Michel, nicknamed Pisseux:[7] "The *savate*," Théophile Gautier wrote in *La Presse* of August 17, 1846,

has long been held to be a kind of dirty fighting reserved for "the pallid hooligan with weakly body and complexion yellow as an old penny." Indeed, practically all that had been seen was frightful bandits in tattered overalls, frayed caps and down-at-heel shoes making mysterious and sinister motions with their hands, the terror of peaceable citizens, and motions with their feet which caused patrolmen caught unawares suddenly to sit down in the gutter.

This "villains' fencing" or "*Cour des Miracles* boxing" was practiced with the guard low and clenched when the hands were merely a defensive weapon; or forward and open to push the opponent's nose up; legwork and the kick to the groin were the main thing. Although codified by Michel and his pupils, and later practiced by the Paris dandies and Sue's friends, this low-life technique still predominated in the low-life districts and drew its main inspiration from them.[8] But news items in the press and the police court files also show that it was the ordinary technique of the Paris workers.

It appears, then, that the workers' appreciation of strength and their habitual violence were not solely matters of the *compagnonnages*. These urban traditions needed, however, to be mentioned in order to explain the changes in *compagnonnage* violence in the Paris environment, its aggravation and its deterioration.

III
Parisian Violence and Compagnonnage *Violence*

Aggravation is the right word in an initial period—to the end of the crisis coinciding with the early years of the July Monarchy—and, after that, deterioration.

In Paris the journeymen associations were permanently at odds not only among themselves, but also with the Parisian trade groups. They brushed shoulders on a narrow labor market, on the same jobs, in the same streets, sometimes even in the same lodging houses. Within the great associations themselves there was fierce competition between the groups. Provinces and departments broke down into cantons and villages. Recalling 1834, a year in which jealousy and hatred flared up between one group and another, Nadaud wrote:

It was in the first place the journeymen making the Tour de France who continued to wage bloody warfare. Among those from the Creuse there were clans from cantons and even communes. If they happened to meet on the same building job, it was a race to see who would best the other and chuck him off the scaffolding. Then began one of those fights which could profit only the boss.[9]

The *compagnonnages* in the provinces inflamed the fights in Paris. "If we had behaved like cowards," Perdiguier wrote, speaking of encounters in the fields and on the highway, "it would certainly have been known in the lodging houses in Paris; collective insults to the corporation of masons could not have gone unpunished at any price." And competition with the Paris workers not only at work, but after work and on holiday, supplemented the rivalry among associations and regional or village groups. In the overcrowded city one lot lived beside the other, or at the other's expense and, in any event, before their eyes. Nadaud's *Mémoires* abound in traces of such encounters and humiliations, the jeers of shop assistants in the rue Saint-Fiacre, roaring with laughter at the masons calling their mates on neighboring scaffoldings by the nicknames of their native place or trade; the attitude of passers-by "when they saw us gathering at evening at the doors of our lodging houses or covered with plaster as we left the job"; and, even more bitterly resented, girls refusing to dance with them at La Courtille. Hence the acts of *compagnonnage* violence recorded in the police reports and narrated by Nadaud. These broke out during the early years of the July Monarchy and differed from any before or after. Violence at work: "His great reputation," Nadaud wrote of one of the journeymen in 1831, "was due to his huge strength. He used to boast that he had never met his match in carrying quarry stones up the ladder, or in wrestling matches taken on for a bet, or in the journeymen's games. It is impossible to realize nowadays how highly feats of strength were prized at that time." Violence on holidays: "Brawls used to break out on Sundays at the barrière Poissonnière between Auvergnats and Limousins. The state of mind and the customs were such that if workers out for a holiday returned to their lodgings without a thorough set-to, they could not say they had enjoyed themselves; we were tough in those days."

The significance of this violence went far beyond mere brawls at work or on holidays. "At that time," wrote Nadaud, "a spirit of pride and independence grew up among the masons from the Creuse which did not permit them to feel inferior to workers in any other trade whatever." Here the history of working-class violence, the everyday tale of brawls, joins a larger history, that of social and political events. "In the district where we lived," says Nadaud,

there was a great deal of wanton violence which lasted for two or three years. The freedom that we wanted and the papers promised us each day inflamed our spirits, and as we had very little education, we balked at the least insult like vigorous mules whipped in open country. We felt we should learn to chastise by sheer strength of arm anyone who had such a poor idea of the chestnut-eaters of Limoges and the Creuse. We pursued each other in gangs. The police seldom intervened.

We need to pay some attention to these acts of violence if we are to understand the general history of Paris at this period, and to pay almost as much heed to the print shops (in which sober workmen—not many, admittedly—created a working-class literature and a working-class press after hours) as to the halls and common lodging rooms where far more workmen came to exercise their muscles. The history of the schools of *chausson* is as important to social and political history as that of the print shops where the *Journal des ouvriers, L'Artisan* and *Le Peuple* were made up—starting in September 1830—and later *L'Atelier*. Physical violence had a political significance. One only has to read Nadaud to realize this.[10] The opening of several schools of *chausson* in the quartier de l'Hôtel-de-Ville and the Cité between 1830 and 1834 reflected a temper recorded in conventional history in different forms. It expressed a new attitude on the part of the working class. It is certainly worth noting that its source was rural, and it was long to retain the stamp of its origin. In the second half of the nineteenth century most of the owners of the physical culture institutes were still former masons or even builders, some of whom worked at both trades, building and fighting.[11] It should be added that the technique of this rural violence was in marked contrast to the Parisian technique of the *savate* we have mentioned. The *chausson* was a clean sport, in which victory went to the more dexterous and better performer and the mark was the face and chest, never the groin.

Gradually, however, these acts of *compagnonnage* violence, like the *compagnonnages* themselves, took on a totally different character in Paris. Just as the journeymen vanished into the mass of the Paris working class, *compagnonnage* violence gradually merged with the proletarian violence already mentioned.

"Communities" and "peer groups": But we must not overlook the durability of these groups, in which modern sociology would readily identify most of the characteristics it attributes to what it now terms "communities" and "peer groups."[12] What is remarkable is the homogeneity, the coherence, the stability over a long period of these closed circles, which were established within the working-class masses, yet remained quite different from them and powerfully defended against them. This was due to their common origin in the same canton or commune (not simply the same department or rural area), and to the fact that they shared the same trades and careers, grew up at the same rate in the same age groups, had the same traditions of migrating at the

same seasons, following the same routes and ending, if not on the same jobs, at least in the same districts, the same hiring places, the same cafés and the same lodgings. From father to son, the Nadauds lodged at 62, rue de la Tisseranderie, kept for generations by the same family.[13] They kept together owing to the same family habits: not only with regard to the complete association of father and son in work, earning, and especially saving, but also with regard to the habits affecting marriage. "Strange was the lot of women who married masons," Nadaud wrote. "Nowadays some of them take their young wives with them; at that period this habit did not exist. Each of the couple had to live alone, sometimes until they were fifty, except for the intervals of the winter season." And they shared the same concerns and the same images; all the talk in the common lodging rooms was of home. "Those who are not married," said Nadaud, "used to tease those who are about the wives they had left solitary. How often homesickness drives the oldest to return home before their time!" There were as many villages as there were common lodging rooms, lost under the eaves of the tall working-class houses in the quartier de la Cité, far from a hostile Paris and solidly defended against it.

During the July Monarchy these defenses weakened and fell. The causes have often been described, but some of them, in our opinion, have a quite special importance. One was the rejuvenation of the population and the growing dissension between the older generation, intolerant guardians of outdated regulations, and the young, who understood little of these strange rites, these outlandish, often cruel, and sometimes obscene, ordeals. Describing the young journeymen who came to Paris after 1830, Nadaud wrote:

They were a score of young chaps from the cantons of Pontarion and Saint-Sulpice-les-Champs, extremely industrious and very polite to each other, who had come to Paris after the 1830 Revolution. They differed entirely in their pleasant conversation, their tastes and their care for their persons, especially coming off the job, from the men of the preceding generation. Our elders had grown up under the gloved hand of the nobles and priests brought back by the armies of the Coalition in 1815. . . . The lower classes had been kept in utter ignorance, and all they had been taught well was the catechism.

More decisive were the causes pertaining specifically to the Parisian environment. The city's ascendancy became more powerful than in the past because the traditional rhythm of migration had been interrupted. From about 1840 on, seasonal migration fell off and no longer functioned as automatically as it had under the Restoration. This first became evident in a species of breakdown of the traditional movement to and from Paris. It still continued, but people ceased to see the use of it and even began to find it burdensome. Martin Nadaud's *Mémoires* clearly reflect the waning of an old tradition, which continued only by the momentum it had acquired. Workers were now reluctant to embark on the long, even dangerous, journey. It was true that post-chaise services were improving, spreading and bringing Paris nearer to the distant provinces; but easier communications seem to have impaired rather than maintained the former custom of returning home from time to time. The post chaise was expensive; and since the provincial could not make use of it, as that would have eaten into his savings, he resigned himself to staying in Paris. The development of communications also operated in the reverse direction. Though the journey was too expensive for workers in Paris to return to the provinces, the expense seldom prevented provincials from going to Paris; they cheerfully bore it in the hope of better earnings. Since this expense was slight compared with the greater ease in leaving home for the city, the movement from country to city increased; and the arrival of newcomers determined to settle in the city forced the earlier seasonal immigrants to settle down permanently too. The spread of railways did the rest. In 1847, out of 9,287 masons, 4,859 were sedentary and 4,428 mobile; 39% lived in homes of their own, 61% in lodgings. "A few return home each year," the Chamber of Commerce inquiry reported, "mostly married workers; but, even so, most of them go back only every two or three years, when they have had a good year." The 1860 inquiry noted some cases of return, but they became fewer and fewer.

The effects of this change on the immigrants' integration with the Paris environment began to be felt at the end of the July Monarchy. The result of the provincials' extended, and soon continuous, sojourn in Paris was to form a working-class mass more uniform in composition, but also more uniform in its poverty. In the past Paris had differed from other great working-class towns such as Lyon, Mulhouse and Lille in its larger variety of workers; the masons had formed a separate group in the labor force as a whole, and only a small proportion of the immigrants had become acclimatized to Paris, while most had returned home after a few years. The colonies from the Creuse, Corrèze and Haute-Vienne, as well as the smaller ones from the eastern departments, were never made up of absolutely the same individuals. Around 1840 the new factor was not the disappearance of these colonies; they continued to exist side by side in the districts, but they were thereafter made up of increasingly stable components. The Lorrainers and the Limousins were still distinguishable from the Parisians, but as they went back more and more seldom to their provinces and were henceforth to be born and die in Paris, they more and more resembled the true Parisians despite their obvious origins and the survival of their customs. Their special districts, patois and traditions survived, but rather as a sign of recognition than as a habitual frame of living. Paris was still the great meeting place for provincials, but all of them began to adopt a less regional mode of life, and the workers among them a class solidarity. We have examined in a previous work the purely occupational aspects of this proletarianization and integration with the urban economic environment.

Causes other than the occupational operated, especially the increase in population, which was not, of course, due to the journeymen alone; but they too were subject, in the same way as the others, to its effects, which we have already described and of which traces are to be found in the best-known *compagnonnage* literature. In this literature too the city was blamed for every ill, in terms similar to those on which we have already commented. In describing the surroundings of the place Maubert, Nadaud dwelt on the same facts as the medical topographies, and as Balzac in *L'Interdiction*.

We were near the rue Saint-Victor, very close to the place Maubert and the many very narrow and unhealthy streets round it, that is to say, in a center where one could see more ragged children, more women besotting themselves in filthy pothouses with their children in their arms or lying on tables or the ground, than anywhere else. These poor little mites would leave this depraved, disgusting, dissolute quarter only to steal in the streets and be picked up by the police and put in jail.[14]

The means whereby the city caused groups to deteriorate were described in the classics of *compagnonnage* literature in precisely the same way as they were everywhere else. These books document the material and moral effects of the urban environment on the inhabitants from both the material and moral point of view no less than the major literary and social works already discussed. They show how the harsh urban environment finally overcame the group, with its rules, its beliefs, its homogeneity and the individuality and pride that membership of a community conferred on each of its members. The general laws of existence of the Paris workers and of the most under-privileged among them, the different conditions of hiring and work, different conditions of daily life, different habits—that is, food, drink, sleep, and recreation—finally prevailed over the laws of the group. And in addition, the consequence of establishment in Paris, namely, the coming of the wives, and hence the break with the village to which there was no longer any reason to return; but also the break with what remained of the village in Paris, because the wives could not live in the common lodging room.

We see this triumph, this bleak triumph, of the Paris environment growing stronger from year to year. "In Paris," George Sand wrote,

compagnonnage is tending increasingly to become lost and dispersed over the great field of work and varied interests. No association could hope to monopolize work in Paris. In any event, the skeptical spirit of a more advanced civilization has put an end to the gothic customs of the *compagnonnage*; too soon, perhaps, for a fraternal association covering all the workers was not yet ready to replace the association. But partisan hatreds have not entirely died out yet in Paris. The joiners in the *compagnons* of liberty group live on the left bank of the Seine; their opponents, the joiners in the *compagnons* wayfarers' group, live on the right bank. They are bound by treaty to work on the side of the river where they live. They fight nevertheless, and the other groups are still intolerant of each other. But, by and large, one may say that *compagnonnage,* with its powers and its passions, has become as it were lost and absorbed into the great movement which is drawing everything toward an independent and sustained progress.

Lost and absorbed, above all, in a uniform condition of poverty, of urban poverty, which Nadaud, recalling the early and the last ten years of the July Monarchy, described in a passage that must be quoted, if only to stress the presence—which was no accident—of the economic and biological themes already discussed:

We saw misery at close quarters in its vast variety and we were able to compare the misery of the countryside with the misery of the towns. The latter is far more terrible; it drains body and spirit, kills the physical and stifles the moral. It is death preceded by long and cruel death throes. It is a slow torture which blunts all the springs of sensibility. In the towns there are no resources when the proletarian's arm lacks employment, no more shelter, no more clothes, no more bread. In his destitution charity, disdainful, insulting, often inadequate, is his sole refuge. I remember seeing workers in Paris gathering on the quais around coffee or potato sellers. Pale of face, barely clothed in a few rags, eating for one or two sous, all those unfortunates thronged the offices of Public Assistance. It was the same in the workhouses and prisons.

Hunger, sickness, death were the themes of the journeymen's misery, just as they were of the Parisian workers' misery. Prison for both. For the journeymen's misery not only blended with Parisian misery, but adopted its behavior—violence. Individual violence assuming forms which were not those of the *compagnonnage*, brawls with knives; "their frequency gives grounds for fearing lest they may be becoming part of lower-class habits."[15] And the relationship between the violent condition and the criminal condition which we have so often noted. At a period when justice was merciless and swift[16] many, many workers were drawn into the criminal condition by the ill-luck of a blow or a knife thrust, by the hazard of a challenge at work, or a drunken brawl, or a mere scuffle.[17] Collective violence, finally, in strikes which the *compagnonnages* conducted; but most of all in the great social and political storms, in which the journeymen no longer took part as such but as members of a broader, suffering and alienated community, and in the same way.

These collective acts of violence must be described, not now in isolation and broken down into their main components, but reconstituted, regrouped and merged into the narrative just as they were in actuality; not their concealed motive forces, but as observed from the outside and in their outward appearance; not taken out of time, but restored to history in its most traditional and essential form. For what we should now do is to narrate the entire history of Paris during the first half of the nineteenth century, since the foregoing detailed discussions have actually been no more than an introduction to a full chronological narrative from which we had to deviate, but only provisionally, the better to return to it; which we had to abandon, but only in appearance and provisionally, the better to assess its value and the need for it. Such detours through statistics, whether economic or demographic, are relevant only if they lead back to the traditional paths of history and merge with them with no more complication than that entailed in trudging through the archives.

We shall not, however, embark upon a narrative of this sort, because to ensure that it was absolutely accurate we should have to undertake further statistical detours of a similar kind in order to identify the specifics of the occupational, the social and in some cases even the demographic characteristics of the population groups which we have measured en masse and to identify, too, the trades, provincial origins and ages of the groups which played the leading part in the strikes, riots and revolutions. Despite the effective influence of the immigration which we have measured, and despite the inevitable aggravation of all the problems, even the political problems, it must undoubtedly have caused, it is by no means certain that this immigration substantially changed the complexion of the most militant sections of the working class and the recruitment of their leaders. Most of those arrested at the time of the disturbances in the earlier and later years of the Restoration were Parisian artisans, according to the statistics compiled at the time and to the police files concerning the events of June 5 and 6, 1832;[18] and it is very probable that the dossiers for June 1848 would, if analyzed, show very much the same result. These small and active groups are so important for the political and social history of Paris and so prominent in the foreground of the scene that the scene itself cannot be definitively described until they themselves have been measured. But that would call for further quantitative analysis of a different type of documentation; not the statistical study of statistical documents (a relatively easy job) but the statistical elaboration of archives, most of which are ill-suited to measurement because the figures are either too few, or too many, or too heterogeneous.

In any event, we shall not embark upon this narrative because it already exists in the many specialized historical studies of the period, which are not diminished or contradicted by our analyses, but are rather confirmed, justified and reinforced by them. To the history of Paris during the Restoration and the July Monarchy as written successively by the political historians, the labor historians and the economic historians, the evaluation of the people involved simply contributes an additional concurrent element, and a more constant and more comprehensive one, that of the crowd. The older description—of electoral battles, labor disputes, riots and revolutions—of social and political groups—of ideas—still stands. But it is heightened by the suggestive findings of demographic evaluation, which, though scattered through this book, can readily be assembled and reconstituted. Instead of the social and political acts of violence, which have been so frequently and so thoroughly studied, though only in relation to crises and to the major groups involved, our type of study is more concerned with other more constant, more complex and more tenacious forms of violence, involving larger numbers and taking on from the rise and weight of the masses their growth, unity and strength. Crisis is perceived to be linked to crisis in a different way. In addition to the great public dramas there were the private, everyday dramas which arose independently of the public dramas, but exacerbated them and used them in the settlement of their own scores. And the weight of the masses changed the nature and significance of those acts of public violence. Going beyond the class struggle and aside from the growth of class consciousness, a purely Parisian problem was settled in this period: that of a population group which tried to find a place for itself in a hostile environment and, failing, gave itself over to hatred, violence and lawlessness of every kind. This was unquestionably a class struggle, but it was carried on by means of a struggle which its contemporaries themselves described as a struggle of race; a conflict between two population groups differing wholly from each other, but above all in body; a difference not merely social but biological.

This was the opinion of contemporaries. But it squared with many of the facts, so much so that the conclusions to which this narrative must lead give good grounds for drawing more far-reaching conclusions, not simply about the biological aspects of the history of Paris during the period, but about the biological bases of social history itself.

GENERAL CONCLUSION
The Biological Bases of Social History

I

We say the biological bases of social history deliberately. Not the biological aspects of social history, nor even the social bases of historical demography, which would amount to two different ways of describing a single study—that of the influence of the economy and society upon the demographic characteristics of populations. We do not in the least deny the importance of such a study, since we have recognized inequality before life and before death as one of the major aspects of the social history of the period. But we shall not devote the general conclusion of this book to the conclusions to be derived from that study. Firstly, because the data in it are so evident both in our analyses and in those of our predecessors that nothing further need be added; and, secondly, because there seems to emerge from our analyses, from those of our predecessors and from the drama of the period itself a conclusion not more important perhaps, but more novel, from which later historical research will derive greater profit.

The influence of the economy and society upon the development of population, or, rather, the influence of the economy upon a social development which blends with the development of population, has been demonstrated so thoroughly that there is no need to revert to it. It was shown by the statisticians of the first half of the nineteenth century, who were the first to recognize and measure inequality before life and death and the harsh conditions which riveted people to this unjust fate. The official report on the cholera epidemic of 1832 expresses the various stages of a discovery which was not dictated in advance by any philosophical bias nor guided by any political or economic prejudice. As to the subsequent verifications of this fundamental determinism—or rather, the systematic or incidental utilization of a materialist hypothesis which was hammered out and came to prevail in the ensuing years—they have been studied in works so important and so numerous that we may consider that, so far as our period is concerned, they have given all that they could: irrefutable evidence of the influence of poverty upon life and death in the Paris of the period. Unless we are simply to go on verifying indefinitely by means of documents readily available what no one disputes any longer, it would seem necessary now to use a different tool, not because the one previously used is to be despised, but because we wish to go further and open up other paths to history. After the economic hypothesis, or parallel and concurrent with it, comes the biological hypothesis. The aim is no longer to discover the influence of economic facts upon demographic facts; it is now to discover the influence of biological facts upon social facts. No longer to describe the economic and social bases of population development but the biological bases of social history. We may well ask whether this hypothesis does not merge in many respects with the other, whether it is not the basis of the other, and whether through it historical materialism itself does not rejoin those purely material models to which, in historical research at any rate, it has by no means attained as yet.

How, especially, could the historian of the Paris population during the first half of the nineteenth century fail to be tempted in observing this period, yet going beyond it, to define the contribution to history made by attention to the biological facts, when those facts cannot but impress him as the most important in the general development of Paris during the period, because he perceives the consequences of the ebb and flow of the people he is describing everywhere and in every form? Let us go even further. Not only does it seem necessary to supplement the study of the economic bases of demographic history with the study of the biological bases of social history; but, within the restricted setting of the Paris of the period, the study of the biological bases of social history is the best justification for the conventional study of the economic bases of human history, which alone has prevailed hitherto. We should explain this: economic and social inequality had such potent repercussions on life and on death simply because, over and beyond the economic facts, a terrible demographic pressure exerted its influence; if it had not, the material conditions would not have had such a vast effect.

II

By the biological bases of social history we mean the influence of the physical characteristics of populations upon the various aspects of individual and collective existence, without a knowledge of which there could be no description of societies either past or present. It so happens that there are methods other than the demographic by which the study of modern societies may now be approached in this way and at this depth. It is quite certain, however, that demography by means of its own subject matter—fertility, mortality, nuptiality, mobility and migration—its documentation and its statistical methods can take biological research further than it could go by using no more than its own techniques, although, of course, it still relies primarily on them. Furthermore, new branches of science, equally concerned with the physical side of man, but dealing in different ways with other aspects of it, have come in to supplement the older disciplines. This is not true of the study of the past. Here demography provides the main, indeed the only, technique, and there is no possible substitute for it, owing to the nature of the documentation. But its findings are just as relevant, at any rate where an exceptionally favorable period such as that we have been studying enables it to be employed in a way which differs from the way it has been used in the past—and from the way in which we have used it ourselves.

The contention that the use of demography is one of the major procedures in social history—in that it reintegrates its principal, though most generally ignored, subject matter, the estimating of population broken down into its components and densities, and even into age, sex and origins—does not go far enough. This merely reduces demography to the role of an ancillary to history. In this contention demography does lend history rather more precision, but it does not transform its documentation, concerns, themes and rhythms; and it still leaves history to treat contemporary descriptions and a sociology in the process of complete transformation with an incomplete program and immutable concepts. Further, the observation that differences in mortality, and even fertility, make it possible to measure other differences and to help to define the contours of classes which are barely delimited in conventional history, and that the history of the past accommodates itself very well with the history of the present in this respect at least, is not sufficient either.

For this again amounts to no more than using demography as an accessory, merely incidentally and from the outside, and to making an unchanged demography merely the handmaiden of an equally unchanged social description. It implies, indeed, a failure to perceive that demographic statistics not only supply history with a further dimension, but extend and transform every part of its program, especially the most relevant part: the study of the relationships between individuals and classes. Henceforth this study can no longer be confined to exceptional events—amid the distorting glare of tumults and revolutions—but now extends to all the incidents of daily life. It is no longer based upon theory, but upon fact; and is now directed not from above, but from below.

What, in fact, is revealed by the experience of the Paris population during this period is the biological content of the attitudes and behavior of people to one another, whether in isolation, in groups or in the mass. The causes first. Through the influence of age, sex and origin; of conditions of life and modes of living, broken down into health, food, fatigue, sleep, work and recreation; and of the communal life of people whose characteristics and constitution are determined by their congregating at the same place and by the crowd they constantly form, for a city perhaps defines itself most precisely by the fact that it is a crowd and this accounts for many of the aspects of urban living. As to the effects, that is, the way in which those attitudes and that behavior are expressed, it is not enough simply to recognize their biological aspects in the public and private acts of violence, the individual and collective settlements of scores which we have described, the brutalities of the street, the workshop and the barricade. We must go further and penetrate into the secret domain in which the body is no less involved, but involved in a different way; involved not by gesture, but by the preparation for gesture, the possibility of gesture, the disposition to act, all of them molded in the same way. For if we had no knowledge of this, we should be totally incapable of understanding the opinion of people about themselves, about others and about things in general.

The doctors, moralists and philosophers of the time gave us ample warning of this, for they agreed in holding the soul to be simply an organic and animal phenomenon, thereby continuing the legacy of the eighteenth century, it is true, but enriching it with the experience of the Revolution and the Empire, and even more with the observations they gathered in the somber Paris hospitals of the first half of the century and set out in documents that have so far been unduly neglected by historical research. In transposing the findings of sociology to history, it is unnecessary to suggest that similar causes have probably had similar effects at every period and that a description of the past could not be more disincarnate than the history of the present. History is self-sufficient and finds within itself the means for its own completion, the secrets for its own perfecting. Even to the present perhaps it contributes more than it takes away when, thanks to a tragic time and a particularly appropriate place—the inhuman Paris almost immediately preceding modern Paris—the carnal depths of a collective experience rise to the surface.

Notes

GENERAL INTRODUCTION
(pp. 1–23)

1. "The number of crimes appears to have risen, particularly in November," reads a police report of January 1827, "and it is to be noted that the increase has apparently been in proportion to the way in which certain newspapers seem to have made a point of assuring malefactors that the authorities are derelict in their duty and impotent. This has led to a positive state of terror in the capital." A report of February 10, 1827, makes a similar observation in similar terms: "Of all the attacks by night the most terrifying was the robbery of M. Pellegrini on January 27." The *Journal des Débats* of February 10, 1827, stated: "All the hearings at the criminal court this week were devoted to the trials of the instigators of some of the dastardly attacks which threw the capital into a panic early this winter."

2. Eugène Sue, *Les Mystères de Paris*, 1963.

3. [A prison used for condemned criminals.—Trans.]

4. Louis-Sébastien Mercier, *Tableaux de Paris*, 12 vols., 1782–88. Restif de la Bretonne, *Les Nuits de Paris*, 1960.

5. Mercier, *op. cit.*

6. [A traveling journeyman who wrote about artisanal life in the 1840's.—Trans.]

7. Comtesse d'Agoult, *Histoire de la Révolution de 1848*, 2 vols., 1862.

8. *Paris incompatible avec la République, plan d'un nouveau Paris où les révolutions seront impossibles*, 1848.

9. Jules-Gabriel Janin, *Paris depuis la révolution de 1830*, 1833.

10. Eugène Roch, *Paris malade, esquisses du jour*, 2 vols., 1832–33.

11. Louis Blanc, *Histoire de dix ans. 1830–1840*, 1841–44.

12. *Extrait de "l'Annuaire statistique de la ville de Paris pour l'année 1880,"* 1881.

BOOK I
Introduction (pp. 27–28)

1. Louis Chevalier, *La formation de la population parisienne au XIXe siècle*, 1949.

2. Letter from Privat d'Anglemont, May 1843: "Yes, our literature is etched in acid. Yes, we use blood and fire where others used tears and tenderness. But we were weaned on brandy, not milk; and we have witnessed on our streets things more terrible, dramas more fearful than we could ever

describe. We have made twenty revolutions in the past forty or fifty years, only to remain where our grandmothers were. If we deal in the terrible, it is because everything around us is terrible. If we are uneasy, uncomfortable in our society, it is because the future is there, more terrible and perhaps more bloody than the past." Correspondence of Eugène Sue, Bibliothèque d'Histoire de la Ville de Paris.

Chapter One (pp. 29–58)

1. Claude Lachaise, *Topographie médicale de Paris,* 1822.

2. Honoré de Balzac, *La Maison du chat qui pelote. La Bal de Sceaux. La Bourse. La Vendetta,* 1853.

3. Bertillon, *op. cit.*

4. Louis René Villermé, *La Mortalité en France dans la classe aisée, comparée à celle qui a lieu parmi les indigents* (n.d.). Adolphe-Lambert-Jacques Quételet, *Sur l'homme et le développement de ses facultés, ou Essai de physique sociale,* 2 vols., 1835.

5. Jules-Jean-Baptiste Anglès, *Observations adressées à M.M. les membres du conseil général des prisons par le prefet de police,* 1819.

6. Archives nationales (hereafter referred to as A.N.) Registres F^{20} 1 and 2.

7. A. N. Registres F^{20} 101.

8. Cf. Jean Sutter, *L'Eugénique,* 1950.

9. In this thesis, *De la statistique appliquée à la pathologie,* Broussais recounted previous attempts to apply statistics to pathology: "The first medical works professedly based largely on statistics in this way are the medical topographies. One of the first is that on Berlin by Formey (1796); many others have been published since; a noteworthy collection can be found in the *Mémoires de médecine militaire.*" After mentioning the work of Louis, Broussais recalled the sensation caused under the Restoration by Dupin's statistical tables on criminality and education by department, the influence of Villermé, Quételet and of the statistical surveys conducted in connection with the cholera epidemic.

10. *Op. cit.*

11. A-J-B Parent-Duchatelet, "Rapport sur le curage des égouts Amelot, de la Roquette, Saint-Martin et autres, demandé par le comte de Chabrol et M. Delavau, préfet de police," *Annales d'Hygiène,* 1820, vol. II.

12. *Histoire de l'Académie des sciences,* 1762, pp. 147 and 337.

13. The following comments by Trébouchet, deploring the interruption in the publication of the death rates in 1824 and 1825, are very pertinent: "We had already been able to observe which diseases give rise to the heaviest mortality among the capital's inhabitants and which of them have the severest effects on children, young people, mature adults and the aged; we had noted a vast difference between the death rates in one arrondissement and another; and we would have been able to express our surprise that certain easily diagnosed diseases almost infallibly susceptible to treatment should cut down so very many children when the cures are perfectly well known. . . . In addition to the data so very interesting to the Paris population, inasmuch as they affect its life and health, to which we were intending to devote further attention once they had attained that degree of certainty with which they may well be invested if similar work is brought to a higher level and sustained for some years, further and possibly even more interesting data

would naturally have come to light. Thus, the great and weighty question of the influence of occupation on health might have found a solution useful to those who practice it and also beneficial to the progress of the arts. A host of local causes of mortality might thus have been discovered. The effect of the Parisian inhabitants' diet and moral behavior on their state of health could have been assessed and determined, at least up to a certain point."

14. François Leuret, Notice historique sur A-J-B Parent-Duchâtelet *Hygiène publique,* or Notice historique sur A-J-B Parent-Duchâtelet *De la Prostitution dans la ville de Paris,* first published 1836.

15. A.N. F^{13} 740.

16. In the *Journal des Débats,* for example: November 12, 1821; May 8, 1822; February 3, 1826.

17. [Laughter on the first floor! Glasses never empty! But in the horrible garret haggard faces that will be dead on the morrow . . . Great ones of the day, take care, for Peter the mason is coming down from his attic. And the mason entered pale as a shroud . . . A flunkey suddenly rushed to the door to stamp on the monstrous woodlouse and the poor mason drenched in sweat is driven from the banquet like an unclean beast.—Trans.]

18. Gilbert-Joseph-Gaspard Chabrol de Volvic, *Recherches statistiques sur la ville de Paris et le département de la Seine,* 4 vols., 1821–29.

19. "M. Benoiston de Châteauneuf," we read in the *Journal des Débats* of December 17, 1822, "has just published a report on the death rate of females aged forty to fifty. The findings he has submitted to the Academy of Sciences by no means confirm received opinion. It would even seem that they run entirely counter to it and that more men than women die at those ages. One of the pieces of evidence M. de Châteauneuf adduces in support of this fact is very curious and shows that if science can help administration, administration can also help science: a table of the decrease in ecclesiastical state pensioners over an average of ten years."

20. *Journal des Débats,* October 18 and 21, 1823.

21. "It is in the most prosperous districts, where there is least prejudice against vaccination, that the epidemic has carried off the fewest victims," commented the *Journal des Débats* on November 27, 1825, "whereas it has disastrous effects in the poor districts where the inhabitants obstinately reject the benefit of vaccination."

22. *Journal des Débats,* November 16, 1826.

23. L. Montigny, *Le Provincial à Paris. Esquisses des moeurs parisiennes,* 1825.

24. Chevalier Gérard Jacob, *Le Frondeur, ou observations sur les moeurs de Paris,* 1829.

25. Sulpice-Paul-Chevalier Gavarni, *Le Diable à Paris,* 2 vols., 1845–46.

26. On prostitution, Sue wrote: "See the invaluable study by Dr. Parent-Duchatelet, the work of a great philosopher and philanthropist" (*Mystères de Paris,* 1844 edition, vol. I, p. 144). There is similar influence by Parent-Duchatelet in the chapter on the Saint-Lazare prison; the slang and nicknames recorded by Sue are those recorded by Parent-Duchatelet. It is also worth noting that the Cité district and the rue aux Fèves are identified by Parent-Duchatelet too as the places where prostitution was densest.

27. A-J-B Parent-Duchatelet, "Mémoire sur les débardeurs de la Ville de Paris," *Annales d'Hygiène,* 1830.

28. M. A. Frégier, *Des classes dangereuses de la population dans les*

grandes villes, et des moyens de les rendre meilleures, 2 vols., Paris, 1840. Frégier's influence is very evident in *Les Mystères de Paris.* "According to M. Frégier, the excellent historian of the dangerous classes of society," wrote Sue, "there live in Paris 30,000 persons whose sole means of support is robbery" (vol. IX, p. 366). Frégier's study seems to have inspired the choice and description of the Cité district, described by Frégier himself in volume I of his book at pp. 135 and 265. A similar influence, too, is seen in Sue's description of ragpickers (Frégier, vol. I, p. 108, and vol. II, p. 139); of the social setback represented by becoming a schoolmaster; of the waifs wandering among the lime kilns (by Frégier, vol. I, p. 98, and by Sue, vol. I, pp. 45 and 46); and of the description of prisons and the study of the problem of solitary confinement (vol. II, p. 413).

29. Cf. Frégier, *op. cit.,* vol. I, pp. 309 and 310.

30. Louis Chevalier, *Les fondements économiques et sociaux de l'histoire politique dans la région parisienne au milieu du XIXᵉ siècle* (in preparation).

Chapter Two (pp. 59–69)

1. Victor-Joseph Etienne de Jouy, *Oeuvres complètes. Essais sur les moeurs,* vols. 1–13, 15, 1823; 25 and 26, 1845–46.

2. Jules Janin, *Un hiver à Paris,* 1845.

3. Review by Janin of *Un grand homme de province à Paris* in the *Revue de Paris,* 1839. Bibliothèque de l'Arsenal, Journal 20445: "M. de Balzac excels in reproducing these frightful details of poverty. But poverty is uniform, it is compounded of the same horrible ingredients everywhere. By dint of playing variations on the everlasting theme of the freezing house, the starving man, the crumbling roof . . . one is bound to end up by repeating oneself." And in another scene, the Palais-Royal: "Here is a terrible description of the Palais-Royal at the time when that seedy mob of publishers and dressmakers still swarmed pell-mell into the wooden galleries; one knows that M. de Balzac excels in filthy descriptions of this sort: the rotting timbers, the stagnant water, the laundry rinsed in wash basins and hung out on lines, a worthy wash for haunts of vice. Nothing escapes him, not a wrinkle, not a sticky scab of this foul tetter. Despite all the power a writer must have to dig so deep, one wonders what pleasure M. de Balzac's readers can find in these hideous details."

4. Janin, *Un hiver à Paris,* p. 201.

5. In his old age, Janin expressed his surprise at the unpardonable levity and culpable cynicism with which the youthful critic of the *Débats*—spoiled child of the Restoration—had greeted and described the Revolution of 1830 and the succeeding tumults year after year thereafter. Actually, and in spite of Janin's later position, these articles contain valuable observations, excellent material for social history. The description of the sacking of Saint-Germain-l'Auxerrois and the looting of the Archbishop's Palace abound in valuable details. Details in Balzac also are worth noting. "After the Revolution of 1830," Balzac wrote in *La messe de l'athée,* "when the people hurled themselves upon the Archbishop's Palace, when republican inspiration impelled them to destroy the golden crosses which rose like shafts of lightning over the immensity of the ocean of houses. . . ." We find these crosses and their significance in Janin, too. "I recounted all I had seen in the crowd," he wrote, "not omitting some revolutionaries bent on the destruction of the

symbols, who, in the clear and sparkling sunlight, tried to throw down the cross on the dome of Saint-Gervais. The sun was as splendid as a sun in spring, the streets were crowded with sightseers, and one after another on the bridge under which flowed so much debris (all the books from the Archbishop's library), straight in front of those shaken domes, one after another or all together came the maskers celebrating the merry Mardi-Gras, the National Guard to the rattle of its drums, the fat ox garlanded with flowers, the young people of the city bearing the tricolor flag and singing *La Parisienne*."

Chapter Three (pp. 70–79)

1. Eugène-François Vidocq, *Les Voleurs*, 1957. Vidocq wrote: "The gentry criminals, the *haute pègre*. Our most prolific novelist, the novelist most apt to interest his readers in the fate of his heroes, speaks in one of his books (*Le Père Goriot*) of an association of malefactors whom he calls the Society of the Ten Thousand because all its members have made it a rule never to do a job worth less than 10,000 francs. The Society of the Ten Thousand never abandons a member who has always loyally observed its articles of incorporation. Giving free rein to his imagination, the ingenious novelist seems to have meant only the *haute pègre*. You find the *pègre de la haute* everywhere, at the outing at the Porte d'Italie and in the stalls at the Théâtre Italien alike. . . . The *pègre de la haute* has on occasion put up the epaulettes of a general officer or the rochet of a prince of the Church. . . . Nowadays the *haute pègre* is made up almost entirely of persons from the lowest classes of society; but in the old days its ranks included people who rubbed shoulders with royalty. Most of them, being above the law because of their rank, took a certain pride in flouting the law."

2. *Le code des gens honnêtes* was published anonymously in 1825; it was reprinted in 1829 under the authorship of "Horace Raisson"; Balzac was named as the author in the 1835 edition.

3. Balzac introduced his description of the dangerous classes in terms of numbers and drew some curious social conclusions from the figures and percentages. "It has been calculated," he wrote, "that there are 20,000 persons on the streets of Paris who rise in the morning with no notion how they will dine. No matter; they do dine, and they dine very well!" He went on: "The Paris garrison is usually some 20,000 strong; it is rather queer to think of 20,000 rogues setting 20,000 snares every morning for their fellow citizens, who have only 20,000 soldiers to protect them from these snares." There is a similar attempt at an estimate in *Splendeurs et misères des courtisanes*: "Again, the population of the world of whores, thieves and murderers in the galleys and prisons amounts to some 60,000 to 80,000 males and females. This world cannot be ignored in any depiction of our manners or in any literal description of our society. About the same number of people are employed by the law, the constabulary and the detective force. This is really rather queer. This hide-and-seek between criminal and law enforcement makes for the vast and highly dramatic duel sketched in this study."

4. "You must realize," Balzac wrote, "that death causes the most frightful ravages in this forgotten class; its manners, its habits, the diseases to which it falls prey, the want of healthy food, the lack of medical care, the abuse of liquor and many, many other passions ceaselessly enervate and consume this pariah caste; death decimates them."

5. "It has been claimed," says Balzac again, "that suicide has been responsible for a sort of write-off of these 20,000 rogues and that the Seine annually took out of circulation, depending on how favorable the rate was, a certain quantity of these gentry forming the 'floating' mass of what is really a social debt. It is true that suicides amounted to 200 to 300 year in, year out; but it is our duty to warn any honest folk and administrators who feel that they can sleep easy on the strength of such a calculation that this assertion is false. It is a rule that a villain never dies by water; and even if he did, there are far more supernumeraries in waiting than villains who go out of business in this way. Besides, the class that suicides belong to has been ascertained and statistics of how they came to grief have been compiled. So the 20,000 snares are still there every morning."

6. At about the same period, Balzac wrote in the *Dictionnaire des enseignes*: "A word to the wise. Louvet, the pubkeeper at No. 9, place de Grève. Connoisseurs of tragedy, hasten to M. Louvet's, order up a bottle and reserve a place at one of the windows of his rooms; it strikes four, the crowd mills, the denouement is at hand; you watch the subject mount the fatal scaffold. . . . Nowadays there are so many sensitive souls that the pubkeepers' rooms, were they as ample as the galleries of the Louvre, would not be able to hold them all on execution days on the place de Grève." Balzac was always careful to eschew any sort of romanticism about capital executions. Thus, he wrote in *Splendeurs et misères des courtisanes*: "Europe took back the newspaper and read with avid eyes all the details of the execution of convicts which the papers have been giving for twenty years; the impressive spectacle, the chaplain who has always converted the subject, the old lag who harangues his former cellmates, the cannon leveled, the convicts on their knees. Followed by the platitudinous reflections which do nothing whatever to change the system of convict prisons in which 18,000 criminals are herded together." Note that Balzac refrained from describing the execution of Tascheron in the *Curé de village*.

7. Henri Monnier, *Scènes populaires dessinées à la plume*, 4 vols., 1835–39.

8. "A quartet of bandits, Claquesous, Gueulemer, Babet and Montparnasse, governed, from 1830 to 1835, the *troisième dessous,* the lower depths of Paris. What was Claquesous? He was the night; and never showed himself till the sky was bedaubed with black. In the evening he emerged from a hole to which he returned before daybreak. Where was this hole? No one knew. In the deepest darkness, when alone with his accomplices, he turned his back when he spoke to them. Was his name Claquesous? No: he said, 'My name is Not-at all.' . . . Montparnasse was a mournful being. . . ." Nothing could be less precise; deliberate imprecision could go no further toward producing the effect of horror or disgust. Whereas, observe the careful identification, the etymological research, the crude light of Balzac's description of a similar social category in *La cousine Bette*. He is describing the actress Olympe, now under the protection of a merchant in the rue Saint-Denis; "She got to know, saving your presence, Madam, a fellow in the claque, the grandnephew of an old mattressmaker in the faubourg Saint-Marceau. This layabout, like all your fine fellows, a pimp for plays, eh?, is the cock of the walk on the boulevard du Temple where he works on the new plays and looks after the actress's entrances, he says. In the morning, he lunches; before the play, he dines to work himself up; and of course he's liked his

liquor and billiards all his life—'That's not what I'd call a situation!' I says to Olympe.—'Too bad, but it is,' said Josepha.—'Well, Olympe had lost her head about the fellow, who, Madam, kept pretty queer company, seeing he was nearly arrested in the pub where the thieves go; but, well, M. Braulard, the head of the *claque,* got him turned loose. Wears gold earrings and lives on doing nothing, sponges on women who're plumb mad for flash fellows like him! He ate up all the money M. Thoul gave the girl. The shop wasn't doing too well; what came in from the embroidery went out on billiards. To go on, the fellow, Madam, had a pretty sister, a good-for-nothing chit, who carried on in the students' quarter just like her brother."

9. This topic has been studied by Jean Savant, author of several books on Vidocq, in particular an excellent edition of Vidocq's Memoirs, published as *Les vrais mémoires de Vidocq,* 1950.

10. *Splendeurs et misères des courtisanes,* part IV.

11. Maurice Alhoy, *Les Bagnes,* 1845.

12. *Journal des Débats,* August 15, 1821: "One Dubois, alias Capon, a notorious robber, sentenced ten or twelve times to deprivation of civil rights in the past twenty years, managed to escape from prison five or six times. He recently arrived in Paris wearing the uniform of a high-ranking officer and several decorations."

Journal des Débats, November 3, 1832: "The police has just arrested a person wearing the decorations of the Legion of Honor, the July Cross and the Order of Saint-Louis, claiming to be an ex-colonel of a line regiment, as he was leaving a gaming house in the Palais-Royal. . . . He is in fact a convict on licence."

13. Victorien Hulot is in despair because his father is ruining himself for Madame Marneffe. "We can have her killed," says Madame Nourrisson. Victor Hulot started, as any honest man would, at these cold-blooded words. The reader, too, is startled at such an unexpected proposal. "Murder!", said he, "And how would you set about it?—'For forty years now, sir, we have been substituting for Providence,' she replied proudly, 'and we have been doing what we would in Paris.' " Victorien shows the horrible and mysterious stranger out. . . . But one of the high officials at the Prefecture of Police, Chapuzot, explains to him the great services the police renders society by allowing this woman to do her worst. And the barrister Victorien Hulot finally goes to ask Vautrin, the head of the criminal police, to send him Madame de Sainte-Estève.

14. *Une double famille.*

Chapter Four (pp. 80–124)

1. *Journal des Débats,* February 26, 1829.

2. It is known that Hugo went to see the performance on October 22, 1828. A journalist published an account of the same scene in the *Gazette des tribunaux* a few days later (October 25, 1828). It has been very rewarding to compare the two accounts and find what Hugo added both to the journalist's account, to Vidocq's and to previous accounts such as Jouy's. What is more striking, however, is their similarity.

3. "At the time the book was written," Hugo wrote, "the author did not think it timely to express outright all that he thought. He preferred to wait until it was appreciated and to see whether it would be. It was. The author can now reveal the political idea, the social idea he had meant to popularize

in this innocent and ingenuous literary form. He declares, therefore, or rather confesses aloud, that *Le dernier jour d'un condamné* is nothing but a plea, direct or indirect, as you please, for the abolition of the death penalty." An interpretation echoed later by Balzac in the *Curé de village.*

4. *Journal des Débats,* January 23, 1833.

5. A.N. BB[18] 1123.

6. *Journal des Débats,* December 4, 1829.

7. The *Courrier des tribunaux* and most of the other papers following it gave many details both of the crime and its perpetrators—when they had done their dastardly deed, they went on to revel for the rest of the night at the pothouse of Marie Labouille, the terrible "mother of the convicts"—and of the execution. This execution was filled with a peculiar horror, mainly because of the behavior of one of the condemned men, Chendelet, who refused the comforts of religion and indulged in the most outrageous conduct. Almost as soon as he mounted the cart, he started a violent diatribe against the police, and then went on to sing:

> *Nous sommes trois bandits ici*
> *Sorti de la forêt de Bondi*
> *Tas de vile canaille!*
> *Pendant que vous nous regardez victimer*
> *Nos amis chez vous font ripaille*
> *Vous feriez mieux d'aller travailler*
> *Tas de vile canaille!*
> *Pour vous acheter des souliers.*

[We are three bandits here come out of the forest of Bondi, you pack of vile scum! While you watch us suffer, our friends are carousing in your homes. You would do better to go to work, pack of vile scum! to buy yourselves shoes.—Trans.]

One more example of the curious relation between poetry and crime, which was later to be embodied so remarkably in Lacenaire.

The *Courrier des tribunaux* gave the following account of the performance: "His movements are precipitate, his gaze bold and penetrating, his voice irate, hoarse and loud. . . . His whole being is shaken by a terrible emotion. . . . His face is pale and haggard. At the Pont-au-Change, by dint of twisting and writhing he managed to get both arms free. When he came to the place de Grève, he shouted: 'Ha! Here we are at the Big Machine!' And then, rising to his feet and turning towards the engine of death as the blade fell on Guérin's neck, he looked on, unmoved, and appeared eager to fling himself beneath it. At this supreme moment the priest attending him addressed a final exhortation: 'Come, my friend, there is still time to reconcile yourself with God' . . . —'No,' replied Chandelet, repulsing him, 'see, see my comrades are happier than I!' With these words, he rushed forward, climbed the stairs at a single bound and flung himself like a madman on the trap. . . . The blade fell and the severed head, bouncing across the basket, rolled across the scaffold leaving a long trail of blood! Soon the cart, carrying off the remains, rolled away; it passed back through the vast crowd which had viewed the men and still wished to view the bodies."

8. The news items gave many examples of these assaults. The *Journal des Débats* of November 17, 1826: "Lerat and Delorme, laborers, who had lived for months in the same room in a lodging house outside the barrière de Fon-

tainebleau, had decided to go back together to the Drôme, their native department. On the evening of the twelfth, after saying good-bye to their comrades, they set out. . . . Not far beyond the barrière, Delorme robbed and murdered his comrade."

9. Lachaise, *op. cit.*

10. [Arrested and executed for conspiracy in 1822.—Trans.]

11. Criticizing the proposal for the abolition of the death penalty, the purpose of which was solely to save Charles X's ministers, Hugo wrote: "If this desirable abolition had been proposed not for four ministers reduced from the Tuileries to Vincennes, but for any ordinary highway robber, one of those *misérables* you hardly look at when they pass you in the street, whom you do not speak to, a brush with whose dusty elbows you instinctively avoid, unfortunates who in their ragged boyhood have run barefoot in the mud of the crossroads, shivering in winter on the edge of the riverbanks, warming themselves at the vents of the kitchens of M. Véfour, at whose restaurant you dine, now and then digging a crust of bread out of a muck-heap and wiping it off before eating it. They scratch with their nails at the gutter all day to find a farthing, having no other amusement than the free spectacle of the King's birthday and the executions on the place de Grève, that other free spectacle; poor devils driven by hunger to stealing and from stealing to all the rest; disinherited children of a stepmother society, prey to the house of correction at twelve, the convict prison at eighteen, the scaffold at forty; unfortunates whom you could have made into good, moral, useful persons, had you given them a school and a workshop, but whom you do not know what to do with, turning them off as a useless burden now into the red anthill of Toulon, now into the silent enclosure of Clamart, cutting off their life after depriving them of liberty. If it had been for one of these that you had proposed to abolish the death penalty, ah, then your sitting would have been truly worthy, great, holy, majestic, venerable!"

12. In the *Journal des Débats* of November 12, 1822, for instance: "For several days subterranean noises have been heard at night in the rue Fromenteau, something like the sound of a printing press or a stamp for making coins or medals. . . . The authorities searched the cellars but found nothing. Engineers are looking at old maps of Paris to see whether there are any quarries in the district." And in the *Journal des Débats* of August 2, 1829: "A muffled thudding has been heard near the Célestins barracks in the Arsenal district. People supposed that a secret counterfeiters' workshop must exist in vast underground workings. It was in fact a cellar communicating with a bakery."

13. Bibliothèque nationale (hereafter referred to as B.N.) Fr. Nouv. Acq. 13379 and 13380.

14. Stern, *op. cit.*

15. *La Ruche populaire,* June 1841, B.N. Lc^2 1463, m.8.

16. As may be seen from the text, which, in the final version, is a fragment of the first draft: "At this period the Gorbeau tenement was, strange to say, inhabited by several persons who had no acquaintance with each other, as is always the case in Paris. All belonged to that indigent class which begins with the last small tradesman in difficulties and sinks from wretchedness to wretchedness down into the lower depths of society, to those two beings to whom all the material things of civilization descend . . . the scavenger and the ragpicker."

17. Hugo's speech was published in a pamphlet entitled *"Douze discours"* in 1851, the speech being entitled *"La Misère."* The official record must be consulted, for Hugo cut it, especially the interruptions. The cuts provided Hugo with a triumph, but gave an entirely false impression of the sitting.

18. Maurice Halbwachs, *La Classe ouvrière et les niveaux de vie, recherches sur la hierarchie des besoins dans les sociétés industrielles contemporaines,* 1913.

19. B.N. 8°, Lc² 1463.

20. Martin Nadaud, *Discours . . . dans la discussion du projet et résolution de la commission chargée de présenter le résumé et l'enquête sur la question du travail agricole et industriel,* 1851.

21. The development of street names has similar characteristics and equal sociological interest. One of the most striking instances, perhaps, is the former rue de la Mortellerie, now the rue l'Hôtel-de-Ville. The street bore its old name for over six centuries—Mortellerie is derived from its former inhabitants the *"morteliers,"* masons and mortar mixers, mainly immigrants from the Limousin. During the 1832 cholera, the inhabitants of the street, which was much ravaged by the epidemic, read *"mort,"* death, into the name and petitioned for it to be changed. In 1835 it was decided to replace the name, dating from 1212, with "rue de l'Hôtel-de-Ville."

22. "When you turn off the rue des Ballets into the rue du Roi-de-Sicile, you find a squalid recess immediately on the right. In the last century there was a house there, only the foundation wall of which remains, a real tenement wall rising to the third storey between the adjoining buildings. This ruin may be recognized by two large square windows still visible; the middle one, nearest to the right-hand gable, is barred by a rotting beam propped as a stay. Through these windows one used to make out a high gloomy wall, which was a piece of the outer wall of the patrol walk of La Force."

23. [At the same instant that the victim fell under four inhuman dagger blows, from the skies above the magnanimous master with his thunder terrified the murderer.—Trans.]

24. "One of the survivors of this exploration," Hugo wrote, "an intelligent workman, very young at that time, used to recount a few years ago the curious details which Bruneseau thought it right to omit in his report to the Prefect of Police as unworthy of the official style."

25. A.N. F⁸ 95.

26. Parent-Duchatelet, *Recherches pour découvrir la cause et la nature d'accidents très graves, développés en mer, à bord d'un bâtiment chargé de poudrette.* This investigation introduced Parent-Duchatelet for the first time to Montfaucon, which was to be the setting of so many of his later investigations.

27. These memories of 1846–1847–1848—the years during which he was writing much of *Les Misérables*—show how well Hugo documented these great criminals. An example is his visit to the Conciergerie in 1846, where he chatted with one of the executioner Sanson's assistants: "M. Sanson lived in an isolated house in the rue du Marais du Temple whose shutters were always closed." Another was his visit to the prison for those condemned to death in 1847: "Situated side by side with and built abutting the Reformatory. The malefactor's beginning and end confront each other . . . a vivid and striking antithesis."

28. "These names," Moreau-Christophe wrote, "are real names. Likewise,

I know the four bandits Gueulemer, Claquesous, Babet and Montparnasse. These four typical bandits formed a sort of parent association in Paris which gained the singular appellation of Patron-Minette in the underworld." In describing Patron-Minette, Moreau-Christophe merely reproduced Hugo's description of them.

29. Lacenaire's poems and memoirs were published in two volumes in 1836. There is a well-known poem by Théophile Gautier, "*La Main de Lacenaire.*"

30. The epic of the Paris urchin appears as early as Delacroix's picture "The Barricade" in 1832, i.e., some thirty years before *Les Misérables.*

31. Antoine François Marius Rey-Dusseuil, *Le Cloître Saint-Méry*, 1832.

32. Alexis de Toqueville, *Sur le droit au travail*, 1848.

33. The places noted by Hugo were the same as those noted by Frégier in 1840: "These children's lives are so ill regulated that they often pass in the space of a few days from comparative comfort to utter destitution. Thus, during the fine weather and when they are without means, it is their habit to sleep out on boats, under the arches of bridges and the girders of markets, in huts and cellars, under carriages, in the quarries and lime kilns, in short wherever they can find shelter; in winter they sleep in the very lowest of lodging houses." Describing Gavroche's hospitality to his two small protégés in the belly of the elephant at the Bastille, Hugo wrote: "Allow us to interrupt our narrative here and remind our readers that we are recording the simple truth, and that twenty years ago a boy who was caught sleeping inside the elephant at the Bastille was brought before the police court on a charge of vagrancy and defacing a public monument."

34. [These honest children who arrive from Savoy every year and whose hands lightly sweep these long pipes blocked with soot.—Trans.]

35. Mercier, *op. cit.*

36. Of the many dossiers on waifs and strays, we select that on the arrest of François Anet, aged eleven, in June 1828 on a charge of selling prints without a permit on a Paris bridge. "The Commune of Ore in the Pyrenees," the defense lawyer wrote, "is one of the poorest in the Saint-Gaudens district. The sole wealth of its inhabitants, herdsmen or very poor farmers, is a very large number of children, and instead of making beggars of them or placing them in the poorhouses, as is the practice in Paris, the fathers put their young children to the trade of print selling and send them all over France and Spain." Such was young François's case: "A zealous policeman who lets loose women and drunkards pass freely on our streets noticed the poor little stall and arrested the child, who has been in the house of detention at La Force consorting with malefactors and fed on the bread and water of criminals. I saw him yesterday and the first thing he said to me, in tears, was that he would not be able to send his poor mother 9 francs for the month of June." A.N. BB[18] 1162 (pièce 749). On child vagrancy, see Fernand Dubief, *La question du vagabondage*, 1911.

38. "If one fact is incontrovertible," Louis Blanc wrote in *L'Organisation du travail*, "it is that population grows far faster in the poor class than in the rich class. According to the *Statistique de la civilisation européenne*, births in Paris are only 1/32nd of the population in the well-to-do districts and 1/26th in the others. This disproportion is a general fact and M. de Sismondi has given a very convincing explanation of it in his book on political economy, attributing it to the fact that day laborers have no expecta-

tions and cannot take heed for the morrow. Only he who is assured of mastery over the morrow can reckon his children against his income; but he who lives from day to day bears the yoke of a mysterious fatality to which he dedicates his race because he was dedicated to it himself. The poorhouses are there, too, threatening to inundate society with hordes of beggars."

39. At the sitting of the Chamber on June 15, 1821, a speaker drew the Assembly's attention to the terrifying yearly increase in the number of abandoned children: "It is true that vaccination and administrative action have contributed a good deal to an apparent increase by reducing the incidence of mortality. But the progressive corruption of morals has caused a real increase, and it is impossible to foresee where it will end. What becomes of the children raised in our foundlings hospitals at such expense? Would it not be more sensible, after all our ill-fated attempts to colonize Madagascar and Senegal, to populate our colonies with these abandoned children? Could we not find a climate similar to that of France somewhere on the coasts of New Holland or Guyana for these children of misfortune? Would not this colonization be more successful than that undertaken by the English at Botany Bay and Port Jackson with transported convicts, whose spirit has been civilized and whose morals at last corrected by religion?"

40. Many examples are to be found in the police court news, such as this from the *Journal des Débats* of October 18, 1821: "The widow Richard, being needy and unable to keep a child of three or four, wished to place it in the orphans' home. She applied to one Maurice and the woman Davaux, both of whom claimed to be employees at the wet-nurses' office and undertook to meet the mother's wishes for 15 francs. But the woman Davaux abandoned the child on a sewer close to the Prefecture of Police that very day. She had tied a small label to its clothes stating the child's age and adding that it was abandoned to the care of God." There are also many examples of the exploitation of children by their parents or by strangers to whom the parents hired them out. There was a notable traffic in children from the Massif Central, as described in many documents, such as *Entretiens sur l'établissement en faveur des jeunes ramoneurs*, 1828.

41. *Journal des Débats,* August 16, 1826: "At the police court a mother with her five children around her was charged with instigating the two eldest, aged ten and thirteen, to theft. They maintained that they alone were guilty and flung themselves at the judges' feet, sobbing: 'Do what you will with us, but save our mother, she is innocent.'" *Journal des Débats,* December 24, 1829: "Theft of a bag containing 120,000 francs in Saint-Roch Church by Lafontaine, aged seventeen, apprentice stable boy, who is so short that he is nicknamed "Highness"; Sauvagnac, seventeen, sweep's assistant; Melchoir, fourteen, house painter's apprentice; Guillaume Sauvagnac, twenty, lamplighter. The Sauvagnacs' mother, a sick-nurse, attended the court in Auvergnat costume."

42. In the *Book of Murder,* published in London in 1839, there is a perfectly serious proposal to stifle all working-class children after the third, the mothers being rewarded for this act of patriotism. "The book," Louis Blanc wrote, "was written in all seriousness by a philosophical publicist; it was commented on and discussed by the most judicious writers in England; it was finally rejected with indignation as an atrocious but by no means ridiculous suggestion." There are many examples of this harshness towards lower-class children and this indifference to their existence. Mrs. Trollope in *Paris and*

the Parisians in 1835 described the Hospice des Enfants Trouvés in the rue d'Enfer (Letter LVIII): "It tends to prevent the unnatural crime of infanticide. . . . One fourth of the innocent creatures, who are deposited at the average rate of above twenty each day, die within the first year of their lives. But this, after all, perhaps is no very just cause of lamentation; one of the ministers of charity who attend at the hospital told me, in reply to an inquiry respecting the education of these immortal but unvalued beings, that the charity extended not its cares beyond preserving their animal life and health . . . and that, unless some lucky and most rare accident occurred to change their destiny, they generally grew up in very nearly the same state as the animals bred upon the farms which received them."

43. "Left to himself on the Paris streets, free from supervision because his parents are kept away from home from morning to night by unremitting toil, he readily throws off the yoke of discipline which he finds onerous. Instead of going to school he often wanders the streets, the quais and the boulevards; attracted by the games of children of his own age, he eagerly mingles with them; he acquires their tastes and habits the more easily in that they, like him, have a natural repugnance to work; finally, when he is sent back to school after playing truant, he is thereafter wholly given over to idleness. However, the parents soon become aware of their child's vicious habits; this leads them to inquire into his conduct at school and they learn that he has been expelled for setting such a bad example. He is soundly thrashed; he flees and fails to return home. The worried parents search for him, but fail to find him. He himself has become totally addicted to the evil company which has corrupted him and he is now thoroughly acquainted with the vagrancy laws."

44. Few of the books of *Les Misérables* were recast so thoroughly as that devoted to Gavroche and the Paris urchins entitled *"Paris étudié dans son atome"* (pp. 668 ff. of the manuscript). The gist of the first chapter (*"Parvulus"*) and the last (*"Gavroche"*) are from the first state of the manuscript; the ten intermediate chapters are from the second, but reproduce many sentences from the first version.

45. "The young vagrants," Frégier wrote, "that is to say, children from seven to sixteen years of age, who live a wandering and idle life, form a sort of corporation whose members have to help each other to evade their parents and apprentice masters when they are looking for them."

46. *Journal des Débats*, January 10, 1828: "Three children, the eldest aged fifteen, arrested in the Hôtel-de-Ville district for shoplifting. Their noms-de-guerre are Cartouche, Mandrin and Tranche-Montagne. A curious and alarming point is that the three children understand and speak thieves' slang and seem to be up to all the thieves' tricks. When 'Cartouche's' mother went to the police station, the young rogue threw his shoe at her head and shouted, 'You're lucky I've been arrested or I'd have killed you tonight!' "

Chapter Five (pp. 125–144)

1. Saint-Simon, *Oeuvres choisies*, 1859, vol. III, p. 274.

2. The only thing of interest to us in the *Nouveau monde industriel* is Fourier's depiction of the proletarians, or what he calls "the misfortune of the industrious." The main elements in this "misfortune" were hunger, disease and the hospital, "the wife and daughter degraded to prostitution by the snares of the wealthy neighbor." It should be emphasized that the docu-

ments, examples and, above all, the statistics he used related to London far
more often than to Paris and far less to Paris than to provincial craftsmen.
His description of poverty and crime was based on the poverty of the London
proletariat. The statistics for the indigent at London were: "117,000 known
paupers a charge on the parish; 115,000 paupers without relief, beggars,
pickpockets, vagabonds; noteworthy among them 3,000 fences, one of whom
is worth 20 million, and 3,000 Jews uttering counterfeit coin and instigating
valets to rob their masters in the city which is the greatest manufacturing
center. France is advancing toward this sort of poverty; Paris has 86,000
known paupers and perhaps as many again unknown. The French workmen
are so poor that in the principal manufacturing provinces such as Picardy,
with Amiens, Cambrai and Saint-Quentin, the peasants have no beds in their
mud huts."

3. Proudhon, *La Guerre et la Paix*, 1861, p. 336: "Poverty is the state
of nature. Pauperism is abnormal poverty. The great cities are one of the
causes of pauperism. Among the unfortunate, the characteristic of pauperism is the 'slow starvation' mentioned by Fourier, hunger at all times, all
the year round, throughout life; hunger which does not kill in a day, but is
all made up of deprivations, of longings; which unendingly saps the body,
impairs the spirit, demoralizes the conscience, bastardizes the race, engenders
every disease and every vice, among them drunkenness and envy, disdain
for work and thrift, baseness of soul, lack of conscience, coarseness of manners, idleness, begging, prostitution and theft. It is this slow starvation that
feeds the working classes' sullen hatred of the comfortable classes, displayed
in times of revolution in strokes of ferocity which terrify the peaceable classes
for long after, bring tyranny in their train and keep the authorities constantly on the alert in normal times."

4. "Let us say that society today hatches out with its impure breath innumerable legions of seceders, unproductive or destructive beings: sharpers,
harlots, vagabonds, beggars, convicts, pickpockets, bandits, whose numbers
are decreasing less than ever. We again accuse society; for will anyone venture to assert that all these unfortunate human creatures would be what they
are if they had been placed in happier circumstances? . . . Were all these
beings predestined, were they born bandits, are they pickpockets, beggars
and harlots by inheritance or by necessity?"

5. "It is not the number of convictions alone that is to be determined
here, but the number of offenses. The work of the criminal courts is merely
one particular piece of machinery which serves to bring out the moral
destruction of humanity under the monopoly system; but this official exposition by no means embraces the extent of the evil. Here are some other figures
which may lead us to a surer approximation. The Paris police courts dealt
with:

> 106,467 cases in 1835
> 128,489 cases in 1836
> 140,247 cases in 1837.

Let us suppose that the increase continued progressively up to 1846 and
that to this total of the cases in the correctional courts we add those at the
assize courts and minor police tribunals and all the unknown or unsolved
crimes, the number of which, according to the officers of the courts, greatly
exceeds the number brought to trial. We shall come to the conclusion that
in one year in the city of Paris more breaches of the law are committed than

there are inhabitants. And since children of seven and under must necessarily be subtracted from the number of persons presumed to have committed these offenses, as they are outside the limits of culpability, we shall have to reckon that every adult citizen is guilty of an offense against the established order three or four times a year."

6. Similarly, Louis Blanc wrote from London in July 1849 in the first number of the *Nouveau monde*: "Order, good God! But what is this order which reconciles itself with poverty, prostitution, theft, murder, with the prisons to be filled and the guillotine they dare not abolish? What is this order which carries us helplessly and incessantly from crisis to crisis, from riot to insurrection and from insurrection to civil war? The family. . . . It needs a purer climate than that in which it is visibly degenerating and dissolving today. We have only to take up the *Gazette des tribunaux* and read." The problem of criminality is thus posited in the very first issue of the *Nouveau monde*.

7. "If the results freeze us with terror, the least we can do is to take the trouble to go back to the causes. Strictly speaking, there is but one, and it is called poverty. When a man is handed over to the executioner nowadays, if you ask why, the answer is: 'Because this man has committed a crime.' And if you go on to ask why this man committed a crime, there is no reply! I was reading the *Gazette des tribunaux* a few days ago, on November 4, 1844; it contained poignantly significant details about a recent murder: 'On July 12 last,' the bill of indictment drawn by Procureur-Général Hébert stated, 'Chevreuil appeared at the police station in the Conservatoire-des-Arts-et-Métiers district and confessed to murdering his woman and forthwith gave particulars of the crime of which he declared himself guilty; he said that his victim, one Caelina-Annette Bronn, was a concubine with whom he had been living for a month past; that, desperate and weary of a life made intolerable by poverty, they had agreed to die together.' The poor girl whom her lover had just stifled under a sheet of cobbler's wax was not a vulgar being, to judge by the evidence at the trial. 'I'll tell you my thoughts,' she had said to her lover one day. 'When I was younger I worked at Saint-Maur, and on fine evenings I used to walk into the fields by myself near the vault of Saint-Maur, in a charming place where I was surrounded by greenery and flowers. I often wept there for the vain dreams I constructed.' "

8. For example, on December 16, 1839 (vol. I, p. 118), Proudhon wrote: "There are 30,000 tailors idle; as many proportionately in other trades; the unemployed are estimated at 150,000. How do they live? It's a mystery. Here is the explanation: it is not always the same people who are without work; they work in turns, one or two days a week, though there is nothing fixed about this rotation. When they have earned 3 francs, 4 francs, 6 francs, the need for refreshment drives them to the outer boulevards." February 12, 1840 (vol. I, p. 184): "The people goes on dying or getting jailed for theft or vagrancy."

9. See in this connection S. L. Puech's studies on Flora Tristan, *La vie et l'oeuvre de Flora Tristan*, 1925.

10. "Many malefactors," Louis Blanc wrote, "have a kind of official position in Paris. The police know them, have their name and address, have a file on their corrupt practices; they follow at their heels in order to take them in the act. The villains strut so long as there is no legal proof of their excesses and remain boldly on the alert for any chance. So that the forces

of repression and the forces of evil constitute two hostile powers within our society, entrenching themselves at their leisure, constantly and openly watching each other, eyeing one another askance, tricking each other and condemning us to look on without rest or respite at the vicissitudes of their everlasting combat. This is comparatively unimportant. Crime was long concerned only with brutal, solitary and personal impulses. But nowadays the murderers and robbers are forming ranks; they obey discipline; they have given themselves a code and a morality; they work in gangs and with well-devised schemes. The criminal court has recently paraded before our eyes the Chapentier gang, which had declared war on middling fortunes; the Courvoisier gang, which had systematized the pillaging of the faubourg Saint-Germain; the Gauthier Perez gang, which robbed the workers' savings; and the gangs of the Auvergnats, the Chloroformers and the Stranglers. Force, inadmissible where labor is concerned, is passing into the camp of crime. And, until we resolve to organize the association of workers, we shall simply look on while the association of assassins organizes itself."

11. Eugène Buret, *De la Misère des classes laborieuses en Angleterre et en France,* 1840.

12. The subject was: "What does distress [*la misère*] consist in, by what signs is it observable in various countries, what are its causes?" Twenty-two essays were submitted. Buret's received the highest award. The essay by Moreau-Christophe, the Inspector-General of Prisons, received an honorable mention.

13. 2 vols., 1840.

14. Buret, *op. cit.*

BOOK II
Introduction (pp. 147–157)

1. Dom Michel Félibien, *Histoire de la ville de Paris,* 5 vols., 1725. Henri Sauval, *Histoire et recherches des antiquités de la ville de Paris,* 1724.

2. In Volume I of his *Tableaux de Paris* (1783), Mercier wrote: "Health is the human benefit to which mankind appears most indifferent. Narrow, badly laid-out streets, houses which are too tall and so impede the free circulation of air, slaughterhouses, fish markets, sewers and cemeteries corrupt the atmosphere, which becomes charged with polluted atoms, and the air thus pent in becomes stagnant and has a malignant influence. The houses are so excessively tall that the people who live on the street level and the first floor are still shrouded in obscurity when the sun is at its height. The houses built on the bridges . . . prevent the draft from sweeping the city from end to end. Citizens who go out in search of pure country air on Sundays and holidays encounter the foul exhalations of night soil and other filth almost as soon as they are beyond the city gates; the filth covers the countryside for half a league around. The stench of cadavers is perceptible in almost every church; that is why many people are turning away from them and refuse to set foot in them. . . . There have been burials in the cemetery of the Innocents for over a thousand years—a fearful thought!"

3. We could cite many examples of these popular beliefs, such as that in the purgative virtues of Seine water. Similarly, at the time of the 1832 cholera epidemic, the inhabitants of Clichy were so convinced of the virtues of the ammoniac atmosphere in which the chemical factories enveloped them that they begged M. Pluvinet not to close down his factory and even offered to contribute any cash he needed to stay open.

4. Delamare says: "The city of Paris, thanks to Providence and the scrupulous observance of all these precautions, has been spared all contagious diseases for nearly a century. Therefore, in order to account for what is invariably observed at all times of this most distressing of all calamities, we have to see the evidence in the fortunate circumstance that appropriate regulations were issued in the distant past." And his review of the regulations of the distant past was dominated by the idea that contagion came from outside the city and that the city could protect itself against it.

5. Delamare's description of contagion is linked with the description of beggary. If a contagious epidemic occurred the thing to do was to expel the infection, which might be caused by the beggars. "Infection is usually the result of a great concourse of poverty-stricken beggars, which has always been regarded as one of the most certain causes of contagious diseases."

6. There are similar observations in *Voyage religieux et sentimental aux quatre cimetières de Paris*, 1809, pp. 156–57.

7. Lachaise, *op. cit.*

8. Moheau, *op. cit.*

9. We shall give only one example from this abundant picturesque literature, *De la salubrité de la Ville de Paris*, by Alphonse L., pedestrian, a pamphlet published in 1826, which has the merit of bringing together all these themes: "One is astounded at the excessive uncleanliness of the public thoroughfares. The provincial and the foreigner ask the Parisian what is the reason for this disorder, this repugnant aspect; they ask whether there are no police regulations concerning a matter of such importance—it seems impossible to go about, to pass from one district to another, without getting covered with black mud and muck. How do you manage to get away from these sloughs, these piles of garbage encountered at every step? This is a matter of much moment to the inhabitants' health. . . . It was realized several years ago that it was a serious drawback to have slaughterhouses and butchers' scalding rooms inside the towns; stockyards were erected at the farthest confines of the faubourgs; large buildings and broad, tree-planted spaces ensure that these establishments are well-ventilated, clean and hygienic. . . . But that took a very long time. The sick? The doctors make their patients move to other districts, order many of them to go and live on the heights of the faubourgs or to leave the city. Garbage of all kinds is flung out on the street from more than 200,000 households every day. The residues from the factories swell these heaps. Horses, carriages, pedestrians pass to and fro over this refuse and debris, and pound it down, converting it into a black mud which is diluted with the foul waters from factories and chemical works, rainwater and household slops; and the men whose job it is take a long time and spend a great deal of hard labor in removing it. Half of it is barely cleared before the other half spreads into the gutters and chokes the flow, and it disappears only when heavy downpours drive it along to block the drains. Foul effluvia and pestilential vapors emanate from the places where this garbage has been deposited from time immemorial, and the mud, too, seeps into the cracks in the paving and stays there. And, even worse, from the gully holes rise fetid, noxious gases even more liable to asphyxiate passers-by, which compel the tenants to evacuate the houses nearest them. The sewage from the drains flows into the Seine and forms a bed of mud beside its banks; this pollutes the water, which is intended for washing and bathing and even to supply drinking water to most

of the city. The heaviest deposits remain in the sewers, and this necessitates frequent scouring; the inlets are then closed and great pools of filthy water spread on the streets and squares, making them impassable. In heavy thunderstorms and thaws the drains cannot carry off the water fast enough and so it invades the cellars and spoils everything in them. . . . Add to this the rotting vegetables deposited by thousands of greengrocers in front of their shops. The mud turns into dust in summer. The narrower streets become impassable. The houses in them are let cheap, and most of those who dwell in them are of a pale and livid complexion, the sign of ill-health and poverty. The result is that people give up even trying to keep themselves and their houses clean after attempting to do so in vain. So we live in a state of filth, with which foreigners, especially those from the north, rightly reproach us." Bibliothèque Sévigné, 12mo.

10. *Les Fous de Paris, Bibliothèque Sévigné,* 2931, 18mo. [The air is cold and heavy, the night has no stars, the waters are all muddy . . . You jostle as you walk a people with black looks. Stay at home, lads, one suffers too much here. In Paris, look you, everything is luxury or poverty. Oh, never come here, for your own sake, for your mother's sake! For the night you leave, a good angel tells you that Paris is accursed!—Trans.]

11. Proudhon, *Correspondance,* vol. I, p. 115.

PART I

Chapter One (pp. 161–174)

1. Chevalier, *La formation de la population parisienne au XIXe siècle.*

2. François Simiand, *Le salaire, l'évolution sociale et la monnaie,* 3 vols., 1932.

Chapter Two (pp. 175–185)

1. Messance, using a technique we shall discuss later, estimated the population at 576,000 in the middle of the century, but admitted that "a current view is that Paris holds over 700,000 souls." Actually, Piganiol de la Force estimated it as between 700,000 and 800,000, and Voltaire as between 700,000 and 750,000.

2. Buffon, *op. cit.*

3. Messance, *Nouvelles recherches sur la population de la France,* 1788.

4. ["The son of my manservant, raised on my farm to useful work, who was taken away from me, goes off to Paris to swell the army of Paris lackeys." —Trans.]

5. Moheau, *op. cit.*

Chapter Three (pp. 186–199)

1. Mercier, *op. cit.*

2. *Journal des Débats,* October 2, 1828: "Between 1809 and 1821 the Highways Administration granted 1,362 permits:

1810:	128	1816:	120
1811:	109	1817:	142
1812:	128	1818:	133
1813:	110	1819:	157
1814:	71	1820:	178
1815:	86		

The building fever then suddenly redoubled, but later died down somewhat. The number of applications for permits was:

1821:	255	1823:	275
1822:	283	1824:	395

and 230 in the first six months of 1825. Thus, in fifteen and a half years 2,800 houses were erected from the ground up or were rebuilt behind their original frontages."

3. *Recherches statistiques sur la Ville de Paris,* vol. IV, 1829.

4. Over 500 orders were published between 1830 and 1848 concerning building lines in Paris streets. In accordance with the method devised by Chabrol, an attempt was made to cut back parts of houses which projected dangerously beyond the ordinary line in thoroughfares with heavy traffic.

5. On this practice by Paris house owners and architects we quote the comments by several architects convened by the Prefect Chabrol in 1828 to investigate the reasons for the fall in land values and the stagnation in real estate transactions. These comments had already been recorded in a memorandum sent in 1829 to the members of the Commission of Inquiry set up by the Ministry of the Interior on July 7, 1828; they deal in part with the height of buildings and attribute the insolvency of the speculators to the architects' strange mania for taking advantage of the full height permitted by the regulations and thereby creating centers of corruption by superimposing too many storeys. In March 1833, the *Edile de Paris,* the house owners' journal, commented on this document: "We are well aware that misconceived personal interest may be an obstacle and that the fees on a three-storey house costing 200,000 francs will not be so productive as they would on the same house with five storeys entailing an outlay of 300,000 francs. We are also aware that the notion that roofing is a single item and that it costs no more to build a roof over the fifth storey than the first will be advanced as an argument by some obstinate and unimaginative builders. As a matter of fact, a comparison of total outlays leads to the conclusion that there has been a deficit whenever buildings have been raised higher than the third storey, whereas the accounts have balanced whenever buildings have not exceeded that height. The more tenants there are in a house, the harder it is to derive the full return from it. It is not uncommon in Paris for a house owner to get less than he had previously earned from renting his main apartments once a building has been enlarged, either because the apartments have become less commodious since their view, air and light have been impaired or because they have lost such conveniences as stables, coach houses and servants' quarters; because, in short, the tenants rightly fear all sorts of unpleasant contacts owing to the excessive number of persons in the building. Lastly, tall great houses of five or six storeys subdivided into a multitude of dwellings are almost always filled with undesirable tenants, since the owners are forced by necessity of getting their money back to let to a crowd of persons unknown to one another and without proper references."

6. The height of buildings was fixed as follows in the letters patent of August 1784:

Width of street	Height of frontage
30 feet and over	54 feet
24 to 30 feet	45 feet
Under 23 feet	36 feet

7. Mrs. Trollope in 1835 described "the profound darkness of every part of the city in which there are not shops illuminated by the owners with gas. This is done brilliantly on the Boulevards . . . but no sooner is this region of light and gaiety left, than you seem to plunge into outer darkness; and there is not a little country town in England which is not incomparably better lighted than any street in Paris which depends for its illumination upon the public regulations of the city." [*Op cit.,* Letter XV.—Trans.]

8. A.N. F.⁸ 239.

Chapter Four (pp. 200–214)

1. Martin-Saint-Léon, *Résumé statistique des recettes et dépenses de la Ville de Paris, de 1797 à 1840,* second edition, 1843.

2.

	1819	1820	1821
Total expenditure:	38,728,000	41,459,000	43,557,000
Hospitals, almshouses, relief:	5,200,000	5,500,000	5,500,000
	1822	1825	1828
Total expenditure:	43,695,000	50,179,000	44,597,000
Hospitals, almshouses, relief:	5,500,000	5,200,000	5,500,000
	1829		
Total expenditure:	48,695,000		
Hospitals, almshouses, relief:	5,813,000		

3. The Saint-Denis canal was opened to traffic on May 14, 1821. In September 1821, the Municipality was authorized to conclude an agreement for the operation and concession of the Saint-Martin canal, to run from the La Villette basin to the ditches at the Bastille; it was finally approved by royal command on August 15. Meanwhile, the work on the Ourcq canal was progressing, and in July 1822 it was navigable from the La Villette basin to Claye. It was opened, though still dry from Claye to the bridge at Beauval below Meaux. On January 21, 1825, the waters of the Ourcq were turned into the new canal and reached La Villette. "Hitherto the reservoir and the Saint-Denis canal had been fed only by the waters of the Beuvronne," the *Journal des Débats* wrote on January 21, 1825. "It had only been navigable from Claye to Paris, but it should soon be open to shipping along the whole of the Ourcq canal from Mareuil to La Villette." And, lastly, the Saint-Martin canal was opened to navigation on November 4, 1825.

4. *Journal des Débats,* September 24, 1828: "The placing of sidewalks in several busy streets has led the Prefect of Police to request eating-house keepers, restaurateurs, café owners and the like to store their garbage in baskets or boxes until the street-cleaning carts pass. It is heartily to be wished that this custom, which has long existed in several large towns, should be established in Paris, where the habit of shooting every kind of garbage into the streets at all hours of the day or night frustrates all the authorities' efforts to keep the city clean."

5. Charles Gourlier, *Résumé chronologique des principales circonstances relatives aux égouts de Paris,* 1852:

In 1660 . . . . 10,034 meters
Sewers built between 1660 and January 1, 1806
(mostly under Louis XV and Louis XVI) . . . . 13,496 meters

Survey of sewers in existence on January 1, 1806 . . . . .25,530 meters
Sewers built between 1806 and 1823 . . . . 9,873 meters
—between 1824 and 1832 . . . . .10,836 meters
Sewers in existence on January 1, 1832, according to Emmery . . . .40,302 meters

6. For example, the section for almshouses and welfare establishments, including grants toward the hospitals' yearly outlay and the services for foundlings and deserted children. The municipal allocations were:

1831	1832	1833	1834	1835	1836
6,379,000	8,066,000	5,329,000	5,328,000	5,339,000	5,295,000

1837	1838	1839	1840	1841	1842
5,388,000	5,142,000	5,347,000	5,591,000	5,487,000	5,413,000

1843	1844	1845	1846	1847	1848
4,712,000	5,791,000	5,595,000	5,965,000	15,166,000	7,387,000.

7. These are to a large extent the sections for major items of civil engineering, such as bridges, highways and waterworks. The allocations and their percentage of total expenditures were:

1831	1832	1833	1834	1835
3,089,467.99	7,329,259.31	1,634,054.36	2,150,983.30	3,510,133.36
5.88%	12.96%	4.28%	5.32%	8.38%

1836	1837	1838	1839	1840
4,352,716.46	5,119,108.25	6,077,123.69	5,677,059.21	5,586,866.95
10.35%	11.39%	14.79%	13.63%	12.63%

1841	1842	1843	1844	1845
—	—			
17.69%	17.59%	17.63%	21.44%	19.53%

1846	1847	1848	1849	1850
15.98%	21.77%	24.04%	18.42%	17.51%.

8. On January 1, 1832, there were only 39,150 meters of conduits, including the encircling aqueduct, besides 217 street taps; on January 1, 1839, there were 134,810 meters of conduits and 1,020 street taps; on January 1, 1842, 165,411 meters and 1,158 street taps; at the end of 1850, 358,000 meters and 1,837 street taps. In 1816, the city water supply was only 8,283 m^3 per day; in 1841, it was 86,400 m^3.

	1816	1841
Arcueil	960 m^3	1,536 m^3
Belleville and Pré-Saint-Gervais	288	384
Seine (Notre-Dame pump)	941	1,920
Seine (fire pump)	5,480	5,760
Seine (prisons)	614	abolished
Ourcq canal		76,800
	8,283 m^3	86,400 m^3

9. In 1840, Emmery published statistics in the *Annales des Ponts et Chaussées* of the Paris water supply and of the distribution of the 4,000 inches supplied by the canal and the 500 inches by the Seine and the old aqueducts. He estimated daily consumption at 100 liters per head. But the consumption by workshops must be subtracted from this.

10. Henri-Charles Emmery de Sept-Fontaines, *Nécrologie,* 1840.

11. P. J. Griard, chief engineer in charge of the Paris municipal service, *Recherches sur les établissements de bains publics à Paris,* 1832.

12. Construction of sewers: 1832–1840, 62,682 meters; 1841–1847, 27,311 meters; 1848–1850, 5,587 meters.

Thus, the length of the sewers as compared with 1660 was:

2½ times as long in 1806	10½ times as long in 1840
4 times as long in 1832	13 times as long in 1847
7½ times as long in 1837	15 times as long in 1852.

Expenditures on new sewers were:

1841	1842	1843	1844
542,000	548,000	416,000	302,000

1845	1846	1847	1848
304,000	187,000	278,000	225,000.

13. Auguste Luchet, *Paris, esquisses dediées au peuple parisien et à M. J.-A. Dulaure . . . ,* 1830.

14. *Annales d'Hygiène,* 1832, vol. VII.

15. Parent-Duchatelet, *Les chantiers d'équarrissage de la ville de Paris,* 1832.

16. A number of official orders issued at the end of the Ancien Régime and during the Revolutionary period, from 1739 on, prohibited the sale of horsemeat and made it an offense to procure it from Montfaucon. In 1811 the police commissioners seized large parcels of this meat (some of them weighing as much as 100 to 140 kilos) at low cookshops situated near places where the indigent assembled, especially in the quartier des Halles and at several places in the faubourg Saint-Marcel, in the rue de la Mortellerie, the rue du Plâtre-Saint-Jacques, the rue de la Huchette and the rue de Saint-Victor. The sale of horsemeat was permitted in and after 1825, but subject to some measure of control. Fresh abuses appeared during periods of extreme poverty. In February 1831, the Health Committee of the quartier de l'Observatoire reported a house full of prostitutes—in which a large quantity of horsemeat for feeding the inhabitants of the district was found—for infringing the sanitary regulations.

17. Most of these reports were summarized in the *Annales d'Hygiène*. See also A. Trébuchet, *Code administratif des établissements dangereux, insalubres ou incommodes,* 1832. The report of the Commission for the Study of Questions Raised by the Agglomeration of Dangerous, Insanitary and Inconvenient Establishments in Paris, May 1856, contains a description of their development from 1847 to 1856.

18. A.N.F[8] 95.

PART II
Chapter One (pp. 217–223)

1. There is no reason to suppose that the death rate in epidemics was any different from that observed in the first half of the nineteenth century, the cholera epidemic of 1832 in particular, when more men than women died in Paris.

2. Moheau, *op. cit.*

3. Mercier, *op. cit.*
4. Dr. Patissier, *Traité des maladies des artisans,* 1822.
5. Number of births:

1770	19,954	1779	20,614	Year I	1793	24,155
1771	18,941	1780	19,617	Year II	1794	24,312
1772	18,713	1787	20,378	Year III	1795	23,937
1773	18,847	1788	20,708	Year IV	1796	18,759
1774	19,353	1789	20,340	Year V	1797	23,558
1775	19,650	1790	20,005	Year VI	1798	23,512
1776	18,919	1791	20,354	Year VII	1799	22,953
1777	22,266	1792	16,269	Year VIII	1800	20,711
1778	21,688	(265 days).				

6. Meister wrote: "I am not the only traveler who has noted that never were so many pregnant women seen in Paris as one sees today."
7. Indeed, in the Year VI, 3,029 of 3,513 babies sent to the Foundlings died; in the Year VII, 3,001 out of 3,777.
8.

Year	Births	Deaths	Surplus of births	Surplus of deaths
1789	20,340	19,962	378	
1790	20,005	19,447	558	
1791	20,354	17,952	2,402	
1792	16,269	17,416		148
1793	24,155	21,167	2,988	
1794	24,312	30,388		6,076
1795	23,937	26,978		3,041
1796	18,759	27,779		9,020
1797	23,558	20,381	2,177	
1798	23,312	20,287	3,025	
1799	22,953	22,932	21	
1800	20,711	19,872	1,339	
TOTAL			13,888	18,285

9. Buffon, *op. cit.*
10. Louis Lazare asserted that the municipal registers go to show that 15,000 wealthy families, or at least 60,000 persons, left Paris between 1789 and 1792.
11. Mercier, vol. II, p. 162.
12. A.N. F^1 3688[7] (Police générale, Seine 1789–1792).

Chapter Two (pp. 224–254)

1. La Bédollière, *Les industriels.*
2. *Paris chez soi,* 1855, p. 254.
3. It so happens that we are able to measure the total immigration into Paris in 1817 and its age distribution for a document published in Volume IV of the *Recherches statistiques* in 1829 (table 53). This document gives the difference by age group between what the Paris population in 1817 should have been in accordance with the number of births and deaths and what it was according to the census.

		Census	Difference (+ represents net emigration)
0–5	85,297	48,824	+36,473
5–10	75,601	46,146	+29,455
10–15	72,072	50,199	+21,873
15–20	68,675	71,412	−2,737
20–25	62,543	73,586	−11,043
30–40	102,192	116,960	−14,768
40–50	85,215	90,929	−5,714
50–60	65,334	73,818	−8,484
60–70	41,615	50,702	−9,087
70–80	17,733	20,331	−2,598
80–90	3,152	4,065	−913
90–100	110	215	−105

4. Frégier, *op. cit.*

5. See also Pierre Mazerolle, *La misère de Paris: Les mauvais gîtes,* 1875.

6. Peuchet had written as early as February 21, 1792, in his official report to the police department with regard to the inspection of hotels and lodging houses: "I have always thought that more importance has been attributed to it than its real utility warrants; it is an imposition for men in no way suspect to be required to state their name and identity simply because business or convenience compels them to rent a furnished room. Any villain can easily find ways of evading the obstacles which this is intended to place in his path."

7. A.N. F⁷ 3873.

8. [See also p. 232.—Trans.]

9. *Annuaire de 1903,* p. 140.

10. *Recherches statistiques,* vol. VI, p. vi.

11. *Population,* April–June 1947, p. 349.

12. Chevalier, *La formation de la population parisienne au XIXᵉ siècle.*

13. The statistics for the importation of freestone into Paris in themselves identify the influence of the immigration of masons upon this increase.

14. Quételet, *op. cit.*

15. Antoine Caillot, *Voyage religieux et sentimental aux quatre cimetières de Paris,* 1809.

16. Lanfranchi, *Voyage à Paris,* 1830.

17. *Population,* October–December, 1952.

18. In *Le cousin Pons,* Remonencq, the moneylender, in a quiet house in the quiet rue de Normandie in the Marais, conceives the idea of poisoning his neighbor Cibot, the tailor and concierge, and offering the beautiful Madame Cibot promotion of this kind: "One morning as he was smoking his pipe, leaning against the jamb of his shop door and dreaming of the fine store on the boulevard de la Madeleine over which Madame Cibot would preside enthroned and superbly gowned, a highly oxidized copper ring happened to catch his eye."

19. In *Les vierges martyres* (1846), for instance, Esquiros wrote of the old women of Paris: "The best protected, those who attach themselves to curés in their old age, finally enter the Salpêtrière, a sort of communal repository wherein society stows away its rags and wrinkles. The others, exposed to the wind and the rain, sell matches, sticks of barleysugar or hanks of yarn on the streets to earn a few sous; many of the old beggarwomen

we meet on the Paris streets, winding a few threads of hemp on their distaff or selling phosphorous matches, are former working women whose strength has long ago given out. There is one of these old women in the rue des Grès behind the Law School, so wrinkled, so bleak, so bony and so cold that winter can do no more to her. When the snow falls in January, when the gutter freezes, you still see her there, sitting on the frozen flagstone, her withered hands turning the handle of an aged bird-organ."

20. Buret, *op. cit.*

21. The affluent districts; eliminating domestic service, the proportion of women falls:

in the Ist, from 53.73% to 51.96% = −1.77
in the IInd, from 53.49% to 51.12% = −2.37.

The poor districts; eliminating domestic service, the decrease in the proportionate female population is less, but not much less:

in the VIIIth, from 50.03% to 49.23% = −0.80
in the VIth, from 50.25% to 49.94% = −1.31.

22.

	Men	Women
rue de l'Hôtel-de-Ville	2,263	1,335
rue des Barres	480	219
rue Geoffroy-l'Asnier	851	720
rue des Nonaindières	357	221
But:		
quai de la Grève	240	291
quai des Ormes	265	297
rue Saint-Antoine	447	463

23. See the tables on pages 253 and 254.

24. *Annuaire statistique de la Ville de Paris*, 1880, p. 152.

BOOK III

PART I

Chapter One (pp. 261–270)

1. Fourier, *Création de l'ordre*, Chapter 3.

2. Simiand, *op. cit.*

3. A.N. F⁷ 677².

4. A.N. F¹¹ 533 and *Recherches statistiques*, vol. II, table 73.

5. A.N. F¹¹ 261.

6. *Journal des Débats*, November 2, 1832.

7. *Journal des Débats*, November 2, 1830.

8. Parent-Duchatelet, *Les Chantiers d'équarrissage*. Alphonse Lescot described in his *Salubrité de la Ville de Paris* (1826) "the humiliating spectacle of unfortunates grubbing for dirty and unhealthy food in the refuse from the rich man's table in the garbage heaps on the streets, and even then having to fight the animals for it."

9. *Journal des Débats*, November 8, 1829.

10. A.N. F¹¹ 261.

11. *Journal des Débats*, February 8, 1828.

12. Proudhon quotes and comments on Hégésippe Moreau's *Ode à la faim* in *La justice dans la Révolution et dans l'Eglise*, vol. III, p. 107.

13. Heinrich Heine, *De la France.*
14. A.N. F²¹, 1290–1293.
15. A.N. F⁷ 6772.
16. In particular, by O. Festy in his study *Le Mouvement ouvrier au début de la Monarchie de Juillet, 1830–1834,* 1908, and by Georges Duveau in his *Eighteen Forty-Eight: The Making of a Revolution,* 1966.
17. A.N. F⁷ 6772.
18. A.N. F²¹ 1, 1290–1293.
19. "Within one month all the beggars not natives of the department of the Seine and the communes of Saint-Cloud, Sèvres and Meudon must leave their territory. They will be issued free of charge with traveling warrants or passports and a bounty for the road to their place of birth or habitual residence."
20. *Journal des Débats,* October 8, 1828: "A child of twelve or thirteen, Louis Brun, was arrested when soliciting charity from passers-by by showing off the tricks of a ferret. . . . When the inspector arrested him, he let the ferret loose in his face and it bit him."
21. The extension of the Villers-Cotteret workhouse and, in December 1829, the opening of a shelter and workhouse for the abolition of beggary at No. 95, rue de l'Oursine.

Chapter Two (pp. 271–292)

1. Vinçard, *Les ouvriers de Paris,* 1863.
2. The example of social success generally cited is that of the house painter Leclaire. Cf. Proudhon, *Les contradictions économiques,* vol. I, p. 245, and Puech, *Flora Tristan,* p. 163.
3. Cf. the statistics for the Morgue published in the *Annales d'Hygiène,* A.N. F⁷ 12243.
4. [A sort of small tower in which deserted babies could be concealed at the doors of institutions for foundlings.—Trans.]
5. Oral report on the sanitary inspection service to the Board of Health for Lyon and the Rhône department in 1826, 1827 and 1828 by Dr. Etienne de Sainte-Marie, member of the Board of Health and of the Lyon Statistical Committee, Paris.
6. *Annales d'Hygiène,* vol. XIII, 1835.
7. *Annales d'Hygiène,* vol. XXI, 1839.
8. *Annales d'Hygiène,* vol. XVI, 1836.
9. Cf. *Annales d'Hygiène,* vol. III, 1830, p. 198.
10. Mercier, *op. cit.*
11. J. F. Reichardt, *Un hiver à Paris, 1802–1803,* published in 1896.
12. In 1700 Thomas Creech, well known for his fine translation of Lucretius, wrote on the margin of the manuscript: "*Nota bene.* I shall have to kill myself when I have finished my book of Lucretius." And, like his favorite author, he kept his word. Voltaire helped considerably to spread this belief by his *Lettres anglaises.* "An Englishman visited me in Paris in 1724; he was ill and he told me he would kill himself if he was not restored to health by July 20. He even gave me his epitaph and handed me 25 louis to raise a small memorial to him at the end of the faubourg Saint-Martin. On July 20 I returned his money and kept his epitaph." The belief was strengthened by the suicide of the poet Chatterton in 1770.

13. Such as *Le diable à Paris* and Mrs. Trollope's visit to the Morgue: "Hatred, revenge, murder, are each terrible; but La Morgue outdoes them all in its power of bringing together in one syllable the abstract of whatever is most appalling in crime, poverty, despair, and death. To the ghastly Morgue are conveyed the unowned dead that are discovered in or near Paris. The Seine is the great receptacle which first receives the victims of assassination or despair." [Letter XXXVII.] Poverty is one of the reasons: "Can we be surprised after this that the Morgue is never empty and that the hand of tender love reaches out to light the stove whose fatal vapor is soon to extinguish the existence of a beloved victim whose life is too precious to continue in a world in which men and even women earn their bread only by the sweat of their brow?"

14. Tissier, *De la manie du suicide, de l'esprit de révolte, de leurs causes et de leurs remèdes,* 1840; Dr. Descuret, *Médecine des passions,* 1845; Dr. Bourdin, *Du suicide considéré comme maladie,* 1845. In 1848 the Academy of Medicine set a competition on the problem of suicide. The winning entry by Dr. Lisle, an alienist, was published in 1856.

15. Many examples of the contagious effects of suicide are to be found in the writings of the nineteenth-century alienists. Dr. Desloges, in practice at Saint-Maurice in the Valais, observed an epidemic of suicides of women in the village of Saint-Pierre-Monjau in 1813; after a woman had hanged herself on a tree, several others went and hanged themselves on it too. Pinel reported that a priest hanged himself near Etampes, and a few days later, two more killed themselves nearby, and several laymen imitated them. The story of the fifteen army pensioners who hanged themselves one after another on a hook in a dark passage in the pensioners' hospital in 1772 is well known; the epidemic ceased only when the hook was removed. At the camp at Boulogne in 1805 a soldier blew out his brains in a sentry box; within a few days others followed his lead in the same sentry box. The emperor ordered it burned and issued an order of the day in which he compared suicide to desertion in the face of the enemy. In 1862 an epidemic of suicides broke out among the juvenile delinquents in the Petite Roquette reformatory; grilles had to be built on either side of the bridge leading to the chapel.

16. For the early years of the Restoration, for example, reports of suicides are to be found in the *Journal des Débats* of August 31, 1821; September 1, 1821; October 4, 1821; July 7, 1822; October 7, 1822; January 2, 1823; July 25, 1823; July 26, 1823; October 15, 1823; January 9, 1824; May 31, 1824; July 4, 1824; and October 2, 1826.

17. The number of attempted or successful suicides in Paris from 1817 to 1826 and from 1839 to 1848 was as follows:

1817	351	1839	670
1818	330	1840	748
1819	376	1841	712
1820	325	1842	670
1821	348	1943	681
1822	317	1844	715
1823	390	1845	745
1824	371	1846	713
1825	396	1847	918
1826	511	1848	698

18. For France alone, the increase was:

	Annual average	No. of suicides per 100,000 inhabitants	Increase in number of suicides (1826–30 = 100)
1826–1830	1,827	50	100
1831–1835	2,119	60	130
1836–1840	2,574	70	148
1841–1845	2,931	80	170
1846–1850	3,446	90	199
1886–1887	8,194	210	471

19. See for example, the list of attempted or successful suicides in the department of the Seine:

	Total no. of suicides	No. of male suicides		Total no. of suicides	No. of male suicides
1817	351	235	1822	317	206
1818	330	192	1823	390	262
1819	376	250	1824	371	239
1820	325	211	1825	396	272
1821	348	236	1826	511	333

Between 1839 and 1848, 4,859 of 7,270 suicides were men.

20. The distribution by age was compiled by Guerry and published in the *Annales d'Hygiène* in 1831, but only for men and only for suicides by hanging and pistol:

Age	Suicides in Berlin	Suicides in Paris (pistol)	Suicides in Paris (hanging)	Suicides in Geneva	Population distribution by age
10–20	224	61	68	53	312
20–30	251	283	51	252	188
30–40	96	182	94		160
40–50	156	150	188		136
50–60	146	161	256	474	100
60–70	77	126	235		68
70–80	41	35	108	221	30
80 and over	9	2	0		6
TOTALS:	1,000	1,000	1,000	1,000	1,000

21. The following table of suicides and attempted suicides in Paris for each month from 1817 to 1825 inclusive is to be found in the Board of Health report, published by *Annales d'Hygiène,* vol. XLIV, 1850:

April	374	September	247
June	336	February	218
May	328	December	217
July	301	January	213
August	296	October	198
March	275	November	181

Foreign suicide statistics:

	Berlin (1812–22)	Hamburg (1816–22)
January, February, March	109	39
April, May, June	155	31
July, August, September	173	41
October, November, December	145	38

A paper in the *Annales médico-psychologiques* (vol. X, p. 131) finds a connection between a rise in the temperature and two suicides in July 1847. Of the 3,084 successful suicides in France in 1845, 922 occurred in June, July and August; 860 in March, April and May; 765 in September, October and November; and 545 in December, January and February.

22. Statistics established by Guerry:

Days of the Week
(Percentage distribution of 6,587 cases throughout the week)

Monday	15.20	Friday	13.71
Tuesday	15.71	Saturday	11.19
Wednesday	14.90	Sunday	13.57
Thursday	15.68		

Time of day*

(*Suicides by hanging*)

Midnight–2 A.M.	77
2–4	45
4–6	45
6–7	135
8–10	110
10–12	123
12–2	32
2–4	84
4–6	104
6–8	77
8–10	84
10–12	71
TOTAL	1,000

* *Annales d'Hygiène*, January 1831.

23. In Paris from 1839 to 1848, 7,270 suicides were divided into the following categories:

Method of suicide		% of total	% per method of suicide	Total males (in 4,859)
Asphyxiation by coal gas	2,065	28.4	21.5	1,045
Asphyxiation by drowning	1,770	24.3	24.1	1,170
Asphyxiation by strangling	1,191	16.4	20.9	1,015
Intentional fall	743	10.2	8.3	402
Cold steel	477	6.6	7.9	382
Firearms	655	9.0	13.4	651
Poison	369	5.1	4.0	194

Thus, asphyxiation by coal comes first in Paris, followed by drowning: *men* (1) drowning, (2) strangling, (3) coal gas; *women* preference for asphyxiation by coal gas (probably, according to the commentators, out of a desire to avoid disfigurement or exposing a bleeding or bedraggled body to the public gaze).

24. Alfred Legoyt, *Le suicide ancien et moderne, étude historique, philosophique et statistique,* 1881.

25. Emile Durkheim, *Le suicide,* 1897.

26. Such as Lacordaire and the abbé Guillon in *Entretiens sur le suicide* (1802 and 1836).

27. Such as Brière de Boismont, in *"De l'influence de la civilisation sur le suicide," Annales d'Hygiène,* 1855: "One of the strongest influences we have observed is the modern melancholy, which no longer has faith, gazes complacently into a dangerous void and prides itself on a total incapacity for action. Next come the democratic idea, that is to say, the general belief that everything is easily attainable, and the cruel disappointments consequent upon it, the exaggeration of the doctrine of material interest, the disasters inseparable from unbridled competition, the frantic excitements of luxury, the consciousness of privation more deeply felt owing to the march of mind, the weakening of religious sentiment, the prevalence of doubt and materialist ideas, and the political upheavals, with their ensuing ruins." Similar ideas also appear in Dr. Descuret, *Médecine des passions.*

28. Esquirol wrote in his article on *"Suicide"* in the *Dictionnaire des Sciences médicales*: "A people among whom life may become an infamy and death a duty (Voltaire) and where public morality and the warnings of religion no longer curb the passions is bound to look upon death as a safe haven from physical pain and mental suffering. Suicide is bound to become far commoner among a people in such straits."

29. Lachaise, *op. cit.*

30. Brone, *"Considérations sur les suicides de notre époque," Annales d'Hygiène,* 1836. Guerry calculated that the ratio in the department of the Seine from 1827 and 1835 was 1 to 2,094.

31. Cf. pp. 471–72.

32. The presumed motives for the total of 7,270 suicides between 1839 and 1848 were as follows:

	Motive for suicide	% of total	Total males	% males in each category
Amorous passion	1,627	22.4	870	17.9
Illness	1,909	26.2	1,308	26.9
Gambling	1,203	16.5	908	18.7
Poverty	1,260	17.3	938	19.3
Motive unknown	1,271	17.5	835	17.2

33. *Annales médico-psychologiques,* vol. X, p. 278.

34. In 1876, per million persons in each category there were 120 suicides in agriculture, 190 in industry, 130 in trade, 290 in domestic service, 550 in the liberal professions and 2,350 persons without occupation or of occupation unknown.

35. Legoyt, *op. cit.,* p. 179.

36. Annual statistics of the Morgue published in the *Annales d'Hygiène.*

Chapter Three (pp. 293–309)

1. "More than two-thirds of Americans," Nathalie Rogoff wrote, "enter an occupational category different from that of their father; of the French only about half. Effective mobility in France is about three-fifths of what it would be if society were completely open. In the United States the corresponding proportion is four-fifths." *Population,* October–December 1950.

2. A.N. F^{20} 434 (Prefects' reports in compliance with the circular of May 10, 1808). F^{20} 435 (in particular, a report of December 1809 on casual laborers working in Paris, such as street porters, messengers, sweeps, crockery menders and shoemenders).

3. See in particular the six volumes of *Le Rôdeur* published in 1816; the *Livre des 101, Paris au XIXe siècle*, an album of sketches by Gavarni, published in 1841. Victor Hugo depicted the Auvergnat in Volume III of *Les Misérables.*

4. La Bédollière, *Les industriels.*

5. "All the provinces send us building workers," wrote La Bédollière, "and in the variegated patois bandied about in the dinner break you recognize the lively tones of the Provençal, the drawl of the Lorrainer and the harsh accent of the Alsatian. Quite recently some masons downed tools on the Paris fortifications because they did not find the beer to their liking (they were Flemings). It is to be noted, however, that a large proportion of the laborers come from Germany, and have been imported so recently that the least ignorant of them have sometimes to act as interpreters for their fellow workers on the building sites."

6. *Journal des Débats,* September 20, 1826.

Chapter Four (pp. 310–319)

1. Lecouturier, *op cit.*

2. "In 1880," said Bertillon, "56,052 live births were registered in Paris by mothers domiciled in Paris (and 1,023 by mothers living outside Paris), of which 14,269 were illegitimate (i.e., 25.45 illegitimates in 100 total births); 2,705 of these were recognized immediately at the time of registration, necessarily by the father, the parent who was physically able to go to the town hall and sign the register. Since 927 children were later formally recognized by the father, this gives a total of 3,632 children born out of wedlock and recognized by their fathers (i.e., 25.44 recognitions by the father in 100 illegitimate births). Further, 2,890 natural children were legitimized by marriage within the year. Several, perhaps many, of them had not been recognized at the time of birth and would have to be added to those recognized by the father; but how many? We cannot even hazard a guess. The figure of 3,632 natural children recognized by their father is therefore a minimum. It may be inferred from this and from the ensuing considerations that we may venture to presume there are at least 4,000 live births each year, the issue of regular cohabitation. For many of the male partners, though they bring up their children properly, do not recognize them; most of them because they simply neglect to do so, but others because they consider the formality unnecessary since they wish to legitimize the child by subsequent marriage (and as we see, there are 2,000 to 3,000 such marriages yearly). Others do not recognize them out of an excessive anxiety to avoid the harsh operation of the present French law in respect of natural children, who, if recognized, can

inherit only a very small portion of their parents' estate. If, then, to keep down to a bare minimum, we assume that there are only 4,000 recognitions or legitimizations yearly and if (against all probability) we assume illicit unions to be as fertile as regular marriages, then since the product of regular marriages is about ten times that of illicit unions yearly (as the same facts recur every year), we should have to conclude that there is one illicit union to 10 regular marriages. And since there were about 825,000 married couples in Paris in 1876, there would be over 82,500 illicit unions! But we should be right in assuming, first, that since the number of births from illicit unions was certainly higher than the number presumed (4,000) and, secondly, that since their presumed fertility (equal to that of married couples) is undoubtedly higher in reality, the two circumstances combined lead us to assume that the number of illicit unions given above is very much lower than the true number." *Annuaire statistique de la Ville de Paris,* 1880.

3. The figures for nonrecognized illegitimate children born at their parents' residence were as follows:

1837:	of 7,271 nonrecognized children,	3,091 born at home—	42.5
1838:	6,998	3,835	54.8
1839:	7,268	3,727	51.3
1840:	7,582	3,455	45.6
1841:	7,641	3,484	45.6
1842:	8,231	3,625	44.0
1843:	8,028	3,537	44.0
1844:	8,282	3,620	43.7
1845:	8,506	3,681	43.3
1846:	8,621	3,585	41.6
TOTAL:	78,428	35,640	45.4

4. The number of illegitimate births relative to total births was as follows:

		Births	Illegitimate births	%
1817 to 1821:	1817	23,750	9,047	38.1
	1818	23,067	8,089	35.1
	1819	24,352	8,641	35.5
	1820	24,858	8,870	35.7
	1821	25,156	8,176	36.5
1827 to 1832:	1827	29,806	10,392	34.9
	1828	29,601	10,475	35.4
	1829	28,521	9,953	34.9
	1830	28,587	10,007	35.0
	1831	29,530	10,378	35.1
	1832	26,283	9,237	35.1
1837 to 1846:	1837	29,192	9,578	32.8
	1838	29,743	9,289	31.2
	1839	30,380	9,471	31.2
	1840	30,213	9,650	31.9
	1841	29,923	9,830	32.8
	1842	31,304	10,286	32.8
	1843	30,616	10,097	33.0
	1844	31,956	10,430	32.6
	1845	32,905	10,626	32.3
	1846	33,387	10,695	32.0

5. Of 3,570 foundlings and abandoned children between 1842 and August 1843: 1,377 were born at the lying-in hospital; 466 were born in hospitals; 912 were born in Paris districts; 88 were born in the banlieue; 16 were born in the provinces; and 711 were born of unknown origin.

6. To take only 1819, 1820 and 1821 here, the arrondissements with hospitals in which the most illegitimate babies were born were:

		At home	In hospital
1819:	Vth	404	30
	IXth	286	83
	XIIth	493	4,163
1820:	Vth	417	49
	VIth	492	9
	IXth	271	80
	XIIth	540	4,219
1821:	Vth	396	113
	VIth	419	9
	IXth	345	96
	XIth	319	29
	XIIth	527	4,298

7. Esquiros, Bibliothèque Sévigné, 616 810,800.

8. The births of illegitimate children were divided by arrondissement as follows:

IXth: Ile Saint-Louis, Cité, Hôtel-de-Ville, Arsenal.	1 illegit. child among 3.49 legit. children
IVth: Saint-Honoré, Louvre, Marchés, Banque.	1 3.79
Vth: Faubourg Saint-Denis, faubourg Saint-Martin, Bonne-Nouvelle, Montorgueil.	1 3.90
IIIrd: Faubourg Poissonnière, Montmartre, Saint-Eustache, Mail.	1 3.96
IInd: Chaussée d'Antin, Palais-Royal, Feydeau, faubourg Montmartre.	1 3.98
XIth: Luxembourg, Ecole médecine, Sorbonne, Palais de Justice.	1 4.26
VIIth: Sainte-Avoye, Mont-de-Piété, Marché Saint-Jean-Arcis.	1 4.28
VIth: Porte-Saint-Denis, Saint-Martin-des-Champs, Lombards, Temple.	1 4.41
XIIth: Saint-Jacques, Saint-Marcel, Jardin du Roi, Observatoire.	1 4.81 (not including births at the lying-in hospital)
Xth: Monnaie, Saint-Thomas, Invalides, faubourg Saint-Germain.	1 5.10
VIIIth: Marais, Popincourt, Saint-Antoine, Quinze-Vingts.	1 5.17
Ist: Roule, Champs-Elysées, Vendôme, Tuileries.	1 6.33

9. For 1828, for example:

	Grand total of recognized and nonrecognized children	Children not recognized at birth	%
I	308	205	66.56
II	481	349	72.56
III	347	240	69.16
IV	353	207	58.64
V	745	472	63.35
VI	565	298	52.74
VII	429	207	48.25
VIII	528	215	40.72
IX	489	360	73.62
X	380	217	57.10
XI	350	248	70.86
XII	5,500	5,166	93.93
TOTAL:	10,475	8,184	78.13

Cf. Rozier, *De la condition sociale des femmes,* 1848.

10. The number of nonrecognized illegitimate children relative to total illegitimate children was as follows:

1817	76.7	1838	71.2
1818	75.3	1839	76.7
1819	77	1840	78.6
1820	76.4	1841	77.7
1827	76.6	1842	80
1829	78.9	1843	79.5
1830	79.0	1844	79.4
1831	79.2	1845	80
1837	75.9	1846	80.6

[*Notes 11 and 12, which take the form of tables, appear at pp. 479 and 480 respectively.*]

13. Frégier, *op. cit.*

14. In 1828, for example, 82 single men in 100 in Paris as against 48 in Corsica.

15. 50% were under thirty years of age.

16. Murphy and Newcomb, for example, have shown that the lineaments of personality are formed when a baby is a few months old, i.e., at a time when there can be no question of deliberate consciousness. The influence of the people round any very young child is the determining factor, i.e., the two or three persons looking after it. The child accepts and imitates the models provided.

17. "One of these bad starts is the breach of the contract of apprenticeship, such as happens from time to time. When parents sacrifice a child's future to their own interests; when they accept his complaints too readily and encourage him in the idea that he is being exploited by his master; when they manage to break the contract binding him to an employer in order to get their hands on a wage he earned in any case only by the sacrifice of the final part of his training for his trade, then the young man only too often comes to believe that he is now being exploited by his father. He leaves

11. The percentage of illegitimate children not recognized at birth was as follows:

Month	1817			1818			1819			1820		
	Total children	Not recognized	%	Total children	Not recognized	%	Total children	Not recognized	%	Total children	Not recognized	%
January	832	657	78.9	724	542		759	589		819	602	
February	800	631	78.9	669	524		781	593		744	582	
March	871	688	78.4	718	526		849	645		894	697	
April	781	602	77.1	680	512		715	526		754	581	
May	836	634	75.8	681	511		702	543		785	599	
June	780	594	76.1	633	505		662	518		692	512	
July	648	480	74.1	589	429		679	531		662	491	
August	586	441	75.2	675	494		684	514		682	506	
September	629	482	76.6	619	456		686	544		700	538	
October	714	543	76.0	690	542		669	522		727	523	
November	786	595	75.7	692	504		729	567		688	529	
December	897	590	75.2	719	549		726	571		723	567	
TOTAL	9,047	6,937	76.7	8,089	6,094	75.3	8,641	6,657	77.0	8,870	6,777	76.4

12. The figures for foundlings:

Month	1827		%	1828		%	1829		%	1837		%
January	897	684		892	681		957	759	79.3	892	687	
February	900	701		977	748		807	644	79.8	879	673	
March	998	799		966	743		883	683	77.3	933	705	
April	911	699		926	733		817	674	82.5	873	655	
May	884	678		860	680		826	668	80.9	878	672	
June	792	619		814	629		739	570	77.1	772	569	
July	819	639		865	686		818	635	77.6	806	790	
August	783	599		790	613		819	647	79.0	754	587	
September	817	630		770	611		756	600	79.4	731	543	
October	865	679		837	659		755	578	76.6	709	572	
November	831	637		818	636		851	668	78.5	613	462	
December	895	720		960	765		925	724	78.3	738	556	
TOTAL	10,392	8,804	77.8	10,475	8,184	78.1	9,953	7,850	78.9	9,578	7,271	

SOURCE: Terme and Monfalcon, *Les enfants trouvés*.

his parents' home, goes off to live in a lodging house, sets up an irregular home with some girl in similar circumstances, has one affair after another, fathers children who die deserted or sick, and thus starts on an ill-starred career. A worker with this background is handicapped in the workshop by having to compete with workmen better trained and more skilled than he, and he comes to envy them. Jealousy of their betters on the part of those who have been unable to obtain or keep a decent job is the most deleterious passion that workingmen can harbor and it is a cause for alarm in industry."

18. In 1829, the 908 persons charged with criminal offenses were divided into the following age groups:

under 16	26	40–45	49
16–21	223	45–50	35
21–25	182	50–55	14
25–30	145	55–60	12
30–35	138	60–65	4
35–40	70		

Chapter Five (pp. 320–349)

1. Messance, *op. cit.*

2. Lachaise, *op. cit.*

3. We have three mortality tables, that by Dupré de Saint-Maur published by Buffon, that by the abbé d'Expilly, and that by Duvillard published in 1806, which seems to have been computed correctly. There are some other tables computed on the basis of particular population groups, which cannot, therefore, be used to characterize the death rate as a whole; the table by Deparcieux in 1748 is of this sort.

4. The commentator on the 1817 census wrote: "We should observe that the figure for infants in the 0–5 group, which is only 48,824, is far lower than one would deduce from the total Paris population, if the known proportions are kept. This difference is due to the large number of children put out to nurse in neighboring villages either by their parents or by the public institutions. The estimates for them are uncertain."

5. L. R. Villermé, "*De la mortalité dans les divers quartiers de la Ville de Paris, et des causes qui la rendent très différente dans plusieurs d'entre eux, ainsi que dans les divers quartiers de beaucoup de grandes villes,*" *Annales d' Hygiène publique et de médecine légale,* vol. III, 1830.

6. Antoine Deparcieux, *Essai sur les probabilités de la durée de la vie humaine,* 1746.

7. The statistics of stillbirths were published in the *Recherches statistiques sur la Ville de Paris et le département de la Seine.* The number of stillbirths per thousand total births (including stillbirths) increased regularly throughout the nineteenth century:

1817–1820	53	1856–1860	72
1821–1825	51	1861–1865	72
1826–1830	53	1866–1870	75
1831–1835	58	1871–1875	74
1836–1840	61	1876–1880	68
1841–1845	65	1881–1885	74
1846–1850	64	1886–1890	69
1851–1855	67	1891–1895	82

The figures are very high and, as Bertillon noted, exceed those for France generally and for other countries.

8. Villermé, *"De l'influence des marais sur la vie,"* Annales d'Hygiène, vol. XI, 1834.

9. Villermé, *"Décès à domicile des enfants dans quelques rues du Ier et du XIIe arrondissements,"* Annales d'Hygiène, vol. III, 1830.

10. Deaths by smallpox:

Arrondisse-ment	1827	1828	1829	1830	1831	1832	1833	1834	1835	1836
Ist	7	2	18	32	29	12	40	36	37	16
IInd	3	3	6	4	7	12	35	26	28	7
IIIrd	6	1	7	4	3	7	25	22	22	
IVth	1	5	6	12	16	19	36	28	25	7
Vth	9	7	9	27	35	28	51	88	81	14
VIth	16	8	22	48	46	18	56	61	64	16
VIIth	2	8	8	45	31	10	46	35	34	13
VIIIth	8	5	32	60	32	32	43	56	56	33
IXth	13	18	29	104	35	14	27	57	56	38
Xth	69	25	94	90	115	127	97	77	76	40
XIth	7	6	13	9	18	10	19	24	24	21
XIIth	45	30	39	79	14	97	126	108	109	26
TOTAL	186	118	283	524	482	386	601	618	613	236

11. [Legally obligatory identification papers for workers.—Trans.]

12. A.N. F^8 124.

13. *Annales d'Hygiène*, vol. XLIV, 1850.

14. "Is it not committing a sin to oppose the will of Heaven?" was the main objection refuted by the author of *Conférences villageoises sur la vaccine* in 1809 (Bibliothèque Sévigné, No. 931984, 12mo.). See also the *Annuaire des cinq départements de l'ancienne Normandie*, 1835, a review of which was published in *Annales d'Hygiène*, vol. XIII, 1835, p. 233, being an account of the prejudices against the vaccine in Normandy and throughout France, except for a few departments such as the Nord, the Bas-Rhin and the Seine.

15. A.N. F^8 124.

16. *Ibid.*

17. *Conférences villageoises*, p. 21.

18. A.N. F^8 124. Four pages printed in German and French entitled *Au Congrès de Rastadt sur l'extirpation de la petite vérole (Über die Ausrottung der Blattern)* ("A sovereign who is resolved to do so can preserve his States from the plague"—Leibnitz).

19. *Manuel pratique de la médecine* by P. J. Bergeron, Doctor of Medicine in the Faculty of Paris, 1821, 12mo., A.N. F^8 124.

20. A.N. F^8 124.

21. A.N. F^8 124.

22. Lachaise, *Topographie médicale*, p. 220.

23. A.N. F^8 124.

24. *Annales d'Hygiène*, vol. IX, 1833.

25. Deparcieux, *op. cit.*

26. Dr. Henri Bayard, *"Mémoire sur la topographie médicale du IVe arrondissement,"* Annales d'Hygiène publique, vol. XXVIII, 1842.

27. La Bédollière, *Les industriels*, p. 66.

28. *Annales d'Hygiène*, vol. I, 1829, p. 351.

29. *Recherches statistiques sur la Ville de Paris*. Draft rejections and their causes: 1816 to 1823, vol. III, tables 66 ff.; 1824, 1825, 1826, vol. IV, tables 85, 86, 87. A.N. F^{20} 438, conscription and rejection, and F^{28} 4401, stature of conscripts.

30. Lachaise, *op. cit.*

31. *Mémoires de l'Académie royale de Médecine*, 1 vol., 1828, p. 72.

32. *Recherches et considérations sur la rivière de Bièvre*, 1822.

33. A.N. F^{12} 208: "The Saint-Denis canal cannot be opened until after the harvest and until the compensation for the value of the land has been settled. . . . As to the Saint-Maur canal, a large number of workmen came to work on it; but since the earth shifting for the tunnel, the part on which the work is now proceeding, requires arduous labor and most of the workmen were little accustomed to this kind of work, they have been forced to give it up because at piece-work rates they did not earn their keep. There had been some question of employing them at daily rates, but since the little work they would have done fell far short of making up the price of a day, the entrepreneurs would have had to be paid compensation, and His Majesty, on being informed of this situation, gave me strict orders at his levee to make no change in the arrangements for carrying out the earth shifting for the Saint-Maur canal and to continue to have it done at piece-work rates." May 15, 1811: "The work on the Saint-Maur canal will be able to employ workers unaccustomed to this kind of work only on the part where the trenches are dug in the open; several have been compelled to give up working in the tunnel because they lacked the necessary strength."

34. Moheau, *op. cit.*

35. A. Chevalier, *"Nécessité de faire de nouvelles recherches sur les maladies qui affligent les ouvriers,"* *Annales d'Hygiène*, vol. XIII, 1835, p. 304. The author stresses the lack of certainty in studies on occupational diseases.

36. Parent-Duchatelet, *"Les ulcères des extrémités inférieures des artisans de Paris,"* *Annales d'Hygiène*, vol. IV, 1830, p. 239.

37. *Annales d'Hygiene*, July 1831.

38. *Annales d'Hygiène*, vol. II, 1834, p. 5.

39. It is hard to tell whether the number of masons in Paris was the same in both years. If it is reasonable to estimate the number of hands employed from the volume of building material brought into the city in 1831 and 1832, the difference could not have been very great, since there was very little difference in the volume of building material brought into Paris.

40.

	Population in 1831	Ratio of deaths to population (per thousand)
rue Saint-Merri	1,551	34
rue des Vieilles-Etuves	322	34
cloître Saint-Merri	392	35
impasse Clairvaux	27	37
rue Maubuée	856	41
rue Simon-le-Franc	787	43
rue Barre-du-Bec	247	44
rue Brise-Miche	91	44
rue du Renard	113	47
rue de la Cour du Maure	40	75

41. Roch; Rey-Dusseuil, *Le cloître Saint-Merri,* 1832.

Conclusion (pp. 350–355)

42. A needy person had to be sixty-five years of age; an indigent household had to have three children; a widow or widower had to have three children; the applicant had to have some serious infirmity which disabled him from working.

43. Buret, *op. cit.*

44. Cf. Lanzac de Laborie, *Paris sous Napoléon,* vol. V, p. 65; and Clavareau, *Mémoire sur les hôpitaux civils de Paris,* An XIII, Bibliothèque Sévigné, 4391, 8vo.

45. *Annales d'Hygiène,* vol. VII, 1832, p. 218.

46. Duchatel, *La charité*: "Let us leave care for the aged to families . . . the aged should not be admitted to the permanent foundations to the detriment of the feelings of nature. . . . To live from one day to the next, to spend all they earn often even before they earn it, is the most usual mode of life of the Paris working class. Any workman who earns enough in three days to exist for the whole week ordinarily spends the other four days in idleness and dissipation."

47. Villermé, *"De la mortalité dans les divers quartiers de la Ville de Paris," Annales d'Hygiène,* vol. III, p. 294.

48. The total numbers of indigent persons were as follows:

Empire and Restoration

1802	97,784	1816	
1803	111,626	1817	
1804	86,936	1818	84,461
1805	90,705	1819	85,357
1806	94,062	1820	82,643
1807	97,914	1821	77,192
1808	116,703	1822	54,371
1809	118,202	1823	60,138
1810	121,801	1824	60,543
1811	116,670	1825	65,293
1812	93,836	1826	66,205
1813	102,806	1827	71,257
1814	115,223	1828	74,789
1815		1829	62,705

July Monarchy

		(ratio of indigent to the total population)		
1830				
1831				
1832	68,896	1	per	11.16
1835	62,539	1	"	12.32
1838	58,500	1	"	15.37
1841	66,486	1	"	13.30
1844	66,148	1	"	13.78
1847	73,901	1	"	13.99

49. A.N. F[7] 6772, December 6, 1828.

50. *Annales d'Hygiène,* vol. XV, 1836. Indigent persons in receipts of relief included:

Men		Women	
Ragpickers	156	Laundresses	703
Cab drivers	194	Ragpickers	141
Porters	1,028	Former domestics	926
Cobblers	703	Charwomen	229
Former domestics	120	Child-nurses	229
Former clerks and scriveners	213	Sick-nurses	173
Second-hand dealers	81	Second-hand dealers	1,351
Building workers	1,749	Needlewomen	2,175
Miscellaneous laborers	5,880	Miscellaneous daily workers	4,086
Water carriers	238	Water carriers	39
Concierges	1,433	Concierges	790
Shoemakers	148	Unspecified	3,720
Tailors	418		
Unspecified	1,338		

51. Statistics of the indigent population. The origins of heads of households in receipt of relief were divided as follows:

	1829	1832	1835	1844	1847
Born in Paris	9,026	9,595	8,945	8,910	11,638
Born outside Paris, but married in Paris	5,686	5,430	4,764	4,660	
Born outside Paris, unmarried or married outside Paris	15,649	16,698	15,260	16,106	19,576

52. In 1835, the ratio of the indigent population (in receipt of relief) to the general population was:

Arrondissement	Population	Indigent persons in receipt of relief	Ratio	
Ist	66,793	3,599	1 in	18
IInd	74,773	2,646	1	28
IIIrd	49,833	2,392	1	20
IVth	44,734	3,129	1	14
Vth	67,756	4,699	1	14
VIth	80,811	6,936	1	11
VIIth	59,415	3,936	1	15
VIIIth	72,800	9,938	1	7
IXth	42,561	4,924	1	8
Xth	83,127	5,073	1	16
XIth	50,227	3,896	1	12
XIIth	77,456	11,357	1	6
TOTAL	770,286	62,539	1	12

[*See p. 486 for balance of this note.*]

	Ist	IInd	IIIrd	IVth	Vth	VIth	VIIth	VIIIth	IXth	Xth	XIth	XIIth
1835												
Heads of household born in Paris	439	323	275	394	591	1,109	529	1,348	712	786	562	1,877
Born outside Paris, but married in Paris	558	194	100	377	372	777	153	681	453	172	272	655
Born outside Paris, unmarried, or married outside Paris	652	774	741	760	1,151	1,288	1,170	1,967	1,161	1,704	1,186	2,697
1847												
Born in Paris	463	314	260	323	697	994	421	1,498	461	760	521	2,127
Born outside Paris, but in the department of the Seine	39	51	23	120	34	100	113	1,819	65	109	154	168
Born outside the department of the Seine	1,350	928	859	736	1,780	1,844	1,672	1,690	1,597	1,985	1,432	3,703
Born abroad	148	114	95	95	162	112	47	52	87	158	86	193
TOTAL	2,000	1,407	1,237	1,278	2,673	3,050	2,253	5,059	2,210	3,012	2,193	6,191

1. Let us look, for instance, at the disturbances in the early years of the Restoration, such as those in the summer of 1820: "Young persons, most of them from outside Paris," the Prefect Chabrol stated in his proclamation of June 8, 1820, "led astray by the enemies of the public peace, have nowhere encountered citizens who do not reprobate their excesses. The estimable artisans who maintain their families by the fruits of their daily industry have distinguished themselves by the propriety of their conduct." Regulations for lodging houses stricter than those previously issued were embodied in an order of June 15.

The disturbances in November 1827 were thus described in the *Journal des Débats* of November 21: "Some five score ragged fellows ran through the streets with their aprons full of stones. They went around the shopping district, smashing windows, breaking down doors, beating up citizens to make them, so they said, illuminate their shops. It is much to be regretted that this mob was not pursued and apprehended by the military."

2. "Our readers will recall the frightful row the Opposition kicked up a few months ago about a word—'barbarians'—we used to describe a class of people kept in a permanent state dangerous to society by their lack of education and their precarious livelihood," the *Journal des Débats* wrote on July 10, 1832.

3. *Journal des Débats*, August 27, 1830: "DUPIN: 'Of the 5 million, two and a half are allocated for building and digging; I demand that preference be given to fathers of families and workmen domiciled in Paris. (*Loud protests.*) The remaining million and a half has not been allocated to any particular object. I propose that 300,000 francs be set aside to assist the printers. Further, the Government should find some way to induce the excessive number of workers in Paris to go back of their own free will to their provinces.' (*Renewed loud protests. A voice:* 'What about liberty?') DUPIN: 'I too am for the maintenance of order, and in demanding that workers domiciled in the capital be given preference . . .' (*Prolonged interruption.*) MESTADIER: 'I rise to protest against a line of argument pernicious to the capital and dangerous to our provinces. M. Dupin has proposed that in sharing out the public works in Paris a distinction be drawn between workers domiciled in Paris and workers from the provinces. I wish to ask this great expert in statistical calculations just how he would go about taking the requisite census for making such an unjust distinction. I have the honor to be deputy from a department which sends 20,000 to 24,000 workers to Paris.' SEVERAL VOICES: 'They do not all come from the Limousin; there are also Lorrainers and Auvergnats.' MESTADIER: 'These workers are no less deserving than those of the capital; they are free among themselves, but they are poorer; that's the whole difference.' VIENNET: 'No one dreams of making any such distinction.' "

4. Stern, *op. cit.*

5. This was the burden of the inquiry ordered in 1848 at the request of the Workers' Commission following the riot of May 15. One of the main questions was: "What means are suggested to halt the migration of rural laborers to the towns and to use the hands not employed by industry on the farms?"

6. Emile Littré, *Dictionnaire de la langue française*, 4 vols., 1863–69.

7. "A man who would only have been an unfortunate proletarian in town became a respected citizen when a yeoman proprietor in the country."

8. "Pauperism is something quite different, a new social malady, as novel as the term used to designate it. It is an English term introduced into France some sixty years ago. It denotes the condition of a number of persons who permanently lack the necessities of life. Pauperism is a novel condition both in its causes and in its characteristics. Its origins are to be found in contemporary industrial organization and in the mode of living and behavior of factory workers."

9. Frégier, *op. cit.* Cf. Proudhon's analysis of the notions of "poor" and "proletarian" in Book IV, chapter III, of *La justice* and Volume II of *La guerre et la paix*.

10. Lecouturier, *Paris incompatible avec la République*.

11. Pierre Marie-Sébastien Bigot de Morogues, *Du pauperisme, de la mendicité et des moyens d'en prevenir les funestes effets*, 1834.

12. Le Play, vol. VI, p. 285.

13. Frégier, *op. cit.*

14. Like the unnamed woman mentioned in the *Journal des Débats* of July 13, 1828: "Having been arrested in a house under construction in the rue des Beaux-Arts where she had been sleeping, she refused to give her name. 'The reason why I am not giving my name is that I am a wealthy ragpicker. I scavenge in my spare time. I am a rich ragpicker and I always have something to butter my bread with. I am always clean when I go out. In the evening I dress up a bit on the unconventional side and go out and pick rags.' "

15. Vidocq, *Quelques mots sur une question à l'ordre du jour. Réflexions sur les moyens propres à diminuer les crimes et les récidives*, 1844.

16. *La Ruche populaire*, 4th and 5th year, p. 372.

17. Mrs. Trollope, *Paris and the Parisians in 1835*, Letter XXXIV.

18. *Revue de la Révolution de 1848*, vol. VII.

Chapter Two (pp. 373–393)

1. *L'Interdiction*.

2. "This illogical route," Balzac wrote in *La cousine Bette*, "was laid out by the logic of the passions, always most inimical to the legs."

3. "A lot of sympathy is being lavished on the fate of the working classes nowadays," he said again in *La cousine Bette*. "They are represented as fleeced by the factory owners; but the State is a hundred times harsher than the most penny-pinching industrialist; so far as salaries are concerned, it exaggerates thrift to a point where it makes no sense at all. If you are a diligent worker, industry pays you in proportion to your work; but what does the State pay hundreds of its humble and devoted workers—the clerks?"

4. Monnier, *op. cit.*

5. A.N. F[20] 435. "*Rapport du préfet de police*," 1807. Detailed information on casual laborers working in Paris, such as street porters, messengers, sweeps, crockery-menders, shoemenders, etc.

6. Mercier, *op. cit.*

7. Arthur Young, *Travels in France*, 2 vols., 1793.

8. Joseph-Marie Audin-Rouvière, *Essai sur la topographie physique et médicale de Paris* (n.d.).

9. ["The Parisian race is the pale hooligan with weakly body and complexion yellow as an old penny. It is this peevish lad one sees at all hours, lazy, strolling far from his home, hitting at the lean dogs and all along the high walls chalking up a thousand indecent designs as he whistles. This lad believes in nothing, he spits on his mother. The name of Heaven is only a bitter farce to him. In brief, it is the epitome of libertinage in a fifteen-year-old face. It is inveterate vice."—Trans.]

10. In *Les secrets de la princesse de Cadignan,* the Princess, married to a man she does not love, tells the story of Michel Chrestien's silent love for her.

11. *Un grand homme de province à Paris.* "When Michel Chrestien died in 1832, Horace Bianchon, Daniel d'Arthez and Léon Giraud went, despite the danger, and carried his body to Saint-Merri to pay him their last homage in defiance of the ardor of politics."

12. "How do you expect," wrote Zulma Carraud to Balzac on September 10, 1832, "that a person who regards the workman merely as a machine, the horny-handed laborer merely as a jailbird . . . ?" Honoré de Balzac, *Correspondance avec Zulma Carraud,* edited by Marcel Bouteron, p. 67.

Chapter Three (pp. 394–408)

1. "It is hard to conceive," Corbon wrote, "what courage a man of the people needs simply to address a bourgeois of any standing by his last name alone, whereas this bourgeois has addressed the workman simply by his last name from the start. If he manages it without too much effort, it means that he is lucky enough to be dealing with outstanding persons who are making an effort to eradicate this prejudice in themselves and in those around them. For I have very good grounds for saying that the prejudice is even more strongly rooted in the working class than in the bourgeoisie. In 1848 it was the progressive bourgeoisie that conceived the idea of sending workers to the Constituent Assembly, though it was the workers whom the right to vote had made the masters of the situation. No, it is not jealousy that makes Parisian workers, like workers elsewhere, reluctant to entrust a mandate of any importance to men of their class. It is, I repeat, because they are still thoroughly imbued with the sense of their inferiority, their incapacity. The people has a long way to go yet before it believes that its redemption has arrived."

2. For example, a letter by Vinçard to Dutacq, the managing editor of *Le Siècle,* on an article by Balzac referring to "the lower classes": "When a crime is committted among the upper classes, the motive is never practically negligible, as it is in the lower classes, where the accused often have a criminal record of convictions and breaches of the law."

3. When the *Courrier français* wrote on September 15, 1842: "The big problem is to get the workingman to abandon his irregular habits and frequenting pothouses; it is to exert a form of moral pressure on him to compel him voluntarily to deposit what he has saved during the week in the savings banks instead of taking it to the pothouses at the barrières every Monday," Vinçard protested: "That is a flat lie; it applies only to a very small minority. . . . Anyway, if the toilers do go to the barrières on Sundays and holidays, is there so much harm in it? Where else do you suppose they can forget the neglect and misery to which they are abandoned? . . . Unless they can go and enjoy a little fresh air outside the walls of the industrial

prisons of our cities which you are walling in like a Bastille, enclosing so much space at such great cost that they will soon have to travel four or five leagues to find a little greenery. . . ." Flora Tristan has left an account of the sitting of the Committee of *La Ruche* on February 18, 1843, at which she read two chapters of *L'union ouvrière*. Vinçard rose to protest against the chapter on women's activities. It dealt with the workers' custom of frequenting pothouses, and Vinçard objected that this would give the bourgeoisie an opportunity to raise their eternal complaints about it. As a matter of fact, he was the only opposing voice when Roly, a carpenter, wrathfully opposed its insertion on the ground that it was an insult to work-ingmen and women. He did not deny that workers went to pothouses, but thought that this vicious habit should be concealed from the bourgeois and should not be stressed by the workers. (See also Puech on this.)

4. For example, J. F. Coeur's song in his book *Chansonnier du prolétaire*: "Wealthy people of Lyon, you who in opulence. . . . But on this day we are without work, have pity on the poor workers," 1843, B.N. Ye 40630, 800.

5. Duquenne wrote a lengthy review of Régis Allier's book, *Le système pénitentiaire et les sociétés de patronage*, in November 1842: "The poor do not, like the rich, enjoy the pleasures of the table or banquets. . . . Lawful or unlawful, they have only one spouse, on whom they concentrate all their joys, all their happiness; with her they all too often forget that work is hard to find, the competition enormous, the landlord merciless, the winter harsh, illness frequent, the pawnshop usurious. . . . To be frank, what have all these revolutions done for the people? Nothing. . . . As things stand now, robbery of the rich by the poor is merely reparation, that is to say, the just and reciprocal transfer of a coin or a piece of bread from the robber to the robbed."

6. "Two girls have just killed themselves with charcoal braziers," *La Ruche* reported in September 1841. "Compelled by poverty to leave their province, they exhausted themslves in Paris, not in working, but in seeking work, situated as they were between prostitution and death. . . . As I was strolling one morning in the ancient and horrible Cité, I came up with some people watching a woman who, from inanition, had fallen in the mud of the street . . . a child at her breast . . . crime and poverty."

7. It was in verse that Roly the carpenter addressed the Sisters of Charity of the Saint-Merri almshouse with reference to slanderous rumors current about them. *La Ruche populaire*, July 1841; "Do you not know, Sisters, how you are being slandered? You are being accused of being unworthy of your calling. Daughters of Saint-Vincent, you Sisters of Charity, you refused to open your door when, groaning in agony, a woman in labor called for help." But he used prose and the fictional character of Paul the locksmith to describe certain aspects of the working-class condition. "It was a Satur-day, a fine evening in the summer of 1840, about the time when rumors of war were current. The many workers living in the faubourg Saint-Martin were returning from their day's work; some were laughing and gossiping outside their landlady's door, others were accosting the working girls of the faubourg or shouting jests at them. . . ." *La Ruche*, September 1842.

8. *La Ruche populaire*, January 1844.

9. "The people," Proudhon wrote, "taught for a long time past by its newspapers, its plays, its songs, its economists . . .", *Correspondance*, vol. I, p. 276. Audiganne too has given a good account of the part played by melo-

drama in working-class culture. *Les populations ouvrières et les industries dans le mouvement social du XIXe siècle,* 1854 (vol. II, p. 162).

10. Victor-Henri-Joseph Ducange, *Les Moeurs, contes et nouvelles,* 2 vols., 1834.

11. A reader wrote to Sue on February 13, 1843: "I had already had the idea of writing to you about your Morel family, an all too realistic depiction, typical, alas, of many miserable lives, to ask you to delete the half-witted old woman in the second edition, as she savors too much of the unnatural, the extravagant, the novelistic, and thus impairs your admirable portrait."

12. A woman reader wrote on August 20, 1843: "We found Rodolphe's grief on the morrow of his daughter's death too calm, too meditative; he displays melancholy rather than despair. We would have wished his grief to be drear, somber, concentrated, without effusions, unprotesting, tearless." On February 15, 1843, a reader wrote: "But I must tell you, Sir, that I have not taken up my pen to pay you compliments. As executive manager of the Poor Relief of the Reformed Church for twenty-five years and resident of the Helvetic Welfare Association in Paris, which has been active for twenty-three, my purpose is naturally more serious. The point is how Fleur-de-Marie is to die. Two solutions suggest themselves: to let her die a saint; that is what everyone expects and consequently it would satisfy no one. Or to let her devote the remainder of her life to managing a large home for poor orphans under the auspices of her august father, to whom she would be an angel of consolation."

13. "It seems to my simple mind," a concierge in the rue Jean-Pain-Mollet wrote to Sue on October 18, 1843, "that an author's merit is to come as close as possible to the truth and that you have painted the portrait of the honest artisan and his privations very well. And to think that he must conceal his poverty; for, if he revealed all of it, he would lose the little confidence to which he is rightly entitled. I foretell immortality for you and your work, and those whose reproaches you incur are, to use a trivial expression, those who wear the cap when it fits." In *Soixante ans de souvenirs,* Legouvé later repeated that this was the chapter that made the greatest impression. He described (p. 377) "the growing success of Sue's works and the development of his influence on the masses. He exercised a species of empire over the people of Paris. The most ardent sympathies, the most grateful enthusiasms greeted each of his chapters and sometimes took a strange and tragic form. One evening as he entered his home, his foot struck something suspended and moving in the dark. He lit a candle, and what did he see? The feet of a man who had managed to get into his hallway, how it was never discovered, and had hanged himself; he was clutching a note which read: 'I am killing myself out of despair; I felt that death would be less harsh if I died under the roof of he who loves and defends us.' This fanatical devotion to Sue dated particularly from the publication of an episode you may perhaps recall, the story of the Morel family." The people of Paris, within which the artisans constituted a large class, had recognized itself in the description of the artisan Morel in *Les Mystères de Paris.*

14. Proudhon, *Correspondance,* vol. I, p. 227, August 3, 1840.

15. *Révolution sociale,* p. 126. There is no need to give further quotations, but Proudhon's analysis of the savage condition in *Les contradictions économiques,* vol. I, p. 161, is well worth looking at.

Chapter Four (pp. 409–417)

1. Toqueville, *op. cit.*

2. Cabanis, *Rapports du physique et du moral*, vol. I, p. 58.

3. Lavater, *L'Art d'étudier les physiognomies*, 1772; *Les fragments physiognomoniques*, 1774.

4. Gall, *Anatomie et physiologie du système nerveux en général et du cerveau en particulier, avec des observations sur la possibilité de reconnaître plusieurs dispositions intellectuelles et morales de l'homme et des animaux, par la configuration de leur tête*, 4 vols., 1818–20; *Sur les fonctions du cerveau*, 6 vols., 1822–25.

5. Eugène Sue, *Les Mystères de Paris*, vol. VIII: "A phrenologist would have observed . . ."

6. Broussais, *Cours de phrénologie*, 1836.

7. For example, Dr. Voisin, chief medical officer at Bicêtre, and Dr. Lauvergne, chief medical officer at the Toulon convict prison and the author of a book, *Les Forçats*.

8. Agricol Perdiguier, *Compagnonnage: la Rencontre de deux frères, scène récente adressé aux compagnons de la France*, 1838.

9. *Le Rivarol de 1842. Dictionnaire satirique des celebrités contemporaines*, par FORTUNATUS. *Variétés politiques et littéraires*, vol. II, Bibliothèque de la Ville de Paris, 12016, 12mo.

10. Gavarni, *op. cit.*

11. Cf. Loys Delteil's illustrated catalogue, *Le peintre graveur illustré*, B.N. Usuel No. 50.

12. *La Caricature*, November 4, 1830, to August 27, 1835.

13. *Le Charivari*, daily paper founded by Philipon on December 1, 1832, to which Daumier contributed. It published the 100 plates on Robert Macaire from August 20, 1836, to November 25, 1838.

14. Charles Menche de Loisne, *L'influence de la littérature française de 1830 à 1850 sur l'esprit public et les moeurs* (B.N. Z 54979, 800).

15. BB[18] 1192: "On October 22, 1830, the bourgeois Abraham, resident in the rue de Paris at Belleville, complains of ill-usage by a gathering of local workmen who pelted him with stones and mud . . . 'for no reason,' he states."

PART III (pp. 419–433)

1. Perdiguier, *op. cit.*

2. "We come to the meadow. The Angevin takes off his waistcoat, trousers and shirt; he is stark naked and displays his vast muscles. Our friends feared for me. 'Look,' I said to him, 'we are near the road, passers-by can see us; let us at least keep our trousers on, they will do as drawers, and let us take care not to tear them, because I am wearing my best.' The Angevin put his trousers on again. Both of us were bare-armed, bare-chested."

3. *Journal des Débats*, October 9, 1823: "The *compagnonnage* associations among workmen of various trades, especially the joiners, often stir up bloody brawls. On September 22 two hostile bands—50 '*compagnons* of liberty' and 50 'of duty'—armed with their own peculiar weapons proposed to fight a pitched battle not far from the barrière de Monceau. The gendarmerie came up. Jean Lamoureux, a member of the 'liberty' band, reproached his comrade Merle for not joining the ranks. Merle said he had

been running a small shop for some time and had given up the trade of joiner. On September 23, Lamoureux stabbed him three times with a pair of iron compasses." *Journal des Débats*, October 25, 1827: "Brawl at Bobinot's wine shop, 6, quai de Bercy, between 60 and 80 joiners; for no motive except the animosity between workmen of the *compagnonnage* persuasion and those who did not accept any kind of 'duty.' The battle was so furious from the start that all the shops shut and everyone fled; the wretches assaulted each other with compasses and cudgels. A hundred gendarmes were called in. But the furious joiners after dispersing, no doubt at a given password, met again at Saint-Mandé, where battle was joined again more hotly than before. The combat lasted five or six hours. One journeyman was killed by a compass thrust through the throat and 8 or 10 others are in a desperate state. These wretches have never before been known to fight so savagely."

4. A.N. F⁷ 4161.

5. *Ibid.*

6. Auguste Luchet, *Les Moeurs d'aujourd'hui*, 1854.

7. Michel, nicknamed Pisseux, born at La Courtille in 1794, classified the moves and devised a theory called The Art of the *Savate*. He opened a school in his district. Later, he left La Courtille and opened another school in the rue Buffaut, faubourg Montmartre. His most eminent pupils are said to have included the duc d'Orléans and Lord Henry Seymour.

8. "The master instructor Leboucher, who had a school at 20, rue du Vert-Bois, and had Deburau as a pupil," Charlemont wrote in *La boxe française*, "virtually revived boxing. His teaching was brutal and instinctive; people went to him chiefly to learn how to defend themselves against prowlers at the barrières and persons of that ilk. He taught you how to defend yourself against a lout and to teach a surly cab driver to mend his ways. He was perfectly acquainted (we do not mean from personal practice, of course) with all these villains' dirtiest tricks; he had unexpected parries and astonishing ripostes and he taught you them remarkably well. He exhorted his pupils to keep their hand in (as he put it) by going to public dances from time to time and trying a bash with a couple of hooligans (it did keep one's hand in)."

9. Nadaud, *Mémoires*.

10. "There was some connection," Nadaud wrote, "between this temper and the opening of a large number of schools of *chausson* in our district. The first *chausson* teacher who gained some fame among us was a certain Toulouse. One of his pupils was Gadoux, who came from my village and gained a reputation as one of the great masters of the art." Nadaud first came to Paris with two "strong men," Vacheron, from le Grand Blessac, and Gadoux. As Nadaud had asked his father if he could attend Gadoux's school and his father had made Gadoux promise never to take him, Nadaud attended Le Mule's school in the rue de la Vannerie.

11. Charlemont described Ducros's career thus: "Ducros was born at Montpellier in 1824. His teacher was a certain Surgis who, orphaned very young, used to sell ticket checks at the doors of the Paris theaters, and later followed the acrobats to fairs. They taught him boxing, the staff and the cudgel. He was short, very muscular and very sturdy; he was one of the few who dared to measure up to the famous English boxer Tom Cribb.

His school was at the corner of the rue Saint-Denis and the rue de Rivoli at Mother Lesage's wine shop, on the spot where the *Pygmalion* draper's store now stands. The school was frequented mainly by market porters from Les Halles and elsewhere; boxing and the staff were much practiced, but especially the cudgel. Surgis died of a chill at the Hôtel-Dieu. Charles Ducros succeeded his teacher and moved to 100, rue Saint-Antoine. Soon afterwards he settled down at 9, rue Beautreillis, where we got to know him. He worked at two trades at once, master builder part of the day, teacher of boxing, staff, etc., in the evening. Tenon, a fencing master, was attached to the establishment."

12. Georges Gurvitch, *La vocation actuelle de la sociologie*, 1950.

13. "Before entering the lodging house where my father was to introduce me to Mme Champesme at 62, rue de la Tisseranderie, he led me to the quai de la Grève beside the Seine to wash my face and hands. . . . Mme Champesme has two daughters. The elder came up at once to kiss me. I lowered my eyes and dared not look at her, and she said to my father: "Why, père Nadaud, you told me your son was so smart, he seems very shy to me."

14. This brings to mind once more Balzac's description: "Today the rue du Fouarre is one of the dirtiest streets in the XIIth arrondissement, the poorest district in Paris, in which two-thirds of the inhabitants lack firewood in winter, the district which sends the most brats to the Foundlings Hospital, the most sick to the Hôtel-Dieu, the most beggars onto the streets, the most ragpickers to the garbage dumps at the corner, the most sick old men to lean against the walls in the sun, the most unemployed workers to the squares, the most indictments to the police courts."

15. A.N. F^7 4163, October 1841.

16. Cf. Plantie, *Contribution à l'étude de la violence en droit pénal.*

17. We give only one example, taken from the *Journal des Débats* of September 6, 1821: "Three workmen were arguing in a pothouse at Petit Mont-Rouge. A quarrel broke out over a sum of 40 francs which one of them owed. Pierre Renauld, a young man of twenty-seven, having attempted to cut his comrade's throat with a knife, was sentenced to forced labor for life and to be branded. He listened to the sentence with most remarkable aplomb."

18. A.N. BB^{18} 1330.

Index

A Note about the Author

Louis Chevalier, professor at the Collège de France and at the Institut d'Etudes Politiques, is by training both an historian and a demographer. Elected to the Collège de France on the basis of his first book about Paris, *La formation de la population parisienne au XIXème siècle*, and of his new methods of social description which it reflects, Professor Chevalier has since devoted himself essentially to the study of the Parisian milieu.

Among his other books are *Les fondements économiques et sociaux de l'histoire politique de la région parisienne, 1848-1870; Le problème démographique nord-africain*, and *Les Parisiens*.